HARCOURT
· TROPHIES ·

A HARCOURT READING/LANGUAGE ARTS PROGRAM

FLORIDA TEACHER'S EDITION

SENIOR AUTHORS
Isabel L. Beck ◆ Roger C. Farr ◆ Dorothy S. Strickland

AUTHORS
Alma Flor Ada ◆ Marcia Brechtel ◆ Margaret McKeown
Nancy Roser ◆ Hallie Kay Yopp

SENIOR CONSULTANT
Asa G. Hilliard III

CONSULTANTS
F. Isabel Campoy ◆ David A. Monti

Orlando   Boston   Dallas   Chicago   San Diego

Visit *The Learning Site!*

www.harcourtschool.com

Acknowledgments appear in the back of this book.

Printed in the United States of America

ISBN 0-15-324983-8

2 3 4 5 6 7 8 9 10   073   10 09 08 07 06 05 04 03 02

Program Authors

SENIOR AUTHORS

Isabel L. Beck
Professor of Education and Senior Scientist at the Learning Research and Development Center, University of Pittsburgh

Research Contributions: Reading Comprehension, Beginning Reading, Phonics, Vocabulary

Roger C. Farr
Chancellor's Professor of Education and Director of the Center for Innovation in Assessment, Indiana University, Bloomington

Research Contributions: Instuctional Assessment, Reading Strategies, Staff Development.

Dorothy S. Strickland
The State of New Jersey Professor of Reading, Rutgers University

Research Contributions: Early Literacy, Elementary Reading/ Language Arts, Writing, Intervention

AUTHORS

Alma Flor Ada
Director of Doctoral Studies in the International Multicultural
Program, University of San Francisco

Research Contributions: English as a Second Language,
Bilingual Education, Family Involvement

Marcia Brechtel
Director of Training, Project GLAD, Fountain Valley School District,
Fountain Valley, California

Research Contributions: English as a Second Language,
Bilingual Education

Margaret McKeown
Research Scientist at the Learning Research and Development Center,
University of Pittsburgh

Research Contributions: Reading Comprehension, Vocabulary

Nancy Roser
Professor, Language and Literacy Studies, University of Texas, Austin

Research Contributions: Early Literacy, Phonics, Comprehension,
Fluency

Hallie Kay Yopp
Professor, Department of Elementary Bilingual and Reading
Education, California State University, Fullerton

Research Contributions: Phonemic Awareness, Early Childhood

SENIOR CONSULTANT

Asa G. Hilliard III
Fuller E. Callaway Professor of Urban Education, Department of Educational Foundations, Georgia State University, Atlanta

Research Contributions: Multicultural Literature and Education

CONSULTANTS

F. Isabel Campoy
Former President, Association of Spanish Professionals in the USA

Research Contributions: English as a Second Language, Family Involvement

David A. Monti
Professor, Reading/Language Arts Department, Central Connecticut State University

Research Contributions: Classroom Management, Technology, Family Involvement

WHAT RESEARCH SAYS ABOUT

PHONEMIC AWARENESS

Research clearly shows that phonemic awareness is one
of the primary predictors of success in learning to read,
and instruction in phonemic awareness significantly
supports students' reading and writing achievement.

Phonemic awareness is the awareness of sounds in spoken language. It is recognizing and understanding that speech is made up of a series of individual sounds, or phonemes, and that the individual sounds can be manipulated. A phonemically aware child can segment and blend strings of isolated sounds to form words. Phonemic awareness falls under the umbrella of phonological awareness, which also includes recognizing and manipulating larger units of sound, such as syllables and words. Phonemic awareness can be difficult for young children to attain because it demands a shift in attention from the *content* of speech to the *form* of speech. It requires individuals to attend to the sounds of speech separate from their meanings. Primary grade teachers will find that a handful of children enter school with well-developed phonemic awareness. Other children have only a rudimentary sense of the sound structure of speech. With extended exposure to a language-rich environment, most children develop phonemic awareness over time.

Research has shown that phonemic awareness is significantly related to success in learning to read and spell. The relationship is one of reciprocal causation or mutual facilitation. That is, phonemic awareness supports reading and spelling acquisition, and instruction in reading and spelling, in turn, supports further understanding of the phonemic basis of our speech. The relationship is so powerful that researchers have concluded the following:

- Phonemic awareness is the most potent predictor of success in learning to read (Stanovich, 1986, 1994).
- The lack of phonemic awareness is the most powerful determinant of the likelihood of failure to learn to read (Adams, 1990).
- Phonemic awareness is the most important core and causal factor separating normal and disabled readers (Adams, 1990).

Phonemic awareness is central in learning to read and spell because English and other alphabetic languages map speech to print at the level of phonemes. Our written language is a representation of the *sounds* of our spoken language. It is critical to understand that our speech is made up of sounds. Without this insight, written language makes little sense.

Direct instruction in phonemic awareness helps children decode new words and remember how to read familiar words. Growth and improvement in phonemic awareness can be facilitated through instruction and practice in phonemic awareness tasks such as these:

- **Phoneme isolation,** which requires students to recognize individual sounds in words. For example, "What is the last sound in *hop*?" (/p/)
- **Phoneme matching,** which requires students to recognize the same sound in different words. For example, "Which two words begin with the same sound—*bed, bike, cat*?" (*bed, bike*)
- **Phoneme blending,** which asks students to form a recognizable word after listening to separately spoken sounds. For example, "What word is /a/ -/p/ -/l/?" (*apple*)
- **Phoneme segmentation,** which has students break a word into its individual sounds. For example, "What sounds do you hear in the word *dog*?" (/d/-/ô/-/g/)
- **Phoneme deletion,** which requires students to identify what word remains when a specific phoneme has been removed. For example, "Say *spin* without /s/." (*pin*)
- **Phoneme addition,** which requires the identification of a word when a phoneme is added. For example, "Say *row* with /g/ at the beginning." (*grow*)

Q What types of phonemic awareness activities or tasks are children exposed to in the program?

A Phonemic awareness instruction in *Trophies* is strongly supported by the finding that phonemic awareness is one of the most potent predictors of success in learning to read. Activities for stimulating phonemic awareness are incorporated throughout the program. There are two types of phonemic awareness instruction in *Trophies*. The first is word-play activities that draw attention to sounds in spoken language, recited poems, and read-aloud literature. The second type is more formal instruction that focuses on single phonemes to prepare students for studying the letter-sound correspondences for those phonemes.

Q What phonemic awareness skills are taught in kindergarten and grade I?

A Phonemic awareness instruction in *Trophies* follows a systematic, developmental sequence progressing in difficulty from an awareness of words, syllables, and onset/rimes to isolating medial phonemes, substituting phonemes, and other manipulating tasks.

> **"** A growing number of studies indicate that phonemic awareness is not simply a strong predictor, but that it is a necessary prerequisite for success in learning to read. **"**
>
> — **Hallie Kay Yopp**
> Professor
> Department of Elementary
> Bilingual and Reading Education,
> California State University,
> Fullerton

Phonemic Awareness Skills Sequence

- Word Segmentation
- Rhyme Recognition and Production
- Syllable Blending
- Syllable Segmentation
- Syllable Deletion
- Onset and Rime Blending
- Initial Phoneme Isolation

- Final Phoneme Isolation
- Medial Phoneme Isolation
- Phoneme Blending
- Phoneme Segmentation
- Phoneme Substitution
- Phoneme Addition
- Phoneme Deletion

Look for

✓ **Daily phonemic awareness lessons in Kindergarten and Grade I**
✓ **Additional Support Activities to Reteach and Extend**
✓ **Point-of-use suggestions for Reaching All Learners**

Q How do the phonemic awareness lessons relate to the phonics lessons in *Trophies*?

A In kindergarten and grade I, each phonemic awareness lesson is tied to a phonics lesson. A phonemic awareness lesson, for example, could focus on blending phonemes in words with the /i/ sound, featuring such words as *sit, lip,* and *if.* The subsequent phonics lesson would be the short sound of the letter *i.*

EXPLICIT, SYSTEMATIC PHONICS

Decoding is the process of translating written words into speech. Phonics instruction gives students the knowledge of letter-sound correspondences and strategies they need to make the translations and to be successful readers.

Explicit, systematic phonics instruction can help children learn to read more effectively. Current and confirmed research shows that systematic phonics instruction has a significant effect on reading achievement. Research findings clearly indicate that phonics instruction in kindergarten and first grade produces a dramatic impact on reading achievement. In phonics instruction letter-sound correspondences are taught sequentially and cumulatively and are then applied. The individual sounds represented by letters are blended to form words, and those words appear in decodable text. At grade 2, more complex letter patterns are introduced and practiced. This type of instruction allows students to continually build on what they learn.

Word Blending and Word Building are essential aspects of phonics instruction. Word Blending is combining the sounds represented by letter sequences to decode and pronounce words. In phonics instruction beginning in kindergarten or first grade, students are explicitly taught the process of blending individual sounds into words. They begin with VC or CVC words, such as *at* or *man,* and progress to words with consonant blends, as in *tent* and *split.* In contrast to Word Blending, which focuses on decoding a particular word, Word Building allows students to practice making words by using previously taught letter-sound relationships. Word Building activities require children to focus attention on each letter in the sequence of letters that make up words. This helps children develop a sense of the alphabetic system of written English.

As students progress through the grades, they receive direct instruction in decoding multisyllabic words. Direct instruction in recognizing syllables will help students develop effective strategies to read longer, unfamiliar words. Research shows that good readers chunk letter patterns into manageable units in order to read a long, unfamiliar word. Effective strategies include

- identifying syllable boundaries
- identifying syllable types
- isolating affixes
- applying phonics knowledge to blend syllables in sequence

Direct instruction in these strategies helps students recognize word parts so they can apply phonics generalizations to decode unfamiliar words.

> **Decoding is important because this early skill accurately predicts later skill in reading comprehension.**
> — **Isabel L. Beck**
> **Professor of Education and Senior Scientist at the Learning Research and Development Center, University of Pittsburgh**

Q **How is Word Blending taught in** *Trophies*?

A The purpose of Word Blending instruction is to provide students with practice in combining the sounds represented by letter sequences to decode words. *Trophies* employs the cumulative blending method, which has students blend sounds successively as they are pronounced.

Q **How does** *Trophies* **use Word Building to help students with decoding (reading) and encoding (spelling)?**

A In the decoding portion of Word Building, teachers first tell students what letters to put in what place. For example, students are told to put *c* at the beginning, *a* after *c,* and *t* at the end. They are asked to read the word *cat* and then are asked to change *c* to *m* and read the new word, *mat.* In Word Building activities that help encoding, students are asked which letter in the word *cat* needs to change to make the word *mat.* This encoding approach is used to build spelling words throughout the first grade program.

Q **How are students taught to decode multisyllabic words?**

A Students are taught to see words as patterns of letters, to identify long words by breaking them down into syllable units, and to blend the syllables to form and read long words. Decoding lessons throughout grades 2–6 directly and explicitly provide students with various strategies, including understanding syllable types and patterns and recognizing such word structures as prefixes, suffixes, and root words, to decode multisyllabic words.

Look for

- ✔ **Phonics and spelling lessons**
- ✔ **Word Blending**
- ✔ **Word Building**
- ✔ **Decoding/Phonics lessons in Grades 2–6**
- ✔ **Additional Support Activities to reteach and extend**

READING ALOUD

Reading aloud to students contributes to their motivation, comprehension, vocabulary, fluency, knowledge base, literary understanding, familiarity with academic and literary terms, sense of community, enjoyment, and perhaps to a lifetime love of literature.

Sharing and responding to books during read-aloud time helps develop communication and oral language skills and improves comprehension. Literature that is read aloud to students serves as the vehicle for developing literary insights, including sensitivity to the sounds and structure of language. Students learn how powerful written language can be when fluent readers read aloud, interpreting a text through appropriate intonation, pacing, and phrasing. Comprehension skills are developed as students ask and answer questions and share their personal understandings. More advanced students who are read to and who get to talk with others about the best of written language learn both to discuss texts knowingly and to interpret their meanings expressively.

Reading aloud exposes students to more challenging texts than they may be able to read independently. Vocabulary development is fostered by listening to both familiar and challenging selections read aloud. Texts read aloud that are conceptually challenging for students can effectively improve language and comprehension abilities. Listening to challenging texts also exposes students to text structures and content knowledge that are more sophisticated than they may encounter in their own reading.

Listening skills and strategies are greatly improved during read-aloud activities. When students are encouraged to respond to stories read aloud, they tend to listen intently in order to recall relevant content. When students listen responsively and frequently to literature and expository texts, they hone critical-thinking skills that will serve them in many other contexts. In sum, reading aloud

- models fluent reading behavior
- builds students' vocabularies and concepts
- creates an interest in narrative structures
- builds background knowledge by introducing children to new ideas and concepts and by expanding on what is familiar to them
- exposes students to different text structures and genres, such as stories, alphabet books, poetry, and informational books

" Sharing literature with children increases their vocabulary and their understanding of how language works. Sharing stories, informational books, and poetry with children has become increasingly valued for its cognitive contribution to children's literary development. **"**

— **Dorothy S. Strickland**
The State of New Jersey
Professor of Reading,
Rutgers University

Q **How does *Trophies* provide opportunities for teachers to read aloud to their students?**

A *Trophies* provides a comprehensive collection of read-aloud selections for all levels of instruction. In kindergarten through grade 2, the program includes read-aloud options for students every day. In grades 3–6, a read-aloud selection accompanies every lesson in the *Teacher's Edition.* Read-aloud selections are available in *Read-Aloud Anthologies* for kindergarten through grade 2, the *Library Books Collections* for kindergarten through grade 6, and several other formats.

Q **What genres can students meet through read-alouds?**

A Students encounter a wide variety of literary genres and expository texts through read-aloud selections in all grades. Expository nonfiction becomes more prevalent as students move up the grades. Other genres include poetry, finger plays, folktales, myths, and narrative nonfiction. In lessons in grades 3-6 with focus skills, such as narrative elements or text structure, the genre of the read-aloud selection matches the genre of the reading selection.

Q **What kind of instruction accompanies read-aloud selections in *Trophies*?**

A In kindergarten and grade 1, the instruction that accompanies Sharing Literature includes three options:
- Build Concept Vocabulary
- Develop Listening Comprehension
- Listen and Respond

In grade 2, options include Develop Listening Comprehension, Set a Purpose, and Recognize Genre. The instructional focus in kindergarten centers on concepts about print and beginning narrative analysis (characters, setting, important events). As students move up the grades, they are taught more complex literary skills, such as following the structure of stories, recognizing their beginnings, middles, and endings, and even occasionally generating alternative endings. In grades 3–6, read-alouds also serve as a vehicle for exploring expository text structures.

Look for

- ✔ **Daily "Sharing Literature" activities in Kindergarten through Grade 2**
- ✔ **Read-aloud selections and instruction with every lesson in Grades 2–6**
- ✔ ***Library Books Collections* at all grades**
- ✔ ***Read-Aloud Anthologies* in Kindergarten through Grade 2**

COMPREHENSION

Reading comprehension is the complex process of constructing meaning from texts. Recent comprehension research has been guided by the idea that the process is strategic and interactive.

Comprehension is the construction of meaning through an interactive exchange of ideas between the text and the reader. Comprehension strategies are interactive processes that allow readers to monitor and self-assess how well they understand what they are reading. These processes include determining the purpose or purposes for reading, such as to obtain information or to be entertained. After the purpose is determined, readers activate prior knowledge about the content of the text and its structure. Research has shown that the more readers know about the content of a particular text, the more likely they will understand, integrate, and remember the new information. Familiarity with the genre or text structure also fosters comprehension.

Most students need explicit instruction in comprehension skills and strategies. Research shows that comprehension skills and strategies are necessary for student success and that they do not develop automatically in most students. Without explicit instruction and guidance, many readers fail to acquire automatic use of these skills and strategies and show little flexibility in applying them to understand a variety of texts. Research shows that poor readers who are directly taught a particular strategy do as well as good readers who have used the strategy spontaneously. Typically, direct instruction consists of

- an explanation of what the skill or strategy is and how it aids comprehension
- modeling how to use the skill or strategy
- working directly with students as they apply the skill or strategy, offering assistance as needed
- having students apply the skill or strategy independently and repeatedly

Students need extensive direct instruction, guidance, and cumulative practice until they can independently determine the method of constructing meaning that works for them.

Students need to learn strategies for comprehending a wide variety of texts, including both fiction and nonfiction. In kindergarten, students should be taught to understand narrative structure. They should learn to identify the beginning, middle, and ending of a story and other literary elements, such as characters and setting. Then they can use their knowledge of these elements to retell stories they have listened to. In first through third grade, readers deepen their knowledge of these narrative elements and interact with others as book discussants and literary meaning makers. They learn to use the specific language of literature study, such as *point of view* and *character trait*. By grades 4–6, students must have the skills, strategies, and knowledge of text structures to comprehend complex nonfiction texts, including those in the classroom content areas. Students need to be explicitly and systematically taught the organizational structure of expository text, e.g., compare/contrast, cause/effect, and main idea and details. These organizational structures should be taught systematically and reviewed cumulatively.

> **❝ One of the fundamental understandings about the nature of reading is that it is a constructive act. Specifically, a reader does not extract meaning from a page, but constructs meaning from information on the page and information already in his/her mind. ❞**
>
> — **Isabel L. Beck**
> **Professor of Education and Senior Scientist at the Learning Research and Development Center, University of Pittsburgh**

Q How does *Trophies* provide explicit instruction in comprehension?

A *Trophies* features systematic and explicit comprehension instruction grounded in current and confirmed research. Comprehension instruction in kindergarten focuses on helping students construct meaning from stories read to them. From the earliest grades, teachers guide students before, during, and after reading in the use of strategies to monitor comprehension. Guided comprehension questions ask students to apply a variety of comprehension skills and strategies appropriate to particular selections. Each tested skill is introduced, reinforced, assessed informally, retaught as needed, reviewed at least twice, and maintained throughout each grade level.

Q How does comprehension instruction in *Trophies* build through the grades?

A Comprehension instruction in *Trophies* is rigorous, developmental, and spiraled. Students gain increasingly sophisticated skills and strategies to help them understand texts successfully. In the instructional components of the earliest grades, emergent and beginning readers develop use of strategies as they respond to texts read by the teacher, and more advanced students begin to apply skills and strategies to texts they read themselves. Students demonstrate their comprehension through asking and answering questions, retelling stories, discussing characters, comparing stories, and making and confirming predictions. As students progress through the grades, they build upon their existing skills and read a more extensive variety of texts.

Q How is instruction in genres and text structures developed in the program?

A The foundation of *Trophies* is a wide variety of fiction and nonfiction selections, including many paired selections to promote reading across texts. Instruction in both the *Pupil Edition* and *Teacher's Edition* helps students develop a thorough understanding of genre characteristics and text structures. In kindergarten, students explore story elements, such as characters, setting, and important events. As students move up the grades, they analyze both literary elements and devices and expository organizational patterns, such as cause/effect and compare/contrast, to understand increasingly difficult texts.

Look for

✓ **Focus Strategies and Focus Skills**
✓ **Diagnostic Checks**
✓ **Additional Support Activities**
✓ **Guided Comprehension**
✓ **Strategies Good Readers Use**
✓ **Ongoing Assessment**
✓ **Comprehension Cards**

WHAT RESEARCH SAYS ABOUT

VOCABULARY

A large and flexible vocabulary is the hallmark of an educated person. The more words students acquire, the better chance they will have for success in reading, writing, and spelling.

Students acquire vocabulary knowledge through extensive reading in a variety of texts. The amount of reading students do in and out of school is a strong indicator of students' vocabulary acquisition. Research supports exposing students to rich language environments through listening to literature and reading a variety of genres independently. Their vocabulary knowledge grows when they hear stories containing unfamiliar words. As students progress through the grades, their reading of books and other materials contributes more significantly to vocabulary knowledge than viewing television, participating in conversations, or other typical oral language activities. In other words, increasing students' volume of reading is the best way to promote vocabulary growth.

Students need multiple encounters with key vocabulary words in order to improve comprehension. Current and confirmed research has shown that students need to encounter a word several times before it is known well enough to facilitate comprehension. Direct instruction in vocabulary has an important role here because learning words from context is far from automatic. After being introduced to new words, students need opportunities to see those words again in their reading and to develop their own uses for the words in a variety of different contexts, in relationship to other words, and both inside and outside of the classroom. For instruction to enhance comprehension, new words need to become a permanent part of students' repertoires, which means instruction must go well beyond providing information on word meanings.

Students can benefit from direct instruction in vocabulary strategies. Although estimates of vocabulary size and growth vary, children likely learn between 1,000 and 5,000 words per year—and the average child learns about 3,000 words. Since wide reading provides a significant source for increasing word knowledge, it is imperative that students learn key strategies to help them learn new words as they are encountered. Vocabulary strategies students should know by third grade include

- using a dictionary and other reference sources to understand the meanings of unknown words
- using context to determine the meanings of unfamiliar words
- learning about the relationships between words (synonyms, antonyms, and multiple-meaning words)
- exploring shades of meaning of words that are synonyms or near-synonyms
- using morphemic analysis—breaking words into meaning-bearing components, such as prefixes and roots

At grades 3 and above, morphemic analysis becomes an even more valuable dimension of vocabulary instruction. For example, learning just one root, *astro,* can help students unlock the meanings of such words as *astronaut, astronomy, astrology,* and *astrological.*

> **Research on vocabulary shows that for learners to come to know words in a meaningful way, they need to engage with word meanings and build habits of attending to words and exploring their uses in thoughtful and lively ways.**
>
> **— Margaret C. McKeown**
> **Research Scientist**
> **Learning Research and Development Center,**
> **University of Pittsburgh**

Q How does *Trophies* provide exposure to a wide variety of texts?

A *Trophies* provides students with a wealth of opportunities to read a rich variety of texts. The *Pupil Editions,* the nucleus of the program in grades 1–6, feature a variety of high-quality literature selections that help students build vocabulary. *Trophies* also provides students with extensive reading opportunities through such components as these:

- *Big Books* (kindergarten and grade 1)
- *Read-Aloud Anthologies* (kindergarten through grade 2)
- *Library Books Collections* (kindergarten through grade 6)
- *Books for All Learners* (grades 1–6)
- *Intervention Readers* (grades 2–6)
- *Teacher's Edition* Read-Aloud Selections (grades 2–6)

Q How does the program provide multiple exposures to key vocabulary?

A Students are given many rich exposures to key vocabulary through the following program features:

- Vocabulary in context on *Teaching Transparencies*
- *Pupil Edition* and *Teacher's Edition* Vocabulary Power pages
- *Pupil Edition* main selections
- Word Study pages of the *Teacher's Edition* (grades 3–6)
- Additional Support Activities in the *Teacher's Edition*
- *Practice Books*
- *Books for All Learners*
- *Intervention Readers*

Q How does *Trophies* facilitate the teaching of vocabulary-learning strategies?

A Lessons include explicit teaching and modeling of vocabulary strategies. Specific lessons in both the *Pupil Edition* and *Teacher's Edition* provide direct instruction that helps enable students to increase their vocabulary every time they read. Strategies include using a dictionary, using context to determine word meaning, and understanding word structures and word relationships.

Look for

- ✔ **Building Background and Vocabulary**
- ✔ *Big Book* lessons
- ✔ **Listening Comprehension**
- ✔ **Word Study (grades 3–6)**
- ✔ **Lessons on word relationships and word structure (grades 3–6)**
- ✔ **Additional Support Activities**

FLUENCY

Research recognizes fluency as a strong indicator of efficient and proficient reading. A fluent reader reads with accuracy at an appropriate rate, attending to phrasing. When the reading is oral, it reflects a speech-like pace.

Oral fluency is reading with speed, accuracy, and prosody—meaning that the reader uses stress, pitch, and juncture of spoken language. Researchers have repeatedly demonstrated the relationship between fluency and reading comprehension. If a reader must devote most of his or her cognitive attention to pronouncing words, comprehension suffers. It follows then that students who read fluently can devote more attention to meaning and thus increase their comprehension. This is why oral reading fluency is an important goal of reading instruction, especially in the elementary grades. Word recognition must be automatic—freeing cognitive resources for comprehending text. If word recognition is labored, cognitive resources are consumed by decoding, leaving little or no resources for interpretation. In kindergarten and at the beginning of grade 1, oral reading may sound less like speech because students are still learning to decode and to identify words. Nevertheless, with appropriate support, text that "fits," and time to practice, students soon begin to read simple texts in a natural, more fluent, manner. By the beginning of grade 2, many students have come to enjoy the sounds of their own voices reading. They choose to read and reread with the natural sounds of spoken language and have few interruptions due to inadequate word attack or word recognition problems.

Fluent readers can
- recognize words automatically
- group individual words into meaningful phrases
- apply strategies rapidly to identify unknown words
- determine where to place emphasis or pause to make sense of a text

Fluency can be developed through directed reading practice, opportunities for repeated reading, and other instructional strategies. The primary method to improve fluency is directed reading practice in accessible texts. Practice does not replace instruction; it provides the reader opportunity to gain speed and accuracy within manageable text. One form of directed reading practice is repeated reading, which gives a developing reader more time and chances with the same text.

Repeated reading
- provides practice reading words in context
- produces gains in reading rate, accuracy, and comprehension
- helps lower-achieving readers

" Children gain reading fluency when they can read at a steady rate, recognizing words accurately and achieving correctness in phrasing and intonation. "

— Nancy Roser
Professor, Language and Literacy Studies
The University of Texas at Austin

Q How does *Trophies* teach and assess oral reading fluency?

A Toward developing fluent readers, *Trophies* provides explicit, systematic phonics instruction to build word recognition skills that enable students to become efficient decoders. (See the Phonics section of these pages for more information.) *Trophies* also provides the following tools that enables teachers to assess student progress on an ongoing basis:

- Oral reading passages in the back of each *Teacher's Edition* (Grades 2–6)
- Guidelines to help teachers use these passages (Grades 2–6)
- *Oral Reading Fluency Assessment*

Q How does *Trophies* provide intervention for students who are not developing oral reading fluency at an appropriate pace?

A In the grades 2–6 Intervention Resource Kit, every day of instruction includes a fluency builder activity. Students are assigned repeated readings with cumulative texts. These readings begin with word lists, expand to include multiple sentences, and eventually become extended self-selected passages. Fluency performance-assessment activities are also provided in the *Intervention Teacher's Guides*.

Q How does *Trophies* provide opportunities for repeated readings?

A In grades 1–6, the Rereading for Fluency features offer a wide variety of engaging activities that have students reread with a focus on expression, pacing, and intonation. These activities include

- **Echo Reading**—Students repeat (echo) what the teacher reads aloud.
- **Choral Reading**—Students read aloud with the teacher simultaneously.
- **Repeated Reading**—The teacher models, and students reread several times until fluency is gained.
- **Readers Theatre**—Students assume roles and read them aloud from the text.

Look for

- ✓ Rereading for Fluency
- ✓ Oral reading passages in the *Teacher's Edition*
- ✓ *Oral Reading Fluency Assessment*
- ✓ *Intervention Teacher's Guides*

ASSESSMENT

Assessment is integral to instruction. By choosing the appropriate assessment tools and methods, you can find out where your students are instructionally and plan accordingly.

Assessment is the process of collecting information in order to make instructional decisions about students. Good decisions require good information and to provide this information, assessment of students and their learning must be continuous. Because the reading process is composed of many complex skills, such as comprehension, word attack, and synthesis of information, no one assessment tool can evaluate completely all aspects of reading. Teachers need to gather information about their students in many ways, both formally and informally. Assessment helps them plan instruction, and ongoing assessments throughout the instructional process should guide their decisions and actions.

Assessment must systematically inform instruction and help teachers differentiate instruction. The first tool the classroom teacher requires is an entry-level assessment instrument to identify students' instructional level and potential for participating in grade-level instruction. This diagnostic instrument should be sensitive to gaps and strengths in student learning. After placement, teachers need differentiation strategies that are flexible and that can be easily adapted according to continual monitoring of student progress.

Assessments for monitoring progress should be used to determine ongoing priorities for instruction. The use of both formal and informal tools and strategies, including formative and summative assessments, provides a comprehensive picture of students' achievement as they progress through an instructional program. Informal assessments encourage teachers to observe students as they read, write, and discuss. These assessments provide immediate feedback and allow teachers to quickly determine which students are having difficulty and need additional instruction and practice. Formal assessments provide opportunities for teachers to take a more focused look at how students are progressing. Whether formal or informal, monitoring instruments and activities should be

- frequent
- ongoing
- easy to score and interpret

Teachers should be provided with clear options for monitoring and clear pathways for providing intervention and enrichment as needed. Less frequent summative assessments may be used to gauge long-term growth.

Student progress needs to be communicated to parents and guardians on a regular basis. As students become more accountable for their learning through standards-based testing, teachers are becoming more accountable not only to administrators but also to families. A complete instructional program should offer means for teachers to communicate with families about how their students are progressing and how families can contribute to

> " Knowing how well a student can use literacy skills such as reading, writing, listening, and speaking is vital to effective instruction. "
>
> — **Roger Farr**
> Chancellor's Professor and Director of the Center for Innovation in Assessment, Indiana University, Bloomington

Q How does *Trophies* integrate entry-level group and individual assessments with instruction?

A The *Placement and Diagnostic Assessment* provides an overview of specific diagnostic information about prerequisite skills for each grade level. In addition, *Reading and Language Skills Assessment* pretests can be used to determine whether students need additional instruction and practice in phonics, comprehension skills, vocabulary, writing, and writing conventions.

Q What monitoring instruments are included with *Trophies*?

A Formative assessments that facilitate monitoring student progress include

- Diagnostic Checks at point of use for immediate assessment of understanding, with follow-up Additional Support Activities in the *Teacher's Edition*
- Ongoing Assessment to assess and model the use of reading strategies, in the *Teacher's Edition*
- *Intervention Assessment Book*
- Performance Assessment activities in the *Teacher's Edition*
- *End-of-Selection Tests* to monitor students' comprehension of each selection

In each theme's *Teacher's Edition*, the Theme Assessment to Plan Instruction section provides a clear road map for using assessment to adapt instruction to student needs.

Q What other assessment instruments are used in *Trophies*?

A The *Reading and Language Skills Assessment*, which includes posttests for end-of-theme assessment and Mid-Year and End-of-Year Tests, provides information about students' mastery of reading skills. Other assessment instruments in *Trophies* include

- *Holistic Assessment*, which uses authentic, theme-related passages and provides a more global, holistic evaluation of students' reading and writing ability
- *Oral Reading Fluency Assessment*, which monitors accuracy and rate
- *Assessment Handbook* (Kindergarten)

Look for

In the *Teacher's Edition*
- ✔ **Diagnostic Checks**
- ✔ **Ongoing Assessment**
- ✔ **Performance Assessment**
- ✔ **Theme Assessment to Plan Instruction**

Other Components
- ✔ ***Placement* and *Diagnostic Assessments***
- ✔ ***Reading and Language Skills Assessment* (Pretests and Posttests)**
- ✔ ***Holistic Assessment***
- ✔ ***Oral Reading Fluency Assessment***
- ✔ ***Assessment Handbook* (Kindergarten)**

WRITING

Good writing skills are critical both to students'
academic achievement and to their future success
in society.

Writing instruction should incorporate explicit modeling and practice in the conventions of written English. All students can benefit from systematic instruction and practice in spelling, grammar, usage, mechanics, and presentation skills, such as handwriting and document preparation. Mastering these conventions enables students to communicate their ideas and information clearly and effectively.

- In kindergarten, children should use their growing knowledge of language structure and the conventions of print to begin expressing their ideas through words and pictures and putting these ideas into writing, with words spelled phonetically.

- In grades 1–3, students should continue to transfer their developing reading skills to writing conventions by using their knowledge of word structure and phonics to spell new words. They should learn and apply the fundamentals of grammar, mechanics, and sentence structure.

- In grades 4–6, instruction should build advanced spelling, grammar, and mechanics skills and should apply them in student writing of narratives, descriptions, and other extended compositions. Students should be systematically taught to apply writing conventions in purposeful writing activities.

Students should learn about and practice the process skills that good writers use. Many students do not realize, until they are told, that most stories and articles are not written in one sitting. Good writers plan, revise, rewrite, and rethink during the process of writing. Instruction in writing processes can spring from author features and interviews with the writers whose works students are reading. The teacher's modeling of effective prewriting, drafting, revising, proofreading, and publishing techniques should build upon this understanding. Particular attention should systematically be paid to revision strategies such as adding, deleting, clarifying, and rearranging text. Students should apply these strategies to their own work repeatedly and should learn new techniques gradually and cumulatively.

Systematic instruction in writer's craft skills should be applied to the process. Students should be taught that, whatever the form of their writing, they must determine a clear focus, organize their ideas, use effective word choice and sentence structures, and express their own viewpoint. These writer's craft skills should be taught through focused exercises and writing tasks and should be reinforced cumulatively in lessons that teach the elements of longer writing forms.

> **Effective writing is both an art and a science. The ability to generate interesting ideas and a pleasing style characterizes the art side; mastering the craft and its conventions characterizes the science side. Good instruction judiciously attends to both.**
>
> — **Dorothy S. Strickland**
> The State of New Jersey
> Professor of Reading,
> Rutgers University

Q **How does *Trophies* provide instruction and practice in the conventions of written English?**

A *Trophies* provides systematic, explicit instruction and abundant practice in spelling, grammar, usage, and mechanics in daily, easy-to-use lessons. Transparencies, activities, and practice sheets are provided for modeling and practice. Presentation skills are also formally taught, with an emphasis on handwriting at the lower grades. Spelling instruction, especially at the primary grades, is closely linked to phonics instruction. All skills of conventions are applied in purposeful writing activities.

Q **How does *Trophies* teach the process of writing?**

A From the earliest grades, students using *Trophies* learn that good writers plan and revise their writing. Students are guided through the prewriting, drafting, revising, and proofreading stages with models, practice activities, graphic organizers, and checklists. Instruction in presentation skills, such as handwriting and speaking, guides the publishing stage. Teacher rubrics for evaluation are provided at point of use, and reproducible student rubrics are provided in the back of the *Teacher's Edition*.

Q **How does *Trophies* apply writer's craft instruction to the writing process?**

A In kindergarten, students begin to write sentences and brief narratives about familiar experiences. Students also engage in shared and interactive writing in kindergarten through grade 2. In grades I and 2, instruction in story grammar and sentence types becomes more sophisticated, with students learning about and applying one component, such as capitalization, at a time. In grades 2–6, explicit writer's craft lessons are built into the writing strand and follow this format:

- Weeks I and 2 of the unit present writer's craft skills, such as organizing, choosing words, and writing effective sentences. Students complete targeted exercises and apply the craft in relatively brief writing forms.
- Weeks 3 and 4 present longer writing forms, emphasizing the steps of the writing process. The writer's craft skills learned in Weeks I and 2 are applied in longer compositions.
- In grades 3–6, Week 5 presents a timed writing test in which students apply what they have learned.

Look for

- ✓ Writer's Craft lessons
- ✓ Writing Process lessons
- ✓ Timed or Tested Writing lessons
- ✓ 5-day grammar and spelling lessons
- ✓ Traits of good writing

LISTENING AND SPEAKING

Increasingly, young people must comprehend, and are expected to create, messages that are oral and visual rather than strictly written. Listening and speaking skills are essential to achievement in both reading and writing.

Listening to narratives, poetry, and nonfiction texts builds thinking and language skills that students need for success in reading and writing. The domains of the language arts (listening, speaking, reading, and writing) are closely connected. Listening instruction and speaking instruction are critical scaffolds that support reading comprehension, vocabulary knowledge, and oral communication skills. Classroom instruction must be focused on these skills and must also strategically address the needs of students with limited levels of language experience or whose language experiences are primarily in languages other than English.

Listening instruction and speaking instruction should progress developmentally through the grades. In the primary grades, instruction should focus on

- listening to and retelling stories, with an emphasis on story grammar (setting, characters, and important events)
- explicit modeling of standard English structures, with frequent opportunities to repeat sentences and recite rhymes and songs
- brief oral presentations about familiar topics and experiences
- developing familiarity with academic and literary terms

As students move up the grades, they should develop increasingly sophisticated listening and speaking skills, including the more complex production skills. By grades 4–6, students should be increasingly capable of

- delivering both narrative and expository presentations using a range of narrative and rhetorical devices
- modeling their own presentations on effective text structures they have analyzed in their reading
- orally responding to literature in ways that demonstrate advanced understanding and insight
- supporting their interpretations with facts and specific examples
- interpreting and using verbal and nonverbal messages
- analyzing oral and visual messages, purposes, and persuasive techniques

❝ Oral response activities encourage critical thinking and allow students to bring their individuality to the process of responding to literature. ❞

— **Hallie Kay Yopp**
Professor
Department of Elementary Bilingual
and Reading Education,
California State University, Fullerton

Q **How does *Trophies* provide rich listening experiences that build understanding of language structures and texts?**

A From the very first day of kindergarten through the end of grade 6, *Trophies* provides abundant and varied texts, support, and modeling for listening instruction. With resources such as *Big Books, Read-Aloud Anthologies,* and Audiotext of the reading selections, the teacher has every type of narrative and expository text available. *Trophies* also provides direct instruction and engaging response activities so that teachers can use each listening selection to its full advantage. The *English-Language Learners Resource Kit* provides additional opportunities for students with special needs to develop an understanding of English language structure, concept vocabulary and background, and listening comprehension skills.

Q **How does *Trophies* develop listening through the grades?**

A Listening is developed through the Sharing Literature features in kindergarten through grade 2 with such options as Build Concept Vocabulary, Develop Listening Comprehension, and Listen and Respond and through the *Read-Aloud Anthologies.* In grades 3–6, read-alouds serve as a vehicle for setting a purpose for listening and develop listening comprehension and listening strategies.

Q **How does *Trophies* provide instruction in speaking and in making presentations?**

A *Trophies* provides instruction to guide students in making both narrative and expository presentations. In kindergarten, each lesson offers formal and informal speaking opportunities through the Share Time feature. In grades 1 and 2, speaking activities are included in the Rereading for Fluency and in the Wrap-Up sections of the lesson. The Morning Message feature in kindergarten through grade 2 provides additional informal speaking opportunities. In grades 3–6, presentation skills become more sophisticated. Students are asked to make such presentations as extended oral reports, multimedia presentations, debates, and persuasive speeches.

Look for

- ✓ **Develop Listening Comprehension**
- ✓ **Daily "Sharing Literature" activities (Kindergarten through Grade 2)**
- ✓ **Read-Aloud selections and instruction with every lesson (Grades 2–6)**
- ✓ **Morning Message (Kindergarten–Grade 2)**
- ✓ **Author's Chair presentations (Kindergarten–Grade 2)**
- ✓ **Rereading for Fluency**
- ✓ **Listening and Speaking Lessons (Grades 3–6)**
- ✓ **Presentation Rubrics (Grades 2–6)**
- ✓ ***Read-Aloud Anthologies* (Kindergarten–Grade 2)**

WHAT RESEARCH SAYS ABOUT

RESEARCH AND INFORMATION SKILLS

Today's increasing amount of accessible information and ideas mandates an explicit approach to research and information skills and strategies.

Information is more widely available to the general public than ever before, and having the skills and strategies to effectively access and produce information is increasingly important. Evaluating and producing electronically transmitted information is becoming a basic literacy skill, as well as a skill that can lead to a more rewarding working life. Students who do not receive instruction in information skills are at a clear disadvantage. The goal of such instruction should be to prepare students to carry these skills into many areas so that students can be independent seekers, consumers, and providers of information throughout their lives.

Instruction in research and information skills should begin at an early age. By grade 2, students should be learning to choose reference sources for specific purposes, such as to clarify word meanings or to find colorful, exact words for their own writing. In grade 3, students should refine their dictionary skills and become familiar with the structure of other reference sources, such as atlases and encyclopedias. In grade 4 and above, students should become more proficient with

- using a variety of print and electronic information media, such as newspapers, almanacs, library catalogs, and other online sources
- basic keyboarding and word processing skills
- computer usage skills, such as efficient Internet searching and document creation
- using tables of contents, indexes, and other document features to locate information
- taking notes efficiently
- evaluating the quality of information
- finding information in a library
- using reference sources as an aid to writing

As students move up the grades, they should learn to produce and deliver increasingly lengthy, well-researched informational reports. Because the language arts domains (reading, writing, listening, and speaking) are closely interrelated, the text structures students learn through their reading become structures they can use to effectively present their own research. Skills such as identifying the main idea of a nonfiction selection should be explicitly incorporated into writing assignments at the upper grades. Students should be able to compose, revise, edit, and publish their research findings by using a computer. Other skills for students in the upper grades include substantive inquiry, framing questions to develop the research logically, identifying and securing multiple reference sources, analyzing and synthesizing information, and summarizing and evaluating the research results.

Q How does *Trophies* provide instruction in using reference sources, including computer-based resources?

A Direct instruction is provided through explicit skill lessons. Instruction includes such skills as recognizing authoritative sources and evaluating information. These lessons include

- Using a Dictionary
- Locating Information: Online Information
- Locating Information: Text Features/Book Parts
- Locating Information: Newspapers, Magazines, and Reference Sources
- Search Techniques

Q What technological resources are available for use by students with *Trophies*?

A *The Learning Site* (www.harcourtschool.com) offers, among many other features, motivating, interactive activities that challenge students to practice and apply skills taught in the *Pupil Edition* and *Teacher's Edition.*

Other resources available for students include

- *Writing Express™ CD-ROMs* (activities that provide reinforcement of language and writing skills)
- *Mission: Comprehension™ Reading Skills Practice* (practice and reinforcement of comprehension skills)
- *Phonics Express™ CD-ROM* (captivating games and activities that reinforce phonics skills)
- *Media Literacy and Communication Skills Package™* (a set of videotapes and accompanying Teacher's Guides that reinforce listening, speaking, viewing and presentation skills)

Q How are students taught to develop research reports and other informational projects?

A In grades 1–2, the Making Connections sections in the *Pupil Edition* and the Cross-Curricular Centers in the *Teacher's Editions* offer activities that require students to gather and present. In grades 3–6, students engage in a full theme's worth of instruction in all stages of writing a research report, including gathering information, note-taking, outlining, drafting, revising, and publishing. Students also have the opportunity to use information and research skills to complete a theme project, which involves formulating research questions and recording and presenting their research findings.

Look for

- ✓ Skill lessons with Teaching Transparencies
- ✓ Research Report Writing lessons
- ✓ Theme Projects
- ✓ Presentation Rubrics
- ✓ Technology Integrated with the lesson plans

REACHING ALL LEARNERS

Students come to school with diverse experiences and language backgrounds. Teachers, who are charged with providing universal access to high-quality instruction, require specially designed plans and materials to help all students meet or exceed grade-level standards.

Curriculum and instruction must be carefully planned to provide for students who need varying levels of intervention and challenge. Students require additional instruction, practice, and extension at different times and in different degrees. Some students need occasional reteaching and slight modifications in pacing, while others are at greater risk and require more intensive intervention. Research shows that students with learning difficulties need more review and practice to perform a new task automatically. Instruction should cumulatively integrate simpler or previously learned tasks with newer, more complex activities. In addition, research shows the following:

- Reading difficulties can stem from inaccuracy in identifying words.
- Intervention should be geared toward a student's level of reading development.
- Diagnostic testing results should show what students know and what they need to know; frequent assessment is critical.
- Instruction should be direct and explicit.

Curriculum and instruction must be structured to meet the needs of English-language learners. The 2000 U.S. Census confirmed what many educators already knew: more and more students do not speak English as their first language. Widely ranging levels of English proficiency in mainstream classrooms present special challenges and opportunities for teachers. Depending on their level of English acquisition and their grade placement, English-language learners need varying degrees of additional support in areas such as oral language, English phonology, vocabulary, background information, and the academic language of school.

Students who already meet or exceed grade-level expectations need opportunities for enrichment or acceleration. They need to be challenged by vocabulary extension study and exposure to sophisticated literature in a variety of genres. Students may also be encouraged to carry out investigations that extend their learning. Such activities should promote sustained investigative skills: raising questions, researching answers, and organizing information. Several research studies have shown the importance of setting high standards for advanced learners. An instructional program that clearly provides for differentiation at a variety of levels can be the tool teachers need to provide universal access to high-level standards.

> **"** In the process of helping students learn, we want to support them in discovering that each person is unique and has a unique contribution to make towards creating a better world for all. **"**
>
> — **Alma Flor Ada**
> Director of Doctoral Studies in the
> International Multicultural Program
> University of San Francisco
>
> — **F. Isabel Campoy**
> Former President, Association of
> Spanish Professionals in the USA

Q **How does *Trophies* provide differentiated instruction at a variety of levels?**

A *Trophies* was designed to accommodate a diverse student population, with tiers of differentiation for different needs. Diagnostic Checks, with brief activities, are positioned at point of use within each lesson in the *Teacher's Edition* so that specific needs of students can be identified and addressed. Additional Support Activities, tied closely to the lessons, are provided for further differentiation. The three types of activities address below-level readers, advanced students, and English-language learners. In addition, Alternative Teaching Strategies are provided for students who perform below level on the *Reading and Language Skills Assessments*. The *Library Books Collections* and the *Books for All Learners* also provide students at all levels with a wealth of reading opportunities in a variety of genres.

Q **What additional support does *Trophies* provide?**

A An *Intervention Resource Kit* and an *English-Language Learners Resource Kit* are available for students with greater needs.

Both kits
- align closely with the core program
- provide rigorous daily lessons
- provide abundant cumulative, spiraled practice

For below-level readers, the *Intervention Resource Kit* preteaches and reteaches the same skills and concepts that are taught in the core program. The *English-Language Learners Resource Kit* builds background, vocabulary and concepts, academic language, comprehension, and language arts. Finally, to guide teachers in making instructional decisions, *Trophies* provides a complete assessment program, with instruments for entry-level assessment, monitoring of progress, and summative assessment. (See the Assessment section of these pages for more information.)

Look for

✓ **Reaching All Learners**
✓ **Diagnostic Checks**
✓ **Additional Support Activities**
✓ **Practice pages for all levels**
✓ *Books for All Learners*
✓ *Intervention Resource Kit*
✓ *English-Language Learners Resource Kit*
✓ *Library Books Collections*
✓ *Placement and Diagnostic Assessments*

The task of managing the classroom is becoming increasingly complex. Teachers are seeking to maximize instructional effectiveness for students with a diverse range of skills and backgrounds.

Classroom management is a critical variable related to student achievement. Research shows that the more time teachers spend dealing with student behavior and interruptions in instruction, the more student achievement suffers. A classroom environment that promotes student growth and learning results from making effective decisions about the organization and scheduling of instruction and the physical arrangement of the classroom.

Effective organization includes differentiating instruction to engage all students in instructional-level activities. Grouping strategies are important for addressing diverse needs, but grouping must never be treated as an aim in itself. Flexible grouping can help ensure that all students meet instructional goals, and it can be effective in helping students participate and contribute in a learning environment. Grouping should be fluid and temporary, varying according to individual students' progress and interests and should allow time for students to function independently and be responsible for their own work. The types of instruction that are most successful in the major grouping patterns include

Whole Group
- Sharing literature
- Developing concepts
- Providing modeling
- Presenting new knowledge

Small Group
- Developing skills
- Practicing processes
- Collaborating on projects
- Providing challenge activities

After flexible work groups are established, effective classroom organization should focus on scheduling classroom activities and creating a classroom arrangement that facilitates learning. Initially, teachers might establish one or two learning centers based on tasks that are familiar to students. Then teachers can develop other centers and routines as needed. Before beginning a routine, teachers should introduce students to the procedures for using each area, ensuring that students understand what they are to do and how much time they should spend in each area. A rotation schedule should be established so that students can easily move from one area to another as tasks are completed. Helping students become familiar with schedules and routines enables the teacher to devote more time to individual and small-group instruction.

> **The organization of the classroom should provide students with many opportunities to share with teachers and other students the things they are reading and writing.**
>
> **— Roger Farr**
> Chancellor's Professor and Director of the Center for Innovation in Assessment, Indiana University, Bloomington

Q How can teachers keep other students engaged in meaningful experiences while providing instruction to students with special needs?

A *Trophies* provides an abundance of productive materials and ideas for independent and small-group work

- Managing the Classroom sections in the back of the *Teacher's Editions* that provide clear instructions in arranging the classroom with centers or stations, using a Work Board with center icons to help organize routines and schedules, and tracking student progress.
- Classroom Management and Reading and Writing Routines sections in the *Teacher's Editions* (grades 1–2) that provide suggestions for individual, whole-group, and small-group activities.
- Cross-Curricular Centers and Stations with pacing suggestions to regulate student participation
- Lesson-specific Workboards to help teachers manage groups and individuals simultaneously
- Integration of content from social studies, science, and other content areas
- *Books for All Learners* to allow students to read independently at their own level
- Practice pages for students with diverse skills and language backgrounds
- Theme Projects for extended group work
- Comprehension Cards, *Library Books Collections,* and other resources to facilitate group and independent reading

Q How does *Trophies* help teachers manage its instructional pathways for classrooms with diverse learners?

A *Trophies* provides a clear, manageable system of diagnostic assessment checkpoints, ongoing formal assessment and performance-based opportunities, and instructional pathways for teachers to follow based on results. In addition to easy-to-use lesson planners that include suggested pacing, the system provides

- Diagnostic Checks and customized activities at point of use
- Additional Support Activities to reinforce, reteach, and extend key concepts in every lesson
- *Intervention Resource Kits* and *English-Language Learners Resource Kits* for more intensive instruction
- Alternative Teaching Strategies for additional options to modify instruction

For more information, see Theme Assessment to Plan Instruction in each *Teacher's Edition.*

Look for

- ✓ Diagnostic Checks
- ✓ Cross-Curricular Centers or Stations
- ✓ Work Boards
- ✓ *Books for All Learners*
- ✓ *Library Books Collections*
- ✓ Practice pages
- ✓ Theme Projects
- ✓ Comprehension Cards
- ✓ Managing the Classroom

Contents

Theme 9: Around the Town

Consonants _Vv, Jj_
Short Vowel _Ee_

Theme 10: Neighborhood Helpers

Consonants _Yy, Zz_

Theme 11: Exploring Our Surroundings

Consonant *Qq*

Short Vowel *Uu*

Theme 12: Under the Ocean

Short Vowels *Aa, Ee, Ii, Oo, Uu*

Reference Materials

Additional Support Activities

Theme Resources

Additional Resources

Around the Town

Children learn about the different places in a town. They will discover how people join together to help one another in their communities.

Theme Resources

READING MATERIALS

Big Book

◀ **The Shape of Things**
by Dayle Ann Dodds illustrated by Julie Lacome

Library Books

◀ **Benny's Pennies** by Pat Brisson
illustrated by Bob Barner

◀ **Good-Bye Hello**
by Barbara Shook Hazen
illustrated by Michael Bryant

Big Book of Rhymes and Songs

◀ **Down by the Bay**

◀ **Old Mister Rabbit**

Read-Aloud Anthology

◀ **The Shoemaker and the Elves**
retold by Anne Rockwell

◀ **Mr. Backward**
by Douglas Florian

◀ **My Pet Spider**
by Jane Simon

◀ **Caps for Sale** by Esphyr Slobodkina

◀ **Sing a Song of People** by Lois Lenski

Independent Readers

▲ **The Lost Dog**   ▲ **Mack and Will Are Friends**   ▲ **A Good Home**

PHONICS

Theme 9 Practice Book

Phonics Practice Book

Decodable Books

▲ **A Big, Big Van**   ▲ **Come In**   ▲ **Hop In!**

Alphabet Patterns

van, jar, egg
pages T10–T12

Phonics Express™ CD-ROM
Level A

Visit *The Learning Site:* www.harcourtschool.com

TEACHING TOOLS

Big Alphabet Cards

Vv, Jj, Ee

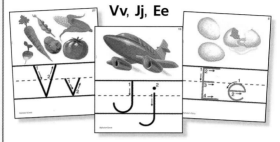

Letter and Sound Charts

Charts 21, 5, and 12

Letter and Sound Chart Sentence Strips

21, 5, 12

Vulture packed vegetables.

High-Frequency Word Cards

look, come

Picture/Word Cards

Teacher's Resource Book

pages 71, 55, 62

Oo-pples and Boo-noo-noos

English-Language Learners Kit

Intervention Kit

MANIPULATIVES

Tactile Letter Cards

v j e

Write-On/Wipe-Off Board Letters and Sounds Place Mat

Word Builder and Word Builder Cards

j e t

Magnetic Letters

Aa Bb Cc

ASSESSMENT

Assessment Handbook

Group Inventory

Theme 9 Test

Big Book ▶

Library Book ▶

Week 1

Week 2

	Week 1	Week 2

• **Sharing Literature**
• **Listening Comprehension**
	Big Book: *The Shape of Things*
	Library Book: *Benny's Pennies*
	Read Aloud-Anthology:
	   "The Shoemaker and the Elves"
	   " Mr. Backward"
		Big Book: *The Shape of Things*
		Library Book: *Good-Bye Hello*
		Read-Aloud Anthology: *"My Pet Spider"*
		Big Book of Rhymes and Songs:
		   "Down by the Bay"

• **Phonemic Awareness** • **Phonics** • **High-Frequency Words**	**Consonant *Vv* T** **Consonant *Jj* T** **Review Consonants *Jj, Vv* T** **High-Frequency Words** look, come **T**	**Short Vowel Ee T** **Blending /e/ - /t/** **Words with /e/ and /t/**
• **Reading**	**Decodable Book 7:** *A Big, Big Van* **Independent Reader 24:** *The Lost Dog*	**Decodable Book 8:** *Come In* **Independent Reader 25:** *Mack and Will Are Friends*

• **Writing**	**Shared Writing**
	   Story
	Interactive Writing
	   List
	   Chart
	Independent Writing
	   Gift
	   Family
		Shared Writing
		   Instructions
		Interactive Writing
		   New Verse
		Independent Writing
		   Description
		   Sentence

• **Cross-Curricular Centers**	🎨 **Art**
	   Shapes of Our Town
	🌐 **Math**
	   Let's Go Shopping
	🎨 **Art**
	   Design Shoes
	👑 **Manipulatives**
	   Long and Short
	🔤 **Letters and Words**
	   Letter Guess
		👑 **Manipulatives**
		   Building Puzzles
		🔤 **Letters and Words**
		   Scrambled Eggs
		🔬 **Science**
		   Spider Prints
		🔤 **Letters and Words**
		   Build Words
		✏️ **Writing**
		   "Look What We Can Do" Books

T = tested skill

Library Book ▶

Week 3

Big Book: *The Shape of Things*

Library Book: *Good-bye Hello*

Read-Aloud Anthology: *"Caps For Sale"* *"Sing a Song of People"*

Big Book of Rhymes and Songs: *"Old Mister Rabbit"*

Review Consonant *Nn*
  Short Vowel *Ee* T

Blending /e/ - /n/

Words with /e/ and /n/

Review Blending /e/ - /n/

Decodable Book 9: *Hop In!*

Independent Reader 26: *A Good Home*

Interactive Writing
  Writing Process

 Block
  Build Two Different Neighborhoods

Math
  Cap Patterns

Sand and Water
  Build a Sand Town

Science
  What Is It?

Literacy
  Favorite Books

Theme Organizer
Half-Day Kindergarten

Use the following chart to help organize your half-day kindergarten schedule. Choose independent activities as time allows during your day.

ORAL LANGUAGE

Morning Message
Phonemic Awareness
Sharing Literature
- Big Book: *The Shape of Things*
- Library Book: *Benny's Pennies*
- Library Book: *Good-Bye Hello*
- Read-Aloud Anthology
- Big Book of Rhymes and Songs

LEARNING TO READ

Phonics
Decodable Books 7–9
- *A Big, Big Van*
- *Come In*
- *Hop In!*

High-Frequency Words

Independent Readers 24–26
- *The Lost Dog*
- *Mack and Will Are Friends*
- *A Good Home*

LANGUAGE ARTS

Shared Writing
Interactive Writing
Independent Writing
Writing Every Day

INDEPENDENT ACTIVITIES

Sharing Literature
  Respond to Literature
Phonics
  Independent Practice
  Handwriting
  Practice Book pages
High-Frequency Words
  Independent Practice
  Practice Book pages

About the
Authors and Illustrators

Dayle Ann Dodds

Author of *The Shape of Things*

Dayle Ann Dodds was inspired to write *The Shape of Things* while helping out in a kindergarten class. Ms. Dodds is the author of several other children's books. She lives in Palo Alto, California.

Julie Lacome

Illustrator of *The Shape of Things*

Julie Lacome is the author-illustrator of *Walking Through the Jungle* and the illustrator of *A Was Once an Apple Pie.* She enjoyed using potato-cut printing in illustrating *The Shape of Things.*

Pat Brisson

Author of *Benny's Pennies*

Pat Brisson, in addition to being a writer, is a reference librarian and an avid gardener. She also travels to schools across the country for author visits. She lives in New Jersey with her husband and their four sons.

Bob Barner

Illustrator of *Benny's Pennies*

Bob Barner has illustrated many picture books, including *The Elevator/Escalator Book,* which he also wrote.

Barbara Shook Hazen

Author of *Good-Bye Hello*

Barbara Shook Hazen has published over two dozen books for children. She spends some of her time in New York City and some in the Berkshire Hills of Massachusetts.

Michael Bryant

Illustrator of *Good-Bye Hello*

Michael Bryant was raised in East Orange, New Jersey. The discovery of his love for art is credited to his mother's never-ending encouragement. Mr. Bryant resides in Newark, New Jersey, with his wife and two daughters.

Theme Assessment

After completing the theme, most children should show progress toward mastery of the following skills:

Concepts of Print
- ❏ Follow words from left to right and from top to bottom on the printed page.
- ❏ Recognize and name all the uppercase and lowercase letters of the alphabet.

Phonemic Awareness
- ❏ Blend vowel-consonant sounds orally to make words or syllables.
- ❏ Count the number of sounds in syllables and syllables in words.

Phonics and Decoding
- ❏ Match all consonant sounds and short-vowel sounds to appropriate letters.
- ❏ Read one-syllable and High-Frequency Words.
- ❏ Understand that as letters of words change, so do the sounds.

Vocabulary and High-Frequency Words
- ❏ Read High-Frequency Words *look* and *come.*
- ❏ Identify and sort common words in basic categories.
- ❏ Understand content words.

Comprehension
- ❏ Locate the title, name of author, and name of illustrator.
- ❏ Connect to life experiences the information and events in the text.
- ❏ Understand the main idea and details.

Literary Response
- ❏ Distinguish fantasy from realistic text.
- ❏ Recognize cause and effect.
- ❏ Identify characters and make judgments about them.

Writing
- ❏ Write consonant-vowel-consonant words.
- ❏ Write sentences using action words.

Listening and Speaking
- ❏ Share information about ideas, speaking audibly in complete, coherent sentences.
- ❏ Relate an experience or creative story in a logical sequence.

Assessment Options

Assessment Handbook
- Group Inventory
- Phonemic Awareness Inventory
- Theme Skills Assessment
- Concepts About Print Inventory
- Observational Checklists

Reaching All Learners

■ BELOW-LEVEL

Levels of Support

Point-of-use Notes in the Teacher's Edition

pp. 23, 35, 39, 43, 45, 49, 53, 55, 59, 61, 63, 65, 69, 73, 83, 87, 91, 95, 99, 103, 107, 109, 110, 115, 119, 129, 133, 137, 141, 149, 155, 161, 165

Additional Support Activities

High-Frequency Words:
pp. S2-S3

Comprehension and Skills:
pp. SI2-SI3, SI8-SI9

Phonemic Awareness:
pp. S4-S5, SI0-SI1, SI4-SI5

Phonics:
pp. S6-S7, S8-S9, SI6-SI7

Intervention Resources Kit

■ ENGLISH-LANGUAGE LEARNERS

Levels of Support

Point-of-use Notes in the Teacher's Edition

pp. 25, 35, 41, 43, 51, 53, 55, 59, 65, 71, 73, 85, 87, 93, 95, 99, 101, 107, 109, 117, 129, 139, 141, 149, 155, 163

Additional Support Activities

High-Frequency Words:
pp. S2-S3

Comprehension and Skills:
pp. SI2-SI3, SI8-SI9

Phonemic Awareness:
pp. S4-S5, SI0-SI1, SI4-SI5

Phonics:
pp. S6-S7, S8-S9, SI6-SI7

 Visit *The Learning Site!* at
www.harcourtschool.com
See Language Support activities

English-Language Learners Resources Kit

■ ADVANCED

Levels of Challenge

Point-of-use Notes in the Teacher's Edition

pp. 39, 51, 55, 59, 61, 63, 69, 73, 87, 91, 95, 99, 101, 103, 109, 115, 119, 129, 131, 133, 137, 145, 147, 149, 153, 155, 161, 163, 165

Additional Support Activities

High-Frequency Words:
pp. S2-S3

Comprehension and Skills:
pp. S12-S13, S18-S19

Phonemic Awareness:
pp. S4-S5, S10-S11, S14-S15

Phonics:
pp. S6-S7, S8-S9, S16-S17

Accelerated Instruction

Use higher-grade-level materials for accelerated instruction.

Theme Project, p. 12

Combination Classrooms
Buddy Reading

Have children spend their independent reading time reading with a partner. Try to include an advanced reader and a beginning reader in each pair, regardless of their age or grade. Encourage each pair to record titles of books they enjoyed.

Students with Special Needs
Minimizing Distractions

In order to keep children focused on the task at hand, situate them in an area of the classroom away from as much visual stimuli as possible. The fewer distractions children are confronted with, the better chance they will have of keeping their attention on what they are doing.

Recommended Reading

Below are suggestions for reading materials that will meet kindergarten children's diverse needs. Books that are on a child's level provide support for new skills. Advanced books give children an opportunity to stretch and challenge their reading potential. Read-aloud books are important because they expose children to story language and vocabulary.

■ BELOW-LEVEL

I Read Signs by Tana Hoban. Morrow, 1987. This wordless book introduces street signs and symbols.

Peter Spier's Rain by Peter Spier. Doubleday, 1982. A wonderful picture book with closely observed details of daily life and the magic of rain.

Town Mouse by Geraldine Dobbie. Todtri Productions, 1999. Set out on an adventure with the town mouse.

Alphabet City by Stephen T. Johnson. Viking, 1995. Make out the shapes of letters A-Z in different parts of the city in this wordless picture book.

■ ON-LEVEL

Window by Jeannie Baker. Greenwillow, 1991. This story shows the changing view from a boy's window as he grows into adulthood.

Things That Go by Anne Rockwell. E. P. Dutton, 1991. Many types of transportation, such as motorcycles, trains, jeeps, sleds, and bicycles, are described in this book.

There Is a Town by Gail Herman. Random House, 1996. In a small town setting, readers learn about a surprise in a special box.

Sing a Song of People by Lois Lenski. Little, Brown & Co., 1987. Rhyming text shows different people all around a busy city.

■ ADVANCED

The House Book by Shirley Frederick. Harcourt Science Instant Reader, 2000. Learn about different types of homes in this book.

City Dog by Karla Kuskin. Clarion, 1994. A city dog gets the chance to learn about the countryside for the first time.

Goldilocks and the Three Bears by Betty Miles. Aladdin, 1998. The familiar tale is told through repetitive text and bright illustrations.

Houses by Ann Morris. GoodYear, 1996. Different homes are explored through photos and text.

■ READ ALOUD

Mitchell Is Moving by Marjorie Sharmat. Simon & Schuster, 1978. Two dinosaur friends realize how much they care about one another when one of them moves away.

The Little House by Virginia Lee Burton. Houghton, 1942. This classic story describes how the city came to a little house in the country.

In the Park by Huy Vuon Lee. Holt, 1998. A boy learns from his mother how to write Chinese words for things they observe in the park.

Lost! by David McPhail. Little, Brown, 1993. A bear who finds himself lost in the big city gets some help from a friendly boy who in turn needs help of his own.

Homework Ideas

Visit The Learning Site: *www.harcourtschool.com • See Resources for Parents and Teachers: Homework Helper*

	Literature	Phonics	Language Arts	Theme	Cross-Curricular
WEEK 1	**Draw a picture** to show what Benny buys with his pennies.	Draw pictures of objects whose names begin with **the /j/ sound.**	Draw and label a picture to show what kinds of **coins** Benny had.	With a family member, take a walk in the neighborhood. Make a list of the different **shapes** you see.	Draw and label **shapes** that you see around your house.
WEEK 2	**Draw a shape.** Add details to it to make an animal or object. Label your picture.	Practice writing **the letters** *Vv, Jj,* and *Ee* on a piece of paper. Circle your best letters.	Write or dictate a list of **stores** and **shops** in your neighborhood. Choose one shop and draw a picture of it.	Draw and write about a **neighborhood worker** in your community.	Work with a family member to **count** different groups of coins.
WEEK 3	Draw and write about someone who has to move to a **new place.**	Work with a family member to write **words with *e* and *n*.**	Draw and label a **map** of your room or a room in your house.	Draw and label a picture of your **favorite neighborhood place.**	With a family member, look at a **map** of your town to find your neighborhood and street.

Come to Our "Town"!

Materials

- Teacher's Resource Book page 19
- butcher paper
- construction paper
- paints and brushes
- crayons and markers
- safety scissors
- masking tape

School-Home Connection

Invite family members to visit the classroom town. Children should conduct tours of the town, pointing out the places pictured in the mural and along their street. Encourage visitors to tell about the things they have seen in towns.

Visit *The Learning Site!* at **www.harcourtschool.com**

Introduce

Tell children they are going to turn the classroom into a small town. Ask them what kinds of things they might find in a town, and list their answers on the board. Tell children they will make roads, street signs, create storefronts, and make a mural to show people and things in a town.

Send home the Family Letter to encourage family members to participate in the project.

Prepare

- Children can create a mural showing the places and people in a town.

- Have groups of children paint roads on butcher paper and "pave" the classroom, while other children make street signs or paint shop fronts to attach to desks along both sides of the paper road.

Share

Before guests arrive, have children line up desks and tables so the painted road can be put in place. Children should attach shop fronts to desks and tables, and be ready to take visitors on a walk through town, pointing out all the sights. Some children can act as shop keepers or police officers, helping guests across the street.

Teacher Notes

Learning Centers

Choose from the following suggestions to enhance your learning centers for the theme Around the Town. (Additional learning centers for this theme can be found on pages 76 and 122)

ART CENTER

3-D Building

Tell children they are going to make a stand-up building. Have children make flaps by folding the short ends of a sheet of white construction paper so they meet in the middle. Then have children turn their paper over and draw a storefront, hospital, fire station, or other town building on it. When children finish, have them unfold the flaps slightly to stand their buildings up. Children can arrange their buildings to make a miniature town.

20 Minutes a day

Materials

- white construction paper
- crayons

WRITING CENTER

Write About Your Town

Give children a sheet of paper, and tell them to write about a place they like to go in their town. Tell children to write the name of the place they like to go and to tell what they like to do there. Invite children to illustrate their sentences and to write a label or a caption for their drawing.

I like to go to the prk.
I like to go on the swings.

We swing in the prk.

20 Minutes a day

Materials

- paper
- pencil
- crayons

SOCIAL STUDIES CENTER

"Places in Town" Poster

Have children look through magazines to find and cut out pictures of places that can be found in a town. Then have children sort the pictures into categories, such as parks, schools, grocery stores, post offices, and hospitals. Have them glue each category of items in its own place on the chart paper and label the category. Display finished posters in the classroom.

Materials

- old magazines
- safety scissors
- glue stick
- chart paper

MANIPULATIVE CENTER

Matching Things and Places

Identify the following pictures of places in a town: clothes store, fire station, grocery store, hospital, pet shop, toy store, and zoo. Arrange the pictures in a row on a table in the center. Then place the selected *Picture Cards* face down in a pile in front of the pictures. Have partners sort the *Picture Cards* according to where they would find each person, thing, or animal: at a clothes store, fire station, grocery store, hospital, pet shop, toy store, or zoo.

Materials

- pictures of the following places: clothes store, fire station, grocery store, hospital, pet shop, toy store, zoo (Patterns T20)
- *Picture Cards:* alligator, bear, carrot, cat, doctor, dog, egg, firefighter, fish, gorilla, hat, jelly, jump rope, kangaroo, kite, ladder, lemon, milk, mitten, nurse, pineapple, puzzle, rabbit, seal, socks, tiger, tomato, vegetables, vest, watermelon, X ray, zebra

DRAMATIC PLAY CENTER

At the Grocery Store

Tell children that they are going to turn the dramatic play center into a grocery store. Have them work together to create displays and stack goods. Then have children take turns being the shop keeper who helps customers find items; check-out clerk who rings up orders, bags goods, and accepts play money from customers; and customers who shop, ask the shop keeper questions, and pay for their purchases.

Materials

- toy shopping cart
- paper bags
- toy canned goods and grocery store items
- toy cash register
- play money or counters

SAND AND WATER CENTER

Plan a Park

Provide a variety of materials in the sand and water center that partners can use to create a miniature park. Partners can talk about the things they like to use in a park, such as a sandbox, slide, picnic benches, soccer field, and wading pool, and then use their imagination to create a small park. Children can complete their park with miniature figures.

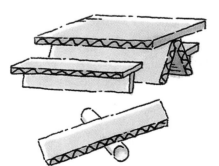

Materials

- sand tray or classroom sandbox
- water
- small dish
- miniature toy trees, figures
- recyclable objects: paper roll, cardboard
- safety scissors

Teacher Notes

Teacher Notes

THEME 9

Week 1

Around the Town

Day 1

Day 2

 15-30 Minutes

ORAL LANGUAGE

- **Phonemic Awareness**

- **Sharing Literature**

Phonemic Awareness, 23
Phoneme Matching and Isolation: Initial

Sharing Literature, 24
 Read
Big Book: *The Shape of Things*

(Skill) **Literature Focus, 25**
Understand Content Words

Phonemic Awareness, 39
Phoneme Isolation: Initial

Sharing Literature, 40
 Read
Library Book: *Benny's Pennies*

(Skill) **Literature Focus, 41**
Dialogue

45 Minutes

LEARNING TO READ

- **Phonics**

- **Vocabulary**

Daily Routines
- **Morning Message**
- **Calendar Language**
- **Writing Prompt**

Phonics, 34 T
Introduce: Consonant *Vv*
Identify/Write **T**

Phonics, 42 T
Review: Consonant Vv

High-Frequency Word, 44
Introduce: *look*

Words to Remember, 45

 15-30 Minutes

LANGUAGE ARTS

- **Writing**
Daily Writing Prompt

 Interactive Writing, 36
Write a Chart

Writing Prompt, 36
Draw and write about your favorite shape.

Share Time, 37
Discuss shapes

 Writing, 46
Write About a Gift

Writing Prompt, 46
Draw and write about self-selected topics.

Share Time, 47
Author's Chair

T = tested skill

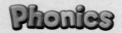 **Phonics**

Consonants *Vv, Jj*

Focus of the Week:
- **HIGH-FREQUENCY WORDS:** *look, come*
- **PHONEMIC AWARENESS**
- **SHARING LITERATURE**
- **WRITING: Chart, Story, List**

Day 3

Phonemic Awareness, 49
Phoneme Blending

Sharing Literature, 50

Read

Read-Aloud Anthology:
"The Shoemaker and the Elves," pp. 87–89

(Skill) **Literature Focus, 51**
Problem-Solution

 Phonics, 52 T
Introduce: Consonant *Jj*
Identify/Write T

High-Frequency Word, 54 T
Introduce: *come*

Words to Remember, 55

✏️ **Shared Writing, 56**
Write a Story

Writing Prompt, 56
Draw and write about someone you want to help.

Share Time, 57
Discuss favorite parts of the story from the Writing activity.

Day 4

Phonemic Awareness, 59
Phoneme Isolation: Initial

Sharing Literature, 60
Read-Aloud Anthology:
"Mr. Backward," p. 23

(Skill) **Literature Focus, 61**
Rhyming Words

 Phonics, 62 T
Review: Consonant Jj

High-Frequency Words, 64 T
Review: *look, come*

Read
DECODABLE BOOK 7
A Big, Big Van

✏️ **Interactive Writing, 66**
Write a List

Writing Prompt, 66
Draw and write about your favorite articles of clothing.

Share Time, 67
Discuss funny things Mr. Backward does.

Day 5

Phonemic Awareness, 69
Phoneme Blending

Sharing Literature, 70

Read

Library Book:
Benny's Pennies

(Skill) **Literature Focus, 71**
Beginning, Middle, Ending

 Phonics, 72 T
Review: Consonants /v/v, /j/j

✏️ **Writing, 74**
Write About Your Family

Writing Prompt, 74
Draw and write about self-selected topics.

Share Time, 75
Share family books.

Day at a Glance
Day 1

WARM UP

Phonemic Awareness
Phoneme Matching and Phoneme Isolation: Initial

Sharing Literature
Big Book:
The Shape of Things

Read

Develop Listening Comprehension

Respond to Literature

Literature Focus: Understand Content Words

Phonics
Consonant *Vv*

Interactive Writing
Chart

MORNING MESSAGE

Kindergarten News

Today the weather is _____.

(Child's name) likes

_____ weather.

Write Kindergarten News Talk with children about today's weather. Ask children what kind of weather they like best.

Use prompts such as the following to guide children as you write the news:

- **What is the weather like today?**
- **Who can point to where I should begin writing this sentence?**
- **What sound do you hear at the beginning of the word *weather*?**
- **Let's clap syllables for the word *weather*. What's the first part? What's the second part?**

As you write the message, invite children to write letters, words, and names they have learned previously. Remind them to use proper spacing, capitalization, and punctuation.

Calendar Language

Point to and read aloud the days of the week. Name the days of the week again, inviting children to join in and clap syllables for the name of each day. Ask what day it is.

Sunday	Monday	Tuesday	Wednesday	Thursday	Friday	Saturday
		1	2	3	4	5
6	7	8	9	10	11	12
13	14	15	16	17	18	19
20	21	22	23	24	25	26
27	28	29	30	31		

FLORIDA STANDARDS/GLEs   FCAT: LA.A.1.1.2.K.5 Phonetic principles; **LA.B.2.1.2.K.1** Record ideas; *Also* **LA.A.1.1.2.K.2** Alphabet; **LA.A.1.1.2.K.3** Sounds; **LA.C.1.1.3.K.1** Conversation rules; **LA.C.3.1.2.K.1** Questions

Phonemic Awareness

PHONEME MATCHING: INITIAL

Identify Beginning Sounds   Say these two words, emphasizing the initial sounds, and have children repeat them: *vegetable, van.*

MODEL *Vegetable* and *van* begin with the same sound. *Vegetable* begins with the /v/ sound and *van* begins with the /v/ sound. They both have the same beginning sound.

Tell children that you will say other groups of words. Have them raise their hand if the words begin with the same sound.

voice, volcano (same)   very, village (same)

sock, wing (not same)   bottle, bunch (same)

gate, gorilla (same)   wing, kitten (not same)

Thumbs ↑
Thumbs ↓

PHONEME ISOLATION: INITIAL

Identify the Initial Sound in Words   Say the following sets of words. Ask: **Which two words begin with the same sound? What is that sound?**

MODEL Listen for the two words that begin with the same sound: *veg- etable, pig, van. Vegetable* and *van* have the same beginning sound: /v/. *Pig* does not. Say *vegetable* and *van* with me. What is the beginning sound? (/v/) Let's listen for more beginning sounds.

- **Which two words begin with the same sound: *kitten, king, wind*?** (*kit- ten, king*) **Say *kitten* and *king* with me. What is the first sound you hear in *kitten* and *king*?** (/k/)

- **Which two words begin with the same sound: *very, vil- lage, tame*?** (*very, village*) **Say *very* and *village* with me. What is the first sound you hear in *very* and *village*?** (/v/)

▲ **Big Book**

OBJECTIVES

- *To listen and respond to a story*
- *To know that print moves left to right across the page*
- *To understand content words*

Materials

- Big Book: *The Shape of Things*
- chart paper
- marker

Sharing Literature

Read The Shape of Things

READ ALOUD/READ ALONG

Before Reading   Display the cover of *The Shape of Things*. Track the print of the title and the author's and illustrator's names while reading the words aloud. Then use these prompts to build background:

- Point to a classroom object in the shape of a square. Ask: **What shape is this?** (square) Point to a circular shape and a triangular shape and ask: **What shape is this?**

- **What do you see on the cover of the book?** (Possible response: a house, children, a dog, trees, the sun)

- **What shapes do you see in the house?** (Possible response: squares, rectangles, circle)

Page through the book, pausing briefly to allow children to preview the illustrations. Encourage children to comment on the pictures.

During Reading   Read the selection aloud. As you read,

- track the print.
- emphasize the name of the shape on each page.
- model for children how to predict which shape will be in the picture.

MODEL   First, I just see a yellow square. Then, on the next page, the yellow square has turned into a house!

FLORIDA STANDARDS/GLEs   FCAT: LA.A.1.1.4.K.1 Comprehension. *Also* **LA.A.1.1.1.K.1** Predictions; **LA.A.1.1.2.K.1** Print organization; **LA.A.2.1.4.K.1** Illustrations; **LA.C.1.1.1.K.2** Oral language

Handwriting

Writing *V* and *v* Write uppercase *V* and lowercase *v* on the board.

Point to the uppercase *V*. **What letter is this?**

Point to the lowercase *v*. **What letter is this?**

MODEL **Watch as I write the letter *V* so that everyone can read it.**

As you give the Letter Talk, trace the uppercase *V*. Use the same modeling procedure for the lowercase *v*.

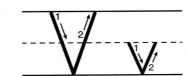

Letter Talk for *V*

Straight line down slant right, straight line up slant right.

Letter Talk for *v*

The lowercase *v* is the same as the uppercase letter, except that it is smaller. Straight line down slant right. Straight line up slant right.

D'Nealian handwriting models are on pages R12–13.

PRACTICE/APPLY

Guided Practice Help children find *Vv* on their *Write-On/Wipe-Off Board*. Have them trace the uppercase *V* with a finger and then write the letter several times. Then have them do the same for lowercase *v*.

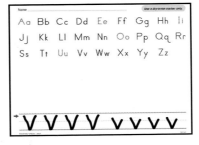

Independent Practice Distribute drawing paper and violet paint. Explain that violet is a shade of purple. Have children print large *V*'s on their papers and then have them trace over the letters with violet paint.

FLORIDA STANDARDS/GLEs **LA.A.1.1.2.K.2** Alphabet; **LA.C.3.1.2.K.1** Questions

BELOW-LEVEL

Provide sand trays and have children write the letter *V* in the sand as they say: *Down slant right, up slant right.*

ENGLISH-LANGUAGE LEARNERS

As you introduce the *Letter Talk* for *Vv*, model each step to make sure children understand the terms *slant* and *right*.

Phonics Resources

Phonics Express™ CD-ROM, **Level A,** Sparkle/Route 1/ Market

Phonics Practice Book pages 95–96 *in class*

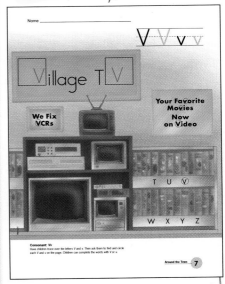

▲ **Practice Book page 7** *h.w.*

Around the Town **35**

OBJECTIVES

- *To share information and ideas, speaking in complete, coherent sentences*

- *To understand the purpose of a chart*

- *To write a chart*

Materials

- chart paper
- marker

Writing
Every Day

Day 1: Chart
Work together to write a chart about shapes.

Day 2: Gift
Have children draw a picture and write about a gift they would like to give someone.

Day 3: Story
Write a story about the shoemaker's elves.

Day 4: List
Work together to make a list of clothes.

Day 5: Family Gift Book
Have children make a book of gifts for family members.

LANGUAGE ARTS

Interactive Writing

Write a Chart

SHAPE TREASURE HUNT

Talk About Charts   Tell children that they are going to go on a Treasure Hunt for things in the classroom that are made from shapes. Ask: **How can we sort and write the things we find during the hunt?** (make a chart)

Write a Chart   Ask: **What shapes will we look for?** (circles, rectangles, triangles, squares, ovals) **Where should I write these shapes on the chart so we can sort and list beneath them the objects we find?** (across the top of the page) **I need to write an uppercase letter for each shape because it is the title of its list. Who would like to help me underline these words?** Invite children to write familiar letters at the beginning and end of words throughout the lesson. If necessary, guide children to find objects in the classroom. Ask: **What do you see in our classroom that is the same shape as a _____?** List objects for one shape at a time.

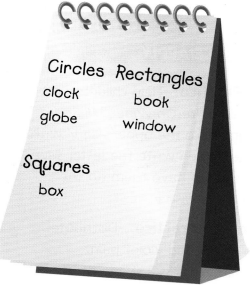

Journal Writing   Have children write and draw about their favorite shape.

FLORIDA STANDARDS/GLEs   FCAT: LA.B.2.1.2.K.1 Record ideas; *Also* **LA.A.1.1.2.K.1** Print organization; **LA.B.1.1.1.K.2** Generate ideas; **LA.B.1.1.2.K.2** Basic formats

WRAP UP # Share Time

Reflect on the Lesson Ask children to point to and name the shapes on chart paper from the Sharing Literature lesson. Have them match pictures with words they listed on their Treasure Hunt chart. Read each shape and object to children.

S.S.R. Have children read silently from a book of their choice.

 ART

Shapes of Our Town

Cut squares, triangles, circles, rectangles, and diamonds from colored construction paper. On each index card, draw a simple shape of a building, a vehicle, or an animal that is familiar to children. Have children choose an index card and reproduce the figure on white construction paper, using the colored shapes. Then have them glue the shapes in place and add a background to their pictures.

Materials

- index cards
- colored construction paper
- white construction paper
- glue
- crayons

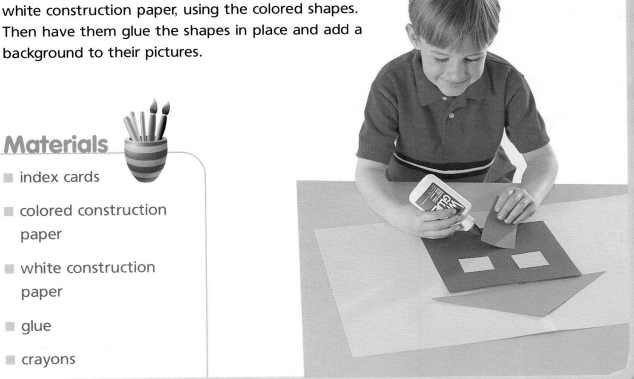

Day at a Glance

Day 2

WARM UP

Phonemic Awareness
Phoneme Isolation: Initial

Sharing Literature
Library Book:
Benny's Pennies

Read

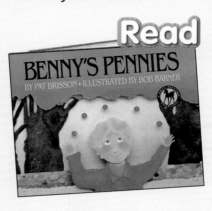

BENNY'S PENNIES
BY PAT BRISSON • ILLUSTRATED BY BOB BARNER

Develop Listening Comprehension

Respond to Literature

Literature Focus: Dialogue

Phonics
Relating /v/ to *v*

High-Frequency Word
look

Writing
Gifts

MORNING MESSAGE

Kindergarten News

(Child's name) has a _____.

(Child's name) would like to

get a _____.

Write Kindergarten News Talk with children about pets they have, pets they know, or ones they would like to have.

Use prompts such as the following to guide children as you write the news:

- **What kind of pet do you have? What kind of pet would you like to have?**
- **What sound do you hear at the beginning of (animal name)?**
- **Who can point to the word *like*?**

As you write the message, invite children to write letters and words they have learned previously. Remind them to use proper spacing, capitalization, and punctuation.

Calendar Language

Tell children you will name a week day. Ask children to raise their hand if you name a school day.

Sunday	Monday	Tuesday	Wednesday	Thursday	Friday	Saturday
		1	2	3	4	5
6	7	8	9	10	11	12
13	14	15	16	17	18	19
20	21	22	23	24	25	26
27	28	29	30	31		

FLORIDA STANDARDS/GLEs FCAT: **LA.A.1.1.2.K.4** Words; **LA.B.2.1.2.K.1** *Also* Record ideas; **LA.C.3.1.2.K.1** Questions

Phonemic Awareness

PHONEME ISOLATION: INITIAL

Listen for /v/ Tell children you will say some words and they will listen for the beginning sound in the words. Say the following sentence:

Vanessa put violins, violets, and vegetables in her van.

Vanessa **begins with /v/. What sound does** *violins* **begin with?** (/v/)

What sound does *violets* **begin with?** (/v/)

What sound does *vegetables* **begin with?** (/v/)

What sound does *van* **begin with?** (/v/)

Let's say the tongue twister together.

What else could Vanessa put in her van whose name begins with /v/?

(Possible responses: vests, vacuum cleaner, vase, vine)

BELOW-LEVEL

Have children say the sentence again, elongating the /v/ sound in the words.

ADVANCED

Have children complete this sentence with a variety of /v/ words: *Victor likes* _____.

FLORIDA STANDARDS/GLEs   **FCAT: LA.A.1.1.2.K.5** Phonetic principles; *Also* **LA.C.1.1.1.K.1** Follow directions; **LA.C.3.1.2.K.1**; Questions **LA.D.2.1.2.K.2** Alliteration

Around the Town   39

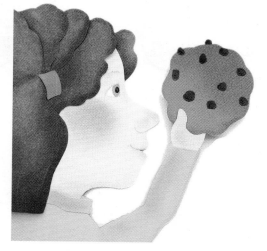

▲ Library Book

OBJECTIVES

- *To listen and respond to a story*
- *To make and confirm predictions*
- *To understand characters*
- *To recognize dialogue*

Materials

■ *Library Book: Benny's Pennies*

Sharing Literature

Read Benny's Pennies

READ ALOUD

Before Reading   Display the cover of *Benny's Pennies*. Track the print of the title as you read it aloud. Ask children what is special about the two words in the title. (They rhyme.) Read the names of the author and the illustrator. Then help children use the cover illustration and the title to make predictions.

- Point to Benny. **This is Benny. He is the main character in this story.**

- **How many pennies do you think Benny will have in this story? Why do you think that?** (Five; there are five pennies in the picture on the cover.)

- **What do you think Benny will do with these pennies?** (Possible response: He will buy something.)

- **What would you buy if you had five pennies to spend?** (Possible response: candy)

During Reading   Read the story aloud. As you read,

- use a different voice for each character.

- pause and point to the number of pennies that Benny gives each person.

- pause to model how to change predictions.

> **MODEL**   **At first I thought that Benny was going to buy something for himself with his pennies. Now I think he is buying gifts for others.**

FLORIDA STANDARDS/GLEs   **LA.A.1.1.1.K.1** Predictions; **LA.A.2.1.4.K.1** Illustrations; **LA.C.1.1.1.K.2** Oral language; **LA.C.3.1.2.K.1** Questions

DEVELOP LISTENING COMPREHENSION

After Reading Have children answer these questions:

- **What does Benny buy that is beautiful?** (a rose)
- **What does Benny buy for his dog?** (a bone)
- **How many pennies does Benny spend on the presents?** (five)
- **What kind of boy is Benny?** (Possible response: He likes to share.)

RESPOND TO LITERATURE

Identifying with a Story Character Have children pretend that they have five pennies to spend, just like Benny. Ask them to share what they would do with the pennies. Invite children to discuss how the story would be different if Benny had spent the pennies on himself or saved them in his piggy bank.

★ Literature Focus

DIALOGUE

Tell children that sometimes words in a story are words that the characters speak. Write the following sentence from the story *Benny's Pennies* on the board: *"What should I buy?" he asked*. Read the sentence aloud and point to the quotation marks.

MODEL These are quotation marks. Quotation marks show that the words are being spoken by someone. The author put quotation marks around these words because Benny says these words.

Read a few sentences with dialogue and ask children to tell who says the words.

Name each object that Benny buys with his pennies. Have children look through the story to find an illustration of each object.

ONGOING ASSESSMENT

As you share *Benny's Pennies*, note whether children

- **listen and respond to the story.**
- **make and confirm predictions.**
- **understand characters.**

FLORIDA STANDARDS/GLEs **FCAT: LA.A.1.1.4.K.1** Comprehension; **LA.A.2.1.1.K.1** Main idea; *Also* **LA.C.1.1.3.K.1** Conversation rules; **LA.C.3.1.2.K.1** Questions

Day 2

OBJECTIVE
To match consonant v to its sound

Materials

- *Letter and Sound Chart 21*
- *Tactile Letter Cards v*
- Teacher's Resource Book p. 71
- *Picture/Word Cards vegetables, violin*
- pocket chart
- paper bags
- scissors
- crayons

▲ **Letter and Sound Chart 21**

Phonics
Relating /v/ to v

ACTIVE BEGINNING

Recite the Rhyme   Teach children "Vroom, Vroom, Vroom." Tell children to listen for the sound /v/ as they recite the rhyme. Then have them pretend to vacuum as they recite the rhyme again.

Vroom, Vroom, Vroom
The vacuum's voice is very noisy.

Vroom, vroom, vroom.

When we want things very clean,

We vroom the vacuum through each room.

by Susan Little

TEACH/MODEL

Introduce Letter and Sound   Display *Letter and Sound Chart 21.*

Touch the letter *V*. **What is the name of the letter? This letter stands for the /v/ sound. When you say /v/, you touch your bottom lip with your top front teeth. Say /vv/.**

Read aloud the rhyme on the *Letter and Sound Chart*, tracking the print. Read the *Vv* words in the rhyme aloud. Then point to each *v*, and have children say the /v/ sound.

Point to the blank. **What *Vv* word will I write?**

Have children join in as you read the rhyme again. Ask them to touch their bottom lip with their top front teeth as they say the /v/v.

FLORIDA STANDARDS/GLEs   FCAT: LA.A.1.1.2.K.5 Phonetic principles; *Also* **LA.A.1.1.2.K.1** Print organization; **LA.A.1.1.2.K.2** Alphabet; **LA.A.1.1.2.K.3** Sounds; **LA.C.3.1.2.K.1** Questions

PRACTICE/APPLY

Guided Practice Distribute *Tactile Letter Cards v*. Then place *Picture/Word Cards vegetables* and *violin* in the pocket chart. Say the names of the pictures as you point to the *v* in each. Have children repeat the words.

Tell children: **Some words begin with v.**

Point to the *v* in *vegetables*. **The /v/ sound is at the beginning of vegetables.**

I'll say some words. If the word begins with the /v/ sound, hold up your v card. If it doesn't begin with the /v/ sound, don't hold up your v card. *Thumbs↑ Thumbs↓*

vine   very   water   vest   lake   violin   pig   vulture

Independent Practice Distribute a paper bag to each child. Help children make a vest by cutting off the bottom of the bag for their heads and by cutting out a hole on each side of the bag for their arms. Ask children to decorate their vests with the letters *Vv* and with pictures of words whose names begin with the /v/ sound. Have children wear and share their "v vests."

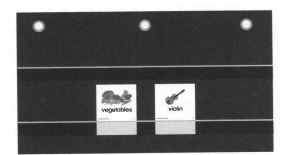

FLORIDA STANDARDS/GLEs   FCAT: LA.A.1.1.2.K.5 Phonetic principles; *Also* **LA.A.1.1.2.K.2** Alphabet; **LA.A.1.1.2.K.3** Sounds

---

BELOW-LEVEL

As you introduce the *Letter and Sound Chart*, have children identify the items near the van. Have them emphasize the /v/ sound as they say each word. For more practice with Consonant *Vv*, see Alternative Teaching Strategies, page T2.

ENGLISH-LANGUAGE LEARNERS

Have children point to each *Picture Card*, say the name of the picture, and make the beginning sound they hear. Then tell children to draw and label an item whose name begins with the /v/ sound.

Phonics Resources

Phonics Express™ CD-ROM, **Level A,** Sparkle/Route I/Park, Harbor, Fire Station

Phonics Practice Book pages 97–98 *class*

▲ **Practice Book page 8** *hw*

Around the Town   43

OBJECTIVE

To read high-frequency
word look

Materials

- Big Book:
  The Shape of Things

- High-Frequency
  Word Card

  look

- Teacher's Resource Book
  p. 139

- High-Frequency Word
  Card files

High-Frequency Word *look* ✔*Introduce*

TEACH/MODEL

Display page 16 of the *Big Book: The Shape of Things*. Track the print as you read the page aloud.

Point to the word *look* on the page and say: **This is the word *look*.** Have children say the word with you. Display *High-Frequency Word Card look*. Ask: **What word is this?** Have children follow along as you track the print and reread the words *look again and see*. Then have a child match the *High-Frequency Word Card look* to the word *look* on the page.

PRACTICE/APPLY

Guided Practice   Make copies of the *High-Frequency Word Card look* in the *Teacher's Resource Book*. Give each child a word card and tell children to point to and say the word *look*. Then ask each child to name an object in the classroom and say: *Look at the (name of object).* Have children point to their word card and read it as they say the sentence.

Independent Practice   Ask children to place their *High-Frequency Word Card look* in their file. Then have children look in their *High-Frequency Word Card* file to find a word card to complete each sentence frame. Say the following sentence frames:

> I _____ to look at flowers. (like)
>
> I can _____ a cloud. (see)
>
> Do you _____ a pet? (have)
>
> _____ at the pictures. (Look)

FLORIDA STANDARDS/GLEs   FCAT: LA.A.1.1.2.K.4 Words; LA.A.1.1.3.K.4 Build vocabulary; LA.C.3.1.3.K.1 Basic vocabulary; *Also* LA.A.1.1.2.K.1 Print organization; LA.A.1.1.3.K.1 Frequent words

WRAP UP # Share Time

Author's Chair Ask children to read their sentence and share their drawing of the gift they would give someone.

S.S.R. *Sustained Silent Reading* Have children read silently from a book of their choice.

 **Centers** **+2 MATH**

Let's Go Shopping

Have each child take five pennies from the bowl. Then children can take turns selecting the items they want to buy. Tell children to take one item at a time and put the correct number of pennies next to that item. Children can shop until they have purchased five items.

Materials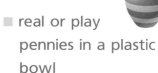

- real or play pennies in a plastic bowl

- small classroom items, such as pencils, erasers, plastic animals, each with a price tag of 1¢

Day at a Glance

Day 3

WARM UP

Phonemic Awareness
Phoneme Blending

Sharing Literature
Read-Aloud Anthology:
"The Shoemaker and the Elves"

Read

KINDERGARTEN
READ-ALOUD
Anthology
≋Harcourt

Develop Concept Vocabulary

Respond to Literature

Literature Focus: Problem-Solution

Phonics
Consonant *Jj*

High-Frequency Word
come

Shared Writing
Story

MORNING MESSAGE

Kindergarten News

I like to _____ with my family.

Sometimes we _____. On week-ends, my family likes to _____.

Write Kindergarten News Talk with children about what they like to do with their families.

Use prompts such as the following to guide children as you write the news:

- **What are some things you like to do with your family?**
- **Who can write the word** *we*?
- **Let's clap syllables for the word** *family*. **How many word parts does it have?**
- **Who can point to each word in the first sentence?**

As you write the message, invite children to write letters or words they have learned previously. Remind them to use proper spacing, capitalization, and punctuation.

Calendar Language

Display a calendar for the current month and read the name of the month. Say: *This month is _____.* Have children repeat the sentence. Then ask several children *What month is this?* and have them answer *This month is _____.*

Sunday	Monday	Tuesday	Wednesday	Thursday	Friday	Saturday
		1	2	3	4	5
6	7	8	9	10	11	12
13	14	15	16	17	18	19
20	21	22	23	24	25	26
27	28	29	30	31		

FLORIDA STANDARDS/GLEs FCAT: **LA.A.2.1.5.K.2** Get information; **LA.B.2.1.2.K.1** Record ideas; *Also* **LA.C.1.1.3.K.1** Conversation rules; **LA.B.1.1.3.K.2** Print direction; **LA.C.3.1.2.K.1** Questions

Phonemic Awareness

PHONEME BLENDING

Blend Sounds Use the rabbit puppet for this blending activity. Tell children to listen to the sounds the rabbit says and guess the word he is saying.

Say: /j/ /a/ /m/ slowly, emphasizing each sound. **Say it with the rabbit: /j/ /a/ /m/.**

Say it again, blending the sounds. /jjaamm/. **Blend the sounds with the rabbit: /jjaamm/.**

Have children blend the sounds with the rabbit and name the word. (/jjaamm/, jam)

Use the same procedure for the following words.

/p/ /e/ /n/ (pen)	/j/ /e/ /t/ (jet)	/v/ /e/ /t/ (vet)
/v/ /a/ /n/ (van)	/j/ /o/ /b/ (job)	/b/ /e/ /d/ (bed)
/j/ /o/ /g/ (jog)	/s/ /i/ /p/ (sip)	/j/ /u/ /g/ (jug)
/k/ /a/ /t/ (cat)	/p/ /i/ /g/ (pig)	/n/ /e/ /t/ (net)

BELOW-LEVEL

Ask children to repeat each phoneme in two letter words such as *at*, *in*, *on* and *if*. Have them slowly blend the sounds with you each time more quickly until the word is said naturally.

/P/I/G/ = PIG

Harcourt

▲ **Read-Aloud
Anthology**

OBJECTIVES

• *To listen to a folktale*

• *To distinguish between
real and make-believe*

• *To make and confirm
predictions*

• *To identify problem and
solution*

Materials

■ *Read-Aloud
Anthology pp. 87–89*

Sharing Literature

Read "The Shoemaker and the Elves"

READ ALOUD

Before Reading Tell children that they are going to listen to a folktale, a story that has been told many times. Read aloud the title in the *Read-Aloud Anthology* and then use these prompts to build background:

• **What is a shoemaker?** (a person who makes shoes)

• **What are elves?** (Possible response: Elves are very little people.)

• **Are elves real or make-believe characters?** (They are make-believe.)

Model how to make a prediction about the story as you show children the pictures.

MODEL **The title of the story is "The Shoemaker and the Elves," and I see pictures of elves. So I think that elves might make the shoes in this story. I'll read to find out.**

During Reading Read the story aloud. As you read,

• use a different voice as you read each character's parts.

• pause to point out the problem and solution at the end of page 88.

MODEL **The problem is that the shoemaker has only enough leather to make one pair of shoes. The solution is that the elves make such a beautiful pair of shoes that the shoemaker makes extra money and can buy more leather.**

FLORIDA STANDARDS/GLEs   **FCAT: LA.A.1.1.2.K.4** Words; **LA.A.1.1.3.K.5** Story elements; **LA.E.1.1.1.K.1** Genres; *Also* **LA.A.1.1.1.K.1** Predictions; **LA.C.3.1.2.K.1** Questions

DEVELOP CONCEPT VOCABULARY

Write the following story words on the chalkboard: *leather, customer, stitch, trousers, stockings*. Point to each word, read it aloud, and then tell children the meaning of each word. Tell children you will give a clue and they will guess the word.

- **Many shoes are made from this material.** (leather)
- **This is another word for *sew*.** (stitch)
- **These are like socks.** (stockings)
- **This is another word for *pants*.** (trousers)
- **This is a person who buys something.** (customer)

RESPOND TO LITERATURE

Discuss the End of the Story   Discuss and confirm predictions children made at the beginning of the story. Ask children if they liked the end of the story. Ask them if they were surprised that the elves don't come back after they get their new clothes.

Literature
Focus

PROBLEM-SOLUTION

Tell children that many stories have a problem that must be solved during the story. Model for children how to state the problem and solution.

MODEL **In "The Shoemaker and the Elves," the shoemaker is poor and doesn't have leather to make shoes. This is the problem. The elves help him solve his problem by making shoes that customers want to buy. Then the shoemaker can get more leather to make shoes. This is the solution.**

Ask children to repeat what the problem is in "The Shoemaker and the Elves." (The shoemaker doesn't have leather to make shoes.) Have children also say how this problem is solved. (Elves make shoes for the shoemaker's customers.) Write these responses in two boxes labeled *Problem* and *Solution*. Place them in a center for children to illustrate.

ADVANCED

Direct children's attention to the three illustrations on pages 88 and 89. Ask them to retell the story by discussing what is happening in each picture.

ENGLISH-LANGUAGE LEARNERS

To help children understand the task of a shoemaker, act out the words *cut*, *stitch*, and *hammer* as you say each word.

ONGOING ASSESSMENT

As you share "The Shoemaker and the Elves," note whether children

- listen for a period of time.
- make and confirm predictions.

FLORIDA STANDARDS/GLEs   **FCAT: LA.A.1.1.3.K.5** Story elements; *Also* **LA.C.3.1.2.K.1** Questions

OBJECTIVES

- *To write uppercase and lowercase Jj independently*

- *To recognize J and j*

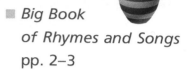

Materials

- *Big Book of Rhymes and Songs pp. 2–3*

- *Music CD*

- *Big Alphabet Card Jj*

- *Write-On/Wipe-Off Boards*

- drawing paper

- crayons

Phonics
Consonant *Jj*  Introduce

ACTIVE BEGINNING

Sing "The Alphabet Song" Display "The Alphabet Song" in the *Big Book of Rhymes and Songs.* Play the *Music CD* and point to each letter as you sing the song with children.

TEACH/MODEL

Introduce the Letter Name
Hold up the *Big Alphabet Card Jj.*

The name of this letter is *j.* Say the name with me.

Point to the uppercase *J.* **This is the uppercase *J.***

Point to the lowercase *j.* **This is the lowercase *j.***

Point to the *Big Alphabet Card* again. **What is the name of this letter?**

Point to the *J* in "The Alphabet Song." **What is the name of this letter?**

Display the letter *j* on page 4 of *The Shape of Things.*

Follow along as I read the page.

Point to the letter *j* in the word *just.* **What is the name of this letter?**

 FLORIDA STANDARDS/GLEs   LA.A.1.1.2.K.1 Print organization; LA.A.1.1.2.K.2 Alphabet; LA.C.1.1.1.K.2 Oral language; LA.C.3.1.2.K.1 Questions

Handwriting

Writing *J* and *j* Write uppercase *J* and lowercase *j* on the board.

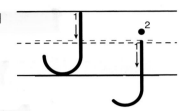

Point to the uppercase *J*. **What letter is this?**

Point to the lowercase *j*. **What letter is this?**

MODEL Model how to write uppercase *J*. **Watch as I write the letter *J* so that everyone can read it.**

Letter Talk for *J*

Straight line down and curve to the left.

As you repeat the Letter Talk, trace the uppercase *J*. Use the same modeling procedure for the lowercase *j*.

D'Nealian handwriting models are on pages R12–13.

Letter Talk for *j*

Straight line down and curve to the left. Dot the top.

PRACTICE/APPLY

Guided Practice Help children find *Jj* on their *Write-On/Wipe-Off Board.* Have them trace the letters and then write the letters several times.

Independent Practice Distribute drawing paper. Have children fold the paper in half and write uppercase *J*'s on one side of the paper and lowercase *j*'s on the other side.

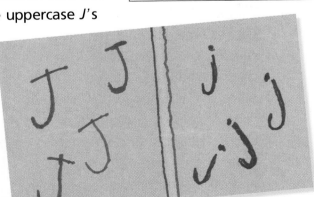

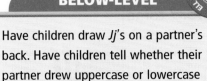

Have children draw *Jj*'s on a partner's back. Have children tell whether their partner drew uppercase or lowercase letters.

ENGLISH-LANGUAGE LEARNERS

As you introduce the *Letter Talk* for *Jj*, model each step to make sure children understand the terms *straight*, *curve*, *left*, and *dot*.

Phonics Resources

Phonics Express™ CD-ROM, Level A, Speedy/Route 5/Harbor

Phonics Practice Book pages 99–100

▲ **Practice Book page 10**

OBJECTIVE

To read high-frequency word come

Materials

- chart paper
- *High-Frequency Word Card* come
- *Teacher's Resource Book* pp. 138, 139, 140
- drawing paper
- crayons
- sentence strips
- marker

High-Frequency Word *come* ✔Introduce

TEACH/MODEL

Copy on chart paper the last line of the rhyme. Recite the rhyme and track the print for the line written on the paper.

Come along with me.

Oh, what fun it will be!

We'll walk and talk, and laugh for a while,

If you come along with me!

Point to the word *come* and say: **This is the word *come*.** Have children say the word. Display *High-Frequency Word Card come.* Ask: **What word is this?** Have children say the rhyme with you. Then have a child match the *High-Frequency Word Card come* to the word *come* in the last sentence of the rhyme.

PRACTICE/APPLY

Guided Practice   Make copies of the *High-Frequency Word Card come* in the *Teacher's Resource Book*. Give each child a card and tell children to point to and say the word *come*. Then tell children to point to their word card as they say the word *come*.

Say to a child: **Come here.** Ask the child to come to where you are and say, *I will come.* Have the child point to the Word Card as he or she says the word *come*.

Independent Practice   Make copies of the *High-Frequency Word Cards Come, to,* and *the* in the *Teacher's Resource Book*. Have children draw a picture of a place they like to go to, and then glue the words *Come to the* above the picture. Have them write the picture name to complete the sentence.

 FLORIDA STANDARDS/GLEs   **FCAT: LA.A.1.1.2.K.4** Words; **LA.A.1.1.3.K.4** Build vocabulary; *Also* **LA.A.1.1.2.K.1** Print organization; **LA.B.1.1.3.K.1** Spelling approximations

Words to Remember

Word Wall

Reading Words Hold up the *High-Frequency Word Card* *come* and have children read it aloud. Ask a child to name the letter at the beginning of the word *come*. Have that child place the word card under the letter *c* of the classroom word chart.

Words in Sentences Have children look closely at their new word, *come*. Ask them to name the letters in the word. Write the following sentences on sentence strips: *I come to _____. We come to _____.* Read each sentence strip with children. Have them frame the word *come*. Have children read the sentences and complete them orally.

Diagnostic Check: High-Frequency Words

If... children have difficulty recognizing the high-frequency word *come*,

Then... have them trace over the letters in the word *come* with a finger on their individual *Word Cards*. Then have them write the word *come* with a finger on their desktop as they say it.

ADDITIONAL SUPPORT ACTIVITIES

BELOW-LEVEL	Reteach, p. S2
ADVANCED	Extend, p. S3
ENGLISH-LANGUAGE LEARNERS	Reteach, p. S3

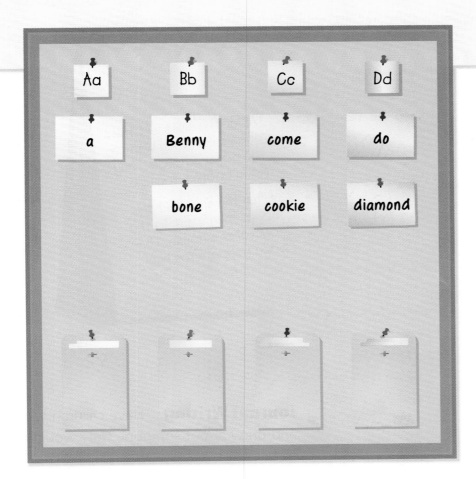

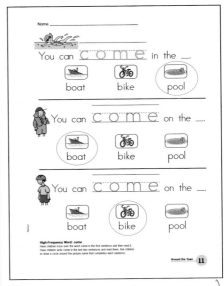

▲ **Practice Book page 11**

FLORIDA STANDARDS/GLEs **FCAT: LA.A.1.1.3.K.4** Build vocabulary; *Also* **LA.A.1.1.2.K.1** Print organization; **LA.A.1.1.3.K.1** Frequent words; **LA.C.1.1.3.K.1** Conversation rules

Around the Town 55

OBJECTIVES

- *To understand story characters*
- *To write a story*

Materials

- chart paper
- marker

Shared Writing

Write a Story

EXTENDING LITERATURE

Talk About Story Characters Remind children that in "The Shoemaker and the Elves," the elves help the shoemaker and his wife by making shoes. Ask children: **What other people could the elves help and what could the elves do for them?** (Possible response: The elves could help my mom make lunches.)

Write a Story Tell children that together you are going to write a story about what the elves do after they leave the shoemaker and his wife. Write this story starter on the chart: *After the elves left the shoemaker, they went to the _____'s house. At night, they made _____ for him (her).* Track the print as you read it aloud. Ask children to name someone and tell what the elves could secretly do for that person. Record their ideas in an ongoing story.

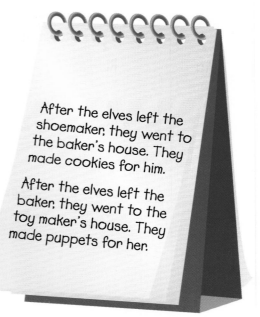

After the elves left the shoemaker, they went to the baker's house. They made cookies for him.

After the elves left the baker, they went to the toy maker's house. They made puppets for her.

Journal Writing Have children write and draw about someone they would like to help.

 FLORIDA STANDARDS/GLEs FCAT: LA.A.1.1.3.K.5 Story elements **LA.B.1.1.2.K.3** Sequence; **LA.B.2.1.2.K.1** Record ideas; *Also* **LA.A.1.1.2.K.1** Print organization

WRAP UP Share Time

Reflect on the Lesson Display the story children created during Shared Writing. Read it aloud to children and then provide an opportunity for children to orally share more sentences.

S.S.R. Have children read silently from a book of their choice.

Centers  ART

Design Shoes

Cut out shoe shapes from white drawing paper. Invite children to draw pictures or patterns on the shapes to design shoes that they would like to wear. Display finished designs around the room.

Materials

- drawing paper
- scissors
- crayons

Day at a Glance
Day 4

WARM UP

MORNING MESSAGE

Kindergarten News

(Child's name) likes to eat _____.

(Child's name)'s favorite food

is _____.

Phonemic Awareness
Phoneme Isolation: Initial

Sharing Literature
Read-Aloud Anthology:
"Mr. Backward"

Read

Respond to Literature

Literature Focus: Rhyming Words

Phonics
Relating /j/ to *j*

Reading
Decodable Book 7: *A Big, Big Van*

Interactive Writing
List

Write Kindergarten News Talk with children about their favorite foods. Encourage them to talk about new foods they have tried.

Use prompts such as the following to guide children as you write the news:

- **What is your favorite food?**
- **What sound do you hear at the beginning of *favorite* and *food*?**
- **What letter should I write first in (child's name)?**
- **Who can point to the word *to*?**

As you write the message, invite children to write letters, words, or names they have learned previously. Remind them to use proper spacing, capitalization, and punctuation.

Calendar Language

Tell children that the days of each month are numbered and the numbers tell the date. Point to and read aloud the date. Name the month and the date. Ask: *What month is this? What is today's date?*

Sunday	Monday	Tuesday	Wednesday	Thursday	Friday	Saturday
		1	2	3	4	5
6	7	8	9	10	11	12
13	14	15	16	17	18	19
20	21	22	23	24	25	26
27	28	29	30	31		

FLORIDA STANDARDS/GLEs FCAT: LA.A.1.1.2.K.4 Words; **LA.A.1.1.2.K.5** Phonetic principles; *Also* **LA.A.1.1.3.K.1** Frequent words; **LA.C.1.1.3.K.1** Conversation rules; **LA.C.3.1.2.K.1** Questions

Phonemic Awareness

PHONEME ISOLATION: INITIAL

Listen for /j/ Teach children the following rhyme and its movements.

Come to the jungle. (Make a "come along" hand gesture.)

Jog along with me. (Jog in place.)

Just see the jolly monkeys, (Shade eyes with hand and look around the room.)

Jump from tree to tree. (Jump in place.)

▲ **"Jim Along, Josie,"** *Oo-pples and Boo-noo-noos: Songs and Activities for Phonemic Awareness*, pages 96–97.

Have children repeat the rhyme several times, emphasizing the /j/ sound in the words. Then tell children you will say some words and they will listen for the beginning sound in those words.

Say: *jungle*. Have children repeat *jungle*.

Say it again, emphasizing the /j/ sound.

Say: **/j/ is the sound I hear at the beginning of *jungle*—/j/.**

Then say the following words from the rhyme. Have children repeat each word and its beginning sound.

jog /j/   **just /j/**   **jolly /j/**   **jump /j/**

Ask children to make the sound they hear at the beginning of the words. (/j/)

REACHING ALL LEARNERS

Diagnostic Check: Phonemic Awareness

If... children have difficulty isolating and identifying the beginning sound /j/,

Then... segment each word for children: /j/-*ump*. Ask them to segment the word with you and then say the word naturally. Have them repeat the word and then its beginning sound: *jump* /j/.

ADDITIONAL SUPPORT ACTIVITIES

BELOW-LEVEL Reteach, p. S4

ADVANCED Extend, p. S5

ENGLISH-LANGUAGE LEARNERS Reteach, p. S5

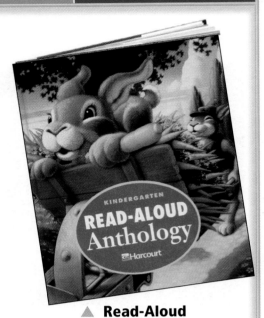

▲ **Read-Aloud Anthology**

OBJECTIVES

• *To listen to a poem*

• *To make predictions*

• *To identify rhyming words*

Materials

■ *Read-Aloud Anthology,* p. 23

■ drawing paper

■ crayons

Sharing Literature

Read "Mr. Backward"

READ ALOUD

Before Reading   Tell children that they are going to listen to a poem. Read aloud the title of the poem "Mr. Backward" in the *Read-Aloud Anthology* and then model how to make predictions:

> **MODEL** I think this is going to be a funny poem. I'm trying to think of what a person could do backward. Maybe Mr. Backward will put on some of his clothes backward.

Invite children to predict what Mr. Backward might do in the poem.

During Reading   Read the poem aloud. As you read,

• react to rhythm and rhyme.

Let's clap the rhythm of the words.

• emphasize prepositions such as *before, inside, on,* and *beneath.*

I'll read the words again and this time, clap when you hear words that rhyme.

During the second reading, pause to explain any words that may be unfamiliar, such as *sauerkraut* and *antifreeze.*

FLORIDA STANDARDS/GLEs   FCAT: LA.A.1.1.3.K.5 Story elements; *Also* **LA.A.1.1.1.K.1** Predictions; **LA.D.1.1.1.K.1** Sound patterns

RESPOND TO LITERATURE

Discuss the Poem Reread aloud lines 2, 3, 8, 13, and 14 of the poem. Ask children to explain what is "backward" about each activity. Have children choose an activity and illustrate it on drawing paper.

Literature Focus

RHYMING WORDS

Say several pairs of rhyming words from "Mr. Backward," and have children repeat them: *town/down, meal/real, sink/ink*. Remind children that rhyming words have the same ending sounds. Then have children make rhyming pairs by substituting a new beginning sound. Give clues such as these:

- **What sounds like *head* and starts with /b/?** (*bed*)
- **What sounds like *toes* and starts with /n/?** (*nose*)
- **What sounds like *spot* and starts with /d/?** (*dot*)
- **What sounds like *rakes* and starts with /b/?** (*bakes*)

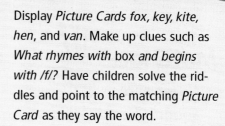

BELOW-LEVEL

Display *Picture Cards fox, key, kite, hen,* and *van.* Make up clues such as *What rhymes with* box *and begins with /f/?* Have children solve the riddles and point to the matching *Picture Card* as they say the word.

ADVANCED

Have pairs of children look through books and magazines and say names of pictured items. Have them try to identify a word that rhymes with the picture name.

ONGOING ASSESSMENT

As you share "Mr. Backward," note whether children

- can listen to a poem for enjoyment.
- can make predictions.
- can identify rhyming words.

FLORIDA STANDARDS/GLEs **FCAT: LA.A.2.1.1.K.1** Main idea; **LA.C.2.1.1.K.1** Main idea; *Also* **LA.D.2.1.2.K.1** Patterned structures

OBJECTIVE

To match consonant j to its sound

Materials

- *Letter and Sound Chart 5*
- *Tactile Letter Card j*
- Teacher's Resource Book p. 55
- *Picture/Word Cards jeep, jet*
- pocket chart
- Jar Pattern (page T11)
- scissors
- crayons
- craft sticks
- tape

J j

A jellyfish juggles
Jars of jelly.
When he's done,
One by one,
He puts them in his belly.

▲ **Letter and Sound Chart 5**

Phonics

Relating /j/ to j

ACTIVE BEGINNING

Recite the Rhyme   Teach children the rhyme "Put on Your Jacket." Have them recite the rhyme again, listening for each /j/ sound. Ask children to repeat the words that begin with the /j/ sound. (jacket, join, jump, jog)

Put on Your Jacket

Put on your jacket

And join us outside.

Jump with a jump rope

Jog to the slide!

by Susan Little

TEACH/MODEL

Introduce Letter and Sound   Display *Letter and Sound Chart 5*.

Touch the letter *J*. **What is the name of the letter?**

This letter stands for the /j/ sound.

Read aloud the rhyme on the *Letter and Sound Chart*, tracking the print. Read aloud the *Jj* words in the rhyme. Then point to each *j* and have children say the /j/ sound.

Have children join in as you read the rhyme again.

FLORIDA STANDARDS/GLEs   FCAT: LA.A.1.1.2.K.5 Phonetic principles; *Also* **LA.A.1.1.2.K.1**; Print organization; **LA.A.1.1.2.K.2**; Alphabet; **LA.A.1.1.2.K.3**; Sounds; **LA.C.3.1.2.K.1**; Questions; **LA.D.2.1.2.K.1** Patterned Structures

PRACTICE/APPLY

Guided Practice Distribute *Tactile Letter Cards j*. Then place *Picture/Word Cards jeep* and *jet* in the pocket chart. Say the names of the pictures as you point to the *j* in each. Have children repeat the words.

Tell children: **Some words begin with *j*.**

Point to the *j* in *jeep*. **The /j/ sound is at the beginning of *jeep*. I'll say some words. If the word begins with the /j/ sound, hold up your *j* card. If it doesn't begin with the /j/ sound, don't hold up your *j* card.**

Thumbs↑ Thumbs↓

jug   box   jar   jiggle   bake   jeans   dog   junk

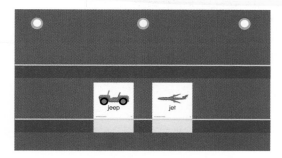

Independent Practice Pass out copies of the Jar Pattern (page T11). Have children draw and label on the jar a picture of an item whose name begins with the /j/ sound. Ask children to whisper the name to you before they draw. Children can cut out the patterns and tape their jar to craft sticks. Encourage them to take turns saying words and people's names that begin with /j/.

FLORIDA STANDARDS/GLEs **FCAT: LA.A.1.1.2.K.5** Phonetic principles; *Also* **LA.A.1.1.2.K.2** Alphabet; **LA.A.1.1.2.K.3** Sounds; **LA.C.1.1.1.K.1** Follow directions

Around the Town   63

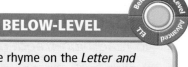

Reread the rhyme on the *Letter and Sound Chart*. Have children take turns framing a word that begins with the letter *j*. Say each word and have children repeat the word and make the /j/ sound. For more practice with Consonant *Jj*, see Alternative Teaching Strategies, page T3.

ADVANCED

Using the *Letter and Sound Chart* illustration as a model, have children draw a jellyfish holding pictures of things that begin with *j*. Tell them to write *Jj* on their pictures.

Phonics Resources

Phonics Express™ CD-ROM, Level A, Speedy/Route 5/ Market, Fire Station

Phonics Practice Book pages 101–102 *class*

▲ **Practice Book page 12**

OBJECTIVE

To read high-frequency words look, come

Materials

- index cards
- *High-Frequency Word Cards*

- *Picture/Word Cards alligator, duck, fox, pig*
- pocket chart
- *Decodable Book 7: A Big, Big Van*

ADVANCED

Have children read *Independent Reader 24: The Lost Dog.*

High-Frequency Words *look, come*

Decodable Book  Review

TEACH/MODEL

Review *look* and *come* On an index card, write the word *at*. Place the index card and *High-Frequency Word Cards Come, look, the* and *Picture/Word Card alligator* in a pocket chart. Add a period at the end. Point to each word slowly and have children read the sentence. Invite children to replace *alligator* with the *Picture/Word Cards duck*, *fox*, and *pig* in the sentence and track the print as children read the new sentences.

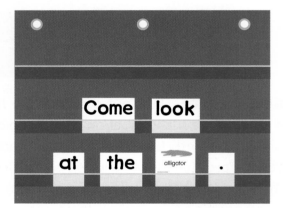

PRACTICE/APPLY

Read the Book Distribute copies of *Decodable Book 7: A Big, Big Van*. Read the title with children, encouraging them to point to each word as they read it. Have children read the book, pointing to each word as they read.

Respond Ask children to draw a picture of a different animal that could be in the box in the van. Have them label their picture.

 FLORIDA STANDARDS/GLEs FCAT: LA.A.1.1.2.K.4 Words; *Also* **LA.A.1.1.2.K.1** Print organization; **LA.A.1.1.3.K.1** Frequent words; **LA.B.1.1.2.K.2** Basic formats; **LA.B.1.1.3.K.1** Spelling approximations; **LA.B.1.1.3.K.2** Print direction; **LA.B.1.1.3.K.3** Punctuation; **LA.B.2.1.4.K.1** Informational texts; **LA.C.1.1.1.K.1** Follow directions

WRAP UP

Share Time

Reflect on the Lesson   Have children talk about the funniest things Mr. Backward does in the poem.

S.S.R.   Have children read silently from a book of their choice.

 **Centers**    **MANIPULATIVES**

Long and Short Sort

Prepare eight to ten picture/word cards by drawing pictures of objects whose names begin with /j/. Label each picture. Draw objects such as jeans, jar, jam, juggler, jet, jump rope, jellyfish, and jug. After children identify each item, ask them to sort the cards into two groups: one with short words and one with long words.

Materials

- index cards
- crayons
- marker

jump rope

Day at a Glance
Day 5

WARM UP

Phonemic Awareness
Phoneme Blending

Sharing Literature
Library Book:
Benny's Pennies

Read

Develop Concept Vocabulary

Respond to Literature

Literature Focus: Beginning, Middle, Ending

Phonics
Consonants *Vv, Jj*

Writing ✏
Your Family

MORNING MESSAGE

Kindergarten News

One classroom rule is _____.

We always _____. We should

never _____.

Write Kindergarten News Talk with children about classroom rules, such as taking turns, listening while others are talking, and respecting other people's belongings.

Use prompts such as the following to guide children as you write the news:

- **What is one of the rules we follow in our class?**
- **What sound do you hear at the beginning of the word *rule*?**
- **Who can point to the word *We*?**
- **How many sentences did I write?**

As you write the message, invite children to write letters and words they have learned previously. Remind them to use proper spacing, capitalization, and punctuation.

Calendar Language

Point to and read aloud the names of the days of the week. Have children identify the first day of the week. (Sunday) Have children identify the last day of the week. (Saturday)

Sunday	Monday	Tuesday	Wednesday	Thursday	Friday	Saturday
		1	2	3	4	5
6	7	8	9	10	11	12
13	14	15	16	17	18	19
20	21	22	23	24	25	26
27	28	29	30	31		

FLORIDA STANDARDS/GLEs **FCAT: LA.A.1.1.2.K.6** Print meaning; *Also* **LA.A.1.1.2.K.1** Print organization; **LA.A.1.1.2.K.3** Sounds; **LA.A.1.1.3.K.1** Frequent words; **LA.C.1.1.3.K.1** Conversation rules; **LA.C.3.1.2.K.1** Questions

Phonemic Awareness

PHONEME BLENDING

Blend Sound   Have children point to the heart shape on Side B of their *Write-On/Wipe-Off Board*. Give each child chips to use with the board. Explain that children will be working with the three boxes next to the heart. Tell children they will place a chip in a box for each sound they hear and will say the word.

MODEL   Say /j/ /e/ /t/ slowly, emphasizing each sound. Place a chip in the first box for /j/. Place a chip in the middle box for /e/. Place a chip in the last box for /t/. Say /j/ /e/ /t/ again, blending the sounds: /jjeett/. Have children blend the sounds with you and name the word: /jjeett/, jet.

Use the same procedure with the following words.

/r/ /e/ /d/ (red)	/v/ /a/ /n/ (van)	/m/ /o/ /p/ (mop)
/j/ /i/ /g/ (jig)	/d/ /o/ /g/ (dog)	/s/ /a/ /t/ (sat)
/j/ /e/ /t/ (jet)	/l/ /e/ /t/ (let)	/j/ /a/ /m/ (jam)
/g/ /i/ /v/ (give)	/v/ /ā/ /s/ (vase)	/s/ /a/ /d/ (sad)

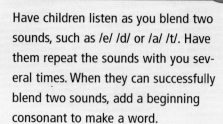

BELOW-LEVEL

Have children listen as you blend two sounds, such as /e/ /d/ or /a/ /t/. Have them repeat the sounds with you several times. When they can successfully blend two sounds, add a beginning consonant to make a word.

ADVANCED

Point out pictures of objects in a picture dictionary. Choose objects whose names are consonant-vowel-consonant words, such as *hen, pig*, and *cat*. Ask children to blend the sounds and have listeners guess the word being said.

BENNY'S PENNIES
BY PAT BRISSON · ILLUSTRATED BY BOB BARNER

▲ **Library Book**

OBJECTIVES

- *To recall story events*
- *To recognize text patterns*
- *To identify the beginning, middle, and ending of a story*

Materials

- *Library Book: Benny's Pennies*
- story props
- chart paper

Sharing Literature

Read Benny's Pennies

READ ALOUD

Before Reading   Show the cover of *Benny's Pennies*. Track the print of the title as you read it aloud. Read the name of the author and ask: **What does an author do?** Read the name of the illustrator and ask: **What does an illustrator do?** Then use these prompts to help children recall story events and to set a purpose for rereading:

- **What is this story about?** (Benny has five pennies. He uses them to buy special presents for his family and pets.)
- **What are the five things Benny buys?** (a rose, a cookie, a hat, a bone, and a fish)

If children cannot remember all the things Benny buys, then tell children that you will read the story again to help them remember the five things Benny buys with his pennies.

During Reading   Reread the story aloud. As you read,

- encourage children to join in on the repetitive phrase *"Will you sell me a _____ for a penny?"*
- pause as you come to rhyming words and model how to anticipate the words.

MODEL   *"Yes, I will," said Mrs.* (pause) *Hill.* **Mrs. Hill is on the last page I read, so I know her name.** *Will* **and** *Hill* **rhyme, so that must be the next word.**

FLORIDA STANDARDS/GLEs   FCAT: **LA.A.1.1.4.K.1** Comprehension; **LA.A.2.1.1.K.1** Main idea; *Also* **LA.D.1.1.1.K.1** Sound patterns

DEVELOP CONCEPT VOCABULARY

 *also*

After Reading   Ask children how many presents Benny buys with his pennies. (five) Begin a word web on the board by writing the word *Presents* in the center circle. Ask children to name the presents as you record them in the web. (rose, cookie, hat, bone, fish) Then ask questions such as these:

- **Which word is the shortest?** (*hat*)
- **Which words have four letters?** (*rose, bone, fish*)
- **Which word rhymes with *dish*?** (*fish*)
- **Which word has two word parts?** (*cookie*)
- **Which word names something that you can wear?** (*hat*)

RESPOND TO LITERATURE

Dramatize the Story   Have a small group of children act out the story. As you retell the story, pause to let children ad-lib their parts and perform appropriate actions. You may want to supply props for the flower, cookie, and hat, and cutout figures for the bone and the fish.

Literature Focus

BEGINNING, MIDDLE, ENDING

Remind children that a story has a beginning, a middle, and an ending. As you model how to identify the parts of a story, record the events in a story map.

MODEL   **In the beginning, Benny doesn't know what to buy with his five pennies. His mother, brother, sister, dog, and cat all give him ideas. In the middle, Benny buys five different gifts with his pennies. At the end, Benny gives everyone a gift.**

Together, retell the beginning, middle, and ending of the story.

ENGLISH-LANGUAGE LEARNERS

As you read and discuss each illustration, point out important pictures and say the words; for example, *newspaper, butcher, meat, boat, fishing pole.*

ONGOING ASSESSMENT

As you share *Benny's Pennies,* note whether children

- can recall story events.
- can recognize text patterns.

FLORIDA STANDARDS/GLEs   **FCAT: LA.A.1.1.2.K.5** Phonetic principles; *Also* **LA.C.3.1.2.K.1** Questions; **LA.C.3.1.4.K.1** Gestures

Around the Town   **71**

OBJECTIVES

- *To recognize uppercase and lowercase Vv and Jj*

- *To match sounds to letters*

Materials

- pocket chart

- *Big Alphabet Cards Vv, Jj*

- *Picture Cards jeep, jelly, jet, jump rope, van, vegetables, vest, violin*

- *Letter and Sound Place Mats*

Phonics

Consonants /v/v, /j/j ✔ Review

ACTIVE BEGINNING

Recite the Rhymes

Display *Big Alphabet Cards Vv* and *Jj*. Ask children to name each letter and to trace the letter with a finger on their desk. Have children recite "Vroom, Vroom, Vroom" (page 42) and "Put on Your Jacket" (page 62).

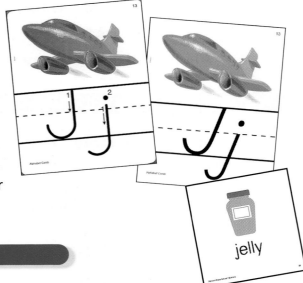

TEACH/MODEL

Discriminate *V* and *J* Hold up *Big Alphabet Card Vv* and ask what letter this is. Point to the picture and say its name. Have children repeat it. (vegetables)

What sound do you hear at the beginning of *vegetables*? /v/ **What letter stands for the /v/ sound in *vegetables*?** (v) Touch the letter and say **/v/.** Touch the letter again and have children say /v/.

Follow the same procedure for *Big Alphabet Card Jj.*

In a pocket chart, place *Alphabet Cards V* and *J* and *Picture Cards violin* and *jelly*. Say each picture name and tell children you need to decide where to put each *Picture Card*.

MODEL **I'll start with the violin. *V—iolin* begins with the /v/ sound. So I'll put the picture of the violin below *Vv*.**

Model the same process with *Picture Card jelly.*

FLORIDA STANDARDS/GLEs FCAT: LA.A.1.1.2.K.5 Phonetic principles; *Also* **LA.A.1.1.2.K.2** Alphabet; **LA.A.1.1.2.K.3** Sounds; **LA.C.3.1.2.K.1** Questions

PRACTICE/APPLY

Guided Practice Place these *Picture Cards* on the chalk ledge: *jeep, jelly, jet, jump rope, van, vegetables, vest, violin*. Tell children that they will now sort some pictures.

Say the picture name. If the beginning sound is /v/, let's put the card below the *Vv*. If the beginning sound is /j/, let's put the card below the *Jj*.

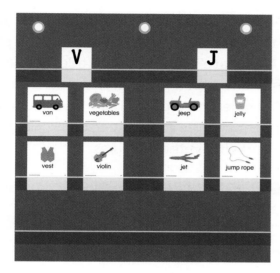

Independent Practice Give each child a *Letters and Sounds Place Mat*.

I'm going to say some words. Listen carefully to the sound you hear at the beginning of the word. Think about the letter that stands for that sound, and point to that letter on your mat.

valentine	jam	jar	vulture	jug	violet	valley
job	junk	vine	velvet	jeans	vase	voice

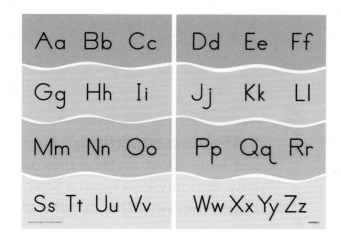

FLORIDA STANDARDS/GLEs **FCAT: LA.A.1.1.2.K.5** Phonetic principles; *Also* **LA.A.1.1.2.K.2** Alphabet; **LA.A.1.1.2.K.3** Sounds; **LA.C.1.1.1.K.1** Follow directions

REACHING ALL LEARNERS

Diagnostic Check: Phonics

If... children cannot identify letter/sound for *Vv* and *Jj* patterns in words,

Then... focus on one letter/sound at a time, saying the names of pictures, saying the initial sound, and tracing the letter on *Tactile Letter Cards*.

ADDITIONAL SUPPORT ACTIVITIES

BELOW-LEVEL	Reteach, p. S6
ADVANCED	Extend, p. S7
ENGLISH-LANGUAGE LEARNERS	Reteach, p. S7

Phonics Resources

Phonics Express™ CD-ROM, **Level A,** Sparkle/Route 1/ Train Station; Speedy/Route 5/ Train Station

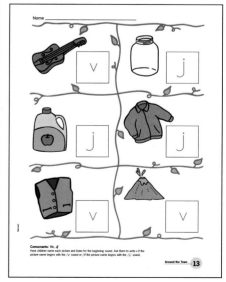

▲ **Practice Book page 13** h.w.

OBJECTIVES

- *To share information and ideas, speaking in complete, coherent sentences*

- *To use letters and phonetically spelled words to write about people and objects*

- *To write labels*

Materials

- drawing paper

- crayons

Writing

Write About Your Family

FAMILY GIFT BOOK

Talk About Family Members   Have children tell a partner about the people in their families. Ask them to name gifts they would like to give to each of their family members.

Write About Your Family   Distribute four pieces of drawing paper to each child. Ask children to fold the paper in half like a book. Then have them write the title "My Gifts" on the front cover and draw a wrapped present. Ask children to draw each of their family members on a page. Then have them go back and draw a gift they would give to each person. Finally, have children label the people and gifts in their pictures.

Writing Every Day

Self-Selected Writing   Have children draw and write about anything they'd like. If they have difficulty thinking of a topic, have them ask two friends what they're going to write about.

FLORIDA STANDARDS/GLEs   FCAT: LA.B.2.1.2.K.1 Record ideas; *Also* **LA.B.1.1.2.K.2** Basic formats; **LA.B.1.1.3.K.1** Spelling approximations; **LA.B.1.1.3.K.2** Print direction

WRAP UP Share Time

Read the Labels When children have completed their books, have them share them with the rest of the class. Ask them to read the labels on their pictures.

S.S.R. Sustained Silent Reading Have children read silently from a book of their choice.

Centers ABC LETTERS AND WORDS

Letter Guess

Place the *Magnetic Letters* in the bag and the *Picture Cards* face up on the table. Have children choose a letter from the bag and then find the *Picture Card* whose name begins with that letter. Ask them to place the *Magnetic Letter* beneath that picture. Encourage children to try the game again, putting the *Picture Cards* in the bag and the *Magnetic Letters* on the table.

Materials

- *Magnetic Letters j, v, b, h, w, l*
- paper bag
- *Picture Cards jelly, vest, baby, horse, watermelon,* and *ladder*

Learning Centers

Choose from the following suggestions to enhance your learning centers for the theme Around the Town.
(Additional learning centers for this theme can be found on pages 14-16 and 122)

MANIPULATIVE CENTER

Build Sentences

Give partners a set of sentence strips. Have them take one sentence strip at a time, read it, and then use *High-Frequency Word Cards*, Alphabet Cards, and punctuation cards to build each sentence. When children finish building one sentence, they should each read it before choosing a new sentence strip to build.

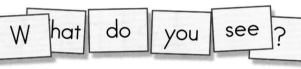

20 Minutes a day

Materials

- sentence strips: Do you see it? I can see it. Can I have it? You can have it. What do you see? Look at it!
- *High-Frequency Word Cards: do, have, I, look, see, what, you*
- *Alphabet Cards D, Y, W, L, a, a, c, i, n, t, t*
- punctuation cards ?, !, .

WRITING CENTER

Write Riddles

Tell partners they are going to play a guessing game. Give each child a paper with sentence frames on it. Tell children to choose a place in town to describe. Children should write their clues—but not mention the place they are describing—in the spaces numbered 1–3. Have children complete the sentence with the name of the place they described. When children finish, have them take turns reading their clues and the final question, *What am I?*, to their partner.

1. I have mal boxes and stamps.
2. You can get stamps frm me.
3. Pepl mal ltrs here.

What am I?

I am a post ofis.

20 Minutes a day

Materials

- paper with the following sentence frames:
  1. _____
  2. _____
  3. _____
  What am I?
  I am a _____
- pencils

Teacher Notes

Teacher Notes

THEME 9

Week 2

Around the Town

Theme 9: Week 2

Day 1

Phonemic Awareness, 83
Phoneme Isolation: Medial

Sharing Literature, 84

Read

Big Book: *The Shape of Things*

(Skill) **Literature Focus, 85**
Main Idea

 **Phonics, 86** T
Introduce: Short Vowel *Ee*
Identify/Write T

 Writing, 88
Write a Description

Writing Prompt, 88
Draw and write about self-selected topics.

Share Time, 89
Describe illustrations from *The Shape of Things*.

Day 2

Phonemic Awareness, 91
Phoneme Segmentation

Sharing Literature, 92

Read

Library Book: *Good-Bye Hello*

(Skill) **Literature Focus, 93**
Setting

 **Phonics, 94** T
Review: Short Vowel Ee
Relating /e/ to *e*

 Writing, 96
Write a Sentence

Writing Prompt, 96
Draw and write about self-selected topics.

Share Time, 97
Share pictures.

ORAL LANGUAGE 15-30 Minutes

- **Phonemic Awareness**

- **Sharing Literature**

45 Minutes
LEARNING TO READ

- **Phonics**

- **Vocabulary**

Daily Routines
- **Morning Message**
- **Calendar Language**
- **Writing Prompt**

15-30 Minutes
LANGUAGE ARTS

- **Writing**
 Daily Writing Prompt

T = tested skill

Phonics

Short Vowel *Ee;*
Blending /e/ - /t/

Focus of the Week:
- **PHONEMIC AWARENESS**
- **SHARING LITERATURE**
- **WRITING Descriptions, Sentences**

Day 3

Phonemic Awareness, 99
Phoneme Blending

Sharing Literature, 100
 Read

Read-Aloud Anthology:
"My Pet Spider," pp. 25–27

(Skill) **Literature Focus, 101**
Cause and Effect

Phonics, 102 T
Blending /e/-/t/

 Shared Writing, 104
Write Instructions

Writing Prompt, 104
Draw and write about your favorite animals.

Share Time, 105
Retell the story using Character Cutouts.

Day 4

Phonemic Awareness, 107
Phoneme Counting

Sharing Literature, 108
Big Book of Rhymes and
Songs: "Down by the Bay,"
pp. 12–13

(Skill) **Literature
Focus, 109**
Visualize

Phonics, 110 T
Review: Short Vowel /e/e

Read

DECODABLE BOOK 8
Come In

 Interactive Writing, 112
Write a New Verse

Writing Prompt, 112
Draw and write about something silly
an animal might do.

Share Time, 113
Read and sing new song verses.

Day 5

Phonemic Awareness, 115
Rhyme Recognition

Sharing Literature, 116
Read

Big Book: *The Shape of
Things*

(Skill) **Literature Focus, 117**
Rhyming Words

Phonics, 118 T
Words with /e/ and /t/

 Writing, 120
Write a Description

Writing Prompt, 120
Draw and write about self-selected
topics.

Share Time, 121
Share favorite pictures of buildings.

Day at a Glance
Day 1

WARM UP

Phonemic Awareness
Phoneme Isolation: Medial

Sharing Literature
Big Book:
The Shape of Things

Read

THE SHAPE OF THINGS
DAYLE ANN DODDS ILLUSTRATED BY JULIE LACOME

Develop Concept Vocabulary
Respond to Literature
Literature Focus: Main Idea

Phonics
Vowel *Ee*

Writing
Description

MORNING MESSAGE

Kindergarten News

There is a (building or location) in our town. (Child's name) saw a (vehicle) in our town.

Write Kindergarten News   Talk with children about the community where they live. Encourage them to talk about the buildings, landmarks, and vehicles they see there.

Use prompts such as the following to guide children as you write the news:

- **Who can name a place in our town?**
- **What letter should I write at the beginning of the word *town*?**
- **Who can point to the end of a word?**
- **Let's count the letters in (child's name).**

As you write the message, invite children to contribute by writing letters, words, and names they have learned previously. Remind them to use proper spacing, capitalization, and punctuation.

Calendar Language

Point to and read aloud the days of the week. Ask what day today is. Ask what day came before today. Point to that day and say: *Yesterday was _____.* Invite children to name yesterday and today.

Sunday	Monday	Tuesday	Wednesday	Thursday	Friday	Saturday
		1	2	3	4	5
6	7	8	9	10	11	12
13	14	15	16	17	18	19
20	21	22	23	24	25	26
27	28	29	30	31		

FLORIDA STANDARDS/GLEs   FCAT: LA.A.2.1.5.K.2 Get information; **LA.B.2.1.2.K.1** Record ideas; *Also* **LA.A.1.1.2.K.2** Alphabet; **LA.A.1.1.2.K.3** Sounds; **LA.C.1.1.3.K.1** Conversation rules; **LA.C.3.1.2.K.1** Questions

Phonemic Awareness

PHONEME ISOLATION: MEDIAL

Listen for /e/   Use the rabbit puppet for this activity. Remind children that the rabbit likes to break words into parts. Tell children the rabbit will say a word and they will listen for the middle sound in the word.

Say: *vet.* /v/ /e/ /t/. **Let's say the word with the rabbit. What sound do you hear in the middle of the word?** I hear /e/ in the middle of *vet.* **Say /e/ with me.**

Tell children that the rabbit is going to say some words. If the rabbit says a word that has the /e/ sound in the middle, children should make the /e/ sound. Guide children by segmenting each word and having them repeat it. Use the following words:

get	/g/ /e/ /t/		not	/n/ /o/ /t/
luck	/l/ /u/ /k/		wet	/w/ /e/ /t/
nap	/n/ /a/ /p/		sell	/s/ /e/ /l/
hen	/h/ /e/ /n/		red	/r/ /e/ /d/
desk	/d/ /e/ /s/ /k/		tip	/t/ /i/ /p/
left	/l/ /e/ /f/ /t/		yet	/y/ /e/ /t/

BELOW-LEVEL

Tell children to listen to the word you say. Say: *web*. Ask: *What sound do you hear in the middle of* web*?* /e/ Say the following words and have children name all sounds they hear in the middle of each word: *jet, can, deck, tell, hop, sled, let.*

▲ **Big Book**

OBJECTIVES

- *To locate the title, name of author, and name of illustrator*

- *To describe how illustrations contribute to the text*

- *To identify the main idea of a story*

Materials

- *Big Book: The Shape of Things*

- chart paper

- marker

Sharing Literature

Read The Shape of Things

READ ALOUD

Before Reading Display the cover of *The Shape of Things.* Ask children to point to the title and read it aloud. Have children point to the name of the author and the illustrator. Ask: **Why are these names here? What did these people do?** Use these prompts to recall the story and set a purpose for rereading:

- **What is this book about?** (how things are made of shapes)

- **What kinds of shapes did we see in this book?** (squares, circles, rectangles, triangles, ovals, diamonds)

- **What were some of the things that were made from these shapes?** (Possible response: A kite was made from a diamond.)

During Reading Read the selection aloud. As you read,

- identify any shapes or items that children forgot to identify.

- point out how the pictures help children understand the words on page 10.

MODEL **I was not sure what shape a rectangle is until I saw the picture. Now I know exactly what it is.**

🦩 **FLORIDA STANDARDS/GLEs**   **FCAT: LA.A.1.1.4.K.1** Comprehension; **LA.A.2.1.1.K.1** Main idea; **LA.E.1.1.1.K.1** Genres;   *Also* **LA.B.2.1.4.K.1** Informational texts; **LA.C.3.1.2.K.1** Questions

DEVELOP CONCEPT VOCABULARY

After Reading Write the words *shape*, *square*, *circle*, and *rectangle* on chart paper. Point to and read each word. Then use each word in a sentence. Ask children to respond to questions by using complete sentences.

I see a <u>shape</u>. Do you see a shape?

I see a door that is a <u>rectangle</u>. Where do you see a rectangle?

I see a clock that is a <u>circle</u>. Where do you see a circle?

I see a block that is a <u>square</u>. Where do you see a square?

RESPOND TO LITERATURE

Find Shapes Have children draw some objects from pages 18–19 in the book. Have them switch papers with a partner and then circle the shapes they find in each other's drawing.

Literature Focus

MAIN IDEA

Remind children that a sentence that tells what a story is about is called the main idea. Sometimes the sentence is in the story, and sometimes we have to figure it out by using the words and pictures.

MODEL **The title of a book can also tell the main idea. The title *The Shape of Things* and the picture on the cover help us form a sentence that tells the main idea:** *Shapes are all around us.*

FLORIDA STANDARDS/GLEs   FCAT: LA.A.1.1.2.K.4 Words; **LA.A.1.1.3.K.5** Story elements; **LA.A.2.1.1.K.1** Main idea; **LA.C.3.1.3.K.1** Basic vocabulary; *Also* **LA.A.1.1.3.K.3** Categorize words; **LA.A.2.1.4.K.1** Illustrations

ENGLISH-LANGUAGE LEARNERS

To give children an opportunity to hear vocabulary and see shapes in the story again, have them listen to the *Audiotext*.

ONGOING ASSESSMENT

As you share *The Shape of Things*, note whether children

- can locate the title and names of author and illustrator.

- understand how illustrations contribute to the text.

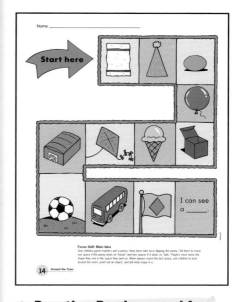

▲ **Practice Book page 14**

Around the Town   **85**

OBJECTIVES

To recognize E and e

*To write uppercase
and lowercase Ee
independently*

Materials

- *Big Book
of Rhymes and Songs*
p. 16

- *Big Alphabet Card Ee*

- *Write-On/Wipe-Off
Boards*

- drawing paper

- crayons

Phonics Resources

Phonics Express™ **CD-ROM,
Level A,** Bumper/Route 2/ Train
Station

Phonics
Vowel Ee ✔*Introduce*

ACTIVE BEGINNING

Recite "Everything Grows" Display "Everything Grows" in the *Big
Book of Rhymes and Songs.* Track the print as you read the rhyme
with children.

EVERYTHING GROWS

Everything grows and grows;
Babies do, animals too.
Everything grows.
Everything grows and grows;
Sisters do, brothers too.
Everything grows.

16

TEACH/MODEL

Introduce the Letter Name Hold up the *Big Alphabet Card Ee.*

The name of this letter is *e*. Say the name with me.

Point to the uppercase *E*. **This is the
uppercase *E*.**

Point to the lowercase *e*.
This is the lowercase *e*.

Point to the *Big Alphabet
Card* again. **What is the
name of this letter?**

Point to an *E* in "Everything
Grows." **What is the name of this letter?**

Follow along as I read the title.

Point to the letter *e*. **What is the name of this letter?**

FLORIDA STANDARDS/GLEs LA.A.1.1.2.K.1 Print organization; LA.A.1.1.2.K.2 Alphabet; LA.C.3.1.2.K.1
Questions; LA.D.2.1.2.K.1 Patterned structures

Handwriting

Writing *E* and *e*   Write uppercase *E* and lowercase *e* on the board.

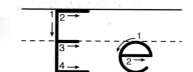

Point to the uppercase *E*. **What letter is this?**

Point to the lowercase *e*. **What letter is this?**

MODEL   **Watch as I write the letter *e* so that everyone can read it.**

Give the Letter Talk as you trace the uppercase *E*. Use the same modeling procedure for lowercase *e*.

Letter Talk for *E*

Straight line down, line across at the top, at the middle, and at the bottom.

Letter Talk for *e*

Curve left, straight line across the middle.

D'Nealian handwriting models are on pages R12–13.

PRACTICE/APPLY

Guided Practice   Help children find *Ee* on their *Write-On/Wipe-Off Board*. Have them trace uppercase *E* with a finger and write the letter several times. Then have them do the same for lowercase *e*.

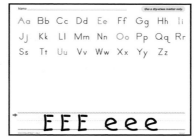

Independent Practice   Distribute drawing paper in the shape of an egg to children. Have them fill their egg with *Ee*'s. Then have them circle their best *E* and *e*.

BELOW-LEVEL

Guide children in writing the letters. Put your hand over their hand and write the letters with them. Then have children write the letters on their own.

ADVANCED

Encourage children to use pencils to write *E* and *e* on lined paper.

ENGLISH-LANGUAGE LEARNERS

As you introduce children to *Ee* letter formation, model each step of the Letter Talk to make sure children understand the terms *straight down*, *top*, *middle*, *bottom*, and *curve left*.

Phonics Practice Book pages 103–104 *Class*

▲ **Practice Book page 15** *hw*

OBJECTIVES

- *To use letters and pho-netically spelled words to write about objects*

- *To write a description*

Materials

- an orange
- chart paper
- drawing paper
- crayons

Writing Every Day

Day 1: Description
Have children choose an object, draw a picture of it, and write a description of it.

Day 2: Sentence
Have children complete a sentence frame by writing and by drawing.

Day 3: Instructions
Work together to write instructions for caring for a pet.

Day 4: New Verse
Work together to write a new verse for "Down by the Bay."

Day 5: Describe Buildings
Have children draw buildings and write shape and color words to tell about their drawings.

LANGUAGE ARTS

Writing

Write a Description

DESCRIBE A CLASSROOM OBJECT

Talk About an Object   Hold up an orange and model for children how to use color, size, and shape to tell about something. As you model, write the sentences on chart paper after you say them.

> **MODEL**   **When we want to tell someone what something looks like, we can tell its color.** *The orange is orange.* **We can tell if it is big or small.** *The orange is small.* **We can tell its shape. The orange is in the shape of a circle if we draw it on paper.** *The orange is a circle.*

Write a Description   Distribute drawing paper and tell children that they are going to choose an object from *The Shape of Things* and write about what it looks like. Page through the *Big Book* to remind children of their choice. Have them choose an object, draw it, and write sentences that tell what it looks like on their paper. Display the chart with the three sentences for children to use as a model.

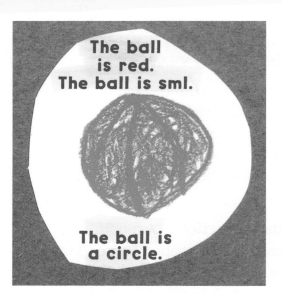

Self-Selected Writing   Have children write and draw about anything they'd like. If they have difficulty thinking of a topic, have them ask two friends what they're going to write about.

FLORIDA STANDARDS/GLEs   **FCAT: LA.A.1.1.2.K.4** Words; **LA.B.2.1.2.K.1** Record ideas;   *Also* **LA.A.1.1.3.K.3** Categorize words; **LA.B.1.1.2.K.2** Basic formats; **LA.B.1.1.3.K.1** Spelling approximations; **LA.B.1.1.3.K.2** Print direction; **LA.B.1.1.3.K.3** Punctuation; **LA.B.2.1.4.K.1** Informational texts; **LA.C.1.1.1.K.1** Follow directions

WRAP UP # Share Time

Reflect on the Lesson Invite children to share their picture and read their sentence. Have a child point to the object in the *Big Book* that is being described.

S.S.R. *Sustained Silent Reading* Have children read silently from a book of their choice.

 **Centers** **MANIPULATIVES**

Building Puzzles

Glue each picture onto a piece of poster board. When the glue is dry, cut the picture into about eight to ten pieces, making most of the pieces squares, rectangles, and triangles. Put pieces of each puzzle into a large envelope. Have children choose an envelope and assemble the puzzle. Ask them to tell what shapes they see in the completed picture.

Materials

- magazine pictures of buildings
- glue
- poster board
- scissors
- large envelopes

FLORIDA STANDARDS/GLEs LA.A.1.1.2.K.1 Print organization; LA.A.2.1.2.K.1 Select materials; LA.E.2.1.1.K.1 Background knowledge

Around the Town **89**

WARM UP

Phonemic Awareness
Segmenting Phonemes

Sharing Literature
Library Book:
Good-bye Hello

GOOD-BYE
hello

Develop Listening Comprehension

Respond to Literature

Literature Focus: Setting

Phonics
Relating /e/ to e

Writing
Writing: Sentence

MORNING MESSAGE

Kindergarten News

(Name) is my friend.

We like to _____.

Write Kindergarten News Talk with children about friends they have and what they like to do with their friends. Help children think about people other than classmates who might be their friends.

Use prompts such as the following to guide children as you write the news:

- **Who is your friend? What do you and your friend do together?**
- **What sound do you hear at the beginning of _____'s name?**
- **Who can point to the word *my*?**
- **Who can write the word *like*?**

As you write the message, invite children to contribute by writing letters, words, and names they have learned previously. Remind them to use proper spacing, capitalization, and punctuation.

Calendar Language

Point to and read aloud the names of the days of the week. Ask what day today is. Ask children what day comes after today. Point to the name of the day and say: *Tomorrow is* _____. **Invite children to name today and tomorrow.**

Sunday	Monday	Tuesday	Wednesday	Thursday	Friday	Saturday
		1	2	3	4	5
6	7	8	9	10	11	12
13	14	15	16	17	18	19
20	21	22	23	24	25	26
27	28	29	30	31		

FLORIDA STANDARDS/GLEs FCAT: LA.A.1.1.2.K.5 Phonetic principles; **LA.A.2.1.5.K.2** Get information; **LA.B.2.1.2.K.1** Record ideas; *Also* **LA.A.1.1.3.K.1** Frequent words; **LA.C.1.1.3.K.1** Conversation rules; **LA.C.3.1.2.K.1** Questions

Phonemic Awareness

SEGMENTING PHONEMES

Listen for /e/ Have children point to the heart shape on Side B of their *Write-On/Wipe-Off Board.* Give each child a disk to use with the board. Explain that they will be working with the three boxes next to the heart.

Whole group - not each child.

MODEL Hold up Side B of the *Write-On/Wipe-Off Board.* **I will listen for /e/ in the word** *bed.* **Say /b/ /e/ /d/. Say** *bed* **with me.** Point to the first box and say: **Do I hear /e/ in the beginning? /b/. No.** Point to the second box. **Do I hear /e/ in the middle? /b/ /e/. Yes. So I will place a disk in the middle box.** Point to the last box. **Do I hear /e/ at the end? /b/ /e/ /d/. No. /bbeedd/. I hear /e/ in the middle, so my disk goes in the middle box.**

Tell children to listen for the /e/ sound and to place their disk in the first, middle, or last box to show where they hear /e/ when they repeat the word.

Say *egg.* **Where is the /e/ sound in** *egg***?** (beginning)

Say *get.* **Where is the /e/ sound in** *get***?** (middle)

Say *bell.* **Where is the /e/ sound in** *bell***?** (middle)

Say *ten.* **Where is the /e/ sound in** *ten***?** (middle)

Say *end.* **Where is the /e/ sound in** *end***?** (beginning)

Say *web.* **Where is the /e/ sound in** *web***?** (middle)

▲ **"A Frog Went A-Courtin'," *Oo-pples and Boo-noo-noos: Songs and Activities for Phonemic Awareness,* pages 76–77.**

BELOW-LEVEL

Have children listen as you say word pairs such as *ten/pan, pen/bet, fed/men, hit/set.* Ask children to tell you which pairs have the same middle sound.

ADVANCED

Have children draw pictures of a mop, a box, a fox, a bed, a pen, a hen. Tell them to cut out the pictures and sort them into *Words with /o/* and *Words with /e/* piles.

Sharing Literature

Read Good-bye Hello

▲ **Library Book**

OBJECTIVES

To use pictures and context to make predictions

To understand characters' feelings

To ask and answer questions about a text

To identify setting

Materials

■ *Library Book: Good-bye Hello*

■ drawing paper

■ crayons

READ ALOUD

Before Reading   Display the cover of *Good-bye Hello*. Ask a child to point to the title as you read it aloud. Then read the names of the author and the illustrator. Help children use the cover illustration and the title to make predictions:

- Point to the girl. **This is the main character in this story.**

- **What do you think is happening in the story?** (Possible response: The girl is moving away.)

Page through the book, pausing briefly to allow children to preview the illustrations. Have children make predictions about the story.

During Reading   Read the story aloud. As you read,

- pause to point to illustrations that show that the girl is sad to leave.

- model how to confirm predictions.

MODEL   **I thought this story would have a happy ending because I noticed that the girl is smiling at the end of the book. Now I know that I was right.**

🍊 **FLORIDA STANDARDS/GLEs   FCAT: LA.A.1.1.4.K.1** Comprehension;   *Also* **LA.A.1.1.1.K.1** Predictions; **LA.A.1.1.2.K.1** Print organization; **LA.A.2.1.4.K.1** Illustrations; **LA.C.1.1.1.K.2** Oral language; **LA.C.2.1.2.K.1** Nonverbal cues; **LA.C.3.1.2.K.1** Questions

PRACTICE/APPLY

Guided Practice Distribute *Tactile Letter Card e* and a *Write-On/Wipe-Off Board* to each child. Have children point to the heart shape on Side B of their *Write-On/Wipe-Off Board*. Explain that they will be working with the three boxes next to the heart. Then place *Picture/Word Cards egg* and *jet* in a pocket chart. Say each word as you point to the e in each. Have children repeat the words.

Tell children: **Some words begin with e and some words have e in the middle.**

Point to the e in *egg*. **The /e/ sound is at the beginning of the word *egg*.** Point to the e in *jet*. **The e is in the middle of the word *jet*.**

I'm going to say some words. If the /e/ sound is at the beginning of a word, put your letter e in the beginning box. If the /e/ sound is in the middle of the word, put your letter e in the middle box.

Model the procedure, using the words *egg* and *jet*. Then say these words:

✱ whole group

edge	**elk**	**engine**	**elephant**
bed	**pet**	**leg**	**ten**	**net**

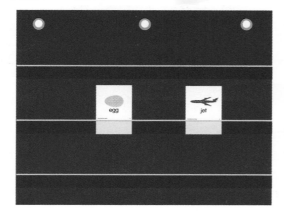

Independent Practice Distribute copies of the Egg Pattern (T12) and drawing paper to children. Have children cut out the egg and the crack and help them attach the egg to their drawing paper with a brass fastener. This will allow the egg to open and close. Ask children to open their eggs and draw a picture of an item whose name has the /e/ sound. Remind them that the picture can't be bigger than the egg. Have them write *Ee* above the egg and label the picture.

FLORIDA STANDARDS/GLEs   FCAT: LA.A.1.1.2.K.5 Phonetic principles; *Also* **LA.A.1.1.2.K.2** Alphabet; **LA.A.1.1.2.K.3** Sounds; **LA.B.1.1.2.K.2** Basic formats; **LA.B.1.1.3.K.1** Spelling approximations; **LA.B.1.1.3.K.2** Print direction

Diagnostic Check: Phonics

If... children cannot match the vowel sound /e/ to letter e,

Then... have them take turns finding on the *Letter and Sound Chart* an *Ee* at the beginning of a word and underlining it, using the clear plastic overlay and a marker. Then say the word and have children repeat it. /e/ *Elephant* /e/

ADDITIONAL SUPPORT ACTIVITIES

BELOW-LEVEL	Reteach, p. S8
ADVANCED	Extend, p. S9
ENGLISH-LANGUAGE LEARNERS	Reteach, p. S9

Phonics Practice Book pages 105–106 *class*

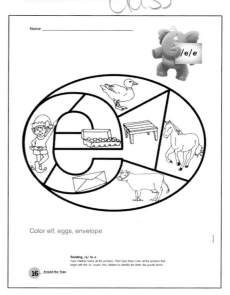

▲ **Practice Book page 16**

h.w.

Around the Town   95

OBJECTIVES

- *To use letters and phonetically spelled words to write about objects*

- *To write a sentence*

Materials

- drawing paper
- crayons

Writing

Write a Sentence

CHARACTER FOCUS

Talk About Sentences   Remind children that a sentence tells a complete thought. Write this sentence on the board: *The girl moved to a new house.* Track the words as you read the sentence. Point out the uppercase letter at the beginning of the sentence and the period at the end.

Write a Sentence   Remind children that in *Good-bye Hello* the girl makes sure she takes her stuffed animal, Fuzzy Bear, with her when she moves. On the board, write the sentence frame *I would take my* _____. Track the words as you read them to the class. Have children copy the words on their paper and finish the sentence by writing the name of something they would take with them to a new place. Have them draw a picture of the item.

SHARE

Read the Sentences   When children have finished, invite them to share the sentence they wrote. Talk with children about why they chose the thing they did.

Self-Selected Writing Have children write and draw about anything they'd like. If they have difficulty thinking of a topic, have them ask two friends what they're going to write about.

FLORIDA STANDARDS/GLEs   FCAT: LA.B.2.1.2.K.1 Record ideas; *Also* **LA.B.1.1.2.K.2** Basic formats; **LA.C.1.1.3.K.1** Conversation rules; **LA.B.1.1.3.K.2** Print direction; **LA.B.1.1.3.K.3** Punctuation; **LA.C.3.1.1.K.1** Speak clearly

Phonemic Awareness

PHONEME BLENDING

Blend Sounds Use the rabbit puppet for this blending activity. Remind children that the rabbit likes to break words into parts. Tell children they will listen to sounds the rabbit says and then will blend the sounds and say the word.

Have the rabbit say: /n/ /e/ /t/ slowly, emphasizing each sound.

Listen as the rabbit blends the sounds. **/nneett/.** Have children blend the sounds with you and name the word. **/nneett/,** *net.*

Use the same procedure with the following words.

/w/ /e/ /t/ (wet)   /s/ /e/ /t/ (set)   /t/ /e/ /l/ (tell)

/r/ /e/ /d/ (red)   /k/ /a/ /t/ (cat)   /t/ /e/ /n/ (ten)

/j/ /o/ /b/ (job)   /b/ /e/ /l/ (bell)   /b/ u/ /g/ (bug)

/v/ /e/ /t/ (vet)   /d/ /o/ /g/ (dog)   /n/ /e/ /t/ (net)

REACHING ALL LEARNERS

Diagnostic Check: Phonemic Awareness

If... children have difficulty blending sounds to make words,

Then... have them look at the *Picture Card cat* and say its name. Then have them say *cat* slowly and segment the word into parts: /c/ /a/ /t/. Have children practice with *Picture Cards dog, fox, hat, hen, jet, pig, sun, van.*

ADDITIONAL SUPPORT ACTIVITIES

BELOW-LEVEL	Reteach, p. S10
ADVANCED	Extend, p. S11
ENGLISH-LANGUAGE LEARNERS	Reteach, p. S11

▲ **Read-Aloud Anthology**

OBJECTIVES

To make predictions

To listen and respond to a poem

To recognize cause and effect

Materials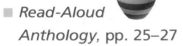

■ *Read-Aloud Anthology*, pp. 25–27

■ chart paper

■ marker

■ *Teacher's Resource Book*, pp. 93–94

■ crayons

■ scissors

■ craft sticks

■ tape

Sharing Literature

Read "My Pet Spider"

READ ALOUD

Before Reading Tell children that you are going to read a poem called "My Pet Spider." It's about a spider who crawls out of her cage to look for some friends. Ask children to guess what kinds of animal friends a spider might have, and list their responses on chart paper. Model how to set a purpose for reading.

MODEL **We listed some animals a spider might have as a friend. Now I'm going to read the poem to see if any of the animals on our list are there.**

During Reading Read the poem aloud. As you read,

• pause to allow children to name the animal whose name rhymes with each place in the story.

• invite children to join in on the phrase *but no one was home so she went back alone*.

• pause to circle on the class list any animals that appear in the poem.

MODEL **The spider went to the log to look for the frog. *Frog* is here on our list. I will circle it because you were right.**

FLORIDA STANDARDS/GLEs   **FCAT: LA.A.1.1.4.K.1** Comprehension; **LA.E.1.1.1.K.1** Genres; **LA.E.1.1.2.K.1** Story elements; *Also* **LA.A.1.1.1.K.1** Predictions; **LA.C.1.1.1.K.2** Oral language

DEVELOP CONCEPT VOCABULARY

After Reading   Remind children that the spider goes places to find friends. Create a word web by writing *Places* in the center circle. Have children name the places where the spider's friends lived. (lake, log, thicket, tree, hole, plant) Help children remember the places by asking questions such as: **Where does the cricket live?** (in a thicket) Explain that a thicket is an area filled with bushes. Then place children into groups of 7. Have each child illustrate, label, and share with the group a place from the story.

RESPOND TO LITERATURE

Act Out the Poem   Have children stay in groups with their illustrations. Give each child a Character Cutout from the *Teacher's Resource Book.* Have children color their cutout and tape it to a craft stick. Discuss the movements each kind of animal makes. Then reread "My Pet Spider" as groups of children act it out with their characters and illustrations.

Literature Focus

CAUSE AND EFFECT

Remind children that in the poem the pet spider crawls out of her cage. Ask: **Why does she crawl out of her cage?** (because she is lonely)

Say: **In poems and stories one thing happens that makes another thing happen. The pet spider is lonely, so she crawls out of her cage to find a friend.**

Discuss other events in the poem that make something else happen. (The spider finds no one home, so she goes back alone; the spider finds the animals at home, so she goes back home with them.)

ADVANCED

Have children work with a partner to write and illustrate a new sentence for the poem that tells about another place and animal. You may want to provide the sentence frame: *She went to the _____ to look for the _____.* When children finish, have them share their sentence.

ENGLISH-LANGUAGE LEARNERS

Show children the animals pictured on the Character Cutouts and name them. Then say each animal name and have children point to the corresponding cutout.

ONGOING ASSESSMENT

As you share "My Pet Spider," note whether children

- can make predictions.
- can listen and respond to a poem.

FLORIDA STANDARDS/GLEs   FCAT: LA.A.1.1.2.K.4 Words; **LA.A.1.1.3.K.5** Story elements; **LA.A.1.1.4.K.1** Comprehension; **LA.C.3.1.3.K.1** Basic vocabulary; **LA.E.1.1.2.K.1** Story elements; *Also* **LA.A.1.1.3.K.2** Nouns and verbs; **LA.B.1.1.2.K.2** Basic formats; **LA.B.2.1.4.K.1** Informational texts; **LA.C.3.1.1.K.1** Speak clearly; **LA.C.3.1.2.K.1** Questions

Around the Town   101

OBJECTIVES

- *To identify and recognize the initial sound of a spoken word*

- *To blend /e/ and /t/*

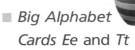

Materials

■ *Big Alphabet Cards Ee and Tt*

■ *Alphabet Cards e, n, p, t*

■ pocket chart

■ sentence strips

Phonics

Blending /e/ - /t/

ACTIVE BEGINNING

Word Hunt Have children sit in a circle. As you read the following verse, have the children echo. Establish a beat and keep it going throughout the verse.

Going on a word hunt.

What's this word?

/n/ /e/ /t/

Together: *Net!*

Continue with the words /b/ /e/ /t/ (*bet*), /s/ /e/ /t/ (*set*), /t/ /e/ /n/ (*ten*).

TEACH/MODEL

Recognize /e/ and /t/ Display *Big Alphabet Card Ee* on the chalk ledge or in a pocket chart.

What letter is this?

What sound does this letter stand for? (/e/)

Have children say /e/ with you as you point to the letter.

Do the same procedure for *Big Alphabet Card Tt*.

Word Blending Explain to children that they are going to blend letters together to read words, such as *pet* and *ten*.

- Place *Alphabet Cards p, e, t* in the pocket chart, separate from each other.

- Point to *p*. Say **/pp/**. Have children repeat the sound after you.
- Point to *e*. Say **/ee/**. Have children repeat the sound after you.
- Point to *t*. Say **/tt/**. Have children repeat the sound after you.

 FLORIDA STANDARDS/GLEs   FCAT: LA.A.1.1.2.K.5 Phonetic principles; *Also* **LA.A.1.1.2.K.2** Alphabet; **LA.A.1.1.2.K.3** Sounds; **LA.C.3.1.2.K.1** Questions

- Slide *e* next to *p*. Say **/ppee/**.

- Slide the *t* next to the *pe*. Move your hand under the letters and blend the sounds, elongating them—**/ppeett/**. Have children repeat after you.

- Then have children read *pet* with you.

PRACTICE/APPLY

Guided Practice   Place the letters *t*, *e*, and *n* in the pocket chart.

- Point to *t* and say **/tt/**. Point to the letter *e* and say **/ee/**. Slide the *e* next to *t*. Move your hand under the letters and blend the sounds, elongating them—**/ttee/**. Have children blend the sounds after you.

- Point to *n*. Say **/nn/**. Have children say the sound.

- Slide the *n* next to the *te*. Slide your hand under *ten* and blend the sounds. Have children blend the sounds as you slide your hand under the word.

- Then have children read the word *ten* along with you.

Follow the same procedure to build and blend *get*, *wet*, and *Ted* with children.

Independent Practice   Write on sentence strips the sentence frame *I have ten _____*. Place one strip in the pocket chart and have children read the sentence frame. Then distribute the sentence strips to children. Have them write a word that completes the sentence. When they have finished, ask them to read their sentence.

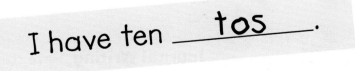

FLORIDA STANDARDS/GLEs   FCAT: LA.A.1.1.2.K.5 Phonetic principles; *Also* LA.A.1.1.2.K.3 Sounds; LA.B.1.1.2.K.2 Basic formats; LA.B.1.1.3.K.1 Spelling approximations; LA.B.1.1.3.K.2 Print direction; LA.B.1.1.3.K.3 Punctuation; LA.B.2.1.4.K.1 Informational texts

Have children use their *Word Builders* and *Word Builder Cards* to blend /e/ and /t/ with you. Follow the procedure used in the Teach/Model section of the lesson. For more practice with Short Vowel *Ee*, see Alternative Teaching Strategies, page T4.

ADVANCED

Place the *Magnetic Letters e, g, j, l, n, t* and a cookie sheet in the Letters and Words Center. Place the *Magnetic Letters e* and *t* on the cookie sheet. Encourage children to make words with *e* and *t*, such as *get* and *ten*.

▲ **Practice Book page 17**

Shared Writing

Write Instructions

OBJECTIVES

To share information and ideas, speaking in complete, coherent sentences

To understand the purpose of instructions

To write instructions, using action words

Materials

- chart paper
- marker

TAKING CARE OF A PET

Talk About Instructions Remind children that instructions help people know how to do things. Talk about the kinds of things that people need instructions for, such as how to do a new dance or how to build a birdhouse.

Write Instructions Tell children that together they are going to write instructions on how to care for a class pet (real or imaginary). Model for children how to use action words to explain how to take care of the pet.

> **MODEL** I know a pet needs to have a clean cage. First, I will clean the cage. I know our pet needs to drink water. I will give it clean water. I know our pet needs to eat. I will give it food.

As children offer suggestions, list their ideas on the chart paper.

Clean the cage.

Give the hamster clean water.

Feed the hamster.

SHARE

Read the Instructions When the instructions are finished, read them with children. Make sure children have included everything necessary for the care of the pet. Then read the sentences again and have children say the action word in each sentence.

Journal Writing Have children write and draw about favorite animals.

FLORIDA STANDARDS/GLEs **FCAT: LA.A.1.1.2.K.4** Words; **LA.A.1.1.2.K.6** Print meaning; **LA.B.1.1.2.K.3** Sequence; **LA.B.1.1.2.K.4** Add details; **LA.B.2.1.2.K.1** Record ideas; *Also* **LA.A.1.1.2.K.1** Print organization; **LA.A.1.1.3.K.2** Nouns and verbs; **LA.B.1.1.2.K.1** Dictate messages; **LA.B.1.1.2.K.2** Basic formats; **LA.B.1.1.3.K.1** Spelling approximations; **LA.B.1.1.3.K.2** Print direction; **LA.B.2.1.1.K.2** Contribute ideas

Phonemic Awareness

PHONEME COUNTING

Isolate Sounds in Words   Use the rabbit puppet for this activity. Distribute disks and Side B of the *Write-On/Wipe-Off Board* to each child. Tell children they can break words into parts just like the rabbit.

MODEL   *Not:* /n/ /o/ /t/. **I'll put a disk in a box for each sound.** /n/ /o/ /t/. **What is the first sound you hear in** /n/ /o/ /t/? I hear /n/. **What is the middle sound?** I hear /o/. **What is the last sound?** I hear /t/. **Let's count the disks. I have three disks. There are three sounds in the word** *not.*

Use the same procedure and the rabbit puppet with the following words:

dot (/d/ /o/ /t/; three)	**red** (/r/ /e/ /d/; three)	**pen** (/p/ /e/ /n/; three)
pet (/p/ /e/ /t/; three)	**Ed** (/e/ /d/; two)	**vet** (/v/ /e/ /t/; three)
at (/a/ /t/; two)	**net** (/n/ /e/ /t/; three)	**men** (/m/ /e/ /n/; three)
dig (/d/ /i/ /g/; three)	**bag** (/b/ /a/ /g/; three)	**in** (/i/ /n/; two)

BELOW-LEVEL

To help children learn to segment sounds, begin by saying words and word parts with only two sounds, such as *at, it, in,* or *ig, en, op.* When children can segment two sounds, add a beginning consonant.

ENGLISH-LANGUAGE LEARNERS

Ask children to say short words in their primary language. Work together to segment the sounds of those words.

/p/ /e/ /t/

Sharing Literature

Read "Down by the Bay"

READ ALOUD

Before Reading   Display "Down by the Bay" in the *Big Book of Rhymes and Songs*. Track the print as you read the title. Set a purpose for rereading the words of the first verse of the song.

MODEL   I remember that the song had different animals in it. I'll read the words of the first verse again so I can find out which animal is in the first verse. Then I'll listen to the rest of the song so I can remember the silly things the animals do.

During Reading   Read the first verse of the song aloud. As you read,

- ask children to point to the beginning of each sentence.
- track the print.
- emphasize the rhyming words: *grow/go; whale/tail; say/bay*.

Then play the song on the *Music CD*. Have children sing the song with you.

Down by the bay,
Where the watermelons grow,
Back to my home,
I dare not go.
For if I do,
My mother will say,
"Did you ever see a whale
With a polka-dot tail,
Down by the bay?"

▲ **Big Book of Rhymes and Songs**

OBJECTIVES

- *To recite a song*
- *To respond creatively to a song through art*
- *To recognize that print is read from left to right across the page*
- *To visualize song scenes*

Materials

- *Big Book of Rhymes and Songs*, pp. 12–13
- *Music CD*
- drawing paper
- crayons

FLORIDA STANDARDS/GLEs   FCAT: LA.E.1.1.1.K.1 Genres; *Also* **LA.A.1.1.2.K.1** Print organization; **LA.C.1.1.1.K.2** Oral language; **LA.D.2.1.3.K.1** Multiple Media; **LA.D.2.1.4.K.1** Media

RESPOND TO LITERATURE

Draw a Picture Review the words about the animals in all the verses: (whale with a polka-dot tail, fly wearing a tie, bear combing his hair, llamas eating their pajamas.) Then ask each child to draw a picture of the animal in his or her favorite verse.

Literature Focus

VISUALIZE

Tell children that you can make pictures in your mind to help you understand a story.

MODEL **The song talks about silly things that aren't real. I need to listen carefully to what the words are saying and then make a picture in my mind. The second verse talks about a fly with a tie. Close your eyes and picture the fly wearing a tie. I picture in my mind a little black fly wearing a little purple tie. What color tie did you picture when you heard the words?**

🌴 **FLORIDA STANDARDS/GLEs** **FCAT: LA.A.1.1.2.K.4** Words; **LA.A.1.1.4.K.1** Comprehension; **LA.E.1.1.1.K.1** Genres; *Also* **LA.D.2.1.1.K.1** Word choice; **LA.E.2.1.1.K.2** Personal interpretations

---

REACHING ALL LEARNERS

Below · On-Level · Advanced · ELL

Diagnostic Check: Comprehension

If... children have difficulty visualizing parts of the story,

Then... ask them to think of a pet they have or want. Say: *Picture your pet purple.* Have them draw the animal with a purple crayon. Say: *Picture your pet on a boat in your backyard.* Have them add to their illustration. Tell children to work with a partner to tell each other make-believe things to draw about their pets.

ADDITIONAL SUPPORT ACTIVITIES

BELOW-LEVEL	Reteach, p. S12
ADVANCED	Extend, p. S13
ENGLISH-LANGUAGE LEARNERS	Reteach, p. S13

ONGOING ASSESSMENT

As you share "Down by the Bay," note whether children

• can recite a song.

• recognize that print is read from left to right across the page.

OBJECTIVE

To decode short vowel /e/e words

Materials

- *Alphabet Cards g, e, t*
- pocket chart
- *Decodable Book 8: Come In*
- drawing paper
- crayons

BELOW-LEVEL

As children read the book, have them frame the words *look, do, the, to* and *come* with their fingers.

ADVANCED

Have children read *Independent Reader 25: Mack and Will Are Friends.*

Phonics

Short Vowel /e/e  Review

TEACH/MODEL

Review Blending   Place *Alphabet Cards e* and *t* next to each other in a pocket chart. Move your hand under the letters, blend them, and say **/eett/—et**. Have children blend the sounds with you.

Place the *Alphabet Card g* in front of *et*. Slide your hand under the letters, blend them, and say the word, **/ggeett/—get**. Have children blend the sounds and say the word.

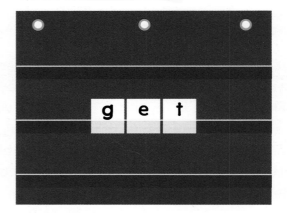

Write this sentence frame on the board: *Come get wet in the _____.* Track the print as children read this sentence and suggest words to finish the sentence, such as *pool, tub, shower, rain.*

PRACTICE/APPLY

Read the Book   Distribute copies of *Come In.* Read the title to children. Have children read the book, pointing to each word as they read.

Respond   Have children draw a picture of Max jumping into the pool.

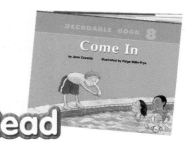

FLORIDA STANDARDS/GLEs   FCAT: LA.A.1.1.2.K.4 Words; **LA.A.1.1.2.K.5** Phonetic principles; *Also* **LA.A.1.1.2.K.1** Print organization; **LA.A.1.1.2.K.3** Sounds; **LA.A.1.1.3.K.1** Frequent words; **LA.C.1.1.1.K.1** Follow directions

Phonemic Awareness

RHYME RECOGNITION

Identify Rhyming Words   Read the following sentences to children and have them repeat them.

Don't touch that pot.

It is hot!

pot–hot, pot–hot

Pot and *hot* have the same ending sounds. They rhyme. Say them again with me: *pot*, *hot*.

Tell children that you are going to say more sentences. Ask them to listen for the rhyming words. After children tell you the rhyming words, have them repeat the phrase with you and add the rhyming words at the end as in the model.

I like jam.

And I like ham.

(jam, ham)

My brother is Sam.

My sister is Pam.

(Sam, Pam)

You can skip,

but do not slip!

(skip, slip)

I have a pig.

She likes to dig.

(pig, dig)

Don't be sad!

Please be glad!

(sad, glad)

I built a pen

for my red hen.

(pen, hen)

Sam   Pam

FLORIDA STANDARDS/GLEs   FCAT: LA.A.1.1.2.K.5 Phonetic principles; *Also* **LA.C.1.1.1.K.1** Follow directions; **LA.D.1.1.1.K.1** Sound patterns

---

BELOW-LEVEL

Show children *Alphabet Cards e* and *t* in a pocket chart. Ask them to say /e/ /t/. Ask them to say /et/ with a /p/ and place *Alphabet Card p* in front of *et* to form *pet*. Have a child take out the *p* and put in a *g:* /g/-*et*. Switch the cards as you say the words fast to show that the ending doesn't change in rhyming words.

ADVANCED

Say short rhyming sentences such as these and have children complete the second sentence with a rhyming word: *I have a cat. She sleeps on the _____.* (mat) *My pillow is red. It's on my _____ .* (bed)

▲ **Big Book**

OBJECTIVES

*To identify the front cover
and back cover of a book*

To recall story events

To identify rhyming words

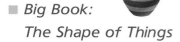

Materials

■ *Big Book:
The Shape of Things*

■ chart paper

■ marker

Sharing Literature

Read **The Shape of Things**

READ ALOUD

Before Reading   Display the *Big Book* and point to the title, *The Shape of Things*. Ask: **What is this?** (the title) Read the title aloud. Have a child point to the front cover and the back cover, using the words *front* and *back*. Use these prompts to set a purpose for rereading:

- **Why do we see shapes in all of these pictures?** (Everything is made with shapes.)

- **What was added to the square to make it into a house?** (a roof, two windows, and a door)

- **What was added to the circle to make it into a Ferris wheel?** (lights and chairs)

Tell children that you will read the story again to find out what was added to each shape to make another object.

During Reading   Reread the selection aloud. As you read,

- emphasize the rhyming words on each page.

- emphasize the words *Until you add* in the rhyme so children can focus on the information that follows.

- to help children keep track of the shapes, pause on each page to summarize what has happened so far.

MODEL   **First, the square was made into a house. Next, the circle was made into a Ferris wheel. Now the triangle is made into a boat.**

FLORIDA STANDARDS/GLEs   **FCAT: LA.A.1.1.2.K.4** Words; **LA.E.1.1.2.K.1** Story elements; *Also* **LA.C.1.1.1.K.2** Oral language

RESPOND TO LITERATURE

Answer a Story Question Display page 19 of the *Big Book* and read the question aloud: *How many can you find?* First, have children take turns pointing to all the squares they can find in the picture. Record their findings on a chart with tally marks. Next, have children take turns pointing out all the rectangles, and record those findings. Continue until all the shapes have been identified. Have children help you count the tally marks to answer the question.

Literature Focus

RHYMING WORDS

Remind children that rhyming words have the same ending sounds. Read the last two lines on page 4 of *The Shape of Things*. Repeat the words *door* and *more*.

MODEL *Door* and *more* have the same ending sounds. So *door* and *more* are rhyming words.

Read the last two lines on each page that tells about a shape. Ask children to name the rhyming words. (*low, go; sky, by; track, back; then, hen; tail, sail*)

ENGLISH-LANGUAGE LEARNERS

Place paper shapes or shape blocks (square, rectangle, circle, triangle, and diamond) in a paper bag. Have children choose a shape from the bag and say its name in English as well as in their primary language.

ONGOING ASSESSMENT

As you share *The Shape of Things*, note whether children

- can identify the front cover and back cover of the book.

- can recall story events.

- can identify rhyming words.

FLORIDA STANDARDS/GLEs FCAT: **LA.A.1.1.2.K.5** Phonetic principles; *Also* **LA.C.3.1.2.K.1** Questions; **LA.D.1.1.1.K.1** Sound patterns

Around the Town **117**

Phonics
Words with /e/ and /t/

OBJECTIVES

- *To build and read simple one-syllable words*

- *To understand that as the letters of words change, so do the sounds*

Materials

- *Alphabet Cards e, l, m, n, p, t*

- *Word Builders*

- *Word Builder Cards e, l, m, n, p, t*

- pocket chart

- *Magnetic Letters*

- cookie sheet

REVIEW LETTERS

ACTIVE BEGINNING

Action Rhyme   Teach children this rhyme and the actions that go with it:

Get the soap, get the sponge. (Pretend to grab items.)

It's bath time—we're all set!

Ten fingers, ten toes. (Wiggle fingers and point to toes.)

They all get soapy and wet! (Pretend to scrub body in a bath.)

TEACH/MODEL

whole group

Blending Words   Distribute *Word Builders* and *Word Builder Cards e, l, m, n, p, t* to children. As you place *Alphabet Cards* in a pocket chart, tell children to place the same *Word Builder Cards* in their *Word Builders.*

- Place *Alphabet Cards l, e,* and *t* in the pocket chart. Have children do the same.

- Point to *l*. Say /ll/. Point to *e*. Say /ee/.
- Slide the *e* next to the *l*. Then move your hand under the letters and blend the sounds, elongating them—/llee/. Have children do the same.

FLORIDA STANDARDS/GLEs   FCAT: LA.A.1.1.2.K.5 Phonetic principles; *Also* LA.A.1.1.2.K.2 Alphabet; LA.A.1.1.2.K.3 Sounds; LA.C.1.1.1.K.1 Follow directions; LA.C.1.1.1.K.2 Oral language; LA.D.2.1.2.K.1 Patterned structures

- Point to the letter *t*. Say /tt/. Have children do the same.
- Slide the *t* next to the *le*. Slide your hand under *let* and blend by elongating the sounds: /lleett/. Have children do the same.
- Then have children read the word *let* along with you.

PRACTICE/APPLY

Guided Practice Have children place *Word Builder Cards* e and t in their *Word Builders*. *whole group*

- **Add *m* to et. What word did you make?**

- **Change *m* to *p*. What word did you make?**

- **Change *t* to *n*. What word did you make?**

- **Change *p* to *t*. What word did you make?**

whole group

Independent Practice Have children use the *Magnetic Letters* e, j, n, p, t, v and a cookie sheet in the Letters and Words Center to build and read *jet*, *net*, *vet*, *pet*, and *ten*.

BELOW-LEVEL

Have children use their *Word Builders* and *Word Builder Cards* to blend /e/ and /t/ with you. Follow the procedure used in the Teach/Model section of the lesson.

ADVANCED

Have children use the *Magnetic Letters e, j, n, p, t* and *High-Frequency Word Cards I, have, a* to build sentences: *I have a net. I have a jet. I have a pet.*

▲ **Practice Book page 18**

h.w.

OBJECTIVES

To share information and ideas, speaking in complete, coherent sentences

To use letters and phonetically spelled words to write about people and objects

To write a description

Materials

■ drawing paper

■ crayons

Writing

Write a Description

BUILD BACKGROUND

Talk About Buildings   Ask children to tell about the houses or apartment buildings where they live. Guide them to tell about the shapes of the buildings.

Write a Description   Have children draw pictures of the outside of the buildings where they live, including shapes such as squares, rectangles, and triangles. Invite them to color their buildings and add background details. Ask them to write the names of the shapes and colors they used in their pictures.

red sqr,
blak tringl

SHARE

Read the Descriptions   When children have finished, invite them to share their pictures and tell about the buildings they drew. You can collect the pictures and staple them together to make a book. Write "Shapes Where We Live" on a cover and place the book in the Literacy Center for children to read.

Self-Selected Writing Have children draw and write about anything they'd like. If they have difficulty thinking of a topic, have them ask two friends what they're going to write about.

FLORIDA STANDARDS/GLEs   **FCAT: LA.B.2.1.2.K.1** Record ideas; *Also* **LA.A.1.1.3.K.3** Categorize words; **LA.B.1.1.2.K.2** Basic formats; **LA.B.1.1.3.K.1** Spelling approximations; **LA.B.1.1.3.K.2** Print direction

WRAP UP # Share Time

Reflect on the Lesson Have children share their pictures of the outside of the building where they live. Compare pictures and discuss the different shapes and colors.

S.S.R. Have children read silently from a book of their choice.

 **Centers**  **WRITING**

Make "Look What We Can Do" Books

Ask children to draw pictures of things they have recently learned how to do. Encourage them to write sentences about their pictures, starting with the words, *I can* _____. After children have completed their drawings, bind them into a book titled "Look What We Can Do!" When you share the book, ask children to read their sentences aloud.

I can mak a bo.

Materials

- drawing paper

- crayons

- paper punch and yarn

FLORIDA STANDARDS/GLEs **FCAT: LA.A.2.1.5.K.2** Get information; **LA.B.2.1.2.K.1** Record ideas; *Also* **LA.A.1.1.2.K.1** Print organization; **LA.A.2.1.2.K.1** Select materials; **LA.B.1.1.2.K.2** Basic formats; **LA.B.1.1.3.K.1** Spelling approximations; **LA.B.1.1.3.K.2** Print direction; **LA.B.1.1.3.K.3** Punctuation

Learning Centers

Choose from the following suggestions to enhance your learning centers for the theme Around the Town. (Additional learning centers for this theme can be found on pages 14-16 and 76)

MATH CENTER

Matching Shapes

Line up a variety of shapes on a table in the math center, such as a circle, square, triangle, rectangle, and oval. Tell children to look through magazines to find and cut out pictures of things in a town. Then have children work as a group to look at each picture and identify the shape it most resembles. For example, a wheel looks like a circle, and a bus has a rectangular shape. Children can sort the pictures according to shape.

Materials

- blocks or shapes such as: circle, square, triangle, rectangle, oval
- old magazines
- safety scissors

LITERACY CENTER

"Adventure in Town" Book

Have children work with a partner. Tell partners they will choose sentences and finish them to write a story about an adventure in town. Tell children to read the sentences and then to choose the ones they want to use for their story. Have them complete each sentence strip, cut it apart, and paste it on a sheet of drawing paper. Children can number the pages, illustrate the sentences, and then reorder the pages before stapling them together to make a book about an adventure in town. Partners can take turns reading their book to each other.

What do you see?
I see a bridg.

Materials

- copies of these sentence strips: What do you see? I see a _____. Come see the _____. Look at the _____. I see it! Come get a _____. Do you have a _____? No, I do not. I do! I have a _____.
- pencils
- safety scissors
- glue sticks
- drawing paper
- crayons
- stapler

Teacher Notes

Teacher Notes

15-30 Minutes

ORAL LANGUAGE

- **Phonemic Awareness**

- **Sharing Literature**

45 Minutes

LEARNING TO READ

- **Phonics**

- **Vocabulary**

Daily Routines
- **Morning Message**
- **Calendar Language**
- **Writing Prompt**

15-30 Minutes

LANGUAGE ARTS

- **Writing**
  Daily Writing Prompt

Day 1

Phonemic Awareness, 129
Phoneme Isolation: Medial

Sharing Literature, 130
 Read

Library Book:
Good-Bye Hello

(Skill) **Literature Focus, 131**
Making Judgments About Characters

Phonics, 132 T
Review: Consonant /n/*n*, Short Vowel /e/*e*

Interactive Writing, 134
Writing Process: Prewrite

Writing Prompt, 134
Draw and write about a special friend.

Share Time, 135
Share your favorite part of the book.

Day 2

Phonemic Awareness, 137
Phoneme Blending

Sharing Literature, 138
 Read

Read-Aloud Anthology:
"Caps for Sale," pp. 73–74

(Skill) **Literature Focus, 139**
Sequence

Phonics, 140 T
Blending /e/ - /n/

 Interactive Writing, 142
Writing Process: Draft

Writing Prompt, 142
Draw and write about self-selected topics.

Share Time, 143
Share questions and illustrations.

T = tested skill

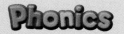 **Phonics**

Review /n/n, /e/e;
Blending /e/ - /n/

Focus of the Week:
- **PHONEMIC AWARENESS**
- **SHARING LITERATURE**
- **WRITING: Classroom Signs (Writing Process)**

Day 3

Phonemic Awareness, 145
Phoneme Deletion: Initial

Sharing Literature, 146
Big Book: *The Shape of Things*

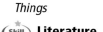 **Literature Focus, 147**
Summarize

Phonics, 148 T
Words with /e/ and /n/

 Interactive Writing, 150

Read

Writing Process: Respond and Revise

Writing Prompt, 150
Draw a picture by following directions.

Share Time, 151
Share favorite parts of the lesson.

Day 4

Phonemic Awareness, 153
Phoneme Substitution

Sharing Literature, 154
Big Book of Rhymes and Songs: "Old Mister Rabbit," pp. 26–27

 Literature Focus, 155
Action Words

Phonics, 156 T
Review: Short Vowel /e/e

Read

DECODABLE BOOK 9
Hop In!

 Interactive Writing, 158
Writing Process: Proofread

Writing Prompt, 158
Draw and write about self-selected topics.

Share Time, 159
Revisit the Decodable book.

Day 5

Phonemic Awareness, 161
Rhyme Recognition

Sharing Literature, 162
Read-Aloud Anthology: "Sing a Song of People," p. 22

Literature Focus, 163
Setting

Phonics, 164 T
Review: Blending /e/ - /n/

 Interactive Writing, 166
Writing Process: Publish

Writing Prompt, 166
Draw and write about a favorite place to visit.

Share Time, 167

Read

Share pictures about the poem.

Day at a Glance
Day 1

WARM UP

Phonemic Awareness
Phoneme Isolation: Medial

Sharing Literature
Library Book:
Good-bye Hello

Read

GOOD-BYE
hello

Develop Concept Vocabulary

Respond to Literature

Literature Focus: Making Judgments About Characters

Phonics

Consonant /n/*n*,
Short Vowel /e/*e*

Interactive Writing

Writing Process: Prewrite

MORNING MESSAGE

Kindergarten News

On the weekend, (Child's name)'s

family _____.

(Child's name) went to _____.

Write Kindergarten News   Talk with children about activities they did over the weekend.

Use prompts such as the following to guide children as you write the news:

- **What did you do this past weekend?**
- **What sound do you hear at the beginning of the word *weekend*?**
- **Who can write the word *to*?**
- **What should I write at the end of this sentence?**

As you write the message, invite children to contribute by writing letters, words, and names they have learned previously. Remind them to use proper spacing, capitalization, and punctuation.

Calendar Language

Point to and read aloud the seasons of the year. Say something that defines each season in terms of weather and seasonal activities. Tell children what season it is. Ask: *What season is it now?*

Sunday	Monday	Tuesday	Wednesday	Thursday	Friday	Saturday
		1	2	3	4	5
6	7	8	9	10	11	12
13	14	15	16	17	18	19
20	21	22	23	24	25	26
27	28	29	30	31		

FLORIDA STANDARDS/GLEs   FCAT: LA.A.1.1.3.K.4 Build vocabulary; **LA.A.2.1.5.K.2** Get information; **LA.B.2.1.2.K.1** Record ideas; *Also* **LA.A.1.1.2.K.2** Alphabet; **LA.A.1.1.3.K.1** Frequent words; **LA.C.1.1.3.K.1** Conversation rules; **LA.C.3.1.2.K.1** Questions

Phonemic Awareness

PHONEME ISOLATION: MEDIAL

Identify Medial Sounds   Tell children to listen for the middle sound in the words of a song. Sing the following words to the tune of "Old MacDonald Had a Farm":

What is the sound in the middle of these words: _hen_ and _let_ and _men_?

/e/ is the sound in the middle of these words: _hen_ and _let_ and _men_.

With an /e/ /e/ here and an /e/ /e/ there,
here an /e/, there an /e/, everywhere an /e/, /e/.
/e/ is the sound in the middle of these words: _hen_ and _let_ and _men_.

Repeat the song, using the following sounds and words, and invite children to sing with you:

tan and **_bag_** and **_cat_** /a/

jet and **_fed_** and **_leg_** /e/

fix and **_sit_** and **_pig_** /i/

rug and **_tub_** and **_bus_** /u/

wet and **_bed_** and **_set_** /e/

dog and **_sock_** and **_fox_** /o/

REACHING ALL LEARNERS

Diagnostic Check: Phonemic Awareness

If... children have difficulty blending sounds to make words,

Then... have them look at the _Picture Card_ cat and say its name. Next, have them say _cat_ slowly and segment the word: /c/ /a/ /t/. Have children practice with _Picture Cards_ dog, fox, hat, hen, jet, pig, sun, van.

ADDITIONAL SUPPORT ACTIVITIES

BELOW-LEVEL   Reteach, p. S14

ADVANCED   Extend, p. S15

ENGLISH-LANGUAGE LEARNERS   Reteach, p. S15

FLORIDA STANDARDS/GLEs   LA.A.1.1.2.K.5 Phonetic principles

▲ **Library Book**

OBJECTIVES

- *To recall story events*

- *To distinguish realistic text from fantasy*

- *To make judgments about characters*

Materials

■ *Library Book: Good-bye Hello*

Sharing Literature

Read Good-bye Hello

READ ALOUD

Before Reading Display the cover of *Good-bye Hello*, ask children where the title is, and read it aloud. Ask children to recall the main character's feelings. Then model a purpose for rereading.

> **MODEL** I remember that this story is about a girl who is moving. I think the girl is sad at the beginning but happy at the end. I'll read the story again to see if I am right.

During Reading Reread the story aloud. As you read,

- pause occasionally to ask children how they would feel.
- model how to tell if the story is real by comparing texts.

> **MODEL** A make-believe story is "The Shoemaker and the Elves." Seeing elves make shoes could not happen in real life. Everything that happens in *Good-bye Hello* could happen in real life. The girl says good-bye to things in her old neighborhood. She moves and says hello to things in her new neighborhood. This story is about something that could really happen.

FLORIDA STANDARDS/GLEs **FCAT: LA.A.1.1.2.K.6** Print meaning; **LA.A.1.1.3.K.5** Story elements; **LA.A.2.1.5.K.2** Get information; *Also* **LA.C.1.1.1.K.2** Oral language; **LA.C.3.1.2.K.1** Questions

DEVELOP CONCEPT VOCABULARY

After Reading Write the words *neighbors* and *neighborhood* on the board. Point to and read each word. Then ask children to respond to the following questions using complete sentences.

The Bells and the Garcias are my neighbors. Who are your neighbors? (Possible response: A girl and her mom live next door to me.)

There is a grocery store and a park in my neighborhood. What is in your neighborhood? (Possible response: There is a pizza shop.)

RESPOND TO LITERATURE

Discuss the Story Have children take turns naming things that the girl says good-bye to and things she says hello to.

Literature Focus

MAKING JUDGMENTS ABOUT CHARACTERS

Remind children that they can use story clues to help them decide if a character is friendly and fun or mean and boring. Have them discuss the girl in *Good-bye Hello*.

MODEL I think the girl is friendly because she says good-bye to lots of neighbors and Jamie in her old neighborhood. I think she likes to have fun because she plays the drum and makes a fort out of boxes. Ask: *Would you like to be friends with the girl in the story? Why?*

ADVANCED

Encourage children to work with a partner to look through other stories such as *Benny's Pennies*. Have them read to find clues that tell a character's feelings.

ONGOING ASSESSMENT

As you share *Good-bye Hello*, note whether children

• can recall story events.

• can distinguish realistic text from fantasy.

FLORIDA STANDARDS/GLEs   FCAT: **LA.A.1.1.2.K.4** Words; **LA.A.1.1.2.K.6** Print meaning; **LA.A.1.1.3.K.4** Build vocabulary; **LA.A.2.1.1.K.1** Main idea; *Also* **LA.E.2.1.1.K.2** Personal interpretations

Around the Town   13'

OBJECTIVES

- *To recognize uppercase and lowercase Ee and Nn*
- *To match sounds to letters*

Materials

- pocket chart
- *Big Alphabet Cards Ee, Nn*
- *Picture Cards egg, nest*
- *Tactile Letter Cards e, n*
- drawing paper
- crayons
- scissors

Phonics

Consonant /n/n
Short Vowel /e/e  Review

ACTIVE BEGINNING

Recite the Rhymes   Display *Big Alphabet Cards Ee* and *Nn*. Ask children to identify each letter. Have children form a circle. Ask a child to stand in the middle of the circle and hold up *Big Alphabet Card Ee*. Have the children walk around the circle as they sing or recite "If I Ever Met an Elephant," on page 94. Follow the same procedure for "No, No, Nancy," which is on p. 524, Volume 1.

TEACH/MODEL

Review Letters and Sounds   Display *Big Alphabet Card Ee* in a pocket chart and ask what letter this is.

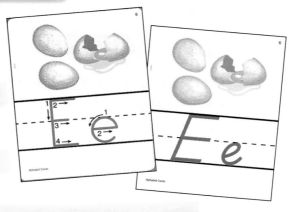

Point to the picture and say its name. Have children repeat it.

What sound do you hear at the beginning of *egg*? (/e/)

What letter stands for the /e/ sound in *egg*? (*Ee*)

Touch the letter and say **/e/**. Touch the letter again and have children say /e/.

Follow the same procedure for *Big Alphabet Card Nn*.

Place *Picture Cards egg* and *nest* on the chalk ledge. Say each picture name and tell children you need to decide where to put each *Picture Card*.

I'll start with the egg. *E—gg* begins with the /e/ sound. So I'll put the picture of the egg below *Ee*.

Model the same process with *Picture Card nest*.

FLORIDA STANDARDS/GLEs   **LA.A.1.1.2.K.1** Print organization; **LA.A.1.1.2.K.2** Alphabet; **LA.A.1.1.2.K.3** Sounds; **LA.C.3.1.2.K.1** Questions; **LA.D.2.1.2.K.1** Patterned structures

PRACTICE/APPLY

Guided Practice   Distribute *Tactile Letter Cards* e and n to each child.

I will say some words that begin with the /e/ sound and some that don't. Hold up your e card if the word begins with the /e/ sound. Thumbs ↑ Thumbs ↓

Confirm the answer for each word by holding up the appropriate *Tactile Letter Card*.

empty   desk   elevator   elf   cup   every

I will say some words that begin with the /n/ sound and some that don't. Hold up your n card if the word begins with the /n/ sound. Thumbs ↑ Thumbs ↓

night   pig   nut   noodle   castle   news

Independent Practice   Have children continue to work with their *Tactile Letter Cards* e and n. Distribute drawing paper that is divided into four sections. Have children draw a picture of an elephant, egg, nest, and nut, one in each section. Have them cut out their pictures. Tell them to name each picture. If the word begins with /e/, place the picture below *Tactile Letter Card* e. If the word begins with /n/, place the picture below *Tactile Letter Card* n.

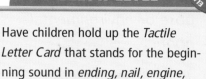

BELOW-LEVEL

Have children hold up the *Tactile Letter Card* that stands for the beginning sound in *ending, nail, engine, everyone, night, note, empty.*

ADVANCED

Have children make their own picture cards for the letters e and n.

Phonics Resources

 Phonics Express™ CD-ROM, Level A, Sparkle/Route 2/Fire Station; Bumper/Route 2/Park

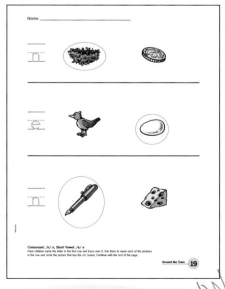

▲ **Practice Book page 19** HW

OBJECTIVES

- *To understand the purpose of environmental print*

- *To brainstorm ideas for signs*

Day 1: Prewrite
Work with children to make a list of ideas for classroom signs.

Day 2: Draft
Work with children to write signs on poster board.

Day 3: Respond and Revise
Reread the signs with children; children make corrections.

Day 4: Proofread
Children check signs carefully to make them better.

Day 5: Publish
Children illustrate and hang signs.

Writing Process

Write Classroom Signs

PREWRITE

Review the Story   Page through *I Read Signs* and point to each sign as you read it aloud. Review the places where each sign might be seen and how the sign can help people around the town you live in.

Make a List of Ideas   Ask children to think about places where it would be helpful to display a sign in their own classroom. Have several children tell their ideas for you to record on chart paper. Help children supply ideas by asking questions such as these:

- **How do we know where to put a writing we want to share?**

- **How can we let others know when we are at the playground?**

- **How can we remind each other to wash our hands in the rest room? Where is the best place to hang the sign?**

- **Where is a good place to hang a sign at the library center?**

- **Where should we remind each other to be neat?**

Share   Track the print as you read the list to children. Encourage children to share what words they think should be on each sign.

Places We Need a Sign

sharing basket
classroom door
rest room sink
bookshelves
art center

Journal Writing   Have children write and draw about a special friend.

FLORIDA STANDARDS/GLEs   FCAT: LA.B.2.1.2.K.1 Record ideas; *Also* **LA.B.1.1.1.K.2** Generate ideas; **LA.B.2.1.1.K.2** Contribute ideas; **LA.B.2.1.4.K.1** Informational texts; **LA.C.1.1.1.K.2** Oral language

- Slide *e* next to *h*. Say /**hhee**/.

- Slide the *n* next to the *he*. Move your hand under the letters and blend the sounds, elongating them —/**hheenn**/. Have children repeat after you.

- Then have children read *hen* with you.

PRACTICE/APPLY

Guided Practice   Place the letters *p*, *e*, and *n* in the pocket chart.

- Point to *p* and say /**pp**/. Point to the letter *e* and say /**e**/. Slide the *e* next to *p*. Move your hand under the letters and blend the sounds, elongating them—/**ppee**/. Have children blend the sounds after you.

- Point to *n*. Say /**nn**/. Have children say the sound.

- Slide the *n* next to the *pe*. Slide your hand under *pen* and blend the sounds. Have children blend the sounds as you slide your hand under the word.

- Then have children read the word *pen* along with you.

Follow the same procedure to build and blend *hen*, *ten*, and *net* with children.

Independent Practice   Write the *en* on an index card and place it and *Alphabet Cards t, h, m, d* in a pocket chart in the Letters and Words Center. Have children place each letter in front of *en* and read each word.

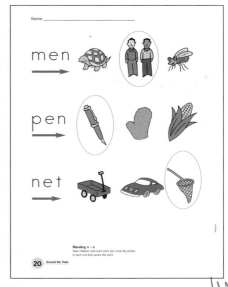

▲ **Practice Book page 20**

FLORIDA STANDARDS/GLEs   FCAT: LA.A.1.1.2.K.5 Phonetic principles; *Also* **LA.A.1.1.2.K.1** Print organization; **LA.A.1.1.2.K.2** Alphabet; **LA.A.1.1.2.K.3** Sounds; **LA.A.1.1.3.K.1** Frequent words

Around the Town   141

OBJECTIVES

- *To write with a purpose*

- *To draft signs for the classroom*

Materials

- list of ideas, p.134
- poster board
- crayons

Writing Process

Write Classroom Signs

DRAFT

Read aloud the list of children's ideas. Choose an idea from the chart and model for children how to write a sign on poster board.

MODEL When I write words on a sign, I will write them big so everyone can see them. I will use uppercase letters for all the words because they all say an important message. Most signs do not use end punctuation.

As children contribute by writing letters, ask the following questions:

- **What word can we write on a sign for a basket where we can put our finished writings? How will this sign help us?**

- **Where should you start writing?**

- **Listen to the beginning sound in the word** *basket*. **What letter stands for that beginning sound?**

When all the letters are written on the sign, explain that you will set it aside so children can help you write the next sign. Continue using the above process until all the signs are written on separate pieces of poster board. After all signs are complete, hold them up and read them aloud to children.

Writing Every Day
My Journal

Self-Selected Writing Have children write and draw about anything they'd like. If they have difficulty thinking of a topic have them ask two friends what they're going to write about.

FLORIDA STANDARDS/GLEs **LA.B.1.1.2.K.4** Add details; *Also* **LA.A.1.1.2.K.1** Print organization; **LA.B.1.1.2.K.1** Dictate messages; **LA.B.1.1.2.K.2** Basic formats; **LA.B.1.1.3.K.2** Print direction; **LA.B.2.1.1.K.2** Contribute ideas

142 **Around the Town**

Phonemic Awareness

INITIAL PHONEME DELETION

Delete Initial Sounds   Tell children that you will say a word. Then you will say the word without the beginning sound.

Say: *pit*.

Now I'll say *pit* without the /p/: *it*.

Now you try it. Say *bed*. Say *bed* without the /b/. (*ed*)

Use the same procedure with the following words.

Say *fox*. Now say *fox* without /f/. (*ox*)

Say *vet*. Now say *vet* without /v/. (*et*)

Say *jam*. Now say *jam* without /j/. (*am*)

Say *den*. Now say *den* without /d/. (*en*)

Say *web*. Now say *web* without /w/. (*eb*)

▲ **"His Four Fur Feet,"** *Oo-pples and Boo-noo-noos: Songs and Activities for Phonemic Awareness*, **pages 83–84.**

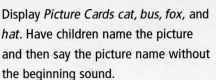

ADVANCED

Display *Picture Cards cat, bus, fox,* and *hat.* Have children name the picture and then say the picture name without the beginning sound.

THE SHAPE OF THINGS

DAYLE ANN DODDS ILLUSTRATED BY JULIE LACOME

▲ **Big Book**

OBJECTIVES

- *To recall story events*

- *To summarize story events*

Materials

- *Big Book:*
  The Shape of Things

- *drawing paper*

- *crayons*

Sharing Literature

Read **The Shape of Things**

READ ALOUD

Before Reading   Display *The Shape of Things* and point to the title as you read it aloud. Use these prompts to set a purpose for rereading:

- **What shape was the Ferris wheel made from?** (a circle)

- **What shape was the sailboat made from?** (triangle)

- **What shape was the house made from?** (square)

Tell children that you will read the story again to find out what shapes were used to make each object.

During Reading   Reread the selection aloud. As you read,

- ask children to name the color of each shape as it is introduced.

- recall the previous shapes after each new shape is introduced.

MODEL **This new shape is called a triangle. The other shapes we have seen in the book so far are a square and a circle.**

FLORIDA STANDARDS/GLEs   **FCAT: LA.A.1.1.4.K.1** Comprehension; **LA.A.2.1.3.K.1** Supportive details; *Also* **LA.A.1.1.2.K.1** Print organization; **LA.C.1.1.1.K.2** Oral language; **LA.C.3.1.2.K.1** Questions

RESPOND TO LITERATURE

Shape Picture Book   Ask each child to draw one of the shapes from the *Big Book*—a square, a circle, a rectangle, a triangle, an oval, or a diamond. Then have children add details to the shape to make it into something else. Have children draw items other than those in the book. Combine all of the pictures into a book titled "Shapes Are All Around Us."

SUMMARIZE

Remind children that summarizing is telling about the most important ideas in a book.

MODEL   *The Shape of Things* shows that many things in the world around us are made from shapes. That is the most important idea of the book.

ADVANCED

Ask children to summarize stories they have read recently, such as "Caps for Sale" and *Benny's Pennies*.

ONGOING ASSESSMENT

As you share *The Shape of Things*, note whether children

• can recall story events.

FLORIDA STANDARDS/GLEs   FCAT: LA.A.1.1.3.K.5 Story elements; LA.A.1.1.4.K.1 Comprehension; LA.A.2.1.1.K.1 Main idea

Around the Town   147

Phonics

Words with /e/ and /n/

OBJECTIVES

- To build and read simple one-syllable words

- To understand that as the letters of words change, so do the sounds

Materials

- Alphabet Cards d, e, n, p, t

- Word Builders

- Word Builder Cards d, e, n, p, t

- pocket chart

- Magnetic Letters

- cookie sheet

REVIEW LETTERS

ACTIVE BEGINNING

Action Rhyme   Teach children this rhyme and the actions that go with it:

Peck, peck, peck,
(Bob your head toward the floor.)

Goes the little hen.

Waddle, waddle, waddle.
(Strut like a hen.)

She goes into her pen.

TEACH/MODEL

whole group

Blending Words   Distribute *Word Builders* and *Word Builder Cards d, e, n, p, t* to children. As you place *Alphabet Cards* in a pocket chart, tell children to place the same *Word Builder Cards* in their *Word Builders*.

- Place *Alphabet Cards p, e,* and *n* in the pocket chart. Have children do the same.

- Point to *p*. Say /**pp**/. Point to *e*. Say /**ee**/.

- Slide the *e* next to the *p*. Then move your hand under the letters and blend the sounds, elongating them: /**ppee**/. Have children do the same.

FLORIDA STANDARDS/GLEs   **FCAT: LA.A.1.1.2.K.5** Phonetic principles; *Also* **LA.A.1.1.2.K.1** Print organization; **LA.A.1.1.2.K.3** Sounds; **LA.C.1.1.1.K.1** Follow directions; **LA.C.2.1.2.K.1** Nonverbal cues

- Point to the letter *n*. Say /nn/. Have children do the same.

- Slide the *n* next to the *pe*. Slide your hand under *pen* and blend by elongating the sounds: /ppeenn/. Have children do the same.

- Then have children read the word *pen* along with you.

PRACTICE/APPLY

Whole Group

Guided Practice Have children place *Word Builder Cards* e and n in their *Word Builders*.

- **Add *d* to *en*. What word did you make?**

- **Change *d* to *p*. What word did you make?**

- **Change *n* to *t*. What word did you make?**

- **Change *p* to *n*. What word did you make?**

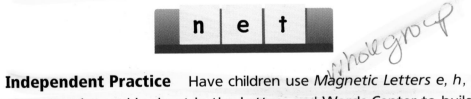

Whole group

Independent Practice Have children use *Magnetic Letters* e, h, m, n, t and a cookie sheet in the Letters and Words Center to build and read *men*, *ten*, *hen*, and *net*.

REACHING ALL LEARNERS

Diagnostic Check: Phonics

If... children cannot relate /e/ to *e*,

Then... have them take turns finding on the *Letter and Sound Chart* an *Ee* at the beginning of a word and underlining it using the clear plastic overlay. Then say the word and have children repeat it. /e/ *Elephant* /e/

ADDITIONAL SUPPORT ACTIVITIES

BELOW-LEVEL	Reteach, p. S16
ADVANCED	Extend, p. S17
ENGLISH-LANGUAGE LEARNERS	Reteach, p. S17

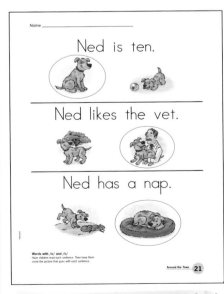

Name _____

Ned is ten.

Ned likes the vet.

Ned has a nap.

Words with /e/ and /n/
Have children read each sentence. Then have them circle the picture that goes with each sentence.

Around the Town **21**

▲ **Practice Book page 21** *HW*

Around the Town **149**

OBJECTIVE

- *To improve a group writing piece through responding and revising*

Materials

- written signs, p.142
- correction tape
- marker

Writing Process

Write Classroom Signs

RESPOND AND REVISE

Reread the Signs Read aloud each completed sign, tracking the words. Ask questions like these:

- Does the sign have all the right words?
- Is there anything that needs to be added to the sign?
- Is there anything that needs to be taken off of the sign?
- What does the sign show us? Where would be a good place to hang this sign?

Make Revisions Allow children to use correction tape to make any changes to the words on the signs.

Writing Every Day

Journal Writing Have children work with a partner and give each other directions to create a simple drawing.

FLORIDA STANDARDS/GLEs **FCAT: LA.A.1.1.2.K.4** Words; **LA.B.1.1.2.K.4** Add details; *Also* **LA.A.1.1.2.K.1** Print organization; **LA.B.2.1.4.K.1** Informational texts; **LA.C.1.1.1.K.2** Oral language; **LA.C.3.1.2.K.1** Questions

Phonemic Awareness

PHONEME SUBSTITUTION

Substitute Initial Sounds   Say the following rhyme and have children repeat it:

Dancing, dancing dinosaur,

Dancing, dancing on the floor,

Dancing, dancing on my shoe.

Dinosaur, I'll dance with you!

Model for children how to change a letter to create a silly poem.

> **MODEL**   Say: *Dancing, dancing dinosaur.* Ask: **What sound do you hear at the beginning of each word in the line?** (/d/) **Instead of saying /d/ at the beginning of the words, I will say /m/.** *Mancing, mancing minosaur.* **Say the silly sentence with me. Now say the whole rhyme using /m/ instead of /d/.**

Replace /d/ in the rhyme with the following sounds:

/v/ makes *Vancing, vancing vinosaur.*

/j/ makes *Jancing, jancing jinosaur.*

/k/ makes *Kancing, kancing kinosaur.*

/g/ makes *Gancing, gancing ginosaur.*

Display *Picture Cards* cat, fish, jet, nail, vest. Have children name each picture and then substitute a new beginning sound to make a new word.

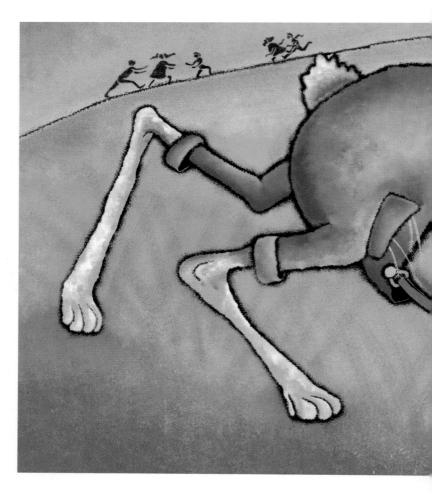

▲ Big Book of Rhymes and Songs

OBJECTIVES
- *To listen and respond to a song*
- *To recognize uppercase letters*
- *To identify action words*

Materials
- *Big Book of Rhymes and Songs, pp. 26–27*
- *Music CD*

Sharing Literature

Read "Old Mister Rabbit"

READ ALOUD

Before Reading   Display "Old Mister Rabbit" in the *Big Book of Rhymes and Songs*. Track the print as you read the title. Ask children to point to the uppercase letters in the title. Then use this model to help children set a purpose for rereading.

MODEL   **I remember this song about the rabbit. I know that the rabbit goes into a garden, but I can't remember what he eats there. I'll find out when we read this again.**

During Reading   Read the song lyrics aloud. As you read,
- clap the rhythm of the words.

Play the *Music CD* and invite children to sing along.

FLORIDA STANDARDS/GLEs   FCAT: LA.A.1.1.2.K.1 Print organization; **LA.C.1.1.1.K.1** Follow directions; **LA.C.3.1.2.K.1** Questions; **LA.C.3.1.4.K.1** Gestures; **LA.C.1.1.3.K.1** Conversation rules; **LA.E.2.1.2.K.1** Patterned structures

RESPOND TO LITERATURE

Change the Lyrics   Reread the last phrase of the song, *and eating all my cabbage.* Have children repeat the phrase several times, each time substituting a different vegetable name such as *carrots, broccoli, spinach, corn.*

Literature Focus

ACTION WORDS

Remind children that action words tell what a person or animal is doing. Point out the action words in "Old Mister Rabbit"—*jumping, eating.* Sing the song again and lead children in pantomiming the actions. Then say these words and have children act them out: *clap, bend, yawn, march, read.*

Diagnostic Check: Comprehension

If... children have difficulty understanding action words,

Then... show children *Picture Cards dinosaur, dog, duck, girl,* and model actions to go with each picture. Dinosaur stomps, dog eats, duck swims, girl writes. Have children repeat the action. As you hold up each picture, ask: *What is the action?*

ADDITIONAL SUPPORT ACTIVITIES

BELOW-LEVEL	Reteach, p. S18
ADVANCED	Extend, p. S19
ENGLISH-LANGUAGE LEARNERS	Reteach, p. S19

ONGOING ASSESSMENT

As you share "Old Mister Rabbit," note whether children

- can listen and respond to a song.
- recognize uppercase letters.

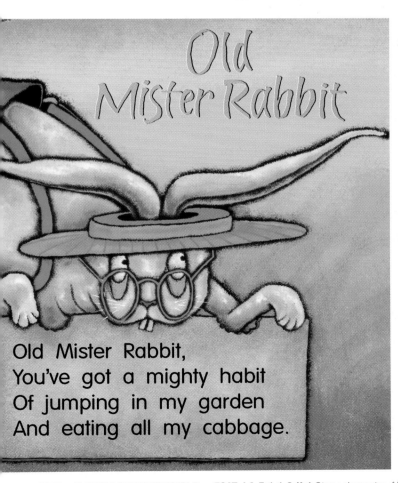

Old Mister Rabbit,
You've got a mighty habit
Of jumping in my garden
And eating all my cabbage.

FLORIDA STANDARDS/GLEs   FCAT: LA.E.1.1.2.K.1 Story elements; *Also* **LA.A.1.1.3.K.2** Nouns and verbs; **LA.D.1.1.1.K.1** Sound patterns; **LA.D.2.1.2.K.1** Patterned structures; **LA.E.2.1.1.K.2** Personal interpretations; **LA.E.2.1.2.K.1** Patterned structures

OBJECTIVE

To decode short vowel /e/e words

Materials

■ *Alphabet Cards G, e, t*

■ index cards

■ pocket chart

■ *Decodable Book 9: Hop In!*

■ drawing paper

■ crayons

ADVANCED

Have children read *Independent Reader 26: A Good Home.*

ENGLISH-LANGUAGE LEARNERS

Page through the book and help children name the kinds of animals in the illustrations. Then review the animals by saying: *Show me a picture of a (goat, cat, dog, fox, pig).*

Phonics

Short Vowel /e/e ✔ *Review*

TEACH/MODEL

Review Blending   Place *Alphabet Cards G, e* and *t* next to each other in a pocket chart. Move your hand under the letters, blend them, and say the word. **/ggeett/—get.** Have children blend the sounds and say the word with you. On index cards, write the words *in my van* and place each one in the pocket chart after the word *Get*. Place a period at the end. Have children read the sentence as you track the print.

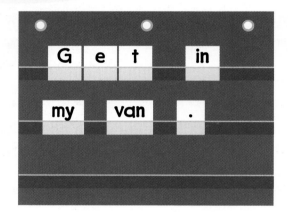

PRACTICE/APPLY

Read the Book   Distribute copies of *Hop In!* Have children read the title. Encourage children to point to each word as they read it. Have children read the book, pointing to each word as they read.

Respond   Have children draw a picture of their favorite animal from the book. Ask them to write the animal's name.

 FLORIDA STANDARDS/GLEs   FCAT: LA.A.1.1.2.K.4 Words; **LA.A.1.1.2.K.5** Phonetic principles; **LA.A.1.1.2.K.6** Print meaning; **LA.D.1.1.1.K.1** Sound patterns; *Also* **LA.A.1.1.2.K.1** Print organization; **LA.A.1.1.2.K.2** Alphabet; **LA.A.1.1.3.K.2** Nouns and verbs

Phonemic Awareness

RHYME RECOGNITION

Identify Rhyming Words Decorate a shoe box to look like a fox, and place a small object or *Picture Card* inside. Tell children they can ask Mr. Fox to give them clues to help them name the picture or object that is inside the box. Model for children how to ask Mr. Fox for clues:

MODEL Children ask:

Mr. Fox,

What's in the box?

What do you hide?

What's inside?

Mr. Fox's reply: **It rhymes with *hen* and *ten* and *men*.**

Maybe it could be a _____.

Children answer: (pen)

Open the box and show children a pen to confirm their answers.
Use the following *Picture Cards* and substitute rhyming words into the rhyme:

(*tear, wear, stare*) bear	(*fan, man, pan*) van
(*log, frog, hog*) dog	(*black, tack, pack*) yak
(*coat, float, vote*) goat	(*wig, twig, fig*) pig
(*sheep, sleep, keep*) jeep	(*cane, lane, mane*) rain
(*see, we, he*) key	(*fun, run, bun*) sun

FLORIDA STANDARDS/GLEs FCAT: LA.A.1.1.2.K.5 Phonetic principles; *Also* **LA.C.1.1.1.K.2** Oral language; **LA.D.1.1.1.K.1** Sound patterns; **LA.D.2.1.2.K.1** Patterned structures

Around the Town 161

Sharing Literature

Read "Sing a Song of People"

READ ALOUD

Before Reading   Show children page 22 in the *Read-Aloud Anthology* and read aloud the title. Tell children that this is a poem about how people get from place to place in a city. Then use these prompts to build background:

- **How do you get from place to place?** (Possible response: in a car.)

- **What are some ways that people get from place to place in the city?** (Possible responses: walk; ride in a bus, car, taxi, train)

During Reading   Read the poem aloud. As you read,

- emphasize the rhythm of the text by swaying back and forth as you read.

- model for children how to listen for rhyming words.

MODEL   I really like the way this poem sounds when I read it out loud. I hear the words *slow/go, go/know* at the end of some lines. These words all have the same ending sound: *slow, go, know.* They are rhyming words.

▲ **Read-Aloud Anthology**

OBJECTIVES

- *To listen for rhythm and rhyme*

- *To identify words that name places and things*

- *To recognize setting*

Materials

- *Read-Aloud Anthology,* p. 22

- drawing paper

- crayons

FLORIDA STANDARDS/GLEs   FCAT: LA.A.1.1.2.K.4 Words; **LA.C.1.1.4.K.1** Sequence; *Also*; **LA.A.1.1.2.K.1** Print organization; **LA.C.1.1.2.K.1** Choose literature; **LA.D.1.1.1.K.1** Sound patterns; **LA.D.2.1.2.K.1** Patterned structures; **LA.E.2.1.2.K.1** Patterned structures

DEVELOP CONCEPT VOCABULARY

After Reading   Remind children that the poem describes many ways that people get from one place to another. Begin a web on the board by writing in the center circle the words *How People Travel*. Track the words and, if necessary, explain the meaning of *travel*. Then have children name the methods of travel in the poem. Add each suggestion to the web.

Then ask questions such as these:

- **Which word names something that has more than 2 seats and that school children ride in the morning?** (bus)

- **Which word names a car that someone else drives for you?** (taxi)

- **Which word names a train that runs under the ground?** (subway)

- **Which word names what you ride in to get from one floor to another in a tall building?** (elevators)

RESPOND TO LITERATURE

Draw and Write About the Poem   Have children choose one of the transportation methods from the web and draw and label it. Display pictures in the classroom under the title "How People Travel."

Literature Focus

SETTING

Remind children that the setting of a story is when and where the story happens.

Point out that poems, like "Sing a Song of People," can also have settings.

MODEL **The setting of this poem is the city. I can tell because there are lots of people, tall buildings, buses, taxis, and subways.**

Ask children to name the settings of *Benny's Pennies* and *Good-bye Hello*.

ADVANCED

Reread the last four lines of the poem. Ask children to talk about the meaning of the final lines, *Sing of city people / you see but never know!*

ENGLISH-LANGUAGE LEARNERS

Reread the poem and stop to explain words such as *umbrellas, sidewalk, buildings,* and *taxis.*

ONGOING ASSESSMENT

As you share "Sing a Song of People," note whether children

- **appreciate the poem's rhythm and rhyme.**

- **identify words that name places and things.**

FLORIDA STANDARDS/GLEs   **FCAT: LA.A.1.1.3.K.4** Build vocabulary; **LA.C.1.1.4.K.1** Sequence; **LA.E.1.1.2.K.1** Story elements

Around

Phonics

Blending /e/ - /n/  *Review*

OBJECTIVES

- *To build and read simple one-syllable words*

- *To understand that as the letters of words change, so do the sounds*

Materials

- *Alphabet Cards d, e, h, m, n, t*

- *Word Builders*

- *Word Builder Cards d, e, h, m, n, t*

- pocket chart

- index cards

- drawing paper

- crayons

REVIEW LETTERS

ACTIVE BEGINNING

Play a Listening Game   Explain to children that they are going to play a game in which they will listen to words that have the /n/ sound. Ask them to stand if the word begins with the /n/ sound and sit if the word ends with the /n/ sound.

train	number	moon	nosy	noodle
fun	nurse	lane	nothing	bean

TEACH/MODEL

Blending Words   Distribute *Word Builders* and *Word Builder Cards d, e, h, m, n, t* to children. As you place *Alphabet Cards* in a pocket chart, tell children to place the same *Word Builder Cards* in their *Word Builders*.

- Place *Alphabet Cards d, e,* and *n* in the pocket chart. Have children do the same.

- Point to *d*. Say /**dd**/. Point to *e*. Say /**ee**/.

- Slide the *e* next to the *d*. Then move your hand under the letters and blend the sounds, elongating them: /**ddee**/. Have children do the same.

- Point to the letter *n*. Say /**nn**/. Have children do the same.

- Slide the *n* next to the *de*. Slide your hand under *den* and blend by elongating the sounds: /**ddeenn**/. Have children do the same.

FLORIDA STANDARDS/GLEs   **FCAT: LA.A.1.1.2.K.5** Phonetic principles; **LA.A.1.1.3.K.4** Build vocabulary; *Also* **LA.A.1.1.2.K.1** Print organization; **LA.A.1.1.2.K.3** Sounds; **LA.C.1.1.1.K.1** Follow directions

- Then have children read the word *den* along with you. Follow the same procedure with these words: *ten, pen, net*.

Have children blend the following phonemes together to say the word: /h/ /e/ /n/, /m/ /e/ /n/, /m/ /e/ /t/, /n/ /e/ /t/.

PRACTICE/APPLY

whole group

Guided Practice Have children place *Word Builder Cards e* and *n* in their *Word Builders*.

- **Add *h* to *en*. What word did you make?**

- **Change *h* to *m*. What word did you make?**

ADVANCED

Have children use the *Magnetic Letters e, h, n, p, t* and *High-Frequency Word Cards You, have, a* to build sentences: *You have a net. You have a pen. You have a hen.*

- **Change *n* to *t*. What word did you make?**

- **Change *m* to *n*. What word did you make?**

Independent Practice Write the words *hen, men,* and *net* on index cards and place them in a pocket chart. Have children read the words. Then have them choose one of the words to write and illustrate on drawing paper.

▲ **Practice Book page 22**

FLORIDA STANDARDS/GLEs **FCAT: LA.A.1.1.2.K.5** Phonetic principles; **LA.A.1.1.3.K.4** Build vocabulary; *Also* **LA.A.1.1.2.K.1** Print organization; **LA.A.1.1.2.K.2** Alphabet; **LA.A.1.1.2.K.3** Sounds; **LA.B.1.1.3.K.2** Print direction; **LA.C.3.1.2.K.1** Questions

OBJECTIVE

- *To illustrate a class writing piece*

Materials

- written signs, p. 158
- crayons

Writing Process

Write Classroom Signs

PUBLISH

Illustrate the Signs Divide the class into groups and distribute a sign to each group. Ask children to illustrate each sign with a border.

Hang the Signs Invite children to place their signs around the classroom in the appropriate locations. Then have children walk around the room to each sign to listen to you read each one. Have children retell the reason why the sign is helpful.

Read Books

Wash Your Hands

Be Neat

Journal Writing Have children draw and label their favorite place to visit in their town or city.

FLORIDA STANDARDS/GLEs   FCAT: **LA.B.2.1.2.K.1** Record ideas; *Also* **LA.A.2.1.4.K.1** Illustrations

THEME 10

Neighborhood Helpers

Children learn about jobs people do, how they work together, and places they go in their neighborhoods.

Theme Resources

READING MATERIALS

Big Book

◀ *The Big Yellow Bus* illustrated by Lorinda Bryan Cauley

Library Books

◀ *Career Day* by Anne Rockwell illustrated by Lizzy Rockwell

◀ *Guess Who?* by Margaret Miller

Big Book of Rhymes and Songs

◀ *The Bus Song*

Read-Aloud Anthology

◀ *Mother, Mother, I Want Another* by Maria Polushkin

◀ *Jamaica's Find* by Juanita Havill

◀ *Franklin in the Dark* by Paulette Bourgeois

◀ *The Town Mouse and the Country Mouse* retold by Lorinda Bryan Cauley

◀ *This Is the Way We Go to School (The Mulberry Bush)*

◀ *Stone Soup* retold by Ann McGovern

Independent Readers

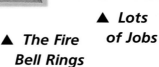

▲ *Neighborhood Friends*

▲ *The Fire Bell Rings*

▲ *Lots of Jobs*

PHONICS

Theme 10 Practice Book

Phonics Practice Book

Decodable Books

▲ *Is It for Me?*

▲ *We Can Fix*

▲ *A Hat I Like*

Alphabet Patterns

yo-yo, zipper
page T13

Phonics Express™ CD-ROM
Level A

Visit *The Learning Site:* www.harcourtschool.com

TEACHING TOOLS

Big Alphabet Cards

Yy, Zz

Letter and Sound Charts

Charts 13 and 15

Letter and Sound Chart Sentence Strips

13, 15

Yak has a yellow yo-yo.

High-Frequency Word Cards

for, me

Picture/Word Cards

Teacher's Resource Book

pages 63, 65

Oo-pples and Boo-noo-noos

English Language Learners Kit

Intervention Kit

MANIPULATIVES

Tactile Letter Cards

y   z

Write-On/Wipe-Off Board
Letters and Sounds Place Mat

Word Builder and Word Builder Cards

y   e   s

Magnetic Letters

Aa Bb Cc

ASSESSMENT

Assessment Handbook

Group Inventory

Theme 10 Test

Big Book ▶

The Big Yellow Bus

Library Book ▶

Career Day

	Week 1	**Week 2**

• **Sharing Literature**
• **Listening Comprehension**
	Big Book: *The Big Yellow Bus*
	Library Book: *Career Day*
	Read-Aloud Anthology:
	  "Mother, Mother, I Want Another"
	Big Book of Rhymes and Songs:
	  "The Bus Song"
		Big Book: *The Big Yellow Bus*
		Library Book: *Guess Who?*
		Read-Aloud Anthology:
		  "Franklin in the Dark"
		  "Jamaica's Find"

• **Phonemic Awareness** • **Phonics** • **High-Frequency Words**	Consonant *Yy* **T** Consonant *Zz* **T** Review Consonants *Yy, Zz* **T** High-Frequency Words *for, me* **T**	Review Consonant *Dd*, Short Vowel *Ee* **T** Blending /e/ - /d/ Words with /e/ and /d/ Review Blending /e/ - /d/
• **Reading**	**Decodable Book 10:** *Is It for Me?* **Independent Reader 27:** *Neighborhood Friends*	**Decodable Book 11:** *We Can Fix* **Independent Reader 28:** *The Fire Bell Rings*

• **Writing**	**Shared Writing**
	  Write About a Job
	Interactive Writing
	  Thank-You Note
	  List
	Independent Writing
	  Write About an Animal
	  Dialogue
		Shared Writing
		  Bus Rules
		  Sentences
		Interactive Writing
		  Description
		Independent Writing
		  Book of Facts
		  Make-Believe Bus

• **Cross-Curricular Centers**	🎨 **Manipulatives**
	  Constructing *Y* and *y*
	🎨 **Art**
	  Yellow Flowers
	🎨 **Art**
	  Zany Zebra
	🎨 **Math**
	  Dots and Numbers
	🎭 **Dramatic Play**
	  Going to the Zoo
		🎭 **Dramatic Play**
		  Going to Work
		🌐 **Social Studies**
		  Workers in Our Town
		✏️ **Writing**
		  "Turtle Fact" Books
		✏️ **Writing**
		  Meeting New Friends
		🎧 **Listening**
		  Listen to the Big Book

T = tested skill

Library Book ▶

Week 3

Big Book: *The Big Yellow Bus*
Library Book: *Guess Who?*
Read-Aloud Anthology:
  "The Town Mouse and the Country Mouse"
  "This Is the Way We Go to School"
  "Stone Soup"

Phonogram -*et*
Phonogram -*en*
Phonogram -*ed*
Build Sentences

Decodable Book 12: *A Hat I Like*
Independent Reader 29: *Lots of Jobs*

Interactive Writing
  Writing Process

 Writing
  Who, What, and Where Silly Sentences
Cooking
  Town Treats and Country Nibbles
Social Studies
  Drive Through "Letter Town"
Listening
  Sing Along
Literacy
  Let's Read

Theme Organizer
Half-Day Kindergarten

Use the following chart to help organize your half-day kindergarten schedule. Choose independent activities as time allows during your day.

ORAL LANGUAGE

Morning Message
Phonemic Awareness
Sharing Literature
• Big Book: *The Big Yellow Bus*
• Library Book: *Career Day*
• Library Book: *Guess Who?*
• Read-Aloud Anthology
• Big Book of Rhymes and Songs

LEARNING TO READ

Phonics
Decodable Books 10–12
• *Is It for Me?*
• *We Can Fix*
• *A Hat I Like*
High-Frequency Words

Independent Readers 27–29
• *Neighborhood Friends*
• *The Fire Bell Rings*
• *Lots of Jobs*

LANGUAGE ARTS

Shared Writing
Interactive Writing
Independent Writing
Writing Every Day

INDEPENDENT ACTIVITIES

Sharing Literature
  Respond to Literature
Phonics
  Independent Practice
  Handwriting
  Practice Book pages
High-Frequency Words
  Independent Practice
  Practice Book pages

About the
Authors and Illustrators

Lorinda Bryan Cauley

Illustrator of *The Big Yellow Bus*
Lorinda Bryan Cauley, a graduate of Rhode Island School of Design, has illustrated many animal folktales. She lives with her husband and son in Escondido, California.

Anne Rockwell

Author of *Career Day*
Anne Rockwell was born in Memphis, Tennessee, and attended the Sculpture Center and Pratt Graphics Arts center. She is a prolific author and illustrator of children's books. Rockwell's ability to remember what it was like to be a child and to look at the world from a child's viewpoint has contributed to her success as an author and illustrator.

Lizzy Rockwell

Illustrator of *Career Day*
Lizzy Rockwell shares her passion for books with her author-mother Anne. No doubt they will be the guests when Lizzy's sons have Career Day in school. The mother-daughter pair have also published *Thanksgiving Day*, *Halloween Day*, and *Show & Tell Day*.

Margaret Miller

Author and Photographer of *Guess Who?*
Margaret Miller is a freelance photographer and the author-photographer of many books for children. Her titles include *Can You Guess?*, *Whose Hat?*, *Who Uses This?*, and *Whose Shoe?* Miller's book *Where Does It Go?* was a *New York Times* Best Illustrated Book in 1992. Miller lives with her family in New York City.

Theme Assessment

After completing the theme, most children should show progress toward mastery of the following skills:

Concepts of Print
- ❑ Identify the front cover, back cover, and title page of a book.
- ❑ Recognize that sentences in print are made up of separate words.

Phonemic Awareness
- ❑ Track isolated phonemes.
- ❑ Track and represent changes in simple syllables and words with two and three sounds as one sound is added, substituted, omitted, shifted, or repeated.

Phonics and Decoding
- ❑ Match all consonant sounds and short-vowel sounds to appropriate letters.
- ❑ Read one-syllable and High-Frequency Words.

Vocabulary and High-Frequency Vocabulary
- ❑ Read High-Frequency Words *for* and *me*.
- ❑ Describe common objects and events in both general and specific language.
- ❑ Understand content words.

Comprehension
- ❑ Use pictures and content to make predictions about story content.
- ❑ Retell familiar stories.
- ❑ Understand the main idea and details.
- ❑ Understand story dialogue.

Literary Response
- ❑ Identify different types of everyday print materials.
- ❑ Identify the characters, settings, and important events.

Writing
- ❑ Write by moving from left to right and from top to bottom.
- ❑ Write about self-selected topics.
- ❑ Use prephonetic knowledge to spell independently.

Listening and Speaking
- ❑ Share information and ideas about careers, speaking audibly in complete, coherent sentences.
- ❑ Describe people, places, things, locations, and actions.

Assessment Options

Assessment Handbook
- Group Inventory
- Phonemic Awareness Inventory
- Theme Skills Assessment
- Concepts About Print Inventory
- Observational Checklists

Reaching All Learners

■ BELOW-LEVEL

Levels of Support

Point-of-use Notes in the Teacher's Edition

pp. 193, 205, 209, 211, 213, 219, 223, 225, 229, 233, 235, 243, 253, 257, 261, 265, 269, 273, 277, 279, 281, 285, 289, 299, 303, 307, 309, 311, 317, 319, 323, 325, 326, 335

Additional Support Activities

Vocabulary:
pp. S20-S21

Comprehension and Skills:
pp. S30-S31, S36-S37

Phonemic awareness:
pp. S22-S23, S28-S29, S32-S33

Phonics:
pp. S24-S25, S26-S27, S34-S35

Intervention Resources Kit

■ ENGLISH-LANGUAGE LEARNERS

Levels of Support

Point-of-use Notes in the Teacher's Edition

pp. 195, 223, 225, 229, 231, 235, 239, 243, 255, 257, 261, 263, 265, 279, 287, 299, 301, 319, 325, 331, 335

Additional Support Activities

Vocabulary:
pp. S20-S21

Comprehension and Skills:
pp. S30-S31, S36-S37

Phonemic Awareness:
pp. S22-S23, S28-S29, S32-S33

Phonics:
pp. S24-S25, S26-S27, S34-S35

Visit *The Learning Site!* at
www.harcourtschool.com
See Language Support activities

English-Language Learners Resources Kit

■ **ADVANCED**

Levels of Challenge

Point-of-use Notes in the Teacher's Edition

pp. 193, 209, 213, 215, 221, 225, 229, 231, 233, 241, 243, 257, 261, 265, 271, 273, 277, 279, 299, 301, 303, 315, 319, 323, 325, 326, 331, 333, 335

Additional Support Activities

Vocabulary:
pp. S20-S21

Comprehension and Skills:
pp. S30-S31, S36-S37

Phonemic Awareness:
pp. S22-S23, S28-S29, S32-S33

Phonics:
pp. S24-S25, S26-S27, S34-S35

Accelerated Instruction

Use higher-grade-level materials for accelerated instruction.

Theme Project, p. 182

Combination Classrooms
Sharing Knowledge

As you build background for the *Big Book*, *Little Books* and other theme literature, invite advanced or older children to share their knowledge with the group. You might identify these students as "information experts" and encourage them to answer questions from the class.

Students with Special Needs
Incorporating Physical Activity

While all children require physical activity and movement, children with special needs may have an especially difficult time sitting still.

Incorporate movement into as many daily activities as possible, such as marching around the classroom during songs, dramatizing stories, and responding through clapping, standing, tapping toes, and so on.

# Recommended Reading

Below are suggestions for reading materials that will meet kindergarten children's diverse needs. Books that are on a child's level provide support for new skills. Advanced books give children an opportunity to stretch and challenge their reading potential. Read-aloud books are important because they expose children to story language and vocabulary.

■ BELOW-LEVEL

Mouse Around by Pat Schories. Farrar Straus Giroux, 1991. Children will have a great time following the mouse around in this wordless picture book.

Snowball Fight by Paul Shipton. Rigby, 2000. A little girl on a walk in her neighborhood gets a few surprises in this wordless picture book.

Let's Go, Teddy Bear by Lynne Bertrand. Firefly, 1998. Teddy leads the way on a touch-smell-discover trip to town with his best friend Kitty.

In the Town by Stephen Caldwell. Barrons Educational Series, 2001. Go exploring with Ben and discover city and country life with easy words and bright pictures.

■ ON-LEVEL

Who Uses This? by Margaret Miller. Mulberry, 1999. Vivid photographs support the guessing-game format.

Whose Hat? by Margaret Miller. Morrow, 1988. Photographs of hats represent a variety of interesting occupations.

Construction Zone by Tana Hoban. Greenwillow, 1999. Construction machines and their operators are featured in bright photographs .

Going Shopping by Alison Hawes. Rigby, 2000. Find out what happens when a little boy goes grocery shopping with his dad.

■ ADVANCED

I Am Lost! by Hans Wilhelm. Scholastic, 1997. A police officer helps a lost dog find his way home again.

The Cow in the House by Harriet Ziefert. Viking, 1997. It takes a lot of noisy animals to convince a man that his house is quieter than he thinks.

One Hole in the Road by W. Nikola-Lisa. Holt, 1996. Workmen rush to fix a hole in the road as passersby looks on.

I Shop with My Daddy by Grace Maccarone. Scholastic, 1998. A girl and her father have a busy day shopping for groceries.

■ READ ALOUD

Good-bye, Curtis by Kevin Henkes. Greenwillow, 1995. A retiring mail carrier gets a surprise when his friends and neighbors throw him a party.

Community Helpers from A to Z by Bobbie Kalman. Crabtree Publishing Co., 1997. This book includes helpers such as veterinarians, firefighters, and sanitation workers.

Teamwork by Ann Morris. Lothrop, 1999. People play and work together in all parts of the world.

Mike Mulligan and His Shovel by Virginia Lee B Houghton, 1939. Mike ar steam shovel, Mary Anne way to keep their jobs.

Neighborhood Helpers

Teacher Notes

Learning Centers

Choose from the following suggestions to enhance your learning centers for the theme Neighborhood Helpers.
(Additional learning centers for this theme can be found on pages 246 and 292)

LITERACY CENTER

This Neighborhood Helper Can . . .

Tell children that they will draw a picture of and write about a neighborhood helper. Give children a sheet of paper with the following sentence frames: *What can the ____ do? The ____ can ____.* Have each child draw a picture of a neighborhood helper. Then have children complete the sentences to tell about their drawing. When children finish, they can take turns showing their pictures and reading their sentences to one another.

What can the firfitr **do?**
The firfitr **can** put out firs.

Materials

- crayons
- paper with the sentence frames: *What can the ____ do? The ____ can ____.*
- pencils

MANIPULATIVE CENTER

Matching Sounds with Letters

Place pictures of neighborhood helpers face down in the Manipulative Center. Have partners take turns choosing and identifying a picture. Then have children choose the Magnetic Letter that represents the initial sound of the neighborhood helper's name and put the letter on the magnetic board.

Materials

- Magnetic Letters and magnetic board
- pictures of firefighter, police, cook, teacher, bus driver, doctor, nurse, truck driver, waiter, farmer

WRITING CENTER

Write a List

Have partners work together to make a list of as many neighborhood helpers as they can. Children can get started by thinking of all the different places in their neighborhood or town where people work. Then have them list other jobs they have heard of. When finished, partners can read their lists to others in the Writing Center.

tchr   nrs   watr

firfiter   farmr   pilet

police   astranot   bus drivr

vet   sientist   mayr

doctr   cook   prezident

20 Minutes a day

Materials

- paper
- pencils

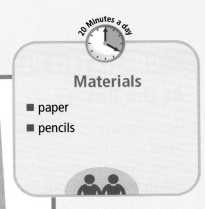

SOCIAL STUDIES CENTER

Neighborhood Workers Collage

Tell children they are going to work together to make a collage of neighborhood workers. Have children look in magazines to find and cut out pictures of neighborhood workers. Have children take turns holding up a picture, identifying it, and then gluing it onto a sheet of chart paper. Display finished collages in the Social Studies Center.

20 Minutes a day

Materials

- old magazines
- safety scissors
- glue sticks
- chart paper

DRAMATIC PLAY CENTER

At the Bakery

Have children put on aprons and role play working in a bakery. Some children can mix pretend ingredients to make bread, cupcakes, or pies. Other children can use a rolling pin to roll out modeling dough or clay to be cut with cookie cutters and placed on baking sheets. Still other children can decorate cakes made from clay.

20 Minutes a day

Materials

- modeling dough or clay
- rolling pin
- cookie cutters
- toy mixing bowls, mixer, spoons, baking pans and sheets
- aprons

MATH CENTER

Helper Puzzle

Tell children they are going to make a puzzle. First have each child look in magazines to find and cut out a large picture of people working. Then have children glue the picture to a sheet of construction paper and cut it into six pieces. Have partners exchange pieces and reassemble the picture. As needed, partners can help each other assemble their picture puzzles.

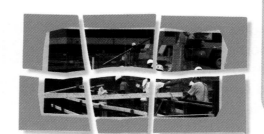

20 Minutes a day

Materials

- old magazines
- glue stick
- construction paper
- scissors

Teacher Notes

Teacher Notes

THEME 10

Week 1

Neighborhood Helpers

Theme 10: Week I

ORAL LANGUAGE
15-30 Minutes

- **Phonemic Awareness**

- **Sharing Literature**

LEARNING TO READ
45 Minutes

- **Phonics**

- **Vocabulary**

Daily Routines
- Morning Message
- Calendar Language
- Writing Prompt

LANGUAGE ARTS
15-30 Minutes

- **Writing**
  Daily Writing Prompt

Day I

Phonemic Awareness, 193
  Phoneme Isolation: Initial

Sharing Literature, 194
  Big Book: *The Big Yellow Bus*

(Skill) **Literature Focus, 195**
  Text Patterns

, **204** T
  Introduce: Consonant *Yy*
  Identify/Write T

Writing, 206
  Write About an Animal

Writing Prompt, 206
  Draw and write about self-selected topics.

Share Time, 207

Read
  Author's Chair

Day 2

Phonemic Awareness, 209
  Phoneme Isolation: Initial

Sharing Literature, 210
Read
  Library Book: *Career Day*

(Skill) **Literature Focus, 211**
  Main Idea/Details

, **212** T
  Relating /y/ to *y*

High-Frequency Word, 214 T
  Introduce: *for*

Words to Remember, 215

Shared Writing, 216
  Write About a Job

Writing Prompt, 216
  Draw and write about a job a friend or family member does.

Share Time, 217
  Discuss the job you would like to have when you are grown up.

T = tested skill

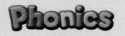 **Phonics**

Consonants *Yy, Zz*

Focus of the Week:
• HIGH-FREQUENCY WORDS: *for, me*
• PHONEMIC AWARENESS
• SHARING LITERATURE
• WRITING: Lists, Dialogue

Day 3

Phonemic Awareness, 219
Phoneme Isolation: Initial

Sharing Literature, 220
Read

Read-Aloud Anthology: "Mother, Mother, I Want Another," pp. 56–57

(Skill) **Literature Focus, 221**
Dialogue

 Phonics, 222 T
Introduce: Consonant *Zz*
Identify/Write **T**

High-Frequency Word, 224 T
Introduce: *me*

Words to Remember, 225

 Writing, 226
Write Dialogue

Writing Prompt, 226
Draw and write about self-selected topics.

Share Time, 227
Retell the Read-Aloud Anthology story with puppets.

Day 4

Phonemic Awareness, 229
Phoneme Isolation

Sharing Literature, 230
Big Book of Rhymes and Songs: "The Bus Song," p. 23

(Skill) **Literature Focus, 231**
Naming Words

 Phonics, 232 T
Relating /z/ to *z*

High-Frequency Words, 234 T
Review: *for, me*

Read
DECODABLE BOOK 10
Is It for Me?

 Interactive Writing, 236
Write a Thank-You Note

Writing Prompt, 236
Write a thank-you note to the person who helps you get to school.

Share Time, 237
Describe a zebra.

Day 5

Phonemic Awareness, 239
Syllable Segmentation

Sharing Literature, 240
Read

Library Book: *Career Day*

(Skill) **Literature Focus, 241**
Summarize

 Phonics, 242 T
Review: Consonants /y/*y*, /z/*z*

 Interactive Writing, 244
Write a List

Writing Prompt, 244
Draw and write about a job you do at home.

Share Time, 245
Describe and discuss jobs in *Career Day.*

Day at a Glance
Day I

Phonemic Awareness
Phoneme Isolation: Initial

Sharing Literature
Big Book:
The Big Yellow Bus

Read

Develop Listening Comprehension

Respond to Literature

Literature Focus: Text Patterns

Phonics
Consonant *Yy*

Writing
Sentences about Animals

MORNING MESSAGE

Kindergarten News

(Child's name) _____

to school.

Write Kindergarten News Talk with children about how they get to school.

Use prompts such as the following to guide children as you write the news:

- **Raise your hand if you ride a bus to school.**
- **What other ways do you come to school?**
- **Who can show me where to begin writing?**
- **What letter will I write first in (child's name)?**
- **Let's count the letters in (child's name). How many?**

As you write the message, invite children to contribute by writing letters, words, or names they have previously learned. Remind them to use proper spacing, capitalization, and punctuation.

Calendar Language

Point to and read aloud the days of the week. Point to and read aloud the days *Monday* through *Friday*. Tell children these are the days they come to school. Have children name the school days with you as you point to each one.

Sunday	Monday	Tuesday	Wednesday	Thursday	Friday	Saturday
		1	2	3	4	5
6	7	8	9	10	11	12
13	14	15	16	17	18	19
20	21	22	23	24	25	26
27	28	29	30	31		

FLORIDA STANDARDS/GLEs **FCAT: LA.A.2.1.5.K.2** Get information; **LA.B.2.1.2.K.1** Record ideas; *Also* **LA.A.1.1.2.K.1** Print organization; **LA.A.1.1.2.K.2** Alphabet; **LA.C.1.1.3.K.1** Conversation rules; **LA.C.3.1.2.K.1** Questions

Phonemic Awareness

PHONEME ISOLATION: INITIAL

Listen for the Initial Sound   Use the rabbit puppet, a basket, and paper carrots for this phoneme isolation activity. Tell children that the rabbit can get a carrot in his basket if they can tell him the beginning sound three times in a word he says.

MODEL I want to put a carrot in the rabbit's basket, so I will listen for the first sound in the word he says. The rabbit says: *yak*. What is the beginning sound in *yak*? /y/ is the beginning sound in yak. Say it with me. The rabbit wants us to say it three times: *yak, /y/-/y/-/y/, yak.* Let's say it with the rabbit. Now who will put a carrot in his basket?

Follow the same procedure for the following words. Invite a different child to put a "carrot" in the basket each time the children say the initial phoneme.

you (/y/)	**wallet** (/w/)	**turtle** (/t/)
yam (/y/)	**paper** (/p/)	**beach** (/b/)
vet (/v/)	**yes** (/y/)	**yellow** (/y/)
jam (/j/)	**hello** (/h/)	**rod** (/r/)
yawn (/y/)	**ring** (/r/)	**gift** (/g/)
fan (/f/)	**carrot** (/k/)	**yesterday** (/y/)

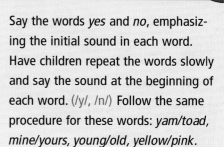

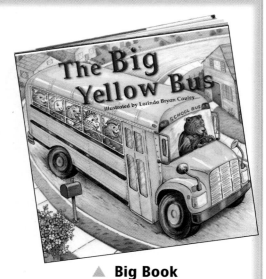

▲ **Big Book**

OBJECTIVES

- *To make predictions*
- *To listen and respond to a story*
- *To act out a story*
- *To understand text patterns*

Materials

■ *Big Book: The Big Yellow Bus*

Sharing Literature

Read The Big Yellow Bus

READ ALOUD

Before Reading   Display *The Big Yellow Bus.* Read the title aloud as you track the print. Use these prompts to help children make predictions.

- **What do you see on the front cover?** (a bus)
- **Who is riding the bus?** (animals) Point to the yak. **This animal is called a yak. A yak is an animal related to a cow or an ox. It is big and has long hair. Which animals can you name?** (Possible responses: zebra, lion, sheep)
- **Where do you think they might be going?** (Possible responses: to school, on a trip, home)

Remind them to think about the title of the story and what they see on the cover to predict what the story is about.

- **What do you think this story is about?** (Possible response: I think it's about going to school.)

During Reading   Read the story aloud. As you read,

- emphasize the repetitive refrain, inviting children to pantomine the animal actions.
- point to the animals and their actions. Invite children to tell what they think about what the animals are doing.
- track the print as you read aloud.

7

FLORIDA STANDARDS/GLEs   FCAT: LA.A.1.1.4.K.1 Comprehension; *Also* **LA.A.1.1.1.K.1** Predictions; **LA.A.1.1.2.K.1** Print organization; **LA.A.2.1.4.K.1** Illustrations; **LA.C.1.1.1.K.2** Oral language; **LA.C.3.1.1.K.1** Speak clearly; **LA.D.1.1.1.K.1** Sound patterns; **LA.E.2.1.2.K.1** Patterned structures

DEVELOP LISTENING COMPREHENSION

After Reading   Have children answer these questions about the story:

- **What is this story about?** (a bus ride to school)
- **Who is going to school on the bus?** (zebras, yaks, lions, sheep)
- **What do the animals do when they get on the bus?** (They each make a different sound.)
- **Why do you think the sheep say "Sh, sh, sh" when they get on the bus?** (Possible response: Maybe it's too noisy.)

RESPOND TO LITERATURE

Act Out the Story   Set up a row of chairs in the front of the room. Ask one child to be the bus driver and to sit in the first chair. Group several children together as zebras, yaks, lions, and sheep. As you reread the story, have each group get on the bus as they are named. Have them pantomime the actions and recite the words the animals say. Allow all children to have a turn acting out the story.

TEXT PATTERNS

Tell children that sometimes the words in a story follow a pattern. Turn to page 4 in *The Big Yellow Bus*. Track the print as you read the text aloud.

down the street; down the street; down the street

The same words on this page are said three times. Let's see if we can find more words that we can say three times.

Read the other pages aloud and ask children: **Which words are repeated on this page?**

ENGLISH-LANGUAGE LEARNERS

Point to each animal in the *Big Book*. Say its name and ask children to repeat the word. Pantomime the actions of each animal as you say the action words. Pretend to zip a jacket as you say "Zip, zip, zip."

ONGOING ASSESSMENT

As you share *The Big Yellow Bus*, note whether children

- make predictions.
- pantomime actions named in the story.
- respond to the story by talking about picture details.

▲ **Practice Book pages 5–6**

FLORIDA STANDARDS/GLEs   FCAT: **LA.A.1.1.4.K.1** Comprehension; **LA.A.2.1.1.K.1** Main idea; *Also*; **LA.C.3.1.1.K.1** Speak clearly; **LA.C.3.1.2.K.1** Questions;

HW

Neighborhood ℙ

The Big Yellow Bus

illustrated by Lorinda Bryan Cauley

The Big Yellow Bus

illustrated by Lorinda Bryan Cauley

Harcourt

Orlando Boston Dallas Chicago San Diego

Visit The Learning Site!
www.harcourtschool.com

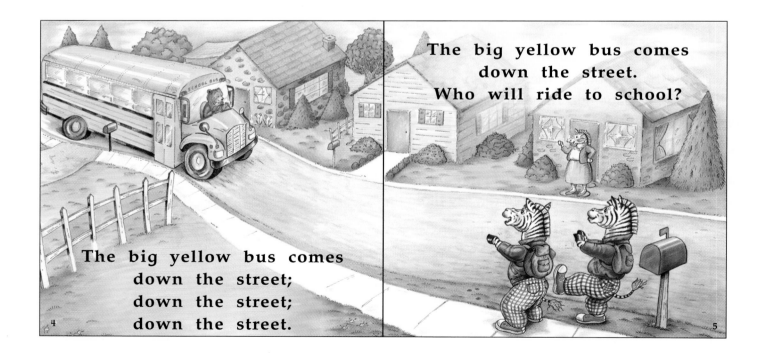

The big yellow bus comes
down the street;
down the street;
down the street.

The big yellow bus comes
down the street.
Who will ride to school?

4

5

The horn on the bus goes
    beep, beep, beep;
    beep, beep, beep;
    beep, beep, beep.

The horn on the bus goes
    beep, beep, beep,
    on the way to school.

7

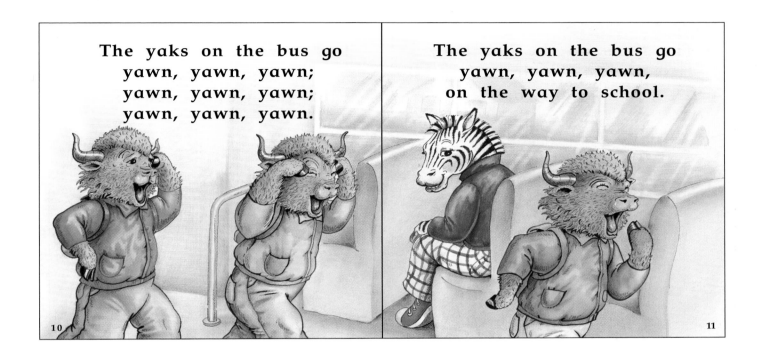

The lions on the bus sing,
"La, la, la;
la, la, la;
la, la, la."

The lions on the bus sing,
"La, la, la,"
on the way to school.

12

13

The animals on the bus go
up and down;
up and down;
up and down.

16

The animals on the bus go
up and down,
on the way to school.

17

The big yellow bus stops
    at the school;
    at the school;
    at the school.

18

The big yellow bus stops
    at the school.
Time for class to start.

19

OBJECTIVES

• To recognize Y and y

• To write uppercase and lowercase Yy independently

Materials

■ Big Book of Rhymes and Songs pp. 2–3

■ Music CD

■ Big Alphabet Card Yy

■ Big Book: The Big Yellow Bus

■ Write-On/Wipe-Off Boards

■ drawing paper

■ crayons or pencils

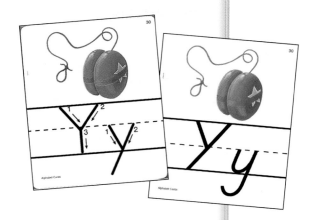

Phonics
Consonant Yy  Introduce

ACTIVE BEGINNING

Sing "The Alphabet Song"   Display "The Alphabet Song" in the *Big Book of Rhymes and Songs*. Point to each letter as you sing the song with children.

▲ **Big Book of Rhymes and Songs, pages 2–3**

TEACH/MODEL

Introduce the Letter Name   Hold up *Big Alphabet Card Yy*.

The name of this letter is *y*. Say the name with me.

Point to the uppercase Y. **This is the uppercase Y.**

Point to the lowercase y. **This is the lowercase y.**

Point to the *Big Alphabet Card* again. **What is the name of this letter?**

Point to the Y in "The Alphabet Song." **What is the name of this letter?**

Display the front cover of *The Big Yellow Bus*.

Follow along as I read the title.

Point to the letter Y. **What is the name of this letter?**

 FLORIDA STANDARDS/GLEs   LA.A.1.1.2.K.1 Print organization; **LA.A.1.1.2.K.2** Alphabet; **LA.C.1.1.1.K.2** Oral language; **LA.C.3.1.2.K.1** Questions

Handwriting

Writing Y and y Write uppercase *Y* and lowercase *y* on the board.

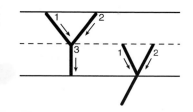

Point to the uppercase *Y*. **What letter is this?**

Point to the lowercase *y*. **What letter is this?**

MODEL **Watch as I write the letter *Y* so that everyone can read it.**

As you give the Letter Talk, trace the uppercase *Y*. Use the same modeling procedure for lowercase *y*.

Letter Talk for *Y*

Slant right down. Slant left down. Straight line down.

Letter Talk for *y*

Slant right down. Slant left down below the other line.

D'Nealian handwriting models are on pages R12–13.

PRACTICE/APPLY

Guided Practice Help children find *Yy* on their *Write-On/Wipe-Off Board*. Have them trace uppercase *Y* with a finger and then write the letter several times. Then have them do the same for lowercase *y*. Tell children to circle their best *Yy*.

Independent Practice Distribute drawing paper and have children fill their paper with *Yys*. Then have them circle their best *Y* and *y*.

Phonics Resources

Phonics Express™ CD-ROM, Level A, Bumper/Route 3/ Harbor

Phonics Practice Book pages 109–110

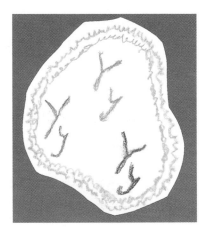

▲ **Practice Book page 7**

OBJECTIVES

- *To innovate on a big book*
- *To create a class book*

Writing Every Day

Day 1: Sentences About Animals

Have children extend the literature *The Big Yellow Bus* by writing sentences to tell about other animals who might ride the big yellow bus.

Day 2: Sentences About Jobs

Have children dictate words to complete sentence frames to tell about jobs they'd like to have.

Day 3: Dialogue

Have children draw a picture of one of the animals from "Mother, Mother, I Want Another," and write what the animal says in a speech bubble.

Day 4: Thank-You Note

Have children write a class thank-you note to the school bus driver.

Day 5: List of Jobs

Have children work together to write a list of jobs they do at home.

LANGUAGE ARTS

Writing

Write Sentences About an Animal

EXTENDING LITERATURE

Talk About Animals   Ask children to name the animals in the story *The Big Yellow Bus*. (zebras, yaks, lions, sheep) Ask children to name other animals who might ride on the big yellow bus and tell what the animals might say. List their responses on chart paper.

Write About an Animal   Model for children on chart paper how to draw and write about animals who ride the bus to school.

MODEL I will choose cats from our list to write about. My sentence will be *The cats go meow, meow, meow.* As I write, I will start my sentence with an uppercase *T*. I will look on the chart to help me spell words. I will put a period at the end.

cow   moo, moo, moo

cat   meow, meow, meow

pig   oink, oink, oink

Compile children's pages into a class book. Include a cover with the title *Animals Go to School.*

The cows go moo, moo, moo.

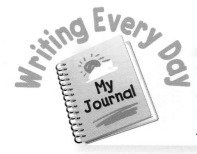

Self-Selected Writing Have children write and draw about anything they'd like. If they have difficulty thinking of a topic, have them ask two friends what they're going to write about.

🏴 **FLORIDA STANDARDS/GLEs   FCAT: LA.B.2.1.2.K.1** Record ideas; *Also* **LA.A.1.1.2.K.1** Print organization; **LA.B.1.1.1.K.2** Generate ideas; **LA.B.1.1.2.K.2** Basic formats; **LA.B.1.1.3.K.1** Spelling approximations; **LA.B.1.1.3.K.2** Print direction; **LA.B.2.1.1.K.1** Familiar experiences; **LA.D.1.1.1.K.2** Language functions

WRAP UP # Share Time

Author's Chair Gather children around an Author's Chair and have them take turns telling about their page in their class book "Animals Go to School." Ask children to name the letter they learned to write.

S.S.R. *Sustained Silent Reading* Have children read silently from a book of their choice.

 **Centers**  **MANIPULATIVE**

Constructing Y and y

Place at the center a variety of materials, and have children construct *Y* and *y* shapes. Invite them to build thick or thin letters using their favorite colors. Tell children to sketch or trace around their *Yy*'s on paper before they put away the materials.

 Materials

- table blocks
- counting rods or cubes
- cut-up drinking straws
- yarn
- crayons

WARM UP

Phonemic Awareness
Phoneme Isolation: Initial

Sharing Literature
Library Book:
Career Day

Read
Career Day
story by
Anne Rockwell
pictures by
Lizzy Rockwell

Develop Listening Comprehension

Respond to Literature

Literature Focus:
Main Idea/Details

Phonics
Relating /y/ to y

High-Frequency Words
for

Shared Writing ✏️
Sentences About Jobs

MORNING MESSAGE

Kindergarten News

When _____ goes to work,

he/she _____.

Write Kindergarten News Talk with children about jobs that family members have.

Use prompts such as the following to guide children as you write the news:

• **What jobs do people in your family have?**

• **Who can show me the top of the page?**

• **Who can show me the bottom of the page?**

• **Who can show me a word?**

As you write the message, invite children to contribute by writing letters, words, or names they have previously learned. Remind them to use proper spacing, capitalization, and punctuation.

····· Calendar Language ·····

Name the days of the week, inviting children to join in and clap for each day. Tell children to count with you the days of the week as you point to each one. Say: *There are seven days in a week.* Ask: *How many days are in a week?*

Sunday	Monday	Tuesday	Wednesday	Thursday	Friday	Saturday
		1	2	3	4	5
6	7	8	9	10	11	12
13	14	15	16	17	18	19
20	21	22	23	24	25	26
27	28	29	30	31		

FLORIDA STANDARDS/GLEs   FCAT: LA.A.1.1.2.K.4 Words; **LA.A.2.1.5.K.2** Get information; **LA.B.2.1.2.K.1** Record ideas; *Also* **LA.C.1.1.3.K.1** Conversation rules; **LA.C.3.1.2.K.1** Questions

Phonemic Awareness

PHONEME ISOLATION: INITIAL

Listen for the Initial Sound Teach children the following rhyme. Say the rhyme aloud, emphasizing the /y/ sound:

A yak with a yellow yo-yo,

Eating yogurt on a yacht,

Yelled, "Yum, yum, Mr. Captain,

This yogurt hits the spot!"

BELOW-LEVEL

Say the rhyme again and have children repeat each line after you. Say the words that begin with /y/, elongating the /y/ sound. Ask children to do the same. Then ask them to say the sound they hear at the beginning of each word. Have children say the rhyme again slowly, elongating the /y/ sound in each word.

ADVANCED

Have children make up a silly sentence about a yellow yo-yo.

Repeat the rhyme and invite children to clap each time they hear a word with the /y/ sound.

Then tell children you will say some words and they will listen for the beginning sound in those words. Say the word **yak**. Have children repeat it. Say it again, emphasizing the /y/ sound.

Say: **/y/ is the sound I hear at the beginning of** *yak*—**/y/.**

Then say the following words. Have children repeat each word and tell the beginning sound.

yellow	**yo-yo**	**yogurt**	**yelled**
yes	**yum**	**yacht**	

Ask children to say the sound they hear at the beginning of the words. (/y/)

FLORIDA STANDARDS/GLEs FCAT: **LA.A.1.1.2.K.5** Phonetic principles; *Also* **LA.C.1.1.1.K.1** Follow directions; **LA.C.3.1.2.K.1** Questions

Neighborhood Helpers **209**

▲ **Library Book**

OBJECTIVES

- *To listen and respond to a story*

- *To connect text to life experiences*

- *To identify details in pictures*

- *To understand main ideas and details*

Materials

■ *Library Book: Career Day*

■ chart paper

■ marker

Sharing Literature

Read Career Day

READ ALOUD

Before Reading Display the cover of *Career Day*. Ask a child to point to the title and the names of the author and the illustrator while you read the words aloud. Tell children that *career* is another word for *job*. Tell children that in some schools, family members and other people from the community come to the classroom to tell about the work they do. Use these prompts to build background:

- **Who is on the front and back covers?** (children)

- **What are the children doing?** (Possible responses: playing dress-up, pretending to be workers)

- **What jobs are they pretending to do?** (Possible responses: construction worker, cook, conductor or ticket taker, firefighter, veterinarian, teacher)

During Reading Read the story aloud. As you read,

- pause on each page to say: **Raise your hand if you know someone who does this job.**

- pause to allow children to point out the tasks the people in the illustrations are doing.

FLORIDA STANDARDS/GLEs **FCAT: LA.A.1.1.4.K.1** Comprehension; *Also* **LA.A.2.1.4.K.1** Illustrations; **LA.C.1.1.1.K.2** Oral language; **LA.C.3.1.2.K.1** Questions

DEVELOP LISTENING COMPREHENSION

After Reading   Have children answer these questions about the story:

- **Where does this story take place?** (Possible response: Mrs. Madoff's kindergarten class)

- **Why do special visitors come to Mrs. Madoff's class?** (to tell about the work they do)

- **Which job do you think is the most interesting? Why?** (Accept reasonable responses.)

RESPOND TO LITERATURE

Talk About Careers   Ask children to name some jobs they might like to do when they grow up. Write their suggestions on chart paper. Ask children to choose a job they would like to pretend to have, and then have them work with a partner to take turns introducing themselves and telling about their jobs.

Literature Focus

MAIN IDEA/DETAILS

Ask children what they think is the main idea of this book. (*Career Day* is about the jobs people have. That is the main idea.)

Model how details tell more about the main idea.

MODEL   **Pablo's father drives a bulldozer. He uses the bulldozer to build a new library.**

Charlie's mother is a judge. She works in a courtroom. She wears a long, black robe. She pounds her gavel if there is too much noise.

ONGOING ASSESSMENT

As you share *Career Day*, note whether children

- **listen for a period of time.**
- **can connect text to life experiences.**
- **can identify details in pictures.**

FLORIDA STANDARDS/GLEs   **FCAT: LA.A.1.1.4.K.1** Comprehension; **LA.A.2.1.1.K.1** Main idea; *Also* **LA.C.1.1.3.K.1** Conversation rules; **LA.C.3.1.2.K.1** Questions

Neighborhood Helpers   211

Phonics
Relating /y/ to y

OBJECTIVE
To match consonant y to its sound

Materials

- *Letter and Sound Chart 13*
- *Tactile Letter Cards y*
- *Picture/Word Cards yak, yarn*
- pocket chart
- yo-yo Pattern (page T13)
- scissors
- crayons
- yarn
- tape

ACTIVE BEGINNING

Recite "Yippee! Yay!" Have children listen for /y/ as they learn the rhyme. Then they can make up motions to recite the rhyme as a cheer.

Yippee! Yay!

Yippee! Yay! Yippee! Yay!

I am six years old today!

Yippee! Yay! Yippee! Yay!

This should be a holiday.

by Susan Little

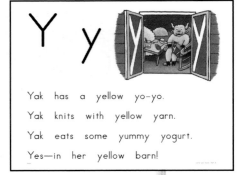

Yak has a yellow yo-yo.
Yak knits with yellow yarn.
Yak eats some yummy yogurt.
Yes—in her yellow barn!

▲ **Letter and Sound Chart 13**

TEACH/MODEL

Introduce Letter and Sound Display *Letter and Sound Chart 13.*

Touch the letter *Y*. **What is the name of the letter?**

This letter stands for the /y/ sound. Say /yy/.

Read aloud the rhyme on the *Letter and Sound Chart*, tracking the print.

Read aloud the *Yy* words in the rhyme. Then point to each *y* and have children say the /y/ sound. Ask: **What letter stands for the /y/ sound?**

Have children join in as you read the rhyme again. Encourage them to emphasize the /y/ sound as they say the /y/y words.

 FLORIDA STANDARDS/GLEs   FCAT: LA.A.1.1.2.K.5 Phonetic principles; *Also* LA.A.1.1.2.K.1 Print organization; LA.A.1.1.2.K.2 Alphabet; LA.A.1.1.2.K.3 Sounds; LA.C.3.1.2.K.1 Questions

PRACTICE/APPLY

Guided Practice   Distribute *Tactile Letter Cards y*. Then place *Picture/Word Cards yak* and *yarn* in a pocket chart. Say the names of the pictures as you point to the *y* in each. Have children repeat the words.

Tell children: **These words begin with y.**

Point to the *y* in *yak*. **The /y/ sound is at the beginning of yak.**

Point to the *y* in *yarn*. **The /y/ sound is at the beginning of yarn.**

I'm going to say some words. If the word begins with the /y/ sound, hold up your y card. If it doesn't begin with the /y/ sound, don't hold up your y card. *Thumbs ↑ Thumbs↓*

yawn   **yell**   **gold**   **yes**   **count**   **yard**   **yet**

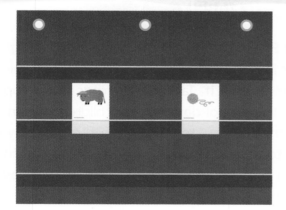

Independent Practice   Distribute yarn and copies of the yo-yo Pattern (page T13). Have children write *Yy* on their yo-yo, decorate it, and cut it out. Ask them to use tape to attach the yellow yarn over the drawn string line on the pattern. They may make the string as long as they like. Have children take turns dropping their yo-yo while pinching the string between two fingers. As they drop their yo-yo, they must say a word that begins with /y/.

BELOW-LEVEL

Display Picture Cards *yak, yellow, yarn,* and *yo-yo*. Say the name and identify the beginning sound as /y/. Continue to point to pictures and have children name the pictures, identify the beginning sound, and identify the letter that makes the /y/ sound. For more practice with Consonant *Yy*, see Alternative Teaching Strategies, page T5.

ADVANCED

Give each child a sheet of drawing paper. Help them fold their papers into four squares. Have children draw and label four pictures of things whose names begin with the /y/ sound.

Phonics Resources

***Phonics Express™* CD-ROM, Level A,** Bumper/Route 3/Fire Station, Market

Phonics Practice Book pages 111–112

Color yolk, yarn, yo-yo

▲ **Practice Book page 8** *HW*

FLORIDA STANDARDS/GLEs   FCAT: LA.A.1.1.2.K.5 Phonetic principles; *Also* **LA.A.1.1.2.K.2** Alphabet; **LA.A.1.1.2.K.3** Sounds; **LA.B.1.1.2.K.2** Basic formats

Neighborhood Helpers   213

OBJECTIVE

• To read the high-frequency word *for*

Materials

- ■ BIG BOOK: *The Big Yellow Bus*
- ■ High-Frequency Word Card
- ■ *Teacher's Resource Book* p. 140
- ■ sentence strips

High-Frequency Word *for* ✔*Introduce*

TEACH/MODEL

Display page 19 of *The Big Yellow Bus*. Read aloud the page. Then reread the sentence *Time for class to start*. Track the print as you read aloud.

Point to the word *for* and say: **This is the word *for*.** Have children say the word. Display *High-Frequency Word Card for*. Ask: **What word is this?** Ask children to say the sentence with you. Have a child match the *High-Frequency Word Card for* to the word *for* in the sentence.

PRACTICE/APPLY

Guided Practice   Distribute copies of the *High-Frequency Word Card for* in the *Teacher's Resource Book*. Tell children to point to the word *for* and say it. Talk about things that happen during different times of the school day. Remind children that in *The Big Yellow Bus*, it was time for class to start when the bus arrived at school. Ask children to take turns saying and finishing the following sentence. Tell them to point to their word card as they say the word *for*.

> It is time for _____.

Independent Practice   Have children copy and complete the following sentence frame to tell who gets a snack. Ask them to point to the word *for* each time they read the sentence.

The _____ is for _____.

🔸 **FLORIDA STANDARDS/GLEs   FCAT: LA.A.1.1.2.K.4** Words; **LA.A.1.1.3.K.4** Build vocabulary; **LA.C.3.1.3.K.1** Basic vocabulary; *Also* **LA.A.1.1.2.K.1** Print organization; **LA.A.1.1.3.K.1** Frequent words; **LA.B.1.1.2.K.2** Basic formats; **LA.B.1.1.3.K.2** Print direction

Word Wall

Reading Words Hold up *High-Frequency Word Card for*. Place the word card under the letter *f* on the classroom word chart and have children read it aloud. Then ask a child to match his or her *High-Frequency Word Card for* to *for* on the word chart.

Find Similarities Have children look closely at their new word *for*. Encourage them to find similarities to other words posted on the chart. Ask the following question to guide them appropriately:

• *For* has three letters. Do any of our other words have three letters? Let's read the other words that have three letters. (*the, you, see*)

▲ **Practice Book page 9** HW

FLORIDA STANDARDS/GLEs FCAT: LA.A.1.1.2.K.4 Words; **LA.A.1.1.3.K.4** Build vocabulary; *Also* **LA.A.1.1.3.K.1** Frequent words

Neighborhood Helpers **215**

OBJECTIVES

• To identify and sort common words in basic categories

• To identify story characters

Materials

■ *Library Book: Career Day*

■ chart paper

■ marker

Shared Writing

Write Sentences About Jobs

COMPLETE SENTENCE FRAMES

Talk About Jobs Have children name jobs they learned about in *Career Day*. As they mention each job, ask them to tell what the person does who has that job.

Write About Jobs Tell children that together they will write about jobs they would like to have when they grow up. Ask them to suggest a job they want to write about.

MODEL Let's pretend we are the people with jobs. I'll write these two sentence frames on chart paper: *I am a (an) _____. I like to _____.* I'll put my finger next to each word I write to make a space.

Ask children to complete the sentence frames by naming the job they would like to have when they grow up and telling what they like about the job they choose. Write their suggestions on chart paper. Read each sentence after you have written it.

I am an artist. I like to draw.

I am a fireman. I like to help put out fires.

Journal Writing Have children draw and write about a job a friend or a family member does.

FLORIDA STANDARDS/GLEs **FCAT: LA.B.1.1.1.K.2** Generate ideas; **LA.B.2.1.2.K.1** Record ideas; **LA.A.1.1.2.K.4** Words; **LA.C.3.1.3.K.1** Basic vocabulary; *Also* **LA.B.1.1.3.K.2** Print direction; **LA.B.2.1.1.K.2** Contribute ideas

WRAP UP Share Time

Read About Jobs   Help children tell about the jobs they would like to have when they grow up by reading the sentences for them from the chart. Encourage children to tell more about these jobs.

S.S.R. *Sustained Silent Reading*   Have children read silently from a book of their choice.

Centers   ART

Yellow Flowers

Place at the center tissue paper and construction paper for each child. Have each child place the pencil eraser in the middle of the tissue paper and wrap the paper around it. Then dip it into glue and press on blue paper. Remove the pencil. Encourage children to make many flowers and then use crayons to create a setting of a garden or a vase.

Materials

- squares of yellow tissue paper
- pencil
- glue
- small squares of blue construction paper
- crayons

FLORIDA STANDARDS/GLEs   **FCAT: LA.A.1.1.2.K.4** Words;   **LA.A.1.1.2.K.6** Print meaning; *Also* **LA.C.1.1.3.K.1** Conversation rules

Neighborhood Helpers   **217**

Day at a Glance
Day 3

Phonemic Awareness
Phoneme Isolation: Initial

Sharing Literature
Read-Aloud Anthology:
"Mother, Mother, I Want Another"

Read

Develop Concept Vocabulary

Respond to Literature

Literature Focus: Dialogue

Phonics
Consonant *Zz*

High-Frequency Words
me

Writing
Dialogue

WARM UP

MORNING MESSAGE
Kindergarten News

(Child's name) likes to listen to

_____ .

Write Kindergarten News Talk with children about their favorite bedtime story. Have children tell why they like this story the best.

Use prompts such as the following to guide children as you write the news:

- **What stories do you like to listen to before you go to bed?**
- **Who can show me a word they know? Count the letters in the word.**
- **Who can show me the beginning of the sentence?**
- **Who can show me the end of the sentence?**

As you write the message, invite children to contribute by writing letters, words, or names they have previously learned. Remind them to use proper spacing, capitalization, and punctuation.

Calendar Language

Point to and read aloud the names of the days of the week. Name the days of the week again, inviting children to join in and clap for each day.

Sunday	Monday	Tuesday	Wednesday	Thursday	Friday	Saturday
		1	2	3	4	5
6	7	8	9	10	11	12
13	14	15	16	17	18	19
20	21	22	23	24	25	26
27	28	29	30	31		

FLORIDA STANDARDS/GLEs **FCAT: LA.A.1.1.2.K.4** Words; **LA.A.2.1.5.K.2** Get information; **LA.B.2.1.2.K.1** Record ideas; **LA.E.1.1.1.K.1** Genres; *Also* **LA.C.1.1.3.K.1** Conversation rules; **LA.C.3.1.2.K.1** Questions

Phonemic Awareness

PHONEME ISOLATION: INITIAL

Tell children you will say some words and they will listen to the beginning sounds in the words. Sing the following to the tune of "The Farmer in the Dell."

Zebra starts with /z/.

Zebra starts with /z/.

I hear /z/ in *zebra*.

Zebra starts with /z/.

Tell children that you will say a new word and they can say the beginning sound. Use the following words and revise the rhyme appropriately:

fish	lion
bus	visitor
water	nurse
cake	teacher
guard	scientist
market	hammer

▲ **"Zany Zaddlepate,"** *Oo-pples and Boo-noo-noos: Songs and Activities for Phonemic Awareness,* page 125.

BELOW-LEVEL

Say the sentence *Zachary Zebra likes zinnias.* Have children repeat the sentence. Say it again, elongating the initial /z/. Have children do the same. Finally have children say the sentence and clap every time they hear /z/.

▲ **Read-Aloud Anthology**

OBJECTIVES

- *To make and check predictions*

- *To use context clues to figure out the meaning of unknown words*

- *To dramatize a story*

- *To understand that characters speak*

Materials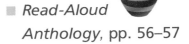

- *Read-Aloud Anthology*, pp. 56–57

- *Teacher's Resource Book*, pp. 82–83

- crayons

- scissors

- glue

- craft sticks

- chart paper

- marker

Sharing Literature

Read "Mother, Mother, I Want Another"

READ ALOUD

Before Reading Turn to page 56 of the *Read-Aloud Anthology* and read aloud the title of the story. Ask children what they remember about "Mother, Mother, I Want Another." Remind children that it is a story about a baby mouse and it takes place at bedtime. Use this model to set a purpose for rereading the story:

MODEL I remember this story is about a baby mouse who wants something from his mother. She does not understand what her baby wants. She tries to get help from lots of mothers. I'll read the story again to find out how Mrs. Mouse solves the problem of getting Baby Mouse what he wants.

Ask: **Do you remember how many mothers helped? Let's read and find out if you're right.**

During Reading Read the story aloud. As you read,

- pause and encourage children to make predictions about what will happen with each mother.

MODEL Now Mrs. Mouse gets Mrs. Donkey. I don't think that a donkey will be able to put a baby mouse to sleep. I think that Baby Mouse will say, "Mother, Mother, I want another."

- encourage children to pretend to be baby mouse and demonstrate how they would say, *Mother, Mother, I want another.*

🔶 **FLORIDA STANDARDS/GLEs FCAT: LA.A.1.1.2.K.4** Words; **LA.A.1.1.4.K.1** Comprehension; *Also* **LA.C.1.1.1.K.2** Oral language; **LA.C.3.1.2.K.1** Questions; **LA.D.2.1.2.K.1** Patterned structures

DEVELOP CONCEPT VOCABULARY

After Reading   Use the following prompts to discuss story vocabulary. Tell children to use all the words in each sentence to figure out the meaning of words they don't know.

Mother Mouse tucks baby mouse into his bed. What does *tuck* mean? (to cover)

Mrs. Duck tells baby mouse not to fret. What does *fret* mean? (to worry, to be upset)

Mrs. Donkey sings a lullaby. What is a *lullaby*? (a bedtime song, a quiet song)

RESPOND TO LITERATURE

Retell the Story   Give each child a copy of the Character Cutouts (*Teacher's Resource Book*, pages 82–83) for this story. Have children color the characters, cut them out, and glue each one to a craft stick. Then ask each child to choose one of the puppets. Place into groups children who have chosen the same character. Reread the story, pausing for each group of children to move their puppets as you read the character's lines.

DIALOGUE

Tell children that characters in stories speak. Remind them that Baby Mouse keeps saying, "Mother, Mother, I want another." Write the words on chart paper. Read the sentence aloud and ask the children to say how they think Baby Mouse says these words. Point out the quotation marks and explain that a writer puts those marks around the words someone speaks. Turn to page 57 in the *Read-Aloud Anthology* and read it aloud. Tell children to listen to what the different characters say. Change the tone and pitch of your voice as you read the dialogue.

ADVANCED

Have children learn the songs the animals sing. Ask them to recite them for the class as they act out the play with their puppets.

ONGOING ASSESSMENT

As you share "Mother, Mother, I Want Another," note whether children

- **make and check predictions.**
- **recognize that characters speak.**
- **can use puppets to dramatize a story.**

OBJECTIVES

- *To recognize Z and z*
- *To write uppercase and lowercase Zz independently*

Materials

- *Big Book of Rhymes and Songs* pp. 2–3
- *Music CD*
- *Big Alphabet Card Zz*
- *Big Book: From Anne to Zach*
- *Write-On/Wipe-Off Boards*
- drawing paper
- crayons or pencils

Phonics
Consonant Zz

ACTIVE BEGINNING

Sing "The Alphabet Song" Display "The Alphabet Song" in *The Big Book of Rhymes and Songs*. Point to each letter as you sing the song with children.

▲ **Big Book of Rhymes and Songs, pages 2–3**

TEACH/MODEL

Introduce the Letter Name Hold up *Big Alphabet Card Zz*.

The name of this letter is *Z*. Say the name with me.

Point to the uppercase *Z*. **This is the uppercase *Z*.**

Point to the lowercase *z*. **This is the lowercase *z*.**

Point to the *Big Alphabet Card* again. **What is the name of this letter?**

Point to the *Z* in *"The Alphabet Song."* **What is the name of this letter?**

Display page 37 of *From Anne to Zach.*

Follow along as I read this sentence. Read page 37.

Point to the letter *Z*. **What is the name of this letter?**

 FLORIDA STANDARDS/GLEs LA.A.1.1.2.K.1 Print organization; **LA.A.1.1.2.K.2** Alphabet; **LA.C.1.1.1.K.2** Oral language; **LA.C.3.1.2.K.1** Questions

Handwriting

Writing Z and z Write uppercase Z and lowercase z on the board.

Point to the uppercase Z. **What letter is this?**

Point to the lowercase z. **What letter is this?**

MODEL **Watch as I write the letter Z so that everyone can read it.**

As you give the Letter Talk, trace the uppercase Z. Use the same modeling procedure for lowercase z.

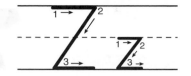

Letter Talk for Z

Straight line across. Slant left and down. Straight line across.

Letter Talk for z

Straight line across. Slant left and down. Straight line across.

D'Nealian handwriting models are on pages R12–13.

PRACTICE/APPLY

Guided Practice Help children find *Zz* on their *Write-On/Wipe-Off Board*. Have them trace the uppercase *Z* with a finger and then write the letter several times. Then have them do the same for lowercase *z*. Tell children to circle their best *Z*.

Independent Practice Distribute drawing paper and have children practice printing *Zz*s. Then have them circle their best *Z* and *z*.

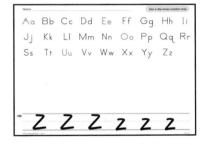

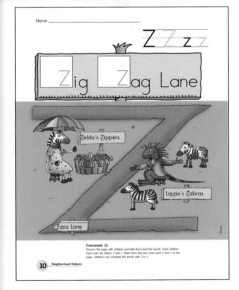

OBJECTIVE

• *To read high-frequency word* me

Materials

■ *Big Book of Rhymes and Songs*, p. 22

■ *High-Frequency Word Card* me

■ *Teacher's Resource Book*, p. 140

High-Frequency Word me ✔ *Introduce*

TEACH/MODEL

Display the rhyme "The Very Nicest Place" in the *Big Book of Rhymes and Songs*. Track the print as you read aloud the poem.

Point to the word *me* and say: **This is the word** *me*. Have children say the word. Display *High-Frequency Word Card* me. Ask: **What word is this?** Have children follow along as you track the print and reread the last phrase. Have children repeat the phrase with you. Then have a child match the *High-Frequency Word Card* me to the word *me* on the page.

PRACTICE/APPLY

Guided Practice   Make copies of the *High-Frequency Word Card* me in the *Teacher's Resource Book*. Give each child a word card. Tell children to point to the word *me* and say it. Then write the following sentence frame on the board. Read the sentence as you track the print. Tell children to point to their word card as they say the word *me*. Invite each child to repeat the sentence, filling in the name of a friend.

_____ can play with me.

Independent Practice   Ask children to place their *High-Frequency Word Card* me in their file. Then have children look in their file to find a word card to match each word you use in a sentence. Say the following sentences:

The cows go moo moo. Find the word *go*.

Have you ever seen a monkey? Find the word *have*.

What is your name? Find the word *what*.

The package is for me. Find the word *for*.

Whole group

FLORIDA STANDARDS/GLEs   FCAT: LA.A.1.1.2.K.4 Words; **LA.A.1.1.3.K.5** Story elements; **LA.C.3.1.3.K.1** Basic vocabulary; *Also* **LA.A.1.1.2.K.1** Print organization; **LA.A.1.1.3.K.1** Frequent words

 Words to Remember

Word Wall

Reading Words Hold up *High-Frequency Word Card me*. Place the word card under the letter *m* on the classroom word chart and have children read it aloud. Then ask a child to match his or her *High-Frequency Word Card me* to *me* on the word chart.

Find Similarities Have children look closely at their new word *me*. Encourage them to find similarities to other words posted on the chart. Ask the following questions to guide them appropriately:

- *Me* has two letters. Do any of our other words have two letters? Let's read the other words that have two letters. *(my, go, we, on, to, do, no)*

- Another word begins with *m* and we use it when we speak about ourselves. Let's read that word. *(my)*

Diagnostic Check: High-Frequency Words

If… children cannot read the word *me* and use the word to respond to sentences,

Then… have children place their *High-Frequency Word Card* on their desk and point to it as they say the word: *me, me, me*. Ask them to repeat this sentence after you and point to the word *me* when they say it: *This treat is for me!*

ADDITIONAL SUPPORT ACTIVITIES

BELOW-LEVEL	Reteach, p. S20
ADVANCED	Extend, p. S21
ENGLISH-LANGUAGE LEARNERS	Reteach, p. S21

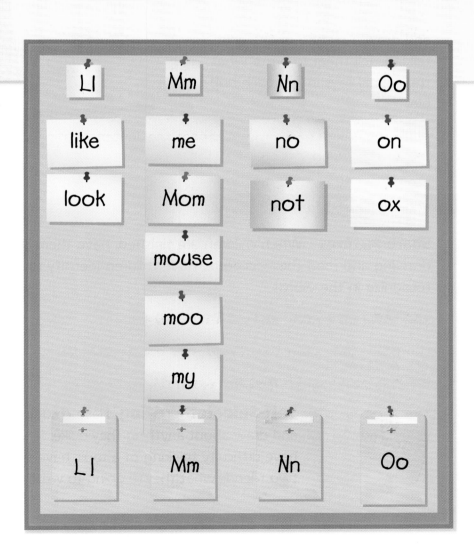

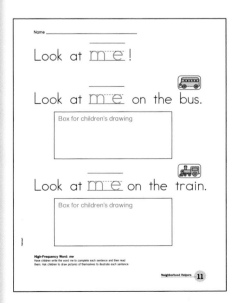

▲ **Practice Book page 11**

FLORIDA STANDARDS/GLEs **FCAT: LA.A.1.1.3.K.4** Build vocabulary; *Also* **LA.A.1.1.2.K.1** Print organization; **LA.A.1.1.2.K.2** Alphabet; **LA.A.1.1.3.K.1** Frequent words; **LA.C.1.1.3.K.1** Conversation rules

OBJECTIVE

- *To discuss sound words*
- *To write dialogue*

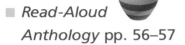

Materials

- *Read-Aloud Anthology* pp. 56–57
- chart paper
- marker
- drawing paper
- crayons or markers

Writing

Write Dialogue

BUILD BACKGROUND

Talk About Dialogue Have children name the animals in "Mother, Mother, I Want Another." (mouse, duck, frog, pig, donkey) Ask them to name the word that tells what each animal says. (mouse/squeak; duck/quack; frog/croak; pig/oink; donkey/hee-haw)

Write Dialogue Tell children they can draw a picture of one of the animals and write what the animal says in a speech bubble. On chart paper, draw a duck and write *Quack!* in the speech bubble. Tell children to choose one of the animals in "Mother, Mother, I Want Another" and draw a picture of the animal talking. Tell them to write what the animal says in a speech bubble.

SHARE

Share Pictures When children are finished, have them share their drawing and read their dialogue. Have children identify letters they recognize in the words.

Self-Selected Writing Have children write and draw about anything they'd like. If they have difficulty thinking of a topic have them ask two friends what they're going to write about.

FLORIDA STANDARDS/GLEs **FCAT: LA.A.1.1.2.K.4** Words; **LA.A.1.1.2.K.5** Phonetic principles; **LA.A.1.1.3.K.4** Build vocabulary; **LA.B.2.1.2.K.1** Record ideas; *Also* **LA.A.1.1.2.K.1** Print organization; **LA.B.1.1.2.K.2** Basic formats; **LA.B.1.1.3.K.1** Spelling approximations; **LA.B.1.1.3.K.2** Print direction; **LA.C.1.1.1.K.1** Follow directions

WRAP UP Share Time

Reflect on the Lesson Have groups of children use their puppets to retell "Mother, Mother, I Want Another." Ask them to tell what they liked best about the story. Have them name the letter they learned to write. (*Zz*)

S.S.R. Have children read silently from a book of their choice.

Centers ART

Zany Zebras

Ask children to draw pictures of zany, or crazy, zebras. Suggest that they use *Zz*s to create the zebras' stripes and then add any other zany details that they want. Direct children to label their zebras with names that begin with the /z/ sound. Create a wall display of Zany Zebras.

Materials

■ drawing paper

■ crayons or markers

■ tape

Day at a Glance
Day 4

Phonemic Awareness
Phoneme Isolation

Sharing Literature
Big Book of Rhymes and Songs: "The Bus Song"

Read
Big Book of Rhymes and Songs

Harcourt

Respond to Literature

Literature Focus:
Naming Words

Phonics
Relating /z/ to *z*

Reading
Decodable Book 10: *Is It for Me?*

Interactive Writing
Thank-You Note

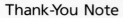

WARM UP

MORNING MESSAGE
Kindergarten News
(Child's name) takes a bus from
_____ to _____.

Write Kindergarten News Talk with children about where they go when they ride a bus. Have them tell other places buses go.

Use the following prompts to guide children as you write the news:

- **What are some places you go by bus?**
- **Who can show me a word?**
- **Who can count the words in the sentence?**
- **Who can show me a word that names a person?**

As you write the message, invite children to contribute by writing letters, words, or names they have previously learned. Remind them to use proper spacing, capitalization, and punctuation.

Calendar Language

Point to the numbers on the calendar. Tell children the days of each month are numbered and the numbers tell the date. Point to and read aloud the month and the date. Ask: *What month is it? What is the date?*

Sunday	Monday	Tuesday	Wednesday	Thursday	Friday	Saturday
		1	2	3	4	5
6	7	8	9	10	11	12
13	14	15	16	17	18	19
20	21	22	23	24	25	26
27	28	29	30	31		

FLORIDA STANDARDS/GLEs FCAT: LA.A.1.1.2.K.4 Words; **LA.A.1.1.2.K.5** Phonetic principles; *Also* **LA.C.1.1.3.K.1** Conversation rules; **LA.C.3.1.2.K.1** Questions

Phonemic Awareness

PHONEME ISOLATION

Listen for /z/   Teach children the following rhyme. Say the rhyme aloud, emphasizing the /z/ sound:

Zoom! To the garden Zany Zebra did go

And ate ten zinnias all in a row.

How many zinnias are now left to grow?

Zero!

Have children repeat the rhyme several times, emphasizing the /z/ sound at the beginning of each *Zz* word. Then tell children you will say some words and they will listen for the beginning sound in those words.

Say: **zero**. Have children repeat *zero*.

Say it again, emphasizing the /z/ sound.

Say: **/z/ is the sound I hear at the beginning of *zero*—/z/.**

Then say the following words. Have children repeat each word and tell the beginning sound.

zebra	**zoo**	**zipped**
zany	**zoom**	**zinnia**

Ask children to say the sound they hear at the beginning of the words. (/z/)

Diagnostic Check: Phonemic Awareness

If... children cannot isolate beginning sound /z/,

Then... have children repeat words that begin with /z/, elongating the initial sound.

ADDITIONAL SUPPORT ACTIVITIES

BELOW-LEVEL   Reteach, p. S22

ADVANCED   Extend, p. S23

ENGLISH-LANGUAGE LEARNERS   Reteach, p. S23

**Big Book of
Rhymes and Songs**

OBJECTIVES

- *To listen and respond to a song*

- *To follow words from left to right and from top to bottom on a printed page*

- *To sing short songs*

- *To identify naming words*

Materials

- *The Big Book of Rhymes and Songs, p. 23*

- *Music CD*

Sharing Literature

Read "The Bus Song"

READ ALOUD

Before Reading Display "The Bus Song" on page 23 of the *Big Book of Rhymes and Songs* and track the print as you read the title aloud. Have children frame the high-frequency word *The*. Use these prompts to build background.

- **Where can you go on a bus?** (Possible responses: school, work, shopping)

- **What story did we read about a bus?** (*The Big Yellow Bus*)

- **What do you remember about this story?** (Possible response: the lions sang, "la"!)

During Reading Read the words to the song aloud. As you read,

- track the print from left to right.

- ask children to point out the high-frequency words *the, on,* and *go*.

Play the song, which is recorded on the *Music CD*. After children listen to the entire song, play the song again and encourage children to join in and sing with you.

BUS

THE BUS SONG

The wheels on the bus
Go round and round,
Round and round,
Round and round,
The wheels on the bus
Go round and round,
All through the town.

23

FLORIDA STANDARDS/GLEs FCAT: LA.A.2.1.1.K.1 Main idea; *Also* **LA.A.1.1.2.K.1** Print organization; **LA.A.1.1.3.K.1** Frequent words; **LA.D.1.1.1.K.1** Sound patterns; **LA.D.2.1.2.K.1** Patterned structures

RESPOND TO LITERATURE

Sing New Verses Sing "The Bus Song" again and have children make up new verses. They can suggest something they might hear or see on a bus and tell what sound it makes.

The door on the bus goes bang, bang, bang.

The brake on the bus goes screech, screech, screech.

The children on the bus go, "La-la-la!"

Literature Focus

NAMING WORDS

Read the first verse of the song aloud, and point to the words *wheels, bus,* and *town*. Tell children these words are naming words. They name people, places, and things. Write the headings *People, Places,* and *Things* on the board. Write several children's names under *People*. Tell children you will write the name of their town or city and the name of their state under *Places*. Then ask children to look around the classroom and name things they see. Write their suggestions under *Things*. Point to each heading and the words listed beneath it as you read the chart aloud to children.

Naming Words

People	Places	Things
Brianna	Los Angeles	desks
Alexandra	California	books
Glenn		chairs
Joseph		pencils

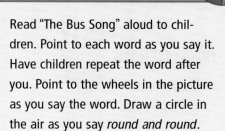

ENGLISH-LANGUAGE LEARNERS

Read "The Bus Song" aloud to children. Point to each word as you say it. Have children repeat the word after you. Point to the wheels in the picture as you say the word. Draw a circle in the air as you say *round and round*.

ADVANCED

Ask children to track the print as they listen to the words to the song on the *Music CD*.

ONGOING ASSESSMENT

As you share "The Bus Song," note whether children

• understand that we read print from left to right and from top to bottom.

• recognize high-frequency words in text.

• can sing the words of a song.

FLORIDA STANDARDS/GLEs FCAT: LA.A.1.1.2.K.4 Words; **LA.A.1.1.4.K.1** Comprehension; *Also* **LA.A.1.1.3.K.2** Nouns and verbs; **LA.D.1.1.1.K.1** Sound patterns; **LA.D.1.1.1.K.2** Language functions; **LA.D.2.1.2.K.1** Patterned structures

OBJECTIVE

To match consonant Zz to its sound

Materials

- *Letter and Sound Chart 15*
- *Tactile Letter Cards z*
- *Picture/Word Cards zipper, zoo*
- pocket chart
- drawing paper
- Zipper Pattern (page T13)
- scissors
- glue
- crayons

Z z

Zig zag,
Play tag.
Zebras zip and zoom
At the zoo.

▲ **Letter and Sound Chart 15**

Phonics

Relating /z/ to z

ACTIVE BEGINNING

Recite "Zip, Zip, Zip" Have children listen for /z/ as they learn the rhyme. Then they can "zip up a jacket" as they say the rhyme again.

Zip, Zip, Zip

Zip, Zip, Zip,

Up it goes.

My zipper zips

Up to my nose.

by Susan Little

TEACH/MODEL

Introduce Letter and Sound Display *Letter and Sound Chart 15.*

Touch the letter *Z.* **What is the name of the letter?**

This letter stands for the /z/ sound. Say /zz/.

Read aloud the sentences on the *Letter and Sound Chart,* tracking the print.

Read aloud the *Zz* words in the sentences. Then point to each *z* and have children say the /z/ sound. Ask: **What letter stands for the /z/ sound?**

Have children join in as you read the rhyme again. Ask them to feel the vibration as they say the words that begin with /z/.

FLORIDA STANDARDS/GLEs   FCAT: LA.A.1.1.2.K.5 Phonetic principles; *Also* **LA.A.1.1.2.K.1** Print organization; **LA.A.1.1.2.K.2** Alphabet; **LA.A.1.1.2.K.3** Sounds; **LA.C.3.1.2.K.1** Questions; **LA.D.2.1.2.K.1** Patterned structures

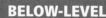

PRACTICE/APPLY

Guided Practice Distribute *Tactile Letter Cards z*. Then place *Picture/Word Cards zipper* and *zoo* in a pocket chart. Say the names of the pictures as you point to the *z* in each. Have children repeat the words.

Tell children: **These words begin with z.**

Point to the *z* in *zipper*. **The /z/ sound is at the beginning of zipper.**

Point to the *z* in *zoo*. **The /z/ sound is at the beginning of zoo.**

I'm going to say some words. If the word begins with the /z/ sound, hold up your z card. If it doesn't begin with the /z/ sound, don't hold up your card. Thumbs ↑ Thumbs ↓

zero   zone   pepper   zucchini   tuna   zigzag   Zachary

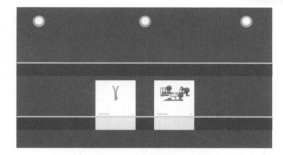

Independent Practice Distribute drawing paper and copies of the Zipper Pattern (page T13). Have children cut out the zipper and glue it to their paper. Ask them to draw a coat around the zipper and decorate it. Have them write the word *zip* and the letters *Zz* on their paper.

BELOW-LEVEL
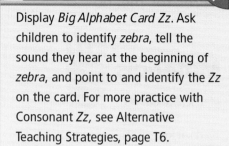

Display *Big Alphabet Card Zz*. Ask children to identify *zebra*, tell the sound they hear at the beginning of *zebra*, and point to and identify the *Zz* on the card. For more practice with Consonant Zz, see Alternative Teaching Strategies, page T6.

ADVANCED

Have children work with partners. Children can take turns creating alliterations with words that begin with the sound /z/.

Phonics Resources

Phonics Express™ **CD-ROM, Level A,** Bumper/Route 5/ Fire Station, Building Site, Park

Phonics Practice Book pages 115–116

▲ **Practice Book page 12** HW

FLORIDA STANDARDS/GLEs FCAT: LA.A.1.1.2.K.5 Phonetic principles; *Also* **LA.A.1.1.2.K.2** Alphabet; **LA.A.1.1.2.K.3** Sounds; **LA.C.1.1.1.K.1** Follow directions

Neighborhood Helpers   233

OBJECTIVE

To read high-frequency words for, me, no

Materials

- index cards
- marker
- *High-Frequency Word Cards* for, me
- pocket chart
- *Decodable Book 10: Is It for Me?*
- drawing paper
- crayons

ADVANCED

Have children read *Independent Reader 27: The Fire Bell Rings.*

LEARNING TO READ

Phonics

High-Frequency Words for, me ✔ *Review*

Read the Decodable Book

TEACH/MODEL

Review High-Frequency Words   Write the words *Is* and *it* on index cards. Place the words *Is* and *it* and the *High-Frequency Word Cards for* and *me* in a pocket chart. Ask children to read them as you place them in the chart. Add a question mark at the end. Have children read the sentence as you point to the words: *Is it for me?* Ask children if they have ever asked this question and why.

PRACTICE/APPLY

Read the Book   Distribute copies of *Is It for Me?* Have children read the title. Encourage children to point to each word as they read it. Have children read the book, pointing to each word as they read.

Respond   Have children draw and label a picture of something they would like to receive in a box in the mail.

 FLORIDA STANDARDS/GLEs   FCAT: LA.A.1.1.2.K.4 Words; *Also* **LA.A.1.1.2.K.1** Print organization; **LA.A.1.1.3.K.1** Frequent words; **LA.B.1.1.2.K.2** Basic formats; **LA.B.1.1.3.K.1** Spelling approximations; **LA.B.1.1.3.K.2** Print directions ;**LA.B.1.1.3.K.3** Punctuation; **LA.B.2.1.4.K.1** Informational texts;   **LA.C.1.1.1.K.1** Follow directions

Decodable Book 10: *Is It for Me?*

It is a red box.
Is it for me?

2

No, it is not.

3

It is a big box.
Is it for me?

4

No, it is not.

5

It is a tan box.
Is it for me?

6

Yes, it is.

7

It is for me.
It is a cap!

8

■ High-Frequency Words

for, me, no

■ Decodable Words

See the list on page T15.

School–Home Connection

Take-Home
Book Version

◄ Decodable Book 10
Is It for Me?

BELOW-LEVEL

Reread the story with children. Ask them to frame the words *for* and *me* on each page.

ENGLISH-LANGUAGE LEARNERS

Point to the picture on the second page and say the words *red box*. Ask children to repeat the words. Then have children read the sentence. Repeat this procedure for the words *big box* and *tan box*.

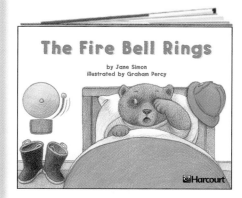

The Fire Bell Rings
by Jane Simon
illustrated by Graham Percy

▲ **Independent Reader 27: The Fire Bell Rings**

OBJECTIVE

To write a thank-you note

Materials

- chart paper
- marker

Interactive Writing

Write a Thank-You Note

SHARE THE PEN

Write a Thank-You Note Use prompts such as the following to help children write words and letters:

Let's write a note to the bus driver to thank him/her for driving us to school. Where do I begin to write? Who can show me? I will write *Dear Bus Driver*. Who can write an uppercase *D*? Who can place a finger next to the word *Dear* to make a space? Who can write an uppercase *B*? Let's write a sentence thanking the bus driver. Who can say the words? I begin to write the sentence here. Point under the *r* in *Dear*. **Who can write an uppercase *T*? Who can write the word *for*?**

Have children write letters and words that they have learned. Have them take turns placing their fingers next to words to mark spaces.

Let's all sign our names on our note. Have children sign their names on the note.

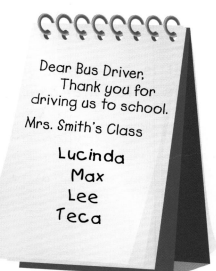

Dear Bus Driver,
Thank you for
driving us to school.
Mrs. Smith's Class

Lucinda
Max
Lee
Teca

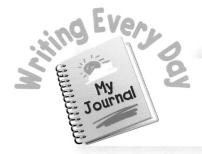

Journal Writing Have children make a thank-you card to the person who helps them get to school in the morning.

 FLORIDA STANDARDS/GLEs **FCAT:** LA.B.2.1.2.K.1 Record ideas; *Also* LA.A.1.1.2.K.2 Alphabet; LA.A.1.1.2.K.3 Sounds; LA.B.1.1.2.K.2 Basic formats; LA.B.1.1.3.K.2 Print direction; LA.B.2.1.1.K.2 Contribute ideas; LA.D.1.1.1.K.2 Language functions

WRAP UP Share Time

Reflect on the Lesson Ask children to say an animal name that begins with the /z/ sound. (zebra) **Have them describe what a zebra looks like. Ask them to tell about their favorite part of today's lessons.**

S.S.R. Have children read silently from a book of their choice.

Centers +2 MATH

Dots and Numbers

Place two counters in one box, three counters in another box, five counters in the third box, and no counters in the fourth box. Place a pile of index cards next to each box. Tell children to count the objects in each box. Tell them to make a dot on the index card for each object they count. Have them count the dots and write the numeral on the back of their cards. Tell them to write a z on the index card for the box that has no objects in it. Tell them z stands for zero.

Materials

- four boxes
- counters or other objects
- index cards
- crayons

FLORIDA STANDARDS/GLEs **FCAT: LA.A.1.1.2.K.5** Phonetic principles; **LA.C.3.1.3.K.1** Basic vocabulary; *Also* **LA.A.1.1.2.K.3** Sounds; **LA.D.2.1.1.K.1** Word choice

Neighborhood Helpers **237**

WARM UP

Phonemic Awareness
Segmentation

Sharing Literature
Library Book:
Career Day

Read

Career Day
story by Anne Rockwell
pictures by Lizzy Rockwell

Develop Concept Vocabulary

Respond to Literature

Literature Focus: Summarize

Phonics
Consonants *Yy, Zz*

Interactive Writing
List of Jobs

MORNING MESSAGE
Kindergarten News
(Child's name)'s classroom

job is _____.

Write Kindergarten News Talk with children about jobs they have in school. Ask them if they enjoy doing one job more than others.

Use prompts such as the following to guide children as you write the news:

• **Who can name the jobs in our class?**

• **What letter will I write first in (child's name)?**

• **Who can show me where (child's name) begins and ends?**

As you write the message, invite children to contribute by writing letters, words, or names they have previously learned. Remind them to use proper spacing, capitalization, and punctuation.

Calendar Language

Point to and read aloud the names of the days of the week. Identify the day of the week. Ask: *What jobs will you do today?*

Sunday	Monday	Tuesday	Wednesday	Thursday	Friday	Saturday
		1	2	3	4	5
6	7	8	9	10	11	12
13	14	15	16	17	18	19
20	21	22	23	24	25	26
27	28	29	30	31		

FLORIDA STANDARDS/GLEs **FCAT: LA.A.1.1.2.K.5** Phonetic principles; **LA.B.2.1.2.K.1** Record ideas; *Also* **LA.A.1.1.2.K.2** Alphabet; **LA.A.1.1.2.K.3** Sounds; **LA.C.1.1.3.K.1** Conversation rules; **LA.C.3.1.2.K.1** Questions

Phonemic Awareness

SEGMENTATION

Track Syllables in Words Remind children that word parts are called syllables. Tell them you will play a game called "Teacher, May We?" Have children stand side by side in a line across the room. Ask two children to help you model how to listen to a word and jump the syllables:

MODEL Let's jump the number of syllables in the word *elephant*. Have children ask: *May we?* **Yes, you may. Repeat** *elephant* **slowly as we jump three times forward.**

Say the following words and have children repeat them and jump for each syllable.

build (build)

courtroom (court-room)

pictures (pic-tures)

bass (bass)

dinosaur (di-no-saur)

newborn (new-born)

worker (work-er)

grandmother (grand-moth-er)

doctor (doc-tor)

manager (man-a-ger)

ENGLISH-LANGUAGE LEARNERS

Place a pencil, a book, and a crayon on a table or desk. Point to each object and say its name. Have children repeat the name. Point to the object again and say its name and clap the syllables. Have children do the same. Ask children to tell how many claps they hear for each word.

di-no-saur

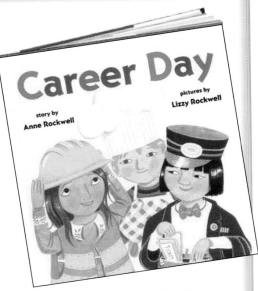

▲ **Library Book**

OBJECTIVES

- *To connect text to life experiences*

- *To ask and answer questions about text*

- *To summarize main ideas*

Materials

■ *Library Book: Career Day*

Sharing Literature

Read Career Day

READ ALOUD

Before Reading   Display the cover of *Career Day* and read the title aloud. Ask children to tell how many words are in the title. Read the title again and ask, **What does the word *career* mean?** ("job") Then use prompts to help children recall the information in the book.

- **What happens on "career day"?** (Possible response: Visitors come to the class to tell about their jobs.)

- **Who can tell me a job that you like or know about in this book?**

Then model how to set a purpose for reading:

MODEL   **I ask questions about a book to see what I might learn about. By looking at the cover, I know that this book is about jobs people do. I also want to know: What jobs does this book tell about? What work do people in those jobs do? I'll read the book again to find out.**

During Reading   Reread the story aloud. As you read,

- model for children how to use pictures and text to find out the meaning of unknown words. After reading pages 13 and 16, think aloud.

MODEL   **By looking at the picture, I see that there are people playing instruments together. They must be part of an orchestra.**

By reading the page, I find out that a paleontologist digs for dinosaur bones.

FLORIDA STANDARDS/GLEs   FCAT: LA.A.1.1.4.K.1 Comprehension; LA.A.2.1.1.K.1 Main idea; *Also* LA.A.2.1.4.K.1 Illustrations; LA.E.2.1.1.K.1 Background knowledge

DEVELOP CONCEPT VOCABULARY

After Reading Tell children to listen to clues about jobs in the book, and name the job.

- **I work with wood to make many things. Who am I?** (a woodworker or carpenter)

- **I take garbage to the dump. I tell people to recycle. Who am I?** (a sanitation worker)

- **I take care of sick animals. Who am I?** (a veterinarian)

RESPOND TO LITERATURE

Draw Pictures Have children draw a picture about a job they think they want to do when they grow up. Tell them to write a sentence about their picture.

I hlp animls get betr.

ADVANCED

Have children interview a worker in your school, such as the principal, art teacher, custodian, nurse, or librarian. Help children prepare one or two questions to ask each worker. Then provide time for children to share with their classmates what they learned.

ONGOING ASSESSMENT

As you share *Career Day*, note whether children

- can listen for an extended period of time.

- connect text to personal experiences.

Literature Focus

SUMMARIZE

Tell children that when you summarize, you tell the important information in the book. Model for children how to summarize *Career Day*:

MODEL *Career Day* is about the jobs people do. At the beginning of the story, a boy introduces his father to the class. His father tells the children about his job as a construction worker. Other people come to tell about jobs, such as a nurse and a judge. The children show the visitors the jobs they do in the classroom.

Have children take turns summarizing *Career Day*.

FLORIDA STANDARDS/GLEs FCAT: **LA.A.1.1.2.K.4** Words; **LA.A.1.1.3.K.5** Story elements; **LA.A.1.1.4.K.1** Comprehension; **LA.A.2.1.1.K.1** Main idea; *Also* **LA.B.1.1.2.K.2** Basic formats; **LA.B.1.1.3.K.2** Print direction; **LA.C.1.1.3.K.1** Conversation rules

Neighborhood Helpers   **241**

LEARNING TO READ

Phonics
Consonants Yy, Zz

 ✔ *Review*

OBJECTIVES

• *To recognize uppercase and lowercase Yy and Zz*

• *To match sounds to letters*

Materials

■ *Big Alphabet Cards Yy, Zz*

■ *pocket chart*

■ *Alphabet Cards Y, Z*

■ *Picture Cards yo-yo, zipper, yak, yarn, yellow, zoo*

■ *Tactile Letter Cards Y, Z*

ACTIVE BEGINNING

Recite the *Y* and *Z* Rhymes Display *Big Alphabet Cards Yy* and *Zz*. Ask children to name each letter and to "write" the letter in the palm of their hands. Then have children join in reciting "Yippee! Yay!" (See page 212.) Then have them recite "Zip, Zip, Zip." (See page 232.)

TEACH/MODEL

Discriminate *Y* and *Z*
Hold up *Big Alphabet Card Y* and ask what letter this is.

Point to the picture and say its name. Have children repeat it. **What sound do you hear at the beginning of *yo-yo*?**

Touch the letter and say /y/. Touch the letter again, and have children say /y/.

Follow the same procedure for *Big Alphabet Card Zz*.

In the pocket chart place *Alphabet Cards Y* and *Z* and *Picture Cards yo-yo* and *zipper*. Say each picture name and tell children you need to decide where to place each *Picture Card*.

MODEL I'll start with the yo-yo. *Y—o-yo* begins with the /y/ sound. So I'll put the picture of the yo-yo below *Y*.

Repeat the process with *Picture Card zipper*.

FLORIDA STANDARDS/GLEs FCAT: LA.A.1.1.2.K.5 Phonetic principles; *Also* **LA.A.1.1.2.K.2** Alphabet; **LA.A.1.1.2.K.3** Sounds; **LA.C.3.1.2.K.1** Questions

PRACTICE/APPLY

Guided Practice Place these *Picture Cards* on the chalkledge: *yak*, *yarn*, *yellow*, *zipper*, *zoo*. Tell children that they will now sort some pictures.

Say the picture name. If the beginning sound is /y/, let's put the card below the *Y*. If the beginning sound is /z/, let's put the card below the *Z*.

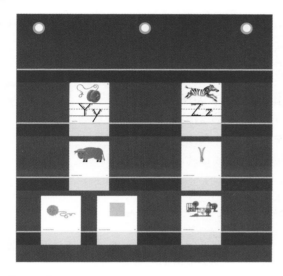

Independent Practice Give each child *Tactile Letter Cards Y* and *Z*.

I'm going to say some words. Listen carefully to the sound you hear at the beginning of each word. Think about the letter that stands for that sound, then hold up the letter card that stands for that sound. *Sign language → y and z*

| zebra | young | zero | yawn | yard | zigzag |
| zoo | you | yell | zip | yeast | zookeeper |

FLORIDA STANDARDS/GLEs FCAT: LA.A.1.1.2.K.5 Phonetic principles; *Also* **LA.A.1.1.2.K.2** Alphabet; **LA.A.1.1.2.K.3** Sounds; **LA.C.1.1.1.K.1** Follow directions

REACHING ALL LEARNERS

Diagnostic Check: Phonics

If... children cannot recognize *y* and *z*,

Then... have them trace over *Tactile Letter Cards y* and *z* and say the sound each letter stands for.

ADDITIONAL SUPPORT ACTIVITIES

BELOW-LEVEL Reteach, p. S24

ADVANCED Extend, p. S25

ENGLISH-LANGUAGE LEARNERS Reteach, p. S25

Phonics Resources

Phonics Express™ CD-ROM, **Level A,** Roamer/Route 1/Park; Bumper/Route 5/Market; Bumper/Route 3/Train Station; Bumper/Route 4/Harbor

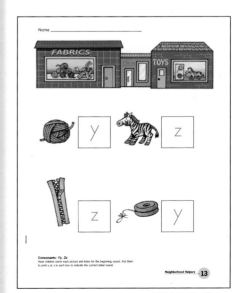

▲ **Practice Book page 13** *HW*

Neighborhood Helpers 24?

OBJECTIVES

- *To discuss a list*
- *To write a list of jobs*

Materials

- chart paper
- markers

Interactive Writing

Write a List of Jobs

SHARE THE PEN

Write a List   Tell children that together you will write a list of jobs they have at home. Use prompts such as the following to help children write with you:

Where should I write the title of our list on the chart paper? Write *Our Jobs.* **What job shall we list first?**

As children suggest ideas for jobs, have them say them in complete sentences. Have them write as many letters and words as they can and point to spaces between words. When the list is complete, read it aloud.

Our Jobs
Set the table.
Clear the table.
Pick up toys.
Make my bed.
Feed my pet.

Journal Writing   Have children draw and write about a job they do at home.

FLORIDA STANDARDS/GLEs   FCAT: LA.A.1.1.2.K.4 Words;   **LA.A.1.1.3.K.4** Build vocabulary;   **LA.B.2.1.2.K.1** Record ideas; *Also* **LA.A.1.1.3.K.3** Categorize words;   **LA.B.1.1.2.K.2** Basic formats;   **LA.B.1.1.3.K.1** Spelling approximations;   **LA.B.1.1.3.K.2** Print direction

WRAP UP Share Time

Reflect on the Lesson Ask children to name words they remember that begin with *y* or *z*. Have them describe the job in *Career Day* they like best.

S.S.R. Have children read silently from a book of their choice.

Centers  DRAMATIC PLAY

Going to the Zoo

Designate areas in the classroom as parts of a zoo, such as ticket booths, animal viewing areas, and food stands. Have children draw on index cards pictures of tickets and food they would like to eat. Have them draw pictures of animals on drawing paper. Place the drawings around the classroom. Hang posters showing the number of tickets needed for each area of the zoo, and have children practice counting out the appropriate number of tickets as they visit the different areas. Children should take turns as zoo workers and as visitors to the zoo.

Materials

■ index cards

■ crayons

■ drawing paper

FLORIDA STANDARDS/GLEs FCAT: LA.A.1.1.2.K.5 Phonetic principles; **LA.A.1.1.4.K.1** Comprehension; **LA.C.3.1.3.K.1** Basic vocabulary; *Also* **LA.A.1.1.2.K.2** Alphabet; **LA.A.1.1.2.K.3** Sounds; **LA.C.1.1.1.K.1** Follow directions

Neighborhood Helpers 245

Learning Centers

Choose from the following suggestions to enhance your learning centers for the theme *Neighborhood Helpers*. (Additional learning centers for this theme can be found on pages 184–186 and 292)

WRITING CENTER

Write About a Neighborhood Helper

Tell children to choose a neighborhood helper they would like to write about. Have them identify their neighborhood helper and write a few sentences to tell what that person does to help others and to explain why the helper is important. Encourage children to use what they know about sounds and letters to spell words. Invite children to draw a picture to illustrate their sentences.

A tchr helps childrn lrn to red and spel.
A tch helps childrn lrn to cnt.
Tchrs help gron ups to.

Materials

- paper
- pencils
- crayons

SOCIAL STUDIES CENTER

Who Uses This?

Place the following *Picture Cards* face down in a pile in the Social Studies Center: *bus, car, hat, helicopter, horse, jet, key, ladder, lunch box, nail, newspaper, telephone, van, vegetables, violin, water, X ray, zipper*. Tell children they are going to play a game called "Who Uses This?" One child at a time takes a *Picture Card*, identifies it, and asks, "Who Uses This?" Then he or she calls on another child to name a worker who uses the object in his or her work.

van

telephone

Materials

- *Picture Cards: bus, car, hat, helicopter, horse, jet, key, ladder, lunch box, nail, newspaper, telephone, van, vegetables, violin, water, X ray, zipper*

Teacher Notes

Teacher Notes

THEME 10

Week 2

Neighborhood Helpers

Day 1

Day 2

ORAL LANGUAGE

15-30 Minutes

- **Phonemic Awareness**

- **Sharing Literature**

Phonemic Awareness, 253
Phoneme Matching and Isolation: Initial

Sharing Literature, 254
 Read

Big Book: *The Big Yellow Bus*

 Literature Focus, 255
Match Words

The Big Yellow Bus

Phonemic Awareness, 261
Phoneme Blending

Sharing Literature, 262
Library Book: *Guess Who?*

 **Literature Focus, 263**
Nonfiction: Text Organization

GUESS WHO? Margaret Miller

LEARNING TO READ

45 Minutes

- **Phonics**

- **Vocabulary**

Phonics, 256 T
Review: Consonant /d/*d*, Short Vowel /e/*e*

Phonics, 264 T
Blending /e/ - /d/

Daily Routines
- **Morning Message**
- **Calendar Language**
- **Writing Prompt**

LANGUAGE ARTS

15-30 Minutes

- **Writing**
  Daily Writing Prompt

 Shared Writing, 258
Bus Rules

Writing Prompt, 258
Draw and write about a rule you follow at school.

Share Time, 259
Compare your ride to school and the bus ride in *The Big Yellow Bus.*

 Writing, 266
Book of Facts

Writing Prompt, 266
Draw and write about self-selected topics.

Share Time, 267
Read

Read the facts from the Writing activity.

T = tested skill

Phonics

Focus of the Week:
- • PHONEMIC AWARENESS
- • SHARING LITERATURE
- • WRITING: Rules, Facts, Descriptions

Review /d/*d*, /e/*e*;
Blending *e - d*

Day 3

Phonemic Awareness, 269
Phoneme Matching: Medial

Sharing Literature, 270

Read

Read-Aloud Anthology:
"Franklin in the Dark,"
pp. 53–55

(Skill) **Literature Focus, 271**
Characters

Phonics, 272 T
Words with /e/ and /d/

 Shared Writing, 274
Write Sentences About a Problem

Writing Prompt, 274
Draw and write about your favorite characters in "Franklin in the Dark."

Share Time, 275
Share sentences about problems.

Day 4

Phonemic Awareness, 277
Phoneme Segmentation

Sharing Literature, 278
Read-Aloud Anthology:
"Jamaica's Find,"
pp. 90–93

(Skill) **Literature Focus, 279**
Retelling the Story

Phonics, 280 T
Short Vowel /e/*e*

Read
DECODABLE BOOK 11
We Can Fix

 Interactive Writing, 282
Write Descriptions

Writing Prompt, 282
Draw and write about something you have lost.

Share Time, 283
Describe a favorite stuffed animal.

Day 5

Phonemic Awareness, 285
Phoneme Isolation: Medial

Sharing Literature, 286
Big Book: *The Big Yellow Bus*

(Skill) **Literature Focus, 287**
Sequence

Phonics, 288 T
Review: Blending /e/-/d/

 Writing, 290
Write About a Make-Believe Bus

Writing Prompt, 290
Draw and write about self-selected topics.

Share Time, 291

Read
Author's Chair

Day at a Glance
Day 1

WARM UP

Phonemic Awareness
Phomeme Matching and Isolation: Initial

Sharing Literature
Big Book:
The Big Yellow Bus

Read

Develop Concept Vocabulary
Respond to Literature
Literature Focus: Match Words

Phonics
Consonant /d/*d*,
Short Vowel /e/*e*

Shared Writing
Bus Rules

MORNING MESSAGE
Kindergarten News

Bus Rules

1._____.

2._____.

Write Kindergarten News   Talk with children about some bus rules. Discuss why bus rules help keep children safe.

Use prompts such as the following to guide children as you write the news:

- **Who can say a rule we should follow when we ride on a bus?**
- **I'll list the bus rules. I'll write the number 1 first.**
- **Who can show me where to write rule number 2?**
- **Who can count the number of spaces between words?**
- **Who can count the number of words in rule 1?**

As you write the message, invite children to contribute by writing letters, words, or numbers they have previously learned. Remind them to use proper spacing, capitalization, and punctuation.

Calendar Language

Point to each day of the week as you say, *Sunday is the first day of the week. Monday is the second day of the week.* Continue in this manner naming all the days. Then name the day of the week using an ordinal number.

Sunday	Monday	Tuesday	Wednesday	Thursday	Friday	Saturday
		1	2	3	4	5
6	7	8	9	10	11	12
13	14	15	16	17	18	19
20	21	22	23	24	25	26
27	28	29	30	31		

FLORIDA STANDARDS/GLEs   FCAT: **LA.A.2.1.5.K.2** Get information; **LA.B.2.1.2.K.1** Record ideas; *Also* **LA.A.1.1.2.K.1** Print organization; **LA.C.1.1.3.K.1** Conversation rules; **LA.C.3.1.2.K.1** Questions

Phonemic Awareness

PHONEME MATCHING: INITIAL

Identify Beginning Sounds Say these two words, emphasizing the initial sounds, and have children repeat them: *dinosaur, doctor*.

> **MODEL** *Dinosaur* and *doctor* begin with the same sound. *Dinosaur* begins with the /d/ sound and *doctor* begins with the /d/ sound. They both have the same beginning sound.

Tell children that you will say another group of words. Have them raise their hand if the words begin with the same sound.

echo, eggplant   empty, end

envelope, deer   jump, mitten

dish, dig   doctor, dance

PHONEME ISOLATION: INITIAL

Identify the Initial Sound in Words Say the following sets of words: Ask: **Which two words begin with the same sound? What is that sound?**

> **MODEL** Listen for the two words that sound the same: *dance, car, doctor. Dance* and *doctor* have the same beginning sound—/d/. *Car* does not. Say *dance* and *doctor* with me. What is the beginning sound?

Let's listen for more beginning sounds.

- Which two words begin with the same sound: *dish, ant, dig*? (dish, dig) **Say *dish* and *dig* with me. What is the first sound you hear in *dish* and *dig*?** (/d/)

- Which two words begin with the same sound: *eggplant, echo, mitten*? (eggplant, echo) **Say *eggplant* and echo with me. What is the first sound you hear in *eggplant* and echo?** (/e/)

- Which two words begin with the same sound: *empty, jump, end*? (empty, end) **Say *empty* and *end* with me. What is the first sound you hear in *empty* and *end*?** (/e/)

- Which two words begin with the same sound: *envelope, dog, deer*? (dog, deer) **Say *dog* and *deer* with me. What is the first sound you hear in *dog* and *deer*?** (/d/)

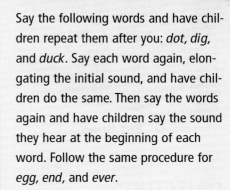

BELOW-LEVEL

Say the following words and have children repeat them after you: *dot, dig,* and *duck*. Say each word again, elongating the initial sound, and have children do the same. Then say the words again and have children say the sound they hear at the beginning of each word. Follow the same procedure for *egg, end,* and *ever*.

Sharing Literature

Read The Big Yellow Bus

▲ **Big Book**

OBJECTIVES

- *To know that print is read from left to right across the page*

- *To develop vocabulary*

- *To describe story scenes*

- *To match words in sentences*

Materials

- ■ *Big Book: The Big Yellow Bus*

- ■ drawing paper

- ■ crayons

- ■ sentence strip

- ■ marker

READ ALOUD

Before Reading Display *The Big Yellow Bus*. Use the following model to review the story and set a purpose for rereading:

> **MODEL** I remember that *The Big Yellow Bus* is a story about animals who go to school on a bus. As the animals get on the bus, they make sounds. I'll read the story again to see what sounds the animals make.

During Reading Read the story aloud. As you read,

- pause at the end of page 6 to point out that you read the text from left to right across a page.

> **MODEL** I read the text on this page from left to right and from top-to-bottom. Then I go to the top of the next page. I read from left to right and from top to bottom.

- invite children to join in by saying the sound words with you.

The zebras on the bus say,
"Zip, zip, zip;
zip, zip, zip;
zip, zip, zip."

FLORIDA STANDARDS/GLEs FCAT: LA.A.1.1.4.K.1 Comprehension; **LA.C.1.1.4.K.1** Sequence; **LA.E.1.1.1.K.1** Genres; **LA.E.1.1.2.K.1** Story elements; *Also* **LA.A.1.1.2.K.1** Print organization; **LA.C.1.1.1.K.2** Oral language; **LA.D.2.1.2.K.1** Patterned structures

DEVELOP CONCEPT VOCABULARY

After Reading Ask children to name the animals that get on the bus in the story. Write each animal name on the board. (zebra, yak, lion, sheep) Ask these questions:

- **Which word names a jungle animal?** (*lion*)
- **Which word names a farm animal?** (*sheep*)
- **Which word names an animal related to the cow?** (*yak*)
- **Which word names an animal that has stripes?** (*zebra*)

RESPOND TO LITERATURE

Draw Favorite Scene Page through *The Big Yellow Bus* and have children describe several scenes. Have them draw their favorite scene from the story. Tell them to write a sentence that tells something about the scene.

Literature Focus

MATCH WORDS

Write this sentence on a sentence strip: *The zebras on the bus go, "Zip, zip, zip," on the way to school.* Turn to the page in the *Big Book* that shows the sentence. Track the print as you read the words aloud. Place the sentence strip in a pocket chart and read the words aloud as you track the print. Tell children they can match the words on the sentence strip to the words in the book. Cut the sentence strip into individual words.

MODEL **Some of the words in this sentence are words you know.** Show *The.* **What word is this? What kind of letter is the letter *T* at the beginning of the word?** (uppercase) **A sentence begins with an uppercase letter. Who can match this card to the word in the sentence on the page?**

Follow the same procedure for the high-frequency words *on*, *go*, and *to*.

FLORIDA STANDARDS/GLEs **FCAT: LA.A.1.1.2.K.4** Words; **LA.A.1.1.3.K.5** Story elements; **LA.B.1.1.2.K.3** Sequence; **LA.E.1.1.2.K.1** Story elements; *Also* **LA.A.1.1.3.K.1** Frequent words; **LA.A.1.1.3.K.2** Nouns and verbs; **LA.B.1.1.2.K.2** Basic formats; **LA.B.1.1.3.K.1** Spelling approximations; **LA.B.1.1.3.K.2** Print direction; **LA.B.2.1.4.K.1** Informational texts; **LA.C.3.1.2.K.1** Questions

ENGLISH-LANGUAGE LEARNERS

Below On-Level Advanced ELL

Turn to the first page in the *Big Book.* Read the text aloud. Point to the bus in the illustration as you say *big yellow bus.* Have children repeat the words. Move your hand from the bus to the street as you say *down the street.* Have children repeat those words. Read the text aloud again and have children repeat the words after you.

ONGOING ASSESSMENT

As you share *The Big Yellow Bus,* note whether children

- **understand that print is read from left to right and from top to bottom.**
- **join in by saying words that are repeated.**

▲ **Practice Book page 14**

Neighborhood Helpers **255**

OBJECTIVES

• To recognize uppercase and lowercase Ee and Dd

• To match sounds to letters

Materials

■ pocket chart

■ Big Alphabet Cards Ee, Dd

■ Alphabet Cards E, D

■ Picture Cards egg, duck

■ Tactile Letter Cards e, d

Phonics
Consonant /d/d
Short Vowel /e/e ✔Review

ACTIVE BEGINNING

Recite the E and D Rhymes Display *Big Alphabet Cards Ee* and *Dd*. Ask children to identify each letter. Have children form a circle. Ask a child to stand in the middle of the circle and hold up *Big Alphabet Card Ee*. Have the children walk around the circle as they recite "If I Ever Met an Elephant." (See page 94.) Follow the same procedure for the rhyme "My Dog." (See page 544, volume 1)

TEACH/MODEL

Review Letters and Sounds Display *Big Alphabet Card Ee* in a pocket chart and ask what letter this is.

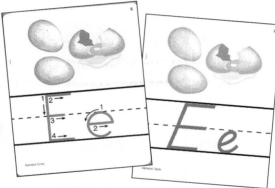

Point to the picture and say its name. Have children repeat it. (*egg*)

What sound do you hear at the beginning of egg? /e/

What letter stands for the /e/ sound in egg? (*Ee*)

Touch the letter and say **/e/**. Touch the letter again and have children say **/e/**.

Follow the same procedure for *Big Alphabet Card Dd*.

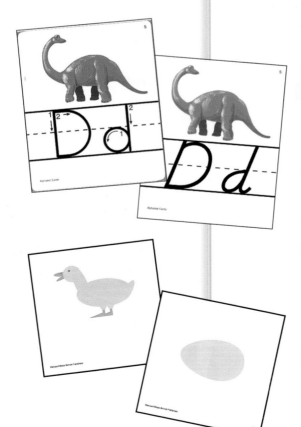

Place in the pocket chart *Picture Cards egg* and *duck*. Say each picture name and tell children you need to decide where to place each picture card.

MODEL I'll start with the egg. *E—gg* begins with the /e/ sound. So I'll put the picture of the egg below *E*.

Model the same process with *Picture Card duck*.

FLORIDA STANDARDS/GLEs FCAT: LA.A.1.1.2.K.5 Phonetic principles; *Also* **LA.A.1.1.2.K.2** Alphabet; **LA.A.1.1.2.K.3** Sounds; **LA.C.3.1.2.K.1** Questions; **LA.D.2.1.2.K.1** Patterned structures

PRACTICE/APPLY

Guided Practice   Distribute *Tactile Letter Cards* e and d to each child.

I will say some words that begin with /e/ and some that don't. Hold up your e card if the word begins with the /e/ sound.

thumbs ↑

Confirm the answer for each word by holding up the appropriate letter card.

| elephant | soap | elevator | eggplant | rain | elbow |

I will say some words that begin with /d/ and some that don't. Hold up your d card if the word begins with the /d/ sound.

thumbs ↑

| dog | yard | dance | dinosaur | help | dinner |

Independent Practice   Have children continue to work with their *Tactile Letter Cards* e and d.

I'm going to say some words. Listen carefully to the sound you hear at the beginning of each word. Think about the letter that stands for that sound, then hold up the letter card that stands for that sound. *Sign language d and e*

| edge | empty | dune | damp | end |
| elk | dim | escalator | dirt | dive |

FLORIDA STANDARDS/GLEs   **FCAT: LA.A.1.1.2.K.5** Phonetic principles; *Also* **LA.A.1.1.2.K.2** Alphabet; **LA.A.1.1.2.K.3** Sounds

---

REACHING ALL LEARNERS

Below · On-Level · ELL · Advanced

Diagnostic Check: Phonics

If... children cannot identify *Dd* and short vowel *Ee*,

Then... have them trace over *Tactile Letter Cards Dd* and *Ee* and say the sounds that the letters stand for.

ADDITIONAL SUPPORT ACTIVITIES

BELOW-LEVEL	Reteach, p. S26
ADVANCED	Extend, p. S27
ENGLISH-LANGUAGE LEARNERS	Reteach, p. S27

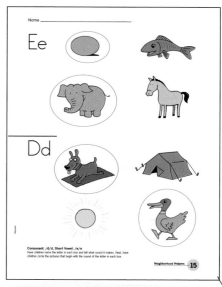

▲ **Practice Book page 15**

Neighborhood Helpers   257

OBJECTIVES

- *To write bus rules*

- *To understand that sentences are made up of words*

- *To understand that a sentence begins with an uppercase letter and ends with a period*

Writing Every Day

Day 1: Bus Rules

Have children dictate a list of rules for riding the bus.

Day 2: Book of Facts

Have each child write a fact about one job from *Guess Who?* Compile their writing into a class book.

Day 3: Sentences about Problems

Have children write about a problem they have had and tell how it was solved.

Day 4: Description

Have children work together to write a description of a lost dog.

Day 5: Caption for a Drawing

Have children draw a picture of a make-believe bus and write a caption to tell where the bus is going.

LANGUAGE ARTS

Shared Writing

Write Bus Rules

EXTEND LITERATURE

Write Sentences Tell children that together you will write a list of rules to follow when they ride on a bus. Write "Bus Rules" on the top of the chart paper. Write the number 1 on the first line. Point to the number and ask children to name it. Tell them you will write numbers beside each bus rule. Write children's suggestions on chart paper. Use these prompts:

If there is a group of children waiting for the bus, what should they do when the bus comes? (Get in line, take turns getting on the bus)

When the bus is moving, what should you do? (stay in your seat)

When can you get out of your seat? (when the bus stops)

Bus Rules
1. Sit in your seat.
2. Stay in your seat until the bus stops.
3. Take turns getting on and off the bus.

SHARE

Read the Bus Rules Read the bus rules aloud to children and have children identify letters and *High-Frequency Words*. Have children count the words and the spaces.

Journal Writing Have children draw and write about a rule they have to follow at school.

FLORIDA STANDARDS/GLEs FCAT: LA.A.1.1.2.K.4 Words; **LA.A.1.1.2.K.6** Print meaning; **LA.B.2.1.2.K.1** Record ideas; **LA.C.3.1.3.K.1** Basic vocabulary; *Also* **LA.A.1.1.2.K.1** Print organization; **LA.A.1.1.2.K.2** Alphabet; **LA.A.1.1.3.K.1** Frequent words; **LA.B.1.1.2.K.1** Dictate messages; **LA.B.1.1.2.K.2** Basic formats; **LA.B.1.1.3.K.1** Spelling approximations; **LA.B.1.1.3.K.2** Print direction; **LA.B.1.1.3.K.3** Punctuation; **LA.B.2.1.1.K.2** Contribute ideas; **LA.C.3.1.2.K.1** Questions

WRAP UP Share Time

Reflect on the Lesson   Ask children to tell how their bus ride to school is the same as or different than the ride the animals go on in the story, *The Big Yellow Bus* . Ask them to name the rules they wrote for riding on a bus and to tell whether or not the animals followed any of the bus rules.

 S.S.R. *Sustained Silent Reading*   Have children read silently from a book of their choice.

Centers  DRAMATIC PLAY

Going to Work

Set up chairs to represent the seats on a bus, making sure to include a special seat for the bus driver. Then ask children to make believe they are going to get on the bus to go to work and to choose props for the work they will do. Each "worker" can introduce himself or herself to the others while getting onto the bus. Tell children to discuss their jobs and their workplaces during the "ride." Children may want to repeat the activity, using different props and assuming different roles.

Materials

- chairs
- hats, briefcases, and other props to indicate various jobs

Day at a Glance
Day 2

WARM UP

Phonemic Awareness
Phoneme Blending

Sharing Literature
Library Book:
Guess Who?

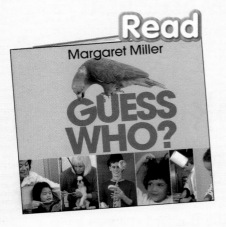

Read
Margaret Miller
GUESS WHO?

Develop Listening Comprehension

Respond to Literature

Literature Focus: Nonfiction: Text Organization

Phonics
Blending /e/-/d/

Writing
Book of Facts

MORNING MESSAGE

Kindergarten News

(Child's name) _____

_____ after school.

Write Kindergarten News Talk with children about places they go after school.

Use prompts such as the following to guide children as you write the news:

- **What do you do after school?**
- **Let's clap the syllables in (child's name) together.**
- **Who can show me where (child's name) ends?**
- **Who can show me a space between words?**

As you write the message, invite children to contribute by writing letters, words, or names they have previously learned. Remind them to use proper spacing, capitalization, and punctuation.

Calendar Language

Point to the numbers on the calendar. Tell children the days of each month are numbered and the numbers tell the date. Point to and read aloud the date. Say: *This is the month of _____.* Ask: *What month is it?* Say: *It is (name the date).*

Sunday	Monday	Tuesday	Wednesday	Thursday	Friday	Saturday
		1	2	3	4	5
6	7	8	9	10	11	12
13	14	15	16	17	18	19
20	21	22	23	24	25	26
27	28	29	30	31		

FLORIDA STANDARDS/GLEs   FCAT: LA.A.2.1.5.K.2 Get information; LA.B.2.1.2.K.1 Record ideas; *Also* LA.A.1.1.2.K.1 Print organization; LA.C.1.1.3.K.1 Conversation rules; LA.C.3.1.2.K.1 Questions

Phonemic Awareness

PHONEME BLENDING

Blend Sounds   Use the rabbit puppet for this blending activity. Tell children they can listen to the sounds the rabbit says and guess the word he is trying to say.

Say /p/ /e/ /t/ slowly, emphasizing each sound.

Say it again, blending the sounds. /ppeett/.

Have children blend the sounds with the rabbit and name the word: /ppeett/, **pet.**

Follow the same procedure with these words:

/m/ /e/ /t/ (*met*)

/s/ /a/ /d/ (*sad*)

/D/ /a/ /n/ (*Dan*)

/J/ /e/ /n/ (*Jen*)

/m/ /u/ /d/ (*mud*)

/w/ /e/ /b/ (*web*)

/g/ /e/ /t/ (*get*)

/d/ /i/ /p/ (*dip*)

REACHING ALL LEARNERS

Diagnostic Check: Phonemic Awareness

If... children cannot blend letters,

Then... have them repeat the following words after you, elongating each sound, and then say the words: *get* and *set*.

ADDITIONAL SUPPORT ACTIVITIES

BELOW-LEVEL   Reteach, p. S28

ADVANCED   Extend, p. S29

ENGLISH-LANGUAGE LEARNERS   Reteach, p. S29

What word am I trying to say?
/zziipp/ /zziipp/

Harcourt

▲ **Library Book**

OBJECTIVES

To ask and answer questions about a text

To understand text that provides information

To understand text organization of a nonfiction selection

Materials

■ *Library Book:
Guess Who?*

Sharing Literature

Read Guess Who?

READ ALOUD

Before Reading Show children the cover of *Guess Who?* Track the print of the title while reading the words aloud. Point to the question mark. Say: **This is a question mark. It comes at the end of words that ask a question.**

Read the title again. Point to *Guess* and say the word. **When you guess something, you try to think of an answer and say it.**

Point to and read aloud the author's name. Tell children that Margaret Miller is a photographer. Ask them what a photographer does. (takes photographs, or pictures, using a camera) Then ask children to describe the photographs on the cover.

During Reading Read the story aloud. As you read,

• encourage children to connect pictures to words and model asking and answering questions about the text.

MODEL **I see seagulls standing on rocks. Do seagulls go to school? I see puppies cuddled together. Do puppies go to school? I see baseball umpires standing at home plate. Do umpires go to school? I see stuffed animals on a shelf. Do they go to school? Who goes to school?** Turn the page. **Children! I see children playing in a classroom.**

• model how to read a word with an exclamation point at the end of page 6.

MODEL **An exclamation point is used to show surprise or excitement. Listen as I read the word and use my voice to show surprise or excitement.** Say: *Children!* in a loud and emphatic tone.

FLORIDA STANDARDS/GLEs **FCAT: LA.A.1.1.2.K.6** Print meaning; **LA.A.1.1.4.K.1** Comprehension; **LA.E.1.1.1.K.1** Genres; *Also* **LA.A.1.1.2.K.1** Print organization; **LA.A.2.1.4.K.1** Illustrations; **LA.C.1.1.1.K.2** Oral language; **LA.C.3.1.2.K.1** Questions

DEVELOP LISTENING COMPREHENSION

After Reading   Have children answer these questions about the book:

- **What is this book about?** (people who do special jobs)
- **Who cleans your teeth?** (a dentist)
- **Who fixes a car?** (a mechanic)
- **What are the names of other workers we read about?** (school children, barber, pilot, baker, letter carrier, photographer)

RESPOND TO LITERATURE

Pantomime the Story   Have children choose one of the workers in the story and act out what he or she does. Invite other children to guess the kind of worker and identify a tool the worker uses.

NONFICTION: TEXT ORGANIZATION

Tell children that words are sometimes arranged in a special way to help the reader understand the information in the book. Turn to page 8 in *Guess Who?* Point to the question.

On this page I read a question: "Who cleans your teeth?"

Point to the photographs on the next page. **On the next page I see four pictures with words. I read the words, but they do not give me the answer to the question.**

Turn the page. **I turn the page and read the word. It is the answer to the question.**

Turn to the next page in the book and point out how the text works: **I read a question; I read four possible answers; I turn the page and read the word that answers the question.**

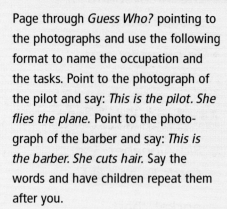

ENGLISH-LANGUAGE LEARNERS

Page through *Guess Who?* pointing to the photographs and use the following format to name the occupation and the tasks. Point to the photograph of the pilot and say: *This is the pilot. She flies the plane.* Point to the photograph of the barber and say: *This is the barber. She cuts hair.* Say the words and have children repeat them after you.

ONGOING ASSESSMENT

As you share *Guess Who?* note whether children

- can join in guessing answers and asking questions.
- understand the purpose of an exclamation point.
- understand that you get information from books.

FLORIDA STANDARDS/GLEs   FCAT: LA.A.1.1.2.K.6 Print meaning; **LA.A.1.1.4.K.1** Comprehension; **LA.A.2.1.1.K.1** Main idea; **LA.A.2.1.3.K.1** Supportive details; **LA.E.1.1.1.K.1** Genres; *Also* **LA.A.2.1.4.K.1** Illustrations; **LA.C.2.1.2.K.1** Nonverbal cues; **LA.E.2.1.1.K.1** Background knowledge; **LA.E.2.1.1.K.2** Personal interpretations

Phonics
Blending /e/ - /d/  *Introduce*

OBJECTIVES

- To identify and recognize the initial sound of a spoken word

- To blend /e/ and /d/

Materials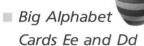

- *Big Alphabet Cards Ee and Dd*

- pocket chart

- *Alphabet Cards e, d, f, I, n, r, T*

- sentence strips

- marker

ACTIVE BEGINNING

Word Hunt Have children sit in a circle. As you read the following verse, have the children echo. Establish a beat and keep it going throughout the verse.

Going on a word hunt.

What's this word?

/d/ /e/ /n/

Together: *Den!*

Continue with the words /b/ /e/ /d/ (*bed*), /f/ /e/ /d/ (*fed*), /l/ /e/ /d/ (*led*).

TEACH/MODEL

Recognize /e/ and /d/ Display *Big Alphabet Card Ee* on the chalk-ledge or in a pocket chart.

What letter is this?

What sound does this letter stand for? (/e/)

Have children say /e/ with you as you point to the letter.

Follow the same procedure for *Big Alphabet Card Dd*.

Word Blending Explain to children that they are going to blend the two letters together to read words, such as *bed* and *den*.

- Place the letters *f, e, d* in the pocket chart, separate from each other.

- Point to *f*. Say **/ff/**. Have children repeat the sound after you.

- Point to *e*. Say **/ee/**. Have children repeat the sound after you.

- Point to *d*. Say **/dd/.** Have children repeat the sound after you.

 FLORIDA STANDARDS/GLEs **FCAT: LA.A.1.1.2.K.5** Phonetic principles; *Also* **LA.A.1.1.2.K.2** Alphabet; **LA.A.1.1.2.K.3** Sounds; **LA.C.1.1.1.K.1** Follow directions; **LA.C.3.1.2.K.1** Questions; **LA.D.2.1.2.K.1** Patterned structures

- Slide the *e* next to the *f.* Say: **/ffee/.**

- Slide the *d* next to the *fe.* Move your hand under the letters and blend the sounds, elongating them —**/ffeedd/.** Have children repeat after you. Then have children blend and read *fed* with you.

PRACTICE/APPLY

Guided Practice Place the letters *r, e,* and *d* in the pocket chart.

- Point to *r* and say **/rr/.** Point to the letter *e* and say **/ee/.** Slide the *e* next to *r.* Move your hand under the letters and blend the sounds, elongating them—**/rree/.** Have children blend the sounds after you.

- Point to *d.* Say **/dd/.** Have children say the sound.

- Slide the *d* next to the *re.* Slide your hands under *red* and blend the sounds. Have children blend the sounds as you slide your hand under the word.

- Then have children read the word *red* along with you.

Follow the same procedure to build and blend *fed, led, Ted,* and *den* with children.

Independent Practice Write on sentence strips the sentence frame *The _____ is red.* Place one strip in the pocket chart and have children read the sentence frame. Then distribute the sentence strips to children. Have them write the name of an object to complete the sentence. When they have finished, ask them to read their sentences.

BELOW-LEVEL

Have children use their *Word Builder* and *Word Builder Cards* to blend /r/ /e/ /d/ with you. Follow the procedure used in the Teach/Model section of the lesson.

ADVANCED

Place *Magnetic Letters b, f, l, n, r, n, t* and a cookie sheet in your Letters and Words Center. Place the *Magnetic Letters e* and *d* on the cookie sheet. Encourage children to make other words with *e* and *d,* such as the names *Ted* and *Ned.*

ENGLISH-LANGUAGE LEARNERS

Before giving each child a sentence strip to complete the Independent Practice, practice reading the sentence frame together. Then, have children say the sentence and fill in the name of the object orally.

▲ **Practice Book page 16**

FLORIDA STANDARDS/GLEs FCAT: LA.A.1.1.2.K.5 Phonetic principles; *Also* LA.A.1.1.2.K.3 Sounds; LA.B.1.1.2.K.2 Basic formats; LA.B.1.1.3.K.1 Spelling approximations; LA.B.1.1.3.K.2 Print direction

Neighborhood Helpers 265

OBJECTIVES

To write a report

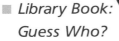

Materials

- *Library Book: Guess Who?*
- drawing paper
- crayons or markers

Writing

Write A Book of Facts

INFORMATIONAL TEXT

Talk About Neighborhood Helpers   Page through *Library Book Guess Who?* and ask children to name the jobs people in the book do. Talk with children about the jobs they think are the most interesting.

Write a Fact   Tell children that they can write a fact about one of the jobs they read about in *Guess Who?* Tell them that facts are true sentences that teach something.

Model for children how to write a fact.

> **MODEL** I want to write a fact about a barber so that I can teach someone what a barber does. A barber cuts hair. I will start this sentence with an uppercase letter and end it with a period.

Have them draw a picture of a worker they learned about in the book. Tell them to write a sentence that tells what the worker does.

A brbr cts har.

Self-Selected Writing Have children write and draw about anything they'd like. If they have difficulty thinking of a topic have them ask two friends what they're going to write about.

FLORIDA STANDARDS/GLEs   FCAT: LA.A.1.1.2.K.6 Print meaning; **LA.B.2.1.2.K.1** Record ideas; *Also* **LA.B.1.1.1.K.2** Generate ideas; **LA.B.1.1.3.K.1** Spelling approximations; **LA.B.1.1.3.K.2** Print direction; **LA.B.1.1.3.K.3** Punctuation; **LA.B.2.1.4.K.1** Informational texts

WRAP UP Share Time

Read the Facts Invite children to take turns displaying and reading their facts. Collect the facts and staple them together. Invite several children to design a cover. Write "All About Jobs" on the cover sheet. Place the book in the classroom library.

S.S.R. Have children read silently from a book of their choice.

SOCIAL STUDIES

Workers in Our Town

Tape a piece of mural paper to the wall and have children draw pictures of people at work. Tell them to think of jobs that they see people do in their neighborhood, as well as jobs that people in their family do. Ask children to name the jobs and label their drawings.

Materials

- mural paper
- tape
- crayons and markers

FLORIDA STANDARDS/GLEs **FCAT: LA.C.3.1.3.K.1** Basic vocabulary; *Also* **LA.A.1.1.2.K.1** Print organization; **LA.A.1.1.3.K.2** Nouns and verbs; **LA.B.1.1.1.K.2** Generate ideas; **LA.B.1.1.3.K.1** Spelling approximations; **LA.B.1.1.3.K.2** Print direction; **LA.B.1.1.3.K.3** Punctuation; **LA.B.2.1.4.K.1** Informational texts; **LA.E.2.1.1.K.1** Background knowledge

Day at a Glance
Day 3

WARM UP

Phonemic Awareness
Phoneme Matching: Medial

Sharing Literature
Read-Aloud Anthology:
"Franklin in the Dark"

Read

Develop Concept Vocabulary

Respond to Literature

Literature Focus: Characters

Phonics
Words with /e/ and /d/

Writing
Sentences about Problems

MORNING MESSAGE

Kindergarten News

(Child's name) can _____.

He/She learned how to _____

by _____.

Write Kindergarten News Talk with children about new things they can do. Ask them to tell how they learned to do these new things.

Use prompts such as the following to guide children as you write the news:

- **Who can tell about something new they can do?**
- **Who can show me the top of the page?**
- **Who can show me the bottom of the page?**
- **Who can point to where to begin reading?**

As you write the message, invite children to contribute by writing letters, words, or names they have previously learned. Remind them to use proper spacing, capitalization, and punctuation.

Calendar Language

Point to and read aloud the names of the days of the week. Ask what day today is. Ask children what day comes after today. Point to the name of the day and say: *Tomorrow is _____.* Ask: *What is today? What is tomorrow?*

Sunday	Monday	Tuesday	Wednesday	Thursday	Friday	Saturday
		1	2	3	4	5
6	7	8	9	10	11	12
13	14	15	16	17	18	19
20	21	22	23	24	25	26
27	28	29	30	31		

FLORIDA STANDARDS/GLEs FCAT: LA.A.2.1.5.K.2 Get information; LA.B.2.1.2.K.1 Record ideas; *Also* LA.A.1.1.2.K.1 Print organization; LA.C.1.1.3.K.1 Conversation rules; LA.C.3.1.2.K.1 Questions

Phonemic Awareness

PHONEME MATCHING: MEDIAL

Listen for Medial Sounds   Tell children you will say some words and they will name the two words that have the same sound in the middle.

Say: jet **/j//e//t/**   bed **/b//e//d/**   mop **/m//o//p/**

Have children say the words with you.

I hear three sounds in *jet*. /j/ /e/ /t/. I hear /e/ in the middle of *jet*. Say /e/ with me. Let's listen for another word with the same /e/ sound in the middle.

Follow the same procedure for *bed* and *mop*.

Say: **jet**   **bed**   **mop**

Which two words have the same middle sound?

Say: **jet. I hear /e/ in the middle.**

Say: **bed. I hear /e/ in the middle.**

Say: **mop. I hear /o/ in the middle.**

Jet **and** ***bed*** **have the same middle sounds.**

Have children follow the same procedure for:

net	tan	fed	met	wig	when
pet	led	nap	set	pot	get
can	man	let	pig	got	dot

▲ **"The Bee and the Pup,"** *Oo-pples and Boo-noo-noos: Songs and Activities for Phonemic Awareness,* **page 58.**

BELOW-LEVEL

Say the word *pet*. Have children repeat it. Say each sound again, raising a finger as you say a sound. /p/ /e/ /t/. Have children do the same. Ask them to name the sound they hear in the middle of pet. Follow the same procedure for *pat* and *mop*.

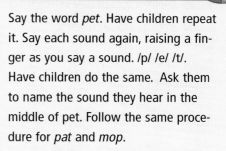

▲ **Read-Aloud Anthology**

OBJECTIVES

- *To use prior knowledge to make predictions*

- *To develop understanding of story vocabulary*

- *To retell the story using puppets*

- *To understand characters*

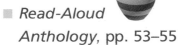

Materials

- *Read-Aloud Anthology*, pp. 53–55

- *Teacher's Resource Book*, p. 95–96

- crayons

- scissors

- craft sticks

- glue

Sharing Literature

Read "Franklin in the Dark"

READ ALOUD

Before Reading Turn to page 53 of the *Read-Aloud Anthology*. Write the story title "Franklin in the Dark" on the board. Read the title aloud as you track the print and tell children this story is about a turtle named Franklin who is afraid of something. Tell children that sometimes they can use what they know to make predictions about a story.

Franklin is a turtle. Let's tell some things we know about turtles.

- **Where do turtles live?** (Possible responses: in ponds, in oceans)
- **What do turtles carry on their backs?** (a shell)
- **Is their shell hard or soft?** (very hard)
- **How does the shell help the turtle?** (The turtle can hide inside the shell.)
- **Do you think it is dark or light inside the shell?** (dark)
- **What might Franklin be afraid of?** (Possible responses: the dark, monsters, insects)

During Reading Read the story aloud. As you read,

- change the tone of your voice as you read the words of different characters.
- pause to talk with children about what each character is afraid of and how they fix the problem.
- pause at the end of page 54 to point out that all the animals are afraid of something.

MODEL **Franklin finds out that the duck is afraid of deep water, the bird is afraid of flying high in the air, and even the the lion and polar bear are afraid of things. Maybe everyone is afraid of something; they just have to figure out what will help them not be afraid.**

 FLORIDA STANDARDS/GLEs **FCAT: LA.A.1.1.4.K.1** Comprehension; **LA.E.1.1.1.K.1** Genres; *Also* **LA.A.1.1.2.K.1** Print organization; **LA.C.1.1.1.K.2** Oral language; **LA.C.3.1.2.K.1** Questions

DEVELOP CONCEPT VOCABULARY

After Reading Use the following prompts to discuss story vocabulary:

The polar bear is afraid of the cold. He wears a snow suit. What is a *snow suit*? (clothing that keeps you warm)

The lion is afraid of loud, scary noises. He wears earmuffs. What are *earmuffs*? (coverings you put on your ears to keep them warm or to keep out noise)

The bird is afraid of flying too high. He uses a parachute. What is a *parachute*? (an umbrella-shaped cloth used to make a slow fall from an airplane)

RESPOND TO LITERATURE

Retell the Story Display the six Character Cutouts from the *Teacher's Resource Book*, and discuss each one. Have children color the characters, cut them out, and make stick puppets by gluing a craft stick to the back of each puppet. Children can take turns or work together to retell "Franklin in the Dark," using the puppets.

Literature Focus

CHARACTERS

Remind children that you can tell about characters by what they say and what they do.

MODEL **Franklin asks a duck, a lion, and a bird for help. Every time he meets an animal he uses the words, "Excuse me." I think Franklin is polite and shows he cares about the other animals by the way he talks to them.**

Turn to page 55 and reread it. After reading, ask children to tell what Franklin's mother says and does. (She listens to Franklin. She helps Franklin see that all the animals are afraid of something.) Tell children that you know that Franklin's mother is kind because of what she says and does.

ADVANCED

Have children choose one of the animals in the story and write in a speech balloon the words the animal might say to Franklin. Have them attach the speech balloon to their puppets and share their animal conversations with a partner.

ONGOING ASSESSMENT

As you share "Franklin in the Dark," note whether children

- **make predictions based on prior knowledge.**
- **join in to talk about each character's problem.**
- **can retell the story using puppets.**

FLORIDA STANDARDS/GLEs **FCAT: LA.A.1.1.2.K.4** Words; **LA.A.1.1.3.K.5** Story elements; **LA.C.3.1.3.K.1** Basic vocabulary; **LA.E.1.1.2.K.1** Story elements; *Also* **LA.E.2.1.1.K.2** Personal interpretations

OBJECTIVES

- To build and read simple one-syllable words

- To understand that as letters of words change, so do the sounds

Materials

- *Alphabet Cards N, b, d, e, n, T, t*
- *Word Builders*
- *Word Builder Cards b, d, e, N, n, T, t*
- pocket chart
- *Magnetic Letters*
- cookie sheet

REVIEW LETTERS

Phonics
Words with /e/ and /d/

ACTIVE BEGINNING

Action Rhyme Teach children this rhyme. Have them clap the syllables as they say the words.

Ed had a red sled.

Ed slid on his sled.

Ed fell on his head.

Ed went to bed.

TEACH/MODEL

Blending Words Distribute *Word Builders* and *Word Builder Cards N, b, d, e, n,* and *t* to children. As you place *Alphabet Cards* in a pocket chart, tell children to place the same *Word Builder Cards* in their *Word Builders.*

- Place *Alphabet Cards N, e,* and *d* in the pocket chart. Have children do the same.

- Point to *N*. Say **/nn/**. Point to *e*. Say **/ee/**.

- Slide the *e* next to the *N*. Then move your hand under the letters and blend the sounds, elongating them—**/nnee/**. Have children do the same.

- Point to the letter *d*. Say **/dd/**. Have children do the same.

- Slide the *d* next to the *Ne*. Slide your hand under *Ned* and blend by elongating the sounds—**/nneedd/**. Have children say and do the same.

FLORIDA STANDARDS/GLEs   FCAT: LA.A.1.1.2.K.5 Phonetic principles; *Also* LA.A.1.1.2.K.2 Alphabet; LA.A.1.1.2.K.3 Sounds

• Then have children blend and read the word *Ned* along with you.

PRACTICE/APPLY

Guided Practice Have children place *Word Builder Cards* e and d in their *Word Builder.*

• **Add *b* to *ed*. What word did you make?**

• **Change *b* to *T*. What word did you make?**

• **Change *d* to *n*. What word did you make?**

• **Change *t* to *d*. What word did you make?**

Independent Practice Have children use *Magnetic Letters* and a cookie sheet in the Letters and Words Center to build and read *Ned, bed, Ted, ten,* and *den.*

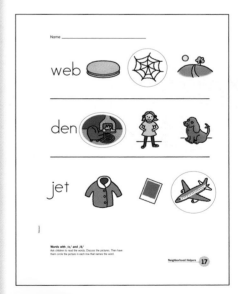

▲ **Practice Book, page 17**

FLORIDA STANDARDS/GLEs   FCAT: LA.A.1.1.2.K.5 Phonetic principles; *Also* LA.A.1.1.2.K.2 Alphabet; LA.A.1.1.2.K.3 Sounds; LA.C.3.1.2.K.1 Questions

Neighborhood Helpers   **273**

OBJECTIVES

To identify a problem and solution

To draw and write sentences about a problem

Materials

■ drawing paper

■ crayons or markers

Shared Writing

Write Sentences About a Problem

PROBLEMS AND SOLUTIONS

Talk About Problems Ask children to describe Franklin's problem in the story "Franklin in the Dark" and tell how he fixes it. (Franklin is afraid of the dark. He puts on his night light.) Explain that stories are often about characters who have a problem and must find a way to fix it. Discuss problems that might happen in the classroom, such as spilling paint or losing something. Talk about what happened to fix each problem.

Write About a Problem Have children draw and write about a problem they have had and how it was fixed. Show children how to fold a sheet of paper in half. On one half of the paper have them write a sentence to tell what the problem is. Have them draw a picture to show how they felt. On the other half have them write a sentence and draw a picture to show how everything worked out in the end. Encourage them to include people who helped them.

I los Max   Sam fond him

Journal Writing Have children draw and label a picture of their favorite character from the story "Franklin in the Dark."

FLORIDA STANDARDS/GLEs **FCAT: LA.B.2.1.2.K.1** Record ideas; *Also* **LA.A.1.1.2.K.1** Print organization; **LA.B.1.1.2.K.2** Basic formats; **LA.B.1.1.3.K.1** Spelling approximations; **LA.B.1.1.3.K.2** Print direction; **LA.B.1.1.3.K.3** Punctuation; **LA.C.1.1.1.K.1** Follow directions; **LA.C.1.1.1.K.2** Oral language; **LA.C.3.1.2.K.1** Questions

WRAP UP # Share Time

Reflect on the Lesson Ask children to tell what Franklin was afraid of. Invite children to share their sentences telling about a problem they have had.

S.S.R. *Sustained Silent Reading* Have children read silently from a book of their choice.

 **Centers** **SCIENCE**

Turtle Fact Books

Place a blank book for each child at the center and ask children to title their book "Turtle Facts." Have children think about what they know or learned today about turtles from the Sharing Literature lesson. Ask them to write one sentence about turtles on each page and illustrate it.

Turtle Facts

 ## Materials

- two pieces of drawing paper folded in half and stapled into a blank book

- crayons

FLORIDA STANDARDS/GLEs LA.B.1.1.1.K.1 Prewriting; LA.B.1.1.2.K.2 Basic formats; LA.B.1.1.3.K.1 Spelling approximations; LA.B.1.1.3.K.2 Print direction; LA.B.1.1.3.K.3 Punctuation; LA.B.2.1.4.K.1 Informational texts; LA.C.1.1.1.K.1 Follow directions; LA.E.2.1.1.K.2 Personal interpretations

Day 4

Phonemic Awareness
Segmentation

Sharing Literature
Read-Aloud Anthology:
"Jamaica's Find"

Read

Respond to Literature

Literature Focus: Retelling the Story

Phonics
Reading
Decodable Book 11: *We Can Fix*

Interactive Writing ✏
Description

ORAL LANGUAGE

WARM UP

MORNING MESSAGE

Kindergarten News

(Child's name) likes to

play with _____.

Write Kindergarten News Talk with children about friends. Ask them to tell about new friends they have made.

Use prompts such as the following to guide children as you write the news:

- **Who can tell about a new friend?**
- **Who can show me where to begin reading?**
- **Who can show me a word?**

As you write the message, invite children to contribute by writing letters, words, or names they have previously learned. Remind them to use proper spacing, capitalization, and punctuation.

Calendar Language

Point to and read aloud the names of the days of the week. Ask what day today is. Say: *Today is _____.* Point to the name of the day before and say: *Yesterday was _____.* Ask: *What day is today? What day was yesterday?*

Sunday	Monday	Tuesday	Wednesday	Thursday	Friday	Saturday
		1	2	3	4	5
6	7	8	9	10	11	12
13	14	15	16	17	18	19
20	21	22	23	24	25	26
27	28	29	30	31		

FLORIDA STANDARDS/GLEs FCAT: LA.A.1.1.2.K.4 Words; **LA.A.2.1.5.K.2** Get information; **LA.B.2.1.2.K.1** Record ideas; *Also* **LA.A.1.1.2.K.1** Print organization; **LA.C.1.1.3.K.1** Conversation rules; **LA.C.3.1.2.K.1** Questions

Phonemic Awareness

SEGMENTATION

Track Syllables in a Word Tell children to listen as you clap the syllables in the word *supper*. Say **supper**, clapping once for each syllable. (sup-per) Say **supper** again, asking children to clap once for each syllable with you. Tell children that these word parts are called syllables.

Say the following words and ask children to repeat them and clap for each syllable. Have children tell how many syllables they hear in each word.

morning (morn-ing)	**ladder** (lad-der)
girl (girl)	**bicycle** (bi-cy-cle)
kitchen (kitch-en)	**welcome** (wel-come)
yesterday (yes-ter-day)	**calendar** (cal-en-dar)
park (park)	**friend** (friend)

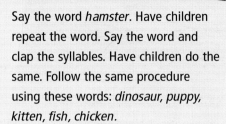

BELOW-LEVEL

Say the word *hamster*. Have children repeat the word. Say the word and clap the syllables. Have children do the same. Follow the same procedure using these words: *dinosaur, puppy, kitten, fish, chicken.*

ADVANCED

Have children work with a partner. Children can take turns saying a name of a person, object, or place. Their partner can clap for the syllables and tell how many syllables they hear.

bi-cy-cle

KINDERGARTEN
READ-ALOUD
Anthology
Harcourt

▲ **Read-Aloud Anthology**

OBJECTIVES

- *To listen and respond to a story*
- *To connect text to life experiences*
- *To understand characters*
- *To retell a story*

Materials

- *Read-Aloud Anthology,* pp. 90–93
- drawing paper
- crayons or pencils
- chart paper
- marker

Sharing Literature

Read "Jamaica's Find"

READ ALOUD

Before Reading   Turn to page 90 of the *Read-Aloud Anthology* and read aloud the title "Jamaica's Find." Ask children to recall what the story is about. Use this model to set a purpose for rereading the story:

MODEL   I remember Jamaica is a little girl. She finds some things at the park. I remember she keeps the stuffed dog and returns the hat to the Lost and Found. But then something happens and she returns the dog also. I'll reread the story to see why Jamaica returns the stuffed dog.

During Reading   Read the story aloud. As you read,

- pause periodically during the story to encourage children to evaluate Jamaica's actions.

MODEL   Jamaica brings the hat to the Lost and Found, but she brings the stuffed dog home. Her mom and dad think she should have brought it to the Lost and Found, too. I agree, because maybe somebody lost the dog and will try to find it.

 FLORIDA STANDARDS/GLEs   FCAT: LA.A.1.1.4.K.1 Comprehension; **LA.C.1.1.4.K.1** Sequence; **LA.E.1.1.2.K.1** Story elements; *Also* **LA.C.1.1.1.K.2** Oral language; **LA.E.2.1.1.K.1** Background knowledge

RESPOND TO LITERATURE

Discuss *Lost and Found*   Ask children to tell what Kristen does when she loses her stuffed dog. (She goes to the Lost and Found in the park.) Have children write and draw about something they have lost or found. Place the drawings on a bulletin board labeled "Lost and Found."

Literature Focus

RETELLING THE STORY

Ask children to name the characters in the story and tell what happens to them. As children share their ideas, record them in a story map on chart paper. Use these prompts to help children retell the story in a logical order:

- **Who is the main character in the story?** (Jamaica)

- **What does Jamaica find at the beginning of the story?** (Jamaica finds a hat and a stuffed dog in the park.)

- **What does Jamaica do with the things she finds?** (She returns the hat to the Lost and Found. She takes the stuffed dog home.)

- **What happens at the end of the story?** (Jamaica returns the dog to the Lost and Found and meets a new friend named Kristen. Kristen finds her lost dog.)

Tell children that a story map can help them retell the story. Read the story map aloud to children. Then ask children to retell the story.

> **First**
> Jamaica finds a hat and stuffed dog in the park.
>
> ↓
>
> **Next**
> Jamaica returns the hat and takes the dog home.
>
> ↓
>
> **Last**
> Jamaica returns the dog to the Lost and Found in the park. Jamaica meets a new friend, Kristen.

REACHING ALL LEARNERS
Below-Level · On-Level · Advanced · ELL

Diagnostic Check: Comprehension

If... children have difficulty retelling the story,

Then... tell them a sentence stating what happens at the beginning, middle, and end of the story. Have them repeat the sentences after you. Then ask them to tell you what happens at the beginning, middle, and end of the story.

ADDITIONAL SUPPORT ACTIVITIES

BELOW-LEVEL	Reteach, p. S30
ADVANCED	Extend, p. S31
ENGLISH-LANGUAGE LEARNERS	Reteach, p. S31

ONGOING ASSESSMENT

As you share "Jamaica's Find," note whether children

- **listen for a period of time.**
- **connect own experiences to text.**
- **understand characters.**

FLORIDA STANDARDS/GLEs   FCAT: LA.A.1.1.4.K.1 Comprehension; **LA.A.2.1.1.K.1** Main idea; **LA.E.1.1.2.K.1** Story elements; *Also* **LA.B.1.1.2.K.2** Basic formats; **LA.B.1.1.3.K.1** Spelling approximations; **LA.B.1.1.3.K.2** Print direction; **LA.B.2.1.4.K.1** Informational texts; **LA.C.3.1.2.K.1** Questions

Neighborhood Helpers   279

Phonics
Short Vowel /e/e  *Review*

OBJECTIVES

To decode short vowel /e/e words

Materials

- *Alphabet Cards b, e, d, a*
- pocket chart
- marker
- index cards
- *Decodable Book 11: We Can Fix*
- drawing paper
- crayons or markers

TEACH/MODEL

Review Blending   Place *Alphabet Cards b, e* and *d* next to one another in a pocket chart. Move your hand under the letters, blend them, and say the word. **/bbeedd/—bed.** Have children blend the sounds and say the word. Add *Alphabet Card a* with a space before *bed*.

Write the words *We, can,* and *fix* on index cards. Place the index cards in the pocket chart in front of *Alphabet Cards a bed*. Add a period at the end. Track the print as children read the words: *We can fix a bed.*

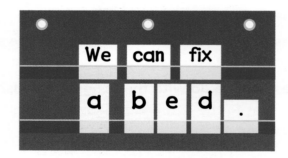

ADVANCED

Have children read *Independent Reader 28: Lots of Jobs.*

PRACTICE/APPLY

Read the Book   Distribute copies of *We Can Fix*. Have children read the title and encourage children to point to each word as they say it. Tell children to point to each word as they read the story.

Respond   Have children draw a picture of something they or a family member can fix.

Read

FLORIDA STANDARDS/GLEs   FCAT: LA.A.1.1.2.K.4 Words; **LA.A.1.1.2.K.5** Phonetic principles; **LA.A.1.1.3.K.4** Build vocabulary; **LA.A.1.1.3.K.5** Story elements; **LA.E.1.1.1.K.1** Genres; *Also* **LA.A.1.1.2.K.3** Sounds; **LA.A.1.1.3.K.1** Frequent words

Decodable Book 11: *We Can Fix*

I can fix a bed.
Tap, tap, tap.

2

I can fix a pet.
Pat, pat, pat.

3

I can fix a van.
Rap, rap, rap.

4

I can fix a rip.
Zip, zip, zip.

5

I can fix a top.
Dab, dab, dab.

6

I can fix a net.
Nip, nip, nip.

7

We can fix it!

8

■ High-Frequency Word

we

■ Decodable Words

See the list on page T15

School-Home Connection

Take-Home Book Version

◄ Decodable Book 11: We Can Fix

BELOW-LEVEL

Write the words *bed, pet, van, rip, top,* and *net* on chart paper. Help children blend the sounds and say the words. Have children read the words with you. Have children reread the book and identify these items in the pictures on each page.

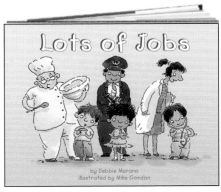

▲ *Lots of Jobs*
Independent Reader 28

OBJECTIVE

To write a description

Materials

■ chart paper

■ marker

Interactive Writing

Write a Description

BUILD BACKGROUND

Talk About the Dog   Reread page 91 in the *Read-Aloud Anthology.* Tell children to listen for the words that tell about the stuffed dog. After reading, ask children to tell what the dog looks like.

Write a Description   Tell children that together you will write a description of the lost dog. Explain that a description tells what something looks like. Use these prompts to help children write:

Where should I write LOST: on the paper? Let's write the word lost in uppercase letters. Who can write uppercase l-o-s-t?

Let's write "A Stuffed Dog." Who can write *A*?

Who can put a finger next to *A* to make a space?

Who can write uppercase *D* and lowercase *o* for the word *Dog*?

Who can show me where to begin writing our next sentence?

Continue in this manner to complete the description. Have children write words and letters as they can.

LOST: A Stuffed Dog

It is gray.

It has black ears.

It has a round white spot for a nose.

Writing Every Day

My Journal

Journal Writing Have children draw and label a picture of something they have lost.

FLORIDA STANDARDS/GLEs **FCAT: LA.B.2.1.2.K.1** Record ideas; **LA.C.3.1.3.K.1** Basic vocabulary; *Also* **LA.A.1.1.2.K.1** Print organization; **LA.B.1.1.2.K.2** Basic formats; **LA.B.1.1.2.K.1** Dictate messages; **LA.B.1.1.3.K.1** Spelling approximations; **LA.B.1.1.3.K.2** Print direction; **LA.B.1.1.3.K.3** Punctuation; **LA.B.2.1.4.K.1** Informational texts

WRAP UP Share Time

Reflect on the Lesson Read the description to children and then ask volunteers to describe a favorite stuffed animal.

S.S.R. Have children read silently from a book of their choice.

Centers  WRITING

Meeting New Friends

Place drawing paper and two speech bubbles for each child at the center. Ask children to draw a picture of themselves and a friend. Have children think about what they may have said to their friend the first time they met. Ask them to write it in a speech bubble and then glue it on their picture. Have them write what their friend may have said back on another speech bubble, and glue the response on the paper.

Materials

■ drawing paper

■ two speech bubbles for each child

■ crayons

■ glue

FLORIDA STANDARDS/GLEs **FCAT: LA.B.2.1.2.K.1** Record ideas; *Also* **LA.B.1.1.2.K.2** Basic formats; **LA.B.1.1.3.K.1** Spelling approximations; **LA.B.1.1.3.K.2** Print direction; **LA.B.1.1.3.K.3** Punctuation; **LA.C.3.1.1.K.1** Speak clearly; **LA.E.2.1.1.K.1** Background knowledge

Day at a Glance
Day 5

Phonemic Awareness
Phoneme Isolation: Medial

Sharing Literature
Big Book:
The Big Yellow Bus

Read

Respond to Literature
Literature Focus: Sequence

Phonics
Blending /e/ - /d/

Writing
Caption about a Make-Believe
School Bus

MORNING MESSAGE

Kindergarten News

Today we will _____.

Write Kindergarten News Talk with children about the activities they will take part in today.

Use prompts such as the following to guide children as you write the news:

• **Today we will (name activities of the day).**

• **Who can tell me one thing we will do today?**

• **Who can point to an uppercase letter? What letter is it?**

• **Who can count the words in the sentence?**

As you write the message, invite children to contribute by writing letters or words they have previously learned. Remind them to use proper spacing, capitalization, and punctuation.

Calendar Language

Point to and read aloud the days of the week. Point to *Sunday* and point to *Saturday*. Ask: *What is the first day of the week? What is the last day of the week?*

Sunday	Monday	Tuesday	Wednesday	Thursday	Friday	Saturday
		1	2	3	4	5
6	7	8	9	10	11	12
13	14	15	16	17	18	19
20	21	22	23	24	25	26
27	28	29	30	31		

FLORIDA STANDARDS/GLEs   FCAT: LA.B.2.1.2.K.1 Record ideas; *Also* LA.A.1.1.2.K.2 Alphabet;LA.A.2.1.5.K.1 Alphabetical order; LA.C.1.1.3.K.1 Conversation rules; LA.C.3.1.2.K.1 Questions

Phonemic Awareness

PHONEME ISOLATION: MEDIAL

BELOW-LEVEL

Listen for Medial Sounds   Tell children to listen for the middle sound in the words of a song. Sing the following words to the tune of "Old MacDonald Had a Farm":

What is the sound in the middle of these words:
set and *mess* and *bed*?
/e/ is the sound in the middle of these words:
set and *mess* and *bed*.
With an /e/ /e/ here and an /e/ /e/ there,
here an /e/, there an /e/,
everywhere an /e/, /e/.
/e/ is the sound in the middle of these words:
set and *mess* and *bed*.

Substitute the following sounds and words into the song and invite children to sing with you:

clam yak map /a/

left fed web /e/

miss fin wig /i/

buzz rub fun /u/

lend wet neck /e/

box lock pot /o/

Tell children they will listen for the sound they hear in the middle of a word. Have each child use Side B of the *Write-On/Wipe-Off* board and disks. Point to the middle box and say: *This is the middle*. Say: *red*. Ask children to repeat the word. Say it again segmenting the sounds: /r/ /e/ /d/ and placing a disk for each sound. Ask children to say the sound they hear in the middle of *red*. (/e/) Follow this procedure for *hen, set, cat*.

What sound do you hear in the middle of *web*?

I hear /e/ in the middle of *web*.

FLORIDA STANDARDS/GLEs FCAT: LA.A.1.1.2.K.5 Phonetic principles; *Also* **LA.C.1.1.1.K.1** Follow directions; **LA.C.1.1.1.K.2** Oral language; **LA.C.3.1.2.K.1** Questions; **LA.D.2.1.2.K.1** Patterned structures

Neighborhood Helpers   285

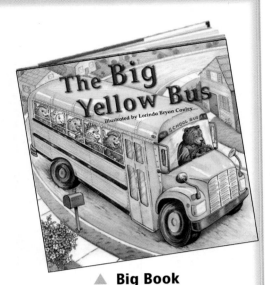
Sharing Literature

Read The Big Yellow Bus

READ ALOUD

Before Reading   Display *The Big Yellow Bus*. Point to the title and track the print as you read it aloud. Point to the name of the illustrator and track the print as you read her name aloud. Ask children what an illustrator does. Model to set a purpose for rereading:

MODEL   I remember this story is about animals riding a bus to school. The pictures help me enjoy the story. Reading the words and looking at the pictures help me understand the story. I'll reread the story and look carefully at the pictures.

During Reading   Read the story aloud. As you read,

- model how the illustrations help you understand the text.

MODEL   The words on the first page tell me that a big yellow bus comes down the street. The question is, "Who will come to school?" By reading the words, I can guess that a school bus is beginning its trip to school. When I look at the pictures, I see an empty bus. I see two zebras waiting for the bus. They are waving at the bus and seem excited and happy.

- ask children to describe other illustrations after you read the text.

▲ **Big Book**

OBJECTIVES

- *To connect illustrations to text*
- *To identify important events*
- *To understand sequence*
- *To connect story events to life experiences*
- *To place story events in logical order*

Materials

- *Big Book: The Big Yellow Bus*
- chart paper
- marker
- drawing paper
- crayons or markers

286   Neighborhood Helpers

FLORIDA STANDARDS/GLEs   **FCAT: LA.A.1.1.2.K.4** Words; **LA.A.1.1.4.K.1** Comprehension; *Also*
LA.A.2.1.4.K.1 Illustrations; **LA.C.1.1.1.K.2** Oral language

RESPOND TO LITERATURE

Connect to Experience Have children tell about a ride they take on a bus. Have them describe the people on the bus. Ask them to tell what happens first, next, and last.

SEQUENCE

Tell children that events in stories happen in a special order. Page through the *Big Book* and work with children to name the story events. Write them on chart paper. Use these prompts:

What happens at the beginning of the story? (The bus comes down the street.)

What animals get on the bus first? (zebras)

What animals get on next? (yaks)

After the list of events is complete, read them aloud, tracking the print. Provide drawing paper and ask children to draw and label one of the story events. Collect the pictures and have groups of children help you assemble them into class books.

1. The bus comes down the street.

2. Zebras get on the bus.

3. Yaks get on the bus.

4. Lions get on the bus.

5. Sheep get on the bus.

6. The bus stops at school.

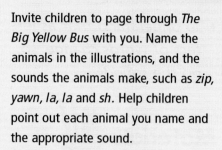

ENGLISH-LANGUAGE LEARNERS

Invite children to page through *The Big Yellow Bus* with you. Name the animals in the illustrations, and the sounds the animals make, such as *zip, yawn, la, la* and *sh*. Help children point out each animal you name and the appropriate sound.

ONGOING ASSESSMENT

As you share *The Big Yellow Bus,* note whether children

• can recall story events.

• use text and illustrations to understand the story.

FLORIDA STANDARDS/GLEs **FCAT: LA.A.1.1.4.K.1** Comprehension; **LA.E.1.1.2.K.1** Story elements; *Also* **LA.B.1.1.2.K.2** Basic formats; **LA.B.1.1.3.K.2** Print direction; **LA.C.1.1.3.K.1** Conversation rules; **LA.C.3.1.1.K.1** Speak clearly; **LA.C.3.1.2.K.1** Questions; **LA.E.2.1.1.K.1** Background knowledge

Neighborhood Helpers **287**

Phonics

Blending /e/ - /d/  *Review*

OBJECTIVES

• To build and read simple one-syllable words

• To understand that as letters of words change, so do the sounds

Materials

■ *Alphabet Cards B, b, d, e, I, n, r*

■ *Word Builders*

■ *Word Builder Cards B, b, d, e, I, n, r*

■ pocket chart

■ index cards

■ drawing paper

■ crayons or markers

REVIEW LETTERS

ACTIVE BEGINNING

Rhyming Sentence   Teach children this sentence and have them clap the syllables as you say it.

Ned led the puppy to the big, red bed!

TEACH/MODEL

Blending Words   Distribute *Word Builders* and *Word Builder Cards b, d, e, I, n,* and *r* to children. As you place *Alphabet Cards* in a pocket chart, tell children to place the same *Word Builder Cards* in their *Word Builders.*

• Place *Alphabet Cards r, e,* and *d* in the pocket chart. Have children do the same.

• Point to *r.* Say **/rr/.** Point to *e.* Say **/ee/.**

• Slide the *e* next to the *r.* Then move your hand under the letters and blend the sounds, elongating them—**/rree/.** Have children do the same.

• Point to the letter *d.* Say **/dd/.** Have children do the same.

• Slide the *d* next to the *re.* Slide your hand under *red* and blend by elongating the sounds—**/rreedd/.** Have children say and do the same.

• Then have children blend and read the word *red* along with you.

FLORIDA STANDARDS/GLEs   **FCAT: LA.A.1.1.2.K.5** Phonetic principles; *Also* **LA.A.1.1.2.K.2** Alphabet; **LA.A.1.1.2.K.3** Sounds; **LA.C.3.1.2.K.1** Questions

PRACTICE/APPLY

Guided Practice Have children place *Word Builder Cards e* and *d* in their *Word Builders.*

• **Add *l* to *ed*. What word did you make?**

• **Change *l* to *b*. What word did you make?**

• **Change *d* to *n*. What word did you make?**

• **Change *B* to *d*. What word did you make?**

Independent Practice Write the words *red, bed, Ned* and *den* on cards and place them in a pocket chart. Have children read the words. Then have them choose one of the words to write on a sheet of paper and illustrate.

BELOW-LEVEL

Display *Alphabet Cards b, e, d*. Point to each letter, say its name and sound. Have children do the same. Place *Alphabet Cards b, e, d* in the pocket chart and use the same procedure in the Teach/Model section of the lesson to have children blend the sounds to read the word.

▲ **Practice Book page 18**

FLORIDA STANDARDS/GLEs FCAT: **LA.A.1.1.2.K.4** Words; **LA.A.1.1.3.K.5** Story elements; **LA.A.2.1.1.K.1** Main idea; **LA.C.3.1.3.K.1** Basic vocabulary; *Also* **LA.A.1.1.3.K.3** Categorize words; **LA.A.2.1.4.K.1** Illustrations

Neighborhood Helpers   289

OBJECTIVE

To draw and write a caption about a make-believe bus

Materials

- drawing paper
- crayons or markers

Writing

Write About a Make-Believe Bus

DRAW AND WRITE

Talk About a Bus   Ask children who ride the bus to school to describe their bus. Have other children describe buses they have been on for field trips. Encourage children to use words to describe the size, shape, and color of the bus. Then tell them to think of make-believe things to add on their bus such as eyes, ears, wings, and hands.

Write About a Bus   Distribute drawing paper and have children draw a picture of a make-believe bus. Ask them to write a sentence to tell where their make-believe bus is going.

My bus wil go to the is crm stor.

Self-Selected Writing Have children write and draw about anything they'd like. If they have difficulty thinking of a topic have them ask two friends what they're going to write about.

FLORIDA STANDARDS/GLEs   FCAT: LA.B.2.1.2.K.1 Record ideas; *Also* **LA.B.1.1.2.K.2** Basic formats; **LA.B.1.1.3.K.1** Spelling approximations; **LA.B.1.1.3.K.2** Print direction; **LA.B.1.1.3.K.3** Punctuation; **LA.B.2.1.4.K.1** Informational texts; **LA.E.2.1.1.K.2** Personal interpretations

WRAP UP Share Time

Author's Chair Have children take turns in the Author's Chair to share their drawings and read their sentences about where their make-believe bus is going.

S.S.R. *Sustained Silent Reading* Have children read silently from a book of their choice.

Centers — LISTENING

Listen to a Story

Play the *Literature Cassette: The Big Yellow Bus.* Have children listen and join in to say the repetitive refrains.

Materials
- *Literature Cassette: The Big Yellow Bus*
- *Cassette player*

FLORIDA STANDARDS/GLEs **LA.A.1.1.2.K.1** Print organization; **LA.C.1.1.1.K.2** Oral language; **LA.C.3.1.1.K.1** Speak clearly; **LA.D.2.1.2.K.1** Patterned structures; **LA.D.2.1.3.K.1** Multiple media

Neighborhood Helpers **291**

Learning Centers

Choose from the following suggestions to enhance your learning centers for the theme Neighborhood Helpers.
(Additional learning centers for this theme can be found on pages 184-186 and 246)

ART CENTER

Make Paper Dolls

Tell children they are going to make "neighborhood helper" paper dolls. Have each child trace the outline of the body of a neighborhood helper on a piece of white construction paper. Have them fill in their figures to look like the person they have chosen as a neighborhood helper—firefighter, police officer, doctor, nurse, teacher. Then have them cut out the figure. When children have cut out their helpers, have them fold them in half and stand up their paper dolls by opening them like a card.

Materials

- "neighborhood helper" (Pattern T23)
- white construction paper
- markers
- safety scissors

SOCIAL STUDIES CENTER

Who Am I?

Tell children to think of a neighborhood helper. Then have them fold a sheet of paper in half. Have them draw a different thing the helper uses or wears in each of the halves. Then have children cut along the fold to make two strips of paper, each with a different picture clue on it. Have children swap their clue strips with a partner, identify the clues, and guess the identity of the neighborhood worker who uses the items.

Materials

- paper
- crayons or markers
- safety scissors

Teacher Notes

ORAL LANGUAGE
15-30 Minutes

- **Phonemic Awareness**

- **Sharing Literature**

LEARNING TO READ
45 Minutes

- **Phonics**

- **Vocabulary**

Daily Routines
- **Morning Message**
- **Calendar Language**
- **Writing Prompt**

LANGUAGE ARTS
15-30 Minutes

- **Writing**
  Daily Writing Prompt

Day 1

Phonemic Awareness, 299
Rhyming Words

Sharing Literature, 300
 Read
Library Book: *Guess Who?*

(Skill) **Literature Focus, 301**
Understanding Content Words

 **Phonics, 302 T**
Introduce: Phonogram -*et*

 Interactive Writing, 304
Writing Process: Prewrite

Writing Prompt, 304
Draw and write about a question and answer.

Share Time, 305
Share a favorite photograph in *Guess Who?*

Day 2

Phonemic Awareness, 307
Phoneme Substitution

Sharing Literature, 308
 Read
Read-Aloud Anthology: "The Town Mouse and the Country Mouse," pp. 83–86

(Skill) **Literature Focus, 309**
Setting

Phonics, 310 T
Introduce: Phonogram -*en*

 Interactive Writing, 312
Writing Process: Draft

Writing Prompt, 312
Draw and write about a favorite food.

Share Time, 313
Author's Chair

T = tested skill

Phonics

Phonograms *-et, -en, -ed*

Focus of the Week:
- PHONEMIC AWARENESS
- SHARING LITERATURE
- WRITING: (Writing Process)

Day 3

Phonemic Awareness, 315
Phoneme Segmentation

Sharing Literature, 316
Big Book: *The Big Yellow Bus*

(Skill) **Literature Focus, 317**
Retell the Story

 Phonics, 318 T
Introduce: Phonogram *-ed*

Interactive Writing, 320
Writing Process: Respond and Revise

Writing Prompt, 320
Draw and write about self-selected topics.

Share Time, 321
 Read
Author's Chair

Day 4

Phonemic Awareness, 323
Phoneme Substitution

Sharing Literature, 324
Read-Aloud Anthology: "This Is the Way We Go to School," p. 121

(Skill) **Literature Focus, 325**
Text Patterns

 Phonics, 326 T
Phonograms *-et, -ed, -en*

Read
DECODABLE BOOK 12
A Hat I Like

Interactive Writing, 328
Writing Process: Edit

Writing Prompt, 328
Draw and write about self-selected topics.

Share Time, 329
Share favorite verses.

Day 5

Phonemic Awareness, 331
Rhyming Words

Sharing Literature, 332
Read
Read-Aloud Anthology: "Stone Soup," pp. 44–47

(Skill) **Literature Focus, 333**
Beginning, Middle, Ending

Phonics, 334 T
Build Sentences

Interactive Writing, 336
Writing Process: Publish

Writing Prompt, 336
Draw and write about ingredients for "Stone Soup."

Share Time, 337
Share what you liked best about the school day.

Day at a Glance
Day I

WARM UP

Phonemic Awareness
Rhyming Words

Sharing Literature
Library Book:
Guess Who?

Read
Margaret Miller

GUESS WHO?

Develop Concept Vocabulary

Respond to Literature

Literature Focus:
Understanding Content Words

Phonics
Phonogram -et

Interactive Writing
Writing Process: Prewrite

MORNING MESSAGE
Kindergarten News

(Child's name) has a _____.

One day, _____.

Write Kindergarten News Talk with children about pets. Ask them to share funny stories about a pet they know about.

Use prompts such as the following to guide children as you write the news:

• **Who can tell a funny story about something that happened to a pet?**

• **Who can show me where to begin writing?**

• **Who can show me where (child's name) begins and ends?**

As you write the message, invite children to contribute by writing letters, words, or names they have previously learned. Remind them to use proper spacing, capitalization, and punctuation.

Calendar Language

Point to and read aloud the months of the year. Ask children how many months are in a year. Read the names again and ask children to repeat them after you. Say: *This is the month of _____.* Ask: *What month is this?*

Sunday	Monday	Tuesday	Wednesday	Thursday	Friday	Saturday
		1	2	3	4	5
6	7	8	9	10	11	12
13	14	15	16	17	18	19
20	21	22	23	24	25	26
27	28	29	30	31		

FLORIDA STANDARDS/GLEs   FCAT: LA.A.1.1.2.K.6 Print meaning; **LA.B.1.1.2.K.3** Sequence; **LA.C.3.1.3.K.1** Basic vocabulary; *Also* **LA.A.1.1.2.K.1** Print organization; **LA.A.1.1.3.K.2** Nouns and verbs; **LA.B.1.1.1.K.2** Generate ideas; **LA.B.1.1.2.K.1** Dictate messages; **LA.B.1.1.3.K.2** Print direction; **LA.B.1.1.3.K.3** Punctuation; **LA.B.2.1.1.K.1** Familiar experiences; **LA.B.2.1.1.K.2** Contribute ideas; **LA.C.3.1.1.K.1** Speak clearly

Phonemic Awareness

RHYMING WORDS

Identify Rhyming Words   Hold up the *Picture Card zoo* and model for children how to rhyme:

MODEL   **Listen as I say words that rhyme with** *zoo:* *zoo, boo, clue, shoe, do, coo, glue, threw.* **The words I said have the same ending sound as /z/-oo. Say /oo/ with me. Now say** *zoo, boo, shoe.* **Let's look at more pictures and say words that rhyme.**

Hold up a *Picture Card* and tell children to look at it and raise their hand if they know a rhyming word that rhymes with the picture name. Use the following *Picture Cards:*

van (*man, can, fan*)

vest (*best, chest, dressed*)

ring (*king, thing, wing*)

nail (*tail, fail, pail*)

moon (*soon, raccoon, noon*)

jet (*bet, set, get*)

hat (*bat, cat, sat*)

bear (*wear, care, share*)

car (*far, jar, star*)

hen (*pen, ten, Jen*)

Diagnostic Check: Phonemic Awareness

If... children cannot identify rhyming words,

Then... have them repeat sets of rhyming words such as *set, bet, net, pet; red, bed, led, fed; map, tap, flap, cap.*

ADDITIONAL SUPPORT ACTIVITIES

BELOW-LEVEL	Reteach, p. S32
ADVANCED	Extend, p. S33
ENGLISH-LANGUAGE LEARNERS	Reteach, p. S33

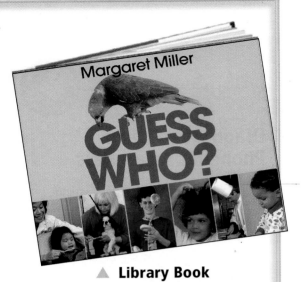

▲ **Library Book**

OBJECTIVES

- *To listen and respond to a story*

- *To describe people, things, and actions*

- *To connect text to life experiences*

- *To understand content vocabulary*

Materials

■ *Library Book: Guess Who?*

Sharing Literature

Read Guess Who?

READ ALOUD

Before Reading Display *Guess Who?* Read the title aloud as you track the print. Ask children to point to and identify the question mark. Ask them to identify other letters they know. Model setting a purpose for rereading:

MODEL I remember that this book is about the jobs people do. I remember there are lots of photographs in this book. I'll reread to find out more about jobs people do.

During Reading Read the story aloud. As you read,

- ask children to respond to each answer choice and then to repeat the correct answer after you read it.

- model how to look at photographs and describe the tasks the people are doing.

MODEL The photograph of the chef shows a man in a chef's hat and coat cutting a vegetable. It looks like an onion. I see food on a plate and pineapple and cabbage on the counter. I see stacks of dishes in front of the chef. I bet that chef is making a delicious meal for people to eat.

FLORIDA STANDARDS/GLEs FCAT: LA.A.1.1.1.K.1 Predictions; **LA.A.1.1.3.K.5** Story elements; **LA.A.1.1.4.K.1** Comprehension; **LA.A.2.1.1.K.1** Main idea; *Also* **LA.A.2.1.4.K.1** Illustrations; **LA.A.1.1.3.K.1** Frequent words

DEVELOP CONCEPT VOCABULARY

After Reading Tell children to listen to the clues you say and guess the name of the job for each clue. Say each sentence and have children give an answer.

I take pictures with a camera. (photographer)

I cut people's hair. (barber)

I deliver the mail. (letter carrier)

I fly a plane. (pilot)

I bake bread and cakes. (baker)

I take care of people's teeth. (dentist)

I fix cars. (mechanic)

RESPOND TO LITERATURE

Have children think of jobs they do in the classroom and jobs adults at your school do. Have children create questions about the jobs such as, Who helps us find new books? Who helps us learn new games? Who helps us learn to read? Who helps clean the animal cages? and Who passes out papers? Have children take turns asking and answering questions.

Literature Focus

UNDERSTANDING CONTENT WORDS

Tell children that in *Guess Who?* readers learn what words mean by looking carefully at the photographs. Point to the photograph of the plumber.

MODEL **I know that a plumber works with pipes under sinks. In the photograph, the plumber is using tools to fix the pipes so the water can run through them into the sink. A plumber is someone who fixes pipes.**

Turn to several more pages and ask children to describe the photograph and use what they know and what they see to tell about the job that person does.

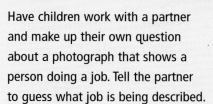

ADVANCED

Have children work with a partner and make up their own question about a photograph that shows a person doing a job. Tell the partner to guess what job is being described.

ENGLISH-LANGUAGE LEARNERS

Page through *Guess Who?*, pausing at several photographs. Read each word as you point to the object in the photograph. Then have children use the following sentence frame to describe the photographs: *I see a _____.*

ONGOING ASSESSMENT

As you share *Guess Who?*, note whether children

- describe people, things, and actions.
- connect text to life experiences.

FLORIDA STANDARDS/GLEs **FCAT: LA.A.1.1.3.K.4** Build vocabulary; **LA.A.1.1.3.K.5** Story elements; **LA.A.1.1.4.K.1** Comprehension; **LA.A.2.1.1.K.1** Main idea; **LA.A.2.1.3.K.1** Supportive details; *Also*: **LA.A.1.1.1.K.1** Predictions; **LA.A.1.1.3.K.2** Nouns and verbs; **LA.A.2.1.4.K.1** Illustrations; **LA.C.3.1.2.K.1** Questions; **LA.E.2.1.1.K.1** Background knowledge

OBJECTIVES

- To find letter patterns in words

- To blend letter patterns to read words

Materials

- Write-On/ Wipe-Off Boards

- chart paper

- marker

Phonics

Phonogram -et ✓ Introduce

ACTIVE BEGINNING

Say a Rhyme Teach children the following rhyme. Have them clap as they say the words.

My wet pet is stuck in a net.

Get the vet for my wet pet.

TEACH/MODEL

Discriminate Sounds Say the words *wet* and *pet* and have children repeat them. Ask how the two words are the same. (They both have /et/; they rhyme.) Tell children that you are going to say some words and that they should give a "thumbs-up" when they hear a word that rhymes with *pet*:

| get | den | fret | red | yet | let |

Build -*et* Words Write the word *pet* on chart paper. Track the print as children read the word. Then write the word *net*. Again, track the print as children read the word. Ask children to read the two words and have them tell how they are the same. (They have *e* and *t*; they rhyme.) Continue by writing the word *jet* and having children read the word.

pet
net
jet

FLORIDA STANDARDS/GLEs FCAT: LA.A.1.1.2.K.5 Phonetic principles; *Also* LA.C.1.1.1.K.1 Follow directions; LA.D.1.1.1.K.1 Sound patterns; LA.D.2.1.2.K.1 Patterned structures

PRACTICE/APPLY

Guided Practice Tell children that you will say some words. If the word rhymes with *get*, ask them to write the word on their *a child* *the chart* *Write-On/Wipe-Off Board*. Have them use the chart with *-et* words as a reference. *whole group*

| rock | net | pet | tip | sell | did | jet |

Independent Practice Distribute to children paper with the sentence frame *I have a _____*. Have children complete the sentence, using one of the words written on the chart paper. Then have them illustrate their sentence.

I have a **jet**.

FLORIDA STANDARDS/GLEs **FCAT: LA.A.1.1.2.K.5** Phonetic principles; **LA.A.1.1.3.K.4** Build vocabulary; **LA.B.2.1.2.K.1** Record ideas; *Also* **LA.A.1.1.3.K.2** Nouns and verbs; **LA.B.1.1.1.K.1** Prewriting; **LA.B.1.1.2.K.2** Basic formats; **LA.B.1.1.3.K.2** Print direction; **LA.B.1.1.3.K.3** Punctuation; **LA.C.1.1.1.K.1** Follow directions

BELOW-LEVEL

Have children use Elkonin boxes to work on sounds they hear in the words. Ask them to move markers into the boxes for *pet*, *net*, *wet*, and *get*.

ADVANCED

Encourage children to write other words that belong in the *-et* family.

early spelling

Have children write in their journals one of the *-et* words from their *Write-On/Wipe-Off Board*.

▲ **Practice Book page 19**

h.w.

Neighborhood Helpers   **303**

OBJECTIVES

- *To discuss a writing topic*

Writing Every Day

Day 1: Prewrite
Help children choose a neighbor-hood helper to describe.

Day 2: Draft
Have children use descriptions from an idea web to create and write sentences.

Day 3: Respond and Revise
Children will work together to add descriptive words to their sentences.

Day 4: Edit
Children will proofread their sentences.

Day 5: Publish
Children will publish the sentences on a poster.

---

works in a bakery shop

likes to make bread

says, "Can I help you?"

Baker

uses an oven

wears an apron and a hat

Writing Process

Write a Description

PREWRITE

Recall Characters   Page through *Guess Who?* and have children name all of the neighborhood helpers in the story. Help them remember the jobs the people do as well as their appearance.

Talk About a Description   Tell children that a description gives clues about something. Play the game "I Spy" with children. Tell them you will give clues and they will listen and try to picture what you are describing.

MODEL   *I see something soft. It likes carrots. It likes to break words into parts.* (the rabbit puppet) **I used what I know about rabbits and also what I know about the rabbit puppet to describe it. I thought about what rabbits feel like and what they eat.**

Hold up the rabbit puppet and ask children to suggest other clues to describe the rabbit.

List Writing Ideas   Tell children that they will write a description about one of the people from *Guess Who?* Ask a child to choose from the Library Book one of the people that he or she thinks the whole class would like to write about. Have children help you describe the job in an idea web. Ask the following questions to help children fill in the web with descriptions:

- Where does the baker work?

- What does the baker wear?

- What does the baker like to do?

- What does a baker like to say to people who come into the bakery?

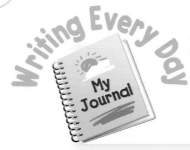

Journal Writing Have children draw and write a question and an answer.

FLORIDA STANDARDS/GLEs   FCAT: LA.A.1.1.2.K.6 Print meaning; **LA.A.1.1.3.K.4** Build vocabulary; *Also* **LA.A.1.1.3.K.1** Frequent words;   **LA.B.1.1.2.K.2** Basic formats; **LA.B.1.1.3.K.2** Print direction; **LA.B.1.1.3.K.3** Punctuation; **LA.B.2.1.1.K.2** Contribute ideas; **LA.C.3.1.2.K.1** Questions

WRAP UP # Share Time

Reflect on the Lesson   Ask children to tell which photograph they liked best in *Guess Who?* Have them explain why. Ask them to tell what they might like to do when they grow up.

S.S.R.   Have children read silently from a book of their choice.

 **Centers**    **WRITING**

Who, What, and Where Silly Sentences

Place P*icture/Word Cards* and drawing paper at the center. Have children choose a *Picture/Word Card* that shows a person and one that shows a place. Ask children to write a silly sentence using the two cards and to illustrate it.

Materials

- *Picture/Word Cards baby, boy, bus, car, doctor, firefighter, gate, girl, helicopter, jeep, jet, king, moon, nest, nurse, queen, van, wagon, water, zoo*

- drawing paper

- crayons

The kng is on the mon.

FLORIDA STANDARDS/GLEs   FCAT: LA.A.1.1.3.K.4 Build vocabulary; **LA.A.1.1.4.K.1** Comprehension; **LA.A.2.1.3.K.1** Supportive details; **LA.B.2.1.2.K.1** Record ideas; *Also* **LA.B.1.1.1.K.1** Prewriting; **LA.B.1.1.2.K.2** Basic formats; **LA.B.1.1.3.K.2** Print direction; **LA.A.1.1.3.K.2** Nouns and verbs; **LA.C.3.1.2.K.1** Questions

Neighborhood Helpers   305

Day 2

Phonemic Awareness
Phoneme Substitution

Sharing Literature
Read Aloud Anthology: "The Town Mouse and the Country Mouse"

Read

KINDERGARTEN
READ-ALOUD
Anthology
Harcourt

Respond to Literature

Literature Focus: Setting

Phonics
Phonogram *-en*

Interactive Writing
Writing Process: Draft

WARM UP

MORNING MESSAGE

Kindergarten News

(Child's name)'s favorite food is

_____ .

Write Kindergarten News Talk with children about favorite foods. Ask them to tell about new foods they have tried.

Use prompts such as the following to guide children as you write the news:

- **Who can name a new food you have tried?**
- **What letter will I write first in (child's name)?**
- **Let's count the letters in (child's name). How many letters are there?**

As you write the message, invite children to contribute by writing letters, words, or names they have previously learned. Remind them to use proper spacing, capitalization, and punctuation.

Calendar Language

Point to and read aloud the months of the year. Tell children there are 12 months in a year. Point to and name the current month. Ask: *What month is it?*

Sunday	Monday	Tuesday	Wednesday	Thursday	Friday	Saturday
		1	2	3	4	5
6	7	8	9	10	11	12
13	14	15	16	17	18	19
20	21	22	23	24	25	26
27	28	29	30	31		

FLORIDA STANDARDS/GLEs FCAT: LA.A.1.1.2.K.6 Print meaning; *Also* LA.A.1.1.2.K.2 Alphabet; LA.A.1.1.3.K.1 Frequent words; LA.A.1.1.3.K.2 nouns and verbs; LA.B.1.1.3.K.2 Print direction; LA.B.2.1.1.K.2 Contribute ideas; LA.C.1.1.3.K.1 Conversation rules; LA.C.3.1.2.K.1 Questions

Phonemic Awareness

PHONEME SUBSTITUTION

Replacing initial phonemes   Say the word *red* and have children tell the sound they hear at the beginning of the word. (/r/)

Say: **Now instead of /r/, say /l/. What is the new word?** (*led*)

Say: *den*. **Now instead of /d/, say /t/. What is the new word?** (*ten*)

Continue in this manner, having children replace initial phonemes and say new words.

Say *wed*. Now instead of /w/, say /f/. What is the new word? (*fed*)

Say *get*. Now instead of /g/, say /v/. What is the new word? (*vet*)

Say *men*. Now instead of /m/, say /p/. What is the new word? (*pen*)

Say *Ben*. Now instead of /b/, say /j/. What is the new word? (*Jen*)

Say *ten*. Now instead of /t/, say /h/. What is the new word? (*hen*)

Sharing Literature

Read "The Town Mouse and the Country Mouse"

READ ALOUD

Before Reading   Turn to "The Town Mouse and the Country Mouse" and read the title aloud. Model for children how to summarize what the story is about:

MODEL   I remember that this story is about two mice who are cousins. One mouse lives in the country. One mouse lives in the city. The mice visit each other.

During Reading   Read the story aloud. As you read,

- pause at the beginning, middle, and ending of the story and have children answer these questions:

What happens in the beginning of the story? (The Town Mouse visits the Country Mouse.)

What happens in the middle of the story? (The Country Mouse goes home with the Town Mouse.)

What happens in the ending of the story? (Possible responses: The Country Mouse goes back to the country; each mouse decides that he likes his own house best.)

▲ **Read-Aloud Anthology**

OBJECTIVES

- *To understand characters*
- *To summarize story events*
- *To share information and ideas, speaking audibly in complete, coherent sentences*
- *To connect to life experiences*
- *To describe locations*
- *To understand setting*

Materials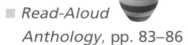

- ■ *Read-Aloud Anthology, pp. 83–86*
- ■ drawing paper
- ■ crayons or markers

FLORIDA STANDARDS/GLEs   FCAT: LA.E.1.1.2.K.1 Story elements; **LA.A.1.1.3.K.5** Story elements; **LA.C.1.1.4.K.1** Sequence; *Also* **LA.C.3.1.2.K.1** Questions; **LA.E.2.1.1.K.1** Background knowledge

RESPOND TO LITERATURE

Draw Favorite Homes Ask children to decide which mouse has a better life, the Town Mouse or the Country Mouse. Discuss the two different homes and ask children to tell why they would prefer to live in one home or the other. Have children draw a picture of the home they prefer. Ask children to write *I like the country* or *I like the town.*

I like the cuntre.

SETTING

Tell children that the setting is where a story takes place. Ask children to name the places in "The Town Mouse and the Country Mouse." (city and country) Use this model to describe the settings.

MODEL In the country, there are fields, a river, and lots of flowers growing. I think that it must be quiet enough that you can hear the birds chirp. In town, there are lots of houses with people, and horses and carriages on the streets. I think that it must be noisy.

BELOW-LEVEL

Invite children to look out the window of your classroom and describe what they see. Tell them that they are describing the setting of the school. Ask them to describe their neighborhood.

ONGOING ASSESSMENT

As you share "The Town Mouse and the Country Mouse," note whether children

- share story events.
- speak using complete sentences.

FLORIDA STANDARDS/GLEs FCAT: LA.A.1.1.2.K.6 Print meaning; **LA.A.1.1.3.K.5** Story elements; **LA.A.1.1.4.K.1** Comprehension; **LA.B.2.1.2.K.1** Record ideas; **LA.E.1.1.2.K.1** Story elements; *Also* **LA.A.2.1.4.K.1** Illustrations; **LA.B.1.1.1.K.2** Generate ideas; **LA.B.1.1.3.K.2** Print direction; **LA.E.2.1.1.K.1** Background knowledge

Phonics

Phonogram -en  Introduce

OBJECTIVES

- *To find letter patterns in words*
- *To blend letter patterns to read words*

Materials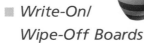

- *Write-On/ Wipe-Off Boards*
- chart paper
- marker

ACTIVE BEGINNING

Say a Rhyme   Teach children the following rhyme. Have them clap as they say the words.

> One hen in a pen.
>
> Two hens in a den.
>
> One hen, two hens
>
> Hen, pen, hens, den!

ten

den

hen

TEACH/MODEL

Discriminate Sounds   Say the words *when* and *men* and have children repeat them. Ask how the two words are the same. (They both have /-en/; they rhyme.) Tell children that you are going to say some words and that they should give a "thumbs-up" when they hear a word that rhymes with *men*:

| then | hat | den | cup | pen | hen |

Build -en Words   Write the word *ten* on chart paper. Track the print as children read the word. Then write the word *den*. Again, track the print as children read the word. Ask children to read the two words and have them tell how they are the same. (They have *e* and *n*; they rhyme.) Continue by writing the word *hen* and having children read the word.

FLORIDA STANDARDS/GLEs   FCAT: LA.A.1.1.2.K.5 Phonetic principles; *Also* **LA.A.1.1.2.K.3** Sounds; **LA.C.3.1.1.K.1** Speak clearly; **LA.D.1.1.1.K.1** Sound patterns; **LA.D.2.1.2.K.1** Patterned structures

PRATICE/APPLY

Guided Practice Tell children that you will say some words. If the word rhymes with *men*, have them write the word on their *Write-On/Wipe-Off Board*. Have them use the chart with *-en* words as a reference.

Whole group

well   hen   den   sap   when   sock   pen

Independent Practice Distribute to children paper with the sentence frame *It is a _____.* Have children complete the sentence, using one of the words written on the chart paper. Then have them illustrate their sentence.

It is a **hen**.

FLORIDA STANDARDS/GLEs   FCAT: **LA.A.1.1.2.K.5** Phonetic principles; *Also* **LA.A.1.1.2.K.1** Print organization; **LA.A.1.1.2.K.2** Alphabet; **LA.A.1.1.2.K.3** Sounds; **LA.A.1.1.3.K.1** Frequent words **LA.B.1.1.2.K.2** Basic formats; **LA.B.1.1.3.K.2** Print direction

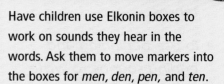

BELOW-LEVEL

Have children use Elkonin boxes to work on sounds they hear in the words. Ask them to move markers into the boxes for *men*, *den*, *pen*, and *ten*.

early spelling

Have children write in their journals one of the *-en* words from their *Write-On/Wipe-Off Board*.

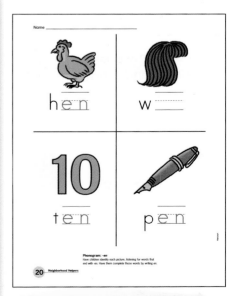

▲ **Practice Book page 20**

hw

Neighborhood Helpers   311

Writing Process

Write a Description

DRAFT

Reread the Description   Hold up the picture of the baker in Guess Who? and have a child point to the baker. Then, reread on page 304 the descriptions in the idea web and remind children of the neighborhood helper they have decided to describe. Model for children how to use the words on the web in a sentence.

MODEL **Let's choose the words *works in a bakery shop* from our web. I will use these words in a sentence: The baker works in a bakery shop. When I write this sentence, I will remember to begin with an uppercase letter and end with a period.**

Have them suggest another phrase from the idea web to write on the chart. If they need help getting started, suggest that they tell who is in the story and when it happens.

Help children orally compose the content of the first sentence; when you are ready to write it, ask questions like these:

- **Where should I start writing on the chart paper?**
- **How shall we begin our first sentence?**
- **Who can write the first word, *The*?**
- **Who can look on the word chart to find the word *like*? Who will write it? What letter stands for the last sound?**
- **Listen to the ending of the word *bread*. What letter stands for the last sound?**
- **Who can make a sentence using other words on the idea web?**

Say each word aloud as you write. Reread the printed sentences often to help children recall the topic. Encourage several different children to take turns telling their ideas about the sentence to use next.

A baker works in a bakery.

A baker wears an apron and a hat.

A baker likes to bake bread.

A baker uses an oven.

A baker says, "Can I help you?"

Writing Every Day

My Journal

Journal Writing   Have children draw and label their favorite food.

FLORIDA STANDARDS/GLEs   FCAT: LA.A.1.1.2.K.4 Words; **LA.A.1.1.2.K.5** Phonetic principles; **LA.A.1.1.3.K.5** Story elements; **LA.A.1.1.2.K.6** Print meaning; *Also* **LA.A.1.1.2.K.1** Print organization; **LA.A.1.1.2.K.2** Alphabet; **LA.A.1.1.2.K.3** Sounds; **LA.A.1.1.3.K.2** Nouns and verbs **LA.B.1.1.1.K.2** Generate ideas; **LA.B.1.1.2.K.2** Basic formats; **LA.B.1.1.3.K.2** Print direction; **LA.B.2.1.1.K.2** Contribute ideas;

WRAP UP Share Time

Author's Chair   Have children read the sentence on their drawing from the Sharing Literature activity. Ask them to tell why they prefer one place over the other.

S.S.R. Sustained Silent Reading   Have children read silently from a book of their choice.

Centers   COOKING

Town Treats and Country Nibbles

Invite children to make snacks that they might share with Town Mouse or Country Mouse. Place each snack into a bowl. On index cards, write the name of the food and place it near the food. Have children make their own combinations of ingredients for a snack. Provide drawing paper for children to write a menu of the snacks they choose to eat.

Note: Food allergies can cause potentially dangerous reactions. Check with parents about possible allergies before working with or offering children food to eat in class.

Materials

- various snacks such as sunflower seeds, popcorn, fish-shaped crackers, raisins, grapes

- bowls and spoons

- drawing paper

- crayons

Popcorn

Grapes

Sunflower Seeds

FLORIDA STANDARDS/GLEs   **FCAT: LA.A.1.1.2.K.4** Words; **LA.A.1.1.2.K.6** Print meaning; **LA.A.1.1.3.K.4** Build vocabulary; **LA.A.1.1.4.K.1** Comprehension; *Also* **LA.A.1.1.3.K.2** Nouns and verbs; **LA.B.1.1.1.K.1** Prewriting; **LA.B.1.1.2.K.2** Basic formats; **LA.C.1.1.3.K.1** Conversation rules

WARM UP

Phonemic Awareness
Phoneme Segmentation

Sharing Literature
Big Book:
The Big Yellow Bus

Read

The Big Yellow Bus
Illustrated by Lorinda Bryan Cauley

Respond to Literature
Literature Focus: Retell the Story

Phonics
Phonogram *-ed*

Interactive Writing
Writing Process: Respond and Revise

MORNING MESSAGE
Kindergarten News

Today is _____.

The weather today is _____.

Write Kindergarten News Talk with children about the weather. Have them describe today's weather.

Use prompts such as the following to guide children as you write the news:

- **Who can tell what the weather is today?**
- **Who can point to where to begin reading?**
- **Who can show me a sentence?**

As you write the message, invite children to contribute by writing letters, words, or names they have previously learned. Remind them to use proper spacing, capitalization, and punctuation.

Calendar Language

Point to and read aloud the days of the week. Have children say the days of the week with you. Say: *Today is _____.* Ask: *What day is today?*

Sunday	Monday	Tuesday	Wednesday	Thursday	Friday	Saturday
		1	2	3	4	5
6	7	8	9	10	11	12
13	14	15	16	17	18	19
20	21	22	23	24	25	26
27	28	29	30	31		

FLORIDA STANDARDS/GLEs   FCAT: LA.A.1.1.2.K.4 Words; **LA.A.1.1.2.K.5** Phonetic principles; *Also* **LA.A.1.1.2.K.1** Print organization; **LA.A.1.1.3.K.1** Frequent words; **LA.B.1.1.3.K.2** Print direction; **LA.B.2.1.1.K.2** Contribute ideas; **LA.C.1.1.3.K.1** Conversation rules; **LA.C.3.1.2.K.1** Questions

Phonemic Awareness

PHONEME SEGMENTATION

Segmenting Sounds   Distribute three disks and Side B of the Write-On/Wipe-Off Board to each child. Have them point to the heart and tell them to use the boxes next to it. Use the rabbit puppet to model for children how to segment phonemes. Tell children they will listen for the sounds they hear in words you say.

MODEL   *pet.* **How many sounds do you hear in** *pet?* *pet* **I hear /p/. I hear /e/. I hear /t/. /p/ /e/ /t/ I hear three sounds in** *pet.* **Place a disk in a box for each sound you hear.** ✳ *hold up a finger for each sound*

Have children repeat the rabbit and follow the same procedure for these words: **ten**   /t/ /e/ /n/   **set**   /s/ /e/ /t/

I hear three sounds in *ten.* **I hear three sounds in** *set.*

fed   /f/ /e/ /d/   **red**   /r/ /e/ /d/

I hear three sounds in *fed.* **I hear three sounds in** *red.*

Tell children to listen as the rabbit says each word. Ask them to say the sounds they hear in each word.

wet	/w/ /e/ /t/	**hen**	/h/ /e/ /n/
bed	/b/ /e/ /d/	**get**	/g/ /e/ /t/
lid	/l/ /i/ /d/	**let**	/l/ /e/ /t/

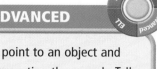

/b/ /e/ /d/

FLORIDA STANDARDS/GLEs   FCAT: LA.A.1.1.2.K.5 Phonetic principles; *Also* **LA.A.1.1.2.K.3** Sounds; **LA.C.1.1.1.K.1** Follow directions

▲ **Big Book**

OBJECTIVES

To listen and respond to a story

To identify setting

To retell the story

Materials

■ *Big Book:*
  The Big Yellow Bus

■ chart paper

■ markers

LEARNING TO READ

Sharing Literature

Read The Big Yellow Bus

READ ALOUD

Before Reading   Display *The Big Yellow Bus.* Track the print as you read the title aloud. Use these prompts to help children identify the story setting:

• **What do the animals ride on?** (a school bus)

> **MODEL** This story happens on a school bus. When the bus stops, animals get on. The bus travels through the town and stops at the school. The setting of this story is on the school bus.

• **When does the story take place?** (in the morning)

During Reading   Read the story aloud. As you read,

• emphasize the rhythm of the story by swaying back and forth.

• pause to point out who and what the zebra sees around him in the setting on the bus.

The big yellow bus comes
down the street;
down the street;
down the street.

4

FLORIDA STANDARDS/GLEs   FCAT: LA.A.1.1.3.K.5 Story elements; **LA.A.1.1.4.K.1** Comprehension; *Also* **LA.A.1.1.2.K.1** Print organization; **LA.C.1.1.1.K.2** Oral language; **LA.C.3.1.2.K.1** Questions; **LA.E.2.1.1.K.1** Background knowledge

RESPOND TO LITERATURE

Make Up a New Verse Tell children they can make up a new verse for the *Big Book.* Ask them to name other animals that might get on the bus, such as a cat, a dog, or a duck. Write the animal names in the verse on chart paper. Have them suggest the sounds the animals make, and write the words in the verse. Read the verse aloud as you track the print. Have children recite the verse with you.

The cats on the bus go,
"Meow, meow, meow,"
on the way to school.

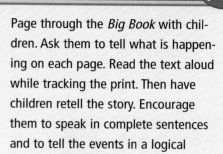

BELOW-LEVEL

Page through the *Big Book* with children. Ask them to tell what is happening on each page. Read the text aloud while tracking the print. Then have children retell the story. Encourage them to speak in complete sentences and to tell the events in a logical order, using the pictures.

ONGOING ASSESSMENT

As you share *The Big Yellow Bus,* note whether children

• listen and understand a story.

• identify features of the story setting.

Literature Focus

RETELL THE STORY

Tell children that when you retell a story, you think about who the characters are and the things that happen. Use these prompts to help children recall story events:

• **Who are the characters in the story?** (bus driver, zebras, yaks, lions, and sheep)

• **What happens first in the story?** (The bus comes down the street.)

• **What happens next?** (The animals get on the bus.)

• **What happens last in the story?** (The bus stops at the school.)

In this story, a school bus comes down the street. First the zebras get on the bus, then the yaks get on the bus, next the lions get on the bus, and finally the sheep get on the bus. All the animals say things as they ride on the bus. At the end of the story, the bus stops at the school.

FLORIDA STANDARDS/GLEs **FCAT: LA.A.1.1.2.K.4** Words; **LA.A.1.1.2.K.6** Print meaning; **LA.A.1.1.4.K.1** Comprehension; **LA.E.1.1.2.K.1** Story elements; *Also* **LA.A.1.1.2.K.1** Print organization; **LA.A.1.1.3.K.1** Frequent words; **LA.C.3.1.2.K.1** Questions; **LA.D.1.1.1.K.1** Sound patterns

Neighborhood Helpers **317**

Phonogram -ed ✔ Introduce

OBJECTIVES

To find letter patterns in words

To blend letter patterns to read words

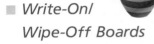

Materials

■ *Write-On/ Wipe-Off Boards*

■ chart paper

■ marker

ACTIVE BEGINNING

Say a Rhyme   Teach children the following silly rhyme. Have them clap as they say the words.

Ned the dog wanted to be fed.

Ned led Ted to a bowl that was red.

Ted fed Ned. They both went to bed.

TEACH/MODEL

Discriminate Sounds   Say the words *sled* and *bed* and have children repeat them. Ask how the two words are the same. (They both have /ed/; they rhyme.) Tell children that you are going to say some words and that they should give a "thumbs-up" when they hear a word that rhymes with *bed*:

led	yes	shed	ear	red	fed

Build *-ed* Words   Write the word *bed* on chart paper. Track the print as children read the word. Then write the word *red*. Again, track the print as children read the word. Ask children to read the two words and have them tell how they are the same. (They have *e* and *d*; they rhyme.) Continue by writing the word *fed* and having children read the word.

bed
red
fed

FLORIDA STANDARDS/GLEs   FCAT: LA.A.1.1.2.K.5 Phonetic principles; *Also* **LA.A.1.1.2.K.3** Sounds; **LA.C.3.1.1.K.1** Speak clearly; **LA.D.1.1.1.K.1** Sound patterns; **LA.D.2.1.2.K.1** Patterned structures

PRACTICE/APPLY

Guided Practice   Tell children that you will say some words. If the word rhymes with *bed*, have them write the word on their *Write-On/Wipe-Off Board*. Have them use the chart with *-ed* words as a reference.

| sit | bed | red | pin | fed | top | tap |

Independent Practice   Distribute to children paper with the sentence frame *The _____ is _____.* Have children complete the sentence, using two of the words written on the chart paper. Then have them illustrate their sentence.

The bed is red

Diagnostic Check: Phonics

If... children cannot blend letters to read *-ed* words,

Then... have them use their Elkonin boxes to segment sounds they hear in the words *bed, red,* and *fed*.

ADDITIONAL SUPPORT ACTIVITIES

BELOW-LEVEL	Reteach, p. S34
ADVANCED	Extend, p. S35
ENGLISH-LANGUAGE LEARNERS	Reteach, p. S35

early spelling

Have children write in their journals one of the *-ed* words from their *Write-On/Wipe-Off Board*.

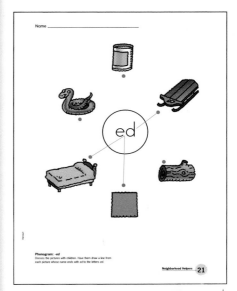

▲ **Practice Book page 21**

Neighborhood Helpers   **319**

OBJECTIVE

To use specific language to describe a neighborhood helper

Materials

- written sentences p. 312
- *Library Book: Guess Who?*
- chart paper
- marker

Writing Process

Write a Description

RESPOND AND REVISE

Make Changes   Reread the description, tracking the words. Ask children to think about the clues that they have used to describe their neighborhood helper. Have children talk about how they could make the clues clearer and more descriptive. Ask questions like these:

- **Is there anything else we need to add to our description?**
- **Instead of repeating the words, *A baker*, what else could we write?**
- **What else could we add to help readers picture the baker?**
- **What can we add to give more information about the baker?**
- **Our description needs a title. Who has an idea for one?**
- **Who will help me write the first uppercase letter?**

Make changes as they are suggested by children. You may want to use a red marker to show the changes on the chart paper. Add a title suggested by the children.

> A Baker at Keely's Bakery
>
> Keely's bakery is near our school.
>
> A baker works there.
>
> He wears an apron and a hat.
>
> He uses an oven to bake bread.
>
> The baker says, "Can I help you?" when you walk to the counter.
>
> I like to eat bread the baker makes at Keely's bakery.

Self-Selected Writing Have children draw and write about anything they'd like. If they have difficulty thinking of a topic, have them ask two friends what they're going to write about.

FLORIDA STANDARDS/GLEs   FCAT: **LA.A.1.1.2.K.4** Words; **LA.A.1.1.3.K.4** Build vocabulary; **LA.A.1.1.3.K.5** Story elements; *Also* **LA.B.1.1.1.K.2** Generate ideas; **LA.B.1.1.2.K.2** Basic formats; **LA.B.1.1.3.K.1** Spelling approximations; **LA.B.1.1.3.K.2** Print direction; **LA.C.3.1.1.K.1** Speak clearly

WRAP UP Share Time

Author's Chair   Invite children to use Author's Chair to share their drawings and sentences about people who help them in the school.

S.S.R. *Sustained Silent Reading*   Have children read silently from a book of their choice.

Centers

LETTERS AND WORDS

Drive Through "Letter Town"

Enlarge and copy the game board and glue it to poster board. Mark the first square *GO* with a green traffic light and the last square *STOP* with a stop sign. On the remaining squares, print the lowercase letters *y, n, e, v, j, x, w, o, k, b, r.* Do the same with uppercase letters. Print the same letters on index cards. Ask children to choose a card and name the letter and its sound. Then have them move their car to the next square that matches that letter. Children can keep drawing cards until their car gets to STOP.

Materials

- *Teacher's Resource Book*, p. 157
- poster board
- glue
- index cards
- toy cars

WARM UP

Phonemic Awareness
Phoneme Substitution

Sharing Literature
Read-Aloud Anthology:
"This Is the Way We Go to School"

Read

Respond to Literature

Literature Focus: Text Patterns

Phonics
Phonograms *-et, ed, en*

Reading
Decodable Book 12: *A Hat I Like*

Interactive Writing ✏️
Writing Process: Edit

MORNING MESSAGE

Kindergarten News

(child's name)'s favorite song is
(name of song).

Write Kindergarten News   Talk with children about their favorite songs.

Use prompts such as the following to guide children as you write the news:

- **Who has a favorite song? What is it?**
- **What letter will I write last in (child's name)?**
- **Who can show me where (child's name) begins and ends?**
- **Let's count the letters in (child's name). How many letters are there?**

As you write the message, invite children to contribute by writing letters, words, or names they have previously learned. Remind them to use proper spacing, capitalization, and punctuation.

Calendar Language

Point to and read aloud the days of the week. Tell children you will name the school days. Point to and read aloud *Monday* through *Friday. Say the schools days with me: Monday, Tuesday, Wednesday, Thursday, and Friday.*

Sunday	Monday	Tuesday	Wednesday	Thursday	Friday	Saturday
		1	2	3	4	5
6	7	8	9	10	11	12
13	14	15	16	17	18	19
20	21	22	23	24	25	26
27	28	29	30	31		

FLORIDA STANDARDS/GLEs   FCAT: LA.A.1.1.2.K.4 Words; **LA.A.1.1.2.K.5** Phonetic principles; *Also*
LA.A.1.1.2.K.1 Print organization; **LA.A.1.1.3.K.1** Frequent words;   **LA.A.1.1.3.K.2** Nouns and verbs;
LA.B.2.1.1.K.2 Contribute ideas; **LA.C.1.1.3.K.1** Conversation rules; **LA.C.3.1.2.K.1** Questions

Phonemic Awareness

PHONEME SUBSTITUTION

Substituting Initial Phonemes Say the word *hen* and have children tell the sound they hear at the beginning of the word. (/h/) Tell children they can say a different sound at the beginning of a word to make a new word.

MODEL *hen.* **What sound do you hear at the beginning of the word?** (/h/)

Change the /h/ to /p/.

What is the new word? pen

Continue in this manner, having children replace initial phonemes and say new words.

Say *red*. Now instead of /r/, say /b/. What is the new word? (*bed*)

Say *Jen*. Now instead of /j/, say /k/. What is the new word? (*Ken*)

Say *led*. Now instead of /l/, say /f/. What is the new word? (*fed*)

Say *vet*. Now instead of /v/, say /m/. What is the new word? (*met*)

Say *Ned*. Now instead of /n/, say /t/. What is the new word? (*Ted*)

BELOW-LEVEL

Say *red* slowly, elongating the sounds, and identifying the sounds you hear in the word: /r/ /e/ /d/. Have children do the same. Then say: *I'll say /b/ instead of /r/: /b/ /e/ /d/.* Have children do the same. *What word did we say?* (bed) Follow the same procedure for *red* and *led*, *red* and *fed*, *red* and *Ted*.

ADVANCED

Have children practice the skill with the words *ten-men-den; set-wet-pet; red-bed-led.*

FLORIDA STANDARDS/GLEs   FCAT: LA.A.1.1.2.K.5 Phonetic principles; *Also* LA.A.1.1.2.K.3 Sounds; LA.C.3.1.1.K.1 Speak clearly

Neighborhood Helpers   323

Sharing Literature

Read "This Is the Way We Go to School"

READ ALOUD

Before Reading   Turn to page 121 of the *Read-Aloud Anthology* and read the title aloud. Tell children they will learn a song about going to school. Use these prompts to build background:

- **How do you get to school?** (Possible response: I ride to school on the bus.)

- **What types of buildings and people do you see on the way to school?** (Possible response: I see the grocery store where my aunt works.)

During Reading   Read the song aloud. As you read,

- have children repeat the lines after you.

- have children clap the syllables with you.

Play the song, which is recorded on the *Music CD*. Encourage children to join in.

▲ **Read-Aloud Anthology**

OBJECTIVES

- *To listen and respond to a song*

- *To innovate on a song*

- *To understand text patterns*

Materials

- *Read-Aloud Anthology* p. 121

- *Music CD*

- chart paper

- marker

FLORIDA STANDARDS/GLEs   FCAT: LA.A.1.1.4.K.1 Comprehension; **LA.A.2.1.1.K.1** Main idea; **LA.E.1.1.1.K.1** Genres;   *Also* **LA.B.2.1.4.K.1** Informational texts; **LA.C.3.1.2.K.1** Questions

RESPOND TO LITERATURE

Innovate on the Song   Have children brainstorm a list of activities children do in school. Write the list on chart paper. Then invite children to make up new verses to "This Is the Way We Go to School," based on some of the activities listed. Encourage them to make up actions to accompany each verse.

Examples might include:

This is the way we build with blocks.

(Put one hand on top of the other.)

This is the way we write our name.

(Write with one finger on the palm of the other hand.)

Read each new phrase aloud; then have children sing and act out the new verse.

This is the way we build with blocks.

This is the way we write our name.

This is the way we read a book.

This is the way we count to ten.

REACHING ALL LEARNERS

Diagnostic Check: Comprehension

If... children cannot identify text patterns,

Then... have children clap with you as you say the repeated words in each verse of the song.

ADDITIONAL SUPPORT ACTIVITIES

BELOW-LEVEL	Reteach, p. S36
ADVANCED	Extend, p. S37
ENGLISH-LANGUAGE LEARNERS	Reteach, p. S37

ONGOING ASSESSMENT

As you share "This Is the Way We Go to School," note whether children

• listen and sing along.

• offer suggestions for innovating on the song.

Literature Focus

TEXT PATTERNS

Sing or play the song again, and have children listen for words they hear over and over. (go to school)

Explain that sometimes words are repeated many times in a song, which makes them easier to remember. Then have children sing the new verses they made up, and identify the words they say over and over.

FLORIDA STANDARDS/GLEs   FCAT: **LA.A.1.1.2.K.4** Words; **LA.A.1.1.3.K.4** Build vocabulary; *Also* **LA.C.1.1.1.K.1** Follow directions; **LA.C.1.1.1.K.2** Oral language; **LA.C.2.1.2.K.1** Nonverbal cues; **LA.D.1.1.1.K.1** Sound patterns

Neighborhood Helpers   325

OBJECTIVE

To decode phonogram words

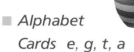

Materials

- *Alphabet Cards e, g, t, a*
- index cards with words *Can, hat, it*
- *High-Frequency Word Cards I, like*
- pocket chart
- *Decodable Book 12: A Hat I Like*

BELOW-LEVEL

Reread the story with children. Have them frame the high-frequency words *I, like, the, my.* Guide them to blend the sounds for *hat, yet, get, Jen, Ted.*

ADVANCED

Have children read *Independent Reader 29: Neighborhood Friends.*

Phonics

Phonograms *-et, -ed, -en*  Review

TEACH/MODEL

Review Blending   Place *Alphabet Cards e* and *t* next to one another in a pocket chart. Move your hand under the letters, blend them, and say **/eett/ -et.** Have children blend the sounds.

Place *Alphabet Card g* in front of *e* and *t.* Slide your hand under the letters, blend them, and say the word: **/ggeett/ get.** Have children blend the sounds and say the word.

Place the index card *Can* and the *High-Frequency Word Card I* in the pocket chart in front of *get.* Place the *Alphabet Card a* and the word cards *hat, like,* and *it* after the word *get,* and add a question mark at the end. Track the print as children read the words: **Can I get a hat like it?**

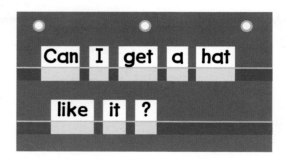

PRACTICE/APPLY

Read the Book   Distribute copies of *A Hat I Like.* Have children read the title and encourage them to point to each word as they read it. Tell children to point to each word as they read the book.

Respond   Have children tell about other kinds of hats that people wear. (Possible responses: chef's hat, hard hat, Western hat, helmet, baseball cap, or magician's hat)

 FLORIDA STANDARDS/GLEs   FCAT: LA.A.1.1.2.K.5 Phonetic principles; *Also* **LA.A.1.1.2.K.1** Print organization; **LA.A.1.1.2.K.3** Sounds; **LA.C.1.1.3.K.1** Conversation rules

Decodable Book 12: *"A Hat I Like"*

I see a hat I like, Dad.
Can I get a hat like it?

2

Not yet, Jen.

3

Look at the hat, Mom.
Can I get a hat like it?

4

Not yet, Ted.

5

I see a hat I like, Dad.
Can I get a hat like it?

6

Not yet, Nan.

7

You can get a hat like me!

8

■ High-Frequency Words

like, see, me, look, the, you

■ Decodable Words

See Word List on page T15.

School–Home Connection

Take-Home Book Version

◀ Decodable Book 12
A Hat I Like

by Alexa Padilla
illustrated by Pat Porter

▲ *Neighborhood Friends*
Independent Reader 29

OBJECTIVES

To locate the beginning and ending of a sentence

To recognize uppercase and lowercase letters and ending punctuation

Materials

- written sentences p. 320
- correction tape
- marker

Writing Process

Write a Description

PROOFREAD

Make Final Changes   Model how to proofread a story by asking questions such as:

- **Who can point to the title? Did we begin each word with an uppercase letter in our title?**

- **Do all of the sentences tell us something about the baker?**

- **Who can find the beginning of a sentence? Did we start the sentence with an uppercase letter? Where is the end of the sentence? Is there a period?**

Have children help you make changes on the chart paper using correction tape and a marker. Talk aloud as they make each change.

Self-Selected Writing Have children draw and write about anything they'd like. If they have difficulty thinking of a topic, have them ask two friends what they're going to write about.

 FLORIDA STANDARDS/GLEs   FCAT: LA.A.1.1.2.K.4 Words; **LA.A.1.1.2.K.6** Print meaning; *Also* **LA.A.1.1.2.K.1** Print organization; **LA.B.1.1.3.K.2** Print direction; **LA.B.1.1.3.K.3** Punctuation; **LA.B.2.1.1.K.2** Contribute ideas;

WRAP UP Share Time

Reflect on the Lesson Ask children to tell which verse they liked best from the Sharing Literature activity. Have them explain why. Ask them to clap the syllables in the phrase of the verse.

 S.S.R. Have children read silently from a book of their choice.

Centers LISTENING

Listen, Clap, and Sing

Have children listen to the song "This Is the Way We Go to School" on the *Music CD*. Have them clap the rhythm and sing the words softly.

 **Materials**

■ *Music CD*

FLORIDA STANDARDS/GLEs FCAT: LA.A.1.1.2.K.4 Words; *Also* **LA.C.3.1.1.K.1** Speak clearly; **LA.C.3.1.4.K.1** Gestures; **LA.D.1.1.1.K.1** Sound patterns; **LA.D.2.1.2.K.1** Patterned structures

Neighborhood Helpers **329**

ORAL LANGUAGE

Day at a Glance
Day 5

Phonemic Awareness
Rhyming Words

Sharing Literature
Read-Aloud Anthology:
"Stone Soup"

Read

Respond to Literature

Literature Focus: Beginning, Middle, Ending

Phonics
Build Sentences

Interactive Writing
Writing Process: Publish

WARM UP

MORNING MESSAGE

Kindergarten News

It is (name the season).

(Child's name)

likes to (name of an activity).

Write Kindergarten News Talk with children about things they like to do in the spring. Encourage them to speak clearly.

Use prompts such as the following to guide children as you write the news:

- **Who can name some activities you do when it is warm outside?**
- **Who can show me a letter?**
- **Who can show me a word?**

As you write the message, invite children to contribute by writing letters, words, or names they have previously learned. Remind them to use proper spacing, capitalization, and punctuation.

Calendar Language

Point to and read aloud the names of the seasons of the year. Have children repeat the seasons of the year with you. Say: *It is spring.* Ask: *What season comes next?*

Sunday	Monday	Tuesday	Wednesday	Thursday	Friday	Saturday
		1	2	3	4	5
6	7	8	9	10	11	12
13	14	15	16	17	18	19
20	21	22	23	24	25	26
27	28	29	30	31		

FLORIDA STANDARDS/GLEs FCAT: LA.A.1.1.2.K.4 Words; **LA.A.1.1.2.K.5** Phonetic principles; *Also* **LA.A.1.1.2.K.1** Print organization; **LA.A.1.1.3.K.1** Frequent words; **LA.B.1.1.3.K.2** Print direction; **LA.B.2.1.1.K.2** Contribute ideas; **LA.C.1.1.3.K.1** Conversation rules; **LA.C.3.1.2.K.1** Questions

Phonemic Awareness

RHYMING WORDS

Listen for Rhyming Words   Tell children to listen for words that rhyme. Remind them that rhyming words have the same ending sounds.

Say: ten   tip   hen

Which two words have the same ending sounds?

I'll say them again.   ten   tip   hen

Ten and *hen* have the same ending sounds.

Ten and *hen* are rhyming words.

Tell children you will say some words. They are to listen for the words that rhyme. Say each set of words, and have children repeat the words and name the words that rhyme.

den, **bag**, **men** *(den, men)*   **Ben**, **Tim**, **Jen** *(Ben, Jen)*

get, **wet**, **sat** *(get, wet)*   **set**, **pet**, **rug** *(set, pet)*

leg, **peg**, **fan** *(leg, peg)*   **fret**, **stop**, **vet** *(fret, vet)*

▲ *"I've Been Workin' on the Railroad,"* Oo-pples and Boo-noo-noos: Songs and Activities for Phonemic Awareness, pages 91–93

ADVANCED

Have children name words that rhyme with *hen* and *get*. Ask them to make up silly rhymes using their rhyming words.

ENGLISH-LANGUAGE LEARNERS

Say the words *ten* and *hen*. Have children repeat each word after you. Say them again, elongating the ending sounds. Have children do the same. Have children repeat each of the following words after you. Have them clap when they hear a word that rhymes with the word *ten*: *Ken, when, what, pen, hip, den, yen, bag, men*.

FLORIDA STANDARDS/GLEs   FCAT: LA.A.1.1.2.K.5 Phonetic principles; *Also* LA.D.1.1.1.K.1 Sound patterns; LA.D.2.1.2.K.1 Patterned structures

Neighborhood Helpers   331

▲ **Read-Aloud Anthology**

OBJECTIVES

- *To listen and respond to a folktale*

- *To understand characters*

- *To act out a story*

- *To understand beginning, middle, and ending*

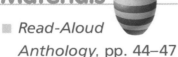

Materials

- *Read-Aloud Anthology*, pp. 44–47

- *Teacher's Resource Book*, p. 86

- crayons

- scissors

- glue

- craft sticks

- chart paper

- marker

Sharing Literature

Read "Stone Soup"

READ ALOUD

Before Reading   Turn to page 45 in the *Read-Aloud Anthology* and read the story title. Remind children that they have heard this story before. Use these prompts to help children recall the story:

- **Who are the characters in this story?** (the young man and the little old lady)

- **Which character has the idea to make stone soup?** (the young man)

- **How does the little old lady help?** (Possible response: She gives him all the ingredients to make soup.)

During Reading   Read the story aloud. As you read,

- invite children to join in as you say, *"Soup from a stone. Fancy that."*

- pause to provide the opportunity for children to discuss how the young man tricks the little old woman.

MODEL **When the young man first comes to the door, the little old woman says that she has no food and nothing in the garden. The young man says that he can make soup from a stone. As the soup cooks, the little old woman gives him all the ingredients to make a tasty soup.**

FLORIDA STANDARDS/GLEs   FCAT: LA.A.1.1.2.K.4 Words; **LA.A.1.1.2.K.6** Print meaning; **LA.A.1.1.3.K.5** Story elements; **LA.A.1.1.4.K.1** Comprehension; **LA.A.2.1.1.K.1** Main idea; *Also* **LA.C.1.1.1.K.2** Oral language; **LA.C.1.1.3.K.1** Conversation rules; **LA.C.3.1.2.K.1** Questions

RESPOND TO LITERATURE

Retell the Story   Distribute copies of the cut-out characters in the *Teacher's Resource Book* to each child. Ask children to color and cut out the characters, the ingredients and the soup pot. Have children glue the characters to craft sticks. Have children work with a partner to retell the story.

Literature Focus

BEGINNING, MIDDLE, ENDING

Write on chart paper the story map shown below. Tell children that they have learned that stories have a beginning, a middle, and an end. Ask the following questions and record children's answers in the story map.

Point to the first box. **What happens in the beginning of "Stone Soup"?** (A young man asks a woman for a stone to make soup.)

Point to the second box. **What happens in the middle of "Stone Soup"?** (The woman gives the young man water, onions, carrots, beef bones, and seasonings.)

Point to the third box: **What happens in the ending of the story?** (The young man and the old woman eat the soup.)

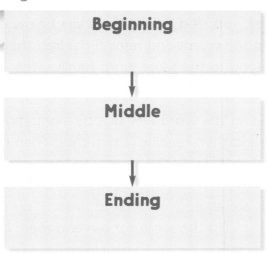

Beginning

↓

Middle

↓

Ending

ONGOING ASSESSMENT

As you share "Stone Soup," note whether children

- understand characters' actions.
- listen and respond to the folk tale.

FLORIDA STANDARDS/GLEs   FCAT: LA.A.1.1.2.K.6 Print meaning; **LA.A.1.1.3.K.5** Story elements; **LA.A.1.1.4.K.1** Comprehension; **LA.C.1.1.4.K.1** Sequence; *Also* **LA.C.1.1.3.K.1** Conversation rules

Neighborhood Helpers   333

OBJECTIVE

To use knowledge of letters, words, and sounds to build and read simple sentences

Materials

- chart paper
- index cards
- sentence strips

Phonics
Build Sentences

✔ *Review*

ACTIVE BEGINNING

Act Out a Nonsense Rhyme Teach children the following rhyme and actions.

Where is my dog Ben? (Look around, with hand at forehead.)

Is he in a deep dark den? (Point, point, point, with index finger.)

No, **he sleeps in his cozy bed** (Place hands together. Place them on the side of your head as if going to sleep.)

TEACH/MODEL

Review *-et, -en, -ed* Copy the chart below onto chart paper. Read aloud the words and remind children that the words in each column belong to the same word family—the *-et* family, the *-en* family, and the *-ed* family.

Model reading the word *wet* first by elongating the sounds, */wweett/*, and then reading it naturally. Then have children elongate the sounds, */wweett/*, and read the word. Continue with the remaining words. Frame the words *wet* and *pet* and ask how the two words are alike. (Possible responses: They rhyme; they both have *e* and *t*.) Do the same for *ten* and *men; bed* and *red*.

wet	ten	bed
pet	men	red

 FLORIDA STANDARDS/GLEs **FCAT: LA.A.1.1.2.K.5** Phonetic principles; **LA.A.1.1.3.K.4** Build vocabulary; *Also* **LA.A.1.1.2.K.1** Print organization; **LA.A.1.1.2.K.3** Sounds; **LA.C.1.1.1.K.1** Follow directions; **LA.D.1.1.1.K.1** Sound patterns

PRACTICE/APPLY

Guided Practice   Write the following words on index cards: *Ten, red, hens, get, wet*. Display the words in a pocket chart as shown.

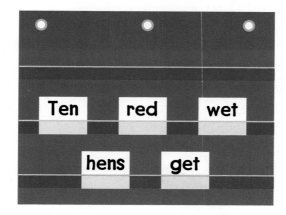

Point to each word and have children read it. Remind them to blend the sounds together to read the word. Then rearrange the cards to make the following sentence:

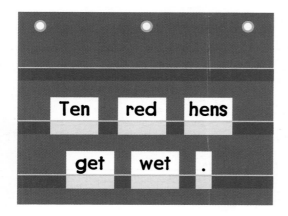

Track the words and have children read the sentence. Then replace *hens* with the word *pens* and have children read the sentence. Continue by replacing one of the words to provide many opportunities for children to read the sentence.

Independent Practice   Have children reread *Decodable Book 12, A Hat I Like*, for more practice reading connected text.

Have children use their *Word Builder* and *Word Builder Cards* to build and blend the following words: *red, fed, ten, pen, get, wet.*

Write the sentences from Guided Practice onto sentence strips. As you read the sentences, make sure children understand the meaning of each word.

early spelling

Have children write one of the words from the Guided Practice sentences in their spelling journal.

▲ **Practice Book page 22**   HW

Neighborhood Helpers   **335**

OBJECTIVES

To discuss recipes

To write a recipe

Materials

- revised sentences p. 328
- glue
- poster board
- crayons or markers

Writing Process

Write a Description

PUBLISH

Make a Hat-Shaped Poster   Read aloud the revised draft to children. Cut the chart apart into separate sentences. Glue the sentences onto a piece of white posterboard cut into the shape of a baker's hat. Have children sign their names around the border of the hat.

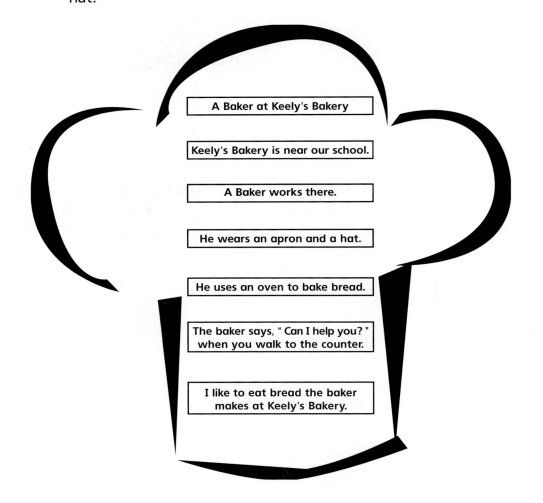

A Baker at Keely's Bakery

Keely's Bakery is near our school.

A Baker works there.

He wears an apron and a hat.

He uses an oven to bake bread.

The baker says, " Can I help you? " when you walk to the counter.

I like to eat bread the baker makes at Keely's Bakery.

My Journal

Journal Writing Have children draw or write ingredients for stone soup.

 FLORIDA STANDARDS/GLEs   **LA.B.2.1.1.K.1** Familiar experiences;   **LA.A.2.1.4.K.1** Illustrations

WRAP UP Share Time

Reflect on the Lesson   Ask children to tell what they liked best about the things they did in school today.

S.S.R. Sustained Silent Reading   Have children read silently from a book of their choice.

Centers   LITERACY

Let's Read

Place the books in the Literacy Center. Tell children to read the books and to choose their favorite one. Ask them to draw and label a picture about their favorite book. Have children write the title of the book on their picture, and then write their name.

Materials

- Decodable Books 10, 11, 12: Is It for Me?; We Can Fix; A Hat I Like

- Little Books: The Big Yellow Bus

- Library Books: Career Day; Guess Who?

FLORIDA STANDARDS/GLEs LA.A.2.1.2.K.1 Select materials; **LA.B.1.1.2.K.2** Basic formats; **LA.B.1.1.3.K.2** Print direction; **LA.C.1.1.1.K.1** Follow directions; **LA.E.2.1.1.K.2** Personal interpretations

Theme Wrap-Up & Review

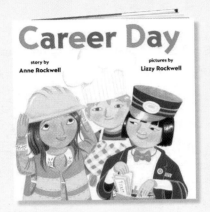

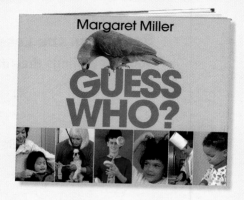

Celebrate *Neighborhood Helpers*

Show children *The Big Yellow Bus*, *Career Day*, and *Guess Who?* Help them summarize or retell each story. Invite comments and personal responses; then ask these questions:

- Which of these books is your favorite? Why?

- What neighborhood jobs have you learned about in this theme?

- What are jobs you might like to do when you grow up?

Teacher Self-Evaluation

As you reflect on the theme *Neighborhood Helpers*, ask yourself:

- Which activities best met my goals for this theme? Which ones did not?

- Have children become more aware of jobs and the people who do them?

- Have I helped children make connections between thematic activities at school and events in their personal life?

------------------------------ **THEME PROJECT** ------------------------------

Neighborhood Songs Concert

Summing Up   During the concert, have children take turns introducing the songs and telling about the neighborhood helpers the songs are about.

REVIEW

Phonics

Bus Ride Set up two rows of five chairs. Write each of the following words on two index cards: *pet, met, vet, pen, hen, ten, Ted, fed, bed, led*. Tape one of the cards to each chair. Invite a child to be the "Bus Driver" and give him or her the other set of index cards. Place *Picture Cards yak, yarn, yellow, yo-yo, zebra, zipper,* and *zoo* on a desk near the first chair. Have children take turns choosing a *Picture Card* and identifying the first letter of the picture name. Children then give the "Bus Driver" the *Picture Card* ticket and the "Bus Driver" gives them a word card. Children read the word and match it to the card that is taped to a chair. Continue until the seats are full. Have the "Bus Driver" pretend to drive the bus as children sing "The Wheels on the Bus."

High-Frequency Words

For Me! Place *High-Frequency Word Cards a, for, me* in a pocket chart. Place *Picture Cards bus, doctor, firefighter, helicopter, newspaper, nurse, yo-yo, zipper* in a box. Have children take turns choosing a *Picture Card* and placing it before *for me*. Tell them to read the phrase.

Comprehension

Understanding Content Words Page through *Library Book Career Day* and pause at several pages. Read the text and have children describe the illustrations and tell about the job. Page through *Library Book Guess Who?* and read several captions on the photographs. Have children describe the photograph and tell about it. Ask children to name jobs they have read about. List the words on the chalkboard and have children tell something they learned about each job.

Writing

Write a Message Have children think about a message they might write to a family member about a job they can do. Tell them to draw a picture about the job and to write a message on the picture.

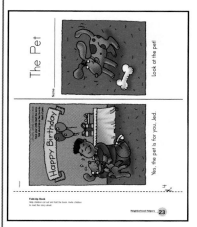

Take–Home Book
Theme 10 Practice Book,
pp. 23–24

ASSESSMENT

Monitoring of Progress

Diagnostic Checks Use the Diagnostic Checks as a point-of-use assessment of children's understanding.

Theme Skills Assessment Use Theme 10 Skills Assessment, pages T 71, 65–66, to monitor a child's understanding of letter recognition, word recognition, sound-symbol relationships, and decoding skills taught in this theme.

• Assessment Handbook

Exploring Our Surroundings

Discovering interesting things about familiar settings helps children appreciate where they live.

Theme Resources

READING MATERIALS

Big Book
◀ *Five Little Ducks* illustrated by Pamela Paparone

Library Books

◀ *Come Along, Daisy!* by Jane Simmons

◀ *What's What?* by Mary Serfozo illustrated by Keiko Narahashi

Big Book of Rhymes and Songs

◀ *The Bear Went Over the Mountain*

◀ *The Little Turtle*

◀ *Kitchen Sink song*

Read-Aloud Anthology

◀ *Bear in There* by Shel Silverstein
◀ *Henny Penny* retold by Judy Sierra
◀ *Chicken Forgets* by Miska Miles
◀ *Blame* by Shel Silverstein

Independent Readers

▲ *Up the Hill* ▲ *Float on the Boat* ▲ *Silly Pig*

PHONICS

Theme 11 Practice Book

Phonics Practice Book

Decodable Books

▲ *Little Cat, Big Cat* ▲ *But I Can* ▲ *Up, Up, Up*

Alphabet Patterns
umbrella
page TI4

Phonics Express™ CD-ROM

Level A

Visit *The Learning Site:* www.harcourtschool.com

TEACHING TOOLS

Big Alphabet Cards
Qq, Uu

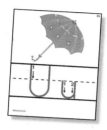

High-Frequency Word Cards
one, little

Picture/Word Cards

English Language Learners Kit

Letter and Sound Charts
Charts 26 and 19

Teacher's Resource Book
pages 76, 69

Intervention Kit

Letter and Sound Chart Sentence Strips
26 and 19

Quiet, quiet, quiet

Oo-pples and Boo-noo-noos

MANIPULATIVES

Tactile Letter Cards

q   u

Write-On/Wipe-Off Board
Letters and Sounds Place Mat

Word Builder and Word Builder Cards

b u t

Magnetic Letters

Aa Bb Cc

ASSESSMENT

Assessment Handbook

Group Inventory

Theme 11 Test

Big Book ▶

Library Book ▶

Week 1

Week 2

	Week 1	Week 2
• **Sharing Literature** • **Listening Comprehension**	**Big Book:** *Five Little Ducks* **Library Book:** *Come Along, Daisy!* **Read-Aloud Anthology:** "Bear in There" **Big Book of Rhymes and Songs:** "The Bear Went Over the Mountain"	**Big Book:** *Five Little Ducks* **Library Book:** *What's What?* **Read-Aloud Anthology:** "Henny Penny" **Big Book of Rhymes and Songs:** "The Little Turtle"
• **Phonemic Awareness** • **Phonics** • **High-Frequency Words**	**Consonant *Qq* T** **Review Consonants *Qq, Yy* T** **Review Consonants *Qq, Zz* T** **Review Consonants *Qq, Xx* T** **High-Frequency Words** *one, little* **T**	**Short Vowel *Uu* T** **Blending /u/ - /t/** **Words with /u/ and /t/**
• **Reading**	**Decodable Book 13:** *Little Cat, Big Cat* **Independent Reader 30:** *Up the Hill*	**Decodable Book 14:** *But I Can* **Independent Reader 31:** *Float on the Boat*
• **Writing**	**Shared Writing** Letter **Interactive Writing** Describing Words Directions **Independent Writing** Sentence Sound Words	**Shared Writing** Story **Interactive Writing** Five Senses How-To Directions **Independent Writing** Question Sentence
• **Cross-Curricular Centers**	**Writing** Sand Letters **Art** A Q Crown **Dramatic Play** In the Kitchen **Social Studies** My Neighborhood **Letters and Words** Pick and Match	**Math** Countdown **Science** What's in the Bag? **Manipulatives** Puzzle Time **Social Studies** Comparing Neighborhoods **Letters and Words** All 26!

T = tested skill

Library Book ▶

Week 3

Big Book: *Five Little Ducks*

Library Book: *What's What?*

Read-Aloud Anthology:
"Chicken Forgets," "Blame"

Big Book of Rhymes and Songs:
"Kitchen Sink-Song"

Review Consonant /n/*n*,
Short Vowel /u/*u* T

Blending /u/ - /n/

Words with /u/ **and** /n/

Review Blending /u/ - /n/

Decodable Book 15: *Up, Up, Up*

Independent Reader 32: *Silly Pig*

Interactive Writing
Writing Process

 Art
Collage Time

 Science
Model Habitats

Listening
Listen to This

Literacy
Favorite Theme Books

Dramatic Play
Class Field Trip

Theme Organizer
Half-Day Kindergarten

Use the following chart to help organize your half-day kindergarten schedule. Choose independent activities as time allows during your day.

ORAL LANGUAGE

Morning Message
Phonemic Awareness
Sharing Literature
- Big Book: *Five Little Ducks*
- Library Book: *Come Along, Daisy!*
- Library Book: *What's What?*
- Read-Aloud Anthology
- Big Book of Rhymes and Song

LEARNING TO READ

Phonics
Decodable Books 13–15
- *Little Cat, Big Cat*
- *But I Can*
- *Up, Up, Up*

High-Frequency Words

 Independent Readers 30–32
- *Up the Hill*
- *Float on the Boat*
- *Silly Pig*

LANGUAGE ARTS

Shared Writing
Interactive Writing
Independent Writing
Writing Every Day

INDEPENDENT ACTIVITIES

Sharing Literature
Respond to Literature
Phonics
Independent Practice
Handwriting
Practice Book pages
High-Frequency Words
Independent Practice
Practice Book pages

About the
Authors and Illustrators

Pamela Paparone

Illustrator of *Five Little Ducks*

Pamela Paparone grew up living both in the United States and abroad. She and her husband now live in Philadelphia, Pennsylvania. She has illustrated many other picture books, including *Who Built the Ark?* and *Firefighters.*

Jane Simmons

Author and Illustrator of *Come Along Daisy!*

Jane Simmons has lived in many countries, including Australia, France, Uganda, Zambia, Malta, and Kuwait. She currently lives on a houseboat in England with two lovebirds, two dogs, and a chicken named Freda. Simmons also wrote *Ebb and Flo and the New Friend.*

Mary Serfozo

Author of *What's What?*

Mary Serfozo says that she was inspired to write children's books after observing a group of children singing along with the local librarian. She has worked as a freelance writer and copywriter, as well as in advertising. Other books include *Who Said Red?*, *Who Wants One?*, *Dirty Kurt*, and *Benjamin Bigfoot.*

Keiko Narahashi

Illustrator of *What's What?*

Keiko Narahashi was born in Japan and moved to the United States when she was young. She received a B.F.A. from the Parsons School of Design. She has illustrated several children's books, and is the author-illustrator of *I Have a Friend, Is That Josie?* and *Two Girls Can!*

Theme Assessment

MONITORING OF PROGRESS

After completing the theme, most children should show progress toward mastery of the following skills:

Concepts of Print
- ❑ Understand that printed materials give information.
- ❑ Distinguish letters from words.

Phonemic Awareness
- ❑ Track and represent changes in simple syllables and words with two and three sounds as one sound is added, substituted, omitted, shifted, or repeated.
- ❑ Count the number of sounds in syllables and syllables in words.

Phonics and Decoding
- ❑ Match all consonant sounds and short-vowel sounds to appropriate letters.
- ❑ Read one-syllable and High-Frequency Words.

Vocabulary and High-Frequency Words
- ❑ Read High-Frequency Words *one* and *little*.
- ❑ Identify and sort common words in basic categories.
- ❑ Understand words associated with the calendar.

Comprehension
- ❑ Retell familiar stories.
- ❑ Ask and answer questions about essential elements of a text.

Literary Response
- ❑ Identify types of everyday print materials.
- ❑ Identify characters, settings, and important events.

Writing
- ❑ Spell independently by using prephonetic knowledge, sounds of the alphabet, and knowledge of letter names.
- ❑ Write "How To" directions.

Listening and Speaking
- ❑ Share information and ideas about favorite books, speaking audibly in complete, coherent sentences.
- ❑ Recite short poems.

Assessment Options

Assessment Handbook
- Group Inventory
- Phonemic Awareness Inventory
- Theme Skills Assessment
- Concepts About Print Inventory
- Observational Checklists

Reaching All Learners

■ BELOW-LEVEL

Levels of Support

Point-of-use Notes in the Teacher's Edition

pp. 363, 365, 373, 377, 381, 383, 387, 391, 393, 397, 401, 402, 407, 411, 421, 423, 425, 429, 433, 437, 441, 445, 447, 453, 457, 467, 471, 475, 477, 483, 487, 493, 499

Additional Support Activities

High-Frequency Words:
pp. S38-S39

Comprehension and Skills:
pp. S48-S49, S54-S55

Phonemic Awareness:
pp. S40-S41, S46-S47, S50-S51

Phonics:
pp. S42-S43, S44-S45, S52-S53

Intervention Resources Kit

■ ENGLISH-LANGUAGE LEARNERS

Levels of Support

Point-of-use Notes in the Teacher's Edition
pp. 379, 381, 389, 393, 397, 402, 411, 433, 437, 441, 447, 448, 455, 479, 487, 493, 494, 499, 503

Additional Support Activities

High Frequency Words:
pp. S38-S39

Comprehension and Skills:
pp. S48-S49, S54-S55

Phonemic Awareness:
pp. S40-S41, S46-S47, S50-S51

Phonics:
pp. S42-S43, S44-S45, S52-S53

Visit *The Learning Site!* at
www.harcourtschool.com
See Language Support activities

English-Language Learners Resources Kit

■ ADVANCED

Levels of Challenge

Point-of-use Notes in the Teacher's Edition

pp. 363, 365, 383, 391, 393, 397, 399, 407, 409, 411, 421, 423, 425, 429, 431, 433, 437, 439, 441, 447, 457, 469, 475, 479, 485, 487, 491, 493, 494, 499, 501, 503

Additional Support Activities

High-Frequency Words:
pp. S38-S39

Comprehension and Skills:
pp. S48-S49, S54-S55

Phonemic Awareness:
pp. S40-S41, S46-S47, S50-S51

Phonics:
pp. S42-S43, S44-S45, S52-S53

Accelerated Instruction

Use higher-grade-level materials for accelerated instruction.

Theme Project, p. 352

Combination Classrooms
Writing Together

After reading the *Library Book: What's what?* pair children to write their own book of riddles. Try to include an advanced writer and a beginning writer in each pair. Encourage children to collaborate on the wording of the riddles, while the advanced writer may act as the scribe for the beginning writer. Both children can draw and label the answers to the riddles on the backs of the pages.

What is cold and wite and fals on the grd?

Students with Special Needs
Organizing Daily Tasks

Many children with special needs have difficulty being organized and staying focused. Create a checklist for each child that indicates what he or she will be expected to accomplish for the day. Discuss the list with the child each day so he or she will know exactly what to do. Remind children to check off each task as they complete it.

Karen
☐ Listen to a story.
☐ Draw a map.
☐ Read a book.
☐ Write a question.

Recommended Reading

Below are suggestions for reading materials that will meet kindergarten children's diverse needs. Books that are on a child's level provide support for new skills. Advanced books give children an opportunity to stretch and challenge their reading potential. Read-aloud books are important because they expose children to story language and vocabulary.

■ BELOW-LEVEL

Black on White by Tana Hoban. Greenwillow, 1993. A wordless board book with simple images.

I Am an Explorer by Amy Moses. Childrens Press, 1990. A child takes a trip to a park and explores an imaginary cave, mountain, jungle, and desert.

Hi, Clouds by Carol Greene. Childrens Press, 1983. Two children watch the changing shapes of clouds.

What a Dog! by Sharon Gordon. Troll, 1989. A dog wants to be walked so little Billy walks him, but he is more than he can handle.

■ ON-LEVEL

Exactly the Opposite by Tana Hoban. Mulberry, 1997. This book pairs brilliant photographs of opposites.

Red Leaf, Yellow Leaf by Lois Ehlert. Harcourt, 1991. This book provides simple information about the life of a sugar maple tree.

Flora McDonnell's A B C by Flora McDonnell. Candlewick, 2001. Both upper-case and lowercase letters are represented by vibrant art in this charming book.

Sidewalk Trip by Patricia Hubbell. Harper, 1999. A young girl has fun exploring her neighborhood with her mother.

■ ADVANCED

Footprints in the Snow by Cynthia Benjamin. Scholastic, 1994. Animals leave their footprints as they head for home during a snowstorm.

Footprints in the Sand by Cynthia Benjamin. Scholastic, 1999. Desert animals leave footprints as they go to their homes.

Rosie's Walk by Pat Hutchins. Simon & Schuster, 1968. Rosie the hen has a fox following her on her walk.

I Like Stars by Margaret Wise Brown. Golden Books, 1998. This poem about stars describes these wonders of the sky.

■ READ ALOUD

Where Do I Live? by the World Wildlife Fund. Cedco, 1998. This book challenges readers to guess where animals live.

The Ugly Vegetables by Grace Kin. Charlesbridge, 1999. A family's garden of Chinese vegetables is a big hit with the neighbors.

The Earth and I by Frank Asch. Harcourt, 1994. A boy tells how he feels about the earth.

Seven Blind Mice by Ed Young. Philomel, 1992. This fable tells of seven blind mice who base their impression of an elephant on its parts.

Homework Ideas

Visit The Learning Site: www.harcourtschool.com • See Resources for Parents and Teachers: Homework Helper

	Literature	Phonics	Language Arts	Theme	Cross-Curricular
WEEK 1	Draw a picture of a **place** you would like to explore.	Look for **the letters** *Qq* in magazines and newspapers.	**Take a walk** in your neighborhood or a park. Talk about what you see as you walk.	Ask different family members to name a **place** they would like **to explore.** Use words or pictures to record their answers.	Talk about three ways that people **travel** from one place to another.
WEEK 2	Write a sentence to tell how the duckling in *Come Along, Daisy!* felt when she got lost.	Practice forming **the letters** *Qq, Uu, Tt,* **and** *Nn* with soft clay or dough.	With a family member, check the upcoming **weather forecast.** Write your prediction about what the weather will be in the next day or two.	Cut out magazine pictures of **places** you would like to **visit.** Label the pictures.	Draw a picture of a make-believe place to explore.
WEEK 3	Make up a **riddle** about an object in your house. Say clues and have a family member solve the riddle.	Draw a picture of three objects whose names have **the /u/ sound.**	Write a list of **words that describe** your pet or a pet you would like to have.	Draw a picture of places in your own **neighborhood** you like to explore.	Think of a **food** you like. Write or dictate words that tell how it tastes, smells, sounds, feels, and looks.

Explorer's Log

Materials

- Teacher's Resource Book page 23
- cover page, titled *Explorer's Log*
- paper
- pencils
- crayons
- glue sticks
- tape

School-Home Connection

Invite family members to visit the classroom to learn about and look at children's Explorer's Logs. Encourage visitors to ask questions about the logs, and remind children to answer politely. Invite visitors to share their observations of nature.

Visit *The Learning Site!* at **www.harcourtschool.com**

Introduce

Tell children they are going to be explorers and keep an "Explorer's Log." Explain that they will draw and label pictures of the things they see in the natural world around them, such as the weather, bugs, and plants. They will go on a nature walk and can add things to their logs every day.

Send home the Family Letter to encourage family members to participate in the project.

Prepare

- Help children make blank Explorer's Logs to bring on a nature walk around the school or in a park. Have children draw pictures of the things they see and collect items such as fallen leaves.

- Back in class, children can tape leaves into their Explorer's Logs, identify them, and label the pictures they drew. Remind children to be alert nature explorers all the time, so they can add to their logs regularly.

Share

As a group, have children take turns telling about their nature walk and the things they included in their Explorer's Logs. Encourage children to read interesting parts aloud for visitors and to let others look at their logs.

Teacher Notes

Learning Centers

Choose from the following suggestions to enhance your learning centers for the theme Exploring Our Surroundings.
(Additional learning centers for this theme can be found on pages 414 and 460)

ART CENTER

This Is What I See

Tell children to draw a picture of a view they see from their classroom or home window, or on their way to or from school. Children should use what they know about sounds and letters to label the people, places, animals, and other objects in their drawing. Encourage children to add a caption to tell the time of day—morning, afternoon, night—they saw the view.

Materials

- paper
- crayons
- markers
- pencils

DRAMATIC PLAY CENTER

I Spy

Have children play a game of "I Spy." Display pictures of natural environments in the dramatic play center for children to use as inspiration. As needed, model how to play "I Spy," saying, "I spy with my little eye, something that is [give a descriptive word]." Tell children to look around the room and identify objects that have the quality you stated. If a child guesses the object, he or she may spy the next object. Otherwise, identify the object for children, and choose a child to be the one who spies.

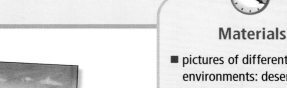

Materials

- pictures of different environments: desert, Arctic, forests, ocean (Patterns T27)

WRITING CENTER

Home Sweet Home

Tell children to choose an animal and write about the place it calls home. Children should write two or three sentences to describe the place where the animal eats, plays, and sleeps. Before children write, encourage them to use what they know about letters and the sounds they stand for. Invite children to draw a picture to illustrate their sentences.

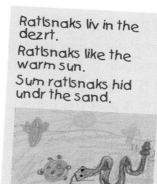

Ratlsnaks liv in the dezrt.
Ratlsnaks like the warm sun.
Sum ratlsnaks hid undr the sand.

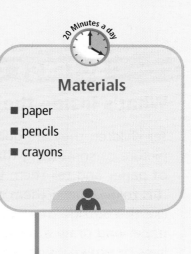

20 Minutes a day

Materials

- paper
- pencils
- crayons

MATH CENTER

Count, Draw, Count

Place *Picture Cards: alligator, bear, duck, egg, fish, nest, rabbit, turtle* and multiple copies of number cards 1–6 facedown in two piles in the math center. Have each child take a number card and a *Picture Card*. Then give children a sheet of paper and have them write the number shown on their number card and then draw an equal number of animals or things shown on their Picture Card. Children can swap drawings and use counters to count each object in the picture.

20 Minutes a day

Materials

- number cards: 1–6
- *Picture Cards: alligator, bear, duck, egg, fish, nest, rabbit, turtle*
- paper
- crayons
- counters or other manipulatives

SCIENCE CENTER

What's Inside the Log?

Tell children they are going to make a paper log and draw a picture of something that lives inside it. Give children a piece of paper and tell them to fold it in half the long way. Once it is folded, have them color the top of the paper to look like the outside of a log. Then have children unfold the paper and draw a picture of something (or some things) that lives or grows inside a log. Children can look inside one another's finished logs to see what's inside.

Materials

- paper
- crayons

SAND AND WATER CENTER

Create a Pond Environment

Have small groups of children work together to create a pond environment in the sand and water center. Children can use a variety of materials to create a pond, including a small dish or container buried in the sand. Pipe cleaners or scraps of felt or cloth can serve as marsh grass or reeds, while toy ducks and other birds can be floated on the pond or placed along the banks of the pond.

Materials

- sand tray or classroom sandbox
- small dish or container filled with water
- miniature toy ducks and other animals
- pipe cleaners
- felt or cloth scraps
- safety scissors

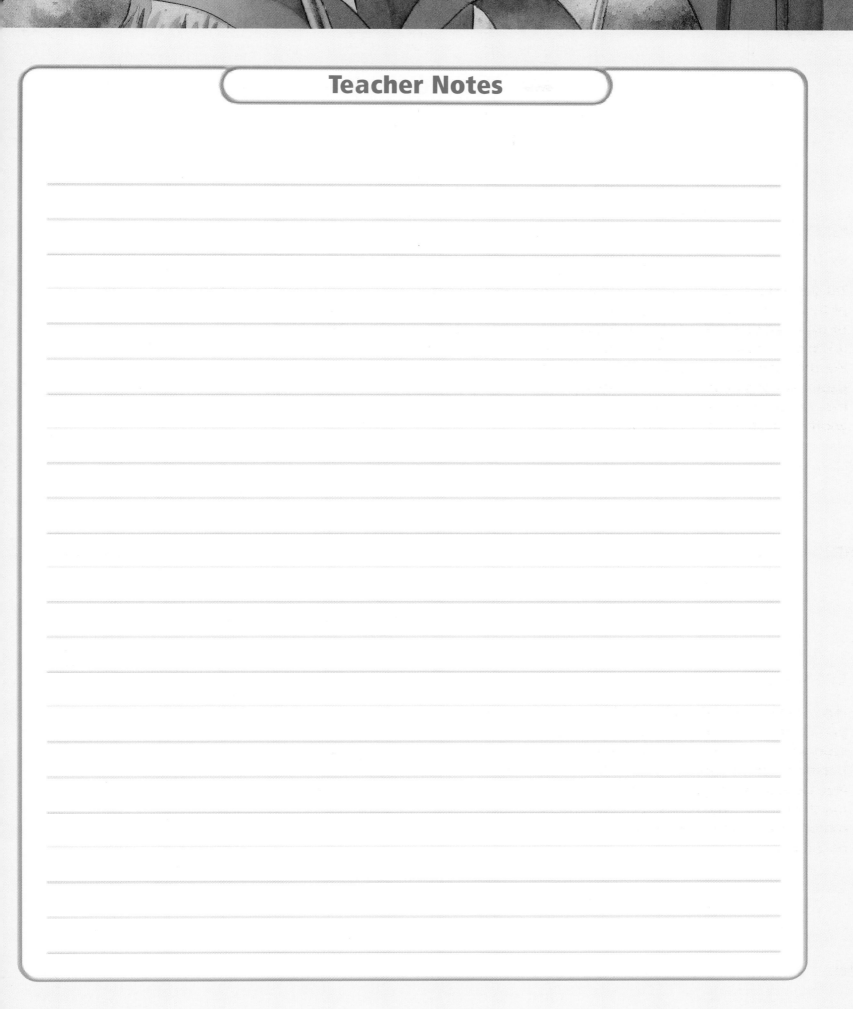

Teacher Notes

Teacher Notes

Week 1
Exploring Our Surroundings

15-30 Minutes

ORAL LANGUAGE

- **Phonemic Awareness**

- **Sharing Literature**

Day 1

Phonemic Awareness, 363
Phoneme Matching and Isolation: Initial

Sharing Literature, 364

 Read

Big Book: *Five Little Ducks*

(Skill) **Literature Focus, 365**
Dialogue

Day 2

Phonemic Awareness, 377
Phoneme Isolation

Sharing Literature, 378
Library Book: *Come Along, Daisy!*

(Skill) **Literature Focus, 379**
Problem-Solution

---

45 Minutes

LEARNING TO READ

- **Phonics**

- **Vocabulary**

Phonics, 372 T
Introduce: Consonant *Qq*
Identify/Write **T**

Phonics, 380 T
Relating /kw/ to *q*

High-Frequency Word, 382 T
Introduce: *one*

Words to Remember, 383

Daily Routines
- **Morning Message**
- **Calendar Language**
- **Writing Prompt**

15-30 Minutes

LANGUAGE ARTS

- **Writing**
  Daily Writing Prompt

 Shared Writing, 374
Write a Letter

Writing Prompt, 374
Draw and write about a favorite game.

Share Time, 375
Discuss parts of a letter.

 Interactive Writing, 384

 Read

Write Describing Words

Writing Prompt, 384
Draw and write about favorite story characters.

Share Time, 385
Share favorite parts of *Come Along, Daisy!*

---

360 **Exploring Our Surroundings**

T = tested skill

Phonics

Consonant *Qq*

Focus of the Week:
- **HIGH-FREQUENCY WORDS:** *one, little*
- **PHONEMIC AWARENESS**
- **SHARING LITERATURE**
- **WRITING: Describing Words, Sentences**

Day 3

Phonemic Awareness, 387
Phoneme Isolation and Matching: Medial

Sharing Literature, 388
Read-Aloud Anthology: "Bear in There," p. 15

(Skill) **Literature Focus, 389**
Action Words

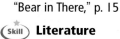 **, 390** T
Review: Consonants /kw/*q*, /y/*y*

High-Frequency Word, 392 T
Introduce: *little*

Words to Remember, 393

 Writing, 394
Write a Sentence

Writing Prompt, 394
Draw and write about self-selected topics.

Share Time, 395

Read

Author's Chair

Day 4

Phonemic Awareness, 397
Phoneme Blending

Sharing Literature, 398
Big Book of Rhymes and Songs: "The Bear Went Over the Mountain," p. 21

(Skill) **Literature Focus, 399**
Text Patterns

 , 400 T
Review: Consonants /kw/*q*, /z/*z*

High-Frequency Words, 402 T
Review: *one, little*

Read

DECODABLE BOOK 13
Little Cat, Big Cat

 Interactive Writing, 404
Write Directions

Writing Prompt, 404
Draw and write about a mountain hike.

Share Time, 405

Read

Author's Chair

Day 5

Phonemic Awareness, 407
Phoneme Counting

Sharing Literature, 408
Library Book: *Come Along, Daisy!*

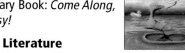

(Skill) **Literature Focus, 409**
Retell the Story

 **, 410** T
Review: Consonants /kw/*q*, /ks/*x*

 Writing, 412
Write Sound Words

Writing Prompt, 412
Draw and write about self-selected topics.

Share Time, 413

Read

Author's Chair

Day at a Glance
Day I

WARM UP

Phonemic Awareness

Phoneme Isolation and
Phoneme Matching: Initial

Sharing Literature

Big Book:
Five Little Ducks

Develop Listening Comprehension

Respond to Literature

Literature Focus: Dialogue

Phonics

Consonant *Qq*

Writing

Shared Writing: Letter

MORNING MESSAGE

Kindergarten News

We like to play _____.

The next school day is _____.

Write Kindergarten News Ask children to talk about their favorite games and to tell why they like them.

Use prompts such as the following to guide children as you write the news:

- **What letter will I write first in the word** *like*?
- **Who can show me the beginning of a word?**
- **Who can point to where to begin reading?**

As you write the message, invite children to contribute by writing letters or words they have previously learned. Remind them to use proper spacing, capitalization, and punctuation.

Calendar Language

Point to and read aloud the days of the week. Then name the school days. Ask what day today is. Ask a child to name the next school day.

Sunday	Monday	Tuesday	Wednesday	Thursday	Friday	Saturday
		1	2	3	4	5
6	7	8	9	10	11	12
13	14	15	16	17	18	19
20	21	22	23	24	25	26
27	28	29	30	31		

FLORIDA STANDARDS/GLEs   FCAT: LA.A.2.1.5.K.2 Get information; **LA.B.2.1.2.K.1** Record ideas; *Also* **LA.A.1.1.2.K.1** Print organization; **LA.A.1.1.2.K.2** Alphabet; **LA.A.1.1.2.K.3** Sounds; **LA.C.1.1.3.K.1** Conversation rules; **LA.C.3.1.2.K.1** Questions

Phonemic Awareness

PHONEME ISOLATION: INITIAL

Continue by repeating the words in each sentence that have the same initial sound. Have children tell what the beginning sound is.

> **MODEL** In the sentence *Yes, I like yams*, the words *yes* and *yams* have the same beginning sound. I hear /y/ at the beginning of *yes*. I hear /y/ at the beginning of *yams*. *Yes* and *yams* begin with /y/. Say the sound with me: /y/.

Ask children to name the beginning sound in the following words:

zebra, zoo (/z/)   **will, went** (/w/)

Jack, jump (/j/)   **quite, question** (/kw/)

Val, van (/v/)

PHONEME MATCHING: INITIAL

Identify the Initial Sound in a Word Tell children you will say a sentence and they are to listen for words that begin with the same sound.

> **MODEL** The queen has a quilt. Say the sentence with me: *The queen has a quilt.* *Queen* begins with the /kw/ sound. *Quilt* begins with the /kw/ sound. *Queen* and *quilt* begin with the same sound: /kw/. Say the words with me: *queen, quilt.*

Tell children that you are going to say some more sentences. Have them name the two words that begin with the same sound.

Yes, I like yams. (Yes, yams)

The zebra is in the zoo. (zebra, zoo)

Jack can jump. (Jack, jump)

Val is in the van. (Val, van)

Will went home. (Will, went)

That is quite a question. (quite, question)

Say two words, such as /zz/-*ip* and /zz/-*oo*, drawing out the beginning sound. Ask children to tell you if they hear the same sound at the beginning of each word. Continue with other word pairs, some of which have the same beginning sound and some of which don't.

ADVANCED

Provide children with two words that have the same beginning sound, and ask them to produce a third word that begins with the same sound.

Sharing Literature

Read Five Little Ducks

▲ **Big Book**

OBJECTIVES

- *To use picture clues and context to make predictions*

- *To listen and respond to a story*

- *To recall story events*

- *To understand dialogue*

Materials

- *Big Book: Five Little Ducks*

- *two sentence strips*

READ ALOUD

Before Reading   Display the cover of *Five Little Ducks*. Track the print as you read the title and the name of the illustrator. Ask children what the ducks are doing in the picture.

As you page through the book, have children examine the illustrations. Model how to make a prediction:

MODEL   **On the cover I see little ducks waddling away and Mother duck watching them. As I turn the pages, I see that some ducks are missing. I wonder if the story will be about those little ducks going away.**

During Reading   Read the story aloud. As you read,
- emphasize the language pattern of repetitive phrases.
- pause during reading. Model how to make predictions during reading.

MODEL   **I predicted the story would be about the little ducks going away. When I read *only four little ducks cam ack*, I see that it *is* about the little ducks going away from Mo er duck. I predict that only three ducks will come back next time.**

FLORIDA STANDARDS/GLEs   FCAT: LA.A.1.1.4.K.1 Comprehension; *Also* **LA.A1.1.1.K.1** Predictions; **LA.A.1.1.2.K.1** Print organization; **LA.A.2.1.4.K.1** Illustrations; **LA.C.1.1.1.K.2** Oral language; **LA.D.1.1.1.K.1** Sound patterns; **LA.D.2.1.2.K.1** Patterned structures; **LA.E.2.1.2.K.1** Patterned structures

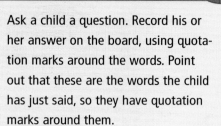

DEVELOP LISTENING COMPREHENSION

After Reading Have children answer these questions about the story:

- **What is this story about?** (little ducks leaving home and then coming back)

- **How do you think Mother duck feels when none of the ducks come back?** (Possible response: She feels sad or lonely.)

- **If you were Mother duck**, **what would you do the next time the ducks wanted to go out?** (Possible response: I would go with my ducks.)

RESPOND TO LITERATURE

Discuss the Story Have children tell what they liked about the story. Ask children to confirm the predictions they made before and during the story.

Literature Focus

DIALOGUE

Write the following on sentence strips: *Mother duck said, "Quack, quack, quack, quack."* Read the sentence aloud and ask the class to repeat the words that Mother duck said. Point out the quotation marks and tell children that a writer puts those marks around the words someone speaks. Direct children to look through the *Big Book* for this sentence.

Mother duck said,	"Quack, quack, quack, quack."

BELOW-LEVEL

Ask a child a question. Record his or her answer on the board, using quotation marks around the words. Point out that these are the words the child has just said, so they have quotation marks around them.

ADVANCED

Have children find dialogue in another book you have shared. Read the dialogue aloud. Then ask them who spoke the words.

ONGOING ASSESSMENT

As you share *Five Little Ducks*, note whether children

- **use picture clues and context to make predictions.**

- **listen for a period of time.**

- **recall story events.**

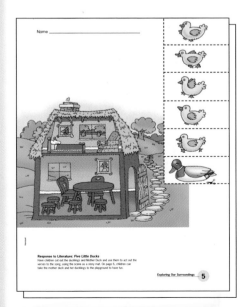

▲ **Practice Book pages 5–6**

FLORIDA STANDARDS/GLEs **FCAT: LA.A.1.1.4.K.1** Comprehension; **LA.A.2.1.1.K.1** Main idea; *Also* **LA.C.3.1.2.K.1** Questions; **LA.E.2.1.1.K.1** Background knowledge

Exploring Our Surroundings **365**

Five little ducks went out one day,
Over the hills and far away.

6

7

Mother duck said,
"Quack, quack, quack, quack."
But only four little ducks
came back.

8

9

Four little ducks went out one day,
Over the hills and far away.

10

11

Mother duck said,
"Quack, quack, quack, quack."
But only three little ducks
came back.

12

13

Three little ducks went out one day,
Over the hills and far away.

14

15

Mother duck said,
"Quack, quack, quack, quack."
But only two little ducks
came back.

16

17

Two little ducks went out one day,
Over the hills and far away.

18

19

Mother duck said,
"Quack, quack, quack, quack."
But only one little duck
came back.

20

21

One little duck went out one day,
Over the hills and far away.

22

23

Mother duck said,
"Quack, quack, quack, quack."
But none of the little ducks
came back.

24

25

Sad mother duck went out one day,
Over the hills and far away.

26

27

Mother duck said,
"Quack, quack, quack, quack."

28

29

And all of her five little ducks
came back!

30

31

OBJECTIVES

- *To recognize Q and q*

- *To write uppercase and lowercase Qq independently*

Materials

- *Big Book:*
  Five Little Ducks

- *Big Alphabet Cards Jj, Qq, Vv, Ww, Xx*

- *Write-On/Wipe-Off Boards*

- drawing paper

- crayons

Consonant Qq ✔ Introduce

ACTIVE BEGINNING

Review the Letters   Have children name each letter as you display the *Big Alphabet Cards Jj, Vv, Ww, Xx.* Then say *violin, window, X ray,* and *jungle,* and have children point to the letter that names the beginning sound in each word.

TEACH/MODEL

Introduce the Letter Name   Hold up the *Big Alphabet Card Qq.*

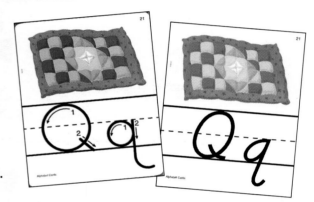

The name of this letter is *q.* Say the name with me. (*q*)

Point to the uppercase *Q.* **This is the uppercase *Q.***

Point to the lowercase *q.* **This is the lowercase *q.***

Point to the *Big Alphabet Card* again. **What is the name of this letter?**

Display page 28 in *Five Little Ducks.*

Follow along as I read the page.

Point to the letter *Q.* **What is the name of this letter?** (*Qq*)

Do the same with lowercase *q.*

FLORIDA STANDARDS/GLEs   FCAT: LA.A.1.1.2.K.1 Print organization; *Also* **LA.A.1.1.2.K.2** Alphabet; **LA.C.1.1.1.K.2** Oral language; **LA.C.3.1.2.K.1** Questions

Handwriting

Writing Q and q Write uppercase Q and lowercase q on the board.

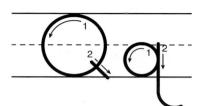

Point to the uppercase Q. **What letter is this?** (Q)

Point to the lowercase q. **What letter is this?** (q)

MODEL **Watch as I write the letter Q so that everyone can read it.**

As you give the Letter Talk, trace the uppercase Q. Use the same modeling procedure for lowercase q.

Letter Talk for Q

Circle. Short slanted line.

Letter Talk for q

Circle. Straight line down. Curve right.

D'Nealian handwriting models are on pages R12-13.

PRACTICE/APPLY

Guided Practice Help children find Qq on their *Write-On/Wipe-Off Board*. Have them trace the uppercase Q with a finger and then write the letter several times. Have them do the same for lowercase q. Tell children to circle their best Q and q.

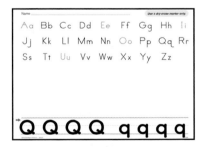

Independent Practice Distribute drawing paper and have children fill the page with Qq's. Ask them to circle their best Q and q.

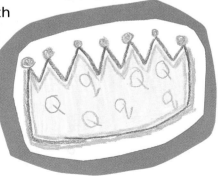

BELOW-LEVEL

Show children matching *Alphabet Cards, Magnetic Letters,* and *Tactile Letter Cards* for the letter *Qq*. Have children trace over each letter with their pointer finger and then write the letters on their paper.

Phonics Resources

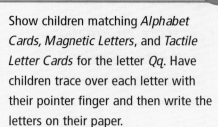

Phonics Express™ CD-ROM, Level A, Sparkle/Route 6/ Market and Harbor

Phonics Practice Book pages 119–120

▲ **Practice Book page 7**

OBJECTIVES

- *To understand the purpose of a letter*

- *To share information and ideas, speaking in complete, coherent sentences*

- *To write a letter*

Materials

- chart paper

- marker

Day 1: Letter
Work together to write a friendly letter.

Day 2: Describing Words
Work together to write describing words about a story character.

Day 3: Sentence
Have children complete a sentence frame by drawing and writing.

Day 4: Directions
Work together to write directions telling the bear how to get over the mountain.

Day 5: Sound Words
Have children write an animal sound in a speech balloon.

Shared Writing

Write a Letter

THINK LIKE A CHARACTER

Talk About Letters   Remind children that people write and send letters to people who are far away. Ask them to share any experiences they have had sending or receiving letters.

Write a Letter   Tell children that together they are going to write a letter from Mother duck to the little ducks. Ask children: **How do I start a letter?** If I am the Mother duck, who am I writing the letter to? Write the greeting, *Dear little ducks,*. Ask children for ideas about what Mother duck might want to tell the little ducks. Record children's suggestions in the body of the letter. Ask children: **How should Mother Duck end her letter? What does this show?** Write the closing, *Love, Mother duck*.

Dear little ducks,
I miss you. Please come home.
Love,
Mother duck

Journal Writing   Have children write and draw about their favorite games.

FLORIDA STANDARDS/GLEs   FCAT: LA.B.2.1.2.K.1 Record ideas; *Also* LA.A.1.1.2.K.1 Print organization; LA.B.1.1.1.K.2 Generate ideas; LA.B.1.1.2.K.1 Dictate messages; LA.B.1.1.2.K.2 Basic formats; LA.B.1.1.3.K.1 Spelling approximations; LA.B.1.1.3.K.3 Punctuation; LA.B.2.1.1.K.1 Familiar experiences; LA.D.1.1.1.K.2 Language functions

WRAP UP  # Share Time

Reflect on the Lesson Read the letter to children. Point to the three parts of the letter and ask: **What does this part of the letter show?**

S.S.R. *Sustained Silent Reading* Have children read silently from a book of their choice.

 **Centers** WRITING

Sand Letters

Have children write *Qq* on a sheet of construction paper. Encourage them to check their letters against those on the *Big Alphabet Card*. Help them trace over the letters with glue, and sprinkle sand onto the glue to form *Qq*.

 Materials

- construction paper
- pencils
- *Big Alphabet Card Qq*
- glue
- sand

Day 2

Phonemic Awareness
Phoneme Isolation

Sharing Literature
Library Book:
Come Along, Daisy!

Read

Come Along, Daisy!
JANE SIMMONS

Develop Listening Comprehension

Respond to Literature

Literature Focus: Problem-Solution

Phonics

Relating /kw/ to q

High-Frequency Word
one

Interactive Writing
Describing Words

ORAL LANGUAGE

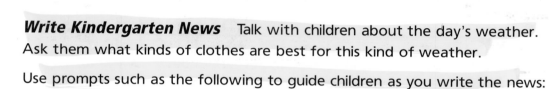

MORNING MESSAGE
Kindergarten News
Today the weather is _____.

We wear _____

and _____.

Write Kindergarten News Talk with children about the day's weather. Ask them what kinds of clothes are best for this kind of weather.

Use prompts such as the following to guide children as you write the news:

- **What is the weather like today?**
- **What did you wear to school?**
- **Who can write the first letter in the word *Today*?**
- **What letter will I write first in the word *weather*?**
- **How many words are in the first sentence?**

As you write the message, invite children to contribute by writing letters or words they have learned previously. Ask children to point out spaces between words.

Calendar Language

Point to the calendar and read aloud the name of the month. Ask: *What month is it?* Have children clap the syllables in the sentence *"Hoorah! It is the month of _____."* with you.

Sunday	Monday	Tuesday	Wednesday	Thursday	Friday	Saturday
		1	2	3	4	5
6	7	8	9	10	11	12
13	14	15	16	17	18	19
20	21	22	23	24	25	26
27	28	29	30	31		

FLORIDA STANDARDS/GLEs **FCAT: LA.A.1.1.2.K.5** Phonetic principles; **LA.A.2.1.5.K.2** Get information; **LA.B.2.1.2.K.1** Record ideas; *Also* **LA.A.1.1.2.K.2** Alphabet; **LA.A.1.1.2.K.3** Sounds; **LA.C.1.1.3.K.1** Conversation rules; **LA.C.3.1.2.K.1** Questions

Phonemic Awareness

PHONEME ISOLATION

Listen for /kw/   Tell children you will say some words and they are to listen for the beginning sound in the words. Say the following sentence:

Queen Quack has quite a quilt.

Queen **begins with /kw/. Say the word** *Queen*.

What sound does *Quack* **begin with?** /kw/ **Say the word** *Quack*.

What sound does *quite* **begin with?** /kw/ **Say the word** *quite*.

What sound does *quilt* **begin with?** /kw/ **Say the word** *quilt*.

Let's say the sentence together.

Now let's say it again, but let's change the last word to another word that begins with /kw/.

Have children take turns saying the sentence and supplying new words that begin with /kw/, such as *question*, *quarter*, *quill*, and *quail*.

FLORIDA STANDARDS/GLEs   **FCAT: LA.A.1.1.2.K.5** Phonetic principles; *Also* **LA.C.1.1.1.K.1** Follow directions; **LA.C.3.1.2.K.1** Questions; **LA.D.2.1.2.K.2** Alliteration

▲ **Library Book**

OBJECTIVES

- *To locate the title and author of a story*

- *To use pictures and context to make predictions*

- *To listen and respond to a story*

- *To connect life experiences to text*

- *To identify problem and solution*

Materials

■ *Library Book: Come Along, Daisy!*

Sharing Literature

Read Come Along, Daisy!

READ ALOUD

Before Reading   Display the cover of *Come Along, Daisy!* Have a child point to the title. Read it aloud. Have a child point to the author's name. Explain that Jane Simmons wrote the story and drew the pictures. Then use these prompts to build background:

- **What do you see on the cover?** (two ducks in a pond and a dragonfly)

- **Who do you think Daisy is?** (Possible response: the yellow duck)

- **Who do you think is saying, "Come along, Daisy!"?** (Possible response: the white duck)

Page through the book, pausing briefly on each page to allow children to preview the illustrations. Have children tell what they think the story will be about.

During Reading   Read the story aloud. As you read,

- use different voices to portray different characters.

- point out how the pictures help the reader understand the story.

- pause periodically to have children make and confirm predictions.

MODEL   Mama Duck tells Daisy to stay close, but Daisy doesn't. I think she might get lost.

378   Exploring Our Surroundings

FLORIDA STANDARDS/GLEs   FCAT: LA.A.1.1.4.K.1 Comprehension; *Also* **LA.A.1.1.1.K.1** Predictions; **LA.A.2.1.4.K.1** Illustrations; **LA.C.1.1.1.K.1** Follow directions; **LA.C.3.1.2.K.1** Questions

DEVELOP LISTENING COMPREHENSION

After Reading   Have children answer these questions about the story:

- **Why does Daisy wander away from Mama Duck?** (Daisy is busy playing.)

- **How does Daisy feel when she is alone? How do you know?** (Possible response: Afraid; she shivers and hides in the reeds.)

- **Where have you gotten lost? How did you feel?** (Possible response: I got lost at the mall. I was afraid.)

RESPOND TO LITERATURE

Discuss the Story   Have children tell what they liked about the story.

Literature Focus

PROBLEM-SOLUTION

Remind children that most stories have a main character who has a problem to solve.

MODEL   The most important character in *Come Along, Daisy!* is Daisy. Her problem is that she gets lost and can't find her mother. Then Mama Duck finds Daisy and everything works out.

Ask children to recall the problem in the *Big Book: Five Little Ducks* and tell how everything works out. (The problem is that one by one the little ducks do not come home. Mother duck goes looking and finds her five little ducks.)

ENGLISH-LANGUAGE LEARNERS

Name the various animals in the book and have children repeat the names. Then say the name of an animal on a page and ask children to point to the corresponding picture. When children become familiar with the animal names, encourage them to take turns naming an animal and asking a partner to point to its picture.

ONGOING ASSESSMENT

As you share *Come Along, Daisy!* note whether children

- can locate the title and author of the story.

- listen for a period of time.

- use pictures and context to make predictions.

FLORIDA STANDARDS/GLEs   FCAT: LA.A.1.1.4.K.1 Comprehension; *Also* **LA.C.3.1.2.K.1** Questions; **LA.E.2.1.1.K.1** Background knowledge

Exploring Our Surroundings   379

OBJECTIVE

To match consonant q to its sound /kw/

Materials

- *Letter and Sound Chart 26*
- *Tactile Letter Cards q*
- *Picture/Word Card queen*
- pocket chart
- *Quilt Pattern (page TI4)*
- scissors
- crayons
- glue

Phonics
Relating /kw/ to q ✔️*Introduce*

ACTIVE BEGINNING

Recite the Rhyme Teach children "A Quick Question." Recite the rhyme and tell them to listen for /kw/. Then have them waddle and quack like ducks after they recite the rhyme again.

A Quick Question

Here's a quick question.

Can you answer back?

What waddles and says

Quack, quack, quack?

TEACH/MODEL

Introduce Letter and Sound Display *Letter and Sound Chart 26.*

Touch the letter *Q.* **What is the name of the letter?**

This letter stands for the /kw/ sound. Say /kw/.

Read aloud the rhyme on the *Letter and Sound Chart,* tracking the print. Read aloud the *Qq* words in the rhyme. Then point to each *q* and have children say the /kw/ sound.

Have children join in as you read the rhyme again.

Quiet, quiet, quiet,
Don't make a peep!
Queen is under the quilt
Fast asleep.

▲ **Letter and Sound Chart 26**

380   Exploring Our Surroundings

FLORIDA STANDARDS/GLEs   FCAT: LA.A.1.1.2.K.5 Phonetic principles; *Also* **LA.A.1.1.2.K.1** Print organization; **LA.A.1.1.2.K.2** Alphabet; **LA.A.1.1.2.K.3** Sounds; **LA.C.1.1.1.K.2** Oral language; **LA.D.2.1.2.K.1** Patterned structures

PRACTICE/APPLY

Guided Practice Distribute *Tactile Letter Cards q.* Then place *Picture/Word Card queen* in the pocket chart. Say the name of the picture as you point to the *q.* Have children repeat the word.

Tell children: **This word begins with *q.***

Point to the *q* in *queen.* **The /kw/ sound is at the beginning of *queen.***

I'll say some words. If the word begins with the /kw/ sound, hold up your *q* card. If it doesn't begin with the /kw/ sound, don't hold up your card. thumbs↑ thumbs↓

page   quick   quiz   carrot   quack   quiet   dish

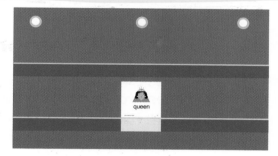

Independent Practice Distribute copies of the Quilt Pattern (page T14). Have children draw and label on the quilt a picture of a word whose name begins with the /kw/ sound. Ask children to whisper the name to you before they draw. Children can cut out their quilt pattern and glue it on drawing paper. Since the quilt is on a bed in the pattern, have children add details to make a scene that looks like their bedroom at home. They can write *Qq*'s around the border. Encourage them to take turns naming other words that begin with *q.*

FLORIDA STANDARDS/GLEs   FCAT: LA.A.1.1.2.K.5 Phonetic principles; *Also* **LA.A.1.1.2.K.2** Alphabet; **LA.A.1.1.2.K.3** Sounds; **LA.B.1.1.2.K.2** Basic formats; **LA.B.1.1.3.K.2** Print direction

Display the *Letter and Sound Chart Sentence Strips* and have children match them to a line on the chart. Ask children to find and frame a word that begins with *q.* Say the word and have the children repeat it. For more practice with Consonant *Qq,* see Alternative Teaching Strategies, page T 7.

ENGLISH-LANGUAGE LEARNERS

Before children draw and label an object whose name begins with the /kw/ sound, have them point to the *Picture Card,* say the name of the picture, and make the beginning sound they hear.

Phonics Resources

Phonics Express™ CD-ROM, **Level A,** Sparkle/Route 6/Park and Harbor

Phonics Practice Book pages 121–122

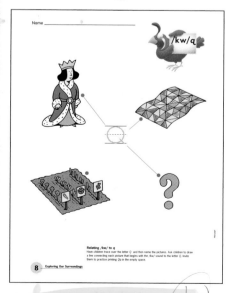

▲ **Practice Book page 8**

High-Frequency Word
one ✔ Introduce

OBJECTIVE

To read high-frequency word one

Materials

- *Big Book: Five Little Ducks*
- *High-Frequency Word Card*
- *Teacher's Resource Book* p. 140
- drawing paper
- crayons

TEACH/MODEL

Display the *Big Book: Five Little Ducks*. Turn to pages 20 and 22. Read these two pages aloud while tracking the print. Place emphasis on the word *one* as you read.

Point to the word *one* in the text and say: **This is the word *one*.** Have children say the word. Display *High-Frequency Word Card one*. Ask: **What word is this?** Reread the sentences in the *Big Book* and have children repeat them after you. Have a child match the *High-Frequency Word Card one* to the word *one* on page 22.

PRACTICE/APPLY

Guided Practice Make copies of the *High-Frequency Word Card one* in the *Teacher's Resource Book*. Have children sit in a circle. Give each child a card and tell children to point to the word *one* and say it. Then have each child complete this sentence, pointing to the word *one* as he or she says it:

I have one _____.

Continue around the circle until all the children have had a turn to complete the sentence.

Independent Practice Have children copy the sentence frame *I have one _____.* on drawing paper and complete it. Ask them to illustrate their sentences.

FLORIDA STANDARDS/GLEs **FCAT: LA.A.1.1.2.K.4** Words; **LA.A.1.1.3.K.5** Story elements; **LA.C.3.1.3.K.1** Basic vocabulary; *Also* **LA.A.1.1.2.K.1** Print organization; **LA.B.1.1.2.K.2** Basic formats; **LA.B.1.1.3.K.2** Print direction; **LA.C.1.1.3.K.1** Conversation rules

Words to Remember
Word Wall

Reading Words   Hold up the *High-Frequency Word Card one* and have children read it aloud. Place the word card under the letter *Oo* on the classroom word chart.

Go on a Word Hunt   Have children look at the words on the word chart. As you give clues such as the following, have children point to and read the words.

- **This word has three letters. It is a number word.** *(one)*
- **This word has four letters. It means "to use your eyes."** *(look)*
- **This word begins with /m/. It means "myself."** *(me)*
- **This word begins with /d/.** *(do)*
- **This word has two letters. It means the opposite of *yes*.** *(no)*

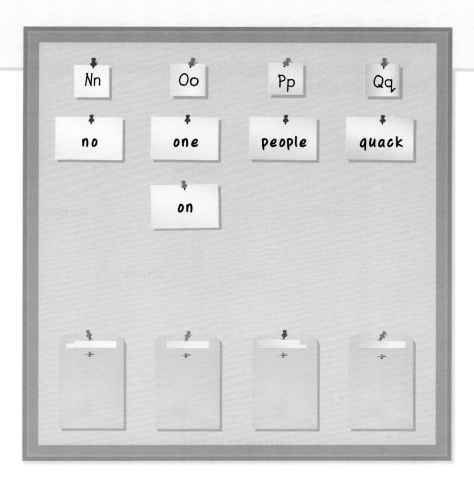

▲ **Practice Book page 9**

FLORIDA STANDARDS/GLEs   FCAT: LA.A.1.1.3.K.4 Build vocabulary; *Also* LA.A.1.1.2.K.3 Sounds; LA.A.1.1.3.K.1 Frequent words

Exploring Our Surroundings   **383**

OBJECTIVES

- *To share information and ideas, speaking in complete, coherent sentences*

- *To understand describing words*

- *To write describing words*

Materials

- *Library Book: Come Along, Daisy!*

- chart paper

- marker

Interactive Writing

Write Describing Words

TELL ABOUT A CHARACTER

Talk About a Story Character Page through *Come Along, Daisy!* with children. Have them talk about what Daisy is like. Remind them that describing words tell what someone or something is like.

Write Describing Words Tell children that together they are going to write describing words about Daisy. On chart paper, write *Daisy* in the center of a word web. Then help children suggest words that tell about Daisy by asking the following questions:

- How did Daisy feel when she heard a noise in the reeds?
- What color is Daisy?
- Is Daisy big or small?

Record their ideas in the word web. As you write, talk about the sounds and letters in words you use. Invite children to contribute by writing letters they know. Have them repeat the sound of each letter as they write it.

Journal Writing Have children write and draw about a favorite story character.

FLORIDA STANDARDS/GLEs FCAT: LA.A.1.1.2.K.4 Words; **LA.A.1.1.3.K.5** Story elements; **LA.B.2.1.2.K.1** Record ideas; **LA.C.3.1.3.K.1** Basic vocabulary; *Also* **LA.B.1.1.2.K.2** Basic formats; **LA.B.1.1.3.K.2** Print direction; **LA.B.2.1.1.K.2** Contribute ideas; **LA.D.1.1.1.K.2** Language Functions

WRAP UP Share Time

Reflect on the Lesson Have children tell about their favorite part of *Come Along, Daisy!* Display the word web they created during Interactive Writing. Read the words they think describe Daisy. Then ask them to tell what word they learned today. (*one*)

S.S.R. Sustained Silent Reading Have children read silently from a book of their choice.

Centers ART

A Q Crown

Have children write *Qq* on a long strip of tagboard. Tell them to draw silly pictures around the *Qq*, showing objects whose names begin with /kw/. Children can decorate their crowns with feathers or glitter. When they have finished, help them tape the two ends of the paper strip together to form a crown that will fit their head.

Materials

- long strips of tagboard with the top cut into points to resemble a crown
- crayons
- feathers
- glitter
- glue
- tape

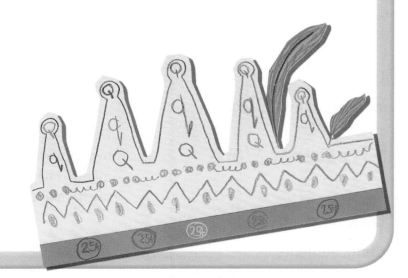

FLORIDA STANDARDS/GLEs **FCAT: LA.A.1.1.2.K.5** Phonetic principles; **LA.A.1.1.3.K.4** Build vocabulary; *Also* **LA.A.1.1.2.K.3** Sounds

Exploring Our Surroundings **385**

Day at a Glance
Day 3

WARM UP

Phonemic Awareness
Phoneme Isolation
Medial

Sharing Literature
Read-Aloud Anthology:
"Bear in There"

Read

KINDERGARTEN
READ-ALOUD
Anthology
Harcourt

Develop Concept Vocabulary

Respond to Literature

Literature Focus: Action Words

Phonics

Consonants /kw/*q*, /y/*y*

High-Frequency Word
little

Writing

Writing: Sentence

MORNING MESSAGE

Kindergarten News

This month is _____.

This month our school _____.

Write Kindergarten News Talk with children about a school event that will be happening this month.

Use prompts such as the following to guide children as you write the news:

- **What will be happening at our school this month?**
- **Who can show me where to begin writing?**
- **What letter will I write first in the word *month*?**
- **Let's count the letters in the word *school*. How many letters are there?**

As you write the message, invite children to contribute by writing letters or words they have learned previously. Remind them to use proper spacing, capitalization, and punctuation.

Calendar Language

Display a calendar for the current month and read the name of the month. Invite children to name the month and count the days.

Sunday	Monday	Tuesday	Wednesday	Thursday	Friday	Saturday
		1	2	3	4	5
6	7	8	9	10	11	12
13	14	15	16	17	18	19
20	21	22	23	24	25	26
27	28	29	30	31		

FLORIDA STANDARDS/GLEs FCAT: LA.A.1.1.2.K.5 Phonetic principles; **LA.A.2.1.5.K.2** Get information; **LA.B.2.1.2.K.1** Record ideas; *Also* **LA.A.1.1.2.K.1** Print organization; **LA.A.1.1.2.K.3** Sounds; **LA.C.1.1.3.K.1** Conversation rules; **LA.C.3.1.2.K.1** Questions

Phonemic Awareness

PHONEME ISOLATION: MEDIAL

Identify the Middle Sound in Words   Tell children you will say a sentence and they are to listen for words that have the same middle sound.

MODEL The fuzzy bug hums in the sun. Say the sentence with me.

The middle sound in *fuzzy* is /u/. Say the word. (*fuzzy*)

The middle sound in *bug* is /u/. Say the word. (*bug*)

The middle sound in *hums* is /u/. Say the word. (*hums*)

The middle sound in *sun* is /u/. Say the word. (*sun*)

Fuzzy, *bug*, *hums*, and *sun* all have the same middle sound, /u/. Say them with me again.

PHONEME ISOLATION: MEDIAL

Say two words to children and have them listen for the middle sound and say it together.

man, **cap** (/a/)	**pet**, **wet** (/e/)
duck, **fun** (/u/)	**cub**, **gum** (/u/)
pig, **six** (/i/)	**fox**, **hot** (/o/)

BELOW-LEVEL

Display the *Picture Cards* sun and bus and have children name the pictures. Tell children the middle sound, then elongate the middle sound in each word, /suun/ and /buus/, and have children do the same. Repeat with these pairs of *Picture Cards*: cat/van, dog/jet, fish/pig, duck/nest, hen/jet.

Sharing Literature

Read "Bear in There"

READ ALOUD

Before Reading   Tell children they will listen to a poem called "Bear in There." Have children tell places where a bear might be. Then ask children if a bear might be in a Frigidaire. Explain that *Frigidaire* is the name of a refrigerator. Then use these prompts to build background:

• **What is a refrigerator?**

• **What is a polar bear? Where do polar bears live?**

After the discussion, ask children to speculate on why a polar bear might be in a refrigerator.

During Reading   Read the poem aloud. As you read,

• emphasize the rhyming words.

• pantomime some of the action words.

• invite children to pantomime the actions of the bear as you read the poem once more.

▲ **Read-Aloud Anthology**

OBJECTIVES

• *To listen and respond to a poem*

• *To make predictions*

• *To understand action words*

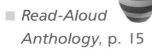

Materials

■ *Read-Aloud Anthology*, p. 15

■ drawing paper

■ crayons

FLORIDA STANDARDS/GLEs   **FCAT: LA.A.1.1.2.K.4** Words; **LA.A.1.1.3.K.5** Story elements; *Also* **LA.C.1.1.1.K.2** Oral language; **LA.C.3.1.2.K.1** Questions; **LA.D.2.1.2.K.1** Patterned structures

DEVELOP CONCEPT VOCABULARY

After Reading   Read the poem once more and ask children to listen for the kinds of food that are in the refrigerator. On chart paper, list their responses in a word web, with *Food* in the center. (*meat, fish, noodles, rice, soda*) Then ask questions such as these:

- **Which food do you like better** *meat* **or** *rice*? **Why?** (*Possible response: I like rice because my mom eats it.*)

- **Which foods could you keep outside the refrigerator?** (*noodles, rice*)

- **Which word names something to drink?** (*soda*)

- **Where else would you find a fish?** (*in a lake*) Ask children to use the word *fish* in a sentence.

RESPOND TO LITERATURE

Draw a Picture About the Poem   Have children draw and label a picture of the polar bear eating something from their refrigerator.

Literature Focus

ACTION WORDS

Remind children that action words tell what a person or animal is doing. As you name each of these action words from the poem, pantomime what the bear is doing: *nibbling, munching, slurping, licking*. Have children repeat the words and the pantomime actions with you.

Ask children to name other action words that tell what a polar bear might do. (*growl, stomp, climb, run*)

ENGLISH-LANGUAGE LEARNERS

Show children pictures of the following objects as you name each one: refrigerator, polar bear, meat, fish, noodles, rice, soda, ice. Have children repeat the words with you. Then point to a picture and ask children to tell you its name.

ONGOING ASSESSMENT

As you share "Bear in There," note whether children

- pantomime action words.
- listen for a period of time.

FLORIDA STANDARDS/GLEs   FCAT: LA.A.1.1.2.K.4 Words; **LA.A.1.1.2.K.5** Phonetic principles; **LA.A.1.1.3.K.5** Story elements; **LA.C.3.1.3.K.1** Basic vocabulary; *Also* **LA.A.1.1.3.K.2** Nouns and verbs; **LA.B.1.1.2.K.2** Basic formats; **LA.B.1.1.3.K.2** Print direction; **LA.B.2.1.4.K.1** Informational texts

OBJECTIVES

• *To recognize uppercase and lowercase Qq and Yy*

• *To match sounds to letters*

Materials

■ pocket chart

■ *Big Alphabet Cards Qq, Yy*

■ *Alphabet Cards Q and Y*

■ *Picture Cards queen, yak, yarn, yellow, yo-yo*

■ *Letters and Sounds Place Mats*

Phonics

Consonants /kw/q, /y/y

 Review

ACTIVE BEGINNING

Recite Rhymes   Display *Alphabet Cards Qq* and *Yy*. Ask children to name each letter and "write" the letter in the palm of a hand. Then have children join in reciting "A Quick Question" (page 380) and "Yippee! Yay!" (page 212).

TEACH/MODEL

Discriminate Q and Y
Display *Big Alphabet Card Q* in a pocket chart and ask for the letter name.

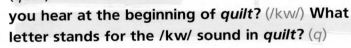

Point to the picture and say its name: (*quilt*). Have children repeat it. (*quilt*) **What sound do you hear at the beginning of *quilt*?** (/kw/) **What letter stands for the /kw/ sound in *quilt*?** (q)

Follow the same procedure for *Big Alphabet Card Yy*.

Place in a pocket chart *Alphabet Cards Q* and *Y* and *Picture Cards queen* and *yarn*. Say each picture name and tell children you need to decide where to put each *Picture Card*.

MODEL   **I'll start with the queen. *Qu—een* begins with the /kw/ sound. So I'll put the picture of the queen below *Qq*.**

Model the same process with *Picture Card yarn*.

 FLORIDA STANDARDS/GLEs   FCAT: LA.A.1.1.2.K.5 Phonetic principles; *Also* **LA.A.1.1.2.K.2** Alphabet; **LA.A.1.1.2.K.3** Sounds; **LA.C.3.1.2.K.1** Questions; **LA.D.2.1.2.K.1** Patterned structures

PRACTICE/APPLY

Guided Practice Place these *Picture Cards* on the chalk ledge: *yellow*, *yo-yo*, *queen*, *yak*, *yarn*. Tell children that they will now sort some pictures.

Say the picture name. If the beginning sound is /kw/, let's put the card below the Q. If the beginning sound is /y/, let's put the card below the Y.

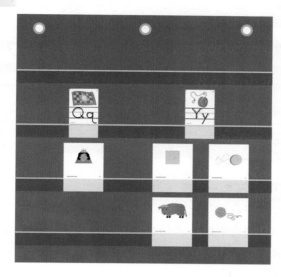

Independent Practice Give each child a *Letters and Sounds Place Mat*.

I'm going to say some words. Listen carefully to the sound you hear at the beginning of the word. Think about the letter that stands for that sound; then point to that letter on your mat.

—Sign language - hold up "sign" or "y sign"

quick	yes	quill	quack	yesterday	yogurt

you	quiet	young	question	yam	quail

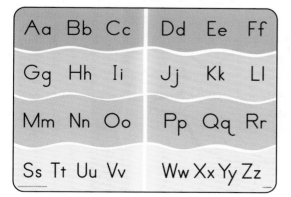 

FLORIDA STANDARDS/GLEs   FCAT: LA.A.1.1.2.K.5 Phonetic principles; *Also* LA.A.1.1.2.K.2 Alphabet; LA.A.1.1.2.K.3 Sounds; LA.C.1.1.1.K.1 Follow directions

BELOW-LEVEL

Have children name the pictures on *Picture Cards* for *q* and *y*, say the sound for each letter, and trace the letter on *Tactile Letter Cards q* and *y*.

ADVANCED

Have children name other words that begin with *q* and *y*. They can make their own picture cards for one or more words.

Phonics Resources

Phonics Express™ CD-ROM, **Level A,** Sparkle/Route 6/Fire Station; Bumper/Route 3/Train Station; Bumper/Route 4/Harbor; Bumper/Route 5/Market

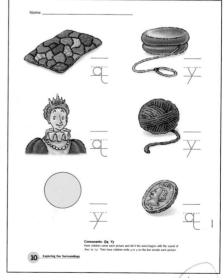

▲ **Practice Book page 10**

Exploring Our Surroundings   391

OBJECTIVE

To read high-frequency word little

Materials

- *Big Book: Five Little Ducks*
- High-Frequency Word Card *little*
- *Teacher's Resource Book* p. 140
- sentence strips
- drawing paper
- crayons
- glue

High-Frequency Word *little* ✔ Introduce

TEACH/MODEL

Display *Five Little Ducks*. Read the title aloud. Then read the first two pages of text while tracking print.

Point to the word *Little* in the title and say: **This is the word *little*.** Point to the word *little* in the text and say: **This is the word *little*.** Have children say the word. Display the *High-Frequency Word Card little*. Ask: **What word is this?** Reread the text and ask children to repeat the sentences after you. Then have one child match the *High-Frequency Word Card little* to the word *little* in each sentence.

PRACTICE/APPLY

Guided Practice Make copies of the *High-Frequency Word Card little* in the *Teacher's Resource Book*. Give each child a card and tell children to point to the word *little* and say it. Ask children to find in the classroom something that is little. Have them say the following sentence, pointing to their *Word Card* as they say the word *little*.

> The _____ is little.

Independent Practice Make copies of the *High-Frequency Word Cards one* and *little* in the *Teacher's Resource Book*. Have children draw a picture of something little and glue the words beside their picture.

 FLORIDA STANDARDS/GLEs FCAT: LA.A.1.1.2.K.4 Words; **LA.A.1.1.3.K.5** Story elements; **LA.C.3.1.3.K.1** Basic vocabulary; *Also* **LA.A.1.1.2.K.1** Print organization; **LA.A.1.1.3.K.1** Frequent words

Words to Remember
Word Wall

Reading Words Hold up the *High-Frequency Word Card little* and have children read it aloud. Have a child place the word card under the letter *Ll* on the classroom word chart.

Words in Sentences Have children look very closely at their new word, *little*. Ask them to name the letters in the word. Then write the following sentence frames on sentence strips: *I see a little _____. I like the little _____.* Ask children to read each sentence strip. Ask two children to frame the word *little*. Then have children take turns completing the sentences, tracking the print as they do so.

I see a little _____.

I like the little _____.

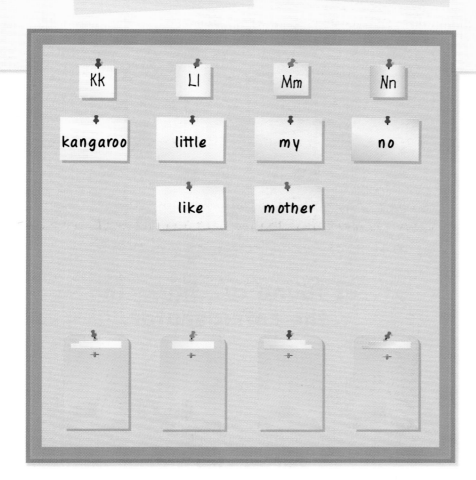

REACHING ALL LEARNERS

Diagnostic Check: High-Frequency Words

If... children cannot recognize and read the high-frequency word *little*,

Then... have them use *Magnetic Letters* or *Letter Cards* to form the word. Have them touch and name each letter in the word and track the print as they read the word. Have children read the word on the *Word Card* and then in text.

ADDITIONAL SUPPORT ACTIVITIES

BELOW-LEVEL	Reteach, p. S38
ADVANCED	Extend, p. S39
ENGLISH-LANGUAGE LEARNERS	Reteach, p. S39

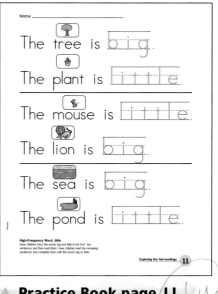

▲ **Practice Book page 11**

FLORIDA STANDARDS/GLEs FCAT: **LA.A.1.1.2.K.4** Words; **LA.A.1.1.3.K.4** Build vocabulary; *Also*; **LA.A.1.1.2.K.1** Print organization; **LA.A.1.1.2.K.2** Alphabet; **LA.A.1.1.3.K.1** Frequent words; **LA.B.2.1.4.K.1** Informational texts; **LA.C.1.1.1.K.1** Follow directions; **LA.C.1.1.3.K.1** Conversation rules

Exploring Our Surroundings **393**

OBJECTIVES

- To share information and ideas, using complete, coherent sentences

- To write sentences

- To write by moving from left to right

- To use letters and phonetically spelled words to write about an event

Materials

- drawing paper
- crayons

Writing

Write a Sentence

DRAW AND WRITE

Talk About the Poem   Ask children to tell you what kind of animal is in the refrigerator in the poem "Bear in There." Have them suggest other animals that would be funny to find in the refrigerator.

Write Sentences   Write the following sentence frame on paper: *I found a _____ in the refrigerator.* Make copies and distribute them to children. Read the sentence frame aloud and have children repeat it with you. Then ask children to draw a picture of another animal that would be funny to find in the refrigerator. Have children finish the sentence by writing the animal's name.

I found a _tigr_ in the refrigerator.

Self-Selected Writing   Have children write and draw about anything they'd like. If they have difficulty thinking of a topic have them ask two friends what they're going to write about.

FLORIDA STANDARDS/GLEs   FCAT: LA.A.1.1.2.K.4 Words; **LA.A.1.1.2.K.5** Phonetic principles; **LA.A.1.1.3.K.4** Build vocabulary; **LA.B.2.1.2.K.1** Record ideas; *Also* **LA.A.1.1.2.K.1** Print organization; **LA.B.1.1.2.K.2** Basic formats; **LA.B.1.1.3.K.1** Spelling approximations; **LA.B.1.1.3.K.2** Print direction; **LA.C.1.1.1.K.1** Follow directions

WRAP UP Share Time

Author's Chair Ask children to talk about the poem they heard today, "Bear in There." Then invite children to share the sentence they wrote during the Writing lesson.

S.S.R. Have children read silently from a book of their choice.

Centers DRAMATIC PLAY

In the Kitchen

Provide kitchen props in the center for children to set up their own kitchen. Use large boxes or a play refrigerator and stove. Have children plan a meal they would like to make. Help them divide up the tasks needed to prepare and serve the food. Encourage children to describe their tasks as they are performing them.

Materials

■ kitchen props, such as pots, pans, spoons, measuring cups, pot holders

■ large boxes or play refrigerator and stove

FLORIDA STANDARDS/GLEs **FCAT: LA.C.3.1.3.K.1** Basic vocabulary; *Also* **LA.A.1.1.2.K.1** Print organization; **LA.E.2.1.1.K.2** Personal interpretations

Exploring Our Surroundings **395**

WARM UP

Phonemic Awareness
Phoneme Blending

Sharing Literature
Big Book of Rhymes and Songs: "The Bear Went Over the Mountain"

Read
Big Book of Rhymes and Songs
Harcourt

Develop Listening Comprehension

Respond to Literature

Literature Focus: Text Patterns

Phonics
Consonants /kw/q, /z/z

Reading
Decodable Book 13: Little Cat, Big Cat

Writing
Interactive Writing: Directions

MORNING MESSAGE

Kindergarten News

(Child's name) will have a special day on _____. (Child's name) will _____ on this special day.

Write Kindergarten News   Talk with children about a day that is special for them. Ask them what they do on that day.

Use prompts such as the following to guide children as you write the news:

- **Do you have a special day coming up? What makes it special?**
- **What letter should I write first in the word *day*?**
- **Let's clap syllables for the word *special*. How many parts do you clap?**
- **What punctuation mark should I put at the end of the sentence?**

As you write the message, invite children to contribute by writing letters, words, or names they have learned previously. Remind them to use proper spacing, capitalization, and punctuation.

Calendar Language

Say the seasons of the year. Have children repeat the seasons of the year with you. Ask: *What season is it after Spring?*

Sunday	Monday	Tuesday	Wednesday	Thursday	Friday	Saturday
		1	2	3	4	5
6	7	8	9	10	11	12
13	14	15	16	17	18	19
20	21	22	23	24	25	26
27	28	29	30	31		

FLORIDA STANDARDS/GLEs   FCAT: LA.A.1.1.2.K.5 Phonetic principles; *Also* **LA.A.1.1.2.K.2** Alphabet; **LA.A.1.1.2.K.3** Sounds; **LA.B.1.1.3.K.3** Punctuation; **LA.C.1.1.3.K.1** Conversation rules; **LA.C.3.1.2.K.1** Questions

Phonemic Awareness

PHONEME BLENDING

Blend Phonemes   Use the rabbit for this blending activity. Tell children they can listen to the sounds the rabbit will say and name the word the rabbit is saying.

MODEL /kw/ /a/ /k/. Say the sounds with the rabbit: /kw/ /a/ /k/. Say the sounds more quickly: /kkwwaakk/. Now say the word *quack*.

Ask children to blend the sounds and say the words to finish each rhyme the rabbit says.

The cat has a /h/ /a/ /t/. (*hat*)

The pet is all /w/ /e/ /t/. (*wet*)

The duck is back. Hear it /kw/ /a/ /k/. (*quack*)

The man drives a /v/ /a/ /n/. (*van*)

It is fun to jump and /r/ /u/ /n/. (*run*)

There is a bug in the /m/ /u/ /g/. (*mug*)

Let's sit. It's time to /kw/ /i/ /t/. (*quit*)

I have six eggs to /m/ /i/ /ks/. (*mix*)

▲ "Down by the Bay," *Oo-pples and Boo-noo-noos: Songs and Activities for Phonemic Awareness*, pages 69–70.

REACHING ALL LEARNERS

Diagnostic Check: Phonemic Awareness

If... children have difficulty blending sounds to say words,

Then... hold up a picture card with letters in its name. Have children say the name, break it into phonemes, and then say the name again.

ADDITIONAL SUPPORT ACTIVITIES

BELOW-LEVEL   Reteach, p. S40

ADVANCED   Extend, p. S41

ENGLISH-LANGUAGE LEARNERS   Reteach, p. S41

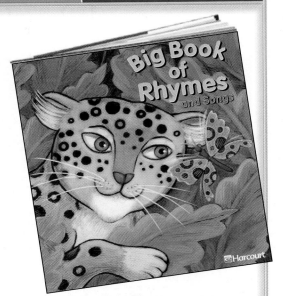

▲ **Big Book of Rhymes and Songs**

OBJECTIVES

- *To recognize the table of contents in a book*

- *To recite a song*

- *To respond to a song through drawing*

- *To recognize text patterns*

Materials

- *Big Book of Rhymes and Songs* p. 21

- *Music CD*

- drawing paper

- crayons

Sharing Literature

Read "The Bear Went Over the Mountain"

READ ALOUD

Before Reading Display the *Big Book of Rhymes and Songs*. Ask a child to turn to the table of contents at the beginning of the book. Ask children what this page lists. Point to the title "The Bear Went Over the Mountain." Ask a child to tell you what page the song is on.

Display page 21 of the *Big Book of Rhymes and Songs* and track the print as you read the title of the song aloud. Set a purpose for rereading the words of the song.

MODEL **I remember that the bear goes over the mountain to see something. I'll read the words again so I can find out what the bear sees.**

During Reading As you read the song aloud,

- track the print.

- emphasize the repeated phrases by having children say them with you.

Then play the song on the *Music CD*. Have children join in on the parts they know and pantomime the movements of a bear going over a mountain.

The Bear Went over the Mountain

The bear went over the mountain,
The bear went over the mountain,
The bear went over the mountain,
To see what he could see.

The other side of the mountain,
The other side of the mountain,
The other side of the mountain,
Was all that he could see.

21

FLORIDA STANDARDS/GLEs **LA.A.1.1.2.K.1** Print organization; **LA.C.1.1.1.K.2** Oral language; **LA.C.3.1.4.K.1** Gestures; **LA.D.1.1.1.K.1** Sound patterns; **LA.D.2.1.2.K.1** Patterned structures; **LA.E.2.1.2.K.1** Patterned structures

DEVELOP LISTENING COMPREHENSION

After Reading   Have children answer these questions about the song:

- **Why does the bear want to go over the mountain?** (to see what is there)

- **What does the bear see when he goes over the mountain?** (the other side of the mountain)

- **How do you think the bear feels when all he sees is the other side of the mountain?** (Possible responses: sad, disappointed)

RESPOND TO LITERATURE

Draw a Different Ending   Distribute drawing paper. Have children draw and label something they think the bear would have liked to have seen on the other side of the mountain.

Literature Focus

TEXT PATTERNS

Sing or play "The Bear Went Over the Mountain" again, asking children to listen for words they hear over and over. Point out that these words are said over and over: *The bear went over the mountain* and *The other side of the mountain*. Remind children that sometimes words are repeated many times in a song, a poem, or a story, which makes them easier to remember. Use children's ideas to create new lines for the song. Write a new line on the board and track the print as you read the line aloud. Have children repeat it three times.

ADVANCED

Ask children to find and name other songs or rhymes in the *Big Book* where words are repeated over and over (such as "Bingo" and "The Kitty Ran Up the Tree").

ONGOING ASSESSMENT

As you share "The Bear Went Over the Mountain," note whether children

- follow along as you track the print.

- recite a song.

FLORIDA STANDARDS/GLEs   FCAT: LA.A.1.1.2.K.5 Phonetic principles; *Also* **LA.B.1.1.2.K.1** Dictate messages; **LA.B.1.1.2.K.2** Basic formats; **LA.B.1.1.3.K.2** Print direction; **LA.C.1.1.1.K.2** Oral language; **LA.C.3.1.2.K.1** Questions

OBJECTIVES

- *To recognize uppercase and lowercase Qq and Zz*

- *To match sounds to letters*

Materials

- pocket chart
- *Big Alphabet Cards Qq, Zz*
- *Picture Cards queen, zebra, zipper, zoo*
- *Letters and Sounds Place Mats*

Phonics

Consonants /kw/q, /z/z ✔ Review

ACTIVE BEGINNING

Recite the Rhymes   Display *Big Alphabet Cards Qq* and *Zz*. Ask children to name each letter and "write" the letter in the palm of a hand. Then have children join in reciting "A Quick Question" (page 380) and "Zip, Zip, Zip" (page 232).

TEACH/MODEL

Discriminate *Q* and *Z*
Display *Big Alphabet Card Z* in a pocket chart and ask for the letter name. (*Zz*)

Point to the picture and say its name: *zebra*. Have children repeat it. (*zebra*)
What sound do you hear at the beginning of *zebra*? (/z/) **What letter stands for the /z/ sound in *zebra*?** (*z*)

Follow the same procedure for *Big Alphabet Card Qq*.

Place in a pocket chart *Alphabet Cards Q* and *Z* and *Picture Cards queen* and *zipper*. Say each picture name and tell children you need to decide where to put each *Picture Card*.

MODEL   **I'll start with the zipper. *Z—ipper* begins with the /z/ sound. So I'll put the picture of the *zipper* below *Z*.**

Model the same process with *Picture Card queen*.

 FLORIDA STANDARDS/GLEs   FCAT: LA.A.1.1.2.K.5 Phonetic principles; *Also* **LA.A.1.1.2.K.2** Alphabet; **LA.A.1.1.2.K.3** Sounds; **LA.C.3.1.2.K.1** Questions; **LA.D.2.1.2.K.1** Patterned structures

PRACTICE/APPLY

Guided Practice Place these *Picture Cards* on the chalk ledge: *zoo, zebra, queen, zipper.* Tell children that they will now sort some pictures.

Say the picture name. If the beginning sound is /kw/, let's put the card below the Q. If the beginning sound is /z/, let's put the card below the Z.

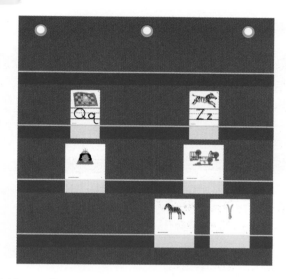

Independent Practice Give each child a *Letters and Sounds Place Mat.*

I'm going to say some words. Listen carefully to the sound you hear at the beginning of the word. Think about the letter that stands for that sound; then point to that letter on your mat.

hold up sign language – "z sign" or "q sign"

zip	quit	zillion	zest	quote	quake
zap	zoom	quick	quarter	zoo	quill

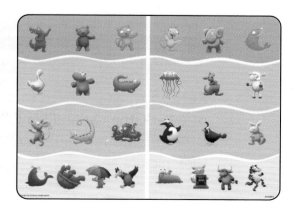

FLORIDA STANDARDS/GLEs **FCAT: LA.A.1.1.2.K.5** Phonetic principles; *Also* **LA.A.1.1.2.K.2** Alphabet; **LA.A.1.1.2.K.3** Sounds; **LA.C.1.1.1.K.1** Follow directions

Have children name the pictures on the *Picture Cards* for *q* and *z*, say the sound for each letter, and "write" the letter in the air with a finger.

Phonics Resources

Phonics Express™ CD-ROM, **Level A,** Sparkle/Route 6/Fire Station; Bumper/Route 5/ Market; Roamer/Route 1/Park; Roamer/Route 2/Train Station

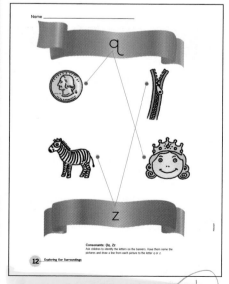

Name _____

Consonants: Qq, Zz
Ask children to identify the letters on the banners. Have them name the pictures and draw a line from each picture to the letter q or z.

12 Exploring Our Surroundings

▲ **Practice Book page 12**

OBJECTIVE

To read high-frequency words one, little

Materials

- *Decodable Book 13: Little Cat, Big Cat*

- *High-Frequency Word Cards* I, little, one, see

- *Picture/Word Cards* cat, fox, dog, pig

- pocket chart

ADVANCED

Have children read *Independent Reader 30: Up the Hill.*

ENGLISH-LANGUAGE LEARNERS

Make sure children understand the concepts of *big* and *little.* Gather a few large and small objects from the classroom and display them as you say: *This is big. This is little.* Have children repeat the sentences with you.

LEARNING TO READ

High-Frequency Words one, *little* ✔ Review

Decodable Book

TEACH/MODEL

Review *one* and *little* Place the *High-Frequency Word Cards* I, *see, one, little,* and the *Picture/Word Card cat* in a pocket chart. Add a period at the end. Point to each word as children read the sentence. Invite children to replace the *Picture/Word Card cat* with *Picture/Word Cards fox, dog,* and *pig* in the sentence and ask them to reread each sentence with the new *Picture/Word Card.*

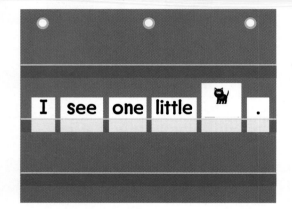

PRACTICE/APPLY

Read the Book Distribute copies of *Little Cat, Big Cat.* Have children read the title encouraging them to point to each word as they say it. Have children read the book pointing to each word as they read.

Respond Ask children to draw a picture of what Little Cat and Big Cat did after Little Cat was rescued. Have them label their picture.

FLORIDA STANDARDS/GLEs FCAT: LA.A.1.1.2.K.4 Words; **LA.E.1.1.1.K.1** Genres; *Also* **LA.A.1.1.2.K.1** Print organization; **LA.A.1.1.3.K.1** Frequent words; **LA.B.1.1.2.K.2** Basic formats; **LA.B.1.1.3.K.1** Spelling approximations; **LA.B.1.1.3.K.2** Print direction; **LA.B.1.1.3.K.3** Punctuation; **LA.B.2.1.4.K.1** Informational texts; **LA.C.1.1.1.K.1** Follow directions

Decodable Book 13: *Little Cat, Big Cat*

I am sad, Pig.
Did you see Little Cat?

2

I did not, Big Cat.
Did Dog see him?

3

I am sad, Dog.
Did you see Little Cat?

4

I did not, Big Cat.
Did Fox see him?

5

I am sad, Fox.
Did you see Little Cat?

6

It is him!
Do you have a net, Fox?

7

I have one, Big Cat.
I can get him.

8

High-Frequency Words

little, you, see, have, one, do

Decodable Words

See List T15.

School-Home Connection

Take-Home Book Version

◄ Decodable Book 13 : *Little Cat, Big Cat*

BELOW-LEVEL

Reread the story with children. Ask them to find and frame the words *little* and *one*.

▲ *Up the Hill* Independent Reader 30

by Malcolm Higgins
illustrated by Holly Cooper

OBJECTIVES

- *To understand the purpose of directions*

- *To write directions*

- *To share information and ideas, speaking in clear, coherent sentences*

Materials

- chart paper

- marker

- Big Book of Rhymes and Songs, page 21

How to Hike
1. PUT ON BOOTS, CLOTHES, AND A HAT.
2. FILL a jug with water.
3. Take your map, binoculars, and walking stick.
4. Go to the mountain.
5. Follow the signs along the trail.

Interactive Writing

Write Directions

Talk About a Hike   Ask children if they've ever taken a long walk or a hike on a trail. Ask: **What types of clothes would I need? How would I know where I am going? What would help me see birds or other animals that are far away?** Help children create a web of items they would need to go on a walking trail.

Write Directions for the Bear   Tell children that together they are going to write directions to tell the bear in the rhyme, "The Bear Went Over the Mountain" how to go hiking over the mountain. Display the poem in the *Big Book of Rhymes and Songs.*

MODEL   **When we want to tell someone how to do something, we can write down directions. The directions have to be in the right order. What should we tell the bear to do first? Let's look at our web and number the words in the order that we will tell bear to use them.**

Invite children to write numerals on the idea web. Then, on chart paper ask children to help you write the title, *How to Hike.* Encourage children to write letters, words, and punctuation they have previously learned. Focus on high-frequency words, medial short vowels, and beginning and ending sounds.

Writing Every Day

Journal Writing   Have children write and draw about something they would like to see on a mountain hike.

🔶 **FLORIDA STANDARDS/GLEs   FCAT: LA.B.1.1.2.K.3** Sequence; **LA.B.2.1.2.K.1** Record ideas; *Also* **LA.A.1.1.2.K.2** Alphabet; **LA.A.1.1.2.K.3** Sounds; **LA.B.1.1.2.K.1** Dictate messages; **LA.B.1.1.2.K.2** Basic formats; **LA.B.1.1.3.K.2** Print direction; **LA.B.2.1.1.K.2** Contribute ideas; **LA.B.2.1.4.K.1** Informational texts; **LA.D.1.1.1.K.2** Language functions

WRAP UP # Share Time

Author's Chair   Gather children around the Author's Chair. Read to children the directions they have suggested for the bear from the Interactive Writing lesson. Invite children to share their picture of what the bear would like to see on the other side of the mountain.

S.S.R. *Sustained Silent Reading*   Have children read silently from a book of their choice.

Centers

SOCIAL STUDIES

My Neighborhood

Have children draw a simple map of their home neighborhood. Have them begin by drawing their own street and house. They can add the houses of friends and neighbors. Other features might include stores, a park, a library, a fire station, and so on. Display children's completed maps on a bulletin board, with the title "Where We Live."

Materials

- drawing paper
- crayons

FLORIDA STANDARDS/GLEs   FCAT: LA.B.1.1.2.K.1 Dictate messages; **LA.B.1.1.3.K.1** Spelling approximations; **LA.B.1.1.3.K.2** Print direction; **LA.D.2.1.2.K.1** Patterned structures; **LA.E.2.1.1.K.1** Background knowledge; **LA.E.2.1.1.K.2** Personal interpretations

Day at a Glance
Day 5

WARM UP

Phonemic Awareness
Phoneme Counting

Sharing Literature
Library Book:
Come Along, Daisy!

Read

Develop Concept Vocabulary

Respond to Literature

Literature Focus: Retell the Story

Phonics
Consonant /kw/q, /ks/x

Writing ✏
Writing: Sound Words

MORNING MESSAGE

Kindergarten News

(Child's name) likes to _____

in the spring. (Child's name) likes to

_____ in the spring.

Write Kindergarten News Talk with children about their favorite spring activities. Encourage them to speak loudly enough for the rest of the class to hear.

Use prompts such as the following to guide children as you write the news:

- **What do you like to do in the spring?**
- **What letter will I write first in (child's name)?**
- **What letter will I write first in the word *spring*?**
- **Let's count the words in the first sentence. How many words are there?**

As you write the message, invite children to contribute by writing letters, words, or names they have learned previously. Remind them to use proper spacing, capitalization, and punctuation.

Calendar Language

Point to the numbers on the calendar. Tell children that the days of each month are numbered and the numbers tell the date. Point to and read aloud the date. Name the month and the date.

Sunday	Monday	Tuesday	Wednesday	Thursday	Friday	Saturday
		1	2	3	4	5
6	7	8	9	10	11	12
13	14	15	16	17	18	19
20	21	22	23	24	25	26
27	28	29	30	31		

FLORIDA STANDARDS/GLEs FCAT: LA.A.1.1.2.K.5 Phonetic principles; **LA.A.2.1.5.K.2** Get information; **LA.B.2.1.2.K.1** Record ideas; *Also* **LA.A.1.1.2.K.2** Alphabet; **LA.A.1.1.2.K.3** Sounds; **LA.C.1.1.3.K.1** Conversation rules; **LA.C.3.1.2.K.1** Questions

Phonemic Awareness

PHONEME COUNTING

Listen for Sounds Remind children how to count the sounds in a word.

MODEL *Ox.* Say the word with me. *Ox.* To count the sounds in the word, I'll say the word like this: /o/ /ks/. Say the sounds: /o/ /ks/. *Ox* has two sounds. I hear /o/ /ks/. *Ox.*

Tell children that you will say some words and they are to listen to hear how many sounds are in each word. Then you will ask them to tell you what those sounds are.

quit (three; /kw/ /i/ /t/)

quill (three; /kw/ /i/ /l/)

up (two; /u/ /p/)

wax (three; /w/ /a/ /ks/)

quack (three; /kw/ /a/ /k/)

sun (three; /s/ /u/ /n/)

mix (two; /m/ /i/ /ks/)

cut (three; /k/ /u/ /t/)

if (two; /i/ /f/)

six (three; /s/ /i/ /ks/)

BELOW-LEVEL

Give children additional practice segmenting the sounds in two-letter words such as *ox, up,* and *Ed.* Then, add a single consonant to those words to form three-letter words such as *box, fox, cup, pup,* and *red, led.*

ADVANCED

Provide children with the *Picture Cards baby, fork, gate, jelly, mitten,* and *nest.* Have them name each picture and then segment the phonemes in the word.

▲ **Library Book**

OBJECTIVES

- *To identify the front and back covers of a book*

- *To recall story events*

- *To understand real and make-believe*

- *To retell the story*

Materials

■ *Library Book: Come Along, Daisy!*

■ chart paper

■ marker

■ drawing paper

■ crayons

Sharing Literature

Read Come Along, Daisy!

READ ALOUD

Before Reading Display the book *Come Along, Daisy!* Ask a child to point to the title as you read it aloud. Have another child show the front of the book and the back of the book. Then use these prompts to help children recall the story:

- **What is Daisy's problem in the story?** (She gets lost.)

- **How is the problem fixed?** (Daisy's mother finds her.)

Help children set a purpose for listening to the story before you reread it.

MODEL I remember that Daisy has a reason for getting lost. I want to read the story again to remember why she does not stay with her mother.

During Reading Reread the story aloud. As you read,

- pause to talk about the setting in the book.

- emphasize the sound words.

- point out that we know this is a make-believe story because the animals talk.

- explain that sometimes an author gives clues about the story in pictures and words.

MODEL When something big stirs under Daisy, she shivers. The author doesn't say that the "something big" is a fish, but I can tell it *is* a fish by looking at the picture. The author doesn't say that Daisy is scared, but I can tell that she *is* scared because she shivers.

FLORIDA STANDARDS/GLEs FCAT: LA.A.1.1.4.K.1 Comprehension; LA.A.2.1.1.K.1 Main idea; LA.C.1.1.4.K.1 Sequence; LA.E.1.1.1.K.1 Genres; LA.E.1.1.2.K.1 Story elements; *Also* LA.A.2.1.4.K.1 Illustrations; LA.C.1.1.1.K.2 Oral language; LA.C.3.1.2.K.1 Questions

DEVELOP CONCEPT VOCABULARY

After Reading Write these words in a word web on chart paper:

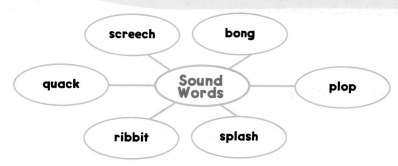

Read each word and have children repeat it. Talk about who makes the sound and what they are doing. (*bong*: Daisy jumping on lily pads; *plop*: the frog jumping on a lily pad; *quack*: Daisy; *ribbit*: the frog; *splash*: the frog jumping in the water; *screech*: big bird in the sky)

RESPOND TO LITERATURE

Draw a Picture of a Favorite Scene Have children draw and label a picture of their favorite part of the story.

RETELL THE STORY

Tell children that they are going to work together to retell the story *Come Along, Daisy!* Lead children to name the characters and tell what happens in the beginning, middle, and ending of the story. Record their ideas on chart paper and review the events to confirm the order.

1. Daisy plays in the pond.
2. She looks for her mother, but Mama Duck is gone.
3. Daisy hides in the reeds.
4. Mama Duck finds Daisy.

FLORIDA STANDARDS/GLEs **FCAT:** LA.A.1.1.2.K.4 Words; LA.A.1.1.3.K.5 Story elements; LA.A.1.1.4.K.1 Comprehension; LA.A.2.1.3.K.1 Supportive details; LA.C.3.1.3.K.1 Basic vocabulary; LA.E.1.1.2.K.1 Story elements; *Also* LA.A.1.1.3.K.3 Categorize words; LA.B.1.1.2.K.1 Dictate messages; LA.B.1.1.2.K.2 Basic formats; LA.B.1.1.3.K.2 Print direction; LA.B.2.1.4.K.1 Informational texts; LA.C.1.1.3.K.1 Conversation rules

ADVANCED

Ask children to retell another story they have heard or read.

ONGOING ASSESSMENT

As you share *Come Along, Daisy!* note whether children

- can identify a character's feelings.
- can recall story events.
- understand real and make-believe.

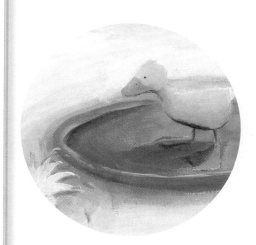

OBJECTIVES

- *To recognize uppercase and lowercase Qq and Xx*
- *To match sounds to letters*

Materials

- pocket chart
- *Big Alphabet Cards Qq, Xx*
- *Alphabet Cards Q and X*
- *Picture Cards fox, lunch box, queen, X ray*
- *Letters and Sounds Place Mats*

Phonics

Consonants /kw/ q, /ks/ x ✓ Review

ACTIVE BEGINNING

Recite the Rhymes Display *Big Alphabet Cards Qq* and *Xx*. Ask children to name each letter and to "write" the letter in the palm of a hand. Then have children join in reciting "A Quick Question" (page 380) and "Fox and Ox" (Vol. 2, page 570).

TEACH/MODEL

Discriminate *Q* and *X*
Display *Big Alphabet Card X* in a pocket chart and ask for the letter name.

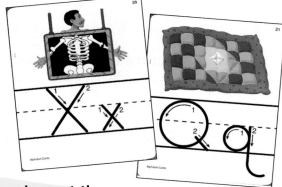

Point to the picture and say its name: (*X ray.*) Have children repeat it. (*X ray*) **What sound do you hear at the beginning of *X ray*?** (/ks/) **What letter stands for the /ks/ sound in *X ray*?** (x)

Follow the same procedure for *Big Alphabet Card Qq*.

Place in a pocket chart *Alphabet Cards Q* and *X* and *Picture Cards queen* and *X ray*. Say each picture name and tell children you need to decide where to put each *Picture Card*.

MODEL **I'll start with the X ray. *X ray* begins with the /ks/ sound. So I'll put the picture of the *X ray* below X.**

Model the same process with *Picture Card queen*.

FLORIDA STANDARDS/GLEs **FCAT: LA.A.1.1.2.K.5** Phonetic principles; *Also* **LA.A.1.1.2.K.2** Alphabet; **LA.A.1.1.2.K.3** Sounds; **LA.C.3.1.2.K.1** Questions; **LA.D.2.1.2.K.1** Patterned structures

PRACTICE/APPLY

Guided Practice   Place these *Picture Cards* on the chalk ledge: *queen, fox, lunch box.* Tell children that they will now sort some pictures.

Say the picture name. If the beginning sound is /kw/, let's put the card below the Q. If the ending sound is /ks/, let's put the card below the X.

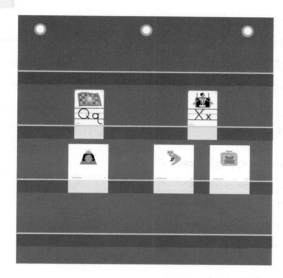

Independent Practice   Give each child a *Letters and Sounds Place Mat.*

I'm going to say some words. Listen carefully to the sound you hear at the beginning of the word. Think about the letter that stands for that sound; then point to that letter on your mat.

had lep jish language for q or x

quick	question	X ray
quiet	quarter	quote

Repeat the procedure for final sounds, using these words.

fox	cat	six
wax	mix	had

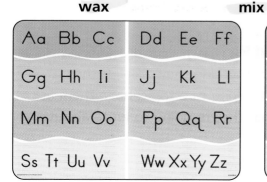

FLORIDA STANDARDS/GLEs   FCAT: LA.A.1.1.2.K.5 Phonetic principles; *Also* **LA.A.1.1.2.K.2** Alphabet; **LA.A.1.1.2.K.3** Sounds; **LA.C.1.1.1.K.1** Follow directions

Exploring Our Surroundings   411

Diagnostic Check: Phonics

If... children cannot recognize and apply /kw/q and /ks/x,

Then... have children focus on one letter at a time. Have them look for a picture whose name begins with /kw/ first. Then have them name *Picture Cards* whose names end with /ks/.

ADDITIONAL SUPPORT ACTIVITIES

BELOW-LEVEL	Reteach, p. S42
ADVANCED	Extend, p. S43
ENGLISH-LANGUAGE LEARNERS	Reteach, p. S43

Phonics Resources

Phonics Express™ CD-ROM, Sparkle/Route 6/Fire Station; Sparkle/Route 5/Building Site

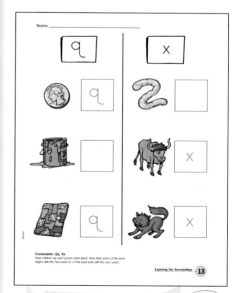

▲ **Practice Book page 13**

OBJECTIVES

- *To write by moving from left to right*

- *To write sound words*

- *To use letters and phonetically spelled words to write animal sounds*

Materials

- ■ crayons
- ■ drawing paper

Writing

Write Sound Words

DRAW AND WRITE

Talk About Sound Words   Display the word web from Develop Concept Vocabulary (p. 409) to review with children the sound words from *Come Along, Daisy!* Have children think of other words that name sounds. Prompt them by asking: **What sound does a bee make?** (*buzz*) **A dog?** (*woof*) **A cow?** (*moo*) **A bird?** (*tweet*).

Write Sound Words   Model for children how to use speech bubbles. Have each child draw a picture of an animal or thing that makes a special sound. Then show children how to draw a speech balloon above the picture. Have them write the sound word inside the balloon.

MODEL   *Buzz* **is the sound a bee makes. I will draw a picture of a bee. A speech bubble shows what sound the bee is making. I will draw it from the bee's mouth.**

SHARE

Read Animal Sounds   Invite children to share the picture they drew.

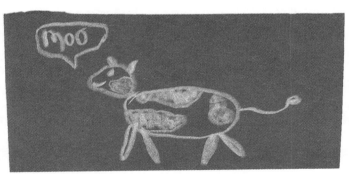

Self-Selected Writing   Have children write and draw about anything they'd like. If they have difficulty thinking of a topic, have them ask two friends what they're going to write about.

FLORIDA STANDARDS/GLEs   FCAT: LA.A.1.1.2.K.4 Words; **LA.A.1.1.3.K.4** Build vocabulary; **LA.C.3.1.3.K.1** Basic vocabulary; *Also* **LA.A.1.1.3.K.3** Categorize words; **LA.B.1.1.1.K.1** Prewriting; **LA.B.1.1.2.K.2** Basic formats; **LA.B.1.1.3.K.1** Spelling approximations; **LA.B.1.1.3.K.2** Print direction

WRAP UP Share Time

Author's Chair Invite children to share the picture they drew as a response to literature, showing their favorite scene from *Come Along, Daisy!* Have each child sit in the Author's Chair to show the picture and explain why they liked that part of the story best.

S.S.R. *Sustained Silent Reading* Have children read silently from a book of their choice.

Centers ABC LETTERS AND WORDS

Pick and Match

Put the *Magnetic Letters* in the bag, and display the *Picture Cards* (or similar pictures). Invite children to reach into the bag without looking and pull out a letter. Have children name the letter and then find the *Picture Card* whose picture name begins with that letter. Encourage children to take several opportunities to pick a letter and find the matching *Picture Card*.

Materials

- *Magnetic Letters e, j, q, v, w, x,* and *y*

- paper bag

- *Picture Cards egg, jump rope, queen, vegetables, water, X ray, yellow*

FLORIDA STANDARDS/GLEs FCAT: LA.A.1.1.2.K.5 Phonetic principles; **LA.C.3.1.3.K.1** Basic vocabulary; *Also* **LA.A.1.1.2.K.2** Alphabet; **LA.A.1.1.2.K.3** Sounds; **LA.C.1.1.1.K.1** Follow directions; **LA.C.1.1.3.K.1** Conversation rules; **LA.C.3.1.1.K.1** Speak clearly

Learning Centers

Choose from the following suggestions to enhance your learning centers for the theme Exploring Our Surroundings.
(Additional learning centers for this theme can be found on pages 354-356 and 460)

MANIPULATIVE CENTER

At Home or In the Wild

Put a pile of the following *Picture Cards* face down in the manipulative center: *alligator, bear, duck, gorilla, hat, jelly, kangaroo, key, lunch box, milk, newspaper, ring, socks, telephone, watch*. Have partners take turns choosing a card, identifying it, and sorting it into the category "At Home" or the category "In the Wild."

Materials

- *Picture Cards: alligator, bear, duck, gorilla, hat, jelly, kangaroo, key, lunch box, milk, newspaper, ring, socks, telephone, watch*

LITERACY CENTER

Read and Seek

Tell children to think of an animal or plant they would like to draw camouflaged, or hidden, in its environment. Then give each child a piece of paper on which is printed the following sentence frames: *I see one little ____. Look for one little ____. Do you see one little ____?* Have children draw their pictures and complete the sentences with the word that identifies the camouflaged plant or animal. Have partners read their sentences to each other and look for the hidden image.

I see one little lizrd.
Look for one little lizrd.
Do you see one little lizrd.

Materials

- paper with the sentence frames: *I see one little ____.*
  Look for one little ____.
  Do you see one little ____?
- pencils
- paper
- crayons

Teacher Notes

Teacher Notes

THEME 11

Week 2
Exploring Our
Surroundings

15-30 Minutes

ORAL LANGUAGE

- **Phonemic Awareness**

- **Sharing Literature**

45 Minutes

LEARNING TO READ

- **Phonics**

- **Vocabulary**

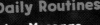

Daily Routines
- **Morning Message**
- **Calendar Language**
- **Writing Prompt**

15-30 Minutes

LANGUAGE ARTS

- **Writing**
  Daily Writing Prompt

Day 1

Phonemic Awareness, 421
Phoneme Isolation and Matching: Medial

Sharing Literature, 422
Read
Big Book: *Five Little Ducks*

 Literature Focus, 423
Number Words

Phonics, 424 **T**
Introduce: Short Vowel *Uu*
Identify/Write **T**

 Shared Writing, 426
Write a Story

Writing Prompt, 426
Draw and write about a special trip.

Share Time, 427
Share the little duck story.

Day 2

Phonemic Awareness, 429
Phoneme Deletion

Sharing Literature, 430
Read
Library Book: *What's What?*

 **Literature Focus, 431**
Reading to Get Information

Phonics, 432 **T**
Relating /u/ to *u*

 Interactive Writing, 434
Write About the Five Senses

Writing Prompt, 434
Draw and write about pets.

Share Time, 435
Discuss *What's What?*

---

418 **Exploring Our Surroundings**

T = tested skill

Phonics

Short Vowel *Uu;*
Blending *t*

Focus of the Week:
- PHONEMIC AWARENESS
- SHARING LITERATURE
- WRITING: Questions, Sentences, Stories

Day 3

Phonemic Awareness, 437
Phoneme Blending

Sharing Literature, 438
Read-Aloud Anthology:
"Henny Penny," pp. 75–77

 (Skill) **Literature Focus, 439**
Sequence

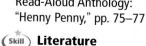**Phonics**, 440 T
Blending /u/–/t/

 Interactive Writing, 442
Read
Write How-to Directions

Writing Prompt, 442
Draw and write about a special place.

Share Time, 443
Share favorite parts of the lesson.

Day 4

Phonemic Awareness, 445
Phoneme Substitution: Initial

Sharing Literature, 446
Big Book of Rhymes and
Songs: "The Little Turtle,"
pp. 24–25

 (Skill) **Literature Focus, 447**
Questions for Research

Phonics, 448 T
Review: Short Vowel /u/*u*

Read
DECODABLE BOOK 14
But I Can

Writing, 450
Write a Question

Writing Prompt, 450
Draw and write about self-selected
topics.

Share Time, 451
Recite "The Little Turtle," and share
questions.

Day 5

Phonemic Awareness, 453
Phoneme Substition: Medial

Sharing Literature, 454
Read
Big Book: *Five Little Ducks*

(Skill) **Literature Focus, 455**
Picture Details

Phonics, 456 T
Words with /u/ and /t/

Writing, 458
Write a Sentence

Writing Prompt, 458
Draw and write about self-selected
topics.

Share Time, 459
Share a sentence about being happy.

Exploring Our Surroundings   **419**

Day at a Glance
Day 1

WARM UP

Phonemic Awareness
Phoneme Isolation and Phoneme Matching: Medial

Sharing Literature
Big Book:
Five Little Ducks

Five Little Ducks
AN OLD RHYME · ILLUSTRATED BY
Pamela Paparone

Develop Concept Vocabulary

Respond to Literature

Literature Focus: Number Words

Phonics
Vowel *Uu*

Shared Writing
Story

MORNING MESSAGE

Kindergarten News

The month is _____.

(Child's name)'s friend is _____.

Write Kindergarten News Ask children to tell about friends and what is special about them.

Use prompts such as the following to guide children as you write the news:

- **Who is your friend? What is special about your friend?**
- **Let's clap the syllables as we say (month).**
- **Who can point to where to begin reading?**
- **Who can show me the letters in _____'s name?**

As you write the message, invite children to contribute by writing letters, words, or names they have previously learned. Remind them to use proper spacing, capitalization, and punctuation.

Calendar Language

Point to and read aloud the names of the current month and the following month. Ask: *What month comes after this one?*

Sunday	Monday	Tuesday	Wednesday	Thursday	Friday	Saturday
		1	2	3	4	5
6	7	8	9	10	11	12
13	14	15	16	17	18	19
20	21	22	23	24	25	26
27	28	29	30	31		

FLORIDA STANDARDS/GLEs **FCAT: LA.A.1.1.2.K.5** Phonetic principles; **LA.B.2.1.2.K.1** Record ideas; *Also* **LA.A.1.1.2.K.1** Print organization; **LA.A.1.1.2.K.2** Alphabet; **LA.C.1.1.3.K.1** Conversation rules; **LA.C.3.1.2.K.1** Questions

Phonemic Awareness

PHONEME ISOLATION: MEDIAL

Identify the Medial Sound in a Word   Say the following sentences. Have children repeat the sentences and pantomime the actions.

Wash a duck in a tub. /u/ is the middle sound in /t/ /u/ /b/.

Rub the suds up and down. /u/ is the middle sound in /r/ /u/ /b/.

Get a brush and fluff her feathers. /e/ is the middle sound in /g/ /e/ /t/.

Have children tell you the middle sound in the following words:

duck (u)   wet (e)

suds (u)   head (e)

bath (a)   tub (u)

BELOW-LEVEL

Simplify the task so that children can grasp the concept. Say two words such as /suun/ and /cuut/, drawing out the medial sound. Have children repeat *sun* and *cut*. Tell them that the two words have the same middle sound. Ask them to say the sound. (/u/) Continue with other word pairs.

ADVANCED

Encourage children to extend what they have learned. As they identify words with the same middle sound, such as *sad* and *math*, ask them to name other words with /a/ as the middle sound.

PHONEME MATCHING: MEDIAL

Model for children how to listen for the middle sound in two words.

> **MODEL**   Listen for /u/: *duck*, *tub*. I hear /u/ in the middle of *duck*. I hear /u/ in the middle of *tub*. Say the words with me: *duck*, *tub*. *Duck* and *tub* have the same middle sound, /u/.

For each of the following sets of words, say: **Listen for /vowel/. Which two words have the same middle sound?**

(**/a/**) **sad, dish, math** (*sad, math*)   (**/o/**) **kick, mop, dot** (*mop, dot*)

(**/u/**) **wish, gum, bus** (*gum, bus*)   (**/u/**) **tent, bug, luck** (*bug, luck*)

(**/u/**) **sub, truck, glad** (*sub, truck*)   (**/e/**) **bet, pot, web** (*bet, web*)

Five Little Ducks
AN OLD RHYME · ILLUSTRATED BY
Pamela Paparone

▲ **Big Book**

OBJECTIVES

• *To recall story events*

• *To identify setting*

• *To recognize number words*

Materials

■ *Big Book:*
  Five Little Ducks

■ index cards

■ drawing paper

■ crayons

Sharing Literature

Read Five Little Ducks

READ ALOUD

Before Reading   Page through *Five Little Ducks,* pausing at each page that starts with a number word. Read the word and have children hold up the appropriate number of fingers. Use these prompts to help children understand the sequence of numbers:

• **How many little ducks are there?** (five)

• **What do you notice about the numbers?** (Possible response: The numbers go down one by one from five to none and then back to five.)

During Reading   Reread the story aloud. As you read,

• model for children how to identify the setting.

> **MODEL** *Five Little Ducks* **takes place in the country. I can tell because I see lots of grass and trees and there are not many houses. So the setting of this story is the country.**

• encourage children to join in by reciting repetitive phrases.

• pause to allow children to count the little ducks in each scene while you frame the number word in the text.

FLORIDA STANDARDS/GLEs   FCAT: LA.A.1.1.2.K.4 Words; **LA.A.1.1.2.K.6** Print meaning; **LA.A.1.1.3.K.5** Story elements, **LA.C.3.1.3.K.1** Basic vocabulary; **LA.E.1.1.1.K.1** Genres; **LA.E.1.1.2.K.1** Story elements; *Also* **LA.A.1.1.2.K.1** Print organization; **LA.A.1.1.3.K.3** Categorize words; **LA.A.2.1.4.K.1** Illustrations; **LA.C.1.1.1.K.2** Oral language; **LA.C.3.1.2.K.1** Questions; **LA.D.2.1.2.K.1** Patterned structures; **LA.E.2.1.2.K.1** Patterned structures

DEVELOP CONCEPT VOCABULARY

After Reading   Write the words *out*, *over*, and *far away* on the board. Point to and read each word. Then use a shoe box and the rabbit puppet to model each word. Use the words in sentences and ask children to answer the questions.

The rabbit goes <u>out</u> of the box. Where did the rabbit go? (out of the box)

The rabbit goes <u>over</u> the box. Where did the rabbit go? (over the box)

The rabbit goes <u>far away</u>. Where did the rabbit go? (far away)

Call on individuals to use *out*, *over*, and *far away* in sentences of their own to tell the rabbit where he should go.

RESPOND TO LITERATURE

Draw and Write About the Story   Ask children to draw and label a place where they think the little ducks go when they leave their mother.

Literature Focus

NUMBER WORDS

Write the words *one, two, three, four,* and *five* on index cards. Tell children they are going to pretend to be the little ducks. As you read the word *one*, hand the matching card to one child and have the child quack once. Repeat the procedure with the other cards and have children quack the appropriate number of times.

BELOW-LEVEL

Visual clues can support children's understanding of the skill. As you display the number word cards one at a time, count the corresponding number of like objects in the classroom: one flag, two doors, and so on.

ADVANCED

Challenge children with an opportunity to extend the skill. Distribute each number word card to a child and have children draw or collect sets of objects that correspond with the number.

ONGOING ASSESSMENT

As you share *Five Little Ducks,* note whether children

• recall story events.

• identify setting.

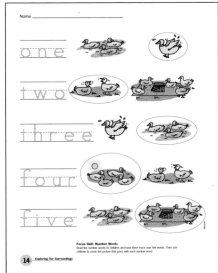

▲ **Practice Book page 14**

🌴 **FLORIDA STANDARDS/GLEs   FCAT: LA.A.1.1.2.K.4** Words; **LA.A.1.1.2.K.6** Print meaning; **LA.A.1.1.3.K.5** Story elements; *Also* **LA.A.1.1.3.K.3** Categorize words; **LA.B.1.1.2.K.2** Basic formats; **LA.B.1.1.3.K.1** Spelling approximations; **LA.B.1.1.3.K.2** Print direction; **LA.B.2.1.4.K.1** Informational texts; **LA.C.3.1.2.K.1** Questions

Exploring Our Surroundings   423

Vowel Uu ✓ Introduce

OBJECTIVES

- *To recognize U and u*

- *To write uppercase and lowercase Uu independently*

Materials

- *Music CD*

- *Big Alphabet Cards Ee, Jj, Uu, Vv, Yy, Zz*

- *Big Book: Five Little Ducks*

- *Write-On/Wipe-Off Boards*

- drawing paper

- crayons

ACTIVE BEGINNING

Play Musical Letters Place *Big Alphabet Cards Ee, Jj, Vv, Yy,* and *Zz* face up on the floor in a large circle. Identify each letter as you put it down. Ask a group of children to march around the outside of the circle as you play a selection on the *Music CD* such as "The Alphabet Song." When you stop the music, have children pick up the card nearest them and say its name.

TEACH/MODEL

Introduce the Letter Name Hold up the *Big Alphabet Card Uu.*

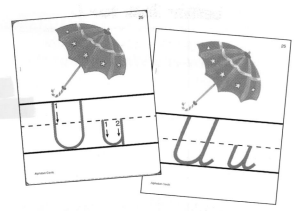

The name of this letter is *u*. Say the name with me.

Point to the uppercase *U*. **This is the uppercase *U*.**

Point to the lowercase *u*. **This is the lowercase *u*.**

Point to the *Big Alphabet Card* again. **What is the name of this letter?**

Display *Five Little Ducks.*

Follow along as I read the title.

Point to the letter *u*. **What is the name of this letter?**

---

424 **Exploring Our Surroundings**

Handwriting

Writing *U* and *u*   Write uppercase *U* and lowercase *u* on the board.

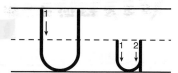

Point to the uppercase *U*. **What letter is this?**

Point to the lowercase *u*. **What letter is this?**

MODEL   **Watch as I write the letter *u* so that everyone can read it.**

As you give the Letter Talk, trace the uppercase *U*. Use the same modeling procedure for lowercase *u*.

Letter Talk for *U*

Straight line down, curve right, and back up.

Letter Talk for *u*

Straight line down, curve right, and back up. Straight line down.

D'Nealian handwriting models are on pages R12–13.

PRACTICE/APPLY

Guided Practice   Help children find *Uu* on their *Write-On/Wipe-Off Board*. Have them trace the uppercase *U* with a finger and then write the letter several times. Then have them do the same for lowercase *u*.

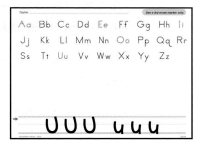

Independent Practice   Distribute drawing paper and have children draw a large umbrella shape and fill the shape with *Uu*s. Then have them circle their best *U* and *u*.

BELOW-LEVEL

Kinesthetic activities can reinforce the skill. Have children practice tracing *U*'s in the sand or tracing over the *Tactile Letter u*.

ADVANCED

Encourage children to use pencils to write *U* and *u* on lined paper.

Phonics Resources

Phonics Express™ **CD-ROM, Level A,** Roamer/Route 4/Train Station

Phonics Practice Book pages 123–124 HW

▲ **Practice Book page 15** HW

FLORIDA STANDARDS/GLEs   **LA.B.1.1.2.K.1** Dictate messages; **LA.A.1.1.2.K.2** Alphabet; **LA.C.1.1.1.K.1** Follow directions; **LA.C.3.1.2.K.1** Questions

Exploring Our Surroundings   425

OBJECTIVE

To write a sequential story

Materials

- Big Book:
  Five Little Ducks
- chart paper
- marker

Writing Every Day

Day 1: Patterned Story

Work together to write a story about the five little ducks.

Day 2: Chart

Work together to write a chart about the five senses.

Day 3: Directions

Work together to write directions telling how to get to the cafeteria.

Day 4: Questions

Have children write a question about an animal.

Day 5: Sentence Frame

Have children complete a sentence frame and draw a picture.

Shared Writing

Write a Story

EXTEND A STORY

Talk About *Five Little Ducks* Talk about the drawings children made as a response to the *Five Little Ducks*. Use their drawings to talk about places where the ducks might go when they leave their mother.

Write a Story Tell children that they are going to write a story to tell where the five little ducks go. Choose one child's drawing of a place. Model for children how to write sentences in sequential order.

MODEL We will write a story about the ducks going to the pond. First, I will write where the ducks go. Next, I will write what the ducks do at the pond. Last, I will write about how they felt at the pond.

Five little ducks go over the hill to the pond. They like to swim. They like to eat bugs. They have fun at the pond.

Have children suggest a sentence for each part of the story and write it on the chart. When the sentences are completed, read aloud the story and ask: Are the sentences in order?

Journal Writing Have children write and draw about a special trip.

FLORIDA STANDARDS/GLEs **FCAT: LA.B.1.1.2.K.3** Sequence; **LA.B.2.1.2.K.1** Record ideas; *Also* **LA.B.1.1.2.K.1** Dictate messages; **LA.B.1.1.2.K.2** Basic formats; **LA.B.1.1.3.K.1** Spelling approximations; **LA.B.1.1.3.K.2** Print direction; **LA.B.2.1.1.K.2** Contribute ideas

WRAP UP Share Time

Author's Chair   Ask children to share their drawings of where they think the ducks go in the *Big Book*. Using the story from the writing activity, have them tell about the ducks at the place in sequential order.

S.S.R.   Have children read silently from a book of their choice.

Centers MATH

Countdown

Have children count out piles of five objects. Demonstrate how to take away one object at a time. Say: **I have five buttons. I take away one button. Now I have four buttons.** Have children count down their own pile of objects by taking away one thing at a time, describing what they are doing each time.

Materials
- math manipulatives

FLORIDA STANDARDS/GLEs   **FCAT: LA.C.3.1.3.K.1** Basic vocabulary; *Also* **LA.A.1.1.2.K.1** Print organization; **LA.A.1.1.2.K.2** Alphabet; **LA.C.1.1.1.K.1** Follow directions; **LA.E.2.1.1.K.1** Background knowledge

Exploring Our Surroundings   **427**

WARM UP

Phonemic Awareness
Phoneme Deletion

Sharing Literature
Library Book:
What's What?

Read

Mary Serfozo
What's what?
A Guessing Game
Illustrated by Keiko Narahashi

Develop Listening Comprehension

Respond to Literature

Literature Focus: Reading to Get Information

Phonics
Relating /u/ to *u*

Interactive Writing ✏
Five Senses

MORNING MESSAGE

Kindergarten News

(Child's name) has a pet_____.

(Child's name) would like to have a

pet _____ .

Write Kindergarten News Talk with children about pets they have or would like to have.

Use prompts such as the following to guide children as you write the news:

- **What kind of pet do you have? What kind of pet would you like to have?**
- **What letter will I write first in the word *pet*?**
- **How many letters are in (child's name)?**
- **Who can show me a word?**

As you write the message, invite children to contribute by writing letters, words, or names they have learned previously. Remind them to use proper spacing, capitalization, and punctuation.

Calendar Language

Have children identify the days of the week. Then ask them to name class activities for some of the days.

Sunday	Monday	Tuesday	Wednesday	Thursday	Friday	Saturday
		1	2	3	4	5
6	7	8	9	10	11	12
13	14	15	16	17	18	19
20	21	22	23	24	25	26
27	28	29	30	31		

FLORIDA STANDARDS/GLEs **FCAT: LA.A.1.1.2.K.5** Phonetic principles; **LA.B.2.1.2.K.1** Record ideas; *Also* **LA.A.1.1.2.K.2** Alphabet; **LA.A.1.1.2.K.3** Sounds; **LA.C.1.1.3.K.1** Conversation rules; **LA.C.3.1.2.K.1** Questions

Phonemic Awareness

PHONEME DELETION

Delete Phonemes Model how to manipulate sounds by deleting initial sounds in words.

MODEL *Cup.* **Say the word:** *cup.* **Listen while I say** *cup* **without the /k/:** *up.* **Say it with me:** *up.*

Tell children you are going to ask them to say some words without certain letters. Use the following:

Say *boat* **without the /b/.** *(oat)*

Say *hut* **without the /h/.** *(ut)*

Say *jack* **without the /j/.** *(ack)*

Say *quail* **without the /kw/.** *(ail)*

Say *zoom* **without the /z/.** *(oom)*

Say *gum* **without the /g/.** *(um)*

Say *tag* **without the /t/.** *(ag)*

Say *tough* **without the /t/.** *(ough)*

Say *can* **without the /k/.** *(an)*

Say *lamb* **without the /l/.** *(amb)*

Say *moon* **without the /m/.** *(oon)*

Say *pool* **without the /p/.** *(ool)*

BELOW-LEVEL

Use this procedure. Say *bus*. Segment the onset and rime: /b/-*us*. Then delete the initial sound: *us*. Have children repeat after you.

ADVANCED

Place *Picture Cards* cat, fish, goat, lamb, queen, and yak face down on a table. Ask children to take turns choosing a *Picture Card*. Have them name the picture and then say the word without the beginning sound. Have them repeat the process, saying each word without the ending sound.

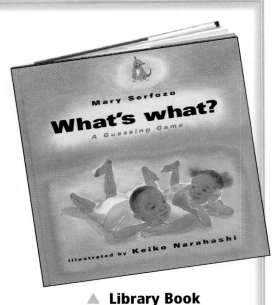

Sharing Literature

Read What's What?

READ ALOUD

Before Reading Display the cover of *What's What?* and track the print of the title and the names of the author and illustrator as you read these aloud. Read the subtitle, *A Guessing Game*, and tell children that the book asks them to guess about something at the end. Use these prompts to build background:

- **What do you see on the cover?** (a dog, a boy, and a girl)

- **What do you think they do in the story?** (Possible response: The boy and girl play with a dog.)

During Reading Read the selection aloud. As you read,

- pause to allow children to answer each question.

- point out the picture clue with each question that helps the reader predict the answer.

  MODEL I see a little picture that goes with each question. As I read the book, I see that those pictures are clues to the answers. So when I see rain and puddles with the question *What's wet?* I think I'll see rain and puddles when I turn the page.

- as each question is asked, pause to allow a child to predict an answer.

▲ **Library Book**

OBJECTIVES

- *To listen and respond to a story*

- *To make and confirm predictions*

- *To read to get information*

Materials

- *Library Book: What's What?*

- chart paper

- marker

FLORIDA STANDARDS/GLEs **FCAT: LA.A.1.1.4.K.1** Comprehension; **LA.A.2.1.3.K.1** Supportive details; *Also* **LA.A.1.1.1.K.1** Predictions; **LA.A.1.1.2.K.1** Print organization; **LA.A.2.1.4.K.1** Illustrations; **LA.C.1.1.1.K.2** Oral language; **LA.C.3.1.2.K.1** Questions

DEVELOP LISTENING COMPREHENSION

After Reading   Have children answer these questions about the selection:

• **Did you guess the answers to the questions?**

• **Can you think of something that is hard? Soft? Warm? Cold?**
(Possible responses: a wall or desk, a blanket or cat, a sweater or mittens, a snowball or ice cube)

• **What do all the words in the book describe?** (a puppy)

RESPOND TO LITERATURE

Discuss the Story   Have children tell their favorite question and answer in the book.

Literature Focus

READING TO GET INFORMATION

Remind children that some books give information. Point out that *What's What?* tells what things are like. Write a chart with two columns on chart paper. In the left-hand column, write the adjectives used in the book: *hard, soft, warm, cold, wet, dry, long, short, light, dark*. Then page through the book and recall with children the things that are described by each word. Record the objects' names in the right-hand side of the chart, opposite the corresponding adjective.

ADVANCED

Ask children to suggest an additional object for each adjective on the chart created during the Literature Focus section of the lesson.

ONGOING ASSESSMENT

As you share *What's What?* note whether children

• listen for a period of time.

• respond to the questions.

• make and confirm predictions.

FLORIDA STANDARDS/GLEs   FCAT: LA.A.1.1.2.K.4 Words; **LA.A.1.1.2.K.6** Print meaning; **LA.A.1.1.3.K.5** Story elements; **LA.A.2.1.3.K.1** Supportive details; **LA.E.1.1.1.K.1** Genres; *Also* **LA.A.1.1.3.K.1** Frequent words; **LA.A.1.1.3.K.3** Categorize words; **LA.B.2.1.4.K.1** Informational texts; **LA.C.3.1.2.K.1** Questions

Exploring Our Surroundings   431

OBJECTIVE

To match vowel Uu to its sound

Materials

- *Letter and Sound Chart 19*
- *Tactile Letter Cards u*
- *Picture/Word Cards umbrella, bus*
- *Umbrella Pattern (page TI4)*
- *scissors*
- *crayons*
- *drawing paper*
- *glue*

Phonics Resources

***Phonics Express*™ CD-ROM, Level A,** Roamer/Route 4/Fire Station, Building Site

U u

Up goes a kite,
Up goes a plane,
Up go your umbrellas
Whenever there is rain.

▲ **Letter and Sound Chart 19**

Phonics
Relating /u/ to u  Introdu

ACTIVE BEGINNING

Recite the Rhyme   Teach children the rhyme "Up and Up and Up." Tell children to listen for the sound /u/ as they learn the rhyme. Then have children say the rhyme again as they act it out.

Up and Up and Up
by Susan Little

Unwinding and unwinding

The long string of my kite.

Up and up and up it goes

Until it's out of sight.

TEACH/MODEL

Introduce Letter and Sound   Display *Letter and Sound Chart 19.*

Touch the letter *U.* **What is the name of this letter?**

This letter stands for the /u/ sound.

Read aloud the rhyme on the *Letter and Sound Chart*, tracking the print. Read aloud the *Uu* words in the rhyme. Then point to each *U* and *u* and have children say the /u/ sound.

Have children join in as you read the rhyme again.

 FLORIDA STANDARDS/GLEs   FCAT: LA.A.1.1.2.K.5 Phonetic principles; *Also* **LA.A.1.1.2.K.2** Alphabet; **LA.A.1.1.2.K.3** Sounds; **LA.C.1.1.1.K.2** Oral language; **LA.C.3.1.2.K.1** Questions; **LA.D.2.1.2.K.1** Patterned structures

PRACTICE/APPLY

Guided Practice Distribute *Tactile Letter Card u* and a *Write-On/Wipe-Off Board* to each child. Have children point to the heart shape on Side B of their *Write-On/Wipe-Off Board*. Explain that they will be working with the three boxes next to the heart. Then place *Picture/Word Cards umbrella* and *bus* in the pocket chart. Say each word as you point to the *u* in each. Have children repeat the words.

Tell children: **Some words begin with *u* and some words have *u* in the middle.**

Point to the *u* in *umbrella*. **The /u/ sound is at the beginning of the word *umbrella*.**

Point to the *u* in *bus*. **The *u* is in the middle of the word *bus*.**

I'll say some words. If the /u/ sound is at the beginning of a word, put your *u* card in the beginning box. If the /u/ sound is in the middle of the word, put your letter *u* in the middle box.

hands on head - beginning   hands on tummy - middle

unlock   cup   fun   uncle   up   dust   under   umpire

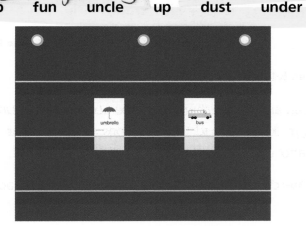

Independent Practice Distribute drawing paper and copies of the Umbrella Pattern (page T14). Have children decorate their umbrellas and write the word *up* on it. Children can cut out the patterns and glue their umbrellas to drawing paper.

FLORIDA STANDARDS/GLEs FCAT: LA.A.1.1.2.K.5 Phonetic principles; *Also* **LA.A.1.1.2.K.2** Alphabet; **LA.A.1.1.2.K.3** Sounds; **LA.B.1.1.2.K.2** Basic formats; **LA.B.1.1.3.K.1** Spelling approximations; **LA.B.1.1.3.K.2** Print direction; **LA.B.2.1.4.K.1** Informational texts

---

Diagnostic Check: Phonics

If... children cannot recognize the letter *Uu* and its related sound,

Then... use the *Letter and Sound Chart Sentence Strips* to show one line of the rhyme at a time. Read aloud the words as you track the print. Have children frame each word to look for words that begin with the letter *Uu*. Read each word they find and emphasize the initial /u/ sound in the word.

ADDITIONAL SUPPORT ACTIVITIES

BELOW-LEVEL   Reteach, p. S44

ADVANCED   Extend, p. S45

ENGLISH-LANGUAGE LEARNERS   Reteach, p. S45

Phonics Practice Book pages 125–126

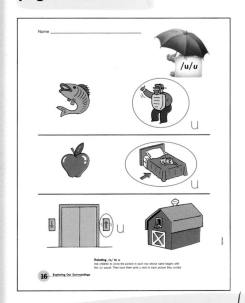

▲ **Practice Book page 16**   HW

Exploring Our Surroundings   433

OBJECTIVES

- To recognize the five senses

- To understand the purpose of a chart

- To share information and ideas, speaking in complete, coherent sentences

Materials

- chart paper
- marker

Interactive Writing

Write About the Five Senses

SHARE THE PEN

Talk About the Five Senses Tell children that we have five senses that we use to explore the world around us: *seeing, hearing, tasting, smelling, feeling.* Have children imagine that they are in a bakery. Ask: **What would you see? Hear? Taste? Smell? Feel?**

Write a Chart Tell children that together they are going to make a chart about the five senses. Ask: **What should the title of our chart be? Where should I write the title?** Write the name of each of the senses at the top of a column on chart paper. Then ask children to name things to go under each sense. As you slowly say the sounds in each word, invite individuals to identify the letters and to come to the chart to write them.

Our Five Senses				
See	**Hear**	**Taste**	**Smell**	**Feel**
sunshine	music	cookies	flowers	puppy
book	bird	apple	grass	pillow

Journal Writing Have children write and draw about a pet they have or would like to have.

FLORIDA STANDARDS/GLEs **FCAT: LA.A.1.1.2.K.4** Words; **LA.A.1.1.3.K.4** Build vocabulary; *Also* **LA.A.1.1.2.K.2** Alphabet; **LA.B.1.1.1.K.2** Generate ideas; **LA.B.1.1.3.K.1** Spelling approximations; **LA.B.1.1.3.K.2** Print direction; **LA.B.2.1.1.K.2** Contribute ideas; **LA.B.2.1.4.K.1** Informational texts; **LA.C.3.1.1.K.1** Speak clearly

WRAP UP Share Time

Reflect on the Lesson Have children tell what they liked in the book *What's What*? Ask them if they were surprised by the ending and why. Ask children to name something they can see, hear, taste, smell, and feel.

S.S.R. *Sustained Silent Reading* Have children read silently from a book of their choice.

Centers — SCIENCE

What's in the Bag?

Place each of the objects in a separate paper bag. Encourage children to reach into a bag and, without looking, use their sense of touch to tell the name of the object to a partner. Allow children to have several turns before placing new objects in the bags.

Materials

- several paper bags

- various objects, such as small erasers, plastic animals or figures, paper clips

Day at a Glance
Day 3

WARM UP

MORNING MESSAGE

Kindergarten News

(Child's name)'s favorite food is

_____ .

(Child's name)'s favorite food is

_____ .

Phonemic Awareness
Phoneme Blending

Sharing Literature
Read-Aloud Anthology:
"Henny Penny"

Read

Develop Listening Comprehension

Respond to Literature

Literature Focus: Sequence

Blending /u/ - /t/

Interactive Writing 🖉
Directions

Write Kindergarten News Talk with children about foods they like best. Ask them to tell why these foods are their favorites.

Use prompts such as the following to guide children as you write the news:

- **What is your favorite food to eat?**
- **Where should I begin to write?**
- **What letter will I write first in the word** *food*?
- **Let's count the words in the first sentence. How many are there?**

As you write the message, invite children to contribute by writing letters, words, or names they have learned previously. Remind them to use proper spacing, capitalization, and punctuation.

Calendar Language

Name the days of the week, inviting children to join in and clap syllables for each day. Tell children to count the days of the week as you point to each one. Ask how many days are in a week.

Sunday	Monday	Tuesday	Wednesday	Thursday	Friday	Saturday
		1	2	3	4	5
6	7	8	9	10	11	12
13	14	15	16	17	18	19
20	21	22	23	24	25	26
27	28	29	30	31		

 FLORIDA STANDARDS/GLEs FCAT: **LA.A.1.1.2.K.5** Phonetic principles; **LA.A.2.1.5.K.2** Get information; *Also* **LA.A.1.1.2.K.1** Print organization; **LA.A.1.1.2.K.2** Alphabet; **LA.A.1.1.2.K.3** Sounds

Phonemic Awareness

PHONEME BLENDING

Blend Phonemes   Tell children they are to listen to the sounds you will say and then they should name the word.

MODEL   /k/ /u/ /t/. Say the sounds after me: /k//u//t/. Now I will blend the sounds: /kkuutt/. Blend the sounds with me: /kkuutt/. Now say the word: cut.

Ask children to blend the sounds and say the words to complete each sentence.

The mother duck says /kw/ /a/ /k/. *(quack)*

In the sky, I see the /s/ /u/ /n/. *(sun)*

I wish you good /l/ /u/ /k/. *(luck)*

I can count to /t/ /e/ /n/. *(ten)*

The answer is /y/ /e/ /s/. *(yes)*

I ride the /b/ /u/ /s/. *(bus)*

REACHING ALL LEARNERS

Diagnostic Check: Phonemic Awareness

If... children cannot blend phonemes to say words,

Then... begin by saying two phonemes, /u/ /p/, and have children repeat them. Blend the phonemes, /uupp/, and have children repeat them. Then say the word naturally, *up*, and have children repeat it. Continue with words with three phonemes.

ADDITIONAL SUPPORT ACTIVITIES

BELOW-LEVEL   Reteach, p. S46

ADVANCED   Extend, p. S47

ENGLISH-LANGUAGE LEARNERS   Reteach, p. S47

▲ **Read-Aloud Anthology**

OBJECTIVES

- *To listen and respond to a story*

- *To make predictions*

- *To ask and answer questions about a text*

- *To tell story events in sequence*

Materials

- *Read-Aloud Anthology, pp. 75–77*

- *Teacher's Resource Book, pp. 97–98*

- crayons

- scissors

- glue

- craft sticks

Sharing Literature

Read "Henny Penny"

READ ALOUD

Before Reading   Read aloud the title "Henny Penny." Tell children that this story is a folktale from long ago that has been told many times. Ask these questions to build background:

- **What is a hen?**

- **Why might a hen be going to see the king?**

During Reading   Read the story aloud. As you read,

- use a different voice for each story character.

- encourage children to say the names of the characters as they are repeated in the text.

- pause after Henny Penny meets each new animal, and let children predict who the next one might be.

FLORIDA STANDARDS/GLEs   FCAT: LA.E.1.1.1.K.1 Genres; **LA.E.1.1.2.K.1** Story elements; *Also* **LA.C.1.1.1.K.2** Oral language; **LA.C.3.1.2.K.1** Questions

DEVELOP LISTENING COMPREHENSION

After Reading   Have children answer these questions about the story:

- **Is the sky really falling?** (Possible response: No, something just hits Henny Penny on the head.)

- **What does Henny Penny do when she thinks the sky is falling?** (She goes to tell the king.)

- **Who tries to trick the animals by showing them a shortcut?** (Foxy Loxy)

- **What does Foxy Loxy want to do?** (eat the animals)

RESPOND TO LITERATURE

Retell the Story   Distribute copies of the Character Cutouts from pages 97–98 of the *Teacher's Resource Book*. Have children color the characters, cut them out, and glue them to craft sticks. Then have small groups retell the story, using their puppets.

Literature Focus

SEQUENCE

Write the words *first, next,* and *last* on the board. Read them and remind children that these words can help them retell the events in a story in the order in which they happened. Model how to retell "Henny Penny," using the order words.

MODEL   **First, Henny Penny gets hit on the head and goes to tell the king that the sky is falling. All the animals follow her. Next, they meet Foxy Loxy, who tells them about a shortcut—right into his den!**

Ask children to tell what happens last. (Cocky Locky tells Henny Penny to run and she escapes from Foxy Loxy.)

ADVANCED

Have children use the words *first, next,* and *last* to retell one of the stories in the Literacy Center.

ONGOING ASSESSMENT

As you share "Henny Penny," note whether children

- **listen for a period of time.**
- **make predictions about the characters.**

FLORIDA STANDARDS/GLEs   FCAT: LA.A.1.1.4.K.1 Comprehension; LA.E.1.1.2.K.1 Story elements; *Also* LA.C.3.1.2.K.1 Questions

Exploring Our Surroundings   **439**

OBJECTIVES

- To identify and recognize the initial sound of a spoken word

- To blend u and t

Materials

- Big Alphabet Cards Uu and Tt

- Alphabet Cards b, c, g, n, r, t, u

- pocket chart

- index cards

Phonics

Blending /u/ - /t/  Introduce

ACTIVE BEGINNING

Word Hunt Have children sit in a circle. As you read the following verse, have the children echo. Establish a beat and keep it going throughout the verse.

Going on a word hunt.

What's this word?

/k/ /u/ /t/

Together: *Cut!*

Continue with the words /b/ /u/ /t/ (*but*), /h/ /u/ /t/ (*hut*), /t/ /u/ /g/ (*tug*).

TEACH/MODEL

Recognize /u/ and /t/ Display *Big Alphabet Card Uu* on the chalk ledge or in a pocket chart.

What letter is this?

What sound does this letter stand for? (/u/)

Have children say /u/ with you as you point to the letter.

Use the same procedure for *Big Alphabet Card Tt.*

Word Blending Explain to children that they are going to blend letters together to read words, such as *nut* and *tug.*

- Place the *Alphabet Cards n, u, t* in the pocket chart, separate from each other.

- Point to *n.* Say **/nn/**. Have children repeat the sound after you.

- Point to *u.* Say **/uu/**. Have children repeat the sound after you.

- Point to *t.* Say **/tt/**. Have children repeat the sound after you.

FLORIDA STANDARDS/GLEs FCAT: LA.A.1.1.2.K.5 Phonetic principles; *Also* LA.A.1.1.2.K.1 Print organization; LA.A.1.1.2.K.2 Alphabet; LA.A.1.1.2.K.3 Sounds; LA.C.3.1.2.K.1 Questions

- Slide *u* next to *n*. Say **/nnuu/**.

- Slide the *t* next to the *nu*. Move your hand under the letters and blend the sounds, elongating them—**/nnuutt/**. Have children repeat after you.

- Then have children blend and read *nut* with you.

PRACTICE/APPLY

Guided Practice   Place the letters *t*, *u*, and *b* in the pocket chart.

- Point to *t* and say **/tt/**. Point to the letter *u* and say **/u/**. Slide the *u* next to *t*. Move your hand under the letters and blend the sounds, elongating them—**/ttuu/**. Have children blend the sounds after you.
- Point to *b*. Say **/bb/**. Have children say the sound.
- Slide the *b* next to the *tu*. Slide your hand under *tub* and blend the sounds. Have children blend the sounds as you slide your hand under the word.
- Then have children read the word *tub* along with you.

Follow the same procedure to build and blend *cut*, *rut*, *but*, and *tug* with children.

Independent Practice   Write the following words on index cards and place them in a pocket chart in the Letters and Words Center: *cut, hut, rut, nut, tub, tug*. Have children track the print as they read each word.

FLORIDA STANDARDS/GLEs   **FCAT: LA.A.1.1.2.K.5** Phonetic principles; *Also* **LA.A.1.1.2.K.1** Print organization; **LA.A.1.1.2.K.3** Sounds

---

BELOW-LEVEL

Say the following sentences and have children name the word you are saying: *What am I saying: /k/-ut? What am I saying: /t/-ub?* For more practice with Short Vowel *Uu*, see Alternative Teaching Strategies, page T8.

ADVANCED

Place the *Magnetic Letters b, c, g, h, t, u* and a cookie sheet in the Letters and Words Center. Place the *Magnetic Letters u* and *t* on the cookie sheet. Encourage children to make other words with *u* and *t*, such as *cut* and *tug*.

ENGLISH-LANGUAGE LEARNERS

Before asking children to read the words in the Independent Practice, review each letter sound with them.

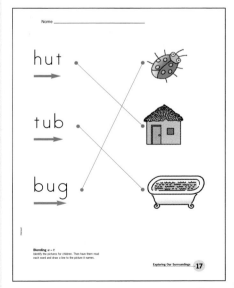

▲ **Practice Book page 17** HW

Exploring Our Surroundings   **441**

OBJECTIVES

- *To understand the purpose of how-to directions*

- *To write how-to directions*

- *To use letters and phonetically spelled words to write about experiences*

Materials

- chart paper

- marker

Interactive Writing

Write How-to Directions

RECALL A STORY

Talk About How-to Directions   Ask children to tell where Henny Penny is going when she meets the other animals. (to see the king) Explain that directions can tell how to get from one place to another.

Write Directions   Tell children that together they are going to write directions that tell how to get from their classroom to the cafeteria.

MODEL   **When we want to tell someone how to get somewhere, we can write down directions. The directions have to be in the right order. What should we write first?**

> How to Go to the Cafeteria
> 1. Go out the door.
> 2. Turn right.
> 3. Walk down the hall to the end.
> 4. Turn left.
> 5. Walk into the cafeteria.

Invite children to write numerals on the chart before you write each sentence. Then, on chart paper ask children to help you write the title, *How to Go to the Cafeteria*. Write each step of the directions as a child explains it. Encourage children to write end punctuation marks and words they have previously learned.

SHARE

Follow the Directions   After the directions are written, read them to children. Then, read the directions aloud again and have children follow each step to walk to the cafeteria.

Writing Every Day

Journal Writing Have children write about a special place they like to go.

FLORIDA STANDARDS/GLEs   FCAT: LA.A.1.1.2.K.6 Print meaning; **LA.B.1.1.2.K.3** Sequence; **LA.B.2.1.2.K.1** Record ideas; *Also* **LA.B.1.1.2.K.1** Dictate messages; **LA.B.1.1.2.K.2** Basic formats; **LA.B.1.1.3.K.1** Spelling approximations; **LA.B.1.1.3.K.2** Print direction; **LA.B.2.1.1.K.2** Contribute ideas; **LA.B.2.1.4.K.1** Informational texts; **LA.E.2.1.1.K.1** Background knowledge

WRAP UP ## Share Time

Reflect on the Lesson Ask children to tell about their favorite part of "Henny Penny." Have them talk about the part of today's lesson they enjoyed the most.

S.S.R. *Sustained Silent Reading* Have children read silently from a book of their choice.

Centers — MANIPULATIVES

Puzzle Time

Glue each picture onto a piece of poster board. When the glue is dry, cut the picture into about ten pieces. Put each puzzle's pieces into a large envelope. Have children choose an envelope and work with a partner to assemble the puzzle. Ask them to describe and discuss the emerging picture as they work.

Materials

- magazine or calendar pictures of outdoor scenes
- glue
- poster board
- scissors
- large envelope

FLORIDA STANDARDS/GLEs **FCAT: LA.C.3.1.3.K.1** Basic vocabulary; *Also* **LA.C.1.1.3.K.1** Conversation rules; **LA.D.1.1.1.K.2** Functions of language

Exploring Our Surroundings **443**

Day at a Glance
Day 4

WARM UP

Phonemic Awareness
Phoneme Substitution: Initial

Sharing Literature
Big Book of Rhymes and Songs:
"The Little Turtle"

Develop Concept Vocabulary

Respond to Literature

Literature Focus: Questions for Research

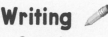

Short Vowel /u/u

Reading
Decodable Book 14: *But I Can*

Writing ✏️
Question

MORNING MESSAGE

Kindergarten News

(Child's name)'s favorite book is

_____ .

(Child's name)'s favorite book is

_____ .

Write Kindergarten News Talk with children about their favorite books. Encourage them to speak loudly enough so that the whole group can hear.

Use prompts such as the following to guide children as you write the news:

• **What is your favorite book? Why?**

• **Let's listen for the beginning sound in (child's name).**

• **What letter will I write first in the word *book*?**

• **Who can point to where to begin reading?**

As you write the message, invite children to contribute by writing letters, words, or names they have learned previously. Remind them to use proper spacing, capitalization, and punctuation.

Calendar Language

Point to and read aloud the days of the week. Name the days of the week again, inviting children to join in and clap syllables for a sentence that includes the name of each day.

Sunday	Monday	Tuesday	Wednesday	Thursday	Friday	Saturday
		1	2	3	4	5
6	7	8	9	10	11	12
13	14	15	16	17	18	19
20	21	22	23	24	25	26
27	28	29	30	31		

FLORIDA STANDARDS/GLEs   FCAT: LA.A.1.1.2.K.5 Phonetic principles; **LA.B.2.1.2.K.1** Record ideas; *Also* **LA.A.1.1.2.K.1** Print organization; **LA.A.1.1.2.K.2** Alphabet; **LA.A.1.1.2.K.3** Sounds; **LA.A.2.1.5.K.1** Alphabetical order; **LA.C.1.1.2.K.1** Choose literature; **LA.C.1.1.3.K.1** Conversation rules; **LA.C.3.1.1.K.1** Speak clearly; **LA.C.3.1.2.K.1** Questions

Phonemic Awareness

PHONEME SUBSTITUTION: INITIAL

Substitute Phonemes   Use the rabbit puppet for the following phoneme substitution activity.

MODEL   Today the rabbit is going to change the beginning sound in a word and then say the new word. Listen as the rabbit says this word: *fun.* Say the word with the rabbit: *fun.* Now the rabbit will change the /f/ in *fun* to /s/. Now the word is *sun*. Say the word: *sun.*

Tell children that the rabbit is going to say some more words and name the sound to be changed. Children are to say the new word.

Change the /k/ in *cut* to /n/. *(nut)*

Change the /t/ in *tub* to /k/. *(cub)*

Change the /z/ in *zip* to /l/. *(lip)*

Change the /m/ in *mug* to /t/. *(tug)*

Change the /l/ in *lock* to /s/. *(sock)*

Change the /f/ in *fan* to /r/. *(ran)*

Change the /t/ in *tug* to /r/. *(rug)*

BELOW-LEVEL

Say a silly rhyme with children. Have them repeat the first line. Then substitute a new initial sound in each word and say the modified line.

/b/ - buzzing bumble bees

/t/ - tuzzing tumble tees

/m/ - muzzing mumble mees

/s/ - suzzing sumble sees

▲ **Big Book of Rhymes and Songs**

OBJECTIVES

- *To respond to a poem*
- *To ask questions for research*

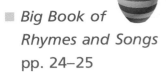

Materials

■ *Big Book of Rhymes and Songs* pp. 24–25

■ *Read-Aloud Anthology* p. 13

■ drawing paper

■ crayons

■ chart paper

■ marker

Sharing Literature

Read "The Little Turtle"

READ ALOUD

Before Reading Display page 24 of the *Big Book of Rhymes and Songs*. Track the print of the title while reading the words aloud. Set a purpose for rereading the poem.

MODEL **I remember that the little turtle tries to catch some things. I'll read the poem again so I can find out what the turtle does.**

Ask children what they would like to find out as you read.

During Reading Read the poem aloud. As you read,

- track the print.
- emphasize the rhyming words.
- perform the actions that go with the poem and ask children to join in with you. (See the *Read-Aloud Anthology* page 13.)

The Little Turtle

There was a little turtle.
He lived in a box.
He swam in a puddle.
He climbed on the rocks.

He snapped at a mosquito.
He snapped at a flea.
He snapped at a minnow.
And he snapped at me.

He caught the mosquito.
He caught the flea.
He caught the minnow.
But he didn't catch me.

Vachel Lindsay

24   25

▲ **Big Book of Rhymes and Songs page 24-25**

FLORIDA STANDARDS/GLEs **FCAT: LA.A.1.1.4.K.1** Comprehension; **LA.E.1.1.1.K.1** Genres; *Also* **LA.A.1.1.2.K.1** Print organization; **LA.C.1.1.1.K.2** Oral language; **LA.D.2.1.2.K.1** Patterned structures; **LA.E.2.1.2.K.1** Patterned structures

DEVELOP CONCEPT VOCABULARY

After Reading Write these action words from the poem on chart paper: *lived, swam, climbed, snapped, caught.* Point to and read each word. Then ask questions such as these:

- **Which word tells something the turtle did with his mouth?** (*snapped*)

- **Which words tell an action that the turtle did and begin with the same sound as *sun*?** (*swam, snapped*)

- **Which words tell an action that the turtle did and begin with the same sound as *castle*?** (*climbed, caught*)

- **Which word tells what the turtle did in a box?** (*lived*)

RESPOND TO LITERATURE

Draw a Picture Ask children: **What does the turtle try to catch?** Have children draw and label a picture of the turtle snapping at one of the creatures mentioned in the poem.

Literature **Focus**

QUESTIONS FOR RESEARCH

Point out to children that the poem gives them some information about real turtles.

Ask children what they know about turtles from reading the poem and from seeing real turtles. Then ask them what they want to know. Organize the information in a K-W-L chart.

K	W	L
They snap. They swim. They climb. They eat bugs.	Do they make any noise? What does the shell feel like?	

Discuss ways children can find answers to their questions, such as by looking in books and magazines, by using television and the Internet, and by watching real turtles. Display the chart in the classroom and write and read aloud the answers as children find them.

REACHING ALL LEARNERS

Diagnostic Check: Comprehension

If... children cannot think of questions to ask for research,

Then... ask children what they know about the topic and what they wonder about it. Help children formulate a question from what they say.

ADDITIONAL SUPPORT ACTIVITIES

BELOW-LEVEL	Reteach, p. S48
ADVANCED	Extend, p. S49
ENGLISH-LANGUAGE LEARNERS	Reteach, p. S49

ONGOING ASSESSMENT

As you share "The Little Turtle," note whether children

- **recite the poem and perform the actions.**

FLORIDA STANDARDS/GLEs FCAT: LA.A.1.1.2.K.4 Words; **LA.A.1.1.2.K.5** Phonetic principles; **LA.A.1.1.3.K.5** Story elements; **LA.A.1.1.4.K.1** Comprehension; *Also* **LA.A.2.1.5.K.3** Stay on topic; **LA.B.1.1.1.K.1** Prewriting; **LA.B.1.1.2.K.2** Basic formats; **LA.B.1.1.3.K.1** Spelling approximations; **LA.B.1.1.3.K.2** Print direction; **LA.B.2.1.4.K.1** Informational texts; **LA.C.3.1.2.K.1** Questions

Phonics

Short Vowel /u/u ✔ Review

Review

OBJECTIVE

To decode short vowel /u/u words

Materials

- Alphabet Cards B, t, u
- High-Frequency Word Card I
- index card
- pocket chart
- Decodable Book 14: But I Can
- drawing paper
- crayons

ADVANCED

Have children read Independent Reader 31: Float on the Boat.

ENGLISH-LANGUAGE LEARNERS

Have children write and illustrate another page for But I Can, using the text pattern Max can not _____, but I can.

TEACH/MODEL

Review Blending Place Alphabet Cards u and t next to each other in a pocket chart. Move your hand under the letters, blend them, and say /uutt/. Have children blend the sounds with you.

Place the Alphabet Card B in front of the u and t. Slide your hand under the letters, blend them, and say the word: /BBuutt/—But. Have children blend the sounds and say the word.

Place the High-Frequency Word Card I and the index card with Can written on it in the pocket chart after But. Track the print as children read the words: But I Can. Have children repeat the words as you track them again.

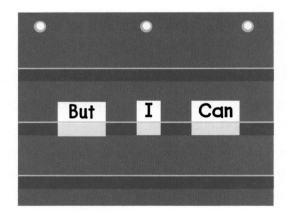

PRACTICE/APPLY

Read the Book Distribute copies of But I Can. Have children read the title. Encourage children to point to each word as they read it.

Have children read the book, pointing to each word as they read.

Respond Have children draw something else the big sister could do that Max couldn't do yet.

FLORIDA STANDARDS/GLEs FCAT: LA.A.1.1.2.K.4 Words; LA.A.1.1.2.K.5 Phonetic principles; LA.E.1.1.1.K.1 Genres; Also LA.A.1.1.2.K.1 Print organization; LA.A.1.1.2.K.3 Sounds; LA.A.1.1.3.K.1 Frequent words

Decodable Book 14: *But I Can*

Max is little. I am big.

2

Max can not hop, but I can.

3

Max can not run, but I can.

4

Max can not get it, but I can.

5

Max can not hit, but I can.

6

Max can not cut, but I can.

7

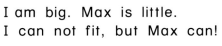

I am big. Max is little.
I can not fit, but Max can!

8

FLORIDA STANDARDS/GLEs   FCAT: LA.A.1.1.2.K.4 Words; **LA.E.1.1.1.K.1** Genres; *Also* **LA.A.1.1.2.K.1** Print organization; **LA.A.1.1.3.K.1** Frequent words

■ **High-Frequency Word**

little

■ **Decodable Words**

See list on page T15.

School-Home Connection

Take-Home Book Version

◄ **Decodable Book 14:** *But I Can*

▲ *Float on the Boat*
Independent Reader 31

Exploring Our Surroundings   449

OBJECTIVES

- *To write by moving from left to right*

- *To write a question*

- *To use letters and phonetically spelled words to write questions about animals*

Materials

- ■ drawing paper

- ■ crayons

Writing

Write a Question

BUILD BACKGROUND

Talk About Animals   Hold up the chart that was created in the Literature Focus lesson. Remind children that even though they knew some things about turtles, they still had some questions about them. Talk about other animals that children are curious about. Ask them to tell the kinds of things they would like to find out about those animals.

Write a Question   Tell children that they are going to write a question about the animal they are curious about. Write these question words on the board to help children get started: *What, Where, Why.* Point to each word as you read it aloud. Model how to write a question with a capital letter at the beginning, and with a question mark at the end: *Why are owls awake at night?* Then distribute drawing paper and have children write and illustrate a question.

Self-Selected Writing Have children write and draw about anything they'd like. If they have difficulty thinking of a topic have them ask two friends what they're going to write about.

FLORIDA STANDARDS/GLEs   FCAT: LA.B.2.1.2.K.1 Record ideas; *Also* **LA.B.1.1.2.K.2** Basic formats; **LA.B.1.1.3.K.1** Spelling approximations; **LA.B.1.1.3.K.2** Print direction; **LA.B.1.1.3.K.3** Punctuation

 **Share Time**

Reflect on the Lesson Invite children to perform the actions as you recite "The Little Turtle" with them. Invite each child to sit in the Author's Chair to ask the question he or she wrote about an animal. Answer the question, if possible.

 S.S.R. Have children read silently from a book of their choice.

  **SOCIAL STUDIES**

Comparing Neighborhoods

Place the pictures in the Social Studies Center. Have children sort the pictures by type of neighborhood (city or country). Encourage children to examine the pictures and to point to things they see that are the same and things they see that are different. Have children find the picture that looks most like their own neighborhood.

 Materials

- magazine pictures of different kinds of neighborhoods (urban/suburban and rural)

FLORIDA STANDARDS/GLEs FCAT: LA.A.2.1.5.K.2 Get information; **LA.C.3.1.3.K.1** Basic vocabulary; *Also* **LA.C.1.1.1.K.1** Follow directions; **LA.C.1.1.3.K.1** Conversation rules

Exploring Our Surroundings 451

Day at a Glance
Day 5

WARM UP

Phonemic Awareness

Phoneme Substitution:
Medial

Sharing Literature

Big Book:
Five Little Ducks

Read

Five Little Ducks
AN OLD RHYME · ILLUSTRATED BY
Pamela Paparone

Respond to Literature

Literature Focus: Picture
Details

Phonics

Words with /u/ and /t/

Writing

Sentence

MORNING MESSAGE

Kindergarten News

Our families are special because

_____

Write Kindergarten News   Talk with children about what is special about their families.

Use prompts such as the following to guide children as you write the news:

- **What is special about your family?**
- **Who can show me a word?**
- **What letter will I write first in the word *special*?**
- **Let's clap the syllables in *families*. How many parts do you clap?**

As you write the message, invite children to contribute by writing letters or words they have previously learned. Remind them to use proper spacing, capitalization, and punctuation.

Calendar Language

Point to and read aloud the seasons of the year. Have children repeat the seasons with you. Ask: *How many seasons are there?*

Sunday	Monday	Tuesday	Wednesday	Thursday	Friday	Saturday
		1	2	3	4	5
6	7	8	9	10	11	12
13	14	15	16	17	18	19
20	21	22	23	24	25	26
27	28	29	30	31		

FLORIDA STANDARDS/GLEs   FCAT: LA.B.2.1.2.K.1 Record ideas; *Also* **LA.A.1.1.2.K.2** Alphabet; **LA.A.1.1.2.K.3** Sounds; **LA.B.1.1.3.K.1** Spelling approximations; **LA.C.3.1.2.K.1** Questions

Phonemic Awareness

PHONEME SUBSTITUTION: MEDIAL

Substitute Phonemes in Words   Use the rabbit puppet for the following phoneme substitution activity.

MODEL   The rabbit is changing the sounds in words again. Today the rabbit is changing the middle sounds in words we know. Listen as the rabbit says this word: *fun.* Say the word with the rabbit: *fun.* Now the rabbit will change the /u/ to /a/. The new word is *fan.* Say the word: *fan.*

Tell children that the rabbit is going to say some more words and the middle sound that will change. Children are to say the new word.

Change the /i/ in *pit* to /a/. (*pat*)

Change the /a/ in *cat* to /u/. (*cut*)

Change the /i/ in *big* to /u/. (*bug*)

Change the /o/ in *not* to /u/. (*nut*)

Change the /u/ in *tug* to /a/. (*tag*)

Change the /a/ in *bat* to /i/. (*bit*)

Change the /a/ in *wag* to /i/. (*wig*)

Change the /a/ in *cap* to /u/. (*cup*)

▲ **"Jennie Jenkins,"** *Oo-pples and Boo-noo-noos: Songs and Activities for Phonemic Awareness,* **pages 94–95.**

BELOW-LEVEL

Have children replace the rime in words rather than the medial phoneme: **Change the *it* in *pit* to *at.*** (*pat*) **Change the *at* in *cat* to *ut.*** (*cut*)

Sharing Literature

Read Five Little Ducks

READ ALOUD

Before Reading Display *Five Little Ducks* and have children tell what they remember about the story. Use these prompts to help children recall what happens.

- **What happens at the beginning of the story?** (The five little ducks go out one day.)
- **What happens in the middle?** (The little ducks don't come back.)
- **What happens at the end?** (Mother duck goes far away and calls the little ducks and they come back.)

During Reading Reread the story aloud. As you read,

- emphasize the language pattern of repetitive phrases.
- invite children to join in when they can.
- before reading the ending of the story, model identifying the problem.

MODEL **What is the problem in this story? The little ducks go away and don't come back.**

Then read on to identify how the problem is fixed and have children tell how in their own words.

Five Little Ducks
AN OLD RHYME · ILLUSTRATED BY
Pamela Paparone

▲ **Big Book**

OBJECTIVES

- *To identify the beginning, middle, and ending of a story*
- *To understand problem and solution*
- *To dramatize story events*
- *To understand picture details*

Materials

- *Big Book: Five Little Ducks*

FLORIDA STANDARDS/GLEs **FCAT: LA.A.2.1.1.K.1** Main idea; **LA.E.1.1.2.K.1** Story elements; *Also*
LA.C.1.1.1.K.2 Oral language; **LA.C.3.1.2.K.1** Questions; **LA.D.2.1.2.K.1** Patterned structures; **LA.E.2.1.2.K.1**
Patterned structures

RESPOND TO LITERATURE

Act Out the Story Suggest that children act out the story by taking the parts of the five little ducks and Mother duck. For each verse, the little ducks can waddle across the classroom, with one more child remaining behind each time.

Literature **Focus**

PICTURE DETAILS

Display pages 8 and 9 of *Five Little Ducks* and read the text. Have children look closely at the pictures. Tell them that they can find out more about stories by looking carefully at the pictures.

MODEL **When I look at the picture of the four ducks coming back, I notice that the ducks live in the country where there are hills and a stream. I also see other animals that live in the country: a moose, a fish, and a skunk. On the next page I notice that Mother duck and the little ducks like to play with water. I see that Mother duck has lots of flowers in her yard.**

Turn to other pages in the book and let children tell you about picture details they notice.

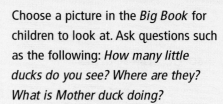
ONGOING ASSESSMENT

As you share *Five Little Ducks*, note whether children

• identify the beginning, middle, and ending of a story.

• understand problem and solution.

FLORIDA STANDARDS/GLEs   FCAT: **LA.A.1.1.4.K.1** Comprehension; **LA.E.1.1.2.K.1** Story elements; *Also* **LA.A.2.1.4.K.1** Illustrations; **LA.D.2.1.2.K.1** Patterned structures; **LA.E.2.1.1.K.2** Personal interpretations

Exploring Our Surroundings   **455**

OBJECTIVES

- *To build and read simple one-syllable words*

- *To understand that as the letters of words change, so do the sounds*

Materials

- *Alphabet Cards b, c, g, n, t, u*

- *Word Builders*

- *Word Builder Cards b, c, g, n, t, u*

- *pocket chart*

- *Magnetic Letters*

- *cookie sheet*

REVIEW LETTERS

Phonics
Words with /u/ and /t/

ACTIVE BEGINNING

Action Sentences   Teach children these sentences and the actions that go with them:

I cut the bread.
(Pantomime slicing bread.)

I spread the peanut butter.
(Pantomime spreading peanut butter on bread.)

I eat it up!
(Pantomime eating a peanut butter sandwich.)

TEACH/MODEL

Blending Words   Distribute *Word Builders* and *Word Builder Cards b, c, g, n, t, u* to children. As you place *Alphabet Cards* in a pocket chart, tell children to place the same *Word Builder Cards* in their *Word Builders*.

- Place *Alphabet Cards c, u,* and *t* in the pocket chart. Have children do the same.

- Point to *c.* Say **/kk/.** Point to *u.* Say **/uu/.**

- Slide the *u* next to the *c.* Then move your hand under the letters and blend the sounds, elongating them—**/kkuu/.** Have children do the same.

FLORIDA STANDARDS/GLEs   FCAT: **LA.A.1.1.2.K.5** Phonetic principles; *Also* **LA.A.1.1.2.K.3** Sounds

- Point to the letter *t*. Say /tt/. Have children do the same.

- Slide the *t* next to the *cu*. Slide your hand under *cut* and blend by elongating the sounds: **/kkuutt/**. Have children do the same.

- Then have children blend and read the word *cut* along with you.

PRACTICE/APPLY

Guided Practice   Have children place *Word Builder Cards u* and *t* in their *Word Builders*.

- **Add *n* to *ut*. What word did you make?**

- **Change *n* to *b*. What word did you make?**

- **Change *t* to *g*. What word did you make?**

- **Change *b* to *t*. What word did you make?**

Independent Practice   Have children use the *Magnetic Letters b, g, h, r, t, u* and a cookie sheet in the Letters and Words Center to build and read *but, hut, rut, tug, tub*.

FLORIDA STANDARDS/GLEs   FCAT: **LA.A.1.1.2.K.5** Phonetic principles; *Also* **LA.A.1.1.2.K.2** Alphabet; **LA.A.1.1.2.K.3** Sounds; **LA.C.3.1.2.K.1** Questions

BELOW-LEVEL

Have children name the letters as they place them in their *Word Builders*. Say the sound and have them repeat it. Have them move their hand under the letters in the *Word Builders* as they blend the sounds with you.

ADVANCED

Have children use the *Magnetic Letters b, h, n, t, u* and *High-Frequency Word Cards I, see, a* to build sentences: *I see a nut. I see a hut. I see a tub.*

▲ **Practice Book page 18**

OBJECTIVES

- *To share information and ideas, speaking in complete, coherent sentences*

- *To write a sentence*

- *To use letters and phonetically spelled words to write about experiences*

Materials

- ■ drawing paper

- ■ crayons

Writing

Write a Sentence

EXPRESS A FEELING

Talk About Happy Times   Remind children that mother duck is happy when the little ducks come back home. Ask children to think about what makes them happy. Have them share their thoughts with the group.

Write About a Happy Time   Write the following sentence frame on the board: *I am happy when I* _____. Read it with children. Then ask them to copy and complete the sentence. Have children draw a picture to illustrate their sentence. Remind children to say the letter sounds slowly as they say each word and write the letters.

 Self-Selected Writing Have children write and draw about anything they'd like. If they have difficulty thinking of a topic, have them ask two friends what they're going to write about.

Writing Every Day

My Journal

FLORIDA STANDARDS/GLEs   FCAT: LA.B.2.1.2.K.1 Record ideas; *Also* **LA.A.1.1.2.K.1** Print organization; **LA.B.1.1.2.K.2** Basic formats; **LA.B.1.1.3.K.1** Spelling approximations; **LA.B.1.1.3.K.2** Print direction; **LA.B.1.1.3.K.3** Punctuation; **LA.B.2.1.1.K.1** Familiar experiences; **LA.C.1.1.1.K.1** Follow directions; **LA.C.3.1.1.K.1** Speak clearly

WRAP UP # Share Time

Author's Chair   Invite children to read the sentences they have written about being happy in the writing activity. Have them describe their illustration.

S.S.R. *Sustained Silent Reading*   Have children read silently from a book of their choice.

Centers   ABC LETTERS AND WORDS

All 26!

Tell children that they have learned to recognize and write all twenty-six letters of the alphabet. Have group members work together to arrange the *Magnetic Letters* in alphabetical order on the cookie sheet. Children can assemble the uppercase alphabet first, then the lowercase alphabet, and finally both forms of each letter.

Materials

- *Magnetic Letters*
- cookie sheet

FLORIDA STANDARDS/GLEs   FCAT: LA.A.1.1.2.K.1 Print organization; **LA.A.1.1.2.K.2** Alphabet; **LA.A.2.1.5.K.1** Alphabetical order; **LA.C.1.1.3.K.1** Conversation rules

Exploring Our Surroundings   459

Learning Centers

Choose from the following suggestions to enhance your learning centers for the theme Exploring Our Surroundings.
(Additional learning centers for this theme can be found on pages 354-356 and 414)

(Additional learning centers for this theme can be found on pages 354-356 and 414)

WRITING CENTER

My Favorite Place

Have children draw a picture of their favorite environment. It can be a familiar one, such as their home or neighborhood, or a place that they have read about, such as a pond or desert. Encourage children to include lots of details that show the plants, animals, and objects in the environment. Have children write a caption that identifies the environment.

I like the forest best

20 Minutes a day

Materials

- paper
- crayons
- pencil

ART CENTER

Torn-Paper Trees

Tell children they are going to make a tree, using torn pieces of paper as leaves and/or flowers. Have children choose a tree, and have them draw its trunk and branches on a sheet of paper. Then have them tear off small pieces of construction paper or tissue paper and glue them to the tree as leaves. If children choose a flowering tree or a fruit tree, have them shape small pieces of paper as flowers or fruit and glue those to the branches. Children can write a label for their trees.

apel tree

20 Minutes a day

Materials

- paper
- crayons
- tissue paper or construction paper of many colors
- glue sticks

Teacher Notes

461

Teacher Notes

Week 3
Exploring Our Surroundings

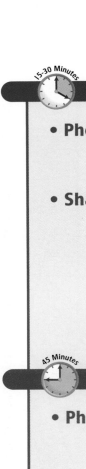

ORAL LANGUAGE — 15–30 Minutes

- **Phonemic Awareness**

- **Sharing Literature**

LEARNING TO READ — 45 Minutes

- **Phonics**

Daily Routines
- **Morning Message**
- **Calendar Language**
- **Writing Prompt**

LANGUAGE ARTS — 15–30 Minutes

- **Writing**
  Daily Writing Prompt

Day 1

Phonemic Awareness, 467
Phoneme Blending

Sharing Literature, 468

Read

Library Book:
What's What?

(Skill) **Literature Focus, 469**
Questions and Statements

Phonics, 470 T
Review: Consonant /n/*n*, Short Vowel /u/*u*

 Interactive Writing, 472
Writing Process: Prewrite

Writing Prompt, 472
Draw and write about a classroom object.

Share Time, 473
Share ideas about ducks.

Day 2

Phonemic Awareness, 475
Phoneme Blending

Sharing Literature, 476

Read

Read-Aloud Anthology:
"Chicken Forgets,"
pp. 51–52

(Skill) **Literature Focus, 477**
Characters

Phonics, 478 T
Blending *u - n*

 Interactive Writing, 480
Writing Process: Draft

Writing Prompt, 480
Draw and write about self-selected topics.

Share Time, 481
Retell "Chicken Forgets."

T = tested skill

 **Phonics**

Review /n/n, /u/u;
Blending *u - n*

Focus of the Week:
- **PHONEMIC AWARENESS**
- **SHARING LITERATURE**
- **WRITING (Writing Process)**

Day 3

Phonemic Awareness, 483
Phoneme Deletion

Sharing Literature, 484
Big Book: *Five Little Ducks*

 Literature Focus, 485
Summarize

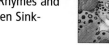**Phonics, 486 T**
Words with /u/ and /n/

 Interactive Writing, 488
Read
Writing Process: Respond and Revise

Writing Prompt, 488
Draw and write about favorite animals.

Share Time, 489
Compare books.

Day 4

Phonemic Awareness, 491
Phoneme Deletion

Sharing Literature, 492
Big Book of Rhymes and Songs: "Kitchen Sink-Song," p. 9

 Literature Focus, 493
Visualizing

Phonics, 495 T
Review: Short Vowel /u/u
Read
DECODABLE BOOK 15
Up, Up, Up

 Interactive Writing, 496
Writing Process: Edit

Writing Prompt, 496
Draw and write about self-selected topics.

Share Time, 497
Discuss the Decodable Book *Up, Up, Up*.

Day 5

Phonemic Awareness, 499
Phoneme Deletion

Sharing Literature, 500
Read
Read-Aloud Anthology: "Blame," p. 14

 Literature Focus, 501
Problem-Solution

Phonics, 502 T
Review blending /u/–/n/

 Interactive Writing, 504
Writing Process: Publish

Writing Prompt, 504
Draw and write about things goats eat.

Share Time, 505
Discuss "Blame."

Exploring Our Surroundings   465

WARM UP

Phonemic Awareness
Phoneme Blending

Sharing Literature
Library Book:
What's What?

Read

Mary Serfozo
What's what?
A Guessing Game

illustrated by Keiko Narahashi

Develop Concept Vocabulary

Respond to Literature

Literature Focus: Questions and Statements

Phonics
Consonant /n/*n*,
Short Vowel: /u/*u*

Interactive Writing ✏
Writing Process: Prewrite

MORNING MESSAGE

Kindergarten News

(Child's name) likes to _____

after school.

(Child's name) likes to _____

after school.

Write Kindergarten News Talk with children about what they like to do after school. Have them name their favorite things to do.

Use prompts such as the following to guide children as you write the news:

- **What do you like to do after school?**
- **What letter did I write last in (child's name)?**
- **Who can point to where to begin reading?**
- **How many words are in the second sentence?**

As you write the message, invite children to contribute by writing letters, words, or names they have learned previously. Remind them to use proper spacing, capitalization, and punctuation.

Calendar Language

Point to and read aloud the months of the year. Count the months with children. Ask them how many months are in the year.

Sunday	Monday	Tuesday	Wednesday	Thursday	Friday	Saturday
		1	2	3	4	5
6	7	8	9	10	11	12
13	14	15	16	17	18	19
20	21	22	23	24	25	26
27	28	29	30	31		

FLORIDA STANDARDS/GLEs FCAT: LA.A.1.1.3.K.4 Build vocabulary; **LA.A.2.1.5.K.2** Get information; **LA.B.2.1.2.K.1** Record ideas; *Also* **LA.A.1.1.2.K.2** Alphabet; **LA.A.1.1.3.K.1** Frequent words; **LA.C.1.1.3.K.1** Conversation rules; **LA.C.3.1.2.K.1** Questions

Phonemic Awareness

PHONEME BLENDING

Blend Phonemes Tell children they are to listen to the sounds you say and guess the word you are saying.

MODEL What word am I saying: /r/ /u/ /n/. Say the sounds with me: /r/ /u/ /n/. This time I'll say the sounds together: /rruunn/. Say the sounds with me: /rruunn/. Say the word: *run*.

Ask children to blend the sounds in these words.

/f/ /u/ /n/ (*fun*)　　　/r/ /u/ /g/ (*rug*)

/t/ /u/ /g/ (*tug*)　　　/kw/ /i/ /z/ (*quiz*)

/b/ /i/ /b/ (*bib*)　　　/h/ /u /m/ (*hum*)

/f/ /o/ /ks/ (*fox*)　　　/z/ /a/ /p/ (*zap*)

/y/ /a/ /k/ (*yak*)　　　/k/ /u/ /p/ (*cup*)

/b/ /u/ /n/ (*bun*)　　　/w/ /a/ /ks/ (*wax*)

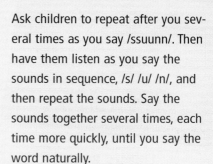

FLORIDA STANDARDS/GLEs　**FCAT: LA.A.1.1.2.K.5** Phonetic principles

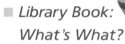

▲ **Library Book**

OBJECTIVES

• *To recognize uppercase letters*

• *To recognize questions and statements*

Materials

■ *Library Book: What's What?*

■ chart paper

■ marker

■ drawing paper

■ crayons

Sharing Literature

Read **What's What?**

READ ALOUD

Before Reading Display the cover of *What's What?* and read aloud the title with children. Point out that the title is a question and it begins with an uppercase letter. Call on a child to identify the uppercase letter (W) and the question mark. Read the title aloud. Use these prompts to recall selection events, and to set a purpose for rereading:

• **What is this book about?** (It is a guessing game about things that are hard, soft, warm, cold, and so on.)

• **Ask children to tell what they like about playing guessing games and asking riddles.**

Tell them you will read the story again to find out the answer to the last riddle.

During Reading Reread the selection aloud. As you read,

• invite children to repeat the question after you. Pause before turning the page to allow children to suggest answers to the question. Then read the answer and show children the picture.

• emphasize the rhyming words.

FLORIDA STANDARDS/GLEs FCAT: **LA.A.1.1.3.K.5** Story elements; **LA.A.2.1.5.K.2** Get information; **LA.E.1.1.1.K.1** Genres; *Also* ; **LA.C.1.1.1.K.2** Oral language; **LA.C.3.1.2.K.1** Questions

DEVELOP CONCEPT VOCABULARY

After Reading   Write these word pairs on chart paper: *hard/soft, warm/cold, wet/dry, long/short, light/dark*. Point to and read each word pair. Tell children that the words in each pair are opposites.

Then say: *Hard, soft.* **Name something that is hard. Name something that is soft.**

Repeat the process with the other pairs of opposites.

RESPOND TO LITERATURE

Draw and Label Opposites   Ask children to choose a word pair from the chart created during the Develop Concept Vocabulary activity. Have them draw and label pictures to show the meaning of the opposites.

QUESTIONS AND STATEMENTS

Display the first page of *What's What?* Read the text and tell children that this is an asking sentence. It asks a question and it has a question mark at the end. Display the next page and read the first sentence. Tell children that this is a telling sentence. It tells the answer to the question and it has a period at the end.

Turn to other pages in the book and read both questions and statements, asking children to identify whether each is an asking sentence or a telling sentence. Remind children to look at the punctuation marks to help them figure out which kind of sentence they are reading.

ADVANCED

Have children look through books in the Literacy Center, identifying asking and telling sentences.

ONGOING ASSESSMENT

As you share *What's What?*, note whether children

- recognize uppercase letters.
- suggest reasonable answers to questions in the book.

FLORIDA STANDARDS/GLEs   **FCAT: LA.A.1.1.2.K.4** Words; **LA.A.1.1.2.K.6** Print meaning; *Also* **LA.A.1.1.3.K.1** Frequent words; **LA.E.2.1.1.K.2** Personal interpretations

Exploring Our Surroundings   **469**

OBJECTIVES

- To recognize uppercase and lowercase Uu and Nn

- To match sounds to letters

Materials

- pocket chart
- Big Alphabet Cards Uu, Nn
- Picture Cards umbrella, newspaper
- Tactile Letter Cards u, n
- drawing paper
- crayons
- scissors

Phonics

Consonant /n/n
Short Vowel /u/u Review

ACTIVE BEGINNING

Recite the Rhymes Display *Big Alphabet Cards Uu* and *Nn*. Ask children to identify each letter. Have children form a circle. Ask a child to stand in the middle of the circle and hold up *Big Alphabet Card Uu*. Have the children walk around the circle as they recite "Up and Up and Up." (See page 432.) Then have them recite "No, No, Nancy." (See Vol. I, page 524.)

TEACH/MODEL

Review Letters and Sounds

Display *Big Alphabet Card Uu* in a pocket chart and ask what letter this is. (*Uu*)

Point to the picture and say its name. Have children repeat it. (*umbrella*)

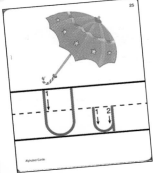

What sound do you hear at the beginning of *umbrella*? (/u/)

What letter stands for the /u/ sound in *umbrella*? (*Uu*)

Touch the letter and say **/u/**. Touch the letter again and have children say /u/.

Follow the same procedure for *Big Alphabet Card Nn*.

Place *Picture Cards umbrella* and *newspaper* on the chalk board ledge. Say each picture name and tell children you need to decide where to put each *Picture Card*.

I'll start with the umbrella. *U—mbrella* begins with the /u/ sound. So I'll put the picture of the umbrella below *Uu*.

Model the same process with *Picture Card newspaper*.

 FLORIDA STANDARDS/GLEs **LA.A.1.1.2.K.1** Print organization; **LA.A.1.1.2.K.2** Alphabet; **LA.A.1.1.2.K.3** Sounds; **LA.C.3.1.2.K.1** Questions; **LA.D.2.1.2.K.1** Patterned Structures

PRACTICE/APPLY

Guided Practice Distribute *Tactile Letter Cards u* and *n* to each child.

I will say some words that begin with /u/ and some that don't. Hold up your *u* card if the word begins with the /u/ sound.

thumbs ↑ thumbs ↓

Confirm answers by holding up *Letter Cards* when appropriate.

table	under	ugly	apple	up	uncle

I will say some words that begin with /n/ and some that don't. Hold up your *n* card if the word begins with the /n/ sound.

thumbs ↑ thumbs ↓

name	mail	nest	rake	nose	number

Independent Practice Provide children with drawing paper that is divided into four sections. Have children draw a picture of an uncle, umbrella, nut, and nine, one in each section. Have them cut out their pictures. Tell children to name each picture. If the word begins with /u/, they should place the picture below *Tactile Letter Card u*. If the word begins with /n/, they should place the picture below *Tactile Letter Card n.*

BELOW-LEVEL

Have children name the pictures on *Picture Cards umbrella* and *newspaper*, say the sound for the beginning letter in each word, and trace the letter on the corresponding *Tactile Letter Card.*

Phonics Resources

Phonics Express™ CD-ROM, Level A, Roamer/ Route 4/Park, Roamer/Route 5/ Building Site, Sparkle/Route 1/ Train Station; Sparkle/Route 2/ Fire Station, Sparkle/Route 3/ Harbor, Sparkle/Route 4/Market

▲ **Practice Book page 19** HW

Exploring Our Surroundings **471**

OBJECTIVES

- *To recall prior knowledge*
- *To generate ideas for an informative writing piece*

Writing Every Day

Day 1: Prewrite
Generate a word web about ducks.

Day 2: Draft
Work together to create sentences from the ideas in the word web.

Day 3: Respond and Revise
Children refine the writing by adding or deleting information.

Day 4: Proofread
Children proofread the sentences for correct punctuation.

Day 5: Publish
Children illustrate the sentences and compile them into a class book.

Writing Process

Write an Informational Book

PREWRITE

Present the Topic   Remind children that they have read two stories with duck characters (*Five Little Ducklings* and *Come Along, Daisy!*). Tell them that they will be writing a class book about real ducks. Explain that their book will be useful to people who want to learn about ducks.

Create a Word Web   Tell children that the first step in writing their book is to think about what they know about ducks. Write the word *ducks* in the center of a piece of chart paper. Tell children that you want to write words about ducks on the paper. Write the word *bird* on the chart and read it to children. Explain that you wrote the word because a duck is a kind of bird. Have children suggest other words that relate to ducks, such as *fly*, *swim*, *feathers*, and *duckling*. Write each word. Draw a circle around each word and draw a line from the word *duck* to each circle.

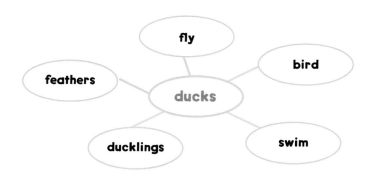

Journal Writing   Have children write and draw about an object in the classroom.

FLORIDA STANDARDS/GLEs   FCAT: LA.B.2.1.2.K.1 Record ideas; *Also* ; **LA.B.1.1.1.K.2** Generate ideas; **LA.B.1.1.3.K.1** Spelling approximations; **LA.B.1.1.3.K.2** Print direction; **LA.B.2.1.1.K.2** Contribute ideas; **LA.B.2.1.4.K.1** Informational texts

WRAP UP # Share Time

Reflect on the Lesson Gather children around the Author's Chair. Have them point to words on the word web created during Writing. Read the words to them. Tell them that they will use the ideas in the web to write about ducks. Have them share what they would like to include in their writing.

S.S.R. Have children read silently from a book of their choice.

 **Centers** ART

Collage Time

Write the following words on chart paper: *soft, hard, wet, dry, warm, cold*. Have children choose one of the words and then cut out of magazines pictures that show things that can be described by this word. Have children glue the pictures onto construction paper to form a collage. Have them copy the word from the chart to label their pictures. You can display children's work on a bulletin board.

 ## Materials

- chart paper
- marker
- magazines
- scissors
- glue
- construction paper

FLORIDA STANDARDS/GLEs **FCAT: LA.A.2.1.3.K.1** Supportive details; *Also* **LA.A.2.1.4.K.1** Illustrations; **LA.C.1.1.1.K.1** Follow directions

Exploring Our Surroundings **473**

Phonemic Awareness
Phoneme Blending

Sharing Literature
Read-Aloud Anthology:
"Chicken Forgets"

Read

KINDERGARTEN
READ-ALOUD
Anthology
Harcourt

Develop Listening Comprehension

Respond to Literature

Literature Focus: Characters

Phonics

Blending /u/-/n/

Interactive Writing
Writing Process: Draft

ORAL LANGUAGE

MORNING MESSAGE

Kindergarten News

(Child's name)'s job at home is ____

_____ .

(Child's name)'s job at home is

_____ .

Write Kindergarten News Talk with children about jobs they have at home. Ask children to tell why they think helping at home is important.

Use prompts such as the following to guide children as you write the news:

• **What jobs do you do at home?**

• **Who can write the word *at*?**

• **Let's count the letters in (child's name)? How many letters are there?**

• **Who can show me the beginning of a word?**

As you write the message, invite children to contribute by writing letters, words, or names they have learned previously. Remind them to use proper spacing, capitalization, and punctuation.

Calendar Language

Point to and read aloud the months of the year. Name the months again, asking children to join in and clap syllables for each month. Ask what month it is now.

Sunday	Monday	Tuesday	Wednesday	Thursday	Friday	Saturday
		1	2	3	4	5
6	7	8	9	10	11	12
13	14	15	16	17	18	19
20	21	22	23	24	25	26
27	28	29	30	31		

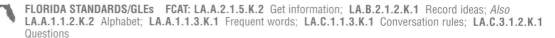
FLORIDA STANDARDS/GLEs   FCAT: LA.A.2.1.5.K.2 Get information; **LA.B.2.1.2.K.1** Record ideas; *Also* **LA.A.1.1.2.K.2** Alphabet; **LA.A.1.1.3.K.1** Frequent words; **LA.C.1.1.3.K.1** Conversation rules; **LA.C.3.1.2.K.1** Questions

Phonemic Awareness

PHONEME BLENDING

Blend Phonemes Tell children you are going to put some sounds together to make a word. Say:

MODEL /t/ /u/ /b/, *tub*. Say it with me: /t/ /u/ /b/. Now say the word: *tub*.

Now you try. What word am I saying: /b/ /u/ /s/? (*bus*)

As you provide these examples, ask children, **What word am I saying?**

/h/ /a/ /m/ (*ham*)	/f/ /i/ /t/ (*fit*)	/b/ /u/ /d/ (*bud*)
/t/ /o/ /p/ (*top*)	/j/ /e/ /t/ (*jet*)	/r/ /e/ /d/ (*red*)
/r/ /u/ /n/ (*run*)	/s/ /u/ /b/ (*sub*)	/d/ /i/ /p/ (*dip*)
/s/ /u/ /n/ (*sun*)	/b/ /u/ /n/ (*bun*)	/n/ /u/ /t/ (*nut*)
/b/ /u/ /g/ (*bug*)	/k/ /a/ /p/ (*cap*)	/f/ /o/ /ks/ (*fox*)
/p/ /e/ /t/ (*pet*)	/f/ /u/ /n/ (*fun*)	/k/ /u/ /p/ (*cup*)

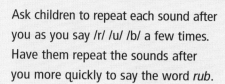

BELOW-LEVEL

Ask children to repeat each sound after you as you say /r/ /u/ /b/ a few times. Have them repeat the sounds after you more quickly to say the word *rub*.

ADVANCED

Have children blend words with consonant blends, such as /p/ /l/ /u/ /g/ (*plug*), /s/ /k/ /i/ /p/ (*skip*), /d/ /r/ /u/ /m/ (*drum*).

Day 2

▲ Read-Aloud Anthology

OBJECTIVES

- *To recognize the problem in a story*
- *To answer questions about a text*
- *To understand characters*

Materials

- *Read-Aloud Anthology, pp. 51–52*

Sharing Literature

Read "Chicken Forgets"

READ ALOUD

Before Reading   Turn to page 51 of the *Read-Aloud Anthology* and read aloud the title of the story. Ask children what they remember about this story. Help children set a purpose for listening before you reread the story.

> **MODEL**   I remember that the chicken has a job to do for his mother. I'll reread the story to find out what that job is and if the chicken does the job.

During Reading   Read the story aloud. As you read,

- vary your voice for each character.
- pause and let children predict what each animal will ask for.
- pause after reading about the goat. Ask children to identify the problem in the story. (The chicken forgets things. He has met two animals who make him forget what he's looking for.)

FLORIDA STANDARDS/GLEs   **FCAT: LA.E.1.1.2.K.1** Story elements; *Also* **LA.C.1.1.1.K.2** Oral language

DEVELOP LISTENING COMPREHENSION

After Reading   Have children answer these questions:

- **Why does the mother hen have to remind the chicken to keep his mind on what he is doing?** (Because sometimes he forgot things.)

- **How does the chicken try to remember what he is supposed to get?** (He repeats the words over and over.)

- **Why is it lucky that the chicken meets the robin last?** (The robin likes blackberries too and helps the chicken remember his job.)

- **How does the mother hen feel when the chicken brings the blackberries home?** (proud)

RESPOND TO LITERATURE

Discuss the Story   Have children suggest what they would tell the little chicken to do to help him remember things.

CHARACTERS

Literature Focus

Remind children that the people and animals in stories are called *characters*. Write the *chicken* and the *mother hen* on the board, and tell what you know about the chicken from the story.

MODEL I learned from the story that the chicken tries hard. He says *Get wild blackberries* over and over so he won't forget his job. Even though he eats some of the blackberries, he saves enough to bring home to the mother hen.

Discuss with children what they learned about the mother hen from the story.

BELOW-LEVEL

Below On-Level Advanced ELL

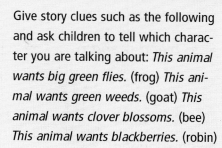

Give story clues such as the following and ask children to tell which character you are talking about: *This animal wants big green flies.* (frog) *This animal wants green weeds.* (goat) *This animal wants clover blossoms.* (bee) *This animal wants blackberries.* (robin)

ONGOING ASSESSMENT

As you share "Chicken Forgets," note whether children

- **recognize the problem in the story.**

- **answer questions about the story.**

FLORIDA STANDARDS/GLEs   FCAT: LA.A.1.1.3.K.5 Story elements; **LA.A.1.1.4.K.1** Comprehension; **LA.E.1.1.2.K.1** Story elements; *Also* **LA.C.3.1.1.K.1** Speak clearly

Exploring Our Surroundings   477

OBJECTIVES

- To identify and recognize the initial sound of a spoken word

- To blend u and n

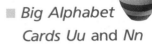

Materials

- Big Alphabet Cards Uu and Nn

- Alphabet Cards b, f, n, r, s, t, u

- pocket chart

- index cards

Phonics

Blending /u/ - /n/  Introduce

ACTIVE BEGINNING

Word Hunt   Have children sit in a circle. As you read the following verse, have children echo. Establish a beat and keep it going throughout the verse.

Going on a word hunt.

What's this word?

/r/ /u/ /n/

Together: *Run!*

Continue with the words /f/ /u/ /n/ (*fun*), /s/ /u/ /n/ (*sun*), /n/ /u/ /t/ (*nut*).

TEACH/MODEL

Recognize *u* and *n*   Display *Big Alphabet Card Uu* on the chalk ledge or in a pocket chart. Ask: **What letter is this?** (Uu) **What sound does this letter stand for?** (/u/)

Have children say /u/ with you as you point to the letter.

Do the same procedure for *Big Alphabet Card Nn.*

Word Blending   Explain to children that they are going to blend letters together to read words, such as *sun.*

- Place the *Alphabet Cards s, u, n* in the pocket chart, separate from each other.

- Point to *s*. Say /**ss**/. Have children repeat the sound after you.
- Point to *u*. Say /**uu**/. Have children repeat the sound after you.
- Point to *n*. Say /**nn**/. Have children repeat the sound after you.

FLORIDA STANDARDS/GLEs   FCAT: LA.A.1.1.2.K.4 Words; **LA.A.1.1.2.K.5** Phonetic principles; *Also* **LA.A.1.1.2.K.2** Alphabet; **LA.A.1.1.2.K.3** Sounds; **LA.C.3.1.1.K.1** Speak clearly; **LA.D.1.1.1.K.1** Sound patterns; **LA.D.2.1.2.K.1** Patterned structures

- Slide the *u* next to *s*. Move your hand under the letters and blend the sounds, elongating them—/**ssuu**/. Have children repeat after you.

- Slide the *n* next to *su*. Move your hand under the letters and blend the sounds, elongating them—/**ssuunn**/. Have children repeat after you.

- Then have children read *sun* with you.

PRACTICE/APPLY

Guided Practice Place the *Alphabet Cards r, u,* and *n* in the pocket chart.

- Point to *r* and say /**rr**/. Point to the letter *u* and say /**u**/. Slide the *u* next to *r*. Move your hand under the letters and blend the sounds, elongating them—/**rruu**/. Have children blend the sounds after you.

- Point to *n*. Say /**nn**/. Have children say the sound.

- Slide the *n* next to the *ru*. Slide your hand under *run* and blend the sounds. Have children blend the sounds as you slide your hand under the word.

- Then have children read the word *run* along with you.

Follow the same procedure to build and blend *bun, fun,* and *nut* with children.

Independent Practice Write the following words on index cards and place them in a pocket chart in the Letters and Words Center: *fun, sun, run, bun, nut*. Have children read each word.

FLORIDA STANDARDS/GLEs FCAT: LA.A.1.1.2.K.5 Phonetic principles; *Also* **LA.A.1.1.2.K.1** Print organization; **LA.A.1.1.2.K.2** Alphabet; **LA.A.1.1.2.K.3** Sounds; **LA.A.1.1.3.K.1** Frequent words

ADVANCED

Place the *Magnetic Letters b, f, n, r, s, t, u* and a cookie sheet in the Letters and Words Center. Place the *Magnetic Letters u* and *n* on the cookie sheet. Encourage children to make other words with *u* and *n*, such as *run* and *nut*.

ENGLISH-LANGUAGE LEARNERS

Before asking children to read the words in the Independent Practice, review each letter sound with them.

▲ **Practice Book page 20**

OBJECTIVES

- *To write informational sentences*

- *To contribute ideas to a writing activity*

Materials

- chart paper
- marker

Writing Process

Write an Informational Book

DRAFT

Review the Topic Display the word web created in the Day 1 Writing activity (page 472). Read each word on the display to children. Tell children that they can use the word web to give them ideas for sentences about ducks. Model selecting a word from the web and writing a sentence about it on chart paper.

MODEL I see we have the word *swim* on our word web. We put it there because ducks swim in the water. I can write a sentence that tells that. I can write *Ducks swim in the water*.

Write Sentences Ask volunteers to select a word from the web and dictate a sentence that relates to it. Write each sentence on the chart paper, allowing children to write known letters, words, and punctuation. Use questions such as the following to guide children:

What kind of letter comes at the beginning of a sentence?

Who can write the first letter of the word _____?

Who can find the word _____ on our chart so we can know how to write it?

Compile a list of sentences on the chart paper, and save the chart paper until the next day's activity.

Ducks fly.

Ducks have feathers.

Ducks swim in the water.

Self-Selected Writing Have children draw and write about self-selected topics in their journals.

FLORIDA STANDARDS/GLEs   **FCAT: LA.B.1.1.2.K.4** Add details; **LA.B.2.1.2.K.1** Record ideas; *Also* **LA.A.1.1.2.K.2** Alphabet; **LA.B.1.1.3.K.1** Spelling approximations; **LA.B.1.1.3.K.2** Print direction; **LA.B.1.1.3.K.3** Punctuation; **LA.B.2.1.1.K.2** Contribute ideas

WRAP UP Share Time

Reflect on the Lesson Have children retell the story "Chicken Forgets." Ask them to think about things the chicken and the mother hen do. Then have them share things they need to remember to do at home.

S.S.R. Have children read silently from a book of their choice.

Centers SCIENCE

Model Habitats

Children can work together to create models of a mountain, a meadow, or a pond. Display books that show the environments and the animals that live there. Encourage children to use natural materials with paper, clay, and plastic animals.

Materials

- box lids
- grass, twigs, small rocks
- glue
- construction paper
- crayons or markers
- plastic animals
- modeling clay

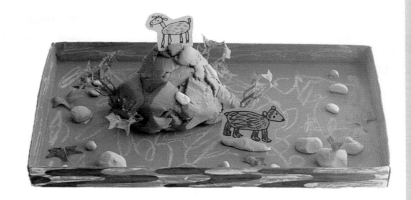

Day at a Glance
Day 3

WARM UP

Phonemic Awareness
Phoneme Deletion

Sharing Literature
Big Book:
Five Little Ducks

Read

Respond to Literature

Literature Focus: Summarize

Phonics
Words with /u/ and /n/

Interactive Writing
Writing Process: Respond and Revise

MORNING MESSAGE

Kindergarten News

Today is a school day. It is

_____.

We like to play

_____.

Write Kindergarten News   Talk with children about the things they like to do when it's time to play.

Use prompts such as the following to guide children as you write the news:

- **What do you like to do during your playtime?**
- **What letter will I write first for the word *Today*?**
- **Who can tell me where to put a period?**
- **How many words are in the second sentence?**

As you write the message, invite children to contribute by writing letters or words they have previously learned. Remind them to use proper spacing, capitalization, and punctuation.

Calendar Language

Point to and read aloud the days of the week. Point to and read aloud *Monday* through *Friday*. Ask children to repeat the names of the school days.

Sunday	Monday	Tuesday	Wednesday	Thursday	Friday	Saturday
		1	2	3	4	5
6	7	8	9	10	11	12
13	14	15	16	17	18	19
20	21	22	23	24	25	26
27	28	29	30	31		

FLORIDA STANDARDS/GLEs   FCAT: LA.A.1.1.2.K.5 Phonetic principles; **LA.A.2.1.5.K.2** Get information; *Also* **LA.A.1.1.2.K.2** Alphabet; **LA.A.1.1.2.K.3** Sounds; **LA.C.1.1.3.K.1** Conversation rules; **LA.C.3.1.2.K.1** Questions

Phonemic Awareness

PHONEME DELETION

Delete Initial Phonemes Say the word *sun* and have children repeat it. Say: Listen while I say *sun* this way: /s//un/. Say it with me: /s//un/.

Listen while I say *sun* without the /s/: *un*. Say it with me: *un*.

Tell children you are going to ask them to say some words without the beginning sound. Use the following words:

Say *nut* without the /n/. (*ut*)   Say *page* without the /p/. (*age*)

Say *run* without the /r/. (*un*)   Say *tug* without the /t/. (*ug*)

Say *quiz* without the /kw/. (*iz*)   Say *quake* without the /kw/. (*ake*)

Sharing Literature

Read Five Little Ducks

READ ALOUD

Before Reading   Browse through *Five Little Ducks*, and ask children to recall the story. Then turn to page 8 and read the dialogue, *"Quack, quack, quack, quack."* Ask:

- **Who says those words?** (Mother duck)
- **How do you know the words are spoken?** (because they have quotation marks around them)
- **Who is Mother duck talking to?** (the little ducks)

During Reading   Reread the story aloud. As you read,

- pause and ask children to identify rhyming words.
- point to spaces between words.
- pause to point out details that show the story is make-believe. Model the first example.

MODEL   As I look at this first picture with Mother duck, I know the story is make-believe. I see the house where the ducks live. There is a toy and a swing set in the yard. Real ducks don't have these things.

Five Little Ducks
AN OLD RHYME · ILLUSTRATED BY
Pamela Paparone

▲ **Big Book**

OBJECTIVES

- *To recall story events*
- *To recognize dialogue*
- *To understand real and make-believe*
- *To compare texts*
- *To summarize a story*

Materials

- *Big Book:*
  Five Little Ducks

FLORIDA STANDARDS/GLEs   FCAT: LA.A.1.1.4.K.1 Comprehension; LA.A.2.1.3.K.1 Supportive details; *Also* LA.A.1.1.2.K.1 Print organization; LA.C.1.1.1.K.2 Oral language; LA.C.3.1.2.K.1 Questions

RESPOND TO LITERATURE

Compare Texts Have children think about *Five Little Ducks* and *Come Along, Daisy!* Talk with them about how the two stories are alike and how they are different. For example, discuss how both stories have ducklings as characters and how one is a rhyming story and the other is not.

Literature Focus

SUMMARIZE

Display *Five Little Ducks*. Page through the book and model how to tell about the beginning, middle, and ending of a story.

MODEL At the beginning of the story, the five little ducks go out. In the middle, one little duck doesn't come back each time. During the ending, Mother duck calls the ducks and they come back.

Ask children to use the words *beginning*, *middle*, and *ending* to summarize the story again.

ADVANCED

Have partners tell about another story they have read, using the words *beginning*, *middle*, and *ending*.

ONGOING ASSESSMENT

As you share *Five Little Ducks*, note whether children

- recall story events.
- recognize dialogue.
- understand real and make-believe.
- compare texts.

FLORIDA STANDARDS/GLEs FCAT: **LA.A.1.1.3.K.5** Story elements; **LA.A.1.1.4.K.1** Comprehension; **LA.A.2.1.1.K.1** Main idea; **LA.E.1.1.2.K.1** Story elements

Exploring Our Surroundings **485**

OBJECTIVES

- *To build and read simple one-syllable words*

- *To understand that as the letters of words change, so do the sounds*

Materials

- *Alphabet Cards f, n, r, s, t, u*

- *Word Builders*

- *Word Builder Cards f, n, r, s, t, u*

- pocket chart

- *Magnetic Letters*

- cookie sheet

REVIEW LETTERS

f r s t

Whole Group

Phonics

Words with /u/ and /n/

ACTIVE BEGINNING

Action Rhyme   Teach children this rhyme and the actions that go with it:

> **Run, run, run.**
>
> **Run like squirrels in the sun!**
> (Run in place.)
>
> **Nuts, nuts, nuts.**
>
> **Eating nuts and having fun!**
> (Pretend to eat peanuts.)

TEACH/MODEL

Blending Words   Distribute *Word Builders* and *Word Builder Cards* f, n, r, s, t, u to children. As you place *Alphabet Cards* in a pocket chart, tell children to place the same *Word Builder Cards* in their *Word Builder.*

- Point to *s.* Say **/ss/.** Point to *u.* Say **/uu/.**

- Slide the *u* next to the *s.* Then move your hand under the letters and blend the sounds, elongating them—**/ssuu/.** Have children do the same.

- Point to the letter *n.* Say **/nn/.** Have children do the same.

- Slide the *n* next to the *su.* Slide your hands under *sun* and blend by elongating the sounds —**/ssuunn/.** Have children do the same.

- Then have children read the word *sun* along with you.

FLORIDA STANDARDS/GLEs FCAT: LA.A.1.1.2.K.5 Phonetic principles. *Also* **LA.A.1.1.2.K.1** Print organization; **LA.A.1.1.2.K.3** Sounds; **LA.C.1.1.1.K.1** Follow directions; **LA.C.2.1.2.K.1** Nonverbal cues; **LA.D.1.1.1.K.1** Sound patterns

PRACTICE/APPLY

Guided Practice   Have children place *Word Builder Cards u* and *n* in their *Word Builder*.

whole group

- **Add *f* to *un*. What word did you make?**

- **Change *f* to *r*. What word did you make?**

- **Change *n* to *t*. What word did you make?**

- **Change *r* to *n*. What word did you make?**

Choose individuals

Independent Practice   Have children use the *Magnetic Letters n, r, s, t,* and *u* in the Letters and Words Center to build and read *sun, run,* and *nut*.

(on board)

REACHING ALL LEARNERS

Diagnostic Check: Phonics

If... children have difficulty blending and reading words,

Then... have them name the letters as they place them in their *Word Builder*. Say the sound and have them repeat the sound. Have them move their hand under the letters in the *Word Builder* as they blend the sounds with you.

ADDITIONAL SUPPORT ACTIVITIES

BELOW-LEVEL   Reteach, p. S52

ADVANCED   Extend, p. S53

ENGLISH-LANGUAGE LEARNERS   Reteach, p. S53

▲ **Practice Book page 21** *HW*

FLORIDA STANDARDS/GLEs FCAT: LA.A.1.1.2.K.5 Phonetic principles; **LA.A.1.1.3.K.4** Build vocabulary. *Also* **LA.A.1.1.2.K.1** Print organization; **LA.A.1.1.2.K.2** Alphabet; **LA.A.1.1.2.K.3** Sounds; **LA.C.3.1.2.K.1** Questions

Exploring Our Surroundings   487

OBJECTIVE

To refine previously written sentences

Materials

■ correction tape

■ marker

Writing Process

Write an Informational Book

RESPOND AND REVISE

Reread the Sentences Display the list of sentences the group created in the Day 2 Writing activity (page 480). Read each sentence to children. Tell children that the next step in writing their book about ducks is to decide how they can improve the sentences they wrote.

Make Revisions Ask children questions such as the following:

Is the information in each sentence correct?

Should we add anything to any of the sentences?

Is there anything else we should add to our book?

Is there anything we do not want to include in our book?

Use correction tape and a marker to replace words that children suggest should be changed. Add new suggestions to the chart. After the changes are made, reread the sentences to children.

Journal Writing Have children draw and write information about their favorite animal.

FLORIDA STANDARDS/GLEs FCAT: LA.A.1.1.2.K.4 Words; **LA.A.2.1.5.K.2** Get information; **LA.B.1.1.2.K.4** Add details; *Also* **LA.A.1.1.2.K.1** Print organization; **LA.B.2.1.4.K.1** Informational texts; **LA.C.3.1.2.K.1** Questions

488   **Exploring Our Surroundings**

WRAP UP Share Time

Reflect on the Lesson   Ask children to tell which was their favorite book—*Five Little Ducks* or *Come Along, Daisy!*—and to tell why they liked it better. Then read aloud the revised sentences about ducks children wrote during Writing.

S.S.R. *Sustained Silent Reading*   Have children read silently from a book of their choice.

Centers   LISTENING

Listen to This

Set up the tape and tape player in the Listening Center. Have children listen to the tape for the different sounds. As they listen, have them draw a picture to show what makes some of the sounds they recognize.

Materials

- tape player

- tape with environmental sounds

- drawing paper

- crayons

FLORIDA STANDARDS/GLEs   **LA.A.1.1.2.K.1** Print organization; **LA.B.1.1.2.K.2** Basic formats; **LA.B.2.1.4.K.1** Informational texts; **LA.E.2.1.1.K.2** Personal interpretations

Day at a Glance
Day 4

Phonemic Awareness
Phoneme Deletion

Sharing Literature
Big Book of Rhymes and Songs: "Kitchen Sink-Song"

Respond to Literature
Literature Focus: Visualize

Phonics
Short Vowel /u/*u*

Reading
Decodable Book 15: *Up, Up, Up*

Interactive Writing
Writing Process: Proofread

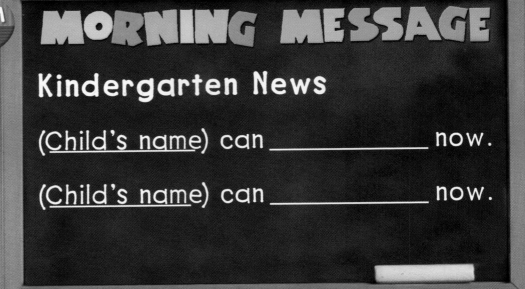

MORNING MESSAGE
Kindergarten News

(Child's name) can _____ now.

(Child's name) can _____ now.

Write Kindergarten News Talk with children about things they can do now that they couldn't do at the beginning of the school year.

Use prompts such as the following to guide children as you write the news:

- **What is something new you can do now?**
- **Where should I begin to write?**
- **How many letters are in (child's name)?**
- **Who can write the word *can*?**

As you write the message, invite children to contribute by writing letters, words, or names they have learned previously. Remind them to use proper spacing, capitalization, and punctuation.

Calendar Language

Point to and read aloud the name of this month. Then point to and read aloud any holidays that are celebrated during this month. Show children on which day each holiday falls.

Sunday	Monday	Tuesday	Wednesday	Thursday	Friday	Saturday
		1	2	3	4	5
6	7	8	9	10	11	12
13	14	15	16	17	18	19
20	21	22	23	24	25	26
27	28	29	30	31		

FLORIDA STANDARDS/GLEs FCAT: LA.A.2.1.5.K.2 Get information; **LA.B.2.1.2.K.1** Record ideas; *Also* **LA.A.1.1.2.K.2** Alphabet; **LA.A.1.1.3.K.1** Frequent words; **LA.C.1.1.3.K.1** Conversation rules; **LA.C.3.1.2.K.1** Questions

490 Exploring Our Surroundings

Phonemic Awareness

PHONEME DELETION

Delete Initial Phonemes   Say the word, delete the initial phoneme, and have children say the new word.

MODEL   Say the word *sit*.

Listen while I say *sit* without the /s/: *it*.

Say the word with me: *it*.

Now say the word *pin*.

What word do we have if we leave the /p/ off the beginning of *pin*?

Say the word *in*.

What word do we have if we leave the /b/ off the beginning of *band*?

Say the word *and*.

Continue with the following words:

What word do we have if we leave

the /d/ off the beginning of *dad*? (*ad*)

the /s/ off the beginning of *sat*? (*at*)

the /g/ off the beginning of *goat*? (*oat*)

the /b/ off the beginning of *bold*? (*old*)

the /s/ off the beginning of *sour*? (*our*)

the /k/ off the beginning of *cup*? (*up*)

ADVANCED

Have children who master deleting initial phonemes practice deleting initial phonemes from words beginning with consonant blends. For example, ask children to say *clap* without the /k/ (*lap*) or *blink* without the /b/ (*link*).

Sharing Literature

Read "Kitchen Sink-Song"

READ ALOUD

Before Reading   Display page 9 of the *Big Book of Rhymes and Songs* and track the print of the title while reading the words aloud. Ask children to name each of the uppercase letters in the title. Then set a purpose for rereading.

MODEL **I know this poem is about sounds in the kitchen. The sink makes some sounds. The title of the poem tells me this. I'll read it again so I can remember what the other sounds are and what makes them.**

During Reading   Read the poem aloud. As you read,

• track the print.

• emphasize the sound words. Pause to allow children to repeat the words.

Read the poem once more, asking children to join in on the sound words.

▲ **Big Book of Rhymes and Songs**

OBJECTIVES

• *To recite a poem*

• *To follow words from top to bottom on a page*

• *To recognize beginning and final sounds*

Materials

■ Big Book of Rhymes and Songs p. 9

Kitchen Sink-Song

Tap goes drip-drip
plip-plip-plink.
Tap goes trickle at the
kitchen sink.
Fridge goes gurgle.
Pan goes slop.
Bin goes flip-flap.
Toast goes POP!

Tony Mitton

FLORIDA STANDARDS/GLEs FCAT: LA.A.1.1.4.K.1 Comprehension; **LA.E.1.1.1.K.1** Genres. *Also* **LA.D.2.1.2.K.1** Patterned structures; **LA.E.2.1.2.K.1** Patterned structures

RESPOND TO LITERATURE

Stage a Dramatic Reading Assign each kitchen object and its sound to a small group. Have groups practice reciting their part with feeling. Then reread the poem, and point to each group when it is their turn.

VISUALIZING

Discuss with children how knowing the way things sound, taste, look, or feel helps them picture details in a story or poem. Model an example for children.

MODEL When I hear the words *drip-drip plip-plip-plink*, I think of water dripping from a faucet. The words name the sounds I hear in my own kitchen when water is dripping in the sink.

Read other sound words from the poem and ask children how the words help them see these things in a kitchen.

Diagnostic Check: Comprehension

If... children cannot visualize objects by the sound words from the poem,

Then... add visuals such as a picture of each item. Show the picture as you reread the poem and say the sound words.

ADDITIONAL SUPPORT ACTIVITIES

BELOW-LEVEL	Reteach, p. S54
ADVANCED	Extend, p. S55
ENGLISH-LANGUAGE LEARNERS	Reteach, p. S55

ONGOING ASSESSMENT

As you share "Kitchen Sink-Song," note whether children

- recite the poem.
- follow words from top to bottom on a page.
- emphasize the sound words

FLORIDA STANDARDS/GLEs **FCAT: LA.C.1.1.4.K.1** Sequence. *Also* **LA.D.1.1.1.K.1** Sound patterns; **LA.D.2.1.2.K.1** Patterned structures; **LA.E.2.1.2.K.1** Patterned structures

Exploring Our Surroundings **493**

OBJECTIVE

To decode short vowel /u/u words

Materials

- *Alphabet Cards u, p*
- pocket chart
- blank sentence strip
- marker
- *Decodable Book 15: Up, Up, Up*
- drawing paper
- crayons

ENGLISH-LANGUAGE LEARNERS

Go through the book, naming each animal as you point to it. Have children repeat the animal names.

ADVANCED

Have children read *Up, Up, Up* on their own. Ask them to track the print as they read. Then have them read *Independent Reader 32: Silly Pig.*

Short Vowel /u/u Review

TEACH/MODEL

Decode Words   Place *Alphabet Cards u, p* in a pocket chart. Move your hand under the letters, blend the sounds, and read the word: **/uupp/, -up.** Have children blend the sounds and read the word.

Write on a sentence strip the sentence *I go up to the top.* Place it in the pocket chart. Slide your hand under the words as children read them.

PRACTICE/APPLY

Read the Book   Distribute copies of *Up, Up, Up.* Have children read the title. Ask what they notice about the title of this book. (It has the same word three times.)

Have children read the book, pointing to each word as they read.

Respond   Have children draw and label pictures of something else the boy and his mother might see on their hike up the mountain.

FLORIDA STANDARDS/GLEs   FCAT: LA.A.1.1.2.K.4 Words; **LA.A.1.1.2.K.5** Phonetic principles; **LA.A.1.1.2.K.6** Print meaning; *Also* **LA.A.1.1.2.K.1** Print organization; **LA.B.1.1.2.K.2** Basic formats; **LA.B.1.1.3.K.2** Print direction; **LA.D.1.1.1.K.1** Sound patterns

Decodable Book 15: *Up, Up, Up*

I go up, up, up.
What do I see?

2

I see a red fox run.
Look at it run, run, run.

3

I see a little bird tap.
Look at it tap, tap, tap.

4

I see a big deer sip.
Look at it sip, sip, sip.

5

I see a tan rabbit hop.
Look at it hop, hop, hop.

6

I see a fat cub nap.
Look at it nap, nap, nap.

7

I am at the top.
I see a big sun set.

8 Look at it set, set, set.

■ High-Frequency Words

go, see, what, the, little, do, look

■ Decodable Words

See Word List on page T15.

School-Home Connection

Take-Home Book Version

◄ Decodable Book 15
Up, Up, Up

▲ **Independent Reader 32:**
Silly Pig

Exploring Our Surroundings **495**

OBJECTIVE

To practice using correct punctuation

Materials

- correction tape
- marker

Writing Process

Write an Informational Book

PROOFREAD

Check Punctuation Display the sentences created in the week's previous Writing activities. Tell children that this is their chance to make their writing better. Direct children to the end mark in each sentence. Read the first sentence and ask: **Should this sentence end with a question mark or a period?**

MODEL **I know this sentence should end with a period because it tells me something about ducks. It is a telling sentence. Telling sentences always end with a period.**

Read the sentence again. Repeat for the remaining sentences. Use correction tape and a marker to fix punctuation that is incorrect.

Writing Every Day

Self-Selected Writing Have children draw and write about anything they'd like. If they have difficulty thinking of a topic, have them ask two friends what they're going to write about.

FLORIDA STANDARDS/GLEs FCAT: LA.B.2.1.2.K.1 Record ideas. *Also* **LA.A.1.1.2.K.1** Print organization; **LA.B.1.1.2.K.2** Basic formats; **LA.B.1.1.3.K.1** Spelling approximations; **LA.B.1.1.3.K.2** Print direction; **LA.B.1.1.3.K.3** Punctuation

WRAP UP  # Share Time

Reflect on the Lesson Ask children what story they learned to read. *(Up, Up, Up)* Have them tell what happens in the story. Then discuss what children remember about walks they have taken with family members.

S.S.R. *Sustained Silent Reading* Have children read silently from a book of their choice.

 **Centers** **LITERACY**

Let's Read

Place the books in the Literacy Center. Tell children to read the books and to choose their favorite one. Ask them to draw and label a picture about their favorite book. Have children write the title of the book on their pictures, and then write their name.

 Materials

■ Decodable Books:
Up, Up, Up

■ Little Books:
Five Little Ducks

■ Library Books:
What's What, Come Along, Daisy

Day at a Glance
Day 5

WARM UP

Phonemic Awareness
Phoneme Deletion

Sharing Literature
Read-Aloud Anthology
"Blame"

Read

Respond to Literature

Literature Focus: Problem-Solution

Phonics
Blending /u/ - /n/

Interactive Writing ✎
Writing Process: Publish

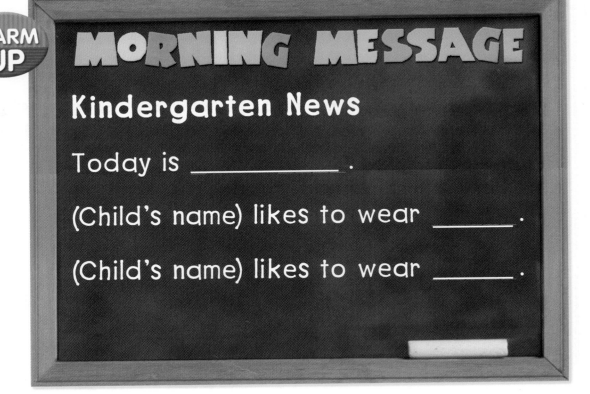

MORNING MESSAGE

Kindergarten News

Today is _____.

(Child's name) likes to wear _____.

(Child's name) likes to wear _____.

Write Kindergarten News Talk with children about their favorite things to wear.

Use prompts such as the following to guide children as you write the news:

- **What do you like to wear to school? At home?**
- **Who can show me where to begin writing?**
- **What letter will I write first in (name of day)?**
- **How many words are in the first sentence? The second sentence? The third sentence?**

As you write the message, invite children to contribute by writing letters, words, or names they have learned previously. Remind them to use proper spacing, capitalization, and punctuation.

Calendar Language

Point to and read aloud the days of the week. Ask what day today is. Ask what day comes after today. Point to the day and say: *Tomorrow is _____.* Invite volunteers to name today and tomorrow.

Sunday	Monday	Tuesday	Wednesday	Thursday	Friday	Saturday
		1	2	3	4	5
6	7	8	9	10	11	12
13	14	15	16	17	18	19
20	21	22	23	24	25	26
27	28	29	30	31		

 **FLORIDA STANDARDS/GLEs** **FCAT: LA.A.2.1.5.K.2** Get information; **LA.B.2.1.2.K.1** Record ideas; *Also* **LA.A.1.1.2.K.2** Alphabet; **LA.A.1.1.3.K.1** Frequent words; **LA.C.1.1.3.K.1** Conversation rules; **LA.C.3.1.2.K.1** Questions

Phonemic Awareness

PHONEME DELETION

Delete Phonemes   Say the word *pan* and have children repeat it. Say:

I'm going to say *pan*, but I'm going to leave out a sound. Listen while I say *pan* without the /p/: *an*. Say it with me: *an*. Now say both words: *pan*, *an*.

Tell children you are going to ask them to say some words and take away letters. Use the following:

Say *rap* without the /r/. (*ap*)

Say *lip* without the /l/. (*ip*)

Say *fog* without the /f/. (*og*)

Say *cab* without the /k/. (*ab*)

Say *bank* without the /b/. (*ank*)

Say *sell* without the /s/. (*ell*)

Say *camp* without the /k/. (*amp*)

Say *cub* without the /k/. (*ub*)

Say *pick* without the /p/. (*ick*)

Say *tug* without the /t/. (*ug*)

Say *tick* without the /t/. (*ick*)

Say *lit* without the /l/. (*it*)

Say *sack* without the /s/. (*ack*)

▲ "The Name Game," *Oo-pples and Boo-noo-noos: Songs and Activities for Phonemic Awareness*, pages 105–111

REACHING ALL LEARNERS

Diagnostic Check: Phonemic Awareness

If... children cannot delete initial phonemes,

Then... have them model the process with disks and *Write-On/Wipe-Off Boards*. Have them place three disks on the board, touch one for each sound in a word, remove the first disk, and say the word without the first sound.

ADDITIONAL SUPPORT ACTIVITIES

BELOW-LEVEL   Reteach, p. S50

ADVANCED   Extend, p. S51

ENGLISH-LANGUAGE LEARNERS   Reteach, p. S51

FLORIDA STANDARDS/GLEs FCAT: LA.A.1.1.2.K.5 Phonetic principles. *Also* **LA.C.1.1.1.K.2** Oral language; **LA.D.1.1.1.K.1** Sound patterns; **LA.D.2.1.2.K.1** Patterned structures

Exploring Our Surroundings   **499**

Sharing Literature

Read "Blame"

READ ALOUD

Before Reading Tell children that you are going to read a poem about a goat and a person who writes a beautiful book. Read the title of the poem, "Blame." Explain that to blame someone or something means to say or think that that person or thing is the reason something went wrong. Ask these questions:

- **What do you know about goats?**
- **What do goats like to eat?**

Tell children to listen to find out what the goat does.

During Reading Read the poem aloud. As you read,

- emphasize the rhyming words.
- point to yourself and to children as you say *I* and *you*.

Read the poem once more, inviting children to chime in and say the final sentence: *Blame the goat!* Reread sets of three and four lines to focus on rhyming words. Ask children to identify the rhyming words.

▲ **Read-Aloud Anthology**

OBJECTIVES

- *To listen and respond to a poem*
- *To identify rhyming words*
- *To identify problem and solution*

Materials

■ *Read-Aloud Anthology p. 14*

FLORIDA STANDARDS/GLEs FCAT: LA.A.1.1.2.K.4 Words; **LA.C.1.1.4.K.1** Sequence; *Also* **LA.A.1.1.2.K.1** Print organization; **LA.C.1.1.2.K.1** Choose literature; **LA.D.1.1.1.K.1** Sound patterns; **LA.D.2.1.2.K.1** Patterned structures; **LA.E.2.1.2.K.1** Patterned structures.

RESPOND TO LITERATURE

Discuss the Poem Talk with children about why the goat ate the first book. What do they think will happen to the second book?

Literature Focus

PROBLEM-SOLUTION

Remind children that characters often have problems to solve. Model how to identify the problem and solution in "Blame."

MODEL The person in the poem wrote a beautiful book, but the goat ate it. That's the problem. How did the person solve that problem? The person wrote another book. That's the solution, or how the problem was fixed.

Invite children to recall a story they have read in this theme such as *Five Little Ducks* or *Come Along, Daisy!*. Ask children to recall the problem and solution.

ADVANCED

Have children revisit some of the books they have read and identify the problem and solution in each.

ONGOING ASSESSMENT

As you share "Blame," note whether children

• listen and respond to a poem.

• identify rhyming words.

FLORIDA STANDARDS/GLEs FCAT: LA.A.1.1.3.K.5 Story elements; **LA.C.1.1.4.K.1** Sequence; **LA.E.1.1.2.K.1** Story elements; *Also* **LA.E.2.1.2.K.1** Patterned structures

OBJECTIVES

- *To build and read simple one-syllable words*

- *To understand that as the letters of words change, so do the sounds*

Materials

- *Alphabet Cards b, f, n, r, s, t, u*

- *Word Builders*

- *Word Builder Cards b, f, n, r, s, t, u*

- pocket chart

- index cards

- drawing paper

- crayons

REVIEW LETTERS

Phonics

Blending /u/-/n/  *Review*

ACTIVE BEGINNING

Sing a Rhyming Words Song   Teach children to sing the following song to the tune of "Mary Wore Her Red Dress." Invite children to answer the question.

> **Do you know a new word,**
>
> **New word, new word,**
>
> **Do you know a new word**
>
> **That rhymes with *sun*?**

Then sing the song again, substituting a rhyming word children have suggested. Continue singing new verses, using words such as *bun*, *fun*, *run*.

TEACH/MODEL

Blending Words   Distribute *Word Builders* and *Word Builder Cards b, f, n, r, s, t, u* to children. As you place *Alphabet Cards* in a pocket chart, tell children to place the same *Word Builder Cards* in their *Word Builder.*

- Place *Alphabet Cards r, u,* and *n* in the pocket chart. Have children do the same.

- Point to *r*. Say /**rr**/. Point to *u*. Say /**uu**/.

- Slide the *u* next to the *r*. Then move your hand under the letters and blend the sounds, elongating them: /**rruu**/. Have children do the same.

FLORIDA STANDARDS/GLEs   **FCAT: LA.A.1.1.2.K.5** Phonetic principles; **LA.A.1.1.3.K.4** Build vocabulary; *Also* **LA.A.1.1.2.K.1** Print organization; **LA.A.1.1.2.K.3** Sounds; **LA.C.1.1.1.K.1** Follow directions; **LA.D.1.1.1.K.1** Sound patterns

- Point to the letter *n*. Say **/nn/**. Have children do the same.
- Slide the *n* next to the *ru*. Slide your hand under *run* and blend by elongating the sounds: **/rruunn/**. Have children do the same.
- Then have children read the word *run* along with you. Follow the same procedure with these words: *fun, sun, nut*.

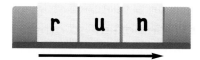

PRACTICE/APPLY

Guided Practice Have children place *Word Builder Cards u* and *n* in their *Word Builders*.

- Add *s* to *un*. What word did you make?

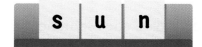

- Change *s* to *b*. What word did you make?

- Change *n* to *t*. What word did you make?

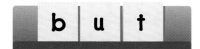

- Change *b* to *n*. What word did you make?

Independent Practice Write the words *sun, run,* and *nut* on index cards and place them in a pocket chart. Have children read the words. Then have them choose one of the words to write and illustrate on drawing paper.

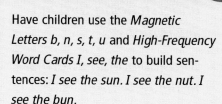

ADVANCED

Have children use the *Magnetic Letters b, n, s, t, u* and *High-Frequency Word Cards I, see, the* to build sentences: *I see the sun. I see the nut. I see the bun.*

ENGLISH-LANGUAGE LEARNERS

Place the *Alphabet Cards f, u, n* in a pocket chart. Point to each card and say the letter name and sound. Have children do the same. Continue with the same procedure in the Teach/Model section.

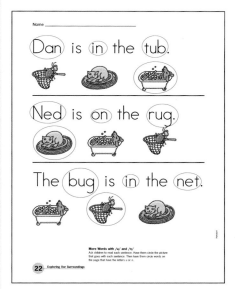

▲ **Practice Book page 22**

FLORIDA STANDARDS/GLEs FCAT: LA.A.1.1.2.K.5 Phonetic principles; LA.A.1.1.3.K.4 Build vocabulary; *Also* LA.A.1.1.2.K.1 Print organization; LA.A.1.1.2.K.2 Alphabet; LA.A.1.1.2.K.3 Sounds; LA.B.1.1.3.K.2 Print direction; LA.C.3.1.2.K.1 Questions

Exploring Our Surroundings 503

OBJECTIVES

• *To demonstrate understanding through illustrations*

• *To complete an informational class book*

Materials

■ sentence strips

■ marker

■ drawing paper

■ crayons

■ construction paper

■ stapler

Writing Process

Write an Informational Book

PUBLISH

Rewrite the Sentences   Display the sentences from the previous Writing activities and read them to children. Tell them that they are going to publish their book about ducks, and that the first step is to write each sentence on a sentence strip as neatly as possible. Explain that writing neatly is important so other people can read what you have written. Invite volunteers to copy letters or words from each sentence on the chart onto a sentence strip. Provide assistance by writing letters or words when necessary.

Illustrate the Sentences   Divide the group into teams, and give each team a large sheet of paper and a sentence strip. Read aloud the sentence strip that you give to each team. Have them draw and color a picture that illustrates the sentence, leaving a space at the bottom large enough to fit the sentence strip.

Publish the Book   Glue each sentence strip to its illustration. Create a cover for the book, and staple the cover onto the book. Place the book in the Reading Center for children to revisit and enjoy.

Writing Every Day

Journal Writing Have children write and draw about something a goat might eat.

FLORIDA STANDARDS/GLEs FCAT: **LA.B.2.1.2.K.1** Record ideas. *Also* **LA.A.2.1.4.K.1** Illustrations

WRAP UP Share Time

Reflect on the Lesson   Ask children to tell what they liked best about the poem "Blame." Read aloud the poem children wrote during Interactive Writing. Ask children if they think goats really eat the things named in both poems.

S.S.R. *Sustained Silent Reading*   Have children read silently from a book of their choice.

 ## Centers DRAMATIC PLAY

Class Field Trip

Tell children that they are going to go on a pretend class field trip. Have them decide on a place they would like to visit, such as a park or a museum. Post mural paper in the center so children can work on drawing a scene showing their destination. Provide chairs that children can arrange to be a "bus." Children can play the roles of bus driver, teacher, and students. Have children board the "bus" and travel to the place they plan to visit. Encourage children to describe their trip as they go.

Materials

- mural paper
- crayons or markers
- chairs

Theme Wrap-Up & Review

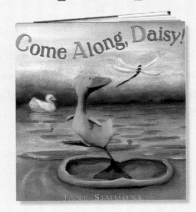

Celebrate *Exploring Our Surroundings*

Show children *Five Little Ducks, Come Along Daisy!* and *What's What?*

Help them summarize or retell each story. Invite comments and personal responses; then ask these questions:

• **Do you think the five little ducks were glad to be home? Why?**

• **What does Daisy see as she explores her surroundings?**

• **What do you like best about where you live?**

Teacher Self-Evaluation

As you reflect on the theme *Exploring Our Surroundings*, ask yourself:

• **Which activities best met my goals for this theme? Which ones did not?**

• **Have children become more aware of their surroundings?**

• **Have I helped children make connections between thematic activities at school and events in their personal life?**

------------------------------ THEME PROJECT ------------------------------

Explorer's Log

Summing Up   After the nature walk, have children list the things they saw and describe the one thing they think is most interesting.

REVIEW

Phonics

Leafy Words Cut leaves from construction paper. Write the following words on the leaves: *hut, cut, nut, bun, fun, run, sun*. Place the leaves face down in a pile. Have children take turns choosing a leaf from the pile and reading the word. Ask them to write it on the board and use it in a sentence.

High-Frequency Words

Word Hunt Place *High-Frequency Word Cards one* and *little* in a pocket chart. Write the words *one* and *little* on several index cards and place them face down on a nearby desk. Have children take turns flipping an index card, reading the word, and placing the card in the pocket chart under the same word.

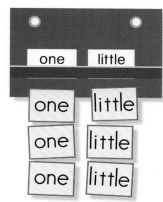

Take–Home Book
Theme 11 Practice Book, pp. 23–24

Comprehension

Characters Page through *Big Book Five Little Duckings* and have children tell about the things they see Mother Duck doing. Have them discuss why they think Mother Duck cares for her five little ducks. Then page through *Library Book Come Along, Daisy!* and ask children to describe the things Daisy does. Ask children to tell why they might like to have Daisy as a friend.

Writing

Write a Description Have children draw and label a picture of their classroom. Ask them to write a sentence telling about something they like to do in the classroom.

ASSESSMENT

Monitoring of Progress

• Assessment Handbook

Diagnostic Checks Use the Diagnostic Checks as a point-of-use assessment of children's understanding.

Theme Skills Assessment Use Theme 11 Skills Assessment, pages T72, 67–68, to monitor a child's understanding of letter recognition, word recognition, sound-symbol relationships, and decoding skills taught in this theme.

Under the Ocean

There are whales, seals, and fish of many sizes and shapes in the ocean! Children will learn about the animals that live there.

Theme Resources

READING MATERIALS

Big Book

◄ *Splash in the Ocean!*
adapted by Mik Zepol
illustrated by Richard Bernal

Library Books

◄ *Fish Faces*
by Norbert Wu

◄ *Swimmy*
by Leo Lionni

Read-Aloud Anthology

◄ *A House by the Sea*
by Joanne Ryder

◄ *There's a Hole in the Middle of the Sea*

◄ *The Seashore Noisy Book*
by Margaret Wise Brown

◄ *If You Ever*
by Charlotte Pomerantz

Big Book of Rhymes and Songs

▼ *The Little Fishes*

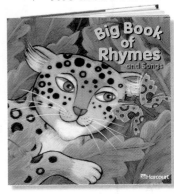

Independent Readers

▲ *At the Beach*   ▲ *Dive in the Ocean*   ▲ *The Best Boat*

PHONICS

Theme 12 Practice Book

Phonics Practice Book

Decodable Books

◄ *Is It a Fish?*

◄ *It Is Fun*

◄ *A Bug Can Tug*

▲ *Sid Hid*

◄ *In a Sub*

Alphabet Patterns

alligator, egg, igloo, octopus, umbrella

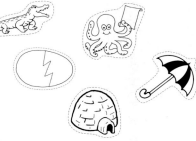

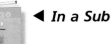

Phonics Express™ CD-ROM
Level A

TEACHING TOOLS

Big Alphabet Cards

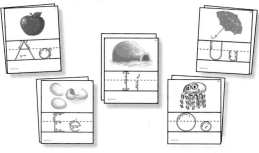

High-Frequency Word Cards

are, here

Picture/Word Cards

English Language Learners Kit

Letter and Sound Charts

Charts 10, 12, 17, 14, and 19

Teacher's Resource Book

pages 60, 62, 67, 64, 69

Intervention Kit

Letter and Sound Chart Sentence Strips

10, 12, 17, 14, and 19

Anteater asked Alligator

Oo-pples and Boo-noo-noos

MANIPULATIVES

Tactile Letter Cards

a e i o u

**Write-On/Wipe-Off Board
Letters and Sounds Place Mat**

Word Builder and Word Builder Cards

b u g

Magnetic Letters

Aa Bb Cc

ASSESSMENT

Assessment Handbook
Group Inventory
Theme 12 Test

Big Book ▶

Library Book ▶

	Week 1	**Week 2**
• **Sharing Literature** • **Listening Comprehension**	**Big Book:** *Splash in the Ocean!* **Library Book:** *Fish Faces* **Read-Aloud Anthology:** "A House by the Sea" **Big Book of Rhymes and Songs:** "The Little Fishes"	**Big Book:** *Splash in the Ocean!* **Library Book:** *Swimmy* **Read-Aloud Anthology:** "There's a Hole in the Middle of the Sea" **Big Book of Rhymes and Songs:** "The Little Fishes"
• **Phonemic Awareness** • **Phonics** • **High-Frequency Words**	Review Consonant /g/*g,* Short Vowel /u/*u* **T** Blending /u/ - /g/ Words with /u/ and /g/ Review Blending /u/ - /g/ High-Frequency Words are, here **T**	Phonogram -*ut* Phonogram -*un* Phonogram -*ug* Build Sentences
• **Reading**	**Decodable Book 16:** *Is It a Fish?* **Independent Reader 33:** *At the Beach*	**Decodable Book 17:** *It Is Fun* **Independent Reader 34:** *The Best Boat*
• **Writing**	**Shared Writing** New Song Verses **Interactive Writing** List **Independent Writing** Sentence Question Description	**Shared Writing** New Verses **Interactive Writing** Story Map List **Independent Writing** Action Words Sentence
• **Cross-Curricular Centers**	**Dramatic Play** Let's Be Animals **Art** Ocean Mural **Block** Houses by the Sea **Math** Subtraction Game **Manipulatives** Go Fish	**Math** Seashell Sort **Letters and Words** Charades **Sand and Water** Sand Sculpture **Letters and Words** Fish Word Puzzles **Science** Science Experiment

T = tested skill

Library Book ▶

Week 3

Big Book: *Splash in the Ocean!*

Library Book: *Swimmy*

Read-Aloud Anthology:
"The Seashore Noisy Book"
"If You Ever"

Review Short Vowels *a, e, i, o, u*

Build Sentences

Decodable Books 18, 19, 20:
A Bug Can Tug
Sid Hid
In a Sub

Independent Reader 35: *Dive in the Ocean*

Interactive Writing
Writing Process

 Art
Fish Prints

ABC Letter and Word
Letter Match

Listening
Sound Effects

ABC Letters and Words
Word Factory

Writing
A Whale of a Tail

Theme Organizer
Half-Day Kindergarten

Use the following chart to help organize your half-day kindergarten schedule. Choose independent activities as time allows during your day.

ORAL LANGUAGE

Morning Message
Phonemic Awareness
Sharing Literature
- Big Book: *Splash in the Ocean!*
- Library Book: *Fish Faces*
- Library Book: *Swimmy*
- Read-Aloud Anthology
- Big Book of Rhymes and Songs

LEARNING TO READ

Phonics
Decodable Books 16–20
- *Is It a Fish?*
- *It is Fun*
- *A Bug Can Tug*
- *Sid Hid*
- *In a Sub*

High-Frequency Words

 Independent Readers 33–35
- *At the Beach*
- *The Best Boat*
- *Dive in the Ocean*

LANGUAGE ARTS

Shared Writing
Interactive Writing
Independent Writing
Writing Every Day

INDEPENDENT ACTIVITIES

Sharing Literature
Respond to Literature
Phonics
Independent Practice
Handwriting
Practice Book pages
High-Frequency Words
Independent Practice
Practice Book pages

About the
Authors and Illustrators

Richard Bernal

Illustrator of *Splash in the Ocean*

Richard Bernal's interest in art began in the second grade, when he started drawing cartoons. He still enjoys cartoons, but of all the illustrating he does, Bernal says, "Children's books are the most fun to do." He lives in St. Louis, Missouri, with his wife, Catherine, and dog, Atticus.

Norbert Wu

Author and Photographer of *Fish Faces*

Norbert Wu says that he knew that he wanted to become a marine biologist by the age of six. Pressured by the advice of others, he studied engineering in college. However, after a short time as an engineer, he took a job as a research diver in Panama. He taught himself the art of underwater photography while living with other researchers on an island. Mr. Wu has dived all over the world, from the Arctic to the tropics. He says, "Photography and learning about ocean wildlife have become my passion and my career."

Leo Lionni

Author and Illustrator of *Swimmy*

Leo Lionni was born into a creative family in Amsterdam, and knew at an early age that he wanted to become an artist. He spent much of his adolescence at art museums teaching himself how to draw. His education, however, did not include art classes. He received a doctorate in economics, while establishing himself as a painter. His career as an author and illustrator began by chance while traveling by train with his grandchildren in the 1950s. To entertain them, he created the story of *Little Blue and Little Yellow*, which has since become a children's classic. Since then, he has written and illustrated numerous award-winning books for children.

Theme Assessment

MONITORING OF PROGRESS

After completing the theme, most children should show progress toward mastery of the following skills:

Concepts of Print
- ❏ Follow words from left to right and from top to bottom on the printed page.
- ❏ Understand that printed material provides information.

Phonemic Awareness
- ❏ Track and represent changes in simple syllables and words with two and three sounds as one sound is added, substituted, omitted, shifted, or repeated.
- ❏ Distinguish orally stated one-syllable words and separate into beginning or ending sounds.

Phonics and Decoding
- ❏ Match all consonant sounds and short-vowel sounds to appropriate letters.
- ❏ Read one-syllable and High-Frequency Words.

Vocabulary and High-Frequency Words
- ❏ Read High-Frequency Words *are* and *here.*
- ❏ Develop concept vocabulary.
- ❏ Understand time concepts today and tomorrow.

Comprehension
- ❏ Emphasize repetitive text.
- ❏ Use picture clues to help understand story content.

Literary Response
- ❏ Distinguish fantasy from realistic text.
- ❏ Compare and contrast story characters.
- ❏ Recognize different genre.

Writing
- ❏ Write by moving from left to right and from top to bottom.
- ❏ Write consonant-vowel-consonant words.
- ❏ Use prephonetic knowledge to spell independently.

Listening and Speaking
- ❏ Recognize and use complete, coherent sentences when speaking.
- ❏ Recite and act out nonsense rhymes.

Assessment Options

Assessment Handbook
- Group Inventory, Form B
- Phonemic Awareness Inventory
- Theme Skills Assessment
- Concepts About Print Inventory
- Observational Checklists

Reaching All Learners

■ BELOW-LEVEL

Levels of Support

Point-of-use Notes in the Teacher's Edition

pp. 531, 533, 543, 547, 553, 559, 561, 563, 567, 569, 571, 575, 577, 579, 593, 597, 602, 605, 607, 609, 611, 615, 617, 619, 625, 635, 639, 645, 647, 651, 653, 655, 657, 659, 661, 663, 667, 671

Additional Support Activities

High-Frequency Words
pp. S56-S57

Comprehension and Skills:
pp. S66-S67, S72-S73

Phonemic Awareness:
pp. S58-S59, S64-S65, S68-S69

Phonics:
pp. S60-S61, S62-S63, S70-S71

Intervention Resources Kit

■ ENGLISH-LANGUAGE LEARNERS

Levels of Support

Point-of-use Notes in the Teacher's Edition

pp. 551, 563, 567, 579, 591, 593, 597, 599, 615, 623, 625, 635, 653, 655, 661

Additional Support Activities

High-Frequency Words:
pp. S56-S57

Comprehension and Skills:
pp. S66-S67, S72-S73

Phonemic Awareness:
pp. S58-S59, S64-S65, S68-S69

Phonics:
pp. S60-S61, S62-S63, S70-S71

 Visit *The Learning Site!* at
www.harcourtschool.com
See Language Support activities

English-Language Learners Resources Kit

■ **ADVANCED**

Levels of Challenge

Point-of-use Notes in the Teacher's Edition

pp. 531, 543, 549, 551, 553, 557, 561, 563, 567, 577, 579, 589, 593, 597, 601, 615, 621, 635, 637, 643, 655, 661, 669, 671

Additional Support Activities

High-Frequency Words:
pp. S56-S57

Comprehension and Skills:
pp. S66-S67, S72-S73

Phonemic Awareness:
pp. S58-S59, S64-S65, S68-S69

Phonics:
pp. S60-S61, S62-S63, S70-S71

Accelerated Instruction

Use higher-grade-level materials for accelerated instruction.

Theme Project, p. 520

Combination Classrooms
Partner Research

Pair an advanced researcher and a beginning researcher who have a common interest in a particular ocean animal. Encourage them to work together to gather information from books, magazines, and if available, the Internet. Children can create a simple report on the ocean animal that includes pictures and text and place it in the Literacy Center for others to read.

Students with Special Needs
Remembering Facts and Information

Children with special needs can often use some help when it comes to remembering information. Make learning facts interesting by creating "study cards" that depict facts or information. Children can work with a partner to quiz each other on the facts.

Recommended Reading

Below are suggestions for reading materials that will meet kindergarten children's diverse needs. Books that are on a child's level provide support for new skills. Advanced books give children an opportunity to stretch and challenge their reading potential. Read-aloud books are important because they expose children to story language and vocabulary.

■ BELOW-LEVEL

An Ocean World by Peter Sis. Greenwillow, 1992. In this nearly wordless book, a whale sails through new seas and makes a new friend.

Eye Spy an Octopus! by Richard Powell. Price Stern Sloan, 1999. See what's looking at you from the deep waters of the ocean.

Barney's Treasure Hunt by Guy Davis. Lyrick Studios, 1997. Barney and his friends seek all kinds of treasures and make discoveries under the sea.

Sea Shapes by Suse MacDonald. Gulliver, 1994. Simple shapes transform into marine life on the next page. A great guessing game and a lesson in drawing.

■ ON-LEVEL

How Many Fish? by Caron Lee Cohen. HarperCollins, 1998. Six fish swimming in the bay meet up with three children who try to count them.

Beach Play by Marsha Hayles. Henry Holt, 1998. A young girl enjoys a day at the beach.

One Fish Two Fish Red Fish Blue Fish by Dr. Seuss. Random House, 1991. Rhyming riddles and Dr. Seuss's fabulous creatures make this an enjoyable reading experience.

At the Beach by Clive Scruton. Rigby, 2000. What kinds of things can you see and do at the beach?

■ ADVANCED

One Seal by John Stadler. Orchard, 1999. A seal and other animals make a pyramid on the beach to help a child save a kite.

On My Beach There Are Many Pebbles by Leo Lionni. Mulberry, 1995. What seem to be ordinary pebbles on the beach actually have hidden pictures for careful readers to find.

Five Silly Fishermen by Roberta Edwards. Random House, 1989. Five fishermen can't count properly and think they have lost one of their group.

Puffins Climb, Penguins Rhyme by Bruce McMillan. Harcourt, 1995. Close-up photos follow penguins and puffins in their natural habitats as rhyming words describe their actions.

■ READ ALOUD

A House for a Hermit Crab by Eric Carle. Simon & Schuster, 1987. A hermit crab begins a journey in search of a new home.

Crab Moon by Ruth Horowitz. Candlewick, 2000. A boy and his mother observe horseshoe crabs spawning at the beach.

Somewhere in the Ocean by J. Ward and T.J. Marsh. Rising Moon, 2000. This counting rhyme describes sea creatures and their offspring.

Wish for a Fish by Bonnie Worth. Random House, 1999. Cat in the Hat takes readers on a tour of the deep-sea, providing plenty of information about its inhabitants.

Homework Ideas

Visit *The Learning Site:* www.harcourtschool.com • See Resources for Parents and Teachers: Homework Helper

	Literature	Phonics	Language Arts	Theme	Cross-Curricular
WEEK 1	Draw and label a picture of the most unusual fish in *Fish Faces.*	Look for words with **the letters** *Gg* and *Uu* on street and store signs in your community.	Write **describing words** that tell about the fish in *Fish Faces.*	Cut out magazine pictures of ocean animals. **Sort** the pictures according to the sizes of the animals.	Use construction paper and yarn to make a **fish mask.**
WEEK 2	Draw a picture of your **favorite ocean animal.**	Play a **letter game.** Have a family member name a letter. Look in newspapers and magazines to find the letter.	**Write questions** about ocean animals. Read the questions to family members and have them supply answers, if possible.	Fold a piece of paper in half. **Draw** two fish faces: a funny fish face and a scary fish face.	Ask a family member to help you learn more about an ocean animal. Draw a picture of the **ocean animal** you study.
WEEK 3	**Retell** the story of *Swimmy* to a friend or family member.	Practice writing **the vowels** *Aa, Ee, Ii, Oo,* and *Uu.* Circle your best letters.	**Make up a story** about a little fish and a big fish. Tell the story to a family member.	**Draw a picture** of another shape Swimmy and his friends could make together.	If possible, visit a pet store that sells fish. **Count** the different kinds of fish you see.

Classroom Aquarium

Materials

- Teacher's Resource Book page 25
- poster board
- paper
- pencils
- construction paper
- safety scissors
- crayons
- paints and brushes
- tape

Introduce

Tell children they are going to turn their classroom into an aquarium by decorating it with underwater scenes they make of animals and plants that live in or near the ocean. Ask children to name animals and plants that live in or near oceans, and write their answers on the board.

Send home the Family Letter to encourage family members to participate in the project.

Prepare

- Children can work in groups to paint and label ocean scenes such as a pod of whales, a school of fish, or seals sunning themselves on rocks.

- Other teams can work together to use a variety of materials to make an octopus and other sea life to decorate chairs and walls.

Share

Children can decorate the classroom with their ocean scenes, taping them to tables and desks. Have children act as underwater guides to take visitors on a tour of their classroom aquarium.

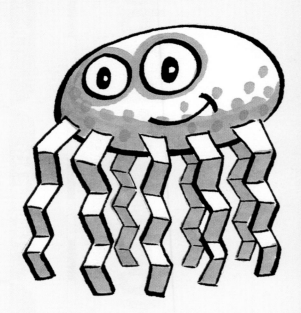

School-Home Connection

Invite family members to tour the classroom aquarium. Encourage children to describe the animals and plants featured in the displays, and to respond to questions and comments. Invite visitors to share their observations of ocean life.

Visit *The Learning Site!* at
www.harcourtschool.com

Teacher Notes

Learning Centers

Choose from the following suggestions to enhance your learning centers for the theme Under the Ocean.
(Additional learning centers for this theme can be found on pages 582 and 628)

ART CENTER

What Do You See?

Have children pretend they are on a submarine. Have them draw a picture of something they see in the ocean. Encourage children to draw pictures of the many plants and animals that live in the ocean. Tell children that they may label the objects in their drawings if they wish.

20 Minutes a day

Materials

- drawing paper
- crayons

SCIENCE CENTER

Ocean Collage

Have children look through magazines to find and cut out pictures of ocean environments, including beaches and animals and plants that live in the ocean or at its shore. Children can glue their pictures onto a sheet of paper to create an ocean collage. Have children label the images they can identify.

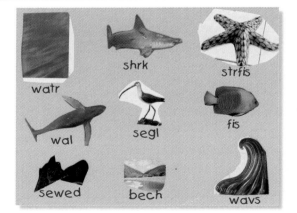

20 Minutes a day

Materials

- old magazines
- safety scissors
- glue sticks
- paper

522   **Under the Ocean**

COOKING CENTER

Ocean Treats

Children should wash their hands before and after working in the cooking center. Tell children they are going to taste some ocean snacks. Identify the seaweed, and tell children that seaweed lives in the ocean and is full of vitamins. People in many parts of the world eat seaweed. Then tell children that the crackers are not from the ocean, but they are shaped like an ocean swimmer: fish! Invite children to sample each of the snacks.

[Note: Food allergies can cause dangerous or fatal reactions. Check with parents about food allergies before allowing children to handle or eat foods in class.]

Materials

- fish-shaped crackers
- seaweed
- paper or plastic plates

MATH CENTER

Go Fish!

Shuffle multiple sets of cards with the numbers 1–6 and place them face down in a pile in the math center. On a surface such as a table, spread numerous brightly colored small construction-paper fish that have been glued to a paper clip. Have children take turns taking a number card, identifying the number, and then using the magnetized fishing rod to fish for the same number of fish as identified on their card. Have children return the fish they "catch" to the fish pond.

Materials

- number cards: 1–6
- paper fish glued to a paper clip (Patterns T29)
- fishing rod made from a craft stick, string, and magnet

WRITING CENTER

Write About an Ocean Animal

Tell children to think of an ocean animal that they would like to write about. Then give children a sheet of paper and have them write two or three sentences that tell what the animal looks like or what it does. Tell children to use what they know about the sounds letters stand for to help them spell words. Invite children to draw a picture to illustrate their sentences.

Whals are big.
They live in the oshun.
Whals breth ar.

 20 Minutes a day

Materials

- paper
- pencils
- crayons

ART CENTER

Make a Starfish

Tell children they are going to make a paper starfish. Have them trace a star onto a piece of construction paper and cut out the star. Children can use sequins, glitter, and markers to decorate their starfish. Encourage children to be fanciful or, if they prefer, to make realistic-looking starfish. If children prefer, allow them to draw a free-form star and cut it out.

 20 Minutes a day

Materials

- cardboard star shape (Patterns T30)
- construction paper
- pencils
- safety scissors
- glue
- glitter or sequins
- markers

Teacher Notes

Teacher Notes

THEME 12

Week 1

Under the Ocean

15-30 Minutes

ORAL LANGUAGE

- **Phonemic Awareness**

- **Sharing Literature**

45 Minutes

LEARNING TO READ

- **Phonics**

- **Vocabulary**

Daily Routines
- Morning Message
- Calendar Language
- Writing Prompt

15-30 Minutes

LANGUAGE ARTS

- **Writing**
  Daily Writing Prompt

Day 1

Phonemic Awareness, 531
Phoneme Isolation and Matching

Sharing Literature, 532
 Read

Big Book: *Splash
in the Ocean!*

(Skill) **Literature Focus, 533**
Compare and Contrast

 **Phonics, 542 T**
Review: Consonant /g/*g*, Short Vowel /u/*u*

 Writing, 544
Write a Sentence

Writing Prompt, 544
Draw and write about self-selected topics.

Share Time, 545
Share favorite ocean animals in *Splash in the Ocean!*

Day 2

Phonemic Awareness, 547
Phoneme Blending

Sharing Literature, 548
Library Book: *Fish Faces*

(Skill) **Literature Focus, 549**
Questions for Research

 Phonics, 550 T
Blending /u/–/g/

High-Frequency Word, 552 T
Introduce: *are*

Words to Remember, 553

Writing, 554
Write a Question

Writing Prompt, 554
Draw and write about self-selected topics.

Share Time, 555

Read

Share questions and answers.

T = tested skill

 **Phonics**

Review /g/*g*, /u/*u*;
Blending *u - g*

Focus of the Week:
- HIGH-FREQUENCY WORDS: *are, here*
- PHONEMIC AWARENESS
- SHARING LITERATURE
- WRITING Sentences, Questions, List

Day 3

Phonemic Awareness, 557
Phoneme Substitution: Initial

Sharing Literature, 558
Read-Aloud Anthology:
"A House by the Sea,"
pp. 116–118

(Skill) **Literature
Focus, 559**
Syllables in Words

 Phonics, 560 T
Words with /u/ and /g/

High-Frequency Word, 562 T
Introduce: *here*

Words to Remember, 563

 Interactive Writing, 564

Read
Write a List

Writing Prompt, 564
Draw and write about a favorite wish.

Share Time, 565
Have children tell what they liked best
about "A House by the Sea."

Day 4

Phonemic Awareness, 567
Syllable Segmentation

Sharing Literature, 568
Big Book of Rhymes and
Songs: "The Little Fishes,"
pp. 28–29

(Skill) **Literature
Focus, 569**
Repetitive Text

 Phonics, 570 T
Review: Short Vowel /u/*u*

Read
DECODABLE BOOK 16
Is It a Fish?

 Shared Writing, 572
Write New Song Verses

Writing Prompt, 572
Draw and write about a pet fish.

Share Time, 573
Discuss the Decodable Book *Is It a Fish?*
and sing new verses for "The Little Fishes."

Day 5

Phonemic Awareness, 575
Phoneme Deletion

Sharing Literature, 576
Read
Library Book: *Fish Faces*

(Skill) **Literature
Focus, 577**
Categorizing

 Phonics, 578 T
Words with /u/ and /g/

Writing, 580
Write a Description

Writing Prompt, 580
Draw and write about self-selected
topics.

Share Time, 581
Share pictures and descriptions of fish
in *Fish Faces*.

Day at a Glance
Day 1

Phonemic Awareness

Phoneme Isolation and Matching: Initial

Sharing Literature

Big Book:
Splash in the Ocean!

Read

Develop Listening Comprehension

Respond to Literature

Literature Focus: Compare and Contrast

Phonics

Consonant /g/g, Vowel /u/u

Writing

Sentence

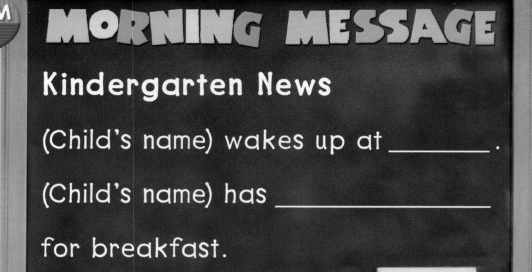

MORNING MESSAGE

Kindergarten News

(Child's name) wakes up at _____.

(Child's name) has _____

for breakfast.

Write Kindergarten News Talk with children about what they do to get ready for school. Have children use complete sentences.

Use prompts such as the following to guide children as you write the news:

- **What do you do in the morning to get ready for school?**
- **Who can show me where to begin writing?**
- **What is the beginning sound in *wakes*?**
- **Let's clap the syllables in *breakfast*. How many parts does it have?**

As you write the message, invite children to contribute by writing letters, words, or names they have previously learned. Remind them to use proper spacing, capitalization, and punctuation.

Calendar Language

Point to the numbers on the calendar. Tell children the days of each month are numbered and the numbers tell the date. Point to and read aloud the date. Name the month and the date.

Sunday	Monday	Tuesday	Wednesday	Thursday	Friday	Saturday
		1	2	3	4	5
6	7	8	9	10	11	12
13	14	15	16	17	18	19
20	21	22	23	24	25	26
27	28	29	30	31		

FLORIDA STANDARDS/GLEs FCAT: LA.A.1.1.2.K.5 Phonetic principles; **LA.B.2.1.2.K.1** Record ideas; *Also* **LA.A.1.1.2.K.1** Print organization; **LA.A.1.1.2.K.3** Sounds; **LA.C.1.1.3.K.1** Conversation rules; **LA.C.3.1.2.K.1** Questions

Phonemic Awareness

PHONEME ISOLATION: INITIAL

Listen for Beginning Sounds   Tell children to listen to the beginning sound in the words you say.

> **MODEL**   *Girl.* Say the word. What sound do you hear at the beginning of *girl*? (/g/) *Gate.* Say the word. What sound do you hear at the beginning of *gate*? (/g/)

Have children repeat the following pairs of words and name the beginning sound in both words.

gum, get (/g/)	**mat, more** (/m/)	**dog, dust** (/d/)	**big, barn** (/b/)
rug, rabbit (/r/)	**house, horn** (/h/)	**game, gift** (/g/)	**cat, cow** (/k/)

PHONEME MATCHING: INITIAL

Listen for Matching Sounds   After children isolate the beginning sounds in two words, have them tell if the two words begin with the same sound.

> **MODEL**   Say the word: *goose.* Say the word: *gift.* What sound do you hear at the beginning of *goose*? (/g/) *gift*? (/g/) *Goose* and *gift* begin with the same sound. Say the words.

As you read the following word pairs, have children repeat the words and tell if they begin with the same sound or not.

give, goose (/g/)	**sun, soap** (/s/)	**us, umbrella** (/u/)
pig, cat	**gas, wax**	**new, top**
game, goat (/g/)	**house, hill** (/h/)	**under, up** (/u/)
dig, dime (/d/)	**umpire, until** (/u/)	**kangaroo, king** (/k/)

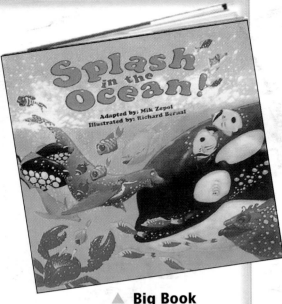

▲ **Big Book**

OBJECTIVES

- *To use the book title and cover illustration to make predictions before reading*

- *To use picture clues and context to make predictions during reading*

- *To sing a song*

- *To compare and contrast*

Materials

- *Big Book: Splash in the Ocean!*

- *Music CD*

- chart paper

- marker

LEARNING TO READ

Sharing Literature

Read Splash in the Ocean!

READ ALOUD

Before Reading   Display the cover of *Splash in the Ocean!* and read the title and the names of the author and illustrator aloud as you track the print. Ask children to describe the illustration on the cover. Use these prompts to help children set a purpose for reading:

- **What do you see on the cover?** (Possible responses: whale, seal, fish, crab)

- **Think about the title and the pictures on the cover. What do you think this story is about?** (Answers will vary.)

Point out the musical notation on the last page of the book. Explain to children that this story is also a song.

During Reading   Read the selection aloud. As you read,

- track the print.

- pause to point to and name the ocean animals in each section.

- pause to encourage children to use picture clues to predict which animal they will read about next. Model making predictions after reading pages 10–11.

> **MODEL** **I see lots of crabs on this page, but in the corner I see some seals swimming into the picture. I think that the next page will be about seals.**

- remind children to check their predictions.

FLORIDA STANDARDS/GLEs **FCAT: LA.A.1.1.4.K.1** Comprehension; *Also* **LA.A.1.1.1.K.1** Predictions; **LA.A.1.1.2.K.1** Print organization; **LA.A.2.1.4.K.1** Illustrations; **LA.C.1.1.1.K.2** Oral language

DEVELOP LISTENING COMPREHENSION

After Reading   Have children answer these questions:

• **What is the story about?** (how ocean animals play together)

• **What ocean animals are in this story?** (whales, seals, fish, crabs)

RESPOND TO LITERATURE

Sing the Song   Play the song on the *Music CD* and invite children to join in and sing along.

Literature Focus

COMPARE AND CONTRAST

Tell children that the animals in the selection are alike because they all live in the ocean. Choose two animals, such as the whale and the seal, and talk about how they are alike and how they are different. Record the comparisons on chart paper.

MODEL   **When I think about what is the same about the seals and the whales, I know they both live in the ocean. What is different is that seals have flippers and whales have fins.**

Then have children suggest ways two other sea animals are alike and different.

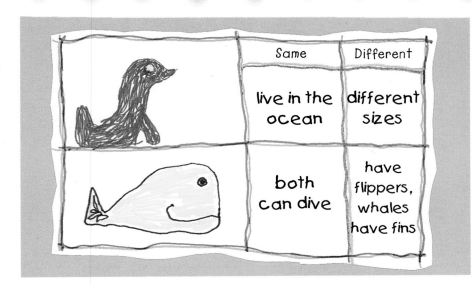

	Same	Different
(seal)	live in the ocean	different sizes
(whale)	both can dive	have flippers, whales have fins

BELOW-LEVEL

Turn to page 4 in *Splash in the Ocean!* Have children point to the brown fish and to the yellow fish. Talk with children about ways the two fish are alike (they both swim under the ocean; both have fins) and ways they are different (one is brown and one is yellow).

ONGOING ASSESSMENT

As you share *Splash in the Ocean!* note whether children

• listen for a period of time.

• use picture clues and context to make predictions.

• join in singing the song.

▲ **Practice Book pages 5–6**

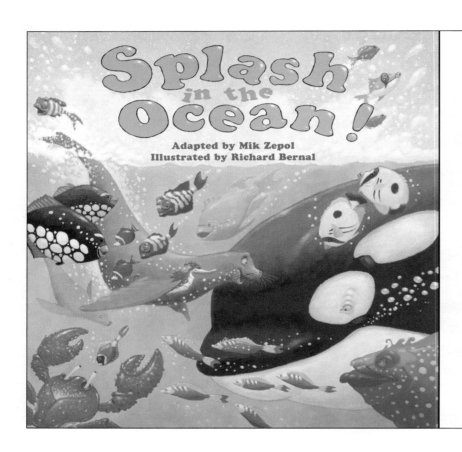

Splash
in the
Ocean!

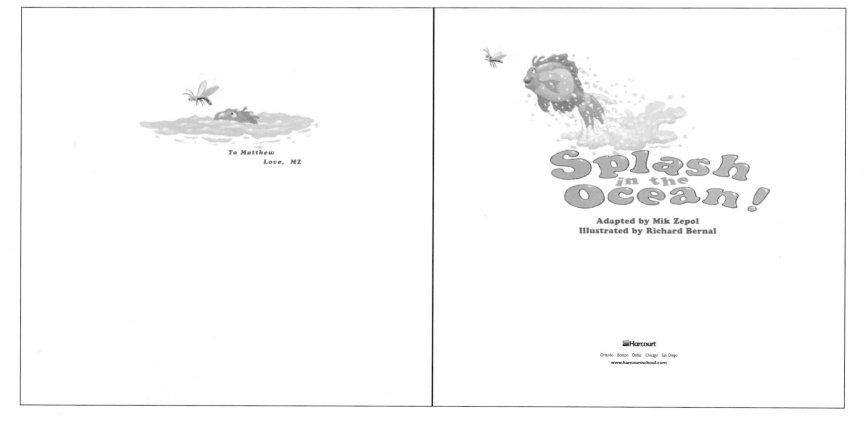

To Matthew
Love, MZ

Splash
in the
Ocean!

Adapted by Mik Zepol
Illustrated by Richard Bernal

Harcourt

Orlando Boston Dallas Chicago San Diego
www.harcourtschool.com

All the fish are
swimming in the ocean,

swimming in the ocean,
swimming in the ocean.

All the fish are
swimming in the ocean,

flippy, flappy, flippy
flappy, splash!

All the crabs are crawling in the ocean,

8

crawling in the ocean, crawling in the ocean.

9

All the crabs are crawling in the ocean,

10

scritchy, scratchy, scritchy scratchy, splash!

11

All the seals are playing in the ocean,

playing in the ocean, playing in the ocean.

All the seals are playing in the ocean,

wibble, wobble, wibble wobble, splash!

All the whales are
jumping in the ocean,

jumping in the ocean,
jumping in the ocean.

16

17

All the whales are
jumping in the ocean,

swishy, swashy, swishy,
swashy, splash!

18

19

All the friends are
splashing in the ocean,

splashing in the ocean,
splashing in the ocean.

20

21

Flippy, flappy

Scritchy, scratchy

Wibble, wobble

Swishy, swashy. . .

22

23

24

25

Phonics

Consonant /g/g, Short Vowel /u/u Review

OBJECTIVES

- *To recognize uppercase and lowercase Uu and Gg*

- *To match sounds to letters*

Materials

- *Big Alphabet Cards Uu, Gg*

- pocket chart

- index card

- marker

- *Picture-Word Card gate*

- *Alphabet Cards U, G*

- *Tactile Letter Cards u, g*

ACTIVE BEGINNING

Recite the U and G Rhymes   Display *Big Alphabet Cards Uu* and *Gg*. Ask children to identify each letter. Have children form a circle. Ask a child to stand in the middle of the circle and hold up *Big Alphabet Card Uu*. Have the children walk around the circle as they recite "Up and Up and Up." (See page 432.) Then have them recite "Goose! Goose!." (See page 42, volume 2.)

TEACH/MODEL

Review Letters and Sounds   Display *Big Alphabet Card Uu* in a pocket chart and ask what letter this is.

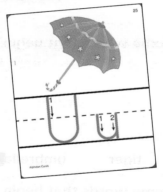

Point to the picture and say its name. Have children repeat it. (*umbrella*)

What sound do you hear at the beginning of *umbrella*? (/u/)

What letter stands for the /u/ sound in *umbrella*? (*Uu*)

Touch the letter and say **/u/**. Touch the letter again and have children say /u/.

Follow the same procedure for *Big Alphabet Card Gg*.

gate

FLORIDA STANDARDS/GLEs   LA.A.1.1.2.K.2 Alphabet; **LA.A.1.1.2.K.3** Sounds; **LA.C.1.1.1.K.2** Oral language; LA.C.3.1.2.K.1 Questions

Draw a picture of an umpire on the index card. In the pocket chart place *Alphabet Cards G* and *U*, the index card with *umpire*, and the *Picture Card* gate. Say each picture name and tell children you need to decide where to place each picture.

MODEL I'll start with the umpire. *U—mpire* begins with the /u/ sound. So I'll put the picture of the umpire below *U.*

Model the same process with *Picture Card* gate.

PRACTICE/APPLY

Guided Practice Distribute *Tactile Letter Cards u* and *g* to each child.

I will say some words that begin with /u/ and some that don't. Hold up your *u* card if the word begins with the /u/ sound.

Confirm the answer for each word by holding up the appropriate letter card. *thumbs ↑ thumbs ↓*

up	tiger	umbrella	under	him	us

I will say some words that begin with /g/ and some that don't. Hold up your *g* card if the word begins with the /g/ sound.

thumbs ↑ Thumbs ↓

go	find	get	like	guess	gone

Independent Practice Have children continue to work with their *Tactile Letter Cards u* and *g*.

I'm going to say some words. Listen carefully to the sound you hear at the beginning of each word. Think about the letter that stands for that sound, then hold up the letter card that stands for that sound. *Sign language "u" or "g"*

umbrella	gas	game	up	gift

under	geese	us	golf	good

FLORIDA STANDARDS/GLEs   **FCAT: LA.A.1.1.2.K.5** Phonetic principles; *Also* **LA.A.1.1.2.K.2** Alphabet; **LA.A.1.1.2.K.3** Sounds

▲ **Practice Book page 7** *HW*

OBJECTIVES

- *To share information and ideas, speaking in complete, coherent sentences*

- *To use letters and phonetically spelled words to write about animals*

- *To write a sentence*

- *To write by moving from left to right*

Writing
Every Day

Day 1: Write a Sentence
Have children complete sentence frames to tell what sea animal they see.

Day 2: Write a Question
Have children write a question about one of the fish from *Fish Faces*.

Day 3: Write a List
Together, children will add to a list of wishes made by the story character in "A House by the Sea."

Day 4: New Song Verses
Using the language pattern from the song "The Little Fishes," have children write new verses for the song.

Day 5: Write a Description
Have children use describing words to draw and write about a fish from the book *Fish Faces*.

Writing

Write a Sentence

COMPLETE A SENTENCE FRAME

Talk About Ocean Animals Remind children that in *Splash in the Ocean!* they read about different ocean animals. Page through the *Big Book* and ask children to name the animals in the selection.

Write a Sentence Tell children that they will write a sentence about ocean animals. Write the sentence frame *I see _____.* on the board and read it aloud. Distribute drawing paper and ask children to copy and complete the sentence frame by writing the name of ocean animals from the story. Encourage children to illustrate their sentence.

I see seals.

Self-Selected Writing Have children write and draw about anything they'd like. If they have difficulty thinking of a topic, have them ask two friends what they're going to write about.

FLORIDA STANDARDS/GLEs   FCAT: LA.B.2.1.2.K.1 Record ideas; *Also* **LA.A.1.1.2.K.1** Print organization; **LA.B.1.1.1.K.2** Generate ideas; **LA.B.1.1.2.K.2** Basic formats

WRAP UP  # Share Time

Reflect on the Lesson To encourage discussion, ask children to talk about their favorite ocean animal in *Splash in the Ocean!* Ask children to share their drawing and read their sentence from today's Writing activity.

S.S.R. *Sustained Silent Reading* Have children read silently from a book of their choice.

 **Centers** **DRAMATIC PLAY**

Let's Be Animals

Display in the center *Splash in the Ocean!* and other books about ocean creatures. Have children choose an ocean animal they would like to pretend to be. Have them draw a picture of the creature and use masking tape to fasten it to the front of their clothing. Have children pretend to swim around the ocean, talking with the other sea animals about what kind of creature they are.

 Materials

- *Big Book: Splash in the Ocean!*
- books about ocean animals
- paper
- crayons
- masking tape

Day at a Glance
Day 2

WARM UP

Phonemic Awareness
Phoneme Blending

Sharing Literature
Library Book:
Fish Faces

Read
FISH FACES

Develop Listening Comprehension

Respond to Literature

Literature Focus: Questions for Research

Phonics
Blending /u/-/g/

High-Frequency Words
are

Writing
Question

MORNING MESSAGE

Kindergarten News

(Child's name) likes to _____

with his/her friend.

(Child's name) likes to _____

with his/her friend.

Write Kindergarten News Talk with children about what they like to do with their friends.

Use prompts such as the following to guide children as you write the news:

- **What do you like to do with your friends?**
- **Let's clap the syllables in (child's name).**
- **What is the first letter in (child's name)?**
- **Who can show me a word?**

As you write the message, invite children to contribute by writing letters, names, or words they have previously learned. Remind them to use proper spacing, capitalization, and punctuation.

Calendar Language

Point to and read aloud the names of the days of the week. Name the days of the week again, inviting children to join in and clap for each day. Ask what day it is.

Sunday	Monday	Tuesday	Wednesday	Thursday	Friday	Saturday
		1	2	3	4	5
6	7	8	9	10	11	12
13	14	15	16	17	18	19
20	21	22	23	24	25	26
27	28	29	30	31		

FLORIDA STANDARDS/GLEs   FCAT: **LA.A.1.1.2.K.4** Words; **LA.A.2.1.5.K.2** Get information; **LA.B.2.1.2.K.1** Record ideas; *Also* **LA.A.1.1.2.K.2** Alphabet; **LA.C.3.1.2.K.1** Questions

Phonemic Awareness

PHONEME BLENDING

Blend Sounds Remind children how to blend sounds to make words.

MODEL Listen as I say the sounds in this word: /b/ /u/ /g/. Now say it with me. /b/ /u/ /g/. Listen as I put together the sounds: /bbuugg/. Say the sounds with me: /bbuugg/. Now say the word: *bug*.

Use the same procedure with the following words.

/g/ /e/ /t/ (get)

/g/ /a/ /s/ (gas)

/g/ /a/ /p/ (gap)

/r/ /u/ /g/ (rug)

/m/ /u/ /g/ (mug)

/h/ /u/ /t/ (hut)

/w/ /a/ /g/ (wag)

/s/ /a/ /t/ (sat)

/t/ /u/ /g/ (tug)

/g/ /u/ /m/ (gum)

/f/ /u/ /n/ (fun)

/h/ /u/ /g/ (hug)

/s/ /u/ /n/ (sun)

/d/ /u/ /g/ (dug)

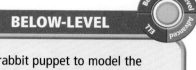

BELOW-LEVEL

Use the rabbit puppet to model the process of blending the sounds: **/uupp/** and saying the word: *up*. Then have children repeat after the rabbit Follow the same procedure for *cup*, *hug*, and *get*.

FISH FACES

NOREEN WU

▲ **Library Book**

OBJECTIVES

- *To listen and respond to a selection*

- *To match photographs with text*

- *To distinguish between stories and information books*

- *To ask questions for research*

Materials

■ *Library Book: Fish Faces*

■ drawing paper

■ crayons

■ chart paper

■ marker

Sharing Literature

Read Fish Faces

READ ALOUD

Before Reading   Display *Fish Faces* and read aloud the title and the name of the author as you track the print. Ask children to repeat the title after you. Ask how many children have seen live fish. Show a few pages in the book. Use these prompts to build background:

- **What do you see on the cover?** (a fish)

- **Is this a photograph or a drawing of a fish?** (a photograph)

- **What do you notice about the pictures in the book?** (They are photographs.)

- **What do you know about fish?** (Answers will vary.)

During Reading   Read the selection aloud. As you read,

- pause to clarify the meaning of unfamiliar words such as *spines*, *periscope*, and *fierce*.

  MODEL *Spines* **are sharp parts poking up out of fish, animals, or plants. A** *periscope* **is a tube you can look through to see things above you.** *Fierce* **means "wild and dangerous."**

- pause to let children match the photographs of fish to the words that describe them.

🔶 **FLORIDA STANDARDS/GLEs   FCAT: LA.A.2.1.3.K.1** Supportive details; *Also* **LA.A.2.1.4.K.1** Illustrations; **LA.C.1.1.1.K.2** Oral language; **LA.C.3.1.2.K.1** Questions

DEVELOP LISTENING COMPREHENSION

After Reading   Have children answer these questions:

• **What is this book about?** (all kinds of fish)

• **Is this a story or a book with information?** (a book with information)

• **What shape can fish be?** (round, flat, long, thin)

RESPOND TO LITERATURE

Draw and Write About Fish   Have children draw and write about their favorite fish in the book. Invite children to share their picture and writing with their classmates.

★ Literature Focus

QUESTIONS FOR RESEARCH

Page through *Fish Faces* and make note of some information the book provides about fish. Then model how to ask questions.

MODEL **This book tells about how fish move. It tells what fish look like—their colors, their mouths, their eyes, their faces. I would like to find out more about fish, such as *What do fish eat?***

Ask children what else they would like to find out about fish. Have them state their suggestions in the form of questions and record the questions on chart paper. Discuss with children how they can get answers to their questions, such as by watching live fish; reading books or magazines; watching videos; searching on the Internet; and taking field trips. As time permits, find answers for some of children's questions.

ADVANCED

Have children write their own questions about fish that they would like to have answered. If possible, help children find the answers.

ONGOING ASSESSMENT

As you share *Fish Faces*, note whether children

• listen for a period of time.

• can match photographs to text as it is read aloud.

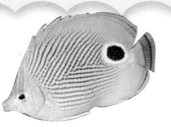

FLORIDA STANDARDS/GLEs   **FCAT: LA.A.1.1.4.K.1** Comprehension; **LA.A.2.1.1.K.1** Main idea. *Also* **LA.B.1.1.3.K.1** Spelling approximations; **LA.B.2.1.1.K.1** Familiar experiences; **LA.C.3.1.2.K.1** Questions

Under the Ocean   549

OBJECTIVES

- *To identify and recognize the initial sound of a spoken word*

- *To blend /u/-/g/*

Materials

- *Big Alphabet Cards Uu and Gg*
- pocket chart
- *Alphabet Cards t, u, g, h, j, r, m*
- index cards
- marker

Phonics
Blending /u/-/g/

ACTIVE BEGINNING

Word Game Sing the following to the tune of "Are You Sleeping?"

What is this word?

What is this word?

/b/ /u/ /g/

/b/ /u/ /g/

The word we made is *bug*!

The word we made is *bug*!

/b/ /u/ /g/, /b/ /u/ /g/.

Continue with the words /t/ /u/ /g/ (*tug*) and /g/ /u/ /m/ (*gum*).

TEACH/MODEL

Recognize *u* and *g* Display *Big Alphabet Card Uu* on the chalk-ledge or in a pocket chart. Ask: **What letter is this?** (u) **What sound does this letter stand for?** (/u/)

Have children say /u/ with you as you point to the letter.

Do the same procedure for *Big Alphabet Card Gg*.

Word Blending Explain to children that they are going to blend letters together to read words, such as *tug*.

- Place the *Alphabet Cards t, u,* and *g* in the pocket chart, separate from each other.

- Point to *t*. Say /**tt**/. Have children repeat the sound after you.
- Point to *u*. Say /**uu**/. Have children repeat the sound after you.
- Point to *g*. Say /**gg**/. Have children repeat the sound after you.

FLORIDA STANDARDS/GLEs   **FCAT: LA.A.1.1.2.K.5** Phonetic principles; *Also* **LA.A.1.1.2.K.2** Alphabet; **LA.A.1.1.2.K.3** Sounds; **LA.C.3.1.2.K.1** Questions

• Slide *u* next to t. Say: /**ttuu**/.

• Slide *g* next to *tu*. Move your hand under the letters and blend the sounds, elongating them—/**ttuugg**/. Have children blend and read *tug* with you.

PRACTICE/APPLY

Guided Practice   Place *Alphabet Cards* h, u, and g in the pocket chart.

• Point to *h* and say /**hh**/. Point to the letter *u* and say /**uu**/. Slide the *u* next to *h*. Move your hand under the letters and blend the sounds, elongating them—/**hhuu**/. Have children blend the sounds after you.

• Point to *g*. Say /**gg**/. Have children say the sound.

• Slide the *g* next to the *hu*. Slide your hand under *hug* and blend the sounds. Have children blend the sounds as you slide your hand under the word.

• Then have children read the word *hug* along with you.

Follow the same procedure to build and blend *jug*, *rug*, and *gum* with children.

Independent Practice   Write the words *mug*, *Gus*, *bug*, *hug*, and *rug* on index cards and place them in a pocket chart in the Letters and Words Center. Ask children to point to each letter and blend the sounds together to read the words.

ADVANCED

Place the *Magnetic Letters b, d, h, g, j, m,* and *u* and a cookie sheet in the Letters and Words Center. Place the *Magnetic Letters u* and *g* on the cookie sheet. Encourage children to make words with *u* and *g*, such as *bug*, *mug*, and *gum*.

ENGLISH-LANGUAGE LEARNERS

Before asking children to read the words in the Independent Practice, review each letter sound with them.

▲ **Practice Book page 9**

OBJECTIVE

To read the high-frequency word are

Materials

- *Big Book:*
  Splash in the Ocean!

- *High-Frequency*
  Word Card   `are`

- *Teacher's Resource Book,*
  p. 140

- sentence strips

- marker

High-Frequency Word *are* ✔ *Introduce*

TEACH/MODEL

Display *Splash in the Ocean!* Turn to the last page featuring the song. Track the print as you read the words: *All the fish are swimming in the ocean.* Write the sentence on the board and read it again.

Point to the word *are* and say: **This is the word *are*.** Have children say the word. Display *High-Frequency Word Card are*. Ask: **What word is this?** Have children listen as you repeat the sentence. Ask a child to match the *High-Frequency Word Card are* to the word *are* in the sentence on the board.

PRACTICE/APPLY

Guided Practice   Make copies of the *High-Frequency Word Card are* in the *Teacher's Resource Book*. Give each child a card and tell children to point to the word *are* and say it. Then ask children to point to the word card as they turn to a classmate and ask this question:

Who are you?

Independent Practice   Have children find the word card *you* in their word file. Model how they can put together the words *Are* and *you* to form the question:

Are you _____?

Have children use the sentence frame to ask questions of one another.

 FLORIDA STANDARDS/GLEs   FCAT: LA.A.1.1.2.K.4 Words; **LA.A.1.1.3.K.4** Build vocabulary; *Also* **LA.A.1.1.3.K.1** Frequent words

552   Under the Ocean

Word Wall

Reading Words Hold up the *High-Frequency Word Card are* and have children read it aloud. Place the word card under the letter *a* on the classroom word chart. Then ask a child to match his or her *High-Frequency Word Card are* to *are* on the word chart.

Words in Sentences Have children look closely at their new word *are*. Ask them to name the letters in the word. Write the following sentence frames on sentence strips: *We are _____. You are _____.* Read each sentence frame with children. Ask a child to come up to frame the word *are*. Have children read the sentence strips, tracking the print and completing the sentences orally.

BELOW-LEVEL

Write short sentences on the board that include the word *are*, such as *We are on the mat.* or *We are in the jet.* Have children frame the word *are* in each sentence.

ADVANCED

Ask children to use the word *are* in a sentence. Provide each child with a sentence strip and have children write the sentence. Tell them to read their sentence to a partner.

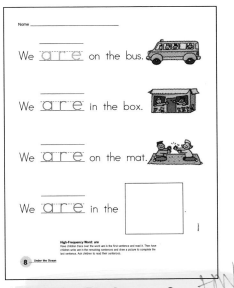

▲ **Practice Book page 8**

FLORIDA STANDARDS/GLEs FCAT: **LA.A.1.1.2.K.4** Words; **LA.A.1.1.3.K.4** Build vocabulary; *Also* **LA.A.1.1.3.K.1** Frequent words

Under the Ocean   553

Writing

Write a Question

USE QUESTION WORDS

Talk About Questions Remind children that a question is a sentence that asks something. Tell them that questions sometimes start with the words *Who*, *What*, *Why*, *Where*, or *When*. As you page through *Fish Faces*, have children think about what they would like to learn about the fish.

Write a Question Tell children they are going to write a question about one of the fish from *Fish Faces*. List the question words *Who*, *What*, *Why*, *Where*, and *When* on the board. Have children choose a question word with which to begin their question and then write the entire question.

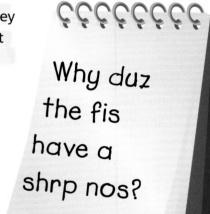

> Why duz
> the fis
> have a
> shrp nos?

Day 2

...s and pho-
...elled words to
write ...out animals

- To write a question

- To write by moving from left to right

Materials

- Library Book: *Fish Faces*

- drawing paper

- crayons or pencils

Writing Every Day

My Journal

Self-Selected Writing Have children write and draw about anything they'd like. If they have difficulty thinking of a topic have them ask two friends what they're going to write about.

FLORIDA STANDARDS/GLEs   LA.B.1.1.1.K.2 Generate ideas; **LA.B.1.1.3.K.1** Spelling approximations; **LA.B.1.1.3.K.2** Print direction; **LA.B.1.1.3.K.3** Punctuation

WRAP UP # Share Time

Reflect on the Lesson Ask children to recall some facts about fish they learned from *Fish Faces*. Invite them to read the questions they wrote during the Writing activity. Answer some of the questions if time permits.

S.S.R. *Sustained Silent Reading* Have children read silently from a book of their choice.

 **Centers** **ART**

Ocean Mural

Set up butcher paper and blue paint in the center. Have children paint a blue ocean background on the butcher paper. Provide materials for children to draw and color fish on the blue background or to make fish out of construction paper and fabric scraps to glue onto the mural. Remind children to add to the mural throughout the theme, as they read about different sea creatures.

Materials

- butcher paper
- blue paint, paintbrushes
- crayons
- construction paper
- fabric scraps
- scissors
- glue

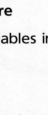

WARM UP

Phonemic Awareness
Phoneme Substitution: Initial

Sharing Literature
Read-Aloud Anthology:
"A House by the Sea"

Read

Develop Concept Vocabulary

Respond to Literature

Literature Focus: Syllables in Words

Phonics
Words with /u/ and /g/

High-Frequency Words
here

Interactive Writing
List

MORNING MESSAGE

Kindergarten News

Today is _____ .

In school today we will _____

_____ .

Write Kindergarten News   Talk with children about what they like to do at school. Encourage them to speak in complete sentences.

Use prompts such as the following to guide children as you write the news:

- **What is something we will do at school today?**
- **Who can show me where to begin writing?**
- **Who can show me a space between words?**
- **What is the first letter in *Today*?**

As you write the message, invite children to contribute by writing letters or words they have previously learned. Remind them to use proper spacing, capitalization, and punctuation.

Calendar Language

Point to and read aloud the names of the days of the week. Ask what day today is. Ask what day comes after today. Point to the name of the day and say: *Tomorrow is _____.* Invite children to name today and tomorrow.

Sunday	Monday	Tuesday	Wednesday	Thursday	Friday	Saturday
		1	2	3	4	5
6	7	8	9	10	11	12
13	14	15	16	17	18	19
20	21	22	23	24	25	26
27	28	29	30	31		

FLORIDA STANDARDS/GLEs   FCAT: LA.A.2.1.5.K.2 Get information; **LA.B.2.1.2.K.1** Record ideas; *Also* **LA.A.1.1.2.K.1** Print organization; **LA.A.1.1.2.K.2** Alphabet; **LA.C.1.1.3.K.1** Conversation rules; **LA.C.3.1.2.K.1** Questions

Phonemic Awareness

PHONEME SUBSTITUTION: INITIAL

Substitute Initial Sounds   Tell children that you are going to say a word. Then explain that you will change the beginning sound to make a new word.

MODEL   *Bug.* **Say the word with me.** *Bug.*

What word would we have if we changed the /b/ in *bug* **to /h/? The new word is** *hug.* **Say the new word:** *hug.*

Now you try it. Say *cut.* **What word would we have if we changed the /k/ in** *cut* **to /n/? Say the new word:** *nut.*

Have children repeat the process with the following words.

Say *run.* **Change the /r/ in** *run* **to /s/. What's the new word?** (*sun*)

Say *pit.* **Change the /p/ in** *pit* **to /f/. What's the new word?** (*fit*)

Say *let.* **Change the /l/ in** *let* **to /n/. What's the new word?** (*net*)

Say *hum.* **Change the /h/ in** *hum* **to /g/. What's the new word?** (*gum*)

Say *sad.* **Change the /s/ in** *sad* **to /b/. What's the new word?** (*bad*)

Say *hop.* **Change the /h/ in** *hop* **to /t/. What's the new word?** (*top*)

▲ "Goin' to the Zoo," *Oo-pples and Boo-noo-noos: Songs and Activities for Phonemic Awareness*, pages 78–79.

ADVANCED

Display the *Picture Cards bus, goat, hen, king, sun,* and *zoo.* Have children name each picture and then substitute a new beginning sound to make a new word.

Sharing Literature

Read "A House by the Sea"

READ ALOUD

Before Reading   Read aloud the title "A House by the Sea." Tell children that this is the title of a rhyming story that you will read aloud. Then use these prompts to build background:

• **What would you see, hear, or touch if you lived near the sea?** (Possible responses: rocks, waves, sand.)

• **What would you do all day if you lived by the sea?** (Possible responses: fish, sail, swim)

During Reading   Read the story aloud. As you read,

• emphasize rhyming words.

• pause to point out details that are make-believe and ask children why they are not real. Model an example:

> **MODEL**   **I just read that the person who lives by the sea washes his face in a cloud and sings to the moon till he laughs out loud. Those things are make-believe because they could not really happen. People cannot wash their faces in a cloud. The moon is not human and cannot laugh.**

• invite children to clap the rhythm of the text as you reread parts of the rhyming story.

▲ **Read-Aloud Anthology**

OBJECTIVES

• *To identify details that are make-believe*

• *To listen and respond to a rhyming story by clapping the rhythm*

• *To respond to a story through art*

• *To identify syllables in words*

Materials

■ *Read-Aloud Anthology*, pp. 116–118

■ chart paper

■ marker

■ drawing paper

■ crayons

FLORIDA STANDARDS/GLEs   FCAT: LA.A.1.1.4.K.1 Comprehension; *Also* **LA.E.2.1.1.K.1** Background knowledge; **LA.E.2.1.2.K.1** Patterned structures

DEVELOP CONCEPT VOCABULARY

After Reading   Write the following words or phrases from the story on chart paper: *frisky seals, star-speckled sky, crest of foam, bobbing*.

Point to each phrase or word and explain its meaning to children.

Frisky means "lively and playful."

Star-speckled means "full of stars."

Crest of foam means "an ocean wave that has some white, bubbly water on the top of it."

Bobbing means "bouncing up and down."

RESPOND TO LITERATURE

Draw a Picture   Have children draw and label a picture that shows what they would do if they lived by the sea. Invite them to also illustrate a concept vocabulary word and then share their work with the class.

Literature Focus

SYLLABLES IN WORDS

Remind children that words have one or more parts, or syllables. Tell children that you will say the names of sea animals. They can repeat the names and clap the number of word parts, or syllables, they hear. Say the words: **seals** (1), **octopus** (3), **whale** (1), **crab** (1), **lobster** (2), **jawfish** (2), **lionfish** (3), **butterflyfish** (4), **eel** (1), **sawfish** (2). Invite individuals to name a sea creature and have the others repeat the name and clap the number of syllables.

FLORIDA STANDARDS/GLEs   **FCAT: LA.A.1.1.2.K.5** Phonetic principles;   **LA.A.1.1.3.K.5** Story elements; *Also* **LA.B.2.1.1.K.1** Familiar experiences

Under the Ocean   **559**

OBJECTIVES

- *To build and read simple one-syllable words*
- *To understand that as letters of words change, so do the sounds*

Materials

- *Alphabet Cards g, h, m, r, u*
- *Word Builders*
- *Word Builder Cards g, h, m, r, u*
- *pocket chart*
- *Magnetic Letters*
- *cookie sheet*

REVIEW LETTERS

h   r   m

Phonics

Words with /u/ and /g/ ✓Introduce

ACTIVE BEGINNING

Action Rhyme   Teach children this rhyme and the actions that go with it:

First the bug gives a tug.
(Pull on an imaginary rope.)
Then the bug gives a hug!
(Give yourself a hug.)
A tug! A hug!
(Repeat both actions.)
That silly bug!
(Shrug your shoulders.)

TEACH/MODEL

Blending Words   Distribute *Word Builders* and *Word Builder Cards* g, h, m, r, u to children. As you place *Alphabet Cards* in a pocket chart, tell children to place the same *Word Builder Cards* in their *Word Builder*.

Whole Group

- Place *Alphabet Cards* h, u, and g in the pocket chart. Have children do the same.

h   u   g

- Point to *h*. Say **/hh/**. Point to *u*. Say **/uu/**.
- Slide the *u* next to the *h*. Then move your hand under the letters and blend the sounds, elongating them—**/hhuu/**. Have children do the same.

h   u   g

- Point to the letter *g*. Say **/gg/**. Have children do the same.

 FLORIDA STANDARDS/GLEs   **FCAT: LA.A.1.1.2.K.5** Phonetic principles; *Also* **LA.A.1.1.2.K.3** Sounds

- Slide the *g* next to the *hu*. Slide your hand under *hug* and blend by elongating the sounds—**/hhuugg/**. Have children do the same.
- Then have children blend and read the word *hug* along with you.

PRACTICE/APPLY

Guided Practice Have children place *Word Builder Cards u* and *g* in their *Word Builders*.

- **Add *r* to *ug*. What word did you make?**

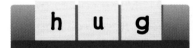

- **Change *r* to *h*. What word did you make?**

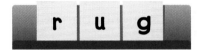

- **Change *g* to *m*. What word did you make?**

- **Change *h* to *g*. What word did you make?**

individuals do on board

Independent Practice Have children use the *Magnetic Letters b, g, m, t,* and *u* and a cookie sheet in the Letters and Words Center to build and read *tug, gum, bug,* and *mug*.

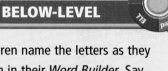

BELOW-LEVEL

Have children name the letters as they place them in their *Word Builder*. Say the sound and have them repeat the sound. Have them move a hand under the letters in the *Word Builder* as they blend the sounds with you.

ADVANCED

Have children use the *Magnetic Letters g, m, r,* and *u* and *High-Frequency Word Cards I, like,* and *my* to build sentences: *I like my mug. I like my gum. I like my rug.*

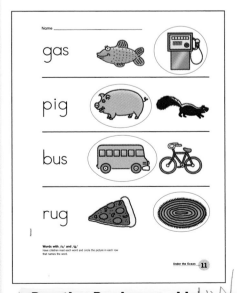

▲ **Practice Book page 11** HW

OBJECTIVE

To read high-frequency word here

Materials

- chart paper
- marker
- *High-Frequency Word Card*
- *Teacher's Resource Book*, p. 140

High-Frequency Word *here* ✓*Introduce*

TEACH/MODEL

Remind children of the rhyming story they heard, "A House by the Sea." Then write the following sentence on chart paper: *I will live here by the sea.* Read the sentence aloud as you track the print.

Point to the word *here* and say: **This is the word *here*.** Have children say the word. Display *High-Frequency Word Card* here. Ask: **What word is this?** Have children listen as you repeat the sentence. Ask a child to match the *High-Frequency Word Card* here to the word *here* in the sentence on the chart.

PRACTICE/APPLY

Guided Practice   Make copies of the *High-Frequency Word Card* here in the *Teacher's Resource Book*. Give each child a card and tell them to point to the word *here* and say it. Explain to children that you will have each of them introduce a classmate by saying: "Here is (classmate's name)." Each time they use the word *here*, they should point to the word card.

Independent Practice   Have children copy the following sentence frame on paper: *Here is my _____.* Ask them to finish the sentence by writing a word to name something that belongs to them and drawing a picture to show what the item looks like.

Here is my _____.

FLORIDA STANDARDS/GLEs   FCAT: LA.A.1.1.2.K.4 Words; *Also* **LA.A.1.1.2.K.1** Print organization; **LA.A.1.1.3.K.1** Frequent words; **LA.B.1.1.3.K.1** Spelling approximations; **LA.B.1.1.3.K.2** Print direction

Word Wall

Reading Words Hold up the *High-Frequency Word Card here* and have children read it aloud. Place the word card under the letter *H* on the classroom word chart. Then ask a child to match his or her *High-Frequency Word Card here* to *here* on the word chart.

Find Similarities Have children look closely at their new word *here*. Ask them to name the letters in the word. Encourage them to find similarities to other words posted on the chart. Ask the following questions to guide them appropriately:

- ***Here begins with h. What other word begins with h?*** *(have)*
- ***Here has four letters. What other words have four letters?***
  (like, have, what, look, come)

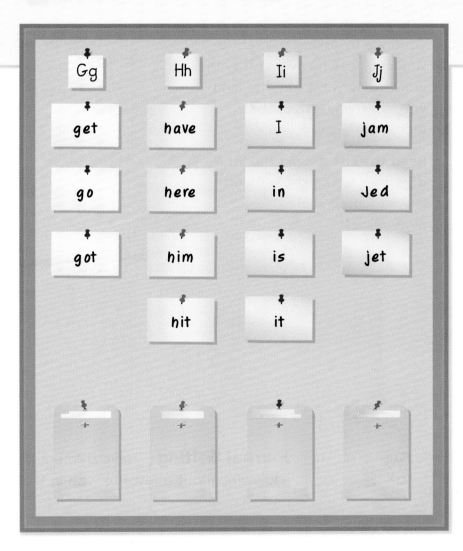

FLORIDA STANDARDS/GLEs **FCAT: LA.A.1.1.3.K.4** Build vocabulary; *Also* **LA.A.1.1.2.K.2** Alphabet; **LA.A.1.1.3.K.1** Frequent words

Diagnostic Check: High-Frequency Words

If... children cannot recognize the high-frequency word *here*,

Then... have children trace the letters of their individual word card with a finger and use *Magnetic Letters* and a cookie sheet to form the word. Using two copies of the word card *here* along with pairs of word cards children know, mix the cards and have children match words that are the same.

ADDITIONAL SUPPORT ACTIVITIES

BELOW-LEVEL	Reteach, p. S56
ADVANCED	Extend, p. S57
ENGLISH-LANGUAGE LEARNERS	Reteach, p. S57

▲ **Practice Book page 10**

Under the Ocean **563**

OBJECTIVES

- *To share information and ideas, speaking in complete, coherent sentences*

- *To write a list*

Materials

- ■ chart paper
- ■ marker

Interactive Writing

Write a List

ADD TO A WISH LIST

Talk About the Story Recall with children that the child in "A House by the Sea" wishes for many unusual things: to live next door to an octopus, to dance with a crab, to sleep on a whale.

Write a List Tell children that together they will write a list of other things the child in the story might wish for. Use prompts such as the following to help children write with you:

What title shall we write? Who can write the *W* in *Wishes*?

What wish shall we list first?

Who will write the letters in the word?

Continue by asking children to suggest ideas for wishes, say the words they want to write, and write as many letters and words as they can.

Read the List ■ Read the list of wishes to the children and allow them to share thier own wishes.

Wishes
eat lunch with a dolphin
dive with a seal
play a game with a whale

Journal Writing Have children draw and write about a favorite wish in their journal.

FLORIDA STANDARDS/GLEs **FCAT: LA.B.2.1.2.K.1** Record ideas; *Also* **LA.B.1.1.3.K.1** Spelling approximations; **LA.B.2.1.1.K.2** Contribute ideas; **LA.B.2.1.4.K.1** Informational text

WRAP UP Share Time

Reflect on the Lesson   Have children tell what they liked best about "A House by the Sea." Ask them what word they learned today. (*here*)

 S.S.R.   Have children read silently from a book of their choice.

Centers   BLOCK

Houses by the Sea

Have children use blocks to build houses and other buildings that they might see by the ocean. Remind children that people live and work near the ocean. Suggest that they build houses and places such as piers, where fishing boats dock to unload their catch.

Materials

■ blocks

■ figures of people

■ plastic boats

FLORIDA STANDARDS/GLEs   **FCAT: LA.A.1.1.4.K.1** Comprehension; *Also* **LA.A.1.1.3.K.1** Frequent words; **LA.C.1.1.1.K.1** Follow directions

Under the Ocean   **565**

Day at a Glance
Day 4

WARM UP

Phonemic Awareness
Syllable Segmentation

Sharing Literature
Big Book of Rhymes and Songs: "The Little Fishes"

Read
Big Book of Rhymes and Songs
Harcourt

Respond to Literature

Literature Focus: Repetitive Text

Reading
Decodable Book 16: Is It a Fish?

Shared Writing
New Song Verses

MORNING MESSAGE

Kindergarten News

(Child's name)'s favorite season

is _____ .

(Child's name) likes to _____

in the (season).

Write Kindergarten News Talk with children about their favorite season and what they like to do in that season.

Use prompts such as the following to guide children as you write the news:

- **Tell about your favorite season. What do you like to do in that season?**
- **Who can show me the first letter in (child's name)?**
- **Let's clap for (child's name). How many parts do you clap?**

As you write the message, invite children to contribute by writing letters, names, or words they have previously learned. Remind them to use proper spacing, capitalization, and punctuation.

Calendar Language

Point to and read aloud the names of the seasons of the year. Have children repeat the season names with you. Ask children to name the season they are in.

Sunday	Monday	Tuesday	Wednesday	Thursday	Friday	Saturday
		1	2	3	4	5
6	7	8	9	10	11	12
13	14	15	16	17	18	19
20	21	22	23	24	25	26
27	28	29	30	31		

FLORIDA STANDARDS/GLEs **FCAT: LA.A.2.1.5.K.2** Get information; **LA.B.2.1.2.K.1** Record ideas; *Also* LA.A.1.1.2.K.2 Alphabet

Phonemic Awareness

SYLLABLE SEGMENTATION

Clap Syllables   Tell children they will say words and clap word parts called syllables.

MODEL   *Swimming*. There are two word parts, or syllables, in *swimming*. Listen as I say each word part and clap for each syllable: *Swim-ming*. Clap each word part as you say the word with me: *swim-ming.*

Say the following words and ask children to repeat the word and clap for each syllable.

little (lit-tle)	**flying** (fly-ing)	**seahorse** (sea-horse)
water (wat-er)	**dolphin** (dol-phin)	**splashing** (splash-ing)
fishes (fish-es)	**move** (move)	**crawling** (crawl-ing)
whale (whale)	**octopus** (oc-to-pus)	**seashell** (sea-shell)
wave (wave)	**seaweed** (sea-weed)	**porpoise** (por-poise)
ocean (o-cean)	**sailboat** (sail-boat)	**angelfish** (an-gel-fish)

REACHING ALL LEARNERS

Diagnostic Check: Phonemic Awareness

If... children cannot segment syllables,

Then... say a word and have children repeat the word. Segment the syllables while clapping and have them do the same. Repeat this procedure several times until children can segment syllables on their own.

ADDITIONAL SUPPORT ACTIVITIES

BELOW-LEVEL   Reteach, p. S58

ADVANCED   Extend, p. S59

ENGLISH-LANGUAGE LEARNERS   Reteach, p. S59

▲ **Big Book of Rhymes and Songs**

OBJECTIVES

- *To sing a song*

- *To connect text to life experiences*

- *To respond to a song through movement*

- *To recognize repetitive text*

Materials

■ *Big Book of Rhymes and Songs*, pp. 28–29

■ *Music CD*

Sharing Literature

Read "The Little Fishes"

READ ALOUD

Before Reading Display the song "The Little Fishes" on pages 28 and 29 of the *Big Book of Rhymes and Songs*. Read the title aloud while you track the print. Point out that the title and the words of the song are written in Spanish as well as English. Then ask these questions to build background:

- **What do you know about fish?** (Possible responses: Fish live in water; they swim; they have fins.)

- **How do fish move?** (They swim, flip, dive; they move quickly through the water.)

During Reading Read aloud the words to the song. As you read,

- read the words rhythmically. Reread and lead children in clapping the rhythm.

- emphasize the repetitive words.

Then play the *Music CD* and have children sing the song with you.

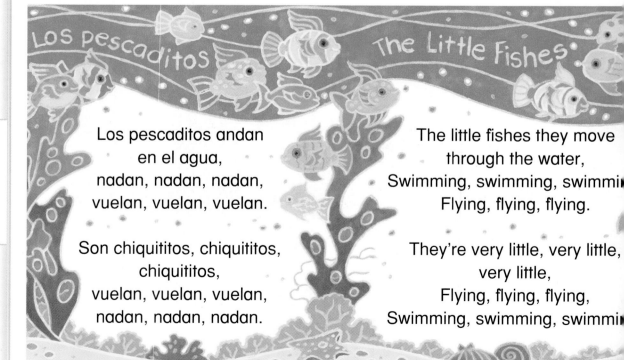

Big Book of Rhyme and Songs. pages 28–29

FLORIDA STANDARDS/GLEs LA.C.1.1.1.K.2 Oral language; LA.C.3.1.2.K.1 Questions; LA.D.2.1.2.K.1 Patterned structures

RESPOND TO LITERATURE

Act Out the Song   Play the song again and have children sing along. Encourage them to use their hands to mimic the fish swimming and "flying" through the water.

Literature Focus

REPETITIVE TEXT

Read the first stanza of the song "The Little Fishes," emphasizing the words *swimming, swimming, swimming,* and *flying, flying, flying.*

MODEL   Sometimes words are said over and over in a song or story. The words in this song tell about the movements the fish are doing. Listen to the first part of the song again. How many times do you hear the word *swimming*? the word *flying*?

Reread the song lyrics and have children join in on the repetitive words. Ask them how many times they hear *very little, flying,* and *swimming* in the second stanza.

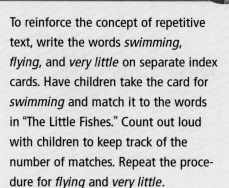
ONGOING ASSESSMENT

As you share "The Little Fishes," note whether children

- can clap the rhythm.
- sing a song.
- respond to the song through movement.

OBJECTIVE

To decode short vowel /u/u words

Materials

- *Alphabet Cards b, u, g*
- index cards
- pocket chart
- *Decodable Book* 16: *Is It a Fish?*
- drawing paper
- crayons

ADVANCED

Have children read *Is It a Fish?* on their own. Ask them to track the print as they read. Then have them read *Independent Reader 33: At the Beach.*

Phonics

Short Vowel /u/u ✔ Review

TEACH/MODEL

Review Blending   Place the *Alphabet Cards b, u,* and *g* in a pocket chart. Move your hand under the letters, blend them, and say the word. **/bbuugg/—bug.** Have children blend the sounds and say the word. Write the words *Is, it,* and *a* on index cards. Write a question mark on an index card. Place them in the pocket chart to form the sentence *Is it a bug?* Point to each word as you read the sentence. Then point to each word slowly, and have children read the sentence. Replace the letter *b* in *bug* with the letter *r* and have children read the new question.

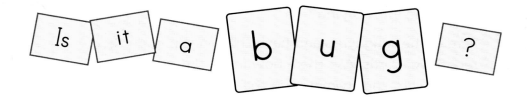

PRACTICE/APPLY

Read the Book   Distribute copies of *Is It a Fish?* Read the title to children, pointing to each word as you say it. Page through the book and ask children to predict which family member will pull a fish out of the glass tank. Then have children read the book, pointing to each word as they read.

Respond   Have children draw a picture of one of the things that a family member pulls out of the glass tank.

FLORIDA STANDARDS/GLEs   FCAT: LA.A.1.1.2.K.4 Words; *Also* **LA.A.1.1.2.K.1** Print organization; **LA.A.1.1.2.K.3** Sounds; **LA.A.1.1.3.K.1** Frequent words

Decodable Book 16: *Is It a Fish?*

Here we are!
Get a rod.

2

Tug, tug, tug.
Is it a fish?
No, it is a man!

3

Tug, tug, tug.
Did Mom get a fish?

4   No, it is a bug!

Tug, tug, tug.
Is it a fish?
No, it is a hen!

5

Tug, tug, tug.
Did Ted get a fish?

6   No, it is a jug!

Tug, tug, tug.
Is it a fish?

7

Come look.
See what Jen got.

8   It is a big fish!

■ High-Frequency Words

here, we, are, no, come, look, see, what

■ Decodable Words

See the Word List on page T15.

School–Home Connection

Take-Home Book Version

◀ **Decodable Book 16**
Is It a Fish?

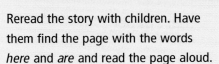

BELOW-LEVEL

Reread the story with children. Have them find the page with the words *here* and *are* and read the page aloud.

▲ **At the Beach**
Independent Reader 33

OBJECTIVES

- To brainstorm ideas for a song
- To write new lyrics to a song
- To write patterned text

Materials

- ■ *Big Book of Rhymes and Songs*, pp. 28–29
- ■ index cards
- ■ pocket chart
- ■ marker
- ■ chart paper

Shared Writing

Write New Song Verses

COMPLETE A SENTENCE FRAME

Talk About the Song
Display the song "The Little Fishes" and read the words. Ask: **Which words in the song describe how fish move?** (*swimming, flying*) Ask children to name other animals and how they move. Record their ideas on index cards and display in a pocket chart.

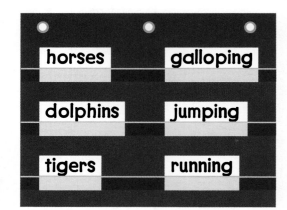

horses	galloping
dolphins	jumping
tigers	running

Write New Song Verses   Tell children that they are going to write new words for the song, "The Little Fishes." Write the following sentence frame on the chart paper:

The _____ they move
Through the _____, _____, _____,
_____.

Have children choose an animal name and action word from the chart and think of where the animal is moving. Write children's ideas to create new verses for the song.

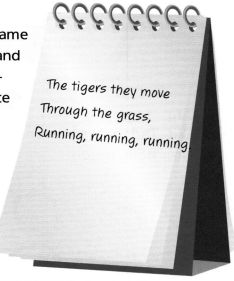

The tigers they move
Through the grass,
Running, running, running

Journal Writing   Have children draw and write about fish they would like to have as pets in their journal.

FLORIDA STANDARDS/GLEs   **LA.B.1.1.1.K.2** Generate ideas; **LA.B.2.1.1.K.1** Familiar experiences; **LA.B.2.1.1.K.2** Contribute ideas; **LA.D.2.1.2.K.1** Patterned structures

WRAP UP **Share Time**

Reflect on the Lesson   Have children tell what they like about the book they read, *Is It a Fish*? Ask them to talk about any parts of the story that surprised them. Then have children sing their new verses for "The Little Fishes."

S.S.R.   Have children read silently from a book of their choice.

Centers   MATH

Subtraction Game

In advance, cut several index cards in half. Make about thirty fish cards by drawing a simple outline of a fish on each card half. To begin, each player gets six fish cards. In turn, each player spins the spinner and reads the number. The player puts that many fish cards into the fish bowl. The player then tells how many fish he or she has left and makes that many marks on a sheet of paper. After everyone has had a turn, players take their fish cards back and play again. When they have played three rounds, children can count the number of marks on their paper.

Materials

- index cards

- spinner with three parts, labeled 1, 2, 3

- clean, dry fish bowl or other container

- writing paper

- markers

WARM UP

Phonemic Awareness
Phoneme Deletion

Sharing Literature
Library Book:
Fish Faces

Read

FISH FACES

NOREEN W...

Develop Concept Vocabulary

Respond to Literature

Literature Focus: Categorizing

Phonics
Words with /u/ and /g/

Writing ✏
Writing: Description

MORNING MESSAGE

Kindergarten News

Today's date is _____.

The weather is _____.

When I go outside, I will _____.

Write Kindergarten News Talk with children about the weather and what they plan to do outdoors.

Use prompts such as the following to guide children as you write the news:

- **What is the weather today? What will you do when you go outdoors today?**
- **Who can show me where to start writing?**
- **Who can name the first letter in *weather*?**

As you write the message, invite children to contribute by writing letters or words they have previously learned. Remind them to use proper spacing, capitalization, and punctuation.

Calendar Language

Point to and read aloud the school days, *Monday* through *Friday*. Ask children to repeat the names of the school days.

Sunday	Monday	Tuesday	Wednesday	Thursday	Friday	Saturday
		1	2	3	4	5
6	7	8	9	10	11	12
13	14	15	16	17	18	19
20	21	22	23	24	25	26
27	28	29	30	31		

FLORIDA STANDARDS/GLEs **FCAT: LA.A.1.1.2.K.6** Print meaning; *Also* **LA.A.1.1.2.K.1** Print organization; **LA.A.1.1.2.K.3** Sounds; **LA.C.1.1.3.K.1** Conversation rules; **LA.C.3.1.2.K.1** Questions

Phonemic Awareness

PHONEME DELETION

Delete Initial Phonemes   Tell children to listen as you say words without the beginning sound. Begin by saying the word *gate* without the /g/.

MODEL   *Gate.* Say the word with me. *Gate.*

I can say *gate* without the /g/.

Gate without the /g/ is *ate.*

Now you say *gate* without the /g/.

Continue with these words:

Say *man* without the /m/. (*an*)   Say *ham* without the /h/. (*am*)

Say *goat* without the /g/. (*oat*)   Say *cat* without the /k/. (*at*)

Say *rug* without the /r/. (*ug*)   Say *sit* without the /s/. (*it*)

Say *get* without the /g/. (*et*)   Say *band* without the /b/. (*and*)

Say *cup* without the /k/. (*up*)   Say *fun* without the /f/. (*un*)

Say *gold* without the /g/. (*old*)   Say *nut* without the /n/. (*ut*)

gold – /g/ = old

BELOW-LEVEL

Modeling the skill for children guides them toward independence. Say the word *go*, emphasizing the sound of /g/, and have children repeat the word after you. Next, tell children that you are going to say the word *go* without the /g/: *o*. Have children repeat /ō/ after you. Repeat the process with other simple words, such as *too, by, me,* and *so.*

Sharing Literature

Read Fish Faces

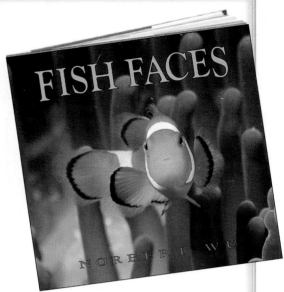

▲ **Library Book**

READ ALOUD

Before Reading Display the cover of *Fish Faces* and point to the title as you read it aloud. Point to the name of the author and remind children that Norbert Wu wrote the words and took the photographs for this book. Page through the book and use these prompts to help children set a purpose for rereading the selection:

- **What is strange-looking about some of the fish in this book?**

- **How does this book teach you about fish?**

MODEL This book doesn't have many words, but there are many colorful photographs of fish. As I read the book again, I want to pay more attention to see what the photographs and the words tell me about fish.

During Reading Reread the selection aloud. As you read,

- point out the details in each photograph that illustrate the words on that page.

- pause for children to describe the fish on each page.

OBJECTIVES

- *To note picture details*

- *To understand action words*

- *To categorize information*

Materials

- *Library Book: Fish Faces*

- paper plates

- scissors

- crayons

- craft sticks

- tape

- chart paper

- marker

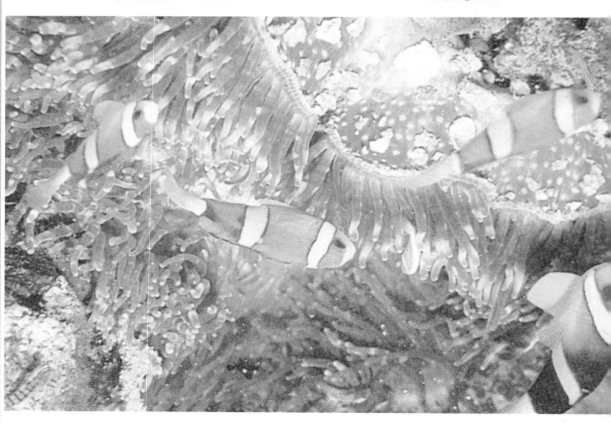

FLORIDA STANDARDS/GLEs **FCAT: LA.A.1.1.4.K.1** Comprehension; **LA.A.2.1.1.K.1** Main idea; *Also* **LA.A.2.1.4.K.1** Illustrations

DEVELOP CONCEPT VOCABULARY

After Reading Tell children to listen as you read pages 5–7 of *Fish Faces*. Then lead children in a discussion by asking: **Which words tell how the fish move?** (*dart, dip, slide, glide*) Demonstrate the meaning of these words by using your hands to represent a fish. Emphasize the difference between the sharp, sudden movements of *dart* and *dip* and the slow, smooth movements represented by *slide* and *glide*.

RESPOND TO LITERATURE

Make Fish Puppets Help children cut out a simple fish shape from paper plates. Have children color the fish shape to look like a fish from *Fish Faces*. Direct them to attach it to a craft stick to make a fish puppet. Encourage children to describe what their fish is like.

Literature Focus

CATEGORIZING

Tell children that there are different ways to describe the fish in *Fish Faces*. Write the following categories on a chart: *Body, Mouth, Nose, Eyes, Face*. Then model how to complete the first column of the chart.

MODEL **One way to think about the fish is to tell how their bodies look. Some fish are flat, some are round, and some are long and thin.**

Record the words that describe the bodies of the fish. Then ask children to recall the other characteristics of the fish and list their responses on the chart. Save this chart for use in today's Writing lesson.

Body	Mouth	Nose	Eyes	Face
flat	wide	long	red	friendly
round	tube	flat	green	fierce
long	beak	sharp	pretend	sad

BELOW-LEVEL

Have children work together to sort wooden blocks by size or shape. When they are finished with one sort, have them sort the blocks in a different way. Ask children to name the categories they used to complete their sorts.

ADVANCED

Have children look through magazines and choose three categories of pictures, for example, animals, people, plants. Tell children to cut out pictures and sort them into groups according to the three categories. When they are finished, have them mix up the pictures and challenge a classmate to sort them.

ONGOING ASSESSMENT

As you share *Fish Faces*, note whether children

• can note picture details.

• can listen for a period of time.

OBJECTIVES

- To build and read simple one-syllable words

- To understand that as letters of words change, so do the sounds

Materials

- Word Builders
- Word Builder Cards b, g, h, j, m, t, u
- Alphabet Cards b, g, h, j, m, t, u
- pocket chart
- index cards
- drawing paper
- crayons

REVIEW LETTERS

Phonics

Words with /u /and /g/ ✔ Review

ACTIVE BEGINNING

Play a Listening Game   Explain to children that they are going to play a game where they will listen to words that have the /g/ sound. Ask them to clap their hands if the word begins with the /g/ sound and stamp their feet if the word ends with the /g/ sound.

| gas | flag | rug | guess | plug |
| snag | girl | guitar | frog | gallon |

TEACH/MODEL

Blending Words   Distribute *Word Builders* and *Word Builder Cards* b, g, h, j, m, t, and u to children. As you place *Alphabet Cards* in a pocket chart, tell children to place the same *Word Builder Cards* in their *Word Builder*.

- Place *Alphabet Cards* m, u, and g in the pocket chart. Have children do the same.

- Point to m. Say **/mm/**. Point to u. Say **/uu/**.
- Slide the u next to the m. Then move your hand under the letters and blend the sounds, elongating them—**/mmuu/**. Have children do the same.

- Point to the letter g. Say **/gg/**. Have children do the same.
- Slide the g next to the mu. Slide your hand under *mug* and blend by elongating the sounds—**/mmuugg/**. Have children do the same.
- Then have children blend and read the word *mug* along with you.

FLORIDA STANDARDS/GLEs   FCAT: LA.A.1.1.2.K.5 Phonetic principles; *Also* LA.A.1.1.2.K.3 Sounds

PRACTICE/APPLY

Guided Practice Have children place *Word Builder Cards u* and *g* in their *Word Builder*.

- Add *t* to *ug*. What word did you make?

- Change *t* to *j*. What word did you make?

- Change *j* to *h*. What word did you make?

- Change *g* to *m*. What word did you make?

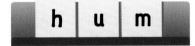

- Change *h* to *g*. What word did you make?

Independent Practice Write the words *dug*, *rug*, *bug*, *gum*, and *tug* on index cards and place them in a pocket chart. Have children read the words. Then have them choose one of the words to write and illustrate on drawing paper.

REACHING ALL LEARNERS

Diagnostic Check: Phonics

If... children have difficulty blending and building words,

Then... have them name the letters as they place them in their *Word Builder*. Say the sound and have them repeat the sound. Have them move their hand under the letters in the *Word Builder* as they blend the sounds with you.

ADDITIONAL SUPPORT ACTIVITIES

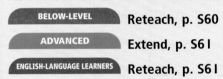

BELOW-LEVEL	Reteach, p. S60
ADVANCED	Extend, p. S61
ENGLISH-LANGUAGE LEARNERS	Reteach, p. S61

▲ **Practice Book page 12**

OBJECTIVES

• *To understand describing words*

• *To write describing words*

• *To write about animals*

Materials

■ chart from Literature Focus lesson (See page 577.)

■ *Library Book: Fish Faces*

■ drawing paper

■ crayons

Writing

Write a Description

DRAW AND WRITE

Talk about Describing Words Remind children that describing words can tell about size, color, and shape. Display the chart that was created in the Literature Focus lesson to list the characteristics of the fish in *Fish Faces*. Read the categories and describing words aloud.

Write a Description Make *Fish Faces* available to children. Have each child choose a fish to describe. Ask children to draw the fish they wish to tell about. Then have them use words from the chart to label their picture.

The fish has red eyes.

Self-Selected Writing Have children draw and write about anything they'd like. If they have difficulty thinking of a topic, have them ask two friends what they're going to write about.

FLORIDA STANDARDS/GLEs FCAT: LA.B.2.1.2.K.1 Record ideas; *Also* **LA.B.1.1.2.K.2** Basic formats; **LA.B.1.1.3.K.1** Spelling approximations; **LA.B.1.1.3.K.2** Print direction

WRAP UP  Share Time

Reflect on the Lesson Ask children to tell what they enjoy more—reading about fish or writing about fish. Have them take turns showing their picture and reading their description of favorite fish in *Fish Faces*.

S.S.R. Have children read silently from a book of their choice.

 Centers  MANIPULATIVES

Go Fish

In advance, cut out several cardboard fish that include a variety of shapes and colors. Attach a paper clip to each fish. Make a fishing pole by attaching a magnet to a length of string at the end of a pointer or yardstick. Place all the fish on the floor in the center. As children fish together, encourage them to describe each fish they catch.

 Materials

- several cardboard fish shapes

- paper clips

- classroom pointer or yardstick

- string

- magnet

Learning Centers

Choose from the following suggestions to enhance your learning centers for the theme Under the Ocean.
(Additional learning centers for this theme can be found on pages 522-524 and 628)

ART CENTER

Clay Fish

Tell children they will use clay or modeling dough to make fish. Ask children to name some different kinds, sizes, shapes, and colors of fish. Then have children choose one kind of fish they would like to make. Remind children that fish have gills and fins. Children can make an imaginary fish or model their creation after a real fish. When children finish, have them show their fish to other children in the art center and tell what kind of fish they made.

Materials
- modeling dough or clay

MANIPULATIVE CENTER

Letters, Sounds, Pictures

Have children fold a sheet of paper in half three times. When they unfold their paper, it will have eight squares on it. Place the following *Alphabet Cards* face down in a pile in the Manipulative Center: *c, d, f, g, o, s, t,* and *w*. One at a time, have children turn a card over and identify the letter on the card and the sound it makes. Have children write the letter in one of the squares on their paper and draw a picture of an ocean animal whose name begins with the letter.

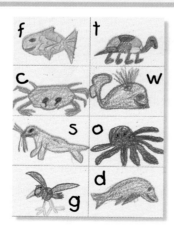

Materials
- Alphabet Cards *c, d, f, g, o, s, t, w*
- paper
- crayons

Teacher Notes

Teacher Notes

THEME 12

Week 2

Under the Ocean

ORAL LANGUAGE
15-30 Minutes

- **Phonemic Awareness**

- **Sharing Literature**

LEARNING TO READ
45 Minutes

- **Phonics**

- **Vocabulary**

Daily Routines
- Morning Message
- Calendar Language
- Writing Prompt

LANGUAGE ARTS
15-30 Minutes

- **Writing**
  Daily Writing Prompt

Day 1

Phonemic Awareness, 589
Rhyme Production

Sharing Literature, 590
 Read

Big Book: *Splash in the Ocean!*

(Skill) **Literature Focus, 591**
Action Words

 Phonics, 592 T
Introduce: Phonogram *-ut*

✏️ **Writing, 594**
Write Action Words

Writing Prompt, 594
Draw and write about self-selected topics.

Share Time, 595
Demonstrate action words and share pictures and sentences.

Day 2

Phonemic Awareness, 597
Rhyme Production

Sharing Literature, 598
 Read

Library Book: *Swimmy*

(Skill) **Literature Focus, 599**
Picture Clues

 Phonics, 600 T
Introduce: Phonogram *-un*

✏️ **Interactive Writing, 602**
Write a Story Map

Writing Prompt, 602
Draw and write about ways you help friends.

Share Time, 603
Retell *Swimmy* and share favorite parts of the story.

T = tested skill

Phonics

Phonograms
-ut, -un, -ug

Focus of the Week:
- PHONEMIC AWARENESS
- SHARING LITERATURE
- WRITING Action Words, Story Map, Sentences

Day 3

Phonemic Awareness, 605
Phoneme Counting

Sharing Literature, 606

 Read

Read-Aloud Anthology:
"There's a Hole in the Middle
of the Sea," p. 141

 Literature Focus, 607
Sequencing

Phonics, 608 T
Introduce: Phonogram *-ug*

 Writing, 610
Write a Sentence

Writing Prompt, 610
Draw and write about self-selected
topics.

Share Time, 611
Share favorite parts of the song and sing
new song verses.

Day 4

Phonemic Awareness, 613
Phoneme Blending

Sharing Literature, 614
Big Book of Rhymes and
Songs: "The Little Fishes,"
pp. 28–29

**Literature
Focus, 615**
Print Concepts

Phonics, 616 T
Review: Short Vowel /u/*u*

Read

DECODABLE BOOK 17
It Is Fun

 Interactive Writing, 618
Write a List

Writing Prompt, 618
Draw and write about favorite animals.

Share Time, 619
Share favorite parts of the Decodable
Book *It Is Fun* and read the list of ocean
animals.

Day 5

Phonemic Awareness, 621
Phoneme Substitution

Sharing Literature, 622

Read

Big Book: *Splash
in the Ocean!*

 **Literature Focus, 623**
Text Patterns

Phonics, 624 T
Build Sentences

 Shared Writing, 626
Write New Verses

Writing Prompt, 626
Draw and write about a trip to the ocean.

Share Time, 627
Share favorite parts of the story and sing
new song verses.

Day at a Glance
Day 1

WARM UP

Phonemic Awareness
Rhyme Production

Sharing Literature
Big Book:
Splash in the Ocean!

Read

Respond to Literature

Literature Focus: Action Words

Phonics
Phonogram *-ut*

Writing
Action Words

MORNING MESSAGE

Kindergarten News

Today is _____.

After school, (child's name) will go

_____.

Write Kindergarten News Talk with children about where they will go and what they will do after school today.

Use prompts such as the following to guide children as you write the news:

• **Tell me what you are going to do after school today.**

• **Who can show me the beginning of a word?**

• **Who can frame a word for me?**

• **How many words are in the second sentence?**

As you write the message, invite children to contribute by writing letters, names, or words they have previously learned. Remind them to use proper spacing, capitalization, and punctuation.

Calendar Language

Point to and read aloud the names of the days of the week. Ask what day today is. Ask what day comes before today. Say: *Yesterday was _____.* Invite children to name yesterday and today.

Sunday	Monday	Tuesday	Wednesday	Thursday	Friday	Saturday
		1	2	3	4	5
6	7	8	9	10	11	12
13	14	15	16	17	18	19
20	21	22	23	24	25	26
27	28	29	30	31		

FLORIDA STANDARDS/GLEs FCAT: LA.A.2.1.5.K.2 Get information; **LA.B.2.1.2.K.1** Record ideas; *Also* **LA.A.1.1.2.K.1** Print organization; **LA.C.1.1.3.K.1** Conversation rules; **LA.C.3.1.2.K.1** Questions

Phonemic Awareness

RHYME PRODUCTION

Generate Rhyming Words As you read the following sentences, ask children to listen for words that rhyme. Remind them that rhyming words are words that sound the same. Say:

The squirrel runs into the hut.

He takes along a big, brown nut.

Hut **is the last word in the first line. What word rhymes with** *hut*?

Say *hut—nut* **with me. The words** *hut* **and** *nut* **have the same middle and ending sound. They are rhyming words.**

Tell children that they are going to listen to some rhymes in which the last word is missing. Ask children to choose the word to complete each rhyme about a silly animal. Then repeat the rhyme, inserting the word.

See the silly pig,

wearing a curly _____.

Choose the word *wig* or *wag*. (*wig*)

The funny cat

put on a _____.

Choose the word *cap* or *hat*. (*hat*)

The flip-flop fish

flaps on the _____.

Choose the word *dish* or *pan*. (*dish*)

Ponies run

because it is _____.

Choose the word *fast* or *fun*. (*fun*)

Rabbit likes to bake

a coconut _____.

Choose the word *cake* or *pie*. (*cake*)

The chickens play

games in the _____.

Choose the word *hay* or *sun*. (*hay*)

Fox hid from ox

under a _____.

Choose the word *box* or *chair*. (*box*)

Six silly sheep

ride in a _____.

Choose the word *car* or *Jeep*. (*Jeep*)

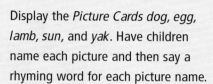

ADVANCED

Display the *Picture Cards dog, egg, lamb, sun,* and *yak*. Have children name each picture and then say a rhyming word for each picture name.

▲ **Big Book**

OBJECTIVES

• *To recall story events*

• *To recognize that print is read from left to right across the page*

• *To respond to a story through movement*

• *To recognize action words*

Materials

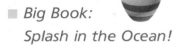

■ *Big Book: Splash in the Ocean!*

■ *self-stick name tags*

■ *marker*

■ *Music CD*

Sharing Literature

Read Splash in the Ocean!

READ ALOUD

Before Reading   Display *Splash in the Ocean!* Ask a child to track the print as you read the title aloud. Use these prompts to help children recall the story.

• **What ocean animals did you see in this story?** (fish, whales, seals, crabs)

• **What did the ocean animals do in the story?** (They played together in the ocean.)

During Reading   Reread the story aloud. As you read,

• invite different children to track the print on each page.

• point to the ocean animals and have children name them.

• pause to point out alliterative word pairs. After reading pages 10–11, focus on the words *scritchy scratchy*, by saying:

MODEL   **The words *scritchy scratchy* describe crabs moving along the bottom of the ocean. Crabs have hard shells that would scrape on rocks and sand. The words are fun to say, because they begin with the same sound. As I read, listen for other word pairs like this.**

FLORIDA STANDARDS/GLEs   **FCAT: LA.A.1.1.2.K.4** Words; **LA.A.1.1.4.K.1** Comprehension; **LA.A.2.1.1.K.1** Main idea; *Also* **LA.C.1.1.1.K.2** Oral language; **LA.C.3.1.2.K.1** Questions; **LA.D.2.1.2.K.2** Alliteration

RESPOND TO LITERATURE

Act Out the Story Make sea animal name tags with the words *fish*, *crab*, *seal*, and *whale* on them. Give each child one of the name tags to wear. Have children with the same animal name tag stand together in groups. Then play the song on the *Music CD*. Encourage children to sing along and move to the words of the song.

Literature Focus

ACTION WORDS

Review with children that some words tell about actions. Read pages 4–5 of *Splash in the Ocean!* Say:

Swimming is an action word. The word *swimming* tells what the fish do. Who can act out the word *swimming*?

Page through the rest of the *Big Book* and point out other action words and the animals doing the action such as *crawling*, *playing*, *jumping*, and *splashing*. Ask children to act out each word as you read it aloud.

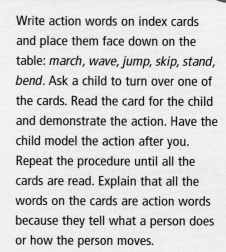

ENGLISH-LANGUAGE LEARNERS

Below / On-Level / Advanced / ELL

Write action words on index cards and place them face down on the table: *march*, *wave*, *jump*, *skip*, *stand*, *bend*. Ask a child to turn over one of the cards. Read the card for the child and demonstrate the action. Have the child model the action after you. Repeat the procedure until all the cards are read. Explain that all the words on the cards are action words because they tell what a person does or how the person moves.

ONGOING ASSESSMENT

As you share *Splash in the Ocean!* note whether children

- **recall story events.**
- **recognize that print is read from left to right across the page.**
- **can respond to a story through song and movement.**

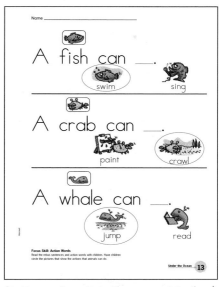

▲ **Practice Book page 13**

FLORIDA STANDARDS/GLEs **FCAT: LA.A.1.1.2.K.4** Words; **LA.A.1.1.3.K.5** Story elements; **LA.C.1.1.4.K.1** Sequence; *Also* **LA.C.1.1.1.K.2** Oral language; **LA.D.2.1.4.K.1** Media; **LA.E.2.1.1.K.2** Personal interpretations

OBJECTIVES

- To find letter patterns in words

- To blend letter patterns to read words

- To write consonant-vowel-consonant words

Materials

- ■ chart paper

- ■ marker

- ■ Write-On/Wipe-Off Boards

- ■ drawing paper

- ■ crayons

 Phonics

Phonogram -ut  *Introduce*

ACTIVE BEGINNING

Say a Rhyme Teach children the following rhyme with the following actions:

> **This is a cozy little hut.**
> (tips of fingers touching to make the shape of a roof)

> **First the door is open.**
> (palms facing away from body)

> **And then it is shut.**
> (palms together)

TEACH/MODEL

Discriminate Sounds Say the words *hut* and *shut* and have children repeat them. Ask how the two words are the same. (They both have /ut/; they rhyme.) Tell children that you are going to say some words and that they should use their fingers to make the shape of the little hut each time they hear a word that rhymes with *hut*:

| but | pig | rut | star | nut | cut |

Build -*ut* Words Write the word *nut* on chart paper. Track the print as children read the word. Then write the word *cut*. Again, track the print as children read the word. Ask children to read the two words and have them tell how they are the same. (They have *u* and *t*; they rhyme.) Continue by writing the word *hut* and having children read the word.

nut
cut
hut

FLORIDA STANDARDS/GLEs **FCAT: LA.A.1.1.2.K.5** Phonetic principles; *Also* **LA.A.1.1.2.K.1** Print organization; **LA.A.1.1.2.K.3** Sounds; **LA.D.1.1.1.K.1** Sound patterns; **LA.D.2.1.2.K.1** Patterned structures

PRACTICE/APPLY

Guided Practice Tell children that you will say some words. If the word rhymes with *shut*, have them write the word on their *Write-On/Wipe-Off Board*. Have them use the chart with *-ut* words as a reference.

thumbs ↑   thumbs ↓

wig   nut   hut   ran   sit   cut   win

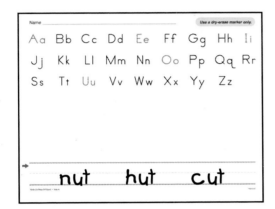

Independent Practice Distribute drawing paper to children and have them fold the paper in half. Have them write a *-ut* word in each half and illustrate it. Encourage them to read the words aloud.

REACHING ALL LEARNERS

Diagnostic Check: Phonics

If... children cannot blend letter patterns to read words,

Then... have them use their *Word Builder* and *Word Builder Cards* to build the word *cut*. Point to each letter and say its sound. Have children do the same. Then blend the sounds to read the word together. Continue with the words *nut, hut, but.*

ADDITIONAL SUPPORT ACTIVITIES

BELOW-LEVEL Reteach, p. S62

ADVANCED Extend, p. S63

ENGLISH-LANGUAGE LEARNERS Reteach, p. S63

early spelling

Early Spelling Have children write one of the *-ut* words from their *Write-On/Wipe-Off Board* in their journal.

▲ **Practice Book page 14**

Under the Ocean   593

OBJECTIVES

- To understand what action words are

- To write action words in sentences

Materials

- drawing paper

- crayons

Writing Every Day

Day 1: Action Words
Have children complete sentence frames to tell about actions they can do.

Day 2: Story Map
Have children work together to create a story map showing events in the book, *Swimmy*.

Day 3: Write Sentences
Have children use patterned language to write sentences to tell about things that can be in the middle of the sea.

Day 4: List
Have children work together to create a list of ocean animals they read about in this theme.

Day 5: New Verses to a Song
Have children complete a sentence frame to add to a Big Book.

LANGUAGE ARTS

Writing

Write Action Words

COMPLETE A SENTENCE FRAME

Talk About Action Words Remind children that an action word tells what someone or something does. Ask children to demonstrate actions such as walking, hopping, and turning as you say the words.

Write Action Words Write the following sentence frame on the board and read it together: *I can _____.* Ask children to think of an action word to complete the sentence. Fill in the blank and read the completed sentence; for example, *I can hop.* Tell children that they are going to write their own sentences with action words. Distribute drawing paper and have children copy and complete the sentence frame *I can _____.* Have children illustrate their sentences.

I can kik.

Self-Selected Writing Have children write and draw about anything they'd like. If they have difficulty thinking of a topic have them ask two friends what they're going to write about.

FLORIDA STANDARDS/GLEs **FCAT: LA.A.1.1.2.K.4** Words; **LA.A.1.1.2.K.6** Print meaning; **LA.A.1.1.3.K.4** Build vocabulary; **LA.B.2.1.2.K.1** Record ideas; *Also* **LA.A.1.1.3.K.2** Nouns and verbs; **LA.B.1.1.2.K.2** Basic formats; **LA.B.1.1.3.K.1** Spelling approximations; **LA.B.1.1.3.K.2** Print direction; **LA.B.1.1.3.K.3** Punctuation; **LA.B.2.1.4.K.1** Informational texts

WRAP UP

Share Time

Reflect on the Lesson   Invite children to demonstrate the actions of the fish, crabs, seals, and whales in Splash in the Ocean! Then ask them to show the picture they drew and read the sentence they wrote about themselves for today's Writing activity.

S.S.R.   Have children read silently from a book of their choice.

 **Centers** **MATH**

Seashell Sort

Ask children to examine a collection of seashells. Suggest various ways for children to sort the shells, such as arranging the shells in order from smallest to largest. Children can also sort the shells by shape and by color. Encourage children to make labels for their piles of shells.

 **Materials**

- seashells of different sizes, shapes, and colors

- index cards

- markers

FLORIDA STANDARDS/GLEs   **LA.A.1.1.2.K.1** Print organization; **LA.B.1.1.2.K.2** Basic formats; **LA.B.1.1.3.K.1** Spelling approximations; **LA.B.1.1.3.K.2** Print direction; **LA.B.2.1.4.K.1** Informational texts

Under the Ocean   **595**

Day at a Glance
Day 2

WARM UP

Phonemic Awareness
Rhyme Production

Sharing Literature
Library Book:
Swimmy

Read

Swimmy
by Leo Lionni

Develop Listening Comprehension

Respond to Literature

Literature Focus: Picture Clues

Phonics
Phonogram -un

Interactive Writing
Story Map

MORNING MESSAGE
Kindergarten News
This weekend (child's name) will

_____ .

Write Kindergarten News   Talk with children about things they like to do on the weekends.

Use prompts such as the following to guide children as you write the news:

- **What is your favorite thing to do on weekends?**
- **Who can show me where to start writing?**
- **Let's clap the syllables in (child's name). How many parts do you clap?**
- **Who can name the sound at the beginning of (child's name)?**

As you write the message, invite children to contribute by writing letters, names, or words they have previously learned. Remind them to use proper spacing, capitalization, and punctuation.

Calendar Language

Point to and read aloud the seasons of the year. Have children repeat the seasons of the year with you. Ask: *What season is it?* Encourage them to speak in complete sentences.

Sunday	Monday	Tuesday	Wednesday	Thursday	Friday	Saturday
		1	2	3	4	5
6	7	8	9	10	11	12
13	14	15	16	17	18	19
20	21	22	23	24	25	26
27	28	29	30	31		

FLORIDA STANDARDS/GLEs   FCAT: LA.A.1.1.2.K.5 Phonetic principles; **LA.B.2.1.2.K.1** Record ideas; *Also* **LA.A.1.1.2.K.1** Print organization; **LA.A.1.1.2.K.3** Sounds;

Phonemic Awareness

RHYME PRODUCTION

Name Rhyming Words   Use the rabbit puppet for the rhyming activity. Remind children that rhyming words are words that sound the same.

The rabbit likes to say words that rhyme. *Dock. Lock.* Say the words with the rabbit. *Dock* and *lock* are words that sound the same. *Dock* and *lock* are rhyming words.

Use the rabbit puppet to say the following rhyme. Ask children to participate by naming words that rhyme with each of the words you have the puppet say. Provide the initial phoneme for children and have them say the word.

Rhyme time!

Rhyme time!

Rabbit says a word—

You make the rhyme!

sun -/f/ (*fun*), /r/ (*run*)

pig -/w/ (*wig*), /j/ (*jig*)

cut -/h/ (*hut*), /n/ (*nut*)

hot -/d/ (*dot*), /g/ (*got*)

wet -/v/ (*vet*), /n/ (*net*)

cap -/t/ (*tap*), /l/ (*lap*)

pat -/h/ (*hat*), /k/ (*cat*)

chick -/p/ (*pick*), /l/ (*lick*)

bid -/k/ (*kid*), /d/ (*did*)

ship -/h/ (*hip*), /s/ (*sip*)

jug -/r/ (*rug*), /m/ (*mug*)

flop -/p/ (*pop*), /t/ (*top*)

▲ **"This Old Man,"** *Oo-pples and Boo-noo-noos: Songs and Activities for Phonemic Awareness*, **page 120.**

REACHING ALL LEARNERS

Diagnostic Check: Phonemic Awareness

If... children cannot name rhyming words,

Then... say the words *run* and *fun*. Tell children that the words rhyme because they have the same ending sound. Ask: **Does *sun* rhyme with *run* and *fun*? Does *bun*? Does *mat*?**

ADDITIONAL SUPPORT ACTIVITIES

BELOW-LEVEL	Reteach, p. S64
ADVANCED	Extend, p. S65
ENGLISH-LANGUAGE LEARNERS	Reteach, p. S65

Sharing Literature

Read Swimmy

READ ALOUD

Before Reading   Display the cover of *Swimmy* and read the title aloud. Point out that Leo Lionni wrote the story and drew the pictures. Then ask a child to turn to the title page. Tell children: **This is the title page. It also tells the title of the book and the name of the author and illustrator.** Provide the following background information.

• **Swimmy is the black fish on the cover.**

• **Fish often travel together in groups called** *schools*.

Ask children: **What do you think this story will be about?**

During Reading   Read the story aloud. As you read,

• pause to let children find Swimmy in each picture.

• point to the appropriate pictures to help children understand story vocabulary such as *medusa*, *lobster*, *eel*, and *sea anemones*.

• pause to make or discuss predictions. Model how children can do this.

MODEL   **After the tuna fish swallows all the little red fish, Swimmy feels lonely and sad. I think he will find some other fish to swim with because the ocean is big and is full of fish.**

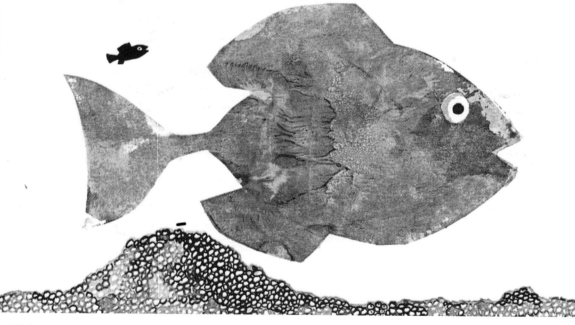

▲ **Library Book**

OBJECTIVES

• *To identify the title page of a book*

• *To make and confirm predictions*

• *To use picture clues to understand text*

Materials

■ *Library Book: Swimmy*

FLORIDA STANDARDS/GLEs   **FCAT: LA.A.1.1.2.K.4** Words; **LA.A.1.1.3.K.5** Story elements; **LA.A.1.1.4.K.1** Comprehension; *Also* **LA.A.1.1.1.K.1** Predictions; **LA.A.1.1.3.K.2** Nouns and verbs; **LA.A.2.1.4.K.1** Illustrations; **LA.C.1.1.1.K.2** Oral language; **LA.C.3.1.2.K.1** Questions

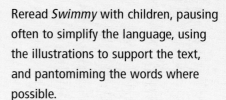

DEVELOP LISTENING COMPREHENSION

After Reading   Have children answer these questions:

- **What happens to the first school of fish Swimmy swims with?** (A tuna fish eats them.)

- **How does this make Swimmy feel?** (scared and lonely)

- **What does Swimmy teach the other fish?** (how to look and swim like a big fish)

RESPOND TO LITERATURE

Discuss the Story   Have children tell what they like about the story. Invite them to refer to illustrations in the book as they comment.

PICTURE CLUES

Remind children that picture clues can help them understand a story better. Point out that Swimmy said he would be the eye of the school of fish. Display the illustration from the story that shows this. Talk about what you can learn from the picture.

MODEL   The author never says why Swimmy would be the eye of the fish. When I look at the picture, I can see that Swimmy is black and the rest of the fish are red, so Swimmy helps make the fish shape look real.

Encourage children to give examples of other parts of the story that they figured out by using picture clues.

ENGLISH-LANGUAGE LEARNERS

Reread *Swimmy* with children, pausing often to simplify the language, using the illustrations to support the text, and pantomiming the words where possible.

ONGOING ASSESSMENT

As you share *Swimmy*, note whether children

- can identify the title page of a book.

- use pictures to help understand text.

- can make and confirm predictions.

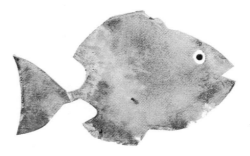

FLORIDA STANDARDS/GLEs   FCAT: LA.A.1.1.4.K.1 Comprehension; **LA.A.2.1.1.K.1** Main idea; **LA.E.1.1.2.K.1** Story elements; *Also* **LA.A.2.1.4.K.1** Illustrations; **LA.C.3.1.2.K.1** Questions

Under the Ocean   599

LEARNING TO READ

Phonics

Phonogram -un ✓ Introduce

ACTIVE BEGINNING

Say a Rhyme   Teach children the following rhyme. Have them run in place as they say the words.

Run, run, run,

Run in the sun!

Run, run, run.

Running is fun!

TEACH/MODEL

Discriminate Sounds   Say the words *run* and *sun* and have children repeat them. Ask how the two words are the same. (They both have /un/; they rhyme.) Tell children that you are going to say some words and that they should clap when they hear a word that rhymes with *run*:

sun   sip   fun   rug   bun   wag

Build -un Words   Write the word *sun* on chart paper. Track the print as children read the word. Then write the word *bun*. Again, track the print as children read the word. Ask children to read the two words and have them tell how they are the same. (They have *u* and *n*; they rhyme.) Continue by writing the word *run* and having children read the word.

sun
bun
run

🗺 **FLORIDA STANDARDS/GLEs   FCAT: LA.A.1.1.2.K.5** Phonetic principles; *Also* **LA.A.1.1.2.K.1** Print organization; **LA.A.1.1.2.K.3** Sounds; **LA.D.1.1.1.K.1** Sound patterns; **LA.D.2.1.2.K.1** Patterned structures

PRACTICE/APPLY

Guided Practice Tell children that you will say some words. If the word rhymes with *fun*, have them write the word on their *Write-On/Wipe-Off Board*. Have them use the chart with *-un* words as a reference. *thumbs ↑ thumbs ↓*

zip   sun   bun   wish   pan   top   run

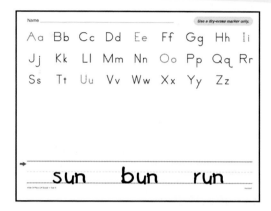

Independent Practice Distribute drawing paper to children with the sentence frame *Look at the* _____. Have children complete the sentence, using one of the words written on the chart paper. Then have them illustrate their sentence.

Look at the sun.

FLORIDA STANDARDS/GLEs FCAT: LA.A.1.1.2.K.5 Phonetic principles; *Also* LA.B.1.1.2.K.2 Basic formats; LA.B.1.1.3.K.2 Print direction; LA.C.1.1.1.K.1 Follow directions;

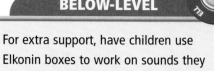

BELOW-LEVEL

For extra support, have children use Elkonin boxes to work on sounds they hear in the words. Ask them to move disks into the boxes for *sun, run, bun,* and *fun.*

ADVANCED

Have children write and draw about something that is fun to do in the sun.

early spelling

Have children write one of the *-un* words from their *Write-On/Wipe-Off Board* in their spelling journal.

▲ **Practice Book page 15** *HW*

OBJECTIVES

- *To describe story events*
- *To write a story map*

Materials

- *Library Book: Swimmy*
- chart paper
- marker

Interactive Writing

Write a Story Map

SHARE THE PEN

Talk About Story Maps Remind children that a story map can help readers remember what happens in a story. A story map tells what happens at the beginning, middle, and ending of a story.

Write a Story Map Draw three large boxes on chart paper and label the boxes: *Beginning, Middle, Ending*. Then use the following prompts to help children write:

Let's write a story map for Swimmy.

We'll write a sentence to tell what happens at the beginning of the story. Who can say the words?

Where do I begin to write? Who can show me?

Who can write a letter they know?

Who can place their finger next to a word to make a space?

Have children write letters and words they know. Have them take turns placing a finger next to a word to mark a space.

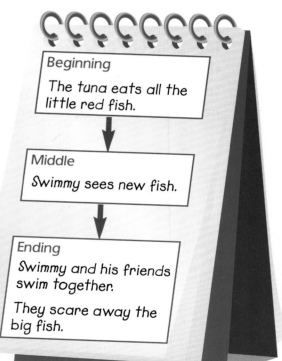

Beginning
The tuna eats all the little red fish.

Middle
Swimmy sees new fish.

Ending
Swimmy and his friends swim together.
They scare away the big fish.

Journal Writing Have children draw and write about something they do to help their friends.

FLORIDA STANDARDS/GLEs FCAT: LA.A.1.1.4.K.1 Comprehension; **LA.B.1.1.2.K.3** Sequence; **LA.B.2.1.2.K.1** Record ideas; **LA.E.1.1.2.K.1** Story elements; *Also* **LA.B.1.1.2.K.2** Basic formats; **LA.B.1.1.3.K.1** Spelling approximations; **LA.B.1.1.3.K.2** Print direction; **LA.B.1.1.3.K.3** Punctuation; **LA.B.2.1.1.K.2** Contribute ideas; **LA.C.3.1.2.K.1** Questions;

WRAP UP Share Time

Reflect on the Lesson Have children retell the story of Swimmy, using the story map. Ask them to tell about their favorite part of the story.

S.S.R. Have children read silently from a book of their choice.

Centers ABC LETTERS AND WORDS

Charades

Write the words *cut, hug, sun, run, tug,* and *cup* on chart paper and post the chart in the center. Write each word on an index card. Children can take turns choosing a word card and reading the word to themselves. Then they can act out the word for others to guess. The child who guesses the word can point to the word on the chart paper and take the next turn.

Materials

- chart paper
- marker
- index cards

FLORIDA STANDARDS/GLEs   FCAT: LA.A.1.1.2.K.4 Words; *Also* **LA.A.1.1.3.K.2** Nouns and verbs; **LA.A.2.1.2.K.1** Select materials; **LA.C.2.1.2.K.1** Nonverbal cues; **LA.C.3.1.1.K.1** Speak clearly; **LA.E.2.1.1.K.2** Personal interpretations

Day at a Glance
Day 3

Phonemic Awareness

Phoneme Counting

Sharing Literature

Read-Aloud Anthology:
"There's a Hole in the Middle of the Sea"

Read

Develop Concept Vocabulary

Respond to Literature

Literature Focus: Sequencing

Phonics

Phonogram *-ug*

Writing

Sentences

MORNING MESSAGE

Kindergarten News

(Child's name)'s favorite nursery

rhyme is _____.

He/she likes it because _____.

Write Kindergarten News Talk with children about their favorite nursery rhymes and why they like them.

Use prompts such as the following to guide children as you write the news:

- **What is your favorite nursery rhyme?**
- **Who can show me where to start writing?**
- **What should I write at the beginning of (child's name)?**
- **Let's count the letters in (child's name).**

As you write the message, invite children to contribute by writing letters, names, or words they have previously learned. Remind them to use proper spacing, capitalization, and punctuation.

Calendar Language

Point to and read aloud the names of the months of the year. Tell children there are twelve months in a year. Point to and name the month. Ask: *What month is it?*

Sunday	Monday	Tuesday	Wednesday	Thursday	Friday	Saturday
		1	2	3	4	5
6	7	8	9	10	11	12
13	14	15	16	17	18	19
20	21	22	23	24	25	26
27	28	29	30	31		

FLORIDA STANDARDS/GLEs   FCAT: LA.A.2.1.5.K.2 Get information; **LA.B.2.1.2.K.1** Record ideas; *Also* **LA.A.1.1.2.K.1** Print organization; **LA.A.1.1.2.K.2** Alphabet; **LA.A.1.1.2.K.3** Sounds; **LA.C.1.1.2.K.1** Choose literature; **LA.C.1.1.3.K.1** Conversation rules; **LA.C.3.1.2.K.1** Questions

Phonemic Awareness

PHONEME COUNTING

Segment Sounds in Words   Tell children they can listen to words you say and tell you what sounds they hear in those words. Use the rabbit puppet for this activity.

MODEL   The rabbit is going to say the word *run* in parts: /r/ /u/ /n/. Say it with the rabbit: /r/ /u/ /n/.

How many sounds do you hear in *run*? (three)

What sounds do you hear in *run*? (/r/ /u/ /n/)

Use the same procedure with the following words.

bug (three; /b/ /u/ /g/)   **on** (two; /o/ /n/)

up (two; /u/ /p/)   **mug** (three; /m/ /u/ /g/)

go (two; /g/ /o/)   **bat** (three; /b/ /a/ /t/)

leg (three; /l/ /e/ /g/)   **sun** (three; /s/ /u/ /n/)

gap (three; /g/ /a/ /p/)   **pup** (three; /p/ /u/ /p/)

ad (two; /a/ /d/)   **sit** (three; /s/ /i/ /t/)

gum (three; /g/ /u/ /m/)   **met** (three; /m/ /e/ /t/)

in (two; /i/ /n/)   **hot** (three; /h/ /o/ /t/)

FLORIDA STANDARDS/GLEs   FCAT: LA.A.1.1.2.K.5 Phonetic principles; **LA.C.1.1.1.K.1** Follow directions; **LA.C.3.1.2.K.1** Questions

Under the Ocean   605

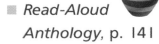

▲ **Read-Aloud
Anthology**

OBJECTIVES

- *To sing a song*

- *To understand real and
make-believe*

- *To recognize cumulative
text*

- *To understand sequence*

Materials

- *Read-Aloud
Anthology*, p. 141

- *Music CD*

- chart paper

- tape

- white drawing paper

- crayons

- diluted blue paint

- paintbrushes

- construction paper shapes

Sharing Literature

Read "There's a Hole in the Middle of the Sea"

READ ALOUD

Before Reading   Turn to page 141 of the *Read-Aloud Anthology* and read the title of the song, "There's a Hole in the Middle of the Sea." Use the following prompts to set a purpose for reading:

- **What do you think you would find in the middle of the sea?**

- **Is there really a hole in the middle of the sea?**

Ask children what they think the song might be about. You may wish to model thinking.

MODEL   **I don't believe there is a hole in the middle of the sea. This song is probably about make-believe things. I'll read the words to the song to find out.**

During Reading   Read the song lyrics aloud. As you read,

- emphasize the rhythm of the words.

- pause after the second verse to call attention to the cumulative pattern of the text, by saying:

MODEL   **Each time I sing a new verse, I add a word and repeat all the other words in the list of things in the hole in the middle of the sea. It's fun to try to remember all the words when I sing the song with the new word each time!**

Repeat the song a time or two, encouraging children to name what comes next. Invite them to clap to the rhythm as they sing.

Then play the *Music CD* and have children sing the song with you.

FLORIDA STANDARDS/GLEs   FCAT: LA.C.1.1.4.K.1 Sequence; **LA.E.1.1.1.K.1** Genres; **LA.E.1.1.2.K.1** Story elements; *Also* **LA.C.1.1.1.K.2** Oral language; **LA.D.1.1.1.K.1** Sound patterns; **LA.D.2.1.2.K.1** Patterned structures; **LA.E.2.1.2.K.1** Patterned structures;

DEVELOP CONCEPT VOCABULARY

After Reading Write the following words from the song on chart paper: *sea, hole, log, bump, frog.* Point to and read each word. Then have children read the words with you. Ask the following questions:

- **Which word means the same thing as the ocean?** (*sea*)
- **Which words rhyme with *bog*?** (*log, frog*)
- **Which words are in the title of the song?** (*hole, sea*)
- **Which word rhymes with *thump*?** (*bump*)

RESPOND TO LITERATURE

Draw a Picture Have children illustrate the song with crayons on white drawing paper. When they are finished, help them brush diluted blue paint over the entire drawing to create an underwater effect.

Literature Focus

SEQUENCING

Remind children that in stories and songs, things happen in a certain order. On chart paper, use tape to attach a large circular piece of blue paper to represent the hole in the middle of the sea. Also cut construction paper shapes for the log with a bump and a frog. As you reread the words to the song, have children tell the order the shapes should be placed: log, bump, frog. Sing the song with children, pointing to each part of the visual as it is mentioned. Tell children that the song would not make sense if the frog came first or if the hole came last.

BELOW-LEVEL

Give children a set of the visuals to represent the objects in the song. Reread the song and help them place the items on the table in the same order as the words in the song.

ONGOING ASSESSMENT

As you share "There's a Hole in the Middle of the Sea," note whether children

- recognize cumulative text by naming what comes next.
- can clap the rhythm of rhymed text.
- can sing a song.

FLORIDA STANDARDS/GLEs **FCAT: LA.A.1.1.2.K.4** Words; **LA.A.1.1.2.K.5** Phonetic principles; **LA.A.1.1.3.K.5** Story elements; **LA.E.1.1.1.K.1** Genres; **LA.E.1.1.2.K.1** Story elements; *Also* **LA.A.1.1.3.K.2** Nouns and verbs; **LA.C.3.1.2.K.1** Questions; **LA.D.1.1.1.K.1** Sound patterns; **LA.E.2.1.2.K.1** Patterned structures

Phonics

Phonogram -ug ✓ Introduce

OBJECTIVES

- To find letter patterns in words
- To blend letter patterns to read words
- To write consonant-vowel-consonant words

Materials

- chart paper
- marker
- *Write-On/Wipe-Off Boards*
- drawing paper
- crayons

ACTIVE BEGINNING

Say a Rhyme Teach children the following rhyme. Say the rhyme twice and then have children join in.

Give your Teddy bear a hug.

Hug, hug, hug.

Give a little bug a hug.

What? Hug a bug? Ugh!

TEACH/MODEL

Discriminate Sounds Say the words *hug* and *bug* and have children repeat them. Ask how the two words are the same. (They both have /ug/; they rhyme.) Tell children that you are going to say some words and that they should hug themselves when they hear a word that rhymes with *hug*:

jug	hit	rug	top	box	tug

Build -ug Words Write the word *mug* on chart paper. Track the print as children read the word. Then write the word *bug*. Again, track the print as children read the word. Ask children to read the two words and have them tell how they are the same. (They have *u* and *g*; they rhyme.) Continue by writing the word *rug* and having children read the word.

mug

bug

rug

FLORIDA STANDARDS/GLEs   FCAT: LA.A.1.1.2.K.5 Phonetic principles; *Also* **LA.A.1.1.2.K.1** Print organization; **LA.A.1.1.2.K.3** Sounds; **LA.D.1.1.1.K.1** Sound patterns; **LA.D.2.1.2.K.1** Patterned structures

PRACTICE/APPLY

Guided Practice   Tell children that you will say some words. If the word rhymes with *jug*, have them write the word on their *Write-On/Wipe-Off Board*. Have them use the chart with *-ug* words as a reference. ~~thumbs↑   thumbs↓~~

| fox | mug | pat | rug | fit | pet | bug |

Independent Practice   Distribute drawing paper to children with the sentence frame *I see a _____.* Have children complete the sentence, using one of the words written on the chart paper. Then have them illustrate their sentence.

FLORIDA STANDARDS/GLEs   **FCAT: LA.A.1.1.2.K.5** Phonetic principles; **LA.B.1.1.2.K.2** Basic formats; **LA.C.1.1.1.K.1;** Follow directions; **LA.D.1.1.1.K.1** Sound patterns

BELOW-LEVEL

For extra support, have children use the word wheel from the *Teacher's Resource Book*, p. 158. On the inside wheel, write *ug*. On the outside wheel, write the letters *b, h, r, m,* and *t*. Have children turn the outside wheel to make words with *-ug*. Help children read aloud the words they make.

ADVANCED

Encourage children to write other words that belong in the *-ug* family.

early spelling

Early Spelling   Have children write one of the *-ug* words from their *Write-On/Wipe-Off Board* in their spelling journal.

▲ **Practice Book page 16**

OBJECTIVES

- *To brainstorm ideas*

- *To write a sentence to add to a song*

Materials

- *Read-Aloud Anthology*, p. 141

- chart paper

- marker

- sentence frames

- drawing paper

- glue

- crayons

Writing

Write a Sentence

ADD VERSES TO A SONG

Talk About the Song Reread the song "There's a Hole in the Middle of the Sea." Ask children to think of other things that could be in the middle of the sea. Record children's ideas on chart paper.

Write a Sentence Duplicate and distribute the following sentence frame to children: *There's a _____ in the middle of the sea.* Have children complete the sentence frame, paste it on a piece of drawing paper and illustrate it. Encourage children to complete more than one sentence frame.

There's a __roc__ in the middle of the sea.

Self-Selected Writing Have children write and draw about anything they'd like. If they have difficulty thinking of a topic have them ask two friends what they're going to write about.

FLORIDA STANDARDS/GLEs **FCAT: LA.B.2.1.2.K.1** Record ideas; *Also* **LA.B.1.1.1.K.2** Generate ideas; **LA.B.1.1.2.K.2** Basic formats; **LA.B.1.1.3.K.1** Spelling approximations; **LA.B.1.1.3.K.2** Print direction; **LA.B.1.1.3.K.3** Punctuation; **LA.C.1.1.1.K.2** Oral language

WRAP UP Share Time

Reflect on the Lesson Have children tell what they like about the song, "There's a Hole in the Middle of the Sea." Use the sentences children wrote during the Writing activity to sing new verses to the song.

S.S.R. Have children read silently from a book of their choice.

 **Centers** **SAND AND WATER**

Sand Sculpture

Dampen sand with water and mix it thoroughly. Have children use their hands or the plastic containers to create different shapes. Encourage children in the center to work together to build a sand castle or other structure. Remind children to wash their hands well afterward.

Materials

- sand table or dishpan filled with sand

- water

- small plastic containers in various shapes and sizes

FLORIDA STANDARDS/GLEs **FCAT: LA.A.2.1.2.K.1** Select materials; **LA.C.1.1.1.K.2** Oral language; **LA.E.2.1.1.K.1** Background knowledge; **LA.E.2.1.1.K.2** Personal interpretations

Day at a Glance
Day 4

Phonemic Awareness

Phoneme Blending

Sharing Literature

Big Book of Rhymes and Songs:
"The Little Fishes"

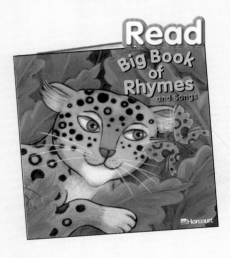

Read
Big Book of Rhymes and Songs

Harcourt

Respond to Literature

Literature Focus: Print Concepts

Phonics

Reading

Decodable Book 17: It Is Fun

Interactive Writing

List

MORNING MESSAGE

Kindergarten News

(Child's name)'s favorite food is

_____. (Name of food) is

good because _____.

Write Kindergarten News Talk with children about their favorite food and why they like it best.

Use prompts such as the following to guide children as you write the news:

- **What is your favorite food?**
- **Who can show me the first letter in the word (name of food)?**
- **Let's clap for (child's name). How many parts do you clap?**
- **Who can point to a word they know and read it?**

As you write the message, invite children to contribute by writing letters, names, or words they have previously learned. Remind them to use proper spacing, capitalization, and punctuation.

Calendar Language

Point to the numbers on the calendar. Tell children that the days of each month are numbered and the numbers tell the date. Point to and read aloud the date. Name the month and the date.

Sunday	Monday	Tuesday	Wednesday	Thursday	Friday	Saturday
		1	2	3	4	5
6	7	8	9	10	11	12
13	14	15	16	17	18	19
20	21	22	23	24	25	26
27	28	29	30	31		

FLORIDA STANDARDS/GLEs **FCAT: LA.A.1.1.2.K.5** Phonetic principles; **LA.A.2.1.5.K.2** Get information; **LA.B.2.1.2.K.1** Record ideas; *Also* **LA.A.1.1.2.K.2** Alphabet; **LA.A.1.1.2.K.3** Sounds; **LA.C.1.1.3.K.1** Conversation rules; **LA.C.3.1.2.K.1** Questions

Phonemic Awareness

PHONEME BLENDING

Blend Sounds Tell children they can listen to the sounds you say and guess the word you are saying. Use the rabbit puppet for this activity.

MODEL Today the rabbit is saying words in parts. Listen as it says this word: /r/ /u/ /g/. What is this word? /r/ /u/ /g/. Say it with the rabbit: /r/ /u/ /g/. Now say the word: *rug*.

Tell children the rabbit is going to say some more words in parts. Have them listen and then say the word.

/s/ /u/ /n/ (*sun*)	/k/ /u/ /t/ (*cut*)	/b/ /u-/g/ (*bug*)
/k/ /a/ /t/ (*cat*)	/p/ /e/ /t/ (*pet*)	/f/ /u/ /n/ (*fun*)
/n/ /o/ /t/ (*not*)	/m/ /a/ /n/ (*man*)	/n/ /e/ /t/ (*net*)
/n/ /u/ /t/ (*nut*)	/h/ /u/ /g/ (*hug*)	/r/ /u/ /g/ (*rug*)
/h/ /a/ /t/ (*hat*)	/t/ /e/ /n/ (*ten*)	/h/ /u/ /t/ (*hut*)
/b/ /u/ /n/ (*bun*)	/s/ /i/ /t/ (*sit*)	/f/ /o/ /ks/ (*fox*)
/h/ /a/ /m/ (*ham*)	/f/ /i/ /n/ (*fin*)	/h/ /u/ /m/ (*hum*)

BELOW-LEVEL

Model the process of blending sounds by saying /u/ /p/. Have children do the same. Then say /uupp/ and have children do the same. Follow the procedure for *run*, *big*, and *hug*.

/n/ /e/ /t/

/b/ /u/ /g/

Day 4

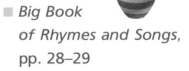

▲ **Big Book of Rhymes and Songs**

OBJECTIVES
- *To sing a song*
- *To use context to understand vocabulary*
- *To recognize that print is read from left to right across the page*
- *To understand print concepts*

Materials
- *Big Book of Rhymes and Songs, pp. 28–29*
- *Music CD*

Sharing Literature

Read "The Little Fishes"

READ ALOUD

Before Reading Display pages 28–29 of the *Big Book of Rhymes and Songs* and read the title aloud while you track the print. Model how to set a purpose for rereading the song lyrics.

MODEL The title reminds me that this song is about little fish. But what do the little fish do? I'll read the words again so I can remember what the fish do.

During Reading Read the song lyrics aloud. As you read,
- invite a child to track the print with you.
- pause to let children frame the repetitive words.
- pause to discuss the meaning of the word *flying* in this song.

MODEL In this song, the word *flying* does not mean "to move through the air like a bird." Sometimes fish jump out of the water and they look as if they are flying.

Then play the *Music CD* and have children sing the song while using their hands to pantomime the fish movements.

LOS pescaditos

Los pescaditos andan
en el agua,
nadan, nadan, nadan,
vuelan, vuelan, vuelan.

Son chiquititos, chiquititos,
chiquititos,
vuelan, vuelan, vuelan,
nadan, nadan, nadan.

28

FLORIDA STANDARDS/GLEs FCAT: LA.A.1.1.2.K.4 Words; **LA.A.1.1.3.K.5** Story elements; **LA.A.1.1.4.K.1** Comprehension; **LA.E.1.1.1.K.1** Genres; *Also* **LA.A.1.1.2.K.1** Print organization; **LA.A.1.1.3.K.2** Nouns and verbs; **LA.C.1.1.1.K.2** Oral language; **LA.C.2.1.2.K.1** Nonverbal cues; **LA.D.2.1.2.K.1** Patterned structures

RESPOND TO LITERATURE

Discuss the Song   Have children tell what they like about the song. Invite children to describe live fish they have seen, telling how the fish looked and moved.

Literature **Focus**

PRINT CONCEPTS

Display the song on pages 28–29 of the *Big Book of Rhymes and Songs*. Point to the words *The Little Fishes* and *Los pescaditos* in each title.

MODEL   The words *The Little Fishes* begin with uppercase letters. That's because the words are the title of the song. If I write the title in Spanish, it would be *Los pescaditos.*

Ask children to point to other words in the song that begin with an uppercase letter. (*The, Swimming, Flying, They're*) Discuss why these words begin with uppercase letters. (The words begin each line of the song.)

Little Fishes

The little fishes they move
through the water,
imming, swimming, swimming,
Flying, flying, flying.

They're very little, very little,
very little,
Flying, flying, flying,
imming, swimming, swimming.

29

REACHING ALL LEARNERS

Diagnostic Check: Comprehension

If... children cannot understand the use of uppercase letters in print.

Then... show several examples of titles, using the poems and rhymes in the *Big Book of Songs and Rhymes*. As you read each title while tracking the print, invite children to take turns identifying the uppercase letters they see. Point out how the first word in each line also begins with an uppercase letter.

ADDITIONAL SUPPORT ACTIVITIES

BELOW-LEVEL   Reteach, p. S66

ADVANCED   Extend, p. S67

ENGLISH-LANGUAGE LEARNERS   Reteach, p. S67

ONGOING ASSESSMENT

As you share "The Little Fishes," note whether children

- recognize that print is read from left to right across the page.
- can sing a song.
- can use context to understand vocabulary.
- use pantomime to respond to the song.

FLORIDA STANDARDS/GLEs   FCAT: LA.C.3.1.3.K.1 Basic vocabulary; *Also* **LA.D.1.1.1.K.2** Functions of language; **LA.E.2.1.1.K.1** Background knowledge

OBJECTIVE

To decode short vowel /u/u words

Materials

- index cards
- marker
- pocket chart
- *High-Frequency Word Card here*
- *Decodable Book 17: It Is Fun*
- drawing paper
- crayons

Phonics

Short Vowel /u/u ✔ Review

TEACH/MODEL

Review Blending Write the word *fun* on an index card and place it in a pocket chart. Move your hand under the letters, blend them, and say the word. **/ffuunn/—fun** Have children blend the sounds and say the word.

Write the words *It* and *is* on index cards. Place the index cards *It is fun* and the *High-Frequency Word Card here* in the pocket chart. Add a period at the end. As you point to the words, have children read them.

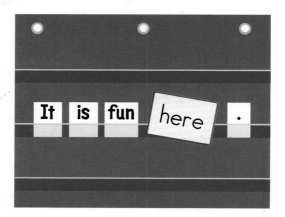

PRACTICE/APPLY

Read the Book Distribute copies of *It Is Fun*. Read the title together, encouraging children to point to each word as they say it. Then have children read the book, pointing to each word as they read.

Respond Have children draw a picture of one of the ways Pam has fun.

🏴 FLORIDA STANDARDS/GLEs FCAT: **LA.A.1.1.2.K.4** Words; **LA.A.1.1.2.K.5** Phonetic principles; **LA.A.1.1.3.K.4** Build vocabulary; **LA.A.1.1.3.K.5** Story elements; **LA.E.1.1.1.K.1** Genres; *Also* **LA.A.1.1.2.K.3** Sounds; **LA.A.1.1.3.K.1** Frequent words

Decodable Book 17: *It Is Fun*

Come on, Sam.
It is fun here.
I like it a lot.

2

I do not like it, Pam.
It is not fun.

3

Look at the bug, Sam.
See, it is fun.

4

I do not like it, Pam.
It is not fun.

5

Look at the net, Sam.
See, it is fun.

6

I do not like it, Pam.
It is not fun.

7

I like it, Pam.
It is fun here.

8

High-Frequency Words

come, the, here, see, like, do, look

Decodable Words

See the list on page T15.

School-Home Connection

Take-Home
Book Version

◄ Decodable Book
It Is Fun

BELOW-LEVEL

Reread the story with children. Have them match *High-Frequency Word Cards* with words in the book.

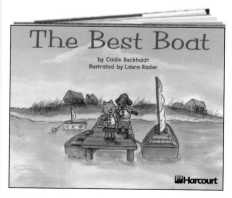

▲ *The Best Boat*
Independent Reader 34

Under the Ocean 617

OBJECTIVES

- *To share information and ideas, speaking in complete, coherent sentences*

- *To write a list*

Materials

- ■ chart paper

- ■ marker

Interactive Writing

Write a List

SHARE THE PEN

Talk About Ocean Animals   Remind children that one way to remember things is to make a list. Help children recall the stories, songs, and poems they have read about in this theme.

Write a List   Tell children that together they will write a list of the different ocean animals they have read about so far in the theme. Use prompts such as the following:

What animal shall we list first?

Who will write the first letter in the word?

Who will write the letters in the word?

Who will write that word?

Adjust the prompts to the task as children suggest animal names. Have children say the word they want to write. Have them write as many letters and words as they can.
Write letters for them as needed.

Ocean Animals

seal
crab
whale
fish
eel
jellyfish

Writing Every Day

My Journal

Journal Writing   Have children draw and write in their journal about a favorite animal. Have children include where the animal lives.

FLORIDA STANDARDS/GLEs   FCAT: LA.A.1.1.2.K.4 Words; **LA.A.1.1.3.K.5** Story elements; **LA.B.2.1.2.K.1** Record ideas; *Also* **LA.A.1.1.3.K.2** Nouns and verbs; **LA.B.1.1.2.K.1** Dictate messages; **LA.B.1.1.2.K.2** Basic formats; **LA.B.1.1.3.K.1** Spelling approximations; **LA.B.1.1.3.K.2** Print direction; **LA.B.1.1.3.K.3** Punctuation; **LA.B.2.1.1.K.2** Contribute ideas; **LA.B.2.1.4.K.1** Informational texts; **LA.C.3.1.2.K.1** Questions

WRAP UP Share Time

Reflect on the Lesson Have children talk about their favorite part of the book It Is Fun. Have them tell what words they learned to read. Display the "Ocean Animals" list that children wrote. Have each child read the word he or she contributed.

↳ Read the List together.

S.S.R. Sustained Silent Reading Have children read silently from a book of their choice.

Centers ABC — LETTERS AND WORDS

Fish Word Puzzles

In advance, cut eight fish shapes from construction paper. Label them with phonograms and beginning sounds, such as *r-un, f-un, s-un, n-ut, t-ug, b-ug, c-ut, h-ut*. Then cut each fish into two puzzle pieces, with one piece containing the beginning sound and the other piece containing the phonogram. Have children fit the puzzles together to make words. Ask them to say the words they make.

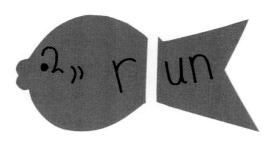

Materials

- construction paper
- marker
- scissors

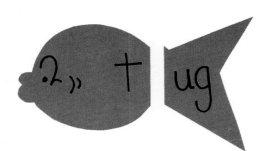

FLORIDA STANDARDS/GLEs **FCAT: LA.A.1.1.2.K.5** Phonetic principles; *Also* **LA.A.1.1.2.K.1** Print organization; **LA.A.1.1.2.K.3** Sounds; **LA.A.1.1.3.K.2** Nouns and verbs; **LA.C.1.1.1.K.1** Follow directions

Under the Ocean **619**

WARM UP

Phonemic Awareness
Phoneme Substitution

Sharing Literature
Big Book:
Splash in the Ocean!

Read

Respond to Literature

Literature Focus: Text Patterns

Phonics
Build and Read Sentences

Shared Writing
New Verses

MORNING MESSAGE

Kindergarten News

Today is _____. It is a

special day for (child's name).

It is special because _____.

Write Kindergarten News Talk with children about why today is a special day. Perhaps it is someone's birthday, or someone made a new friend.

Use prompts such as the following to guide children as you write the news:

- **Who has special news today?**
- **Does anyone have a birthday today?**
- **Who can show me where to begin writing?**
- **Who can show me a space between words?**
- **Let's count the number of words in the first sentence.**

As you write the message, invite children to contribute by writing letters, names, or words they have previously learned. Remind them to use proper spacing, capitalization, and punctuation.

Calendar Language

Point to and name the day of the week. Ask what today is. Ask children to name the next school day.

Sunday	Monday	Tuesday	Wednesday	Thursday	Friday	Saturday
		1	2	3	4	5
6	7	8	9	10	11	12
13	14	15	16	17	18	19
20	21	22	23	24	25	26
27	28	29	30	31		

FLORIDA STANDARDS/GLEs **FCAT: LA.A.2.1.5.K.2** Get information; **LA.B.2.1.2.K.1** Record ideas; *Also* **LA.A.1.1.2.K.1** Print organization; **LA.C.1.1.3.K.1** Conversation rules; **LA.C.3.1.2.K.1** Questions

Phonemic Awareness

PHONEME SUBSTITUTION

Substitute Initial Sounds   Tell children that you are going to say a word. Then explain that you will change the first sound to make a new word.

MODEL   *Tug.* I'm going to change the /t/ in *tug* to /r/. The new word is *rug.* Say it with me. Now you try it. Say *sit.* Now change the /s/ in *sit* to /f/. What's the new word? *(fit)*

Have children repeat the process with the following words.

Say *man.* Change the /m/ to /v/. What's the new word? *(van)*

Say *dot.* Change the /d/ to /p/. What's the new word? *(pot)*

Say *bell.* Change the /b/ to /t/. What's the new word? *(tell)*

Say *miss.* Change the /m/ to /k/. What's the new word? *(kiss)*

Say *hut.* Change the /h/ to /b/. What's the new word? *(but)*

Say *cup.* Change the /k/ to /p/. What's the new word? *(pup)*

ADVANCED

Display the *Picture Cards boy, fish, gate, hen, nail,* and *queen.* Have children say each picture name and then say a new word by replacing the beginning sound with a different sound.

FLORIDA STANDARDS/GLEs   **FCAT: LA.A.1.1.2.K.5** Phonetic principles; *Also* **LA.C.1.1.1.K.1** Follow directions; **LA.C.3.1.2.K.1** Questions

Under the Ocean   **621**

▲ **Big Book**

OBJECTIVES

• *To recognize that book titles are made up of separate words*

• *To participate in a rereading by naming pictures and pantomiming actions*

• *To recognize text patterns*

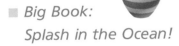

Materials

■ *Big Book: Splash in the Ocean!*

■ *chart paper*

■ *marker*

Sharing Literature

Read Splash in the Ocean!

READ ALOUD

Before Reading   Display *Splash in the Ocean!* and point to the title as you read it aloud. As you track the print, ask children to count the words in the title with you. Have children name any words they recognize. Then use these prompts to recall the selection.

• **What are the ocean animals doing in this story?** (They are playing together.)

• **Do the animals all make the same sounds?** (No, they make different sounds.)

During Reading   Reread the story aloud. As you read,

• invite children to say the animal names as you point to the pictures and pantomime the actions as you read the action words.

• talk about picture details. Encourage children to describe what they see by providing an example.

MODEL **I see that the animals in this story enjoy playing together. I can tell that the animals are happy by looking at the pictures—the animals are all smiling.**

FLORIDA STANDARDS/GLEs   **FCAT: LA.C.2.1.1.K.1** Main idea; **LA.E.1.1.2.K.1** Story elements; *Also* **LA.A.1.1.2.K.1** Print organization; **LA.A.2.1.4.K.1** Illustrations; **LA.C.1.1.1.K.2** Oral language; **LA.C.2.1.2.K.1** Nonverbal cues

RESPOND TO LITERATURE

Make Up Animal Sounds   Have children make up other phrases like *flippy, flappy, splash* and *wibble, wobble, splash* that describe how sea animals move. Some examples can be *teeter, totter, splash* for penguins and *wiggle, waddle, splash* for ducks.

TEXT PATTERNS

Turn to pages 4–11 in *Splash in the Ocean!* and read the text aloud. Point out that many of the words are the same. Write the following on chart paper: *All the _____ are _____ in the ocean.* Page through the book to frame and read this phrase each time it is repeated. Tell children that when a story has text that repeats, they can predict some of the words they will see on each page.

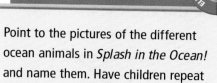

ENGLISH-LANGUAGE LEARNERS

Point to the pictures of the different ocean animals in *Splash in the Ocean!* and name them. Have children repeat the animal names with you.

ONGOING ASSESSMENT

As you share *Splash in the Ocean!*, note whether children

• participate in a rereading by naming pictures and pantomiming actions.

• can describe picture details.

FLORIDA STANDARDS/GLEs   **FCAT: LA.A.1.1.2.K.4** Words; **LA.A.1.1.4.K.1** Comprehension; **LA.C.1.1.4.K.1** Sequence; *Also* **LA.A.1.1.3.K.2** Nouns and verbs; **LA.D.2.1.1.K.1** Word choice; **LA.E.2.1.2.K.1** Patterned structures

OBJECTIVE

To use knowledge of letters, words, and sounds to read simple sentences

Materials

- chart paper
- marker
- index cards
- pocket chart
- *Decodable Books 16, 17: Is It a Fish? It Is Fun*

Phonics
Build Sentences

ACTIVE BEGINNING

Repeat a Rhythmic Rhyme   Teach children the following rhyme and clapping patterns:

A bug sat in the sun, (clap, clap)

It was having lots of fun! (clap, clap)

A bug sat in a hut, (clap, clap)

Eating a crunchy nut! (clap, clap)

TEACH/MODEL

Review *-ut, -un, -ug*   Copy the chart below onto ~~chart paper.~~ board
Read aloud the words and remind children that the words in each column belong to the same word family—the *-ut* family, the *-un* family, and the *-ug* family.

Model reading the word *hut* first by elongating the sounds /hhuutt/ and then reading it naturally. Then have children elongate the sounds /hhuutt/ and read the word. Continue with the remaining words. Frame the words *hut* and *nut* and ask how the two words are alike. (Possible responses: They rhyme; they both have *u* and *t*.) Do the same for *sun* and *run* and *bug* and *rug*.

hut	sun	bug
nut	run	rug

FLORIDA STANDARDS/GLEs   **FCAT: LA.A.1.1.2.K.5** Phonetic principles; *Also* **LA.A.1.1.2.K.3** Sounds; **LA.C.1.1.1.K.2** Oral language; **LA.D.1.1.1.K.1** Sound patterns; **LA.D.2.1.2.K.1** Patterned structures

PRACTICE/APPLY

Guided Practice   Write the following words on index cards: *The, the, is, in, bug, hut, nut, sun, rug, jug*. Display the words in a pocket chart as shown.

Point to each word and have children read it. If necessary remind them to blend the sounds together to read the word. Then rearrange the cards and add a period card to make the following sentence:

Track the words as you assist children in reading the sentence. Then replace *hut* with the word *nut* and have children read the sentence. Continue by substituting different words to provide many opportunities for children to read the sentence.

Independent Practice   Have children reread the *Decodable Books Is It A Fish?* and *It Is Fun* for more practice reading connected text.

FLORIDA STANDARDS/GLEs   FCAT: LA.A.1.1.2.K.5 Phonetic principles; *Also* **LA.A.1.1.2.K.1** Print organization; **LA.A.1.1.2.K.3** Sounds; **LA.A.1.1.3.K.1** Frequent words

Under the Ocean   625

BELOW-LEVEL

Have children use their *Word Builders* and *Word Builder Cards* to build and blend the following words: *fun, run, hug, cut.*

ENGLISH-LANGUAGE LEARNERS

Write the sentences from Guided Practice onto sentence strips. As you read the sentences, make sure children understand the meanings of *hut, nut, sun, rug,* and *jug.*

early spelling

Have children write one of the words from the Guided Practice sentences in their spelling journal. Ask children to draw a picture to describe that word.

Name _____	
I	come
see	the
bug	Here
sun	at

Read and Build Sentences
Have children cut out the word cards. Ask them to use the words on both sides of the cards to make sentences. Have children read the sentences to a partner.

Under the Ocean **17**

▲ **Practice Book pages 17–18**

OBJECTIVES

- To brainstorm ideas
- To write new lyrics to a song

Materials

- *Big Book: Splash in the Ocean!*
- chart paper
- marker

Shared Writing

Write New Verses

ADD TO A SONG

Talk About the Song   Recall with children the ocean animals in *Splash in the Ocean!* Page through the book and point out the repeating text pattern: *All the _____ are _____ in the ocean.* Have children name other sea animals that could be moving about in the ocean.

Write New Verses   Tell children that together they will write some new sentences for the song. On the chart paper, write the sentence frame *All the _____ are _____ in the ocean.* Read the sentence frame, tracking the print. Then ask children to respond by saying words for you to write in the two blanks; for example, *All the sea turtles are diving in the ocean.*

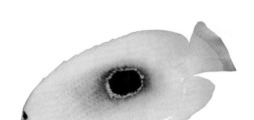

All the jellyfish are spinning in the ocean.

All the lobsters are creeping in the ocean.

Journal Writing   Have children draw and write in their journals about a real or make-believe trip to the ocean.

FLORIDA STANDARDS/GLEs   FCAT: LA.A.1.1.2.K.4 Words; *Also* **LA.A.1.1.2.K.1** Print organization; **LA.A.1.1.3.K.2** Nouns and verbs; **LA.B.1.1.1.K.2** Generate ideas; **LA.B.1.1.2.K.2** Basic formats; **LA.B.1.1.3.K.1** Spelling approximations; **LA.B.1.1.3.K.2** Print direction; **LA.B.2.1.1.K.1** Familiar experiences; **LA.B.2.1.1.K.2** Contribute ideas; **LA.B.2.1.4.K.1** Informational texts

WRAP UP Share Time

Reflect on the Lesson Have children discuss their favorite part of *Splash in the Ocean!* Display the sentences children suggested about ocean animals during Shared Writing. Use the sentences to sing new verses of the song.

S.S.R. Sustained Silent Reading Have children read silently from a book of their choice.

Centers

SCIENCE

Science Experiment

Have children take turns with a partner choosing an object from an assortment of items such as coins, a pencil, a cork, a shell. As children work in the center, they should name the object and predict whether it will sink or float. Then have children place the object in the tub of water to confirm the prediction.

Materials

- small waterproof items that will sink or float, such as corks, pencils, coins, plastic toys, shells, Ping Pong balls

- large plastic basin of water

FLORIDA STANDARDS/GLEs FCAT: LA.A.2.1.2.K.1 Select materials; **LA.C.1.1.1.K.1** Follow directions; **LA.D.2.1.2.K.1** Patterned structures; **LA.E.2.1.1.K.1** Background knowledge; **LA.E.2.1.2.K.1** Patterned structures

Under the Ocean 627

Learning Centers

Choose from the following suggestions to enhance your learning centers for the theme Under the Ocean.
(Additional learning centers for this theme can be found on pages 522–524 and 582)

WRITING CENTER

Ocean Rhymes

Tell children they will work with a partner to write a rhyme or poem about the ocean. Have partners fold a piece of paper in half, and tell partners to list words that describe the ocean and marine life in one column. In the other column, children can write words that rhyme with the ocean words. Have children use the rhymes from their list to write and illustrate an ocean poem.

sea	me be
fish	dish wish
crab	grab
shark	bark hark

The sea is big to me.

Materials

- lined paper
- pencils
- crayons

LITERACY CENTER

Describe a Drawing

Give each child a sheet of paper, and have children draw a picture of animals that live near or in the ocean. Then have children exchange pictures with a partner. Give each child a sentence strip. Have them complete the sentence with the names of the animals they see in the picture. Children can glue the sentence to the back of the picture it describes and then read it to their partner.

Materials

- paper
- crayons
- sentence strip: Here are
  ____, ____, ____, and
  ____.
- pencils
- glue sticks

Teacher Notes

Teacher Notes

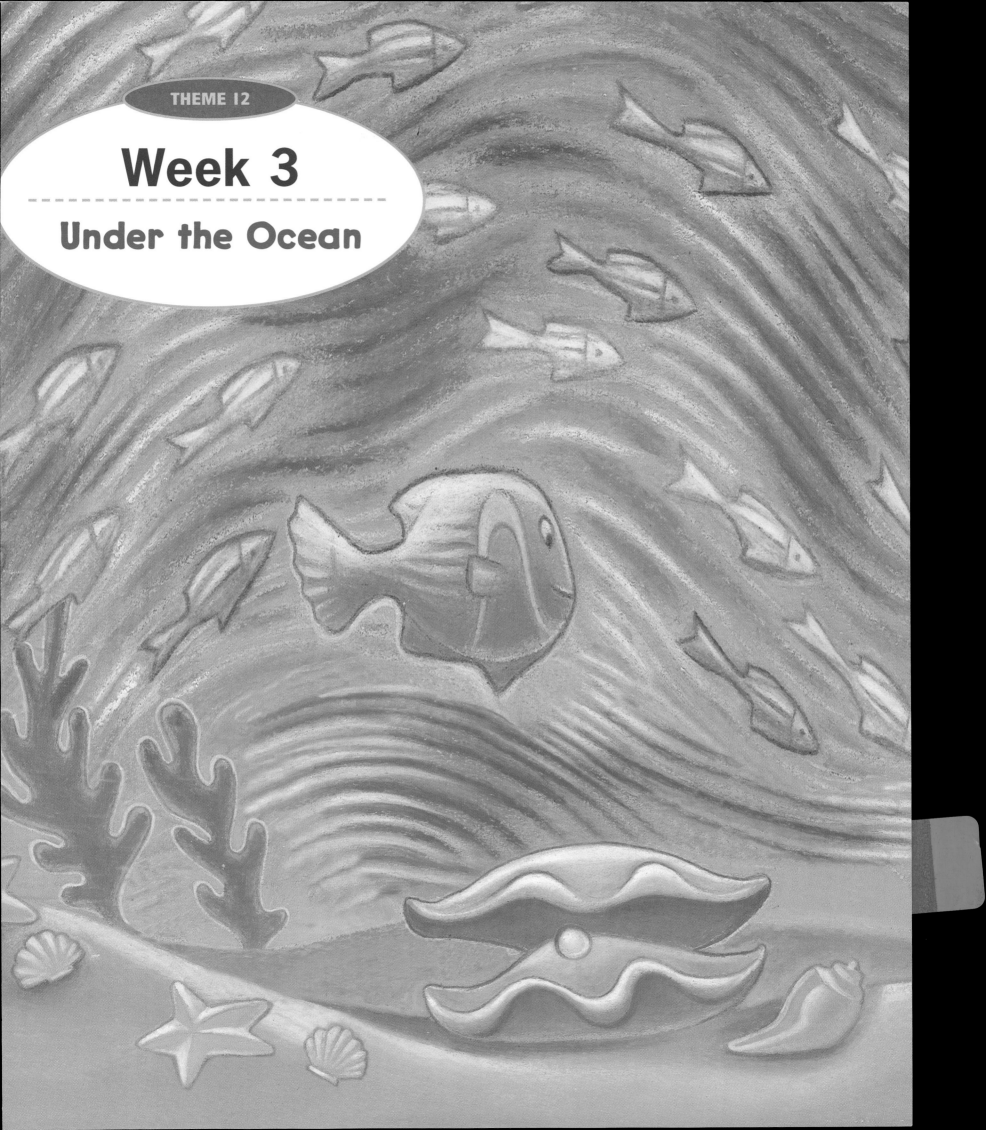

Week 3

Under the Ocean

15–30 Minutes

ORAL LANGUAGE

- **Phonemic Awareness**

- **Sharing Literature**

45 Minutes

LEARNING TO READ

- **Phonics**

- **Vocabulary**

Daily Routines
- Morning Message
- Calendar Language
- Writing Prompt

15–30 Minutes

LANGUAGE ARTS

- **Writing**
  Daily Writing Prompt

Day 1

Phonemic Awareness, 635
Phoneme Substitution

Sharing Literature, 636
 Read
Library Book: *Swimmy*

(Skill) **Literature Focus, 637**
Comparing Genres

 **Phonics, 638 T**
Review: Short Vowels /a/*a*, /e/*e*, /i/*i*, /o/*o*, /u/*u*

 Interactive Writing, 640
Writing Process: Prewrite

Writing Prompt, 640
Draw and write about self-selected topics.

Share Time, 641
Share story summaries and discuss book preferences.

Day 2

Phonemic Awareness, 643
Phoneme Blending

Sharing Literature, 644
Read-Aloud Anthology: "The Seashore Noisy Book," pp. 112–115

 (Skill) **Literature Focus, 645**
Visualizing

 Phonics, 646 T
Review: Short Vowels /a/*a*, /e/*e*, /i/*i*, /o/*o*, /u/*u*

 Read
DECODABLE BOOK 18
A Bug Can Tug

 Interactive Writing, 648
Writing Process: Draft

Writing Prompt, 648
Draw and write about the five senses.

Share Time, 649
Share favorite parts of the lesson and read the class poem.

T = tested skill

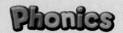 **Phonics**

Review /a/a, /e/e, /i/i, /o/o, /u/u

Focus of the Week:
- PHONEMIC AWARENESS
- SHARING LITERATURE
- WRITING: (Writing Process)

Day 3

Phonemic Awareness, 651
Phoneme Deletion

Sharing Literature, 652
Big Book: *Splash in the Ocean!*

 Literature Focus, 653
Picture Details

 Phonics, 654 T
Review: Short Vowels /a/a, /e/e, /i/i, /o/o, /u/u

Read
DECODABLE BOOK 19
Sid Hid

Interactive Writing, 656
Writing Process: Respond and Revise

Writing Prompt, 656
Draw and write about self-selected topics.

Share Time, 657

Read
Author's Chair

Day 4

Phonemic Awareness, 659
Phoneme Deletion

Sharing Literature, 660
Read-Aloud Anthology: "If You Ever," p. 30

 Literature Focus, 661
Making Inferences

Phonics, 662 T
Review: Short Vowels /a/a, /e/e, /i/i, /o/o, /u/u

Read
DECODABLE BOOK 20
In a Sub

Interactive Writing, 664
Writing Process: Edit

Writing Prompt, 664
Draw and write about animals.

Share Time, 665
Retell the Decodable Book *In a Sub* and share journal writings.

Day 5

Phonemic Awareness, 667
Phoneme Addition

Sharing Literature, 668
Read

Read-Aloud Anthology: "The Seashore Noisy Book," pp. 112–115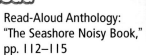

 Literature Focus, 669
Questions for Research

Phonics, 670 T
Build Sentences

Interactive Writing, 672
Writing Process: Publish

Writing Prompt, 672
Draw and write about favorite kindergarten activities.

Share Time, 673
Share pictures of Muffin.

Day at a Glance
Day 1

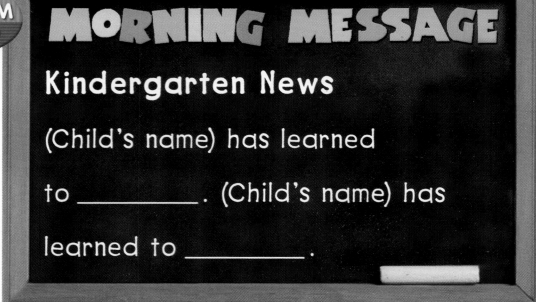

Phonemic Awareness
Phoneme Substitution

Sharing Literature
Library Book:
Swimmy

Read

Develop Concept Vocabulary

Respond to Literature

Lilterature Focus:
Comparing Genres

Phonics
Short Vowels *a, e, i, o, u*

Interactive Writing
Writing Process: Prewrite

MORNING MESSAGE

Kindergarten News

(Child's name) has learned

to _____. (Child's name) has

learned to _____.

Write Kindergarten News   Talk with children about new things they can do. Talk about how much fun it is to try new things.

Use prompts such as the following to guide children as you write the news:

- **Tell about something new you have learned to do.**
- **Who can show me the top of the page?**
- **Let's listen for the beginning sound in (child's name).**
- **How many words are there in the first sentence?**

As you write the message, invite children to contribute by writing letters, names, or words they have previously learned. Remind them to use proper spacing, capitalization, and punctuation.

Calendar Language

Point to and read aloud the names of the days of the week. Name the days of the week again. Invite children to join in and clap for each day. Ask: *What day is it?*

Sunday	Monday	Tuesday	Wednesday	Thursday	Friday	Saturday
		1	2	3	4	5
6	7	8	9	10	11	12
13	14	15	16	17	18	19
20	21	22	23	24	25	26
27	28	29	30	31		

FLORIDA STANDARDS/GLEs   FCAT: LA.A.1.1.3.K.4 Build vocabulary; **LA.A.2.1.5.K.2** Get information; **LA.B.2.1.2.K.1** Record ideas; *Also* **LA.A.1.1.2.K.2** Alphabet; **LA.A.1.1.3.K.1** Frequent words; **LA.C.1.1.3.K.1** Conversation rules; **LA.C.3.1.2.K.1** Questions

Phonemic Awareness

PHONEME SUBSTITUTION

Substitute Middle Sounds   Tell children that you are going to say a word. Then explain that you will change the middle sound to make a new word.

MODEL   *But.* Say the word with me. What word will we have if we change the /u/ in *but* to /a/? The new word is *bat.* Say the word. Now you try it. Say *fin.* Now change the /i/ to /u/. What's the new word? *(fun)*

Have children repeat the process with the following words.

Say *ten.* Change the /e/ to /a/. What's the new word? *(tan)*

Say *ran.* Change the /a/ to /u/. What's the new word? *(run)*

Say *tug.* Change the /u/ to /a/. What's the new word? *(tag)*

Say *pin.* Change the /i/ to /e/. What's the new word? *(pen)*

Say *hop.* Change the /o/ to /i/. What's the new word? *(hip)*

Say *bag.* Change the /a/ to /u/. What's the new word? *(bug)*

REACHING ALL LEARNERS

Diagnostic Check: Phonemic Awareness

If... children cannot substitute middle sounds,

Then... assign each of four children one of the following sounds: /h/, /u/, /t/, /a/. Have the first child say /h/, the second child say /u/, and the third child say /t/. Have children say the word, *hut.* Then repeat the procedure, replacing the second child with the fourth child (who says /a/) and have children say the new word, *hat.*

ADDITIONAL SUPPORT ACTIVITIES

BELOW-LEVEL   Reteach, p. S68

ADVANCED   Extend, p. S69

ENGLISH-LANGUAGE LEARNERS   Reteach, p. S69

▲ **Library Book**

OBJECTIVES

- *To locate the title and name of the author of a story*

- *To use pictures to understand story words and story action*

- *To compare genres*

Materials

- *Library Book: Swimmy*

- drawing paper

- crayons

- *Library Book: Fish Faces*

Sharing Literature

Read Swimmy

READ ALOUD

Before Reading   Display the cover of *Swimmy*. Have a child point to the title. Ask: **How many words are in this title?** (one) Ask a child to point to the name *Leo Lionni.* Remind children that this is the name of the author and illustrator. Help children set a purpose for listening to the story as you reread it.

MODEL **The big fish wants to eat Swimmy and his friends. I think Swimmy saves his friends from the big fish. I'll read the story again to find out if I am right.**

During Reading   Reread the story aloud. As you read,

- point to the picture details that illustrate story words and tell more about what is happening.

- discuss ways Swimmy is different from other fish.

MODEL **Swimmy is a different color than the other fish in the school. He is also different because he swims faster than his brothers and sisters. Swimmy is smart and clever. He thinks of a way to chase the big, scary fish away.**

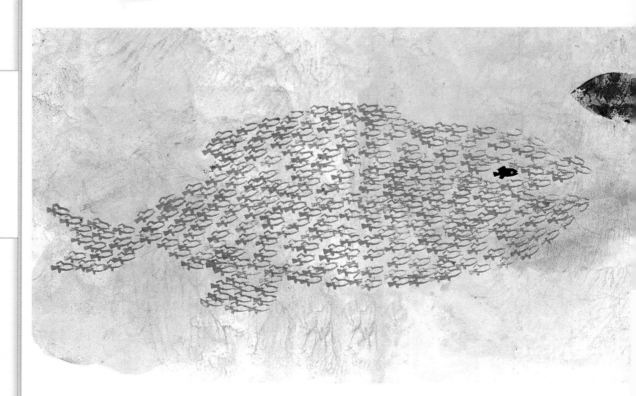

FLORIDA STANDARDS/GLEs   FCAT: LA.A.1.1.2.K.6 Print meaning; **LA.A.1.1.3.K.5** Story elements; **LA.A.2.1.5.K.2** Get information; **LA.E.1.1.1.K.1** Genres. *Also* **LA.A.2.1.4.K.1** Illustrations; **LA.C.1.1.1.K.2** Oral language; **LA.C.3.1.2.K.1** Questions

DEVELOP CONCEPT VOCABULARY

After Reading   Write the following words on the board: *tuna*, *medusa*, *lobster*, *eel*, *sea anemones*. Read the words aloud and have children repeat them with you. Explain that these are the names of sea creatures that Swimmy sees in the ocean. Have a child point to the picture of each ocean animal as you talk about it.

- *Tuna* is the big fish that eats all the little red fish.
- A *medusa* is a type of jellyfish. Some jellyfish can be poisonous.
- A *lobster* is a shellfish that many people like to eat.
- An *eel* is a long, slippery fish that looks like a snake.
- *Sea anemones* are ocean animals that look like plants.

RESPOND TO LITERATURE

Draw and Write About the Story   Have children draw and label a picture that shows their favorite part of the story.

COMPARING GENRES

Display *Swimmy* and *Fish Faces*. Point to *Swimmy* and tell children that this book tells a story that is make-believe.

MODEL In this story, Swimmy **talks to other fish. He teaches them to swim together to trick the big fish. In real life, fish don't talk, so this story is make-believe.**

As you page through *Fish Faces* have children tell how this book is different, even though it too is about fish. (This book gives facts about fish. It is an information book. It has photographs of fish instead of illustrations.) Confirm that children can learn something about real fish by reading this book.

ADVANCED

Challenge children to transfer the skill they have just learned. Have children work in pairs. Direct them to choose a book in the Literacy Center that they have read, and tell whether it is a story or a book with real information.

ONGOING ASSESSMENT

As you share *Swimmy*, note whether children

- can locate the title and name of the author of a story.
- use pictures to understand story words and story action.

FLORIDA STANDARDS/GLEs   FCAT: LA.A.1.1.2.K.4 Words; **LA.A.1.1.2.K.6** Print meaning. *Also* **LA.E.2.1.1.K.2**
Personal interpretations

Under the Ocean   637

OBJECTIVE

To match vowels a, e, i, o, u to their sounds

Materials

- *Letter and Sound Charts 10, 12, 14, 17, 19*

- *Tactile Letter Cards a, e, i, o, u*

- *Write-On/Wipe-Off Boards*

- *Picture/Word Cards alligator, cat, egg, hen, inchworm, pig, dog, umbrella, bus*

- teacher-made picture/word card *olive*

- pocket chart

- *Picture Cards alligator, cat, hat, yak, egg, jet, nest, inchworm, pig, milk, fox, dog, umbrella, bus, sun*

- teacher-made picture card *ox*

Phonics

Short Vowels *a, e, i, o, u* ✔ Review

ACTIVE BEGINNING

Recite "Apples"
Review with children the rhyme "Apples." As you recite the rhyme have children listen for /a/. Then have them clap to the rhythm as they say the rhyme together.

Apples

Adam and Alice

Alex and Ann

Eat juicy red apples

As much as they can.
by Susan Little

TEACH/MODEL

Review Letter and Sound   Display *Letter and Sound Chart 10.*

Touch the letter *a.* **What is the name of the letter?**

This letter stands for the /a/ sound. When you say this letter, your mouth stays open. Say /a/ /a/ /a/.

Read aloud the rhyme on the *Letter and Sound Chart*, tracking the print. Read aloud the *Aa* words in the rhyme. Then point to each *a* and have children say the /a/ sound.

What letter stands for the /a/ sound?

Have children join in as you read the rhyme again. Ask them to open their mouth as they say the /a/ sound. Repeat the procedure to review the letters *e, i, o,* and *u.*

FLORIDA STANDARDS/GLEs   FCAT: LA.A.1.1.2.K.5 Phonetic principles; *Also* **LA.A.1.1.2.K.1** Print organization; **LA.A.1.1.2.K.3** Sounds; **LA.C.3.1.2.K.1** Questions; **LA.D.1.1.1.K.1** Sound patterns

PRACTICE/APPLY

Guided Practice Distribute *Tactile Letter Card a* and *Write-On/Wipe-Off Boards*. Children will use the three-box grid on side B of the board. Then place the *Picture/Word Cards alligator* and *cat* in a pocket chart. Say the names of the pictures as you point to the *a* in each. Have children repeat the words.

Tell children: **Some words begin with *a* and some words have *a* in the middle.**

Point to the *a* in *alligator*. **The /a/ sound is at the beginning of *alligator*.**

Point to the *a* in *cat*. **The /a/ sound is in the middle of *cat*.**

I'm going to say some words. If the /a/ sound is at the beginning of the word, put your letter *a* in the beginning box. If the /a/ sound is in the middle of the word, put your letter *a* in the middle box.

Model the procedure, using the words *ant* and *fan*. Next, say these words:

ax   hat   apple   ant

Follow the same procedure for *e* as in *egg* and *hen*; *i* as in *inchworm* and *pig*; *o* as in *olive* and *dog*; and *u* as in *umbrella* and *bus*.

Independent Practice Distribute the *Picture Cards alligator, cat, hat, yak, umbrella, bus, sun, egg, jet, nest, inchworm, pig, milk, fox, dog,* and the teacher-made picture card, *ox*. Tell children to look at each *Picture Card*, say the word aloud, and decide what vowel sound they hear at the beginning or in the middle of each word. Then have them sort the *Picture Cards* into piles according to the vowel sound.

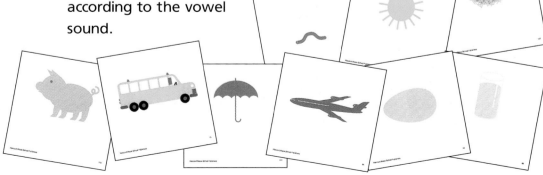
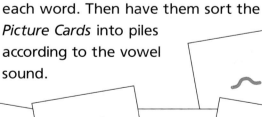

BELOW-LEVEL

Display the *Picture Cards egg, alligator, umbrella, inchworm,* and the teacher-made card *ox*. Say the name of each picture, emphasizing the initial sound. Next, say /a/ and have children point to the *Picture Card* whose name begins with *a*. Continue with the vowels *e, o, i,* and *u*.

▲ **Practice Book pages 19–20**

Under the Ocean 639

OBJECTIVES

- *To recall characteristics of a poem*

- *To generate ideas about a topic*

Writing Every Day

Day 1: Prewrite

Talk about what a poem is. Have children create a list of ocean animals.

Day 2: Draft

Have children choose a topic for a poem and write a draft of a poem about an ocean animal.

Day 3: Respond and Revise

Have children change or add words to revise a poem.

Day 4: Proofread

Have children check the poem they have written for capital letters and punctuation.

Day 5: Publish

Have children create a poem poster.

Writing Process

Writing a Poem

PREWRITE

Generate Ideas for Writing   Reread the poems "The Little Fishes" on pages 28–29 in the *Big Book of Rhymes and Songs* and "Down by the Bay" on pages 12–13. Talk with children about what a poem is. Ask how a poem is different from regular sentences they write. (A poem often rhymes while regular sentences do not; the lines of a poem are not always complete sentences.) Reread "Down by the Bay" and have children name rhyming words they hear. (*grow, go, say, bay, whale, tail*) Mention that some poems, like "Down by the Bay," are turned into songs. Frame lines in the poem "The Little Fishes" to show how some lines repeat words.

Make a List   Ask children what the two poems tell about. (sea animals) Have children name other animals that live in the ocean. As children respond, list the animal names on chart paper.

> fish
> whale
> crab
> seal
> octopus
> shark
> jellyfish

Writing Every Day
My Journal

Self-Selected Writing Have children write and draw about anything they'd like. If they have difficulty thinking of a topic have them ask two friends what they're going to write about.

FLORIDA STANDARDS/GLEs   FCAT: LA.B.2.1.2.K.1 Record ideas; **LA.E.1.1.1.K.1** Genres. *Also* **LA.B.1.1.1.K.2** Generate ideas; **LA.B.1.1.3.K.1** Spelling approximations; **LA.B.1.1.3.K.2** Print direction; **LA.B.2.1.1.K.2** Contribute ideas; **LA.E.2.1.2.K.1** Patterned structures

WRAP UP Share Time

Reflect on the Lesson   Invite children to share the pictures they drew and labeled that show their favorite part of the story, *Swimmy*. Have children talk about which book they liked best—*Swimmy* or *Fish Faces*.

S.S.R. Sustained Silent Reading   Have children read silently from a book of their choice.

Centers ABC LETTER AND WORD

Letter Match

Have partners place all the vowel cards face up on a table. Children can take a turn to choose a card, name the letter, and find its lowercase or uppercase match. Children can place the matching letters in the pocket chart and write both letters on the *Write-On/Wipe-Off Board*. Children should continue this activity until all the letters have been matched.

Materials

- sets of *Word Builder Cards A, a, E, e, I, i, O, o, U, u*
- pocket chart
- *Write-On/Wipe-Off Board*
- marker

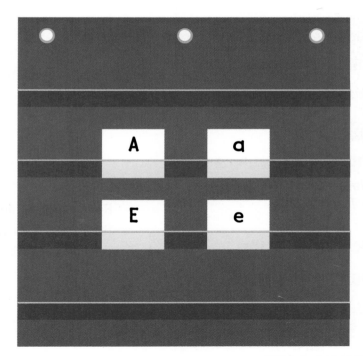

FLORIDA STANDARDS/GLEs   **FCAT: LA.E.1.1.2.K.1** Story elements. *Also* **LA.A.2.1.4.K.1** Illustrations; **LA.C.1.1.1.K.1** Follow directions

Under the Ocean   **641**

Day at a Glance
Day 2

WARM UP

Phonemic Awareness
Phoneme Blending

Sharing Literature
Read-Aloud Anthology:
"The Seashore Noisy Book"

Read

KINDERGARTEN
READ-ALOUD
Anthology
Harcourt

Develop Listening Comprehension

Respond to Literature

Literature Focus: Visualizing

Phonics
Reading
Decodable Book 18: *A Bug Can Tug*

Interactive Writing ✏️

Writing Process: Draft

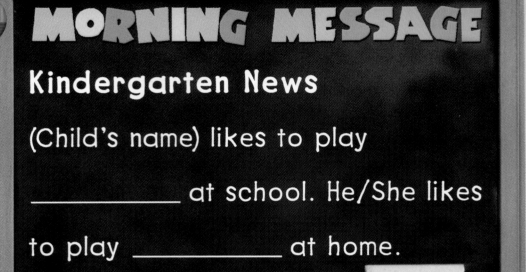

MORNING MESSAGE

Kindergarten News

(Child's name) likes to play

_____ at school. He/She likes

to play _____ at home.

Write Kindergarten News Talk with children about the games they like to play at home and at school.

Use prompts such as the following to guide children as you write the news:

• **What games do you like to play at school? at home?**

• **Who can point to where to begin reading?**

• **Let's count the letters in *school*. How many?**

• **Who can point to a word they know and read it?**

As you write the message, invite children to contribute by writing letters, names, or words they have previously learned. Remind them to use proper spacing, capitalization, and punctuation.

Calendar Language

Have children identify the day of the week. Then ask them to name the class activities for the day.

Sunday	Monday	Tuesday	Wednesday	Thursday	Friday	Saturday
		1	2	3	4	5
6	7	8	9	10	11	12
13	14	15	16	17	18	19
20	21	22	23	24	25	26
27	28	29	30	31		

FLORIDA STANDARDS/GLEs FCAT: LA.A.2.1.5.K.2 Get information; **LA.B.2.1.2.K.1** Record ideas; *Also* **LA.A.1.1.2.K.2** Alphabet; **LA.A.1.1.3.K.1** Frequent words; **LA.C.1.1.3.K.1** Conversation rules; **LA.C.3.1.2.K.1** Questions

Phonemic Awareness

PHONEME BLENDING

Blend Sounds   Use the rabbit puppet for this activity. Tell children they can listen to the sounds the rabbit says and guess the word.

MODEL   The rabbit says this word in parts: /y/ /a/ /k/.

Say the sounds /y/ /a/ /k/.

What is this word /y/ /a/ /k/?

The word is *yak*. **Say it with the rabbit.**

Tell children that the rabbit is going to say some more words in parts. Have them listen and figure out the word the rabbit is saying.

/k/ /a/ /n/ (*can*)	**/n/ /o/ /t/** (*not*)	**/b/ /e/ /d/** (*bed*)
/p/ /i/ /g/ (*pig*)	**/d/ /u/ /k/** (*duck*)	**/m/ /a/ /t/** (*mat*)
/r/ /u/ /g/ (*rug*)	**/n/ /e/ /t/** (*net*)	**/w/ /i/ /n/** (*win*)
/k/ /a/ /p/ (*cap*)	**/h/ /i/ /d/** (*hid*)	**/n/ /u/ /t/** (*nut*)
/l/ /e/ /g/ (*leg*)	**/m/ /o/ /p/** (*mop*)	**/j/ /o/ /b/** (*job*)

FLORIDA STANDARDS/GLEs   FCAT: LA.A.1.1.2.K.5 Phonetic principles

ADVANCED

Ask children to blend words with consonant blends such as /k/ /l/ /a/ /m/ (*clam*), /f/ /r/ /o/ /g/ (*frog*), /s/ /l/ /u/ /g/ (*slug*).

/y/ /a/ /k/

Harcourt

Under the Ocean   643

Sharing Literature

Read "The Seashore Noisy Book"

READ ALOUD

Before Reading   Tell children you are going to read "The Seashore Noisy Book." Then use these prompts to set a purpose for reading.

• **What is it like at the seashore?**

• **What noises do you think you would hear at the seashore?**
(Answers will vary but may include seagulls, waves crashing, people laughing on the beach.)

During Reading Read the story aloud. As you read,

• point out the words and phrases that describe the seashore.

• emphasize the sound words.

• pause after questions to let children predict answers, then read on to let children confirm their predictions.

MODEL   When I read *Scree Scree Scree. What was that?* I predict that it is the sound of birds. I have heard birds screeching near the ocean before. I listen to the next sentence to see if I am right. The author writes, *White birds flying in the air.* I am right!

▲ **Read-Aloud Anthology**

OBJECTIVES

• *To connect text to life experiences*

• *To make and confirm predictions*

• *To recognize setting*

• *To answer questions about a text*

• *To use visualizing to understand text*

Materials

■ *Read-Aloud Anthology, pp. 112–115*

 FLORIDA STANDARDS/GLEs   FCAT: LA.E.1.1.2.K.1 Story elements; *Also* **LA.C.1.1.1.K.2** Oral language

DEVELOP LISTENING COMPREHENSION

After Reading Have children answer these questions about the story:

- **Where does this story take place?** (at the seashore)

- **What does Muffin hear at sea?** (Possible responses include: waves, foghorn, a bell buoy, a motorboat, ship's horn)

- **What makes the splashing sound at the end of the story?** (It is Muffin swimming and splashing in the sea.)

RESPOND TO LITERATURE

Retell the Story Have children retell the story of the adventures Muffin has in "The Seashore Noisy Book."

VISUALIZING

As you reread the story, have children close their eyes and think about the way things look, taste, feel, smell, and sound at the seashore. You may want to model visualizing:

MODEL When I hear the description of Muffin walking along in the warm soft sand, I think about what the sand feels like. I have been to the beach, and I know what sand feels like when it is warm. Thinking about the sand helps me understand this part of the story.

Invite children to name experiences that help them understand parts of the story.

BELOW-LEVEL

If some children hesitate to contribute in large-group discussions, read the story to them ahead of time. Model how to answer the questions posed in the text. Point out the good guesses they make. Suggest that they might share that idea when the whole group reads the story.

ONGOING ASSESSMENT

As you share "The Seashore Noisy Book," note whether children

- **connect text to life experiences.**

- **can make and confirm predictions.**

FLORIDA STANDARDS/GLEs **FCAT: LA.A.1.1.3.K.5** Story elements; **LA.A.1.1.4.K.1** Comprehension; **LA.E.1.1.2.K.1** Story elements; *Also* **LA.C.3.1.1.K.1** Speak clearly

OBJECTIVE
To decode short-vowel words

Materials

- index cards
- marker
- pocket chart
- *High-Frequency Word Card A*
- *Decodable Book 18: A Bug Can Tug*
- drawing paper
- crayons

ADVANCED

Have children read *A Bug Can Tug* on their own. Ask them to track the print as they read. Then have them read *Independent Reader 35: Dive in the Ocean*.

Phonics

Short Vowels *a, e, i, o, u* ✔ *Review*

TEACH/MODEL

Decode Words   Write the words *bug, can,* and *tug* on index cards and place them in a pocket chart. As you point to each word, have children blend the sounds and read the word.

Place the *High-Frequency Word Card A* in the pocket chart. Add a card with a period to form the sentence *A bug can tug.* Track the print as children read the words.

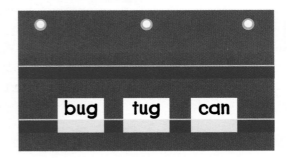

PRACTICE/APPLY

Read the Book   Distribute copies of *A Bug Can Tug.* Read the title together, encouraging children to point to each word as they say it. Then have children read the book, pointing to each word as they read.

Respond   Have children draw a picture of one of the boats that could not tug the dog's boat.

FLORIDA STANDARDS/GLEs   FCAT: LA.A.1.1.2.K.4 Words; **LA.A.1.1.2.K.5** Phonetic principles; *Also* **LA.A.1.1.2.K.2** Alphabet; **LA.A.1.1.2.K.3** Sounds; **LA.C.3.1.1.K.1** Speak clearly; **LA.D.1.1.1.K.1** Sound patterns; **LA.D.2.1.2.K.1** Patterned structures

Decodable Book 18: *A Bug Can Tug*

My boat can not go.
I did not get gas.
I can not fix it.

2

Cat, can you tug me?
I can not tug you, Dog.
My boat is not big.

3

Pig, can you tug me?
I can not tug you, Dog.
My boat is not big.

4

Fox, can you tug me?
I can not tug you, Dog.
My boat is not big.

5

I can tug you, Dog.
A bug can not tug.

6

I am little, but my boat is big.

7

A bug can tug!

8

High-Frequency Words

my, me, go, little, you

Decodable Words

See the list on page T15.

School–Home Connection

Take-Home
Book Version

◄ Decodable Book 18:
A Bug Can Tug

BELOW-LEVEL

Reread the story with children. Have them match *High-Frequency Word Cards* with words in the book.

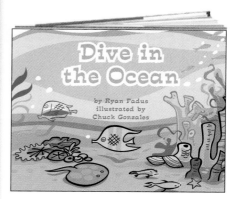

▲ *Dive in the Ocean*
Independent Reader 35

Writing Process

Writing a Poem

DRAFT

OBJECTIVE

• *To work together to write a poem*

Materials

■ list of animal names p.640

■ chart paper

■ marker

Choose an Idea for a Poem Tell children that together they will write a poem about an animal that lives in the ocean. Read the list of animal names children suggested during prewriting. Have children vote to choose the animal they will write about in a poem.

Have children suggest an opening sentence for the poem. If they need help getting started, suggest that they finish the sentence: *If I lived in the ocean, I would want to be a _____.*

Help children orally compose the content of the first sentence; when you are ready to write it, ask questions like these:

• **Where should I start writing on the chart paper?**

• **What is the last word in the first line? Let's think of some words that rhyme with it.**

• **The first word in each line starts with an uppercase letter. Who will write the letter for us?**

Have children come to the chart paper to write letters and words they know. Other children can use a finger to help show spaces between words. Make certain each child has an opportunity to help with the writing.

If I lived in the ocean,
I would want to be
a whale.

I would have a long body
and a great big tail.

When I come up for air,
I spray water like a
spout.

When people run to see me,
they shout.

Journal Writing Have children draw and write about things they hear, smell, see, taste, and touch at school.

FLORIDA STANDARDS/GLEs **FCAT: LA.B.1.1.2.K.4** Add details; **LA.B.2.1.2.K.1** Record ideas; **LA.E.1.1.1.K.1** Genres. *Also* **LA.A.1.1.2.K.2** Alphabet; **LA.B.1.1.3.K.1** Spelling approximations; **LA.B.1.1.3.K.2** Print direction; **LA.B.1.1.3.K.3** Punctuation; **LA.B.2.1.1.K.2** Contribute ideas **LA.C.1.1.1.K.1** Follow directions

WRAP UP

Share Time

Reflect on the Lesson Have children talk about their favorite part of "The Seashore Noisy Book." Display and read the draft of the poem children wrote during Writing. Read it aloud to children. Ask them to tell what they enjoyed most about today's lesson.

S.S.R. Sustained Silent Reading Have children read silently from a book of their choice.

Centers — LISTENING

Sound Effects

Have children make up a story and create sound effects to go with it. Direct children to make a tape recording of their story, including the sound effects. Remind children that they can make up words to stand for different sounds. Invite children to listen to the recording and draw a picture to illustrate the story.

Materials

- tape recorder
- tape cassette
- microphone
- drawing paper
- crayons

WARM UP

MORNING MESSAGE

Kindergarten News

One of our classroom rules is

_____. Another rule is _____.

Following the rules helps us _____.

Phonemic Awareness
Phoneme Deletion

Sharing Literature
Big Book:
Splash in the Ocean!

Read

Respond to Literature

Literature Focus: Picture Details

Phonics

Reading
Decodable Book 19: *Sid Hid*

Interactive Writing ✏
Poem

Writing Process: Respond and Revise

Write Kindergarten News Talk with children about classroom rules, such as taking turns, being good listeners, and putting things where they belong.

Use prompts such as the following to guide children as you write the news:

- **Who can explain some of our classroom rules?**
- **Why is it important to have rules?**
- **Who can name the beginning sound in *rules*?**
- **How many words are in the last sentence?**

As you write the message, invite children to contribute by writing letters or words they have previously learned. Remind them to use proper spacing, capitalization, and punctuation.

Calendar Language

Point to the numbers on the calendar. Tell children the days of each month are numbered and the numbers tell the date. Point to and read aloud the date. Name the month and the date.

Sunday	Monday	Tuesday	Wednesday	Thursday	Friday	Saturday
		1	2	3	4	5
6	7	8	9	10	11	12
13	14	15	16	17	18	19
20	21	22	23	24	25	26
27	28	29	30	31		

FLORIDA STANDARDS/GLEs FCAT: LA.A.1.1.2.K.5 Phonetic principles; **LA.A.2.1.5.K.2** Get information; **LA.B.2.1.2.K.1** Record ideas; *Also* **LA.A.1.1.2.K.2** Alphabet; **LA.A.1.1.2.K.3** Sounds; **LA.C.1.1.3.K.1** Conversation rules; **LA.C.3.1.2.K.1** Questions

Phonemic Awareness

PHONEME DELETION

Delete Initial Phonemes Ask children to listen carefully as you remove the initial phoneme in words.

MODEL *Tin.* **Say the word with me. What word would we have if I left the /t/ off the beginning of** *tin*? *Tin* **without the /t/ is** *in*. **Now you say** *tin* **without the /t/:** *in*.

Continue with these words:

Say *can* without the /k/. (*an*)

Say *his* without the /h/. (*is*)

Say *net* without the /n/. (*et*)

Say *big* without the /b/. (*ig*)

Say *fox* without the /f/. (*ox*)

Say *hut* without the /h/. (*ut*)

Say *gum* without the /g/. (*um*)

Say *had* without the /h/. (*ad*)

Say *rat* without the /r/. (*at*)

Say *bed* without the /b/. (*ed*)

Say *sit* without the /s/. (*it*)

Say *cup* without the /k/. (*up*)

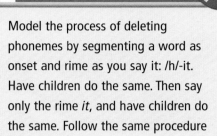

BELOW-LEVEL

Model the process of deleting phonemes by segmenting a word as onset and rime as you say it: /h/-it. Have children do the same. Then say only the rime *it*, and have children do the same. Follow the same procedure for *ran, cup, let, fox*.

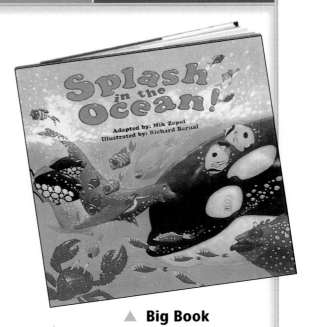

▲ **Big Book**

OBJECTIVES

- *To locate the title and the name of the author of a story*

- *To respond to story text through movement.*

- *To note picture details*

Materials

■ *Big Book: Splash in the Ocean!*

Sharing Literature

Read Splash in the Ocean!

READ ALOUD

Before Reading Display *Splash in the Ocean!* Point to the title and ask: **What is this?** Track the print as you read the title. Tell children that the mark at the end of the title is an exclamation mark and it means that you read the title with excitement in your voice. Ask another child to point to the name of the author as you read the name. Then use these prompts to set a purpose for rereading the selection:

- **Which ocean animal is your favorite?** (Possibe responses: fish, crab, whale, seal)

- **Which ocean animal in the story is the biggest? the smallest?** (whale, tiny fish)

During Reading Reread the story aloud. As you read,

- have children pretend to move like the different animals in the story.

- allow children to chime in on repetitive phrases.

- note the sequence of story events by asking which animals come next before turning the page.

FLORIDA STANDARDS/GLEs **FCAT: LA.A.1.1.4.K.1** Comprehension; **LA.E.1.1.1.K.1** Genres; **LA.E.1.1.2.K.1** Story elements. *Also* **LA.A.1.1.2.K.1** Print organization; **LA.A.2.1.4.K.1** Illustrations; **LA.C.1.1.1.K.2** Oral language; **LA.C.3.1.2.K.1** Questions

RESPOND TO LITERATURE

Describe Story Illustrations Have children take turns choosing their favorite story scene. Have them turn to the illustration in the *Big Book*. Tell them to point to the animal as they name it. Ask them to describe how the animal looks (its color and its size), how it moves, and the sounds it makes.

PICTURE DETAILS

Display pages 8 and 9 of *Splash in the Ocean!* Point out that sometimes pictures help readers understand words. Frame the word *crabs* and say the word. Point to the illustration of a crab.

MODEL When I hear the word *crab*, I'm not really sure what a crab is. I see these animals on the same page as the word *crab*, so I know that this is what a crab looks like.

Then page through the book, having children frame the names of the ocean animals and point to the corresponding pictures.

BELOW-LEVEL

After discussing picture details, have children point to and name the ocean animals in each picture. Help them recall the actions of each animal.

ENGLISH-LANGUAGE LEARNERS

Show children magazine pictures of ocean animals like the ones in *Splash in the Ocean!* Point out the animals and say the names for children to repeat.

ONGOING ASSESSMENT

As you share *Splash in the Ocean!* note whether children

- can locate the title and the name of the author of a story.
- respond to the story through movement.
- can use story illustrations to make predictions.

FLORIDA STANDARDS/GLEs FCAT: LA.A.1.1.3.K.5 Story elements; **LA.A.1.1.4.K.1** Comprehension; **LA.A.2.1.1.K.1** Main idea; **LA.E.1.1.2.K.1** Story elements; *Also* **LA.A.2.1.4.K.1** Illustrations

Materials

- *Alphabet Cards S, i, d*
- pocket chart
- blank sentence strip
- marker
- *Decodable Book 19: Sid Hid*
- drawing paper
- crayons

Phonics

Short Vowels *a, e, i, o, u* ✔ *Review*

TEACH/MODEL

Decode Words Place *Alphabet Cards S, i, d* next to one another in a pocket chart. As you move your hand under the letters, have children blend the sounds and read the word. Write the words *is not in it.* on a sentence strip. Place it after the word *Sid*. Track the print as children read the sentence *Sid is not in it*.

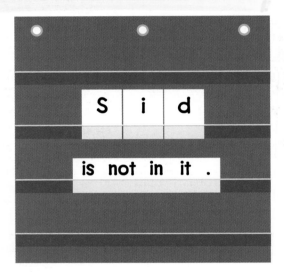

PRACTICE/APPLY

Read the Book Distribute copies of *Sid Hid*. Have children read the title and encourage children to point to each word as they read it. Ask children what they notice about the two words in the title. (They rhyme.) Then have children read the book, pointing to each word as they read.

Respond Have children draw a picture of one of the places the crab looked for Sid. Have them turn their paper over and draw a picture of where Sid was hiding.

FLORIDA STANDARDS/GLEs **FCAT: LA.A.1.1.2.K.5** Phonetic principles; *Also* **LA.A.1.1.2.K.1** Print organization; **LA.A.1.1.2.K.3** Sounds; **LA.C.1.1.1.K.1** Follow directions; **LA.C.2.1.2.K.1** Nonverbal cues; **LA.D.1.1.1.K.1** Sound patterns

Decodable Book 19: *Sid Hid*

Sid hid.
I can not see him.

2

Did you look in the big box?
I did. Sid is not in it.

3

Did you look in the red bag?
I did. Sid is not in it.

4

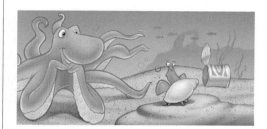

Did you look in the tin can?
I did. Sid is not in it.

5

Did you look in the big pot?
I did. Sid is not in it.

6

Did you look in his little shell?
I did not.

7

Sid is in it.
Sid is in his shell!

8

FLORIDA STANDARDS/GLEs **FCAT: LA.A.1.1.2.K.5** Phonetic principles; **LA.A.1.1.3.K.4** Build vocabulary; *Also* **LA.A.1.1.2.K.1** Print organization; **LA.A.1.1.2.K.2** Alphabet; **LA.A.1.1.2.K.3** Sounds; **LA.C.3.1.2.K.1** Questions

Under the Ocean 655

■ High-Frequency Words
see, the, you, little, look

■ Decodable Words
See the list on page T15.

School-Home Connection

Take-Home Book Version

◀ Decodable Book 19 Sid Hid

REACHING ALL LEARNERS

Diagnostic Check: Phonics

If... children cannot decode words in text,

Then... have children point to each word as they read aloud. Help children decode challenging words by sounding out the letters with them.

ADDITIONAL SUPPORT ACTIVITIES

BELOW-LEVEL Reteach, p. S70

ADVANCED Extend, p. S71

ENGLISH-LANGUAGE LEARNERS Reteach, p. S71

OBJECTIVES

- *To revise a poem*

- *To use descriptive words in sentences*

- *To write a title*

Materials

- *class poem p.648*

- *red marker*

Writing Process

Writing a Poem

RESPOND AND REVISE

Make Changes Reread the poem aloud, tracking the words. Ask children questions like these:

- Is there anything else we need to add to our poem?

- Do we tell what the animal looks like and how it lives?

- Would you like to add words or change any of the words we used?

- Our poem needs a title. Who has an idea for one?

Make changes as they are suggested by children. Invite children to come up and write words and letters they know. You may want to use a red marker to show the changes on the chart paper. Add a title suggested by the children.

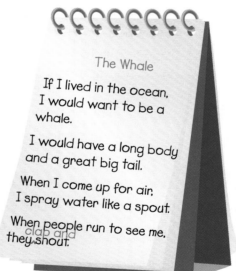

The Whale

If I lived in the ocean,
I would want to be a whale.

I would have a long body and a great big tail.

When I come up for air,
I spray water like a spout.

When people run to see me,
they shout.
clap and

Self-Selected Writing Have children write and draw about anything they'd like. If they have difficulty thinking of a topic have them ask two friends what they're going to write about.

FLORIDA STANDARDS/GLEs **FCAT: LA.A.1.1.2.K.4** Words; **LA.A.2.1.5.K.3** Stay on topic; **LA.B.1.1.2.K.4** Add details; *Also* **LA.A.1.1.2.K.1** Print organization; **LA.C.3.1.2.K.1** Questions; **LA.D.2.1.2.K.1** Patterned structures; **LA.D.2.1.2.K.2** Alliteration

WRAP UP Share Time

Reflect on the Lesson Ask children what they liked about the book *Sid Hid.* Have children take turns using the Author's Chair to share their drawing showing one of the places the crab looked for Sid.

 S.S.R. Have children read silently from a book of their choice.

Centers ABC LETTERS AND WORDS

Word Factory

Have children place the *High-Frequency Word Cards* face down on the table. Each child takes a card, turns it over, and reads the word. Next, the child uses the *Magnetic Letters* to spell out the word on a cookie sheet. Encourage the child to name the letters one by one as he or she places them on the cookie sheet.

Materials

- *High-Frequency Word Cards* see, you, look, the, little, my, go, you, me
- *Magnetic Letters*
- cookie sheet

FLORIDA STANDARDS/GLEs **FCAT: LA.A.1.1.2.K.4** Words; *Also* **LA.B.1.1.1.K.2** Generate ideas; **LA.E.2.1.1.K.2** Personal interpretations

Under the Ocean   **657**

Day at a Glance
Day 4

WARM UP

Phonemic Awareness
Phoneme Deletion

Sharing Literature
Read-Aloud Anthology:
"If You Ever"

Read

KINDERGARTEN
**READ-ALOUD
Anthology**
Harcourt

Respond to Literature

Literature Focus: Making Inferences

Reading
Decodable Book 20: *In a Sub*

Interactive Writing ✏

Writing Process: Proofread

MORNING MESSAGE

Kindergarten News

(Child's name) has a _____ for a

pet. The pet's name is _____.

The pet likes to eat _____.

Write Kindergarten News Talk with children about a pet they have or a pet they would like to have. Encourage them to speak loudly enough for classmates to hear what they have to say.

Use prompts such as the following to guide children as you write the news:

- **What pet do you have? What pet would you like to have?**
- **What letter will I write first in (child's name)?**
- **Who can name the first letter in (name of pet)?**
- **Let's clap the syllables for (child's name). How many parts do you clap?**

As you write the message, invite children to contribute by writing letters, names, or words they have previously learned. Remind them to use proper spacing, capitalization, and punctuation.

Calendar Language

Point to and read aloud the names of the days of the week. Have children identify the first day of the week. (Sunday) **Have children identify the last day of the week.** (Saturday)

Sunday	Monday	Tuesday	Wednesday	Thursday	Friday	Saturday
		1	2	3	4	5
6	7	8	9	10	11	12
13	14	15	16	17	18	19
20	21	22	23	24	25	26
27	28	29	30	31		

FLORIDA STANDARDS/GLEs **FCAT: LA.A.2.1.5.K.2** Get information; **LA.B.2.1.2.K.1** Record ideas; *Also* **LA.A.1.1.2.K.2** Alphabet; **LA.A.1.1.3.K.1** Frequent words; **LA.C.1.1.3.K.1** Conversation rules; **LA.C.3.1.2.K.1** Questions

Phonemic Awareness

PHONEME DELETION

Delete Initial Phonemes Ask children to listen as you take away the beginning sound in a word.

MODEL *Team.* Say the word with me. What part of the word will we have if I say *team* without the /t/? *Team* without the /t/ is *eam.* Now you say *team* without the /t/.

Continue with these words:

Say *boot* without the /b/. (*oot*)   Say *seal* without the /s/. (*eal*)

Say *plain* without the /p/. (*lain*)   Say *runt* without the /r/. (*unt*)

Say *seem* without the /s/. (*eem*)   Say *fork* without the /f/. (*ork*)

Say *tool* without the /t/. (*ool*)   Say *beet* without the /b/. (*eet*)

Say *moon* without the /m/. (*oon*)   Say *bat* without the /b/. (*at*)

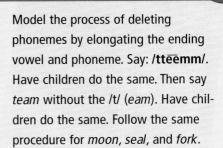

Sharing Literature

Read "If You Ever"

READ ALOUD

Before Reading   Turn to page 30 in the *Read-Aloud Anthology*. Tell children that you are going to read a poem called "If You Ever." Explain that the poem tells about meeting a whale. Then use these prompts to build background:

• **What does a whale look like?**

• **Do you think whales are friendly? Why do you think so?**

During Reading   Read the poem aloud. As you read,

• emphasize the rhyming words *whale* and *tail*.

• reread the poem and lead children as they clap the rhythm of the repetitive text.

Read the poem once more and have children shake a finger each time the word *ever* is repeated and shake their head back and forth each time the word *never* is repeated.

▲ **Read-Aloud Anthology**

OBJECTIVES

• *To listen to a poem for enjoyment*

• *To respond to a poem through movement and drama*

• *To use information from a text to make inferences*

Materials

■ *Read-Aloud Anthology, p. 30*

■ *Teacher's Resource Book, p. 100*

■ scissors

■ crayons

■ craft sticks

■ tape

FLORIDA STANDARDS/GLEs   FCAT: LA.A.1.1.4.K.1 Comprehension; **LA.E.1.1.1.K.1** Genres; *Also* **LA.C.3.1.4.K.1** Gestures; **LA.D.2.1.2.K.1** Patterned structures; **LA.E.2.1.2.K.1** Patterned structures

Act Out the Poem Have children use the Character Cutouts on page 100 of the *Teacher's Resource Book* to act out the poem. After children have cut out and colored the characters, have them use tape to attach the figures to craft sticks to make puppets. As you reread the poem have children use their puppets to mimic the actions of the characters.

Literature Focus

MAKING INFERENCES

Remind children that sometimes authors and poets don't tell the reader everything he or she needs to know about the story or poem. They want the reader to use information in the text and what they already know to figure things out. Reread the poem and discuss what the poet is trying to tell readers about whales.

MODEL The poet says that if you touch a whale's tail, you will never see another whale. I can figure out what the poet means. A whale is a very big animal. If you touched the whale's tail and upset the whale, it might splash a great deal of water on you to let you know it is unhappy. Then you'll learn never to touch another whale.

REACHING ALL LEARNERS

Diagnostic Check: Comprehension

If... children are not able to make inferences,

Then... repeat the important details from the poem or story. Have children think of a similar experience they have had and tell what happened to them. Then relate children's experiences to what happened to the characters they are reading about.

ADDITIONAL SUPPORT ACTIVITIES

BELOW-LEVEL	Reteach, p. S72
ADVANCED	Extend, p. S73
ENGLISH-LANGUAGE LEARNERS	Reteach, p. S73

ONGOING ASSESSMENT

As you share "If You Ever," note whether children

• listen to a poem for enjoyment.

• can respond to a poem through movement and drama.

FLORIDA STANDARDS/GLEs FCAT: LA.A.1.1.4.K.1 Comprehension; **LA.E.1.1.1.K.1** Genres; *Also* **LA.C.3.1.4.K.1** Gestures; **LA.D.2.1.2.K.1** Patterned structures; **LA.E.2.1.2.K.1** Patterned structures

Under the Ocean 661

OBJECTIVE
To decode short vowel words

Materials

- index cards
- marker
- pocket chart
- *Decodable Book 20: In a Sub*
- drawing paper
- crayons

Phonics

Short Vowels *a, e, i, o, u* ✔ *Review*

TEACH/MODEL

Decode Words   Write the word *sub* on an index card and place it in a pocket chart. Move your hand under the letters and have children blend the sounds to read the word.

Write the words *I, am, in,* and *a* on index cards. Place them in the pocket chart in front of *sub*. Add a period to form the sentence *I am in a sub.* Track the print as children read the words.

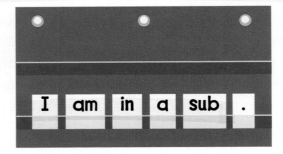

PRACTICE/APPLY

Read the Book   Distribute copies of *In a Sub*. Read the title together, encouraging children to point to each word as they say it. Ask them what they know about subs and have them predict what someone might see from inside a sub. Then have children read the book, pointing to each word as they read.

Read

▲ *In a Sub*
Decodable Book 20

Respond   Have children draw a picture of one of the sights that the little girl sees from her sub.

FLORIDA STANDARDS/GLEs   FCAT: LA.A.1.1.2.K.4 Words; **LA.A.1.1.2.K.5** Phonetic principles; **LA.A.1.1.2.K.6** Print meaning; *Also* **LA.A.1.1.2.K.1** Print organization; **LA.B.1.1.2.K.2** Basic formats; **LA.B.1.1.3.K.2** Print direction; **LA.D.1.1.1.K.1** Sound patterns

Decodable Book 20: *In a Sub*

I am in a sub.
What can I see?

2

Look! It is a red fish.
It can zip. Go, red fish!

3

It is a shark!
It has a big fin.
4 Can you see the tip?

It is a crab.
It can dig.
Look at it go! 5

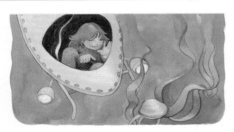

It is a clam.
The clam is little.
6 I can not fit in it.

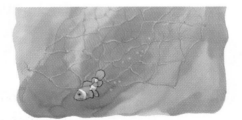

Look at the fish!
It is not in a net.

7

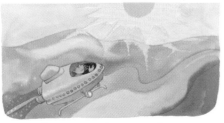

I go up in a sub.
I can see the sun.
8 I had fun!

■ High-Frequency Words

what, see, look, go, you, the, little

■ Decodable Words

See the list on page T15.

School–Home Connection

Take-Home Book Version

◀ Decodable Book 20
In a Sub

BELOW-LEVEL

Reread the story with children. As you name high-frequency words, have children find and point to the words in the book.

OBJECTIVES

- *To share information and ideas, speaking in complete, coherent sentences*

- *To begin each line in a poem with an uppercase letter*

- *edit punctuation*

Materials

- class poem
  p.656

- chart paper

- marker

Writing Process

Writing a poem

PROOFREAD

Make Final Changes   Model how to proofread a poem by asking questions such as:

- **Who can point to the poem title? Did we use uppercase letters in our title?**

- **Who can find the first word in each line. Did we start each line of the poem with an uppercase letter?**

- **Does our poem have sentences? Did we end a sentence with a mark such as a period?**

- **What other things make a whale special?**

If children answered "no" to any of the questions, make changes on the chart paper. Talk aloud as you make each change.

The Whale

If I lived in the ocean,
I would want to be a
Whale.

I would have a long body
And a great big tail.

When I come up for air,
I spray water like a spout.

When People run to see me,
They shout. *clap and*

Journal Writing   Have children draw and write about a large animal they would like to see up close.

FLORIDA STANDARDS/GLEs   FCAT: LA.E.1.1.1.K.1 Genres; *Also* **LA.D.1.1.1.K.1** Sound patterns; **LA.D.1.1.2.K.1** Formal language; **LA.D.2.1.2.K.1** Patterned structures; **LA.D.2.1.2.K.2** Alliteration; **LA.E.2.1.2.K.1** Patterned structures

WRAP UP · Share Time

Reflect on the Lesson Invite children to retell the story *In a Sub*. Have them tell what words they learned to read. Invite children to share their journal writing for today.

S.S.R. Sustained Silent Reading Have children read silently from a book of their choice.

 **Centers**  **WRITING**

A Whale of a Tale

Place in the center several copies of a large, simple outline of a whale shape. Direct children to cut out the whale shape and write their own whale story on it. Have children share their story with their classmates.

 **Materials**

- copies of a whale shape
- scissors
- crayons or pencils

Wnde Whale wuz loking for hur mom. She swam and swam. Haylie

WARM UP

Phonemic Awareness
Phoneme Addition

Sharing Literature
Read-Aloud Anthology:
"The Seashore Noisy Book"

Read

Develop Concept Vocabulary

Respond to Literature

Literature Focus: Questions for Research

Phonics
Build Sentences

Interactive Writing
Writing Process: Publish

MORNING MESSAGE

Kindergarten News

(Child's name) likes kindergarten

because _____. His/Her favorite

kindergarten activity is _____.

Write Kindergarten News   Have children discuss what they like about Kindergarten. Have them describe their favorite Kindergarten activities.

Use prompts such as the following to guide children as you write the news:

- **What is your favorite thing to do in kindergarten?**
- **How many letters are in (child's name)?**
- **Who can point to a word they know and read it?**

As you write the message, invite children to contribute by writing letters, names, or words they have previously learned. Remind them to use proper spacing, capitalization, and punctuation.

Calendar Language

Point to and read aloud the names of the seasons of the year. Have children repeat the season names with you. Ask: *What season is it? What season comes next?*

Sunday	Monday	Tuesday	Wednesday	Thursday	Friday	Saturday
		1	2	3	4	5
6	7	8	9	10	11	12
13	14	15	16	17	18	19
20	21	22	23	24	25	26
27	28	29	30	31		

FLORIDA STANDARDS/GLEs   FCAT: LA.A.2.1.5.K.2 Get information; **LA.B.2.1.2.K.1** Record ideas; *Also* **LA.A.1.1.2.K.2** Alphabet; **LA.A.1.1.3.K.1** Frequent words; **LA.C.1.1.3.K.1** Conversation rules; **LA.C.3.1.2.K.1** Questions

Phonemic Awareness

PHONEME ADDITION

Add Initial Phonemes to Words Tell children to listen carefully as you add sounds to words to say new words.

MODEL Say the word *row*. What word would we have if I added /g/ to the beginning of *row*? The new word is *grow*. Say the word *grow*.

Continue by asking children to say the new words when the following sounds are added:

Add /g/ to *lad*. (*glad*)   Add /p/ to *ant*. (*pant*)

Add /d/ to *rag*. (*drag*)   Add /t/ to *rash*. (*trash*)

Add /k/ to *lamp*. (*clamp*)   Add /b/ to *each*. (*beach*)

Add /p/ to *lane*. (*plane*)   Add /t/ to *ray*. (*tray*)

Add /t/ to *art*. (*tart*)   Add /s/ to *weep*. (*sweep*)

Add /s/ to *tick*. (*stick*)   Add /t/ to *wig*. (*twig*)

Add /s/ to *pill*. (*spill*)   Add /b/ to *lock*. (*block*)

Add /p/ to *out*. (*pout*)   Add /s/ to *tub*. (*stub*)

Add /k/ to *luck*. (*cluck*)   Add /k/ to *rush*. (*crush*)

▲ "Burgalesa," *Oo-pples and Boo-noo-noos: Songs and Activities for Phonemic Awareness*, pages 59–60

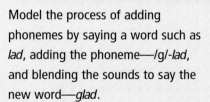
BELOW-LEVEL

Model the process of adding phonemes by saying a word such as *lad*, adding the phoneme—/g/-*lad*, and blending the sounds to say the new word—*glad*.

FLORIDA STANDARDS/GLEs **FCAT: LA.A.1.1.2.K.5** Phonetic principles; *Also* **LA.C.1.1.1.K.2** Oral language; **LA.D.1.1.1.K.1** Sound patterns

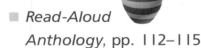
▲ **Read-Aloud
Anthology**

OBJECTIVES

- *To recall story events*

- *To recognize the beginning, middle, and ending of a story*

- *To recognize sound words*

- *To ask questions for research*

Materials

- *Read-Aloud Anthology*, pp. 112–115

- drawing paper

- crayons

- chart paper

- marker

Sharing Literature

Read "The Seashore Noisy Book"

READ ALOUD

Before Reading   Turn to pages 112–113 in the *Read-Aloud Anthology* and read the story title aloud. Then use these prompts to help children recall the story.

- **Who is Muffin?** (the dog in the story)

- **What does Muffin do?** (He goes on a sailboat and learns about the sea.)

- **How does Muffin learn about the sea?** (through sight, taste, touch, smell, sound)

During Reading   Reread the story aloud. As you read,

- pause after each question *What was that?* to allow children to predict the answer.

- pause before reading the story ending to model how to recall the beginning and middle of the story.

MODEL   **At the beginning of the story, Muffin goes to sea on a big sailboat. In the middle of the story, he learns about the sea through sight, taste, smell, touch, and sound. Let's read on to find out how the story ends.**

FLORIDA STANDARDS/GLEs   **FCAT: LA.A.1.1.4.K.1** Comprehension; *Also* **LA.A.1.1.2.K.1** Print organization; **LA.C.1.1.2.K.1** Choose literature

DEVELOP CONCEPT VOCABULARY

After Reading   Remind children that there are many sound words in the story. As you read the following words, ask children to identify what makes the sound.

- *Putt Putt putt putt putt* (boat's motor)
- *Sssswishsh-shshshshshshshsh* (little birds' wings)
- *Flip flop flip flop* (fish jumping in the bottom of a boat)
- *lapping slapping slap lap lap* (the water against the side of the boat)
- *Scree Scree Scree* (white birds flying in the air)
- *Whoooo Whoooo Whoooo Whooo* (ocean liner whistle)

RESPOND TO LITERATURE

Draw and Write About the Story   Have children draw and label pictures of things Muffin saw, smelled, tasted, heard, or felt while he was at sea.

Literature Focus

QUESTIONS FOR RESEARCH

Reread parts of "The Seashore Noisy Book," and point out some of the questions from the story.

MODEL   **As I read "The Seashore Noisy Book," the author asks many questions, such as *What was that grayness?* or *Muffin took a big drink of sea water. But he didn't like it. Why was that?* These questions make me wonder other things about the ocean. I would like to find out the answers to all of these questions.**

Ask children what they learned about the ocean from this story. Find out what else they would like to know about the ocean, encouraging children to state their ideas in the form of questions. Record the questions on chart paper. As time permits, research answers to some of the questions.

ADVANCED

Provide children with a few informational books about the ocean. Help them each find one interesting fact and share it with the class.

ONGOING ASSESSMENT

As you share "The Seashore Noisy Book," note whether children

- can recall story events.
- can identify the beginning, middle, and ending of a story.
- predict answers to each question *What was that?*

FLORIDA STANDARDS/GLEs   FCAT: LA.A.1.1.3.K.5 Story elements; **LA.C.1.1.4.K.1** Sequence; **LA.E.1.1.2.K.1** Story elements; *Also* **LA.E.2.1.2.K.1** Patterned structures

Phonics

Build Sentences  Review

OBJECTIVE

To use knowledge of letters, words, and sounds to read simple sentences

Materials

- chart paper
- marker
- index cards
- pocket chart
- *Decodable Books 18–20: A Bug Can Tug, Sid Hid, In a Sub*

ACTIVE BEGINNING

Act Out a Nonsense Rhyme   Teach children the following rhyme and actions.

> The pig has a wig.
> (Pat top of head.)
>
> The cat has a hat.
> (Put hands on head.)
>
> The fox is in a box!
> (Turn round and round.)
>
> The pet is all wet!
> (Shake head and body to get dry.)

TEACH/MODEL

Review *-ig, -ox, -et*   Copy the chart below onto chart paper. Read aloud the words and remind children that the words in each column belong to the same word family—the *-ig* family, the *-ox* family, and the *-et* family.

Model reading the word *pig* first by elongating the sounds /ppiigg/ and then reading it naturally. Then have children elongate the sounds /ppiigg/ and read the word. Continue with the remaining words. Frame the words *pig* and *wig* and ask how the two words are alike. (Possible responses: They rhyme; they both have *i* and *g*.) Do the same for *fox* and *box* and *pet* and *wet*.

pig	fox	pet
wig	box	wet

FLORIDA STANDARDS/GLEs   FCAT: LA.A.1.1.2.K.5 Phonetic principles; **LA.A.1.1.3.K.4** Build vocabulary; *Also* **LA.A.1.1.2.K.1** Print organization; **LA.A.1.1.2.K.2** Alphabet; **LA.C.1.1.1.K.1** Follow directions; **LA.D.1.1.1.K.1** Sound patterns

PRACTICE/APPLY

Guided Practice   Write the following words on index cards: *pig,
wig, fig, box, fox, has, a, The.* Display the words in a pocket chart
as shown.

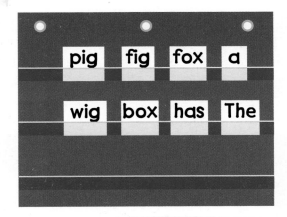

Point to each word and have children read it. If necessary remind
them to blend the sounds together to read the word. Then
rearrange the cards to make the following sentence:

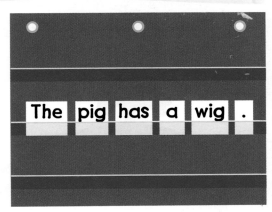

Track the words as you assist children in reading the sentence. Then
replace *pig* with the word *fox* and have children read the sentence.
Continue by substituting different words to provide many opportunities for children to read the sentence.

Independent Practice   Have children reread the *Decodable
Books 18–20, A Bug Can Tug, Sid Hid,* and *In a Sub* for more practice
reading connected text.

early spelling

Have children write one of the
words from the Guided Practice sentences in their spelling journal. Ask
children to draw a picture to describe
that word.

Name	
are	a
dig	hat
mud	in
We	hop

22 Under the Ocean

▲ **Practice Book pages 21–22**

FLORIDA STANDARDS/GLEs   FCAT: LA.A.1.1.2.K.5 Phonetic principles; LA.A.1.1.3.K.4 Build vocabulary; *Also*
LA.A.1.1.2.K.1 Print organization; LA.A.1.1.2.K.2 Alphabet; LA.A.1.1.2.K.3 Sounds; LA.B.1.1.3.K.2 Print direction

OBJECTIVES

- To publish a poem
- To read high-frequency words
- To illustrate the poem

Materials

- class poem p.664
- butcher paper
- drawing paper
- crayons

Writing Process

Writing a Poem

PUBLISH

Make a Poetry Poster   Read the poem aloud, tracking the print. Pause to allow children to read the words *I*, *in*, *the*, *a*, *to*, *see*, *come*, and *me*. Display the poem on a sheet of butcher paper near the Art Center. Encourage each child to draw a whale to create an ocean scene.

The Whale

If I lived in the ocean, I would want to be a whale.

I would have a long body and a great big tail.

When I come up for air, I spray water like a spout.

When people run to see me, they clap and shout.

OK if time

Journal Writing   Have children draw and write about their favorite kindergarten activities.

FLORIDA STANDARDS/GLEs   **FCAT: LA.A.2.1.3.K.1** Supportive details; *Also* **LA.A.2.1.4.K.1** Illustrations

WRAP UP # Share Time

Reflect on the Lesson   Invite children to share the picture they drew of Muffin. Ask them to tell which one of the five senses Muffin is using in the drawing.

S.S.R. Sustained Silent Reading   Have children read silently from a book of their choice.

 **Centers**  **ART**

Fish Prints

 No

...the shape of fish and ocean plants. Pour tempera ...have two or three colors to choose from. Direct ...and make prints on paper. Tell children to ...create an ocean scene with several fish ...

Materials

- ...sponges cut into a variety of fish and ocean plant shapes

- paint trays

- tempera paint

- light-colored construction paper

- paper towels

FLORIDA STANDARDS/GLEs   **FCAT: LA.C.1.1.4.K.1** Sequence; *Also* **LA.B.1.1.3.K.2** Print direction; **LA.C.1.1.1.K.1** Follow directions; **LA.C.1.1.1.K.2** Oral language; **LA.E.2.1.2.K.1** Patterned structures

Under the Ocean   **673**

Theme Wrap-Up & Review

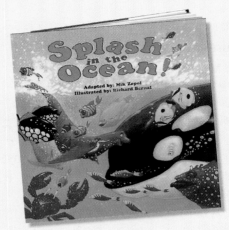

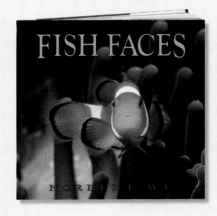

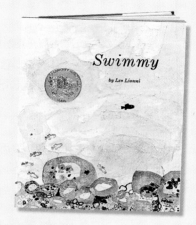

Celebrate *Under the Ocean*

Show children *Splash in the Ocean*, *Fish Faces*, and *Swimmy*. Help them summarize or retell each story. Invite comments and personal responses; then ask these questions:

- **What animals are in *Splash in the Ocean!*?**

- **What might happen if Swimmy and his friends met the animals in *Splash in the Ocean!*?**

- **What sea animals did you learn about in *Fish Faces*? What did you learn about them?**

Teacher Self-Evaluation

As you reflect on the theme *Under the Ocean*, ask yourself:

- **Which activities best met my goals for this theme? Which ones did not?**

- **Have children become more aware of ocean life?**

- **Have I helped children make connections between thematic activities at school and events in their personal life?**

---- **THEME PROJECT** ----

Classroom Aquarium

Summing Up   During the tour of the "Classroom Aquarium," have children tell facts they have learned about life under the ocean.

Lots of fish liv in the ocen.

REVIEW

Phonics

Octopus Word Game In advance, draw a giant octopus and post it on a bulletin board. Gather five boxes and mark them *a, e, i, o, u.* Write these words on index cards: *map, tap, can, fan, van, red, bed, den, hen, men, did, big, pig, dig, pin, hot, pot, top, mop, cub, rub, hum, dug, bug.* Place the cards in the appropriate box. Tell children the octopus needs words to read on his tentacles. Provide beanbags and have children take turns tossing a beanbag into a box. They can take a card from the box, read the word, and post it on the octopus.

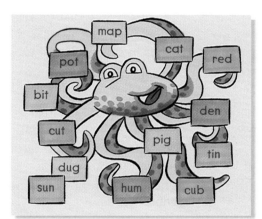

High-Frequency Words

Word Match Make two sets of word cards for *one, little, are, here.* Tell children to turn the cards face down in rows on a table or desk. Have them take turns flipping a card, naming the word, and flipping another card to find a matching word. If the word does not match, children should turn both cards face down and another child takes a turn. If the words match, the child keeps the word set and takes another turn.

Comprehension

Real and Make-Believe Display Library Books *Swimmy* and *Fish Faces.* Point to *Swimmy* and ask children to recall what the story is about. Remind children that the things in this story cannot happen in real life. Fish do not talk and act like humans.

Point to *Fish Faces.* Page through the book, pointing out the photographs and reading some of the information. Ask children how this book is different from *Swimmy.*

Writing

Sea Animals Have children draw and label their favorite sea animal. Ask them to write a fact about the animal.

Take-Home Book
Theme 12 Practice Book, pp. 23–24

ASSESSMENT

• Assessment Handbook

Monitoring of Progress
Diagnostic Checks Use the Diagnostic Checks as a point-of-use assessment of children's understanding.

Theme Skills Assessment Use Theme 12 Skills Assessment, pages T72, 69–70, to monitor a child's understanding of letter recognition, word recognition, sound-symbol relationships, and decoding skills taught in this theme.

Summative Assessment

Administer the Group Inventory, Form B, in the Assessment Handbook, pages 13–26.

Administer the Phonemic Awareness Inventory in the Assessment Handbook, pages 27–38.

**These benchmark statements represent a continuum of learning.
The highlighted column describes observable behaviors most of your children
should exhibit by the end of the school year.**

CONCEPTS ABOUT PRINT

Grade K

Identify the front cover, back cover, and title page of a book.

Follow words from left to right and from top to bottom on the printed page.

Understand that printed materials provide information.

Recognize that sentences in print are made up of separate words.

Distinguish letters from words.

Recognize and name all uppercase and lowercase letters of the alphabet.

Grade I

Match oral words to printed words.

Identify the title and author of a reading selection.

Identify letters, words, and sentences.

PHONEMIC AWARENESS

Grade K

Track and represent the number of two and three isolated phonemes.

Track and represent the sameness/difference of two and three isolated phonemes.

Track and represent the order of two and three isolated phonemes.

Track (move sequentially from sound to sound) and represent changes in simple syllables and words with two and three sounds as one is added, substituted, shifted, or repeated.

Blend vowel-consonant sounds orally to make words or syllables.

Identify rhyming words in response to an oral prompt.

Produce rhyming words in response to an oral prompt.

Separate words into beginning sounds.

Separate words into ending sounds.

Track auditorily each word in a sentence and each syllable in a word.

Count the number of sounds in syllables.

Count the number of syllables in words.

Sequentially segment individual sounds in 2–3 phoneme words.

Grade I

Distinguish initial, medial, and final sounds in single-syllable words.

Distinguish long- and-short-vowel sounds in orally stated single-syllable words.

Create and state a series of rhyming words, including consonant blends.

Add, delete, or change target sounds to change words.

Blend two to four phonemes into recognizable words.

These benchmark statements represent a continuum of learning.
The highlighted column describes observable behaviors most of your children
should exhibit by the end of the school year.

VOCABULARY AND CONCEPT DEVELOPMENT

Grade K

Identify and sort common words in basic categories (e.g., color, shapes, foods).

Describe common objects and events in both general and specific language.

Grade I

Classify grade-appropriate categories of words (e.g., concrete collections of animals, foods, toys).

STRUCTURAL FEATURES, COMPREHENSION, AND TEXT ANALYSIS

Grade K

Locate the title, table of contents, name of author, and name of illustrator.

Use pictures and context to make predictions about story content.

Connect to life experiences the information and events in texts.

Retell familiar stories.

Ask and answer questions about essential elements of a text.

Distinguish fantasy from realistic text.

Identify types of everyday print materials (e.g., storybooks, poems, newspapers, signs, labels).

Identify characters, settings, and important events.

Grade I

Identify text that uses sequences or other logical order.

Respond to who, what, when, where, and how questions.

Follow one-step written instructions.

Use context to resolve ambiguities about word and sentence meanings.

Confirm predictions about what will happen next in a text by identifying key words.

Relate prior knowledge to textual information.

Retell the central ideas of simple expository or narrative passages.

Identify and describe the elements of plot, setting, and character(s) in a story, as well as the story's beginning, middle, and ending.

Describe the roles of authors and illustrators and their contributions to print materials.

Talk about books read during the school year.

Write about books read during the school year.

WRITING

Grade K

Use letters and phonetically spelled words to write about experiences, stories, people, objects, or events.

Write consonant-vowel-consonant words (i.e., demonstrate the alphabetic principle).

Write by moving from left to right and from top to bottom.

Write uppercase and lowercase letters of the alphabet independently, attending to the form and proper spacing of the letters.

Grade I

Select a focus when writing.

Use descriptive words when writing.

Print legibly and space letters, words, and sentences appropriately.

Write brief narratives (e.g., fictional, autobiographical) describing an experience.

Write brief expository descriptions of a real object, person, place, or event, using sensory details.

These benchmark statements represent a continuum of learning. The highlighted column describes observable behaviors most of your children should exhibit by the end of the school year.

ENGLISH LANGUAGE CONVENTIONS

Grade K	Grade 1
Recognize and use complete, coherent sentences when speaking.	Speak in complete, coherent sentences.
Spell independently by using pre-phonetic knowledge, sounds of the alphabet, and knowledge of letter names.	Write in complete, coherent sentences.
	Identify and correctly use singular and plural nouns in speaking and writing.
	Identify and correctly use contractions in writing and speaking.
	Identify and correctly use singular possessive pronouns in writing and speaking.
	Distinguish between declarative, exclamatory, and interrogative sentences.
	Use a period, exclamation point, and question mark at the end of sentences.
	Use knowledge of the basic rules of punctuation and capitalization when writing.
	Capitalize the first word of a sentence, names of people, and the pronoun I.
	Spell three- and four-letter short-vowel words and grade-level-appropriate sight words correctly.

LISTENING, SPEAKING, AND VIEWING

Grade K	Grade 1
Understand and follow one- and two-step oral directions.	Listen attentively.
Share information and ideas, speaking audibly in complete, coherent sentences.	Ask questions for clarification and understanding.
Describe things, people, places/locations, actions, and experiences.	Give, restate, and follow simple two-step directions.
Recite rhymes, songs, and poems.	Stay on the topic when speaking.
Make up a creative story.	Use descriptive words when speaking about people, places, things, and events.
Relate an experience in sequence.	Recite poems, rhymes, songs, and stories.
Relate a creative story in sequence.	Retell stories using basic story grammar and relating the sequence of story events by answering who, what, when, where, why, and how questions.
	Relate an important life event or personal experience in a simple sequence.
	Provide descriptions with careful attention to sensory detail.

Additional Support Activities

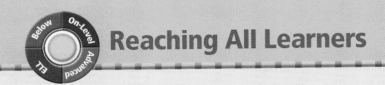
Additional Support Activities
High-Frequency Words

■ BELOW-LEVEL

Reteach: Match Words

Write the word *look* on three self-stick notes and the word *come* on three self-stick notes. Distribute one word to each child. Then write the following sentences on chart paper.

I can look at the sky.

Will you come with me?

Please come to my party.

Let's look at this book together.

Why don't you come over for lunch?

We like to look at the flowers.

Read the sentences aloud, tracking the print. Then reread the first sentence and call on a child who has the word *look* to place the self-stick note over the word *look* in the sentence. Follow the same procedure with the other sentences.

For More Intensive Instruction

See Intervention Resource Kit, Lesson 24 for additional **preteach** and **reteach** activities.

■ ADVANCED

Extend: Write a Sentence

Distribute copies of the *High-Frequency Word Cards Come, to,* and *the.* Have children read the words aloud. Then ask them to glue the words onto drawing paper and complete the sentence, adding a picture to illustrate their work.

■ ENGLISH-LANGUAGE LEARNERS

Reteach: Say a Sentence

Display the *High-Frequency Word Card come* and read it with children. Use the word in a sentence, such as *Can you come to my house?* Then pass the card to a child. The child should use the word *come* in a sentence, and then pass the card on to the next child. Allow each child to have a turn sharing a sentence. Then follow the same procedure with the high-frequency word *look.*

For More Language Development

See English-Language Learners Resource Kit, Lesson 24 for additional **reteach** activities.

Additional Support Activities
Phonemic Awareness

For More Intensive Instruction

See Intervention Resource Kit, Lesson 24 for additional **preteach** and **reteach** activities.

■ BELOW-LEVEL

Reteach: Listen for /j/

Tell children that you will say some words and each time they hear a word that begins with the /j/ sound, they should jump in the air. Say these words: *jungle, pizza, jelly, jeep, march, juice, Japan, lion.*

■ ADVANCED

Extend: Naming /j/ Words

Have children chant the following rhyme with you:

Jiggle, jiggle, jump, jump,

j, j, j.

The word (juice) *begins with* j.

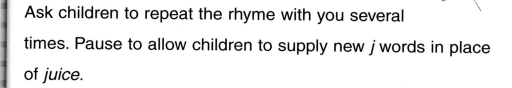

Ask children to repeat the rhyme with you several times. Pause to allow children to supply new *j* words in place of *juice.*

■ ENGLISH-LANGUAGE LEARNERS

Reteach: Which Word Begins with /j/?

Tell children you will say some words and you want them to listen for the /j/ sound at the beginning of the words. Say: *piano, jump.* Ask: *Who can tell me which word begins with /j/?* Follow the same procedure using these word pairs: *jug/name, janitor/home, rooster/jeans, whale/job, jewelry/uncle, butter/jet.*

For More Language Development

See English-Language Learners Resource Kit, Lesson 24 for additional **reteach** activities.

Additional Support Activities
Phonics

■ **BELOW-LEVEL**

Reteach: Name That Picture

Gather pictures of objects whose names begin with *j* and *v*, such as *jack-in-the-box, jar, vacuum, jewelry, volcano, vitamins, jacket, valentine* and tape them in a row to the chalkboard. Call on children to name each picture and write the beginning letter of the picture name below the picture.

For More Intensive Instruction

See Intervention Resource Kit, Lesson 24 for additional **preteach** and **reteach** activities.

■ ADVANCED

Extend: *J* and *V* Pictures

Divide children into two groups, assigning one group the letter *j* and the other group the letter *v*. Provide each group with a large sheet of butcher paper and have them make a decorative border using their letter. Then have the groups cut out magazine pictures whose names begin with their letter and glue them onto the butcher paper. When children have finished, ask them to display and describe their work.

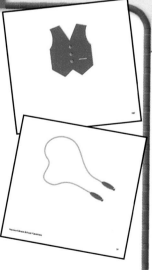

■ ENGLISH-LANGUAGE LEARNERS

Reteach: Picture Sort

Display the *Picture Cards jeep, jelly, vest, jump rope, van, violin, jet,* and *vegetables* on the chalk ledge. Label two boxes with self-stick notes, *j* and *v*. Ask children to help you put the pictures in the correct boxes. Have a child name the first picture, name the beginning letter, and place the *Picture Card* in the correct box. Repeat the procedure until all the *Picture Cards* have been sorted into the appropriate boxes.

For More Language Development

See English-Language Learners Resource Kit, Lesson 24 for additional **reteach** activities.

Additional Support Activities
Phonics

For More Intensive Instruction

See Intervention Resource Kit, Lesson 25 for additional **preteach** and **reteach** activities.

■ BELOW-LEVEL

Reteach: **Listen for Short Vowel /e/**

Tell children you will say some words and you want them to listen to the beginning sound in each word. Every time they hear a word that begins with the /e/ sound, they should write the letter *e* on their paper. Say the words *end, inch, echo, enter, umbrella, excellent.* Follow the same procedure for medial *e*, using the words *sent, left, give, when, fish, bed.*

■ ADVANCED

Extend: Name *e* Words

Hold up the *Big Alphabet Card Ee* and ask children to identify the letter. Tell them that as you pass the card to each one of them, they should say a word that begins with *e* or has *e* in the middle. Record children's words on chart paper and then have individuals come to the chart and circle the *e* in each word.

■ ENGLISH-LANGUAGE LEARNERS

Reteach: Write *e*

Have children work with their *Write-on/Wipe-off Boards*. Say the word *edge* and ask: *Does* edge *begin with the /e/ sound?* When children respond *yes*, have them write the letter *e* on their board. Tell children you will say some more words and if they hear the /e/ sound at the beginning, they are to write the letter *e* on their board. Then say the following words: *empty, ostrich, after, elephant, exit.* Repeat the procedure for words with medial *e*, using these words: *ten, get, mix, best, pan.*

For More Language Development

See **English-Language Learners Resource Kit, Lesson 25** for additional **reteach** activities.

Additional Support Activities
Phonemic Awareness

**For More
Intensive Instruction**

**See Intervention
Resource Kit, Lesson 25**
for additional **preteach**
and **reteach** activities.

■ BELOW-LEVEL

Reteach: Blend the Sounds

Ask children to listen carefully to the following sounds and name the word you are trying to say: /h/ /i/ /t/. Continue with the following words:

/h/ /u/ /g/	/p/ /e/ /n/
/m/ /i/ /s/	/t/ /a/ /g/
/v/ /e/ /t/	/j/ /o/ /g/
/f/ /e/ /l/	/k/ /i/ /k/

■ ADVANCED

Extend: Blending Picture Names

Distribute one of the *Picture Cards bus, cat, dog, fox, jet, pig, sun,* and *yak* to each child. Ask a child to keep his or her card hidden from view and to say each sound in the picture name (such as /b/ /u/ /s/). The rest of the group should name the picture, which can be confirmed by the child displaying the *Picture Card.* Continue until all children have provided their picture names.

■ ENGLISH-LANGUAGE LEARNERS

Reteach: Blending Sounds

Ask children to repeat these sounds after you (pause after each phoneme): /s/ /e/ /t/. Then say the sounds a little more quickly, again having children repeat them after you, until you say the word *set.* Follow the same procedure for the words *ten, red, pig, hot, let, fun.*

For More Language Development

See English-Language Learners Resource Kit, Lesson 25 for additional **reteach** activities.

Additional Support Activities
Comprehension and Skills

For More Intensive Instruction

See Intervention Resource Kit, Lesson 25 for additional **preteach** and **reteach** activities.

■ **BELOW-LEVEL**

Reteach: Show the Number of Syllables

Tell children that you will say a word and you want them to clap the number of syllables they hear in the word. Once they know how many syllables are in the word, they should hold up that number of fingers. Say the word *mother*. Have children repeat the word and clap the syllables, then hold up the corresponding number of fingers. Repeat the procedure with the words *wait, castle, drum, thunder, imagine, inchworm*.

■ ADVANCED

Extend: One or Two Syllables?

Write the words *pet* and *spider* on the board and read them with children. Have partners work together to figure out which word has one syllable and which word has two. Continue with these word pairs: *week/lonely, Monday/lake, cricket/frog, longer/mole, flea/alone, home/thicket.*

■ ENGLISH-LANGUAGE LEARNERS

Reteach: Clap the Syllables

Say the word *day* and clap once. Have children do the same. Tell children that *day* has one syllable. Follow the same procedure for the words *grow, classroom, hammer, instrument,* and *telephone.*

For More Language Development

See English-Language Learners Resource Kit, Lesson 25 for additional **reteach** activities.

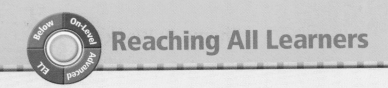
Additional Support Activities
Phonemic Awareness

■ BELOW-LEVEL

Reteach: Listen for the Middle Sound

Display the *Picture Cards bus, yak*, and *duck* on the chalk ledge. Ask children to name each picture. Then ask: *Which two words have the same middle sound?* Take away the *Picture Card yak* and ask: *What sound do you hear in the middle of* bus *and* duck? Follow the same procedure with these sets of *Picture Cards: van, nest, lamb; milk, hen, jet; dog, socks, vest; hat, fish, pig; yak, fox, hat.*

For More Intensive Instruction

See Intervention Resource Kit, Lesson 26 for additional **preteach** and **reteach** activities.

■ ADVANCED

Extend: What's in the Middle?

Divide the group into two teams. Ask the first team member to listen carefully as you say three words: *tell, fix, red.* Ask: *Which two words have the same middle sound? What is the middle sound you hear in* tell? Award one point for each correct answer. Continue with sets of words such as the following:

clap, mad, sit	trick, mop, hill
bump, deck, jug	truck, fox, pop
snap, web, bench	miss, peg, hen

■ ENGLISH-LANGUAGE LEARNERS

Reteach: Naming Middle Sounds

Say the words *bed* and *net* and have children repeat them with you. Say: bed *and* net *have the same middle sound—/e/. Say the middle sound with me—/e/, /e/, /e/.* Follow the same procedure using the words *fun/hum, fish/six, dad/pass, dot/job.*

For More Language Development

See English-Language Learners Resource Kit, Lesson 26 for additional **reteach** activities.

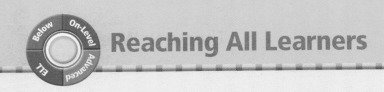
Additional Support Activities
Phonics

**For More
Intensive Instruction**

**See Intervention
Resource Kit, Lesson 26**
for additional **preteach**
and **reteach** activities.

■ **BELOW-LEVEL**

Reteach: Read the Words

Write the following words on index cards: *den, ten, men, net, Ned, hen, pen*. Display each card and ask a child to say the name of the middle letter and read the word.

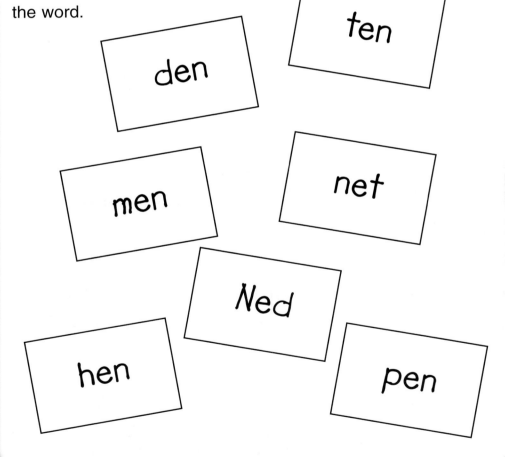

■ ADVANCED

Extend: Word Clues

Write the following words on the board: *hen, pen, ten, men, net, den*. Have children read the list of words. Then provide a clue, such as *This word is a number*, and call on a child to read and circle the answer. Continue until all of the words have been read and circled.

■ ENGLISH-LANGUAGE LEARNERS

Reteach: Words with *e* and *n*

Distribute one *Alphabet Card h, e, n* to each of three children and ask them to stand side by side. Then point to the letters as you read the word, *hen*. Have children read the word with you. Follow the same procedure for *men, ten, net, den, pen*.

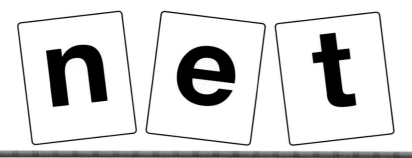

For More Language Development

See English-Language Learners Resource Kit, Lesson 26 for additional **reteach** activities.

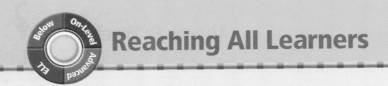

Additional Support Activities
Comprehension and Skills

For More Intensive Instruction

See Intervention Resource Kit, Lesson 26 for additional **preteach** and **reteach** activities.

■ BELOW-LEVEL

Reteach: Act Out the Poem

Read the following line from the poem "Mr. Backward" on page 23 of the *Read-Aloud Anthology: He eats dessert before his meal.* Ask a child to act out the sentence. Then read the sentence again and ask children to name the action word. Follow the same procedure with other lines from the poem that lend themselves to being acted out.

■ ADVANCED

Extend: Charades

Write the following action words on index cards and place them in a large box: *eat, drink, hop, skip, fish, swim, walk, sleep.* Have a child draw a card from the box and read the word to himself or herself. (Provide assistance as needed). Tell the child to act out the word on the card and have the rest of the group guess the word. Continue the game until all the cards have been used.

drink   hop   fish

■ ENGLISH-LANGUAGE LEARNERS

Reteach: Act Out the Story

Retell the story "Caps for Sale" to children and have them act out the action words. For example, you might say: *The peddler **carried** caps on his head. Can you show me how to **carry** caps on your head? The peddler **walked** to town. Can you show me how to **walk**?* and so on.

For More Language Development

See English-Language Learners Resource Kit, Lesson 26 for additional reteach activities.

Additional Support Activities
High-Frequency Words

■ BELOW-LEVEL

Reteach: **A Sentence About Me**

me

Display the *High-Frequency Word Card me* and a personal possession. Say: *This (hat) belongs to me*, pointing to the word card *me* as you say the word. Then pass the word card to a child and invite the child to share a personal possession, using the sentence frame *This _____ belongs to me.* Continue passing the word card until all children have had a chance to say a sentence.

For More Intensive Instruction

See Intervention Resource Kit, Lesson 27 for additional **preteach** and **reteach** activities.

■ ADVANCED

Extend: Write Sentences

Have children copy the following sentences from the board: *Look at me. I can _____.* Ask them to complete the second sentence and draw a picture to illustrate it. Allow children to share their work with the group.

Look at me.
I can _____.

■ ENGLISH-LANGUAGE LEARNERS

Reteach: Spell Words

Place the *Alphabet Cards m, e* in a pocket chart. As you point to each letter, say: m–e *spells* me—me. Point to the letters again and have children repeat the sentence with you. Repeat the procedure with the word *for*.

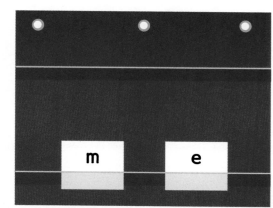

For More Language Development

See English-Language Learners Resource Kit, Lesson 27 for additional **reteach** activities.

Additional Support Activities
Phonemic Awareness

For More Intensive Instruction

See Intervention Resource Kit, Lesson 27 for additional **preteach** and **reteach** activities.

■ BELOW-LEVEL

Reteach: The *z* Zone

Tell children that only words beginning with the /z/ sound can go in the *z* Zone. Ask children to signal thumbs up when they hear a word that can go in the *z* Zone. Say these words: *seal, zipper, rabbit, zoom, zero, gold, zap, zig zag, doughnut.*

FLORIDA STANDARDS/GLES FCAT: LA.A.1.1.2.K.5 Phonetic principles

■ ADVANCED

Extend: Words with *z*

Tell children that Zach Zebra only likes words that begin with /z/. Ask: *Will Zach Zebra like the word* zipper? After children respond, ask the same question again, using these words: *zap, supper, zip, zoom, place, zero, camp, zany.*

■ ENGLISH-LANGUAGE LEARNERS

Reteach: Which Word Begins with *z*?

Say the following pairs of words. Ask children to name the word in each pair that begins with the /z/ sound.

zero/race	horse/zipper
garden/zoom	zebra/tiger
zap/middle	forest/zone
curtain/zoo	zip/lunch

For More Language Development

See **English-Language Learners Resource Kit, Lesson 27** for additional **reteach** activities.

Additional Support Activities
Phonics

For More Intensive Instruction

See Intervention Resource Kit, Lesson 27 for additional **preteach** and **reteach** activities.

■ BELOW-LEVEL

Reteach: Write the Letter

Have children work with their *Write-on/Wipe-off Boards*. Say the word *zoo* and ask a child to name the beginning letter in the word. Have each child write the letter *z* on their board. Ask children to listen carefully to the following words (as you say them one at a time) and write the beginning letter on their board: *yes, zipper, zero, young, zoom, yard, yesterday, zap*. Have children hold up their board after each word so you can confirm their answers.

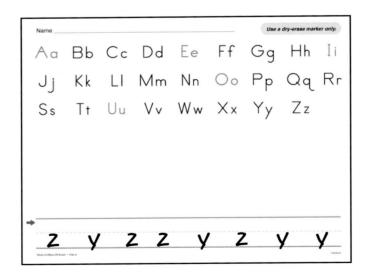

■ ADVANCED

Extend: Name *y* and *z* Words

Display the *Big Alphabet Cards y* and *z*. Tell children that as you hold up each card, you want them to name the letter and say a word that begins with that letter. For example, if you hold up the *y* card, children should say *y* and provide a word such as *yellow*. Hold up each card a few times so that children have several chances to generate words.

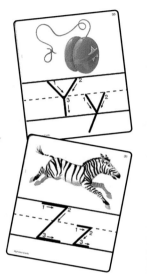

■ ENGLISH-LANGUAGE LEARNERS

Reteach: Is It *y* or *z*?

Divide children into two groups. Give one group the *Big Alphabet Card y* and the other group the *Big Alphabet Card z*. Have each group name their letter. Then ask children to listen carefully as you display the *Picture Card yellow* and name it. Ask: *Which group gets this picture—the* y *group or the* z *group?* Continue with the *Picture Cards yo-yo, zebra, zoo, yak, zipper, yarn.*

For More Language Development

See English-Language Learners Resource Kit, Lesson 27 for additional **reteach** activities.

Additional Support Activities
Phonics

■ BELOW-LEVEL

Reteach: Name That Picture

Gather pictures of objects whose names begin with *e* and *d*, such as *elephant, egg, elf, elevator, doctor, dinosaur, doll, daisy* and tape them in a row to the chalkboard. Call on children to name each picture and write the beginning letter of the picture name below the picture.

For More Intensive Instruction

See Intervention Resource Kit, Lesson 28 for additional **preteach** and **reteach** activities.

■ ADVANCED

Extend: Duck and Elephant Words

Draw the simple outline of a duck and an elephant on chart paper. Ask children to suggest words and names that begin with *d* and record their ideas inside or around the duck. Do the same thing for *e* words in or around the elephant.

dinosaur
dog
Dave
dig

■ ENGLISH-LANGUAGE LEARNERS

Reteach: Write Beginning Letters

Say the word *deer* and ask children to repeat it with you. Ask: *Who can write the beginning letter in* deer? Have a child write the letter on the board.

Then continue the procedure with these words: *doll, empty, edge, duck, dumpling, every, dark, egg*.

d

For More Language Development

See English-Language Learners Resource Kit, Lesson 28 for additional **reteach** activities.

Additional Support Activities
Phonemic Awareness

■ BELOW-LEVEL

Reteach: Word Cheer

Divide children into three groups and tell them that they are going to cheer a word together. Tell the first group that their part of the word is /y/. Have them practice it, /y/ /y/ /y/. Tell the second group that their part of the word is /e/. Have them practice it, /e/ /e/ /e/. Tell the third group that their part of the word is /s/. Have them practice it, /s/ /s/ /s/. Tell children you will lead them in the cheer; that as you point to each group, they are to say their part of the word. Point from the first group to the second group to the third group so that children cheer the word *yes*. Follow the same procedure for other words.

For More Intensive Instruction

See Intervention Resource Kit, Lesson 28 for additional **preteach** and **reteach** activities.

■ ADVANCED

Extend: What's the Word?

Group children in threes. Call one group to the front of the room and assign each child a sound in the word *hen*. Have the children stand in the order of the letters and say the sounds in order (/h/ /e/ /n/). Ask the rest of the children to name the word. Follow the same procedure with other groups and other words.

■ ENGLISH-LANGUAGE LEARNERS

Reteach: Blending Sounds

Have children say the following chant with you:

/t/ /e/ /n/, /t/ /e/ /n/,

The sounds /t/ /e/ /n/ make ten.

Repeat the chant, using the following words: *bed, wig, top, jet, cap, duck.*

For More Language Development

See English-Language Learners Resource Kit, Lesson 28 for additional **reteach** activities.

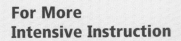
Additional Support Activities
Comprehension and Skills

**For More
Intensive Instruction**

**See Intervention
Resource Kit, Lesson 28**
for additional **preteach**
and **reteach** activities.

■ **BELOW-LEVEL**

Reteach: Retell a Story

Read aloud "Stone Soup" on pages 44–47 of the *Read-Aloud
Anthology*. As you read, stop after the beginning of the story
and ask children to tell you what just happened. Do the same
thing for the middle and end of the story. Be sure that children
mention the characters as they tell about each part.

■ ADVANCED

Extend: Retelling with Pictures

Group children in threes. Assign them a story from the theme or a familiar *Decodable Book*. Also, assign the parts of beginning, middle, and ending to children. Have children draw and label their part of the story.

They can share their

pictures and retell the story

to the class.

■ ENGLISH-LANGUAGE LEARNERS

Reteach: What's the Story All About?

Recall with children a familiar story, such as "The Shoemaker and the Elves," "The Hare and the Tortoise," or "The Ants and the Grasshopper." Ask

children to name the

story characters. Then

guide them to recall what

happened in the

beginning, middle,

and ending of the story.

**For More
Language Development**

**See English-Language
Learners Resource Kit,
Lesson 28** for additional
reteach activities.

Additional Support Activities
Phonemic Awareness

■ BELOW-LEVEL

Reteach: Listen for Rhyming Words

Tell children you will say two words at a time. If the two words rhyme, children should signal thumbs up. Use these words:

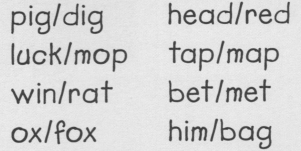

pig/dig	head/red
luck/mop	tap/map
win/rat	bet/met
ox/fox	him/bag

For More Intensive Instruction

See Intervention Resource Kit, Lesson 29 for additional **preteach** and **reteach** activities.

■ ADVANCED

Extend: Name Rhyming Words

Divide children into two teams. Alternating teams, say a word, such as *bed*, and ask the team member to name a rhyming word. Teams score one point for each rhyming word they provide.

■ ENGLISH-LANGUAGE LEARNERS

Reteach: Do They Rhyme?

Ask children to listen carefully as you say *cat* and *sat*. Then ask: *Do* cat *and* sat *have the same ending sounds?* Have children indicate thumbs up if the answer is *yes*. Tell them that *cat* and *sat* are rhyming words. Continue with the words *pen/ten, dig/pig, sad/run, hop/mop, cut/fin, bell/tell.*

For More Language Development

See English-Language Learners Resource Kit, Lesson 29 for additional **reteach** activities.

Additional Support Activities
Phonics

■ BELOW-LEVEL

Reteach: **Read Words with -ed**

Place the *Alphabet Cards r, e, d* in a pocket chart and ask children to read the word. Continue the procedure with these words: *Ted, bed, Ned, fed, led.*

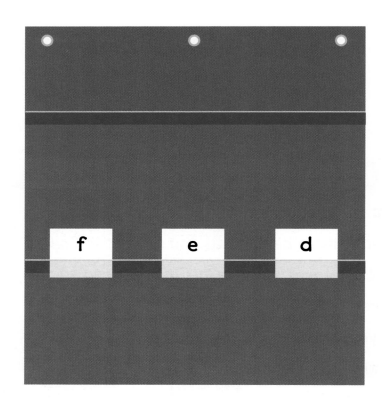

For More Intensive Instruction

See Intervention Resource Kit, Lesson 29 for additional **preteach** and **reteach** activities.

■ ADVANCED

Extend: Make a Word Ladder

Distribute word ladder patterns to children. Ask them to write one *-ed* word on each step of the ladder. (Tell them that they can use names with *-ed*.) Then they can trade papers with a partner and read each other's word ladders.

fed
bed
Ned
Ted
red

■ ENGLISH-LANGUAGE LEARNERS

Reteach: Read *-ed* Words

Place the *Alphabet Cards e, d* in a pocket chart and read the phonogram with children. Then as you place each of the following letters in front of *-ed*, call on children to read the words: *r (red), b (bed), l (led), f (fed)*.

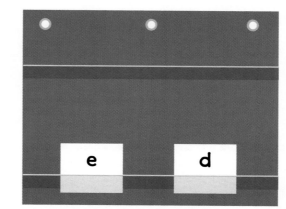

For More Language Development

See English-Language Learners Resource Kit, Lesson 29 for additional **reteach** activities.

Additional Support Activities
Comprehension and Skills

■ BELOW-LEVEL

Reteach: What Comes Next?

Display "The Bus Song" on page 23 of the *Big Book of Rhymes and Songs* and sing the first verse. Then repeat just the first line, *The people in the bus go up and down.* Ask children to continue the verse on their own. You may wish to continue in the same manner with the other verses.

For More Intensive Instruction

See Intervention Resource Kit, Lesson 29 for additional **preteach** and **reteach** activities.

■ ADVANCED

Extend: Write Patterned Text

Work with children to generate a short verse that has patterned text; for example, *Ms. Potter's class reads a book, reads a book, reads a book. Ms. Potter's class reads a book every day.* Record the verse on chart paper and read it several times with children.

■ ENGLISH-LANGUAGE LEARNERS

Reteach: Recognizing Text Patterns

Display pages 2–3 of *Big Book The Big Yellow Bus* and read the words aloud. Ask children to tell you which words they hear over and over. Follow the same procedure using some of the other pages in the *Big Book*.

For More Language Development

See English-Language Learners Resource Kit, Lesson 29 for additional **reteach** activities.

Additional Support Activities
High-Frequency Words

■ BELOW-LEVEL

Reteach: Say a Sentence

Display the *High-Frequency Word Card little* and say a sentence, such as *A baby is little*. Pass the word card to a child and ask him or her to say a sentence using the word *little*. Continue passing the word card until all children have had a chance to say a sentence.

For More Intensive Instruction

See Intervention Resource Kit, Lesson 30 for additional **preteach** and **reteach** activities.

■ ADVANCED

Extend: Write a Sentence

Distribute copies of the *High-Frequency Word Cards I, see, one, little* from *Teacher's Resource Book*, p. T17. Have children read the words aloud. Then ask them to glue the words onto drawing paper and complete the sentence, adding a picture to illustrate their work.

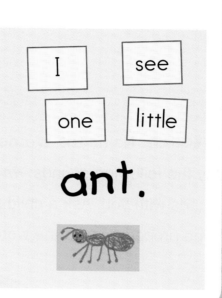

■ ENGLISH-LANGUAGE LEARNERS

Reteach: Can You Guess?

Play a guessing game with children. Display the *High-Frequency Word Card little* and give a clue for something in the classroom, such as *I see something that is little. It is square and red.* (block) Point to the word card as you say *little*. Continue to describe other little objects. Allow any children who feel comfortable doing so to take a turn giving a clue.

For More Language Development

See English-Language Learners Resource Kit, Lesson 30 for additional **reteach** activities.

Additional Support Activities
Phonemic Awareness

**For More
Intensive Instruction**

**See Intervention
Resource Kit, Lesson 30**
for additional **preteach**
and **reteach** activities.

■ **BELOW-LEVEL**

Reteach: Name the Words

Say the following sounds: /m/ /u/ /d/. Have children say the sounds with you. Ask a child to name the word. Follow the same procedure with the words *sad, fun, lot, ten, mix.*

■ ADVANCED

Extend: Blending Picture Names

Distribute one of the *Picture Cards duck, fish, hat, hen, lamb, socks, van,* and *vest* to each child. Ask a child to keep his or her card hidden from view and to say each sound in the picture name (such as /d/ /u/ /k/). The rest of the group should name the picture, which can be confirmed by the child displaying the *Picture Card.* Continue until all children have provided their picture names.

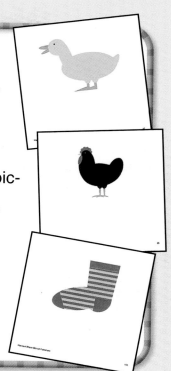

■ ENGLISH-LANGUAGE LEARNERS

Reteach: Blending Sounds

Have children repeat each sound as you say: */bbb/ /uuu/ /ggg/, bug.* Continue with the following sounds, asking children to supply the word when they can.

/fff/ /iii/ /ttt/, fit	/jjj/ /ooo/ /bbb/, job
/nnn/ /uuu/ /ttt/, nut	/yyy/ /eee/ /lll/, yell
/kkk/ /aaa/ /nnn/, can	/rrr/ /uuu/ /bbb/, rub
/ggg/ /ooo/ /ttt/, got	/ppp/ /aaa/ /nnn/, pan

For More Language Development

See English-Language Learners Resource Kit, Lesson 30 for additional **reteach** activities.

Additional Support Activities
Phonics

**For More
Intensive Instruction**

**See Intervention
Resource Kit, Lesson 30**
for additional **preteach**
and **reteach** activities.

■ BELOW-LEVEL

Reteach: Listen for *q* and *x*

Distribute *Tactile Letter Cards q* and *x* to children. Tell them
you will say some words and if they hear the /kw/ sound at
the beginning, they should hold up their *q* card. Say these
words: *quarter, bank, question, quiz, queen, lemon, quiet, hill.*
Then tell children you will say some words with the /ks/ sound
at the end. If they hear the sound they should hold up their *x*
card. Use these words: *clock, wax, six, chin, fix, club, mix,
box.*

■ ADVANCED

Extend: Make Picture Cards

Provide each child with four large index cards. Ask them to make two picture cards for words beginning with *q* and two picture cards for words ending with *x*. Have children write the picture name on the back of each card. Small groups can shuffle their cards together and then sort them into a *q* pile and an *x* pile.

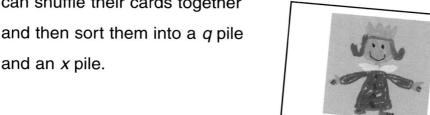

■ ENGLISH-LANGUAGE LEARNERS

Reteach: Letters and Sounds

Write the letter *q* on the board, saying the Letter Talk as you write: *Circle around, straight down, curve right.* Have children write several q's on a sheet of paper. Then say: *Queen Quail is quick.* Have children repeat *Queen Quail is quick* with you. Follow the same procedure for *x*, using the sentence *Fox is in the box.*

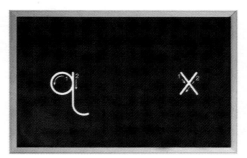

For More Language Development

See English-Language Learners Resource Kit, Lesson 30 for additional **reteach** activities.

Additional Support Activities
Phonics

■ BELOW-LEVEL

Reteach: Does It Have *u*?

Tell children you will say some words and you want them to listen to the beginning sound in each word. Every time they hear a word that begins with the /u/ sound, they should write the letter *u* on their paper. Say the words *under, over, umpire, ugly, into, umbrella*. Follow the same procedure for medial *u*, using the words *rug, hum, wag, jump, rock, plum*.

For More Intensive Instruction

See Intervention Resource Kit, Lesson 31 for additional **preteach** and **reteach** activities.

■ ADVANCED

Extend: Name *u* Words

Hold up the *Big Alphabet Card u* and ask children to identify the letter. Tell them that as you pass the card to each one of them, they should say a word that begins with *u* or has *u* in the middle. Record children's words on chart paper and then have individuals come to the chart and circle the *u* in each word.

ⓤnder
ⓤmpire
jⓤmp
ⓤmbrella
rⓤn

■ ENGLISH-LANGUAGE LEARNERS

Reteach: Listen for *u*

Tell children you will say some words and you want them to listen for the beginning sound. If the word begins with the /u/ sound, children should raise their hand. Say the following words, recording those with initial *u* on chart paper (after children have identified them): *apple, under, up, ox, umbrella, until.* Read the words on the chart paper and ask individuals to circle the letter *u* in each word. Follow the same procedure for words with medial *u*, using these words: *duck, sun, pot, win, cup, nut.*

ⓤnder
ⓤp
ⓤmbrella
ⓤntil

For More Language Development

See English-Language Learners Resource Kit, Lesson 31 for additional **reteach** activities.

Additional Support Activities
Phonemic Awareness

**For More
Intensive Instruction**

**See Intervention
Resource Kit, Lesson 31**
for additional **preteach**
and **reteach** activities.

■ **BELOW-LEVEL**

Reteach: Word Cheer

Divide children into three groups and tell them that they are going to cheer a word together. Tell the first group that their part of the word is /k/. Have them practice it, /k/ /k/ /k/. Tell the second group that their part of the word is /u/. Have them practice it, /u/ /u/ /u/. Tell the third group that their part of the word is /t/. Have them practice it, /t/ /t/ /t/. Tell children you will lead them in the cheer; that as you point to each group, they are to say their part of the word. Point from the first group to the second group to the third group so that children cheer the word *cut*. Follow the same procedure for other words.

■ ADVANCED

Extend: What's the Word?

Group children in threes. Call one group to the front of the room and assign each child a sound in the word *tub*. Have the children stand in the order of the letters and say the sounds in order (/t/ /u/ /b/). Ask the rest of the children to name the word. Follow the same procedure with other groups and other words.

■ ENGLISH-LANGUAGE LEARNERS

Reteach: Blending Sounds

Ask children to repeat these sounds after you (pause after each phoneme): /l/ /u/ /k/. Then say the sounds a little more quickly, again having children repeat them after you, until you say the word *luck*. Follow the same procedure for the words *pat, fin, log, bus, when, map*.

luck

For More Language Development

See English-Language Learners Resource Kit, Lesson 31 for additional **reteach** activities.

Additional Support Activities
Comprehension and Skills

For More Intensive Instruction

See Intervention Resource Kit, Lesson 31 for additional **preteach** and **reteach** activities.

■ **BELOW-LEVEL**

Reteach: Asking Questions

Read aloud a simple nonfiction book to children. Then write these question words on the board and read them: *What, When, Where, Why, How.* Encourage children to state questions they would like to have answered about the book, using one of the question words on the board.

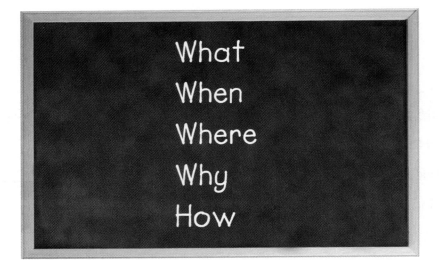

■ **ADVANCED**

Extend: **Writing Questions**

Read aloud a simple nonfiction book to children. When you have finished, ask each child to write one question they would like to have answered about the book. Gather the questions and read them aloud, one at a time. As time permits, answer as many questions as possible.

■ **ENGLISH-LANGUAGE LEARNERS**

Reteach: **Questions About Animals**

Ask children to choose one of the animals from the Theme Literature that they would like to find out more about. Have them suggest questions and record their ideas on chart paper. Then answer, or find answers for, as many questions as possible.

**For More
Language Development**

See **English-Language Learners Resource Kit, Lesson 31** for additional **reteach** activities.

Additional Support Activities
Phonemic Awareness

■ BELOW-LEVEL

Reteach: Sounds in Picture Names

Display the *Picture Card fish* and have children name it. Model how to say *fish* without the /f/ (*ish*) and how to say *fish* without the /sh/ (*fi*). For each of the *Picture Cards bus, fox, goat, jeep, kite, seal*, say: *Say [picture name] without the [initial sound]. Say [picture name] without the [final sound].*

For More Intensive Instruction

See Intervention Resource Kit, Lesson 32 for additional **preteach** and **reteach** activities.

■ ADVANCED

Extend: Sounds in Names

Remind children that the little duck in *Come Along, Daisy!*
was named *Daisy*. Model for them how to
say *Daisy* without the /d/ (*aisy*) and
how to say *Daisy* without the /ē/ (Dais).
Tell each child in turn: *Say [child's
name] without the [initial sound]. Say
[child's name] without the [final sound].*

■ ENGLISH-LANGUAGE LEARNERS

Reteach: Take Away Sounds

Display the *Picture Card cat*. Say: *If I say* cat *without the* /k/, *I
get* at. *Say it with me*—at. *If I say* cat *without the* /t/, *I get* ca.
Say it with me—ca. Repeat the procedure with the *Picture
Cards hat, jet, moon, mouse, nail, sun.*

For More Language Development

**See English-Language
Learners Resource Kit,
Lesson 32** for additional
reteach activities.

Additional Support Activities
Phonics

**For More
Intensive Instruction**

**See Intervention
Resource Kit, Lesson 32**
for additional **preteach**
and **reteach** activities.

■ **BELOW-LEVEL**

Reteach: **Read Words with *u* and *n***

Place the *Alphabet Cards f, u, n* in a pocket chart. Ask children to read the word with you. Repeat the procedure with the words *run, sun, bun, nut, net.*

■ ADVANCED

Extend: Word Clues

Write the following words on the board: *sun, fun, nut, run, bun*. Have children read the list of words. Then provide a clue, such as *This word means having a happy time*, and call on a child to read and circle the answer. Continue until all of the words have been read and circled.

■ ENGLISH-LANGUAGE LEARNERS

Reteach: Write Words with *u* and *n*

Have children work with their *Write-on/Wipe-off Boards*. Tell children that together you are going to write words with the letters *u* and *n*. Say the word *run* and ask: *Who can tell me the first sound you hear in* run? When a child responds, have all the children write *r* on their board. Continue in the same manner to elicit the second and third sounds in *run*, having children write each letter to complete the word. Follow the same procedure for the words *fun, sun, nut*.

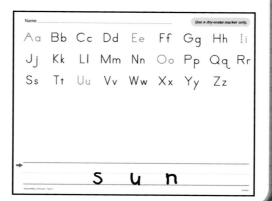

For More Language Development

See English-Language Learners Resource Kit, Lesson 32 for additional **reteach** activities.

Additional Support Activities
Comprehension and Skills

**For More
Intensive Instruction**

**See Intervention
Resource Kit, Lesson 32**
for additional **preteach**
and **reteach** activities.

■ BELOW-LEVEL

Reteach: Name the First and Last Sound

Divide children into two teams. Alternate showing a *Picture Card* to each team. Each team member must name the picture as well as the first and last sound in the picture name. A point is scored for each sound identified. Use the *Picture Cards bus, dog, duck, fox, goat, hen, kite, queen, seal, yak.*

■ ADVANCED

Extend: Bingo

Create nine-grid Bingo cards containing lowercase letters. Distribute the Bingo cards and game markers to children. Then play "Beginning Sound Bingo." As you say a list of words, ask children to listen for the first sound in each and to place a marker on each letter they hear. Use words such as *tiger, gate, dinosaur, wood, laugh,* and so on. Children can win by getting three markers in a row. Play "Final Sound Bingo" using words such as *planet, rain, sub, truck, pool,* and so on.

t

g

d

l

■ ENGLISH-LANGUAGE LEARNERS

Reteach: What Comes First and Last?

Ask children to listen carefully as you say the word *bus*. Ask: *Who can write the first sound you hear in* bus*?* and have a child write the letter on the board. Then ask: *Who can write the last sound you hear in* bus? and have a child write the letter on the board. Repeat the procedure with other words.

b   *s*

For More Language Development

See English-Language Learners Resource Kit, Lesson 32 for additional **reteach** activities.

Additional Support Activities
High-Frequency Words

■ BELOW-LEVEL

Reteach: Match Up Words

Write the word *here* on three self-stick notes and the word *are* on three self-stick notes. Distribute one word to each child. Then write the following sentences on chart paper.

I am here at home.

Please put the book over here.

We are in Kindergarten.

The clock is here on the wall.

You are my best friend.

Where are the cookies?

Read the sentences aloud, tracking the print. Then reread the first sentence and call on a child who has the word *here* to place the self-stick note over the word *here* in the sentence. Follow the same procedure with the other sentences.

For More Intensive Instruction

See Intervention Resource Kit, Lesson 33 for additional **preteach** and **reteach** activities.

■ ADVANCED

Extend: Concentration®

Have partners shuffle two sets of the *High-Frequency Word Cards no, see, look, come, for, me, one, little, are, here.* Have them place the cards face down on the table and play Concentration, keeping word cards that match after they have read the word.

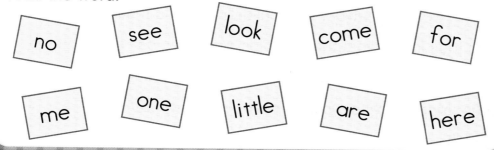

■ ENGLISH-LANGUAGE LEARNERS

Reteach: Find the Words

Distribute the *High-Frequency Word Cards are* and *here* to children. Ask them to read each word and then point to the matching word on the word pattern wall. You may want to review previous high-frequency words in the same way.

For More Language Development

See English-Language Learners Resource Kit, Lesson 33 for additional **reteach** activities.

Additional Support Activities
Phonemic Awareness

**For More
Intensive Instruction**

**See Intervention
Resource Kit, Lesson 33**
for additional **preteach**
and **reteach** activities.

■ **BELOW-LEVEL**

Reteach: **Listen for Syllables**

Say the word *homework*. Ask children to raise their hand
when they know what the syllables are. Then call on a child to
name the syllables. Follow the same procedure for these
words: *toothpaste, pancake, inside, rainbow, bathtub,
goldfish*.

■ ADVANCED

Extend: Break Words into Syllables

Group children in pairs. Whisper one of the following words to each pair: *firehouse, backseat, doorbell, wheelchair, mailbox, outside, barnyard, bluebird.* Have partners determine the two syllables in their word. Then ask one partner to say the first syllable and the other partner to say the second syllable. Have the group name the word.

■ ENGLISH-LANGUAGE LEARNERS

Reteach: Name the Syllables

Say the word *baseball*, clapping for each syllable. Have children do the same. Say: baseball *has two syllables*, base *and* ball. Then say and clap the syllables for the following words and ask children to name the syllables: *suitcase, beehive, backyard, downtown, doghouse, sailboat.*

For More Language Development

See English-Language Learners Resource Kit, Lesson 33 for additional **reteach** activities.

Additional Support Activities
Phonics

**For More
Intensive Instruction**

**See Intervention
Resource Kit, Lesson 33**
for additional **preteach**
and **reteach** activities.

■ **BELOW-LEVEL**

Reteach: Read the Words

Write the following words on index cards: *hug, rug, bug, jug, gum, get, gas.* Display each card and ask a child to read the word and use it in a sentence.

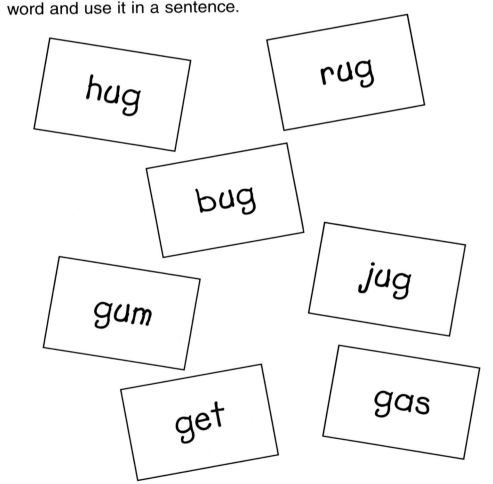

■ ADVANCED

Extend: Build Words

Distribute *Word Builder Cards a, b, g, h, m, r, s, u* and *Word Builders.* Tell children you will give them a clue and you want them to spell the word that names the answer, using their *Word Builder Cards.* Give a clue such as *This word begins with* g. *It's something people put in their cars to make them go.* (gas) Provide clues for other *u* and *g* words, such as *hug, rug, gum, mug, bug,* and have children build the words.

■ ENGLISH-LANGUAGE LEARNERS

Reteach: Name the Picture

Draw a simple picture of a bug and have children identify it. Write the word *bug* below the picture. Do the same thing for the words *rug, jug,* and *gum.* Then point to each word and ask children to read it.

For More Language Development

See English-Language Learners Resource Kit, Lesson 33 for additional **reteach** activities.

Additional Support Activities
Phonics

■ **BELOW-LEVEL**

Reteach: Build and Read Words

Distribute *Word Builder Cards b, c, h, n, t, u* and *Word Builders* to children. Ask them to build and read the following words: *cut, nut, hut, but.*

**For More
Intensive Instruction**

**See Intervention
Resource Kit, Lesson 34**
for additional **preteach**
and **reteach** activities.

■ ADVANCED

Extend: Write Words with -ut

Write the phonogram -ut on the board four times and read it with children. Call on children, one at a time, to come to the board and write a letter in front of each phonogram to make a word (such as *but, cut, nut, hut*). Have children read the completed list of -ut words and use each one in a sentence.

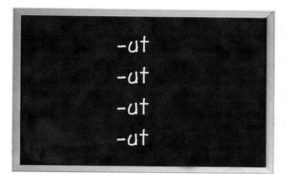

■ ENGLISH-LANGUAGE LEARNERS

Reteach: Read -ut Words

Place the *Alphabet Cards c, u, t* in a pocket chart and read the word with children. Then replace the *c* with *n* and ask children to read the new word. Continue by replacing the initial letter with *h* and *b*.

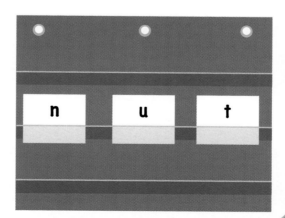

For More Language Development

See English-Language Learners Resource Kit, Lesson 34 for additional reteach activities.

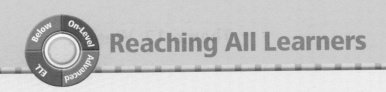
Additional Support Activities
Phonemic Awareness

■ BELOW-LEVEL

Reteach: **What Rhymes?**

Display the *Picture Card hen* and ask a child to name it. Then ask children to name some rhyming words for *hen*. Continue with the *Picture Cards goat, hat, kite, mouse, seal, van*.

For More Intensive Instruction

See Intervention Resource Kit, Lesson 34 for additional **preteach** and **reteach** activities.

■ ADVANCED

Extend: Rhyming Bee

Divide the group into two teams and hold a rhyming bee. Alternate saying a word to each team, for which players must name a rhyming word. Each correct answer scores one point.

■ ENGLISH-LANGUAGE LEARNERS

Reteach: Listen for Rhyming Words

Say the following rhyme:

Sun, sun, sun.

Who can name a word that rhymes with sun?

As children respond, repeat their answers; for example, fun *rhymes with* sun; run *rhymes with* sun.

Follow the same procedure with other words.

For More Language Development

See English-Language Learners Resource Kit, Lesson 34 for additional **reteach** activities.

Additional Support Activities
Comprehension and Skills

■ BELOW-LEVEL

Reteach: Find the Uppercase Letters

On chart paper, write these sentences from "There's a Hole in the Middle of the Sea" on page 141 of the *Read-Aloud Anthology*.

> There's a hole in the middle of the sea.
>
> There's a log in the hole in the middle of the sea.
>
> There's a bump on the log in the hole in the middle of the sea.

Read the sentences with children. Then call on children to circle the uppercase letter in each sentence. Ask them why these words begin with uppercase letters, prompting them as necessary.

For More Intensive Instruction

See Intervention Resource Kit, Lesson 34 for additional **preteach** and **reteach** activities.

■ ADVANCED

Extend: Fix the Sentences

Write the following sentences on the board. Have children read them, one at a time, and tell you what is wrong with each sentence. Call on volunteers to correct the sentences.

> the cat can run.
> my dog is here.
> we are in the hut.
> can you see me?
> i have a cap?
> what can you do?

■ ENGLISH-LANGUAGE LEARNERS

Reteach: Beginning Words in Sentences

Display pages 4–5 of the *Big Book Splash in the Ocean!* and read the sentence aloud. Ask a child to point to the uppercase letter in the sentence. Remind children that sentences always begin with an uppercase letter.

Then display other pages in the *Big Book* and have children point to the uppercase letters.

For More Language Development

See English-Language Learners Resource Kit, Lesson 34 for additional **reteach** activities.

Additional Support Activities
Phonemic Awareness

BELOW-LEVEL

Reteach: Sounds in Picture Names

Display the *Picture Card cat* and have children name it. Model how to replace the middle sound /a/ with /u/ (*cut*). Use the following *Picture Cards* and elicit the new words from children by having them change the middle sound:

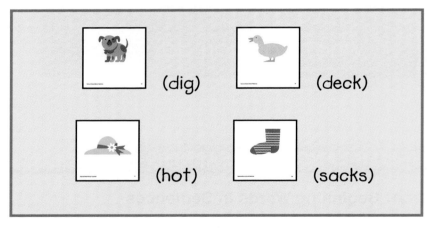

(dig) (deck)

(hot) (sacks)

**For More
Intensive Instruction**

**See Intervention
Resource Kit, Lesson 35**
for additional **preteach**
and **reteach** activities.

■ ADVANCED

Extend: What's the New Word?

Divide the group into two teams. Ask alternate team members questions such as, *What word do you get if you change the /e/ in* bed *to /a/?* Each correct answer scores one point.

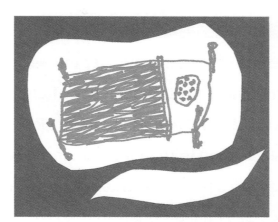

■ ENGLISH-LANGUAGE LEARNERS

Reteach: Change the Middle

Ask children to listen to the middle sound in this word as you elongate it: */tooop/.* Tell them that now you will change the /o/ sound to the /a/ sound. Say the new word, again elongating the middle sound: */taaap/.* Ask children to name the new words as you change /miiiks/ to /maaaks/, /seeet/ to /saaat/, /buuut/ to /baaat/, and /pooot/ to /peeet/.

tap

For More Language Development

See English-Language Learners Resource Kit, Lesson 35 for additional reteach activities.

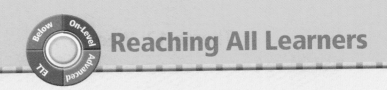

Additional Support Activities
Phonics

■ BELOW-LEVEL

Reteach: Point Out Repetitive Text

Write the repetitive sentences from *Sid Hid* on the board: *I did. Sid is not in it.* Read them aloud, tracking the print. Then ask children to read the sentences with you. Tell them that they will see these sentences several times in the book, *Sid Hid*. Call on individuals to read aloud each page of *Sid Hid*.

For More Intensive Instruction

See Intervention Resource Kit, Lesson 35 for additional **preteach** and **reteach** activities.

 **ADVANCED**

Extend: Read Story Parts

Assign children the parts of the hermit crab, fish, starfish, octopus, clam, and jellyfish. Then have them read aloud their part of *Sid Hid*. If necessary, prompt children when it is their turn to read.

■ **ENGLISH-LANGUAGE LEARNERS**

Reteach: Read the Story Aloud

Ask children to read aloud *Sid Hid* to you. If they come to a high-frequency word they don't know, ask: *Can you find the word on the word chart? Who knows what this word is?* If children come to a decodable word they can't read, guide them to sound out each letter in the word and then blend the sounds.

For More Language Development

See English-Language Learners Resource Kit, Lesson 35 for additional **reteach** activities.

Additional Support Activities
Comprehension and Skills

**For More
Intensive Instruction**

**See Intervention
Resource Kit, Lesson 35**
for additional **preteach**
and **reteach** activities.

■ BELOW-LEVEL

Reteach: Figuring Out Feelings

Reread the *Big Book Splash in the Ocean!* to children. Tell them that the author doesn't say how the story characters feel about one another, but they can use story clues to figure it out. Ask children if they think the characters like each other and to give reasons for why they think so.

■ ADVANCED

Extend: Think About the Story

Recall the book *Swimmy* with children. Remind them that in the end, the little red fish and Swimmy chase the big fish away. Discuss with children how they think Swimmy and the little fish feel after they chase the big fish away.

■ ENGLISH-LANGUAGE LEARNERS

Reteach: How Do They Feel?

Ask children to listen as you tell this story: *Bob went fishing one day. He sat by the lake all afternoon, but he didn't catch one fish.* Then ask: *How do you think Bob felt?* Accept reasonable responses from children. You can follow the same procedure with other simple stories.

For More Language Development

See **English-Language Learners Resource Kit, Lesson 35** for additional **reteach** activities.

Theme Resources

Theme Resources

Consonant Vv

Review the Letter Name

Hold up *Alphabet Card Vv*. Tell children the following:

The name of this letter is *Vv*. Say the name with me.

(Point to the uppercase *V*.) **This is the uppercase *V*.**

(Point to the lowercase *v*.) **This is the lowercase *v*.**

(Point to the *Alphabet Card* again.) **What is the name of this letter?**

Write the Letter

Write uppercase *V* and lowercase *v* on the board. Ask children the following:

(Point to the uppercase *V*.) **What letter is this?**

(Point to the lowercase *v*.) **What letter is this?**

Watch as I write the letter *Vv* so that everyone can read it. (Write *V* and *v*.)

Guided Practice

Distribute *Tactile Letter Cards Vv*. Have students trace the letter *Vv* on the card. Then have them write the letter several times and circle their best *V* and *v*.

Review the Letter Sound

Hold up *Alphabet Card Vv*. Tell children the following:

The letter *v* stands for the /v/ sound. Say /vv/.

(Point to the *Alphabet Card*.) **The letter *v* stands for /vv/.**

(Point to the *Alphabet Card*.) **What sound does this letter stand for? Say the sound each time I touch the card.** (Touch the card several times, each time having children say /v/.)

Guided Practice

Give each child a *Vv Word Builder Card*. Tell children that you will say a word, and that, if the word starts with /v/, they should hold up their card. If it does not, they should not hold up their card.

vegetables	vest	violin	wind
van	seal	vet	watch
violet	sun	vanilla	wagon

Sorting *Vv*s

Place *Word Builder Cards Vv*, *Ww*, and *Dd* in a paper bag. Place *Picture Cards van*, *vegetables*, *vest*, *violin*, *wagon*, *watch*, *water*, *watermelon*, *dinosaur*, *doctor*, *dog*, *duck* in another paper bag. Tell children to empty the paper bags and to match the pictures to the letters. Tell them to name the letter and say the sound each picture name begins with. VISUAL/AUDITORY/KINESTHETIC

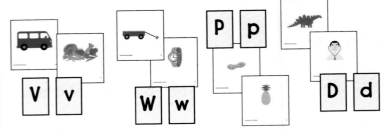

V Game

Write *Vv* on a self-stick note and place it on a volleyball. Have students sit in a circle. Point to the volleyball and tell children

This is a volleyball. Listen to the words I say. If the word begins with /v/, pass the volleyball to the person next to you. If the word does not begin with /v/, don't pass the ball.

Use these words:

violin	west	castle	verb	very
vet	dance	village	vase	visit

AUDITORY/KINESTHETIC

Sound Off!

Distribute strips of paper divided into six sections. Tell children to listen to the words you say and to write the letter that stands for the sound they hear at the beginning of the words. Say these words: **vanilla**, **violets**, **turtle**, **valentine**, **nurse**, **vacuum**. AUDITORY/VISUAL

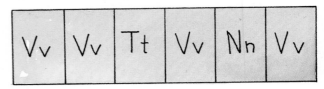

T2 FLORIDA STANDARDS/GLES FCAT: LA.A.1.1.2.K.5 Phonetic principles. *Also* LA.A.1.1.2.K.2 Alphabet, LA.A.1.1.2.K.3 Sounds

ALTERNATIVE TEACHING STRATEGIES

Consonant *Jj*

Review the Letter Name

Hold up *Alphabet Card Jj*. Tell children the following:

The name of this letter is *Jj*. Say the name with me.

(Point to the uppercase *J*.) **This is the uppercase *J*.**

(Point to the lowercase *j*.) **This is the lowercase *j*.**

(Point to the *Alphabet Card* again.) **What is the name of this letter?**

Write the Letter

Write uppercase *J* and lowercase *j* on the board. Ask children the following:

(Point to the uppercase *J*.) **What letter is this?**

(Point to the lowercase *j*.) **What letter is this?**

Watch as I write the letter *Jj* so that everyone can read it. (Write *J* and *j*.)

Guided Practice

Distribute *Tactile Letter Cards Jj*. Have children trace the letter *Jj* on the card. Then have them write the letter several times and circle their best *J* and *j*.

Review the Letter Sound

Hold up *Alphabet Card Jj*. Tell children the following:

The letter *j* stands for the /j/ sound. Say /jj/.

(Point to the *Alphabet Card*.) **The letter *j* stands for /jj/.**

(Point to the *Alphabet Card*.) **What sound does this letter stand for? Say the sound each time I touch the card.** (Touch the card several times, each time having children say /j/.)

Guided Practice

Give each child a *Jj Word Builder Card*. Tell children that you will say a word, and that, if the word starts with /j/, they should hold up their card. If it does not, they should not hold up their card.

jeep	jelly	jet	girl	goat
jump	junk	horse	hen	jacks
jog	jingle	seal	socks	jam

Jumping *Jj*'s

Ask children to stand in a straight line on one side of the room. Tell them to make one jump forward if the word you say begins with /j/ and to make one jump backwards if the word does not begin with /j/. When the line has moved to the other side of the room, the game is over. Say these words:

jump	jeep	cow	fork	join	just
goat	jelly	jam	jar	jet	jog

AUDITORY/KINESTHETIC

Jungle Journey

Place several chairs in a row. Distribute one index card to each child. Tell them these are tickets for a jungle journey. Ask them to write *Jj* on one side of the ticket and to think of a word that begins with the /j/ sound and line up. Have students whisper their /j/ word to you and write it on the back of their "ticket." Tell children to sit in their jungle journey chairs. Ask one child to be the "bus driver." Have students chant these words as they go on their journey: **/j/ is for jungle. Look what I can see! /j/ is for jaguar. It's coming after me! /j/ is for jeep. That's what I'm riding in. /j/ is for jingle jangle jungle. Something is creeping up my skin! Jump!** AUDITORY/VISUAL/KINESTHETIC

J Squares

Distribute square pieces of paper divided into nine three-inch squares. Tell children you will say a word and they can write the letter that stands for the sound they hear at the beginning of the word. Say the following words: **jam, jet, jelly, girl, bus, jungle, judge, jar, fish.** AUDITORY/VISUAL

Jj	Jj	Jj
Gg	Bb	Jj
Jj	Jj	Ff

Short Vowel *Ee*

Review the Letter Name

Hold up *Alphabet Card Ee.* Tell children the following:

The name of this letter is *Ee.* Say the name with me.

(Point to the uppercase *E.*) **This is the uppercase *E.***

(Point to the lowercase *e.*) **This is the lowercase *e.***

(Point to the *Alphabet Card* again.) **What is the name of this letter?**

Write the Letter

Write uppercase *E* and lowercase *e* on the board. Ask children the following:

(Point to the uppercase *E.*) **What letter is this?**

(Point to the lowercase *e.*) **What letter is this? Watch as I write the letter *Ee* so that everyone can read it.** (Write *E* and *e.*)

Guided Practice

Distribute *Tactile Letter Cards Ee.* Have students trace the letter *Ee* on the card. Then have them write the letter several times and circle their best *E* and *e.*

Review the Short Vowel Letter Sound

Hold up *Alphabet Card Ee.* Tell children the following:

The letter *e* stands for the /e/ sound. Say /e/ /e/.

(Point to the *Alphabet Card.*) **The letter *e* stands for /e/ /e/.**

(Point to the *Alphabet Card.*) **What sound does this letter stand for? Say the sound each time I touch the card.** (Touch the card several times, each time having children say /e/.)

Guided Practice

Give each child an *Ee Word Builder Card.* Tell children that you will say a word, and that, if the word starts with /e/, they should hold up their card. If it does not, they should not hold up their card.

egg	elephant	elf	alligator
empty	elk	octopus	echo
edge	apple	elevator	otter

Good Eggs

Distribute egg-shaped patterns for each child. Have children trace the patterns onto yellow construction paper and cut them out. Tell children to draw a belt across the egg's middle. Have them write *Ee* below the belt and draw a happy face above the belt. Children can add arms and legs by cutting out strips of construction paper and gluing them to the eggs. Punch holes in the top of the eggs and loop yarn through to make eggheads to hang in the room. VISUAL/KINESTHETIC

Modeling Ee

Distribute *Tactile Letter Cards E* and *e* and modeling dough. Have children place *Tactile Letter Cards Ee* on their desks and trace the upper and lowercase letters with their fingers chanting /e/, /e/, /e/ as they work. Then ask them to roll their dough into long snakes and make uppercase *Es* and lowercase *es* with their modeling dough. VISUAL/AUDITORY/KINESTHETIC

Ee Escalator

Distribute strips of paper divided into six sections. Make sure the sections are large enough for them to write an uppercase *E* and a lowercase *e.* Tell them to listen to the words you say. If the word begins with the /e/ sound, they can write *Ee* in a section. Use these words: *echo, end, edge, mitten, elbow, egg, elephant.* Have them fold their sections first one forward, next one backward, and so on to make their *Ee* escalators. AUDITORY/VISUAL/KINESTHETIC

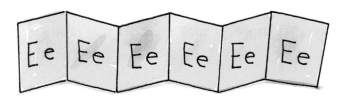

FLORIDA STANDARDS/GLES FCAT: LA.A.1.1.2.K.5 Phonetic principles. *Also* LA.A.1.1.2.K.2 Alphabet, LA.A.1.1.2.K.3 Sounds

ALTERNATIVE TEACHING STRATEGIES

Consonant Yy

Review the Letter Name

Hold up *Alphabet Card Yy*. Tell children the following:

The name of this letter is Yy. Say the name with me.

(Point to the uppercase *Y*.) **This is the uppercase Y.**
(Point to the lowercase *y*.) **This is the lowercase y.**
(Point to the *Alphabet Card* again.) **What is the name of this letter?**

Write the Letter

Write uppercase *Y* and lowercase *y* on the board. Ask children the following:

(Point to the uppercase *Y*.) **What letter is this?**
(Point to the lowercase *y*.) **What letter is this? Watch as I write the letter Yy so that everyone can read it.** (Write *Y* and *y*.)

Guided Practice

Distribute *Tactile Letter Cards Yy*. Have children trace the letter *Yy* on the card. Then have them write the letter several times and circle their best *Y* and *y*.

Review the Letter Sound

Hold up *Alphabet Card Yy*. Tell children the following:

The letter y stands for the /y/ sound. Say /yy/.
(Point to the *Alphabet Card*.) **The letter y stands for /y/.**
(Point to the *Alphabet Card*.) **What sound does this letter stand for? Say the sound each time I touch the card.** (Touch the card several times, each time having children say /y/.)

Guided Practice

Give each child a *Yy Word Builder Card*. Tell children that you will say a word, and that, if the word starts with /y/, they should hold up their card. If it does not, they should not hold up their card.

yak	yellow	yo-yo	wet
yarn	yell	van	yes
net	yawn	wagon	yodel

Sorting *Yy*s

Place *Word Builder Cards Yy, Vv,* and *Ww* in a paper bag. Place *Picture Cards yak, yarn, yellow, yo-yo, van, vegetables, vest, violin, wagon, watch, water, watermelon* in another paper bag. Tell children to empty the paper bags and to match the pictures to the letters. Tell them to name the letter and say the sound each picture name begins with. VISUAL/AUDITORY

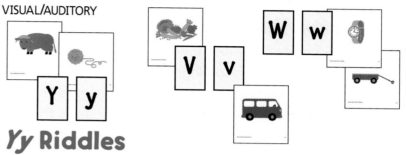

Yy Riddles

Distribute drawing paper. Tell children you are going to say some riddles and they can draw a picture to answer the riddles.

Say: **The answers to these riddles all begin with the letter Yy. Listen to the first riddle: I am the color of the sun. What color am I?** (yellow)
Color a yellow sun. Listen to the second riddle: I am a place to play. I am near a house. What am I? (a yard) **Draw a yard.**

Tell children to label their pictures. VISUAL/AUDITORY

Y Squares

Distribute square pieces of paper divided into nine three-inch squares. Tell children you will say a word and they can write the letter that stands for the sound they hear at the beginning of the word. Say the following words: **yet, yak, yes, water, winter, yellow, year, yard, dog.** AUDITORY/VISUAL

Yy	Yy	Yy
Ww	Ww	Yy
Yy	Yy	Dd

ALTERNATIVE TEACHING STRATEGIES

FLORIDA STANDARDS/GLES **FCAT: LA.A.1.1.2.K.5** Phonetic principles. *Also* **LA.A.1.1.2.K.2** Alphabet, **LA.A.1.1.2.K.3** Sounds

T5

Consonant Zz

Review the Letter Name

Hold up *Alphabet Card Zz.* Tell children the following:

The name of this letter is *Zz.* Say the name with me.

(Point to the uppercase *Z.*) **This is the uppercase *Z.***
(Point to the lowercase *z.*) **This is the lowercase *z.***
(Point to the *Alphabet Card* again.) **What is the name of this letter?**

Write the Letter

Write uppercase *Z* and lowercase *z* on the board. Ask children the following:

(Point to the uppercase *Z.*) **What letter is this?**
(Point to the lowercase *z.*) **What letter is this?**
Watch as I write the letter *Zz* so that everyone can read it. (Write *Z* and *z.*)

Guided Practice

Distribute *Tactile Letter Cards Zz.* Have children trace the letter *Zz* on the card. Then have them write the letter several times and circle their best *Z* and *z.*

Review the Letter Sound

Hold up *Alphabet Card Zz.* Tell children the following:

The letter *z* stands for the /z/ sound. Say /zz/.
(Point to the *Alphabet Card.*) **The letter *z* stands for /z/.**
(Point to the *Alphabet Card.*) **What sound does this letter stand for? Say the sound each time I touch the card.** (Touch the card several times, each time having children say /z/.)

Guided Practice

Give each child a *Zz Word Builder Card.* Tell children that you will say a word, and that, if the word starts with /z/, they should hold up their card. If it does not, they should not hold up their card.

zebra	zipper	zoo	socks
zigzag	zip	seal	nest
zucchini	zinnia	fox	zero

Zipping *Zz*s

Distribute strips of construction paper divided into five sections. Tell children you will say a word and if the word begins with the /z/ sound they can write *Zz* in a section of their paper. Say these words: **zipper, zero, lemon, zip, zoom, zebra.** Have students hold their "zippers" in front of them and pantomime zipping as they say: **Zip, zip, zip, the zipper goes up! Zip, zip, zip, the zipper goes down!**
AUDITORY/VISUAL/KINESTHETIC

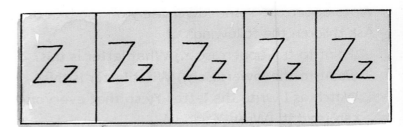

Colorful *Zz*s

Provide small amounts of various colors of finger paint on cookie sheets. Have students wear smocks. Tell them to write *Z* and *z* in their palms. Then have them write *Z* and *z* in the finger paint.
VISUAL/KINESTHETIC

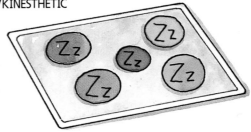

Sleeping Zebras/Buzzing Bees

Write a row of *zzzz*s on the chalkboard. Tell children that *zzz*s sometimes stand for the sound made when someone is asleep snoring or the sound made by a bee buzzing. Distribute drawing paper and tell children to draw a zebra sleeping and to write lots of *zzz*s on their pictures. Tell them they can add a bee buzzing and write lots of *zzz*s for the bee. VISUAL

FLORIDA STANDARDS/GLES   FCAT: LA.A.1.1.2.K.5 Phonetic principles. *Also* LA.A.1.1.2.K.2 Alphabet, LA.A.1.1.2.K.3 Sounds

ALTERNATIVE TEACHING STRATEGIES

Consonant *Qq*

Review the Letter Name

Hold up *Alphabet Card Qq.* Tell children the following:

> **The name of this letter is *Qq*. Say the name with me.**
>
> (Point to the uppercase *Q*.) **This is the uppercase *Q*.**
>
> (Point to the lowercase *q*.) **This is the lowercase *q*.**
>
> (Point to the *Alphabet Card* again.) **What is the name of this letter?**

Write the Letter

Write uppercase *Q* and lowercase *q* on the board. Ask children the following:

> (Point to the uppercase *Q*.) **What letter is this?**
>
> (Point to the lowercase *q*.) **What letter is this?**
>
> **Watch as I write the letter *Qq* so that everyone can read it.** (Write *Q* and *q*.)

Guided Practice

Distribute *Tactile Letter Cards Qq.* Have children trace the letter *Qq* on the card. Then have them write the letter several times and circle their best *Q* and *q*.

Review the Letter Sound

Hold up *Alphabet Card Qq.* Tell children the following:

> **The letter *q* stands for the /kw/ sound. Say /kw/.**
>
> (Point to the *Alphabet Card*.) **The letter *q* stands for /kw/.**
>
> (Point to the *Alphabet Card*.) **What sound does this letter stand for? Say the sound each time I touch the card.** (Touch the card several times, each time having children say /kw/.)

Guided Practice

Give each child a *Qq Word Builder Card.* Tell children that you will say a word, and that, if the word starts with /kw/, they should hold up their card. If it does not, they should not hold up their card.

queen	quack	quick	carrot
quiz	king	quilt	lamb
quiet	kite	ladder	quarter

Q Track

Use masking tape to make a large uppercase *Q* and a large lowercase *q* on the table. Have children take turns tracing the letters with their fingers as they chant the following: ***Q* is for *queen*, *Q* is for *quilt*, *Q* is for *quart*, *Q* is for *quiet*.**
VISUAL/AUDITORY/KINESTHETIC

Qq Crowns

Distribute a long strip of yellow construction paper that has a straight edge on one side and zigzag edge on the other side. Have them place the strip on the table or desk with the straight edge near them. Tell them to write *Qq* along the strip to make their *Q* crown. Help them tape the ends together to make the crown. Tell them to tiptoe quietly around the room wearing their crowns and saying words that begin with /kw/. (*queen, quiet, quick, quack*) AUDITORY/VISUAL/KINESTHETIC

Q Quarters

Fold paper into four sections and distribute one to each child. Tell children they can make *Q*-Quarters. Have them draw a big circle in each section of the paper. Have them write *Qq* on each quarter and color the quarters in. Have them cut out their quarters and write *Qq* on the back and color that side of the quarter. They can place their quarters in a box and use them for money in appropriate class activities. VISUAL/KINESTHETIC

ALTERNATIVE TEACHING STRATEGIES

Short Vowel *Uu*

Review the Letter Name

Hold up *Alphabet Card Uu.* Tell children the following:

The name of this letter is *Uu.* Say the name with me.

(Point to the uppercase *U.*) **This is the uppercase *U.***
(Point to the lowercase *u.*) **This is the lowercase *u.***
(Point to the *Alphabet Card* again.) **What is the name of this letter?**

Write the Letter

Write uppercase *U* and lowercase *u* on the board. Ask children the following:

(Point to the uppercase *U.*) **What letter is this?**
(Point to the lowercase *u.*) **What letter is this?**
Watch as I write the letter *Uu* so that everyone can read it. (Write *U* and *u.*)

Guided Practice

Distribute *Tactile Letter Cards Uu.* Have students trace the letter *Uu* on the card. Then have them write the letter several times and circle their best *U* and *u.*

Review the Short Vowel Letter Sound

Hold up *Alphabet Card Uu.* Tell children the following:

The letter *u* stands for the /u/ sound. Say /u/ /u/.
(Point to the *Alphabet Card.*) **The letter *u* stands for /u/.**
(Point to the *Alphabet Card.*) **What sound does this letter stand for? Say the sound each time I touch the card.** (Touch the card several times, each time having children say /u/.)

Guided Practice

Give each child a *Uu Word Builder Card.* Tell children that you will say a word, and that, if the word starts with /u/, they should hold up their card. If it does not, they should not hold up their card.

umbrella	up	otter	egg
end	ant	under	elephant

Umbrellas

Distribute umbrella-shaped patterns. Have children trace the umbrellas on various colors of construction paper. Tell them to write uppercase *U* and lower case *u* several times on the umbrella. Have students cut out their umbrellas and help them glue the umbrellas to a craft stick. Have students take turns giving these directions:

Put your umbrellas up! Children stand tall and raise their umbrellas over their heads.

Put your umbrellas down. Children squat and put their umbrellas near the floor. VISUAL/KINESTHETIC

Modeling *Uu*

Distribute *Tactile Letter Cards U* and *u* and modeling dough. Have children place *Tactile Letter Cards Uu* on their desks and trace the upper and lowercase letters with their fingers, chanting /u/, /u/, /u/ as they work. Then ask them to roll their dough into long snakes and make uppercase *U*'s and lowercase *u*'s with their modeling dough. VISUAL/AUDITORY/KINESTHETIC

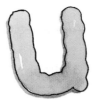

A Rainbow of *Uu*s

Distribute long strips of paper divided into four sections. Tell children to listen to the words you say. If the word begins with the /u/ sound, they can write *Uu* in a section. Use these words: *up, under, end, umbrella.* Tell children to use rainbow colors and color in their paper strips. Staple the strips together and drape the long strip across a corner of the room. Tell children to stand *under* their rainbow of *Uu*s. Tell them to look *up* and name colors they see. AUDITORY/VISUAL/KINESTHETIC

FLORIDA STANDARDS/GLES   FCAT: LA.A.1.1.2.K.5 Phonetic principles. *Also*
LA.A.1.1.2.K.2 Alphabet, LA.A.1.1.2.K.3 Sounds

ALTERNATIVE TEACHING STRATEGIES

Correlating Your Themes

Theme	Big Books	Library Books	Pre-decodable/ Decodable Books	Center Activities
Animals/Pets	*Five Little Ducks*	*Fish Faces*	*Little Cat, Big Cat* *A Bug Can Tug* *Sid Hid*	At Home or in the Wild
Careers	*The Big Yellow Bus*	*Career Day*	*Come In* *Is It for Me?* *A Hat I Like*	At the Grocery Store At the Bakery Who Uses This?
Colors	*The Big Yellow Bus*		*A Hat I Like*	
Day and Night	*The Big Yellow Bus*		*Come In* *But I Can* *Up, Up, Up* *Is It a Fish?*	Home Sweet Home
Families		*Benny's Pennies*	*Little Cat, Big Cat* *But I Can*	Home Sweet Home
Five Senses			*Up, Up, Up*	Matching Sounds with Letters This Is What I See I Spy
Helping/Cooperation			*We Can Fix* *Is It a Fish?* *It Is Fun* *A Bug Can Tug* *Sid Hid*	This Neighborhood Helpers Can . . . Write a List Helper Puzzle
Imagination			*Is It for Me?* *A Hat I Like* *But I Can* *Is It a Fish?* *In a Sub*	What's Inside the Log? What Do You See?
Neighborhoods	*The Big Yellow Bus* *Splash in the Ocean*	*Career Day* *Guess Who?*	*Is It for Me?* *We Can Fix* *A Hat I Like* *Little Cat, Big Cat* *Up, Up, Up* *Is It a Fish?* *Sid Hid*	3-D Building Write About Your Town "Places in Town" Poster "Adventure in Town" Book This Neighborhood Helpers Can . . .
Numbers	*Five Little Ducks*	*Benny's Pennies*	*Hop In!*	Count, Draw, Count
Ocean	*Splash in the Ocean*	*Fish Faces* *Swimmy*	*It Is Fun* *A Bug Can Tug* *Sid Hid* *In a Sub*	Ocean Collage Ocean Treats Go Fish! Write About an Ocean Animal Ocean Rhymes
School	*The Big Yellow Bus*	*Career Day*		
Seasons	*The Big Yellow Bus*		*Come In* *Is It a Fish?*	This Is What I See
Travel	*Splash in the Ocean*		*Up, Up, Up* *A Bug Can Tug* *In a Sub*	My Favorite Place
Weather	*Splash in the Ocean*		*Come In*	This Is What I See

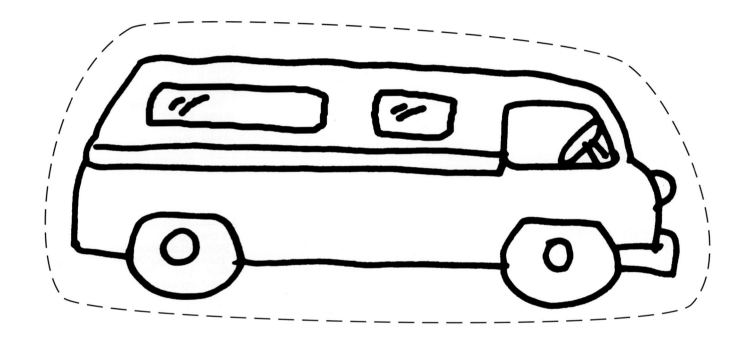

ALPHABET PATTERNS

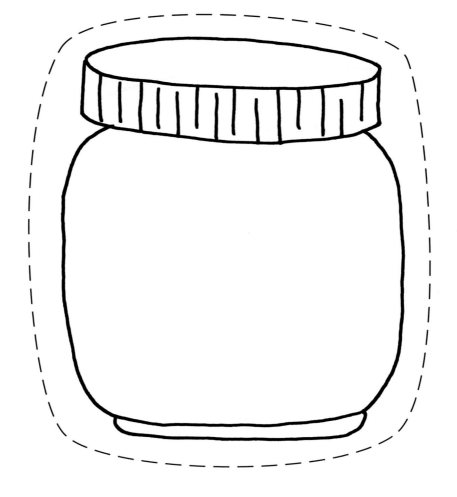

ALPHABET PATTERNS

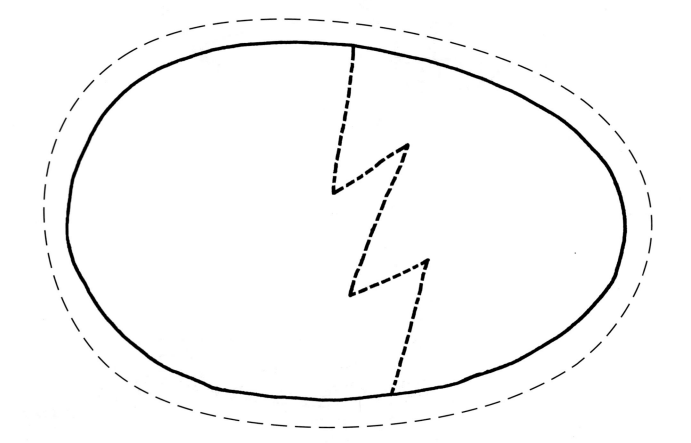

ALPHABET PATTERNS

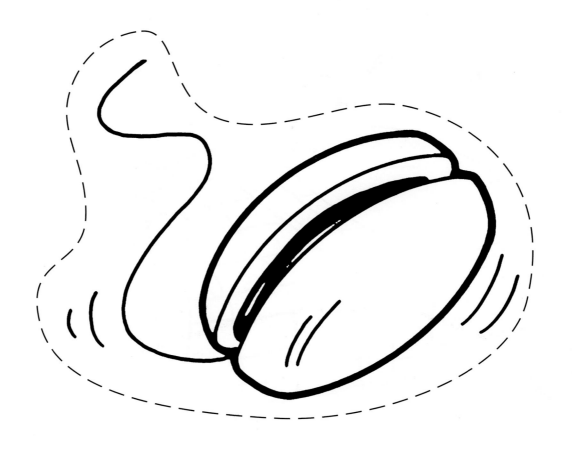

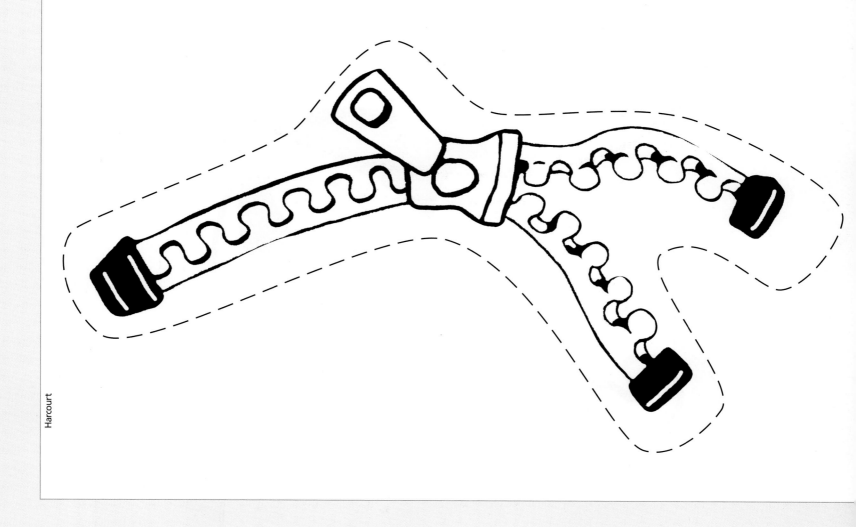

ALPHABET PATTERNS

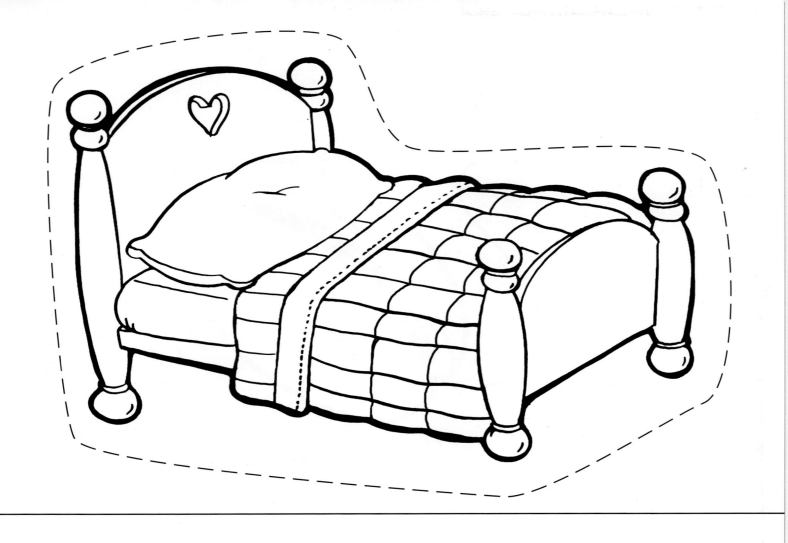

ALPHABET PATTERNS

Story-by-Story Word Lists

The following words appear in the *Pre-decodable* and *Decodable Books* in Themes 9–12.
High-Frequency Words are followed by an asterisk. Story Words are printed in italics. All other
words listed are decodable. Words appearing for the first time in that story are in red.

A Big, Big Van

a
at
big
box
can
cat
come*
dad
Dan
I
in
is
look*
Pam
pat
Sal
see*
the*
van

Come In

a
at
can
come*
do*
dog
get
got
hot
in
is
it
Jim
look*
Max
Meg
not
Pat
pool
Ron
the*
to*
wet

Hop In!

Bev
can
do*
Dot
get
go*
hop
I

in
Jed
Jon
Lil
my*
Nat
not
Pam
the*
Tim
to*
van
what*
you*

Is It for Me?

a
big
box
cap
for*
is
it
me*
no*
not
red
tan
yes

We Can Fix

a
bed
can
dab
fix
I
it
net
nip
pat
pet
rap
rip
tap
top
van
we*
zip

A Hat I Like

a
can
dad
get
hat
I

it
Jen
like*
look*
me*
mom
Nan
not
see*
Ted
the*
yet
you*

Little Cat, Big Cat

a
am
at
big
can
cat
did
do*
dog
fox
get
have*
him
I
in
is
it
little*
net
not
one*
pig
sad
see*
you*

But I Can

am
big
but
can
cut
fit
get
hit
hop
I
is
it
little*

Max
not
run

Up, Up, Up

a
am
big
bird
can
cub
deer
fat
fox
go*
hop
I
little*
nap
rabbit
red
run
see*
set
sip
sun
tan
tap
the*
top
up
what*

Is It a Fish?

a
are*
big
bug
come*
did
fish
get
got
hen
here*
is
it
Jen
jug
look*
man
mom
no*
rod
see*
Ted
tug

we*
what*

It Is Fun

a
at
bug
come*
do*
fun
here*
I
is
it
like*
look*
lot
net
not
on
Pam
Sam
see*
the*

A Bug Can Tug

a
am
big
boat
bug
but
can
cat
dog
fix
fox
go*
I
is
it
little*
me*
my*
not
pig
tug
you*

Sid Hid

bag
big
box
can
did
hid

him
his
I
in
is
it
little*
look*
not
pot
red
see*
shell
Sid
the*
tin
you*

In a Sub

a
am
at
big
can
clam
crab
dig
fin
fish
fit
fun
get
go*
had
has
I
in
is
it
little*
look*
net
not
red
see*
shark
sub
sun
the*
tip
up
what*
you*
zip

Cumulative Word List: Themes 1–12

The following words appear in the *Pre-decodable* and *Decodable Books* in Themes 1–12. High-Frequency Words are followed by an asterisk. Story Words are printed in italics. All other words listed are decodable. Words appearing for the first time in this volume are in red.

a
am
ant
are*
at
bag
bat
bed
Bev
big
bird
boat
box
bug
but
can
cap
cat
clam
come*
crab
cub
cut
dab
dad
Dan
deer
did
dig
do*
dog
Dot
fat
fin
fish

fit
fix
for
fox
frog
fun
get
go*
got
had
has
hat
have*
hen
here*
hid
him
his
hit
hop
hot
I
in
is
it
Jed
Jen
Jim
Jon
jug
Kip
lid
like*
Lil
little*

look*
lot
man
map
mat
Max
me*
Meg
mom
my*
Nan
nap
Nat
net
nip
no*
not
on
one*
Pam
pat
pet
pig
pool
pop
pot
rabbit
ram
rap
red
rip
rod
Ron
run
sad

Sal
Sam
sat
see*
set
shark
shell
Sid
sip
sit
snake
so
sub
sun
tan
tap
Ted
the*
Tim
tin
tip
to*
top
tug
up
van
we*
wet
what*
yes
yet
you*
zip

Theme 9	**Theme 11**
look	one
come	little

Theme 10	**Theme 12**
for	are
me	here

Harcourt

Phonics Sequence and High-Frequency Words

THEME 1: Getting To Know You

Phonics Skills Alphabet Introduction, Early Literacy Skills

High-Frequency Words (none)

Pre-decodable Book 1
First Day at School

Pre-decodable Book 2
Where's My Teddy?

THEME 2: I Am Special

Phonics Skills Consonant Mm Consonant Ss Consonant Rr Consonant Tt

High-Frequency Words *a, my, the*

Pre-decodable Book 3
Pet Day

Pre-decodable Book 4
My Bus

Pre-decodable Book 5
The Party

THEME 3: Around the Table

Phonics Skills Consonant Pp Consonant Cc Short Vowel Aa

High-Frequency Words *I, like*

Pre-decodable Book 6
The Salad

Pre-decodable Book 7
I Am

Pre-decodable Book 8
The Mat

THEME 4: Silly Business

Phonics Skills Consonant Nn Consonant Dd

High-Frequency Words *go, we*

Pre-decodable Book 9
We Go

Pre-decodable Book 10
I Nap

Pre-decodable Book 11
Tap, Tap, Tap

THEME 5: Family Ties

Phonics Skills Consonant Gg Consonant Ff Short Vowel Ii

High-Frequency Words *on, to*

Pre-decodable Book 12
The Park

Pre-decodable Book 13
Sit on My Chair

Pre-decodable Book 14
My Pig

THEME 6: Animal Families

Phonics Skills Consonant Ll Consonant Hh

High-Frequency Words *you, have*

Pre-decodable Book 15
I Have, You Have

Pre-decodable Book 16
Soup

Pre-decodable Book 17
The Dig

THEME 7: Bug Surprises

Phonics Skills Consonant Bb Consonant Kk Short Vowel Oo

High-Frequency Words *do, what*

Decodable Book 1
Kip the Ant

Decodable Book 2
The Big Ram

Decodable Book 3
What Can Hop?

THEME 8: Animal Adventures

Phonics Skills Consonant Ww Consonant Xx

High-Frequency Words *no, see*

Decodable Book 4
I Can See It

Decodable Book 5
What's in the Box?

Decodable Book 6
Hop on Top

THEME 9: Around the Town

Phonics Skills Consonant Vv Consonant Jj Short Vowel Ee

High-Frequency Words *look, come*

Decodable Book 7
A Big, Big Van

Decodable Book 8
Come In

Decodable Book 9
Hop In!

THEME 10: Neighborhood Helpers

Phonics Skills Consonant Yy Consonant Zz

High-Frequency Words *for, me*

Decodable Book 10
Is It for Me?

Decodable Book 11
We Can Fix

Decodable Book 12
A Hat I Like

THEME 11: Exploring Our Surroundings

Phonics Skills Consonant Qq Short Vowel Uu

High-Frequency Words *one, little*

Decodable Book 13
Little Cat, Big Cat

Decodable Book 14
But I Can

Decodable Book 15
Up, Up, Up

THEME 12: Under the Ocean

Phonics Skills Short Vowels a, i, o, e, u

High-Frequency Words *are, here*

Decodable Book 16
Is It a Fish?

Decodable Book 17
It Is Fun

Decodable Book 18
A Bug Can Tug

Decodable Book 19
Sid Hid

Decodable Book 20
In a Sub

PATTERNS: Learning Center (page 15)

Harcourt

PATTERNS: Benny's Pennies

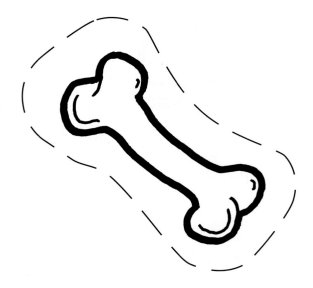

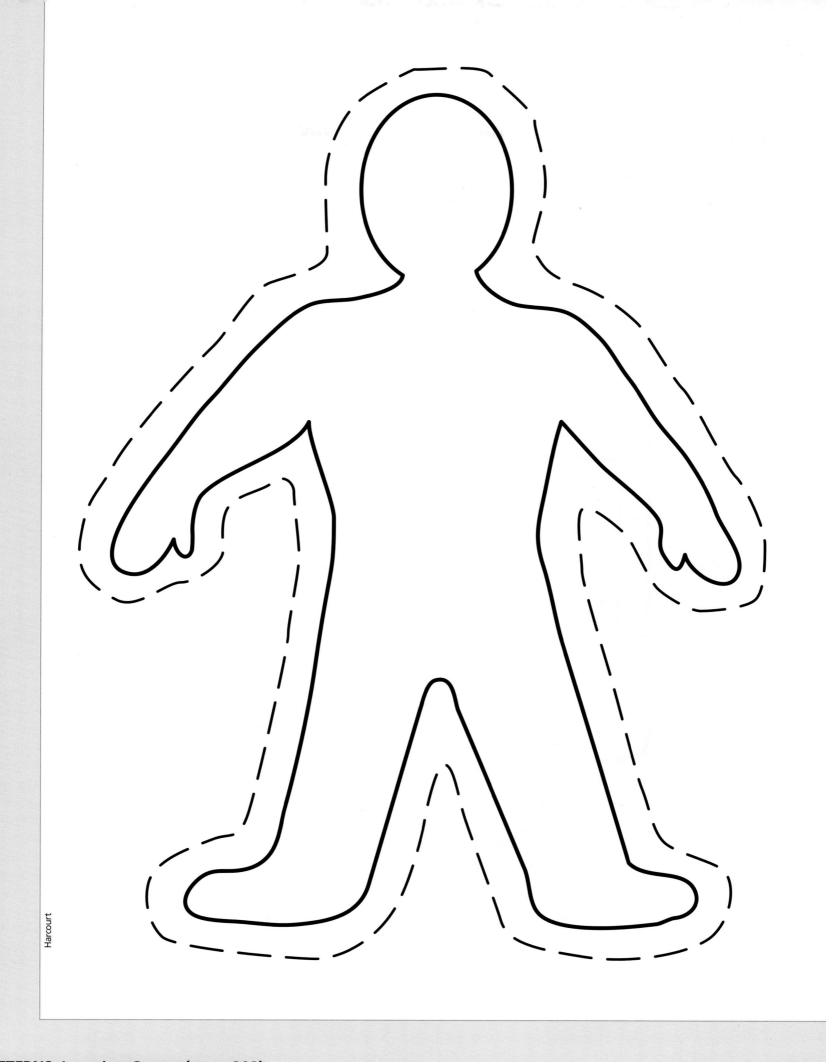

Harcourt

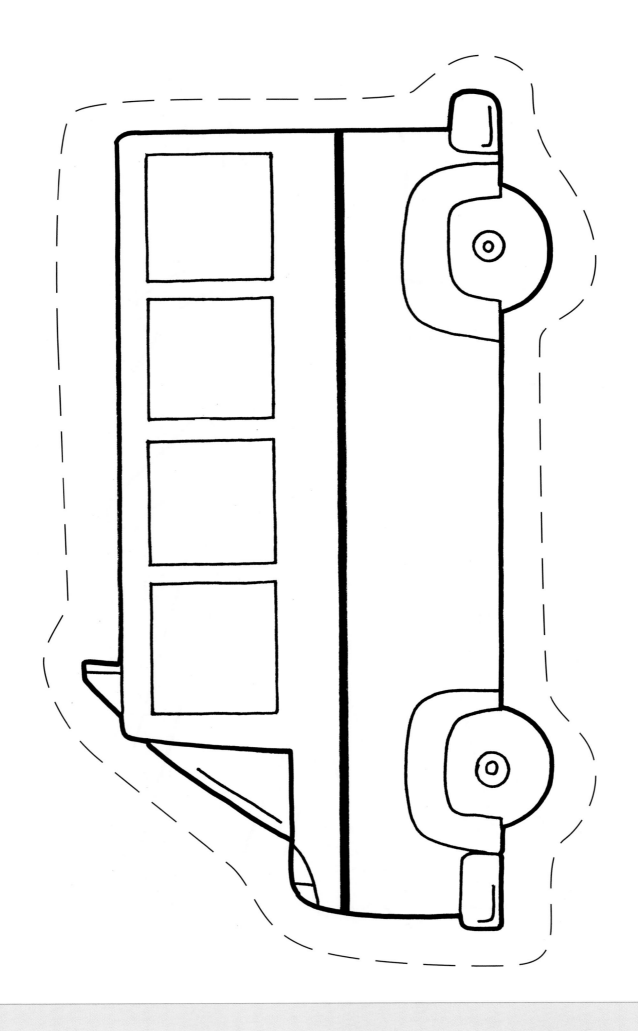

PATTERNS: The Big Yellow Bus

Harcourt

PATTERNS: Career Day

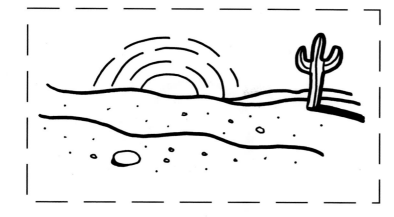

PATTERNS: Learning Center (page 354)

Harcourt

PATTERNS: Five Little Ducks

Harcourt

PATTERNS: Learning Center (page 523)

Harcourt

Additional Resources

Additional Resources

Managing the Classroom
Setting the Stage

Designing a Space

One of the keys to productive learning is the physical arrangement of your classroom. Each classroom has unique characteristics, but the following areas should be considered in your floor plan.

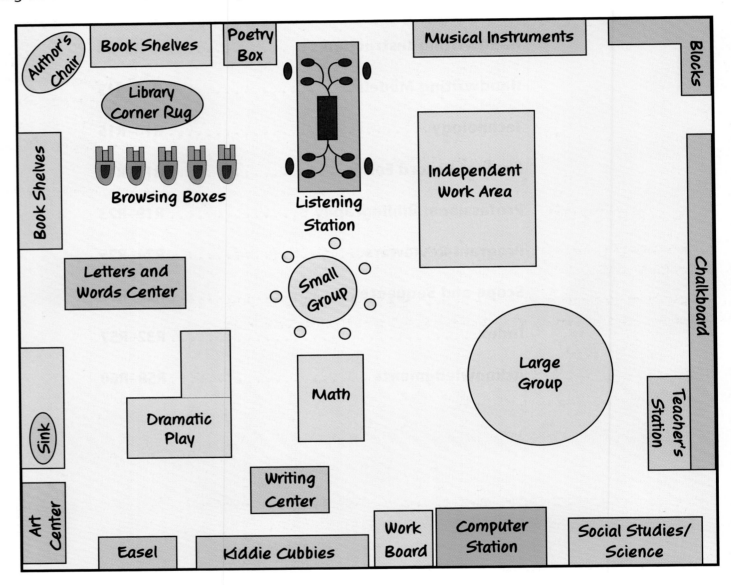

When arranging your classroom, consider traffic patterns and usage of areas. Place quiet centers near small group and independent work areas. Provide some private spaces for children to work.

Tip: A three-sided cardboard divider can instantly become a "private office" or a portable learning center.

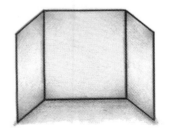

Organizing Materials

- Make certain each work area has the supplies needed to perform the required tasks. Add new supplies as activities change.

- Plan for the accommodation of complete and incomplete tasks and materials storage.

three-sided box for supplies or work

bins, tins, and plastic storage bags

> ## Tips
>
> **Keeping the Room Organized**
>
> - Clean and resupply each center as needed.
>
> - Get children into the habit of returning materials to their proper places.
>
> - Determine the placement of items and centers by usage. For example, you'll need a wastebasket in the Art Center. Art Centers need to be located nearest the sink.
>
> - Set aside time once a day for room cleaning. Assign specific tasks for each child.

Introducing the Centers

Before beginning a routine, acquaint children with procedures for and use of each area.

- Label each center with its name, its icon (see pages T22–T27 in Volume 1), and a symbol to indicate the number of children who can use the center.

- Help children understand how much time they will spend in a center. For example, they can read several books from the Browsing Boxes, listen to one tape recording in the Listening Center, and play one phonics game in the Letters and Words Center.

- Show children how to use the tape recorder, computer, headphones, and overhead projector. Demonstrate proper usage of art supplies.

Beginning a Routine

Establish Flexible Work Groups

In order for you to work with small groups without interruption, the other class members must clearly understand what they are to do. To plan a series of tasks that the other children can do independently, establish small work groups. These are hetero-geneous groups of children who are scheduled for the same center activities on a daily basis. You can change these groups as often as you like.

Introduce a Work Board

One way to schedule classroom activity is with a Work Board. A typical Work Board includes the names of small group mem-bers and icons that represent independent tasks. This sample Work Board is a pocket chart with cards. The Work Board can also be a cork board, a peg board with hooks, or a magnetic board. Its design should be flexible, enabling you to move cards on a daily basis.

Carrie Joshua Derek Suwanna Dillon	Mickey Dante Maritza Ty Karla
ABC Letters and Words Center	Science Center
Science Center	Math Center
Art Center	ABC Letters and Words Center

Introduce the Icons Icons are simple shapes that children can easily recognize and connect with a center in the classroom. Make icons consistent throughout the year. Label each activity center with the icon.

Organize the Work Board One way to set up your Work Board is to place groups of names as shown in the sample above. Near each group, place icons to represent activities for the day. Rotate group cards each day, giving each group a new set of activities. Further options are provided by using an icon that represents "free choice" of three or more additional activities. At the end of the week, change the icons to provide a new set of activities for the next week.

Tracking Progress

There are various ways to keep track of what children are doing during the course of a day.

Kid Watching   Observe children throughout the day. Determine which children are unable to finish all the activities for the day, but are working to capacity, and which children are not completing tasks because they are spending too much time in one center. Visit the centers. Note activities that work well and those that do not.

Portfolios   Have children store products they take from center activities in a portfolio created from a file folder, carton, or even a paper bag with handles. These products can be shared during conferences with children.

Conferencing   Set up a conference schedule to spend ten minutes each week looking through children's portfolios and talking with them about activities they have enjoyed, books they have read, games they have played, art they have created, and so on.

Setting Up Centers

Planning Activities for Classroom Centers

Many of the materials for ongoing centers are at your fingertips. Base center activities on literacy skills children are learning throughout the year. The following are suggestions for particular centers.

Reading Center

This center is a large area in your classroom that can include the following:

Listening Station   Include a tape recorder and headsets. Provide *Audiotexts* and a variety of commercial tapes and tapes recorded by volunteers and children. If you are providing text with a tape, make multiple copies and store the tape and books in a plastic bag. Suggest an extension activity following listening.

Poetry Box   Arrange a large box with copies of poems, rhymes, and finger plays that have been shared during reading time. The poems can be presented as large or small posters, in small books, as puzzles, or as copies for children to illustrate and take home.

Browsing Boxes   Provide boxes of books for each small reading group. Use color-coded boxes or bins that hold fifteen or more books. Provide multiple copies if possible. Books can include those that have been shared during group sessions and books that are appropriate for independent reading. Children can choose books to read from their assigned box.

Classroom Library   One corner of your room can house books children can freely choose and enjoy on their own. Include books of all kinds: Big Books, library books, and books children have made.

ABC Letters and Words Center

Organize this center on a table in one corner of the classroom. Include activities for building and reading words. Children can use an overhead projector and plastic or cardboard letter shapes to form words to project on the wall. Provide write-on/wipe-off boards for writing words and word building pocket charts with letters and cards. Provide supplies for making rhyming words flip books, word slides, word wheels, and phonics game boards.

Computer Center

Children can write with the computer by using word processing software, interact with literature software, or practice phonics activities with the *Phonics Express™* CD-ROM. See references throughout the lessons.

Writing Center

This should be a clearly defined space where writing materials are stored. Your classroom display of learned words might also be nearby for handy reference. Organize all materials in labeled containers.

Other materials might include an alphabet chart and picture dictionaries.

blank books	a variety of paper	stationery and envelopes
stickers	rubber stamps	poster board
pencils	markers	staplers and staple remover
glue	hole punch and yarn	date stamp

Curriculum Centers

Provide reading and writing activities in curriculum centers. Ideas are suggested with each day's instruction and before each theme. Provide materials as needed for children to

- create graphs in the Math Center.

- perform an experiment in the Science Center.

- make a map in the Social Studies Center.

- create new verses to perform a song in the Music Center.

- create artwork in the Art Center in response to stories.

Handwriting

Individual children come to kindergarten at various stages of readiness for handwriting, but they all have the desire to communicate effectively. To learn correct letter formation, they must be familiar with concepts of:

- **position (top, middle, bottom, etc.).**
- **size (tall, short).**
- **direction (left, right, up, down, etc.).**
- **order (first, next, last).**
- **color (red, yellow, green).**
- **same and different.**

Getting to Know You, the first theme in *Trophies,* includes lessons that teach and practice these skills in familiar contexts so that children learn this vocabulary before formal handwriting lessons begin.

Stroke and Letter Formation

The shape and formation of the letters in *Trophies* are based on the way experienced writers write their letters. Most letters are formed with a continuous stroke, so children do not often pick up their pencils when writing a single letter. Letter formation is simplified through the use of letter talk—an oral description of how the letter is formed. Models for manuscript and D'Nealian handwriting are used in this program to support different writing systems.

Learning Modes

A visual, kinesthetic, tactile, and auditory approach to handwriting is used throughout *Trophies.* To help children internalize letter forms, each letter is taught in the context of how it looks, the sound that it stands for, and how it is formed. Suggested activities also include opportunities for children to use their sense of touch to "feel" a letter's shape before and after they practice writing the letter.

Position for Writing

Establishing the correct posture for writing, pencil grip, and paper position will help children form letters correctly and help prevent handwriting problems later on.

Posture Children should sit with both feet on the floor and with hips to the back of the chair. They can lean forward slightly but not slouch. The writing surface should be smooth and flat and at a height that allows the upper arms to be perpendicular to the surface and the elbows to be under the shoulders.

Writing Instrument An adult-sized number two lead pencil is a satisfactory writing tool for most children. However, use your judgment in determining what type of instrument is most suitable for a child, given his or her level of development.

Paper Position and Pencil Grip To determine each child's hand dominance, observe him or her at play and note which hand is the preferred hand. Activities such as stringing beads, rolling a ball, building a block tower, or turning the pages in a book will help you note hand dominance.

Left Hand A left-handed child slants the paper from right (top) to left (bottom) so that the paper  is slanted along the line of the left arm toward the elbow. While writing, the child puts his or her right hand toward the top of the paper to hold it in place. The child holds the pencil slightly above the paint line—about 1 1/2 inches from the lead tip—between the thumb and index finger. The other fingers curve slightly to form a pad on which to slide across the paper. The pencil rests in the crook between.

Right Hand A right-handed child slants the paper from the left (top) to right (bottom) so that the paper is slanted along the line of the right arm toward the elbow. While writing, the child places the left hand on the left, toward the top of the paper to hold it still. He or she holds the pencil at the paint line—about 1 inch from the lead tip. The pencil is held between the thumb and index finger and rests against the third finger. The last two fingers curve slightly under to form a pad on which to slide across the paper. The pencil rests in the crook between the thumb and index finger.

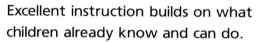

Reaching All Learners

Excellent instruction builds on what children already know and can do. Given the tremendous range of children's access to writing materials and experiences prior to kindergarten, a variety of approaches are suggested throughout *Trophies* as viable alternatives for reaching all learners.

Extra Support For children with limited print concepts, one of the first and most important understandings is that print carries meaning and that writing has real purpose. Whenever possible, include opportunities for writing in natural settings such as learning centers. For example, children can:

- make shopping lists in the creative dramatics center.
- record observations in the science center.
- write and illustrate labels for materials in the art area.

ESL English–Language Learners can participate in the same kinds of meaningful print experiences as their classmates. These might include

- writing signs, labels, and simple messages.
- labeling pictures.
- writing or dictating stories about one's own picture.
- shared writing experiences.

Challenge To ensure children's continued rapid advancement as confident writers, give them:

- exposure to a wide range of reading materials.
- opportunities for independent writing on self-selected and assigned topics.
- explicit instruction in print conventions (punctuation, use of capital letters, and so on) when children need them.

The handwriting strand in *Trophies* teaches correct letter formation using a variety of materials to help all children become fluent, confident writers. These materials include:

- multi-modal activities in the *Teacher's Edition*
- *Big Alphabet Cards* showing correct stroke
- *Write-On/Wipe-Off Board*
- *Tactile Letter Cards*
- *Magnetic Letters,* capital and lowercase
- handwriting practice in Practice *Books* and the *Phonics* Practice *Book*

HANDWRITING

Handwriting
Capital Manuscript Alphabet

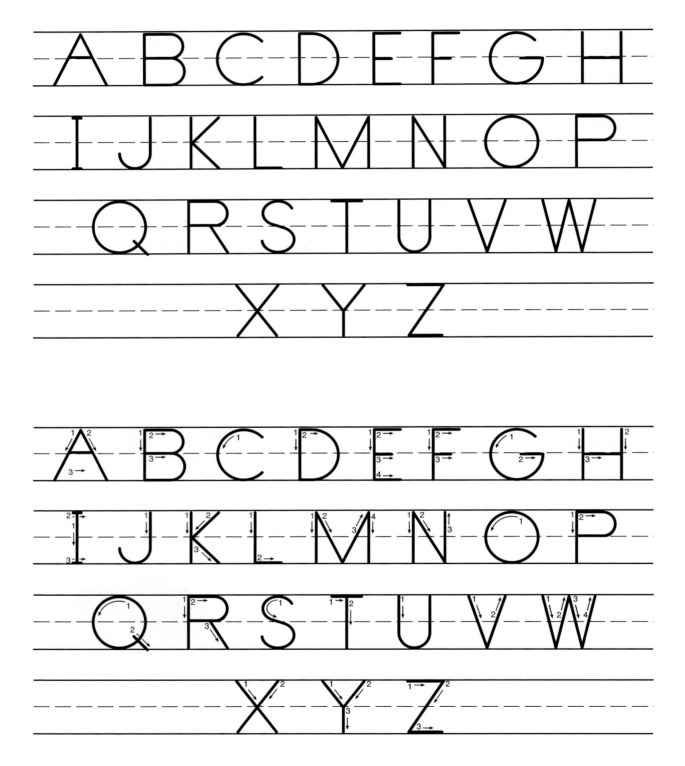

HANDWRITING MODEL

Handwriting
Lowercase Manuscript Alphabet

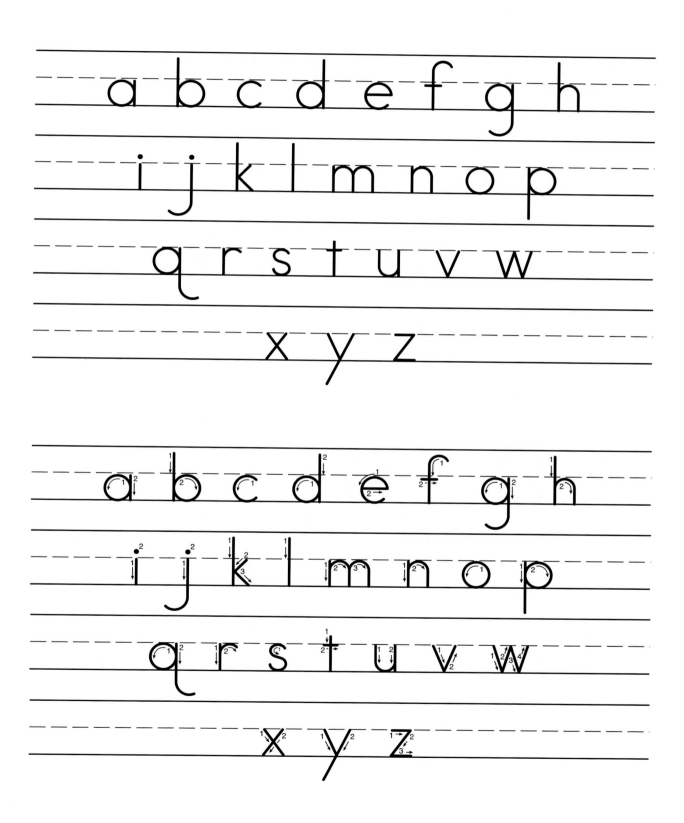

Handwriting
D'Nealian Capital Alphabet

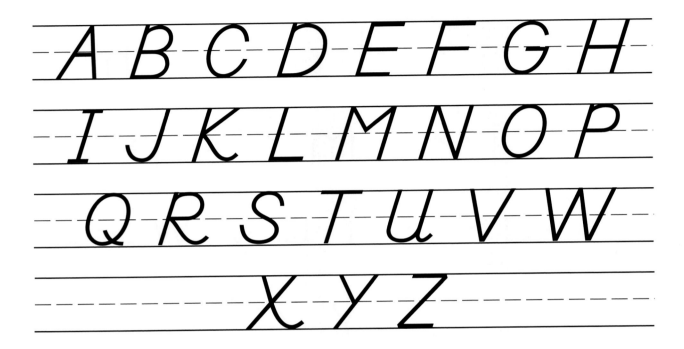

Handwriting
D'Nealian Lowercase Alphabet

a b c d e f g h
i j k l m n o p
q r s t u v w
x y z

My Rules for Internet Safety

I agree that

- **I will never give out private information,** such as my last name, my address, my telephone number, or my parents' work addresses or telephone numbers on the Internet.

- **I will never give out the address or telephone number** of my school on the Internet without first asking an adult's permission.

- **I understand which sites I can visit** and which ones are off-limits.

- **I will tell an adult right away** if something comes up on the screen that makes me feel uncomfortable.

- **I will never agree to meet in person** with anyone I meet online.

- **I will never e-mail a person any pictures** of myself or my classmates without an adult's permission.

- **I will tell an adult** if I get an inappropriate e-mail message from anyone.

- **I will remember that going online** on the Internet is like going out in public, so all the safety rules I already know apply here as well.

- **I know the Internet is a useful tool,** and I will always use it as a responsible person.

- **I will follow these same rules when I am at home,** in school, at the library, or at a friend's.

X _____   _____
     (Student signs here)   (Parent/Guardian signs here)

Visit *The Learning Site!*
www.harcourtschool.com

Harcourt

Traveling on the Internet

There are so many things to see and do on the Internet that new users may wish they had a "tour guide" to help them see the most interesting sites and make sure they don't miss anything. There are many ways to become a savvy Web traveler—one is by learning the language. Here are some common terms.

bookmark A function that lets you return to your favorite Web sites quickly.

browser Application software that allows you to navigate the Internet and view a Web site.

bulletin board/newsgroup Places to leave an electronic message or to share news that anyone can read and respond to.

chat room A place for people to converse online by typing messages to each other. Once you're in a chat room, others can contact you by e-mail. Some online services monitor their chat rooms and encourage participants to report offensive chatter. Some allow teachers and parents to deny children access to chat rooms altogether.

cookie When you visit a site, a notation known as a "cookie" may be fed to a file in your computer. If you revisit the site, the cookie file allows the Web site to identify you as a return guest—and offer you products tailored to your interests or tastes. You can set your online preferences to limit or let you know about cookies that a Web site places on your computer.

cyberspace Another name for the Internet.

download To move files or software from a remote computer to your computer.

e-mail Messages sent to one or more individuals via the Internet.

filter Software that lets you block access to Web sites and content that you may find unsuitable.

ISP (Internet Service Provider) A service that allows you to connect to the Internet.

junk e-mail Unsolicited commercial e-mail; also known as "spam."

keyword A word you enter into a search engine to begin the search for specific information or Web sites.

links Highlighted words on a Web site that allow you to connect to other parts of the same Web site or to other Web sites.

listserv An online mailing list that allows individuals or organizations to send e-mail to groups of people at one time.

modem An internal or external device that connects your computer to a phone line that can link you to the Internet.

password A personal code that you use to access your Internet account with your ISP.

privacy policy A statement on a Web site describing what information about you is collected by the site and how this information is used.

search engine A function that helps you find information and Web sites. Accessing a search engine is like using the catalog in a library.

URL (Uniform Resource Locator) The address that lets you locate a particular site. For example, **http://www.ed.gov** is the URL for the U.S. Department of Education. All government URLs end in **.gov**. Nonprofit organizations and trade associations end in **.org**. Commercial companies now end in **.com**, and non-commercial educational sites end in **.edu**. Countries other than the United States use different endings.

virus A file maliciously planted in your computer that can damage files and disrupt your system. Antivirus software is available.

Web site An Internet destination where you can look at and retrieve data. All the Web sites in the world, linked together, make up the World Wide Web or the "Web."

 Visit *The Learning Site!* www.harcourtschool.com

Harcourt

Using the Student Record Form

Using the Student Record Form

The record form on the following pages is a tool for tracking each student's progress toward grade-level standards. In addition to formal records on assessment results and instructional plans, you may also wish to complete this form several times yearly for each student. Make one copy of the form for each student. Record the date at the top of the column, and use the codes provided to record student progress. You may wish to add comments at the bottom or on the back of the form.

Sharing Student Progress with Family Members

The record form can be one vehicle for communicating with families about how students are making progress toward grade-level standards. Explain that students are expected to master the standards toward the end of the school year. Therefore, a code of B, or Beginning, at the start of the year is expected for most students. After that time, most students should be receiving a P for Making Progress, and by the end of the year they should meet or exceed each standard.

Students who are not making progress, of course, require intervention and frequent assessment to monitor progress and adapt instruction. Explain to family members the levels of support offered by *Trophies* and how you are using these tools to help their students succeed. On the other hand, some students may begin to meet or exceed the standards early in the year. For these families, you can explain how you are using *Trophies* to extend and accelerate progress. (For more information about levels of support in *Trophies*, see Theme Assessment to Plan Instruction at the beginning of each theme.)

Encouraging Family Involvement

Besides explaining student progress, there are several things you can do to encourage parents and guardians to support their students' achievement:

- Use the School-Home Connections pages in the Theme Resources section to suggest activities and reading materials on a weekly basis.
- Copy the Additional Homework Ideas pages at the beginning of each theme, and send them home with students. Encourage family members to use at least one activity per day.
- Have students use My Reading Log (provided in this tabbed section) daily, to record their reading outside of class. Stress repeatedly that sustained daily reading is essential to student growth. Request that parents or guardians sign off on the My Reading Log form, to encourage them to monitor students' reading.
- Above all, offer praise and recognition for all efforts that family members make to support students' literacy.

Student Record Form

Student _____ Teacher _____ Grade _____

	Date____	Date____	Date____	Date____	Date____	Date____
WORD ANALYSIS, FLUENCY, AND SYSTEMATIC VOCABULARY DEVELOPMENT						
Identify the front cover, back cover, and title page of a book.						
Follow words from left to right and from top to bottom on the printed page.						
Understand that printed materials provide information.						
Recognize that sentences in print are made up of separate words.						
Distinguish letters from words.						
Recognize and name all uppercase and lowercase letters of the alphabet.						
Track (move sequentially from sound to sound) and represent the number, sameness/difference, and order of two and three isolated phonemes.						
Track (move sequentially from sound to sound) and represent changes in simple syllables and words with two and three sounds as one sound is added, substituted, omitted, shifted, or repeated.						
Blend vowel-consonant sounds orally to make words or syllables.						
Identify and produce rhyming words in response to an oral prompt.						
Distinguish orally stated one-syllable words and separate into beginning or ending sounds.						
Track auditorily each word in a sentence and each syllable in a word.						
Count the number of sounds in syllables and syllables in words.						
Match all consonant and short-vowel sounds to appropriate letters.						
Read simple one-syllable and high-frequency words.						
Understand that as letters of words change, so do the sounds.						
Identify and sort common words in basic categories.						
Describe common objects and events in both general and specific language.						
READING COMPREHENSION						
Locate the title, table of contents, name of author, and name of illustrator.						
Use pictures and context to make predictions about story content.						
Connect to life experiences the information and events in texts.						
Retell familiar stories.						
Ask and answer questions about essential elements of a text.						
LITERARY RESPONSE AND ANALYSIS						
Distinguish fantasy from realistic text.						
Identify types of everyday print materials.						
Identify characters, settings, and important events.						

Harcourt

WRITING STRATEGIES

Use letters and phonetically spelled words to write about experiences, stories, people, objects, or events.						
Write consonant-vowel-consonant words.						
Write by moving from left to right and from top to bottom.						
Write uppercase and lowercase letters of the alphabet independently, attending to the form and proper spacing of the letters.						

WRITTEN AND ORAL ENGLISH LANGUAGE CONVENTIONS

Recognize and use complete, coherent sentences when speaking.						
Spell independently by using pre-phonetic knowledge, sounds of the alphabet, and knowledge of letter names.						

LISTENING AND SPEAKING STRATEGIES

Understand and follow one- and two-step oral directions.						
Share information and ideas, speaking audibly in complete, coherent sentences.						
Use descriptive words when speaking about people, places, things, and events.						

SPEAKING APPLICATIONS
(Genres and Their Characteristics)

Describe people, places, things, locations, and actions.						
Recite short poems, rhymes, and songs.						
Relate an experience or creative story in a logical sequence.						

Comments:

Key:

B = Beginning

P = Making Progress

M = Meets Standard

E = Exceeds Standard

Harcourt

Professional Bibliography

Adams, M. J. 1990. *Beginning to Read: Thinking and Learning About Print.* Cambridge: Massachusetts Institute of Technology Press.

Adams, M. J., et al. 1998. "The Elusive Phoneme: Why Phonemic Awareness Is So Important and How to Help Children Develop It," *American Educator: The Unique Power of Reading and How to Unleash It,* Vol. 22, Nos. 1 and 2, 18–29.

Adams, M. J.; R. Treiman; and M. Pressley. 1998. "Reading, Writing, and Literacy," in *Handbook of Child Psychology: Child Psychology in Practice* (Fifth edition). Vol. 4. Edited by I. E. Sigel and K. A. Renninger. New York: Wiley.

Allen, L. 1998. "An Integrated Strategies Approach: Making Word Identification Instruction Work for Beginning Readers," *The Reading Teacher,* Vol. 52, No. 3, 254–68.

American Association of School Librarians and the Association of Educational Communications and Technology. 1998. *Information Power: Building Partnerships for Learning.* Chicago: American Library Association.

Anderson, R. C., et al. 1985. *Becoming a Nation of Readers: The Report of the Commission on Reading.* Washington, D.C.: National Academy of Education, Commission on Education and Public Policy.

Anderson, R. C.; P. T. Wilson; and L. G. Fielding. 1988. "Growth in Reading and How Children Spend Their Time Outside of School," *Reading Research Quarterly,* Vol. 23, No. 3, 285–303.

Anderson, R. C., and W. E. Nagy. 1991. "Word Meanings," in *Handbook of Reading Research.* Vol. 2. Edited by R. Barr, et al. New York: Longman.

Ball, E. W., and B. A. Blachman. 1991. "Does Phoneme Awareness Training in Kindergarten Make a Difference in Early Word Recognition and Developmental Spelling?" *Reading Research Quarterly,* Vol. 26, No. 1, 49–66.

Barinaga, M. 1996. "Giving Language Skills a Boost," *Science,* Vol. 271, 27–28.

Baumann, J. F., and E. J. Kame'enui. 1991. "Research on Vocabulary Instruction: Ode to Voltaire," in *Handbook of Research on Teaching the English Language Arts.* Edited by J. Flood, J. J. D. Lapp, and J. R. Squire. New York: Macmillan.

Beck, I., et al. 1996. "Questioning the Author: A Year-Long Classroom Implementation to Engage Students with Text," *The Elementary School Journal,* Vol. 96, 385–414.

Beck, I., et al. 1998. "Getting at the Meaning: How to Help Students Unpack Difficult Text," *American Educator: The Unique Power of Reading and How to Unleash It,* Vol. 22, Nos. 1 and 2, 66–71, 85.

Beck, I., et al. 1997. *Questioning the Author: An Approach for Enhancing Student Engagement with Text.* Newark, Del.: International Reading Association.

Berninger, V. W., et al. 1994. "Developmental Skills Related to Writing and Reading Acquisition in the Intermediate Grades," *Reading and Writing: An Interdisciplinary Journal,* Vol. 6, 161–96.

Berthoff, A. E. 1984. "Recognition, Representation, and Revision," in *Rhetoric and Composition: A Sourcebook for Teachers and Writers.* Edited by R. Graves. Portsmouth, N.H.: Boynton Cook.

Blachman, B. A., et al. 1994. "Kindergarten Teachers Develop Phoneme Awareness in Low-Income, Inner-City Classrooms," *Reading and Writing: An Interdisciplinary Journal,* Vol. 6, 1–18.

Blachowicz, C. L. Z., and P. Fisher. 1996. *Teaching Vocabulary in All Classrooms.* Englewood Cliffs, N.J.: Merrill/Prentice Hall.

Bloom, B. S., ed. 1985. *Developing Talent in Young People.* New York: Ballantine Books.

Bus, A. G.; M. H. vanIJzendoorn; and A. D. Pellegrini. 1995. "Joint Book Reading Makes for Success in Learning to Read: A Meta-Analysis on Inter-generational Transmission of Literacy," *Review of Educational Research,* Vol. 65, 1–21.

Byrne, B., and R. Fielding-Barnsley. 1995. "Evaluation of a Program to Teach Phonemic Awareness to Young Children: A One- and Three-Year Follow-Up and a New Preschool Trial," *Journal of Educational Psychology,* Vol. 87, No. 3, 488–503.

California Department of Education. 1996c. *Connect, Compute, and Compete: The Report of the California Education Technology Task Force.* Sacramento: California Department of Education.

California Department of Education. 1994. *Differentiating the Core Curriculum and Instruction to Provide Advanced Learning Opportunities.* Sacramento: California Department of Education.

California Department of Education. 1998a. *English-Language Arts Content Standards for California Public Schools, Kindergarten Through Grade Twelve.* Sacramento: California Department of Education.

California Department of Education. 1995. *Every Child a Reader: The Report of the California Reading Task Force.* Sacramento: California Department of Education.

California Department of Education. 1998b. *Fostering the Development of a First and a Second Language in Early Childhood.* Sacramento: California Department of Education.

California Department of Education. 1999c. *Reading/Language Arts Framework for California Public Schools: Kindergarten Through Grade Twelve.* Sacramento: California Department of Education.

California Department of Education. 1996a. *Recommended Readings in Literature, Kindergarten Through Grade Eight* (Revised annotated edition). Sacramento: California Department of Education.

Calkins, L. 1996. "Motivating Readers," ERIC Clearinghouse on Assessment and Evaluation (No. SP525606), *Instructor,* Vol. 106, No. l, 32–33.

Campbell, F. A., and C. T. Ramsey. 1995. "Cognitive and Social Outcomes for High-Risk African American Students at Middle Adolescence: Positive Effects of Early Intervention," *American Educational Research Journal*, Vol. 32, 743–72.

Carlisle, J. F., and D. M. Nomanbhoy. 1993. "Phonological and Morphological Awareness in First-Graders," *Applied Psycholinguistics,* Vol. 14, 177–95.

Carnine, D.; J. Silbert; and E. J. Kame'enui. 1990. *Direct Instruction Reading.* Columbus, Ohio: Merrill Publishing Company.

Chall, J.; V. Jacobs; and L. Baldwin. 1990. *The Reading Crisis: Why Poor Children Fall Behind.* Cambridge: Harvard University Press.

Cornwall, A., and H. Bawden. 1992. "Reading Disabilities and Aggression: A Critical Review," *Journal of Learning Disabilities,* Vol. 25, 281–88.

Corson, D. 1995. *Using English Words.* Dordrecht, Netherlands: Kluwer.

Cunningham, A. E., and K. E. Stanovich. 1993. "Children's Literacy Environments and Early Word Recognition Subskills," *Reading and Writing: An Interdisciplinary Journal,* Vol. 5, 193–204.

Cunningham, A. E., and K. E. Stanovich. 1998. "What Reading Does for the Mind," *American Educator: The Unique Power of Reading and How to Unleash It,* Vol. 22, Nos. 1 and 2, 8–15.

Cunningham, P. M. 1998. "The Multisyllabic Word Dilemma: Helping Students Build Meaning, Spell, and Read 'Big' Words," *Reading and Writing Quarterly,* Vol. 14, 189–218.

Daneman, M. 1991. "Individual Differences in Reading Skills," in *Handbook of Reading Research* (Vol. 2). Edited by R. Barr, M. L. Kamil, P. B. Mosenthal, and P. D. Pearson. New York: Longman.

Defior, S., and P. Tudela. 1994. "Effect of Phonological Training on Reading and Writing Acquisition," *Reading and Writing,* Vol. 6, 299–320.

Delpit, L. D. 1986. "Skills and Other Dilemmas of a Progressive Black Educator," *Harvard Educational Review,* Vol. 56, 379–85.

Dickinson, D. K., and M. W. Smith. 1994. "Long-Term Effects of Preschool Teachers' Book Readings on Low-Income Children's Vocabulary and Story Comprehension," *Reading Research Quarterly,* Vol. 29, No. 2, 104–22.

Dillard, A. 1998. "What Reading Does for the Soul: A Girl and Her Books," *American Educator: The Unique Power of Reading and How to Unleash It,* Vol. 22, Nos. 1 and 2, 88–93.

Ediger, M. 1988. "Motivation in the Reading Curriculum," ERIC Clearinghouse on Assessment and Evaluation (No. CS009424).

Ehri, L. 1994. "Development of the Ability to Read Words: Update," in *Theoretical Models and Processes of Reading.* Edited by R. Ruddell, M. Ruddell, and H. Singer. Newark, Del.: International Reading Association.

Ehri, L. C., and S. McCormick. 1998. "Phases of Word Learning: Implications for Instruction with Delayed and Disabled Readers," *Reading and Writing Quarterly,* Vol. 14, 135–63.

Ehri, L. C. 1991. "Development of the Ability to Read Words," in *Handbook of Reading Research* (Vol. 2). Edited by R. Barr, et al. New York: Longman.

Ehrlich, M. F.; B. Kurtz-Costess; and C. Loridant. 1993. "Cognitive and Motivational Determinants of Reading Comprehension in Good and Poor Readers," *Journal of Reading Behavior,* Vol. 25, No. 4, 365–81.

Eisenberg, M., and R. Berkowitz. 1990. *Information Problem Solving: The Big Six Skills Approach to Library and Information Skills Instruction.* Norwood, N.J.: Ablex.

Englert, C. S., et al. 1995. "The Early Literacy Project: Connecting Across the Literacy Curriculum," *Learning Disability Quarterly,* Vol. 18, 253–75.

Epstein, J. L. 1995. "School-Family-Community Partnerships: Caring for Children We Share," *Phi Delta Kappan,* Vol. 76, No. 9, 701–2.

Felton, R. H., and P. P. Pepper. 1995. "Early Identification and Intervention of Phonological Deficits in Kindergarten and Early Elementary Children at Risk for Reading Disability," *School Psychology Review,* Vol. 24, 405–14.

Fielding, L. G., and Pearson, P. D. 1994. "Synthesis of Research—Reading Comprehension: What Works," *Educational Leadership,* Vol. 51, No. 5, 62–7.

Fielding-Barnsley, R. 1997. "Explicit Instruction in Decoding Benefits Children High in Phonemic Awareness and Alphabet Knowledge," *Scientific Studies of Reading,* Vol. 1, No. 1, 85–98.

Fitzgerald, J. 1995. "English-as-a-Second-Language Learners' Cognitive Reading Processes: A Review of Research in the U.S.," *Review of Educational Research,* Vol. 65, 145–90.

Flower, L. 1985. *Problem-Solving Strategies for Writing.* New York: Harcourt Brace Jovanovich.

Foorman, B., et al. 1998. "The Role of Instruction in Learning to Read: Preventing Reading Failure in At-Risk Children," *Journal of Educational Psychology,* Vol. 90, 37–55.

Foster, K. C., et al. 1994. "Computer-Assisted Instruction in Phonological Awareness: Evaluation of the DaisyQuest Program," *Journal of Research and Development in Education,* Vol. 27, 126–37.

Fuchs, L. S., et al. 1993. "Formative Evaluation of Academic Progress: How Much Growth Can We Expect?" *School Psychology Review,* Vol. 22, No. 1, 27–48.

Gambrell, L. B., et al. 1996. *Elementary Students' Motivation to Read.* Reading Research Report No. 52. Athens, Ga.: National Reading Research Center.

Gardner, H. 1983. *Frames of Mind: The Theory of Multiple Intelligences.* New York: Basic Books.

Gersten, R., and J. Woodward. 1995. "A Longitudinal Study of Transitional and Immersion Bilingual Education Programs in One District," *Elementary School Journal,* Vol. 95, 223–39.

Giles, H. C. 1997. "Parent Engagement As a School Reform Strategy," ERIC Clearinghouse on Urban Education (Digest 135).

Goldenberg, C. N., and R. Gallimore. 1991. "Local Knowledge, Research Knowledge, and Educational Change: A Case Study of Early [First-Grade] Spanish Reading Improvement," *Educational Researcher,* Vol. 20, No. 8, 2–14.

Goldenberg, C. 1992–93. "Instructional Conversations: Promoting Comprehension Through Discussion," *The Reading Teacher,* Vol. 46, 316–26.

Good, R. III; D. C. Simmons; and S. Smith. 1998. "Effective Academic Interventions in the United States: Evaluating and Enhancing the Acquisition of Early Reading Skills," *School Psychology Review,* Vol. 27, No. 1, 45–56.

Greene, J. F. 1998. "Another Chance: Help for Older Students with Limited Literacy," *American Educator: The Unique Power of Reading and How to Unleash It,* Vol. 22, Nos. 1 and 2, 74–79.

Guthrie, J. T., et al. 1996. "Growth of Literacy Engagement: Changes in Motivations and Strategies During Concept-Oriented Reading Instruction," *Reading Research Quarterly,* Vol. 31, 306–25.

Hanson, R. A., and D. Farrell. 1995. "The Long-Term Effects on High School Seniors of Learning to Read in Kindergarten," *Reading Research Quarterly,* Vol. 30, No. 4, 908–33.

Hart, B., and T. R. Risley. 1995. *Meaningful Differences in the Everyday Experience of Young American Children.* Baltimore: Paul H. Brookes Publishing Co.

Hasbrouck, J. E., and G. Tindal. 1992. "Curriculum-Based Oral Reading Fluency Norms for Students in Grades 2 Through 5," *Teaching Exceptional Children,* Vol. 24, 41–44.

Hiebert, E. H., et al. 1992. "Reading and Writing of First-Grade Students in a Restructured Chapter I Program," *American Educational Research Journal,* Vol. 29, 545–72.

Hillocks, G., Jr. 1986. *Research on Written Composition: New Directions for Teaching.* Urbana, Ill.: National Council for Teachers of English.

Honig, B.; L. Diamond; and L. Gutlohn. 2000. *Teaching Reading Sourcebook for Kindergarten Through Eighth Grade.* Emeryville, CA: CORE, Consortium on Reading Excellence.

Honig, B.; L. Diamond; and R. Nathan. 1999. *Assessing Reading: Multiple Measures for Kindergarten Through Eighth Grade.* Emeryville, CA: CORE, Consortium on Reading Excellence.

Hoover-Dempsey, K. V., and H. M. Sandler. 1997. "Why Do Parents Become Involved in Their Children's Education?" *Review of Educational Research,* Vol. 67, No. 1, 3–42.

Hunter, M., and G. Barker. 1987. "If at First . . . : Attribution Theory in the Classroom," *Educational Leadership,* Vol. 45, No. 2, 50–53.

Jimenez, R. T.; G. E. Garcia; and P. D. Pearson. 1996. "The Reading Strategies of Latina/o Students Who Are Successful Readers: Opportunities and Obstacles," *Reading Research Quarterly,* Vol. 31, 90–112.

Juel, C. 1991. "Beginning Reading," in *Handbook of Reading Research* (Vol. 2). Edited by R. Barr, M. L. Kamil, P. B. Mosenthal, and P. D. Pearson. New York: Longman.

Juel, C. 1988. "Learning to Read and Write: A Longitudinal Study of 54 Children from First Through Fourth Grades," *Journal of Educational Psychology,* Vol. 80, 437–447.

Kame'enui, E. J. 1996. "Shakespeare and Beginning Reading: 'The Readiness Is All,'" *Teaching Exceptional Children,* Vol. 28, No. 2, 77–81.

Kuhn, M. R., and S. A. Stahl. 1998. "Teaching Children to Learn Word Meanings from Context: A Synthesis and Some Questions," *Journal of Literacy Research,* Vol. 30, No. 1, 119–38.

Lance, K. C.; L. Welborn; and C. Hamilton-Pennell. 1993. *The Impact of School Library Media Centers on Academic Achievement.* San Jose, Calif.: Hi Willow Research and Publishing.

Leather, C. V., and L. A. Henry. 1994. "Working Memory Span and Phonological Awareness Tasks as Predictors of Early Reading Ability," *Journal of Experimental Child Psychology,* Vol. 58, 88–111.

Levy, B. A.; A. Nicholls; and D. Kohen. 1993. "Repeated Readings: Process Benefits for Good and Poor Readers," *Journal of Experimental Child Psychology,* Vol. 56, 303–27.

Liberman, I. Y.; D. Shankweiler; and A. M. Liberman. 1991. "The Alphabetic Principle and Learning to Read," in *Phonology and Reading Disability: Solving the Reading Puzzle.* Edited by D. Shankweiler and I. Y. Liberman. Ann Arbor: University of Michigan Press.

Lie, A. 1991. "Effects of a Training Program for Stimulating Skills in Word Analysis in First-Grade Children," *Reading Research Quarterly,* Vol. 26, No. 3, 234–50.

Lipson, M. Y., and K. K. Wixson. 1986. "Reading Disability Research: An Interactionist Perspective," *Review of Educational Research,* Vol. 56, 111–36.

Louis, K. S.; H. M. Marks; and S. Kruse. 1996. "Teachers' Professional Community in Restructuring Schools," *American Educational Research Journal* (Vol. 33).

Lundberg, I.; J. Frost; and O. P. Petersen. 1988. "Effects of an Extensive Program for Stimulating Phonological Awareness in Preschool Children," *Reading Research Quarterly,* Vol. 23, 263–284.

Lyon, G. R. 1995. "Toward a Definition of Dyslexia," *Annals of Dyslexia,* Vol. 45, 3–27.

Lyon, G. R., and V. Chhabra. 1996. "The Current State of Science and the Future of Specific Reading Disability," *Mental Retardation and Developmental Disabilities Research Reviews,* Vol. 2, 2–9.

Markell, M. A., and S. L. Deno. 1997. "Effects of Increasing Oral Reading: Generalization Across Reading Tasks," *The Journal of Special Education,* Vol. 31, No. 2, 233–50.

McCollum, H., and A. Russo. 1993. *Model Strategies in Bilingual Education: Family Literacy and Parent Involvement.* Washington, D.C.: United States Department of Education.

McGuinness, D.; C. McGuinness; and J. Donahue. 1996. "Phonological Training and the Alphabetic Principle: Evidence for Reciprocal Causality," *Reading Research Quarterly,* Vol. 30, 830–52.

McWhorter, J. 1998. *The Word on the Street: Fact and Fable about American English.* New York: Plenum.

Moats, L. C. 1995. *Spelling: Development, Disability, and Instruction.* Baltimore: York Press.

Moats, L. C. 1998. "Teaching Decoding," *American Educator: The Unique Power of Reading and How to Unleash It,* Vol. 22, Nos. 1 and 2, 42–49, 95–96.

Moffett, J., and B. J. Wagner. 1991. *Student-Centered Language Arts, K-12.* Portsmouth, N.H.: Boynton Cook.

Morrow, L. M. 1992. "The Impact of a Literature-Based Program on Literacy, Achievement, Use of Literature, and Attitudes of Children from Minority Backgrounds," *Reading Research Quarterly,* Vol. 27, 250–75.

Mosenthal, P. 1984. "The Problem of Partial Specification in Translating Reading Research into Practice," *The Elementary School Journal,* Vol. 85, No. 2, 199–227.

Mosenthal, P. 1985. "Defining Progress in Educational Research," *Educational Researcher,* Vol. 14, No. 9, 3–9.

Mosteller, F.; R. Light; and J. Sachs. 1996. "Sustained Inquiry in Education: Lessons from Skill Grouping and Class Size," *Harvard Educational Review,* Vol. 66, No. 4, 797–842.

National Center to Improve the Tools of Educators. 1997. *Learning to Read, Reading to Learn—Helping Children to Succeed: A Resource Guide.* Washington, D.C.: American Federation of Teachers.

National Research Council. 1998. *Preventing Reading Difficulties in Young Children.* Edited by M. S. Burns, P. Griffin, and C. E. Snow. Washington, D.C.: National Academy Press.

National Research Council. 1999. *Starting Out Right: A Guide to Promoting Children's Reading Success.* Edited by M. S. Burns, P. Griffin, and C. E. Snow. Washington, D.C.: National Academy Press.

Neuman, S. B. 1996. "Children Engaging in Storybook Reading: The Influence of Access to Print Resources, Opportunity, and Parental Interaction," *Early Childhood Research Quarterly,* Vol. 11, 495–513.

O'Connor, R. E.; J. R. Jenkins; and T. A. Slocum. 1995. "Transfer Among Phonological Tasks in Kindergarten: Essential Instructional Content," *Journal of Educational Psychology,* Vol. 87, 202–17.

Pearson, P. D., et al. 1992. "Developing Expertise in Reading Comprehension," in *What Research Says to the Teacher.* Edited by S. J. Samuels and A. E. Farstrup. Newark, Del.: International Reading Association.

Pearson, P. D., and K. Camperell. 1985. "Comprehension in Text Structures," in *Theoretical Models and Processes of Reading.* Edited by H. Singer and R. B. Ruddell. Newark, Del.: International Reading Association.

Perfetti, C. A., and S. Zhang. 1995. "The Universal Word Identification Reflex," in *The Psychology of Learning and Motivation* (Vol. 33). Edited by D. L. Medlin. San Diego: Academic Press.

Phillips, L. M.; S. P. Norris; and J. M. Mason. 1996. "Longitudinal Effects of Early Literacy Concepts on Reading Achievement: A Kindergarten Intervention and Five-Year Follow-Up," *Journal of Literacy Research,* Vol. 28, 173–95.

Pinnell, G. S., and L. C. Fountas. 1997. *Help America Read: A Handbook for Volunteers.* Portsmouth, N.H.: Heinemann.

Pressley, M.; J. Rankin; and L. Yokoi. 1996. "A Survey of Instructional Practices of Primary Teachers Nominated as Effective in Promoting Literacy," *The Elementary School Journal,* Vol. 96, 363–84.

Purcell-Gates, V.; E. McIntyre; and P. Freppon. 1995. "Learning Written Storybook Language in School: A Comparison of Low-SES Children in Skills-Based and Whole-Language Classrooms," *American Educational Research Journal,* Vol. 32, 659–85.

Robbins, C., and L. C. Ehri. 1994. "Reading Storybooks to Kindergartners Helps Them Learn New Vocabulary Words," *Journal of Educational Psychology,* Vol. 86, No. 1, 54–64.

Rosenshine, B., and C. Meister. 1994. "Reciprocal Teaching: A Review of the Research," *Review of Educational Research,* Vol. 64, No. 4, 479–530.

Ross, S. M., et al. 1995. "Increasing the Academic Success of Disadvantaged Children: An Examination of Alternative Early Intervention Programs," *American Educational Research Journal,* Vol. 32, 773–800.

Ruddell, R.; M. Rapp Ruddell; and H. Singer, eds. 1994. *Theoretical Models and Processes of Reading* (Fourth edition). Newark, Del.: International Reading Association.

Ryder, R. J., and M. F. Graves. 1994. "Vocabulary Instruction Presented Prior to Reading in Two Basal Readers," *Elementary School Journal,* Vol. 95, No. 2, 139–53.

Sacks, C. H., and J. R. Mergendoller. 1997. "The Relationship Between Teachers' Theoretical Orientation Toward Reading and Student Outcomes in Kindergarten Children with Different Initial Reading Abilities," *American Educational Research Journal,* Vol. 34, 721–39.

Samuels, S. J. 1979. "The Method of Repeated Reading," *The Reading Teacher,* Vol. 32, 403–08.

Sanacore, J. 1988. "Linking Vocabulary and Comprehension Through Independent Reading," ERIC Clearinghouse on Assessment and Evaluation (No. CS009409).

Shefelbine, J. 1991. *Encouraging Your Junior High Student to Read.* Bloomington, Ind.: ERIC Clearinghouse on Reading, English, and Communication.

Shefelbine, J. L. 1990. "Student Factors Related to Variability in Learning Word Meanings from Context," *Journal of Reading Behavior,* Vol. 22, No. 1, 71–97.

Shore, W. J., and F. T. Durso. 1990. "Partial Knowledge in Vocabulary Acquisition: General Constraints and Specific Detail," *Journal of Educational Psychology,* Vol. 82, 315–18.

Shore, B. M., et al. 1991. *Recommended Practices in Gifted Education: A Critical Analysis.* New York: Teachers College Press.

Simmons, D. C., and E. J. Kame'enui. 1996. "A Focus on Curriculum Design: When Children Fail," in *Strategies for Teaching Children in Inclusive Settings.* Edited by E. Meyen, G. Vergason, and R. Whelan. Denver: Love Publishing.

Simmons, D. C., and E. J. Kame'enui, eds. 1998. *What Reading Research Tells Us About Children with Diverse Learning Needs: Bases and Basics.* Mahwah, N.J.: Lawrence Erlbaum Associates.

Sindelar, P. T.; L. Monda; and L. O'Shea. 1990. "Effects of Repeated Readings on Instructional- and Mastery-Level Readers," *Journal of Educational Research,* Vol. 83, 220–26.

Slavin, R. E.; N. L. Karweit; and B. A. Wasik, eds. 1993. *Preventing Early School Failure: Research, Policy, and Practice.* 1993. Boston: Allyn and Bacon.

Snider, V. E. 1995. "A Primer on Phonological Awareness: What It Is, Why It's Important, and How to Teach It," *School Psychology Review,* Vol. 24, 443–55.

Spear-Swerling, L., and R. J. Sternberg. 1998. "Curing Our 'Epidemic' of Learning Disabilities," *Phi Delta Kappan,* Vol. 79, No. 5, 397–401.

Spear-Swerling, L., and R. J. Sternberg. 1996. *Off Track: When Poor Readers Become Learning Disabled.* Boulder, Colo.: Westview Press.

Stanovich, K. E. 1986. "Matthew Effects in Reading: Some Consequences of Individual Differences in the Acquisition of Literacy," *Reading Research Quarterly,* Vol. 21, 360–407.

Stanovich, K. E. 1994. "Constructivism in Reading Education," *The Journal of Special Education,* Vol. 28, 259–74.

Stanovich, K. E. 1993–94. "Romance and Reality," *The Reading Teacher,* Vol. 47, 280–90.

Sulzby, E., and W. Teale. 1991. "Emergent Literacy," in *Handbook of Reading Research* (Vol. 2). Edited by R. Barr, M. L. Kamil, P. B. Mosenthal, and P. D. Pearson. New York: Longman.

Topping, K. 1998. "Effective Tutoring in America Reads: A Reply to Wasik," *The Reading Teacher,* Vol. 52, No. 1, 42–50.

Torgesen, J. K. 1998. "Catch Them Before They Fall: Identification and Assessment to Prevent Reading Failure in Young Children," *American Educator: The Unique Power of Reading and How to Unleash It,* Vol. 22, Nos. 1 and 2, 32–39.

Treiman, R. 1985. "Onsets and Rimes as Units of Spoken Syllables: Evidence from Children," *Journal of Experimental Child Psychology,* Vol. 39, 161–81.

Treiman, R.; S. Weatherston; and D. Berch. 1994. "The Role of Letter Names in Children's Learning of Phoneme-Grapheme Relations," *Applied Psycholinguistics,* Vol. 15, 97–122.

Vandervelden, M. C., and L. S. Siegel. 1995. "Phonological Recoding and Phoneme Awareness in Early Literacy: A Developmental Approach," *Reading Research Quarterly,* Vol. 30, 854–73.

Vellutino, F. R., et al. 1996. "Cognitive Profiles of Difficult-to-Remediate and Readily Remediated Poor Readers: Early Intervention as a Vehicle for Distinguishing Between Cognitive and Experiential Deficits as Basic Causes of Specific Reading Disability," *Journal of Educational Psychology,* Vol. 88, 601–38.

Wagner, R. K., et al. 1993. "Development of Young Readers' Phonological Processing Abilities," *Journal of Educational Psychology,* Vol. 85, 83–103.

Walberg, H. J. 1984. "Families as Partners in Educational Productivity," *Phi Delta Kappan,* Vol. 65, No. 6, 397–400.

Wasik, B. A., and R. E. Slavin. 1993. "Preventing Early Reading Failure with One-to-One Tutoring: A Review of Five Programs," *Reading Research Quarterly,* Vol. 28, 178–200.

Wells, G. 1986. *The Meaning Makers: Children Learning Language and Using Language to Learn.* Portsmouth, N.H.: Heinemann.

White, T. G.; M. F. Graves; and W. H. Slater. 1990. "Growth of Reading Vocabulary in Diverse Elementary Schools: Decoding and Word Meaning," *Journal of Educational Psychology,* Vol. 82, 281–90.

Whitehurst, G. J., et al. 1994. "Outcomes of an Emergent Literacy Intervention in Head Start," *Journal of Educational Psychology,* Vol. 86, 542–55.

Yopp, H. K. 1988. "The Validity and Reliability of Phonemic Awareness Tests," *Reading Research Quarterly,* Vol. 23, No. 2, 159–77.

Program Reviewers

Sarah Armstrong
Reading Coordinator
O'Toole Elementary School
Chicago, Illinois

Dr. Judylynn Baily-Mitchell
Principal
West Salisbury
Elementary School
Salisbury, Maryland

Dr. Judith F. Barry
Coordinator of Reading/
Language Arts
Taunton Public Schools
Taunton, Massachusetts

Carol Berman
Lead Teacher
Crestview Elementary School
Miami, Florida

Angela Berner
Language Arts Staff Developer
Huntington Unified
School District
Administration Offices
Huntington Station, New York

Sue Birch
Teacher
Dunns Corners
Elementary School
Westerly, Rhode Island

Candace Bouchard
Teacher
Sanburg Elementary School
San Diego, California

Dr. Carolyn Reedom
Principal
Vanderberg Elementary School
Henderson, Nevada

Sandra Carron
Teacher
Moreno Valley Unified
School District
Moreno Valley, California

Loretta Cudney
Teacher
Riverside Unified School District
Riverside, California

Justyne Davis
Teacher
Wallbridge Community
Education Center
St. Louis, Missouri

Dr. Ann Dugger
Reading Teacher/Title I
Will Rogers Elementary School
Stillwater, Oklahoma

Rosemary Foresythe
Reading Specialist
West Pottsgrove
Elementary School
Pottstown, Pennsylvania

Stanley Foster
Teacher
Magnolia Avenue School
Los Angeles, California

Kimberly Griffith
Teacher
Fulton Elementary
Aurora, Colorado

Jeffrey Guerra
Teacher
Westchase Elementary School
Tampa, Florida

Anne Henry
Teacher
Northern Hills
Elementary School
Edmond, Oklahoma

Carol Hookway
Teacher
Memorial Elementary School
Natick, Massachusetts

Arlene Horkey
Curriculum Specialist
Belleair Elementary School
Clearwater, Florida

Carolyn M. Horton
District Reading Facilitator
Cedar Rapids Community
School District,
Educational Service Center
Cedar Rapids, Iowa

Patty Jacox
Teacher
Lansing Elementary
Aurora, Colorado

Beverly Keeley
Teacher
Grant Foreman
Elementary School
Muskogee, Oklahoma

Rebecca L. Kelly
Teacher
Wekiva Elementary School
Longwood, Florida

Lisa Leslie
Teacher
Costello Elementary School,
Troy Public Schools
Troy, Michigan

Arlene D. Loughlin
Student Achievement Specialist
Curlew Creek
Elementary School
Palm Harbor, Florida

Christin Machado
Teacher
Jefferson Elementary School
Burbank, California

Alicia L. Marsh
Teacher
Pearl Sample
Elementary School
Culpepper, Virginia

Gail Martin
Teacher
JEB Stuart Elementary School
Richmond, Virginia

Anne M. Merritt
Teacher
Citrus Glen Elementary School
Ventura, California

Joan Miller
Teacher
Carlton Hills Elementary School
Santee, California

Bobbie A. Overbey
Teacher
Carillon Elementary School
Oviedo, Florida

Katherin Pagakis
English Teacher
Washington Elementary School
Waukegan, Illinois

Barbara Pitts
Administrator
Joy Middle School
Detroit, Michigan

Sundee Preedy
Teacher
Aloma Elementary School
Winter Park, Florida

Dorina Rocas
Teacher
Corono-Norco Unified
School District
Corona, California

Josephine Scott
Language Arts
Curriculum Director
Columbus City School District,
Northgate Center
Columbus, Ohio

Renee Siefert
Teacher
Serrano Elementary School
Moreno Valley, California

Gayle E. Sitter
Mathematics Resource
Teacher ELC-7
Orlando, Florida

Linda Smolen
Director of Reading
Buffalo City School District,
427 City Hall
Buffalo, New York

Gail Soft
Teacher
Vermillion Primary School
Maize, Kansas

Alejandro Soria
Teacher
Leo Politi Elementary
Los Angeles, California

Jan Strege
Vice-Principal
Schlegel Road
Elementary School
Webster, New York

Dahna Taylor
Teacher
Chavez Elementary School
San Diego, California

Dr. Sandra Telfort
Teacher
Palmetto Elementary School
Miami, Florida

Dana Thurm
Teacher
Olivenhain Pioneer
Elementary School
Carlsbad, California

Geralyn Wilson
Literacy Coordinator
James McCosh Intermediate
Chicago, Illinois

John L. York
Teacher
Cedar Heights
Elementary School
Cedar Falls, Iowa

Maureen A. Zoda
Reading Specialist Coordinator
Meadow Brook
Elementary School
East Longmeadow,
Massachusetts

KINDERGARTEN REVIEWERS

Janice Allocco
Teacher
Klem Road South
Elementary School
Webster, New York

Irma A. Barr
Teacher
Embassy Creek
Elementary School
Cooper City, Florida

Dikki Cie Chanski
Teacher
Troy Public Schools,
Martell Elementary School
Troy, Michigan

Rosemary Gaskin
Teacher
Broad Rock Elementary School
Richmond, Virginia

Carol Grenfell
District Language
Arts Specialist
Ventura Unified School District
Ventura, California

Cathleen Hunter
Teacher
Peterson Elementary
Huntington Beach, California

Karen A. Kuritar
Teacher
Allen Elementary School
Dayton, Ohio

Charlotte Otterbacher
Teacher
Troy Public Schools,
Hamilton Elementary
Troy, Michigan

Gwendolyn Perkins
Teacher
Ginter Park Elementary School
Richmond, Virginia

Kelly Schmidt
Teacher
Public School #225 Seaside
Rockaway Parkway, New York

Corene Selman
Teacher
Westwood Early
Childhood Center
Woodward, Oklahoma

Laureen B. Stephens
Teacher
Mountainview
Elementary School
Saycus, California

Pam Styles
Teacher
Residence Park Primary School,
World of Wonder Academy
Dayton, Ohio

Scope and Sequence

	GR K	GR 1	GR 2	GR 3	GR 4	GR 5	GR 6
Reading							
Concepts about Print							
Understand that print provides information	░						
Understand how print is organized and read	░						
Know left-to-right and top-to-bottom directionality	░						
Distinguish letters from words	░						
Recognize name	░						
Name and match all uppercase and lowercase letter forms	░						
Understand the concept of word and construct meaning from shared text, illustrations, graphics, and charts	░						
Identify letters, words, and sentences	░	░					
Recognize that sentences in print are made up of words	░	░					
Identify the front cover, back cover, title page, title, and author of a book	░	░					
Match oral words to printed words	░	░					
Phonemic Awareness							
Understand that spoken words and syllables are made up of sequences of sounds	░	░					
Count and track sounds in a syllable, syllables in words, and words in sentences	░	░	░				
Know the sounds of letters	░	░					
Track and represent the number, sameness, difference, and order of two or more isolated phonemes	░	░					
Match, identify, distinguish, and segment sounds in initial, final, and medial position in single-syllable spoken words	░	░	░				
Blend sounds (phonemes) to make words or syllables	░	░	░				
Track and represent changes in syllables and words as target sound is added, substituted, omitted, shifted, or repeated	░	░					
Distinguish long- and short-vowel sounds in orally stated words	░	░	░				
Identify and produce rhyming words	░	░					
Decoding: Phonic Analysis							
Understand and apply the alphabetic principle	░	░					
Consonants: single, blends, digraphs in initial, final, medial positions	●	●	●	░			
Vowels: short, long, digraphs, r-controlled, variant, schwa		●	●	░			
Match all consonant and short-vowel sounds to appropriate letters	●	●					
Understand that as letters in words change, so do the sounds	●	●					
Blend vowel-consonant sounds orally to make words or syllables	●	●	░				
Blend sounds from letters and letter patterns into recognizable words		░	░				
Decoding: Structural Analysis							
Inflectional endings, with and without spelling changes: plurals, verb tenses, possessives, comparatives-superlatives		●	●				
Contractions, abbreviations, and compound words		●	●				
Prefixes, suffixes, derivations, and root words			●	●	●	●	●
Greek and Latin roots					●	●	●
Letter, spelling, and syllable patterns	░	░	░				
Phonograms/word families/onset-rimes	░	░	░				
Syllable rules and patterns			░	●			

Key

Shaded area Explicit Instruction/Modeling/Practice and Application

● Tested

Assessment resources include: Kindergarten Assessment Handbook; Placement and Diagnostic Assessments, Grades 1, 2, and 3–6; Reading and Language Skills Assessments, Grades 1–6; Holistic Assessments, Grades 1–6; End-of-Selection Tests, Grades 1–6; and Oral Reading Fluency Assessment, Grades 1–6

	GR K	GR 1	GR 2	GR 3	GR 4	GR 5	GR 6
Decoding: Strategies							
Visual cues: sound/symbol relationships, letter patterns, and spelling patterns							
Structural cues: compound words, contractions, inflectional endings, prefixes, suffixes, Greek and Latin roots, root words, spelling patterns, and word families							
Cross check visual and structural cues to confirm meaning							
Syllabication rules and patterns							
Word Recognition							
One-syllable and high-frequency words	●	●	●				
Common, irregular sight words	●	●	●				
Common abbreviations			●				
Lesson vocabulary		●	●	●	●	●	●
Fluency							
Read aloud in a manner that sounds like natural speech		●	●				
Read aloud accurately and with appropriate intonation and expression		●		●			
Read aloud narrative and expository text with appropriate pacing, intonation, and expression				●	●	●	●
Read aloud prose and poetry with rhythm and pace, appropriate intonation, and vocal patterns							
Vocabulary and Concept Development							
Academic language							
Classify-categorize		●		●		●	
Antonyms			●	●	●		
Synonyms			●	●	●		
Homographs				●	●		
Homophones			●	●		●	
Multiple-meaning words			●	●		●	
Figurative and idiomatic language							●
Context/context clues			●	●	●	●	●
Content-area words							
Dictionary, glossary, thesaurus				●	●		
Foreign words							
Connotation-denotation						●	●
Word origins (acronyms, clipped and coined words, regional variations, etymologies, jargon, slang)							
Analogies							
Word structure clues to determine meaning			●	●	●	●	●
Inflected nouns and verbs, comparatives-superlatives, possessives, compound words, prefixes, suffixes, root words			●	●	●	●	●
Greek and Latin roots, prefixes, suffixes, derivations, and root words					●	●	●
Develop vocabulary							
Listen to and discuss text read aloud							
Read independently							
Use reference books							
Comprehension and Analysis of Text							
Ask/answer questions							
Author's purpose				●	●	●	●
Author's perspective						●	●
Propaganda/bias							●

Key

Shaded area   Explicit Instruction/Modeling/Practice and Application

●   Tested

Assessment resources include: Kindergarten Assessment Handbook; Placement and Diagnostic Assessments, Grades 1, 2, and 3–6; Reading and Language Skills Assessments, Grades 1–6; Holistic Assessments, Grades 1–6; End-of-Selection Tests, Grades 1–6; and Oral Reading Fluency Assessment, Grades 1–6

SCOPE AND SEQUENCE

	GR K	GR I	GR 2	GR 3	GR 4	GR 5	GR 6
Background knowledge: prior knowledge and experiences						•	•
Cause-effect			•	•	•	•	•
Compare-contrast			•	•	•	•	•
Details		•	•	•	•	•	•
Directions: one-, two-, multi-step	•	•	•	•	•		
Draw conclusions				•	•	•	•
Fact-fiction							
Fact-opinion				•	•	•	•
Higher order thinking							
Analyze, critique and evaluate, synthesize, and visualize text and information							
Interpret information from graphic aids			•	•	•	•	•
Locate information		•	•	•	•	•	•
Book parts				•			•
Text features				•		•	
Alphabetical order		•					
Main idea: stated/unstated		•	•	•	•	•	•
Main idea and supporting details				•	•	•	•
Make generalizations							
Make inferences			•	•	•	•	•
Make judgments							
Make predictions/predict outcomes							
Monitor comprehension							
Adjust reading rate, create mental images, reread, read ahead, set/adjust purpose, self-question, summarize/paraphrase, use graphic aids, text features, and text adjuncts							
Paraphrase/restate facts and details				•	•	•	•
Preview							
Purpose for reading							
Organize information							
Alphabetical order							
Numerical systems/outlines							
Graphic organizers							
Referents							
Retell stories and ideas							
Sequence		•	•	•	•	•	•
Summarize			•	•	•	•	•
Text structure							
Narrative text			•	•	•	•	•
Informational text (compare and contrast, cause and effect, sequence/chronological order, proposition and support, problem and solution)					•	•	•
Study Skills							
Follow and give directions			•	•	•		
Apply plans and strategies: KWL, question-answer-relationships, skim and scan, note taking, outline, questioning the author, reciprocal teaching							
Practice test-taking strategies							

Key

Shaded area Explicit Instruction/Modeling/Practice and Application

•   Tested

      Assessment resources include: Kindergarten Assessment Handbook; Placement and Diagnostic Assessments, Grades 1, 2, and 3–6; Reading and Language Skills Assessments, Grades 1–6; Holistic Assessments, Grades 1–6; End-of-Selection Tests, Grades 1–6; and Oral Reading Fluency Assessment, Grades 1–6

Research and Information	GR K	GR 1	GR 2	GR 3	GR 4	GR 5	GR 6
Use resources and references							
Understand the purpose, structure, and organization of various reference materials							
Title page, table of contents, chapter titles, chapter headings, index, glossary, guide words, citations, end notes, bibliography				•			•
Picture dictionary, software, dictionary, thesaurus, atlas, globe, encyclopedia, telephone directory, on-line information, card catalog, electronic search engines and data bases, almanac, newspaper, journals, periodicals			•	•	•	•	•
Charts, maps, diagrams, timelines, schedules, calendar, graphs, photos			•	•			•
Choose reference materials appropriate to research purpose							•

Viewing/Media	GR K	GR 1	GR 2	GR 3	GR 4	GR 5	GR 6
Interpret information from visuals (graphics, media, including illustrations, tables, maps, charts, graphs, diagrams, timelines)			•	•	•	•	•
Analyze the ways visuals, graphics, and media represent, contribute to, and support meaning of text							
Select, organize, and produce visuals to complement and extend meaning							
Use technology or appropriate media to communicate information and ideas							
Use technology or appropriate media to compare ideas, information, and viewpoints							
Compare, contrast, and evaluate print and broadcast media							
Distinguish between fact and opinion							
Evaluate the role of media							
Analyze media as sources for information, entertainment, persuasion, interpretation of events, and transmission of culture							
Identify persuasive and propaganda techniques used in television and identify false and misleading information							
Summarize main concept and list supporting details and identify biases, stereotypes, and persuasive techniques in a nonprint message							
Support opinions with detailed evidence and with visual or media displays that use appropriate technology							

Literary Response and Analysis

Genre Characteristics	GR K	GR 1	GR 2	GR 3	GR 4	GR 5	GR 6
Know a variety of literary genres and their basic characteristics			•	•	•	•	•
Distinguish between fantasy and realistic text							
Distinguish between informational and persuasive texts							
Understand the distinguishing features of literary and nonfiction texts: everyday print materials, poetry, drama, fantasies, fables, myths, legends, and fairy tales			•	•	•	•	•
Explain the appropriateness of the literary forms chosen by an author for a specific purpose							

Literary Elements	GR K	GR 1	GR 2	GR 3	GR 4	GR 5	GR 6
Plot/Plot Development							
Important events		•	•	•	•	•	•
Beginning, middle, end of story		•	•				
Problem/solution			•				
Conflict				•			
Conflict and resolution/causes and effects					•	•	•
Compare and contrast							
Character							
Identify		•					
Identify, describe, compare and contrast			•	•	•	•	•
Relate characters and events					•	•	•

Key

Shaded area   Explicit Instruction / Modeling / Practice and Application

•   Tested

Assessment resources include: Kindergarten Assessment Handbook; Placement and Diagnostic Assessments, Grades 1, 2, and 3–6; Reading and Language Skills Assessments, Grades 1–6; Holistic Assessments, Grades 1–6; End-of-Selection Tests, Grades 1–6; and Oral Reading Fluency Assessment, Grades 1–6

	GR K	GR 1	GR 2	GR 3	GR 4	GR 5	GR 6
Traits, actions, motives				•	•	•	•
Cause for character's actions					•		
Character's qualities and effect on plot							•
Setting							
Identify and describe		•	•	•	•	•	•
Compare and contrast			•	•	•	•	•
Relate to problem/resolution							
Theme							
Theme/essential message				•	•	•	•
Universal themes							
Mood/Tone							
Identify							•
Compare and contrast							•

Literary Devices/Author's Craft

	GR K	GR 1	GR 2	GR 3	GR 4	GR 5	GR 6
Rhythm, rhyme, pattern, and repetition							
Alliteration, onomatopoeia, assonance, imagery							
Figurative language (similes, metaphors, idioms, personification, hyperbole)				•	•	•	•
Characterization/character development				•		•	
Dialogue				•	•	•	•
Narrator/narration					•	•	•
Point of view (first-person, third-person, omniscient)					•	•	•
Informal language (idioms, slang, jargon, dialect)							

Response to Text

	GR K	GR 1	GR 2	GR 3	GR 4	GR 5	GR 6
Relate characters and events to own life							
Read to perform a task or learn a new task							
Recollect, talk, and write about books read							
Describe the roles and contributions of authors and illustrators							
Generate alternative endings and identify the reason and impact of the alternatives							
Compare and contrast versions of the same stories that reflect different cultures							
Make connections between information in texts and stories and historical events							
Form ideas about what had been read and use specific information from the text to support these ideas							
Know that the attitudes and values that exist in a time period or culture affect stories and informational articles written during that time period							
Explore origin and historical development of words and changes in sentence patterns over the years							

Self-Selected Reading

	GR K	GR 1	GR 2	GR 3	GR 4	GR 5	GR 6
Select material to read for pleasure							
Read a variety of self-selected and assigned literary and informational texts							
Use knowledge of authors' styles, themes, and genres to choose own reading							
Read literature by authors from various cultural and historical backgrounds							

Cultural Awareness

	GR K	GR 1	GR 2	GR 3	GR 4	GR 5	GR 6
Connect information and events in texts to life and life to text experiences							
Compare language, oral traditions, and literature that reflect customs, regions, and cultures							
Identify how language reflects regions and cultures							
View concepts and issues from diverse perspectives							
Recognize the universality of literary themes across cultures and language							

Key

Shaded area   Explicit Instruction/Modeling/Practice and Application

•   Tested

    Assessment resources include: Kindergarten Assessment Handbook; Placement and Diagnostic Assessments, Grades 1, 2, and 3–6; Reading and Language Skills Assessments, Grades 1–6; Holistic Assessments, Grades 1–6; End-of-Selection Tests, Grades 1–6; and Oral Reading Fluency Assessment, Grades 1–6

SCOPE AND SEQUENCE

Writing	GR K	GR 1	GR 2	GR 3	GR 4	GR 5	GR 6
Writing Strategies							
Writing process: prewriting, drafting, revising, proofreading, publishing							
Collaborative, shared, timed writing, writing to prompts		•	•	•	•	•	•
Evaluate own and others' writing							
Proofread writing to correct convention errors in mechanics, usage, punctuation, using handbooks and references as appropriate				•	•	•	•
Organization and Focus							
Use models and traditional structures for writing							
Select a focus, structure, and viewpoint							
Address purpose, audience, length, and format requirements							
Write single- and multiple-paragraph compositions			•	•	•	•	•
Revision Skills							
Correct sentence fragments and run-ons					•	•	•
Vary sentence structure, word order, and sentence length							
Combine sentences					•	•	•
Improve coherence, unity, consistency, and progression of ideas							
Add, delete, consolidate, clarify, rearrange text							
Choose appropriate and effective words: exact/precise words, vivid words, trite/overused words						•	•
Elaborate: details, examples, dialogue, quotations							
Revise using a rubric							
Penmanship/Handwriting							
Write uppercase and lowercase letters							
Write legibly, using appropriate word and letter spacing							
Write legibly, using spacing, margins, and indention							
Writing Applications							
Narrative writing (stories, paragraphs, personal narratives, journal, plays, poetry)		•	•	•	•	•	•
Descriptive writing (titles, captions, ads, posters, paragraphs, stories, poems)		•	•	•	•	•	•
Expository writing (comparison-contrast, explanation, directions, speech, how-to article, friendly/business letter, news story, essay, report, invitation)			•	•	•	•	•
Persuasive writing (paragraph, essay, letter, ad, poster)						•	•
Cross-curricular writing (paragraph, report, poster, list, chart)							
Everyday writing (journal, message, forms, notes, summary, label, caption)							
Written and Oral English Language Conventions							
Sentence Structure							
Types (declarative, interrogative, exclamatory, imperative, interjection)		•	•	•	•	•	•
Structure (simple, compound, complex, compound-complex)		•	•	•	•	•	•
Parts (subjects/predicates: complete, simple, compound; clauses: independent, dependent, subordinate; phrase)		•	•	•	•	•	•
Direct/indirect object							
Word order		•					
Grammar							
Nouns (singular, plural, common, proper, possessive, collective, abstract, concrete, abbreviations, appositives)		•	•	•	•	•	•
Verbs (action, helping, linking, transitive, intransitive, regular, irregular; subject-verb agreement)		•	•	•	•	•	•
Verb tenses (present, past, future; present, past, and future perfect)		•	•	•	•	•	•
Participles; infinitives							

Key

Shaded area   Explicit Instruction/Modeling/Practice and Application

•   Tested

Assessment resources include: Kindergarten Assessment Handbook; Placement and Diagnostic Assessments, Grades 1, 2, and 3–6; Reading and Language Skills Assessments, Grades 1–6; Holistic Assessments, Grades 1–6; End-of-Selection Tests, Grades 1–6; and Oral Reading Fluency Assessment, Grades 1–6

SCOPE AND SEQUENCE

	GR K	GR 1	GR 2	GR 3	GR 4	GR 5	GR 6
Adjectives (common, proper; articles; comparative, superlative)		•	•	•	•	•	•
Adverbs (place, time, manner, degree)				•	•	•	•
Pronouns (subject, object, possessive, reflexive, demonstrative, antecedents)		•	•		•	•	•
Prepositions; prepositional phrases					•	•	•
Conjunctions							
Abbreviations, contractions				•	•	•	•
Punctuation							
Period, exclamation point, or question mark at end of sentences		•	•	•	•	•	•
Comma			•	•	•	•	•
Greeting and closure of a letter			•	•	•	•	•
Dates, locations, and addresses			•	•	•	•	•
For items in a series			•	•	•	•	•
Direct quotations							
Link two clauses with a conjunction in compound sentences					•	•	•
Quotation marks			•	•	•	•	•
Dialogue, exact words of a speaker				•	•	•	•
Titles of books, stories, poems, magazines						•	•
Parentheses/dash/hyphen					•	•	•
Apostrophes in possessive case of nouns and in contractions				•	•	•	•
Underlining or italics to identify title of documents					•	•	•
Colon					•	•	•
Separate hours and minutes					•	•	•
Introduce a list					•	•	•
After the salutation in business letters						•	•
Semicolons to connect independent clauses							
Capitalization							
First word of a sentence, names of people, and the pronoun *I*	•	•	•	•	•	•	•
Proper nouns, words at the beginning of sentences and greetings, months and days of the week, and titles and initials of people		•	•	•	•	•	•
Geographical names, holidays, historical periods, and special events							•
Names of magazines, newspapers, works of art, musical compositions, organizations, and the first word in quotations when appropriate							•
Use conventions of punctuation and capitalization							
Spelling							
Spell independently by using pre-phonetic knowledge, sounds of the alphabet, and knowledge of letter names							
Use spelling approximations and some conventional spelling							
Common, phonetically regular words		•	•	•	•	•	•
Frequently used, irregular words		•	•	•	•	•	•
One-syllable words with consonant blends			•	•	•	•	•
Contractions, compounds, orthographic patterns, and common homophones				•	•	•	•
Greek and Latin roots, inflections, suffixes, prefixes, and syllable constructions					•	•	•
Use a variety of strategies and resources to spell words							
Listening and Speaking							
Listening Skills and Strategies							
Listen to a variety of oral presentations such as stories, poems, skits, songs, personal accounts, or informational speeches							
Listen attentively to the speaker (make eye contact and demonstrate appropriate body language)							

Key

Shaded area   Explicit Instruction/Modeling/Practice and Application

  •   Tested

       Assessment resources include: Kindergarten Assessment Handbook; Placement and Diagnostic Assessments, Grades 1, 2, and 3–6; Reading and Language Skills Assessments, Grades 1–6; Holistic Assessments, Grades 1–6; End-of-Selection Tests, Grades 1–6; and Oral Reading Fluency Assessment, Grades 1–6

	GR K	GR 1	GR 2	GR 3	GR 4	GR 5	GR 6
Listen for a purpose							
Follow oral directions (one-, two-, three-, and multi-step)	▨	▨	▨	▨	▨	▨	▨
For specific information	▨	▨	▨	▨	▨	▨	▨
For enjoyment	▨	▨	▨	▨	▨	▨	▨
To distinguish between the speaker's opinions and verifiable facts				▨	▨	▨	▨
To actively participate in class discussions	▨	▨	▨	▨	▨	▨	▨
To expand and enhance personal interest and personal preferences	▨	▨	▨	▨	▨	▨	▨
To identify, analyze, and critique persuasive techniques					▨	▨	▨
To identify logical fallacies used in oral presentations and media messages						▨	▨
To make inferences or draw conclusions			▨	▨	▨	▨	▨
To interpret a speaker's verbal and nonverbal messages, purposes, and perspectives				▨	▨	▨	▨
To identify the tone, mood, and emotion			▨	▨	▨	▨	▨
To analyze the use of rhetorical devices for intent and effect					▨	▨	▨
To evaluate classroom presentations		▨	▨	▨	▨	▨	▨
To respond to a variety of media and speakers		▨	▨	▨	▨	▨	▨
To paraphrase/summarize directions and information			▨	▨	▨	▨	▨
For language reflecting regions and cultures				▨	▨	▨	▨
To recognize emotional and logical arguments					▨	▨	▨
To identify the musical elements of language	▨	▨	▨	▨	▨	▨	▨
Listen critically to relate the speaker's verbal communication to the nonverbal message				▨	▨	▨	▨
Speaking Skills and Strategies							
Speak clearly and audibly and use appropriate volume and pace in different settings	▨	▨	▨	▨	▨	▨	▨
Use formal and informal English appropriately	▨	▨	▨	▨	▨	▨	▨
Follow rules of conversation	▨	▨	▨	▨	▨	▨	▨
Stay on the topic when speaking		▨	▨	▨	▨	▨	▨
Use descriptive words		▨	▨	▨	▨	▨	▨
Recount experiences in a logical sequence		▨	▨	▨	▨	▨	▨
Clarify and support spoken ideas with evidence and examples		▨	▨	▨	▨	▨	▨
Use eye contact, appropriate gestures, and props to enhance oral presentations and engage the audience				▨	▨	▨	▨
Give and follow two-, three-, and four-step directions		▨	▨	▨	▨	▨	▨
Recite poems, rhymes, songs, stories, soliloquies, or dramatic dialogues	▨	▨	▨	▨	▨	▨	▨
Plan and present dramatic interpretations with clear diction, pitch, tempo, and tone				▨	▨	▨	▨
Organize presentations to maintain a clear focus			▨	▨	▨	▨	▨
Use language appropriate to situation, purpose, and audience				▨	▨	▨	▨
Make/deliver							
Oral narrative, descriptive, informational, and persuasive presentations				▨	▨	▨	▨
Oral summaries of articles and books					▨	▨	▨
Oral responses to literature				▨	▨	▨	▨
Presentations on problems and solutions					▨	▨	▨
Presentation or speech for specific occasions, audiences, and purposes				▨	▨	▨	▨
Vary language according to situation, audience, and purpose				▨	▨	▨	▨
Select a focus, organizational structure, and point of view for an oral presentation				▨	▨	▨	▨
Participate in classroom activities and discussions	▨	▨	▨	▨	▨	▨	▨

Key

Shaded area   Explicit Instruction/Modeling/Practice and Application

• Tested

Assessment resources include: Kindergarten Assessment Handbook; Placement and Diagnostic Assessments, Grades 1, 2, and 3–6; Reading and Language Skills Assessments, Grades 1–6; Holistic Assessments, Grades 1–6; End-of-Selection Tests, Grades 1–6; and Oral Reading Fluency Assessment, Grades 1–6

SCOPE AND SEQUENCE

Index

B

C

Classic selections,
  A Birthday Basket for Tía, by Pat
    Mora, **K-2:** 40–41, 70–71
  Caps for Sale, by Esphyr Slobodkina,
    K-3: 138–139
  "Chicken Forgets," by Miska Miles,
    K-2: 270–271; **K-3:** 476–477
  "The Fearsome Beast," retold by
    Judy Sierra, **K-2:** 476–477
  Five Little Ducks: An Old Rhyme,
    illustrated by Pam Paparone, **K-3:**
    364–371, 422–423, 454–455,
    484–485
  "Franklin in the Dark," by Paulette
    Bourgeois, **K-3:** 270–271
  "The Gingerbread Man," retold by
    Anne Rockwell, **K-1:** 354–355
  "Going on a Bear Hunt," **K-2:**
    662–663
  "The Hare and the Tortoise," by
    Aesop, **K-2:** 670–671
  "Old Mister Rabbit," **K-3:** 154–155
  "The Rooster Who Went to His
    Uncle's Wedding," retold by Alma
    Flor Ada, **K-2:** 558–559
  "The Seashore Noisy Book," by
    Margaret Wise Brown, **K-3:**
    644–645
  "The Shoemaker and the Elves,"
    retold by Anne Rockwell, **K-3:**
    50–51
  "Stone Soup," retold by Ann
    McGovern, **K-1:** 452–453; **K-3:**
    332–333
  Swimmy, by Leo Lionni, **K-3:**
    598–599, 636–637
  "The Terrible Tragadabas," retold by
    Joe Hayes, **K-1:** 620–621
  "The Town Mouse and the Country
    Mouse," retold by Lorinda Bryan
    Cauley, **K-2:** 308–309; **K-3:**
    308–309

Classify,
  See **Comprehension**

Classroom management, K-1: R2–R7;
  K-2: R2–R7; **K-3:** R2–R7

Colors, K-2: 485, 549
  See also **Early literacy skills**

Come Along, Daisy! by Jane Simmons,
  K-3: 378–379, 408–409

Common words, reading,
  See **High-frequency words**

Compare and contrast,
  See **Comprehension, Focus skills**

Compare oral traditions,
  See **Comprehension, Focus skills**

Comparing texts,
  See **Comprehension, Focus skills**

Comprehension,
  anticipating text, **K-2:** 501
  ask and answer questions **K-1:** 33, 57,
    91, 107, 123, 165, 189, 231, 281, 341,
    355, 365, 398, 407, 453, 509, 523,
    575, 621; **K-2:** 25, 41, 93, 139, 195,

211, 221, 263, 309, 365, 379, 389,
423, 431, 439, 533, 549, 559, 601,
609, 647, 671; **K-3:** 25, 41, 93, 195,
211, 263, 365, 379, 399, 431, 439,
447, 477, 533, 549, 599, 645, 669

beginning, middle, ending, **K-1:**
  124–125, 262, 281, 365, 398, 523,
  624; **K-2:** 41, 93, 309, 646, 671; **K-3:**
  71, 279, 287, 308, 333, 454, 485, 602,
  668

categorize, **K-1:** 176, 199, 241, 258,
  289, 445, 582–583, 613, 645; **K-3:**
  577

cause and effect, **K-3:** 101

character traits, **K-2:** 41, 609, 647, 670

characters, **K-1:** 122–123, 340, 384–385,
  460, 543, 566; **K-2:** 25, 50, 84, 92,
  101, 116, 147, 162, 220, 286, 477,
  559, 579, 647; **K-3:** 131, 332, 477

character's actions, **K-2:** 24, 70, 84, 116,
  130, 139, 162, 221, 532, 592, 670

character's feelings, **K-1:** 281, 340; **K-2:**
  40, 93, 240, 241, 549, 670; **K-3:** 92,
  130, 270, 271

classify, **K-1:** 231

compare and contrast, **K-1:** 165, 258,
  566–567; **K-2:** 85, 308; **K-3:** 533, 637

compare oral traditions, **K-2:** 559

comparing texts, **K-2:** 163

connect life experiences to text, **K-1:** 91,
  107, 181, 188, 189, 230, 231,
  272–273, 280–281, 384, 430–431,
  628–629; **K-2:** 41, 70, 108, 130, 154,
  270, 388; **K-3:** 241, 278, 287, 301,
  309, 379, 468, 568, 644

context clues, **K-3:** 92, 138, 220, 364,
  378, 430, 532, 598, 644

dramatic interpretation, **K-1:** 33, 199,
  354–355, 423, 430–431, 461, 469,
  477, 509, 533, 644–645; **K-2:** 105,
  147, 163, 227, 231, 309, 395, 439,
  477, 605, 609, 625, 659, 671, 675;
  K-3: 71, 101, 139, 195, 263, 569

drawing conclusions, **K-1:** 281, 355,
  575, 645; **K-2:** 211, 309, 389, 549,
  600, 609

fact and fantasy, **K-2:** 647

illustrations in picture books, **K-2:** 255

main idea and details, **K-1:** 230–231,
  272–273; **K-2:** 263, 379, 431; **K-3:** 85,
  211

make inferences, **K-1:** 198, 281, 365,
  509, 523; **K-2:** 40, 41, 241, 447, 579;
  K-3: 661

make judgments, **K-1:** 354–355; **K-3:**
  131

make predictions, **K-1:** 32, 33, 56,
  106–107, 122–123, 164, 165, 180,
  181, 281, 340–341, 364–365,
  398–399, 508–509, 522–523,
  574–575; **K-2:** 40, 50, 92, 100, 108,
  138, 146, 194, 210, 262, 271, 365,
  388, 438, 446, 476, 500, 532, 568,
  600, 608, 662, 670; **K-3:** 40, 50, 60,

92, 100, 138, 194, 220, 270, 364, 378,
430, 476, 532, 598, 606, 644, 668

matching words, **K-2:** 325, 493

picture details, **K-1:** 32, 56–57,
  106–107, 164–165, 180–181,
  208–209, 340, 364–365, 385, 431;
  K-2: 84, 116, 117, 254, 262, 300, 316,
  364, 378, 408, 430, 468, 532, 592,
  593, 600, 638, 654; **K-3:** 455, 576,
  599, 652, 653

problem/solution, **K-1:** 553, 620–621;
  K-2: 51, 130, 131, 558, 592, 609; **K-3:**
  51, 220, 379, 454, 501

questions for research, **K-2:** 109

reading to get information, **K-2:** 301

real and make-believe, **K-1:** 122–123,
  355, 460, 508–509, 612–613,
  628–629; **K-2:** 211, 220, 484, 558;
  K-3: 50, 130, 290, 408, 484, 558, 606

retelling the story, **K-2:** 67, 71, 105,
  143, 147, 163, 221, 227, 231, 275,
  309, 329, 333, 378, 395, 439, 451,
  477, 549, 565, 601, 609, 621, 625,
  639, 647, 651, 659, 667, 671

sequence, **K-1:** 181, 280–281, 407,
  476–477; **K-2:** 101, 139, 162, 220,
  221, 378, 379, 476; **K-3:** 71, 139, 279,
  287, 308, 439, 454, 607, 652

setting, **K-1:** 208–209, 522, 566,
  574–575; **K-2:** 92, 532, 624, 625; **K-3:**
  93, 163, 309

summarize, **K-1:** 57, 91, 165, 231, 235,
  272–273, 289, 340–341, 354, 384,
  398, 406, 444, 449, 509, 552; **K-2:** 41,
  93, 139, 365, 379, 388, 408, 469, 533,
  548; **K-3:** 71, 116, 147, 195, 211, 220,
  241, 263, 308, 332, 365, 379, 399,
  439, 477, 485, 533, 549

text patterns, **K-2:** 50, 100, 154, 194,
  286, 316, 324, 332, 364, 422, 423,
  476, 484, 558, 616, 646, 654, 655

use illustrations to make predictions,
  K-1: 32, 56, 90, 258, 340, 364–365,
  508; **K-2:** 92, 210, 262, 364, 532, 600;
  K-3: 194, 286, 364, 378, 430, 532

using prior knowledge, **K-2:** 60, 70, 84,
  92, 116, 130, 138, 154, 194, 195, 210,
  220, 230, 270, 278, 324, 332, 364,
  388, 398, 430, 438, 446, 468, 476,
  492, 500, 592, 608, 616, 646, 662

visualizing, **K-2:** 155

Concepts of print,
  capitalization, **K-1:** 30, 46, 56, 68–69,
    74, 88, 104, 112, 120, 162, 178, 186,
    196, 206, 220, 222, 228, 236, 246,
    256, 270, 278, 286, 296, 306, 338,
    352, 362, 372, 382, 396, 404, 412,
    414, 420, 428, 442, 450, 458, 466,
    468, 474, 506, 520, 530, 540, 543,
    550, 564, 572, 580, 588, 596, 610,
    618, 626, 634, 642; **K-2:** 22, 38, 46,
    48, 58, 68, 82, 90, 98, 106, 112, 114,
    128, 134, 136, 144, 152, 158, 160,
    192, 206, 208, 218, 228, 238, 252,

532–533, 542–543, 552, 566–567, 574, 582–583, 590, 598–599, 612, 620, 628–629, 636–637, 644; **K-2**: 25, 41, 51, 61, 71, 85, 93, 101, 109, 117, 131, 139, 147, 155, 163, 195, 211, 212–213, 221, 231, 241, 255, 263, 271, 279, 287, 301, 309, 317, 325, 333, 365, 379, 389, 399, 409, 423, 431, 439, 447, 455, 469, 477, 485, 493, 501, 533, 549, 559, 569, 579, 593, 601, 609, 617, 625, 639, 647, 655, 663, 671; **K-3**: 25, 41, 51, 61, 71, 85, 93, 109, 117, 131, 139, 147, 155, 163, 195, 211, 221, 231, 241, 255, 263, 271, 279, 287, 301, 309, 317, 325, 333, 379, 399, 409, 423, 431, 439, 447, 455, 469, 477, 485, 501, 533, 559, 569, 577, 591, 599, 607, 615, 623, 637, 645, 653, 661, 669

Directions, following, K-1: 108–109, 189, 341

>   *See also* **Early literacy skills, Focus skills**

D'Nealian handwriting model, K-1:
>   R12–R13; **K-2:** R12–R13; **K-3:** R12–13

Does a Kangaroo Have a Mother, Too?
>   by Eric Carle, **K-2:** 194–203, 254–255, 286–287, 316–317

Drafting,
>   *See* **Process writing**

Dramatic play center,
>   *See* **Learning centers**

Draw and label,
>   *See* **Respond to Literature, Writing**

Drawing conclusions,
>   *See* **Comprehension, Focus skills**

Early Literacy Skills
>   alphabet, **K-1:** 48–49, 50–51, 52, 174, 190, 274, 348, 366, 400, 516,
>   colors, **K-1:** 42–43
>   environmental print, **K-1:** 100–101
>   first names, **K-1:** 134–135
>   following oral directions, **K-1:** 108–109
>   listening to a story, **K-1:** 124–125
>   lowercase letters, **K-1:** 78–79
>   numbers 1–5, **K-1:** 116–117
>   printed names, **K-1:** 26–27
>   uppercase letters, **K-1:** 68–69

Elmer, by David McKee, **K-2:** 548–549, 578–579

English-Language Learners, activities for, **K-1:** 23, 25, 33, 51, 55, 57, 69, 77, 101, 107, 115, 165, 175, 181, 183, 203, 209, 223, 225, 231, 239, 249, 259, 281, 289, 291, 297, 302, 309, 339, 355, 365, 375, 377, 378, 385, 401, 417, 421, 424, 429, 431, 445, 453, 461, 470, 477, 479, 517, 521, 527, 543, 546, 577, 593, 601, 613, 619, 629, 643, 645; **K-2:** 51, 53, 65, 71, 83, 87, 103, 111, 117, 141, 163, 165, 195, 211, 213, 223, 231, 233, 235, 241, 263,

265, 281, 287, 289, 326, 365, 373, 377, 389, 399, 431, 439, 441, 448, 453, 475, 494, 501, 503, 533, 543, 559, 561, 579, 591, 601, 603, 609, 625, 627, 647; **K-3:** 25, 35, 41, 43, 51, 53, 65, 71, 85, 87, 93, 101, 107, 117, 139, 141, 156, 163, 195, 223, 231, 235, 239, 255, 263, 265, 287, 301, 331, 335, 379, 381, 389, 402, 441, 448, 455, 479, 494, 503, 551, 591, 599, 623, 625, 653

Environmental print, K-1: 22, 30, 46, 54, 74, 88, 90–99, 100–101, 104, 112, 120, 162, 178, 186, 196, 206, 220, 228, 236, 246, 256, 270, 278, 286, 296, 306, 338, 352, 362, 372, 382, 396, 404, 412, 420, 428, 442, 450, 458, 466, 474, 506, 520, 530, 540, 550, 564, 572, 580, 588, 596, 610, 618, 626, 634, 642; **K-2:** 22, 38, 48, 58, 68, 82, 90, 98, 106, 114, 128, 136, 144, 152, 160, 192, 208, 218, 228, 238, 252, 260, 268, 276, 284, 298, 306, 314, 322, 330, 362, 376, 386, 396, 406, 420, 428, 436, 444, 452, 466, 474, 482, 490, 498, 530, 546, 556, 566, 576, 590, 598, 606, 614, 622, 636, 644, 652, 660, 668; **K-3:** 22, 38, 48, 58, 68, 82, 90, 98, 106, 114, 128, 136, 144, 150, 152, 160, 166, 192, 208, 218, 228, 238, 252, 260, 268, 276, 284, 298, 306, 314, 322, 330, 336, 362, 376, 386, 396, 406, 420, 428, 436, 444, 452, 466, 474, 482, 490, 498, 530, 546, 556, 566, 574, 588, 596, 604, 612, 620, 634, 642, 650, 658, 666

>   *See also* **Early literacy skills**

Explicit instruction,
>   *See* **Direct instruction**

Extra support,
>   *See* **Reaching All Learners**

Fable selections,
>   "The Ants and the Grasshopper," by Aesop, **K-2:** 388–389
>   "The Hare and the Tortoise," by Aesop, **K-2:** 670–671
>   "The Town Mouse and the City Mouse," retold by Lorinda Bryan Cauley, **K-3:** 308–309

Fact and fantasy,
>   *See* **Comprehension, Focus skills**

Fiction,
>   *Are you there, Baby Bear?* by Catherine Walters, **K-2:** 210–211, 240–241
>   *Benny's Pennies,* by Pat Brisson, **K-3:** 40–41, 70–71
>   *The Big Yellow Bus,* **K-3:** 194–203, 254–255, 286–287
>   *A Birthday Basket for Tía,* by Pat Mora, **K-2:** 40–41, 70–71

Bunny Cakes, by Rosemary Wells, **K-1:** 364–365, 384–385
Caps for Sale, by Esphyr Slobodkina, **K-3:** 138–139
"Chicken Forgets," by Miska Miles, **K-2:** 270–271; **K-3:** 476–477
Come Along, Daisy! by Jane Simmons, **K-3:** 378–379, 408–409
The Crayon Box that Talked, by Shane DeRolf, **K-1:** 522–523, 552–553
Dear Juno, by Soyung Pak, **K-2:** 92–93, 130–131
Elmer, by David McKee, **K-2:** 548–549, 578–579
"Emily's House," by Niko Scharer, **K-1:** 644–645
Five Little Ducks, An Old Rhyme, illustrated by Pam Paparone, **K-3:** 364–371, 422–423, 454–455, 484–485
"Franklin in the Dark," by Paulette Bourgeois, **K-3:** 270–271
Good-Bye hello, by Barbara Shook Hazen, **K-3:** 92–93, 130–131
"Grandfather and I," by Helen E. Buckley, **K-2:** 154–155
Hello Toes, Hello Feet! by Ann Whitford Paul, **K-1:** 180–181, 208–209
I Took My Frog to the Library, by Eric Kimmel, **K-1:** 574–575, 612–613
"Jamaica's Find," by Juanita Havill, **K-2:** 138–139; **K-3:** 278–279
Jazzbo and Googy, by Matt Novak, **K-1:** 122–123
"Let's Go, Froggy!" by Jonathan London, **K-2:** 50–51
Look Out Kindergarten, Here I Come! by Nancy Carlson, **K-1:** 106–107
Moo Moo, Brown Cow, by Jakki Wood, **K-1:** 32–33, 34–41, 45, 114–115
"Mother, Mother, I Want Another," by Maria Polushkin, **K-1:** 280–281; **K-3:** 220–221
Off We Go! by Jane Yolen, **K-2:** 24–33, 84–85, 116–117, 146–147
Peanut Butter and Jelly, by Nadine Bernard Westcott, **K-1:** 340–347, 350–351, 430–431, 460–461
"The Rooster Who Went to His Uncle's Wedding," retold by Alma Flor Ada, **K-2:** 558–559
"The Seashore Noisy Book," by Margaret Wise Brown, **K-3:** 644–645
So Say The Little Monkeys, by Nancy Van Laan, **K-2:** 600–601, 638–639
Splash in the Ocean! adapted by Mik Zepol, **K-3:** 532–541, 590–591, 622–623, 652–653
Swimmy, by Leo Lionni, **K-3:** 598–599, 636–637

Learning Site, The,
    See **Technology**
Letter and Sound Charts, K-1: 182–183,
    200–201, 282–283, 356–357, 376–377,
    408–409, 524–525; **K-2:** 42–43, 62–63,
    94–95, 212–213, 232–233, 380–381,
    400–401, 432–433, 550–551, 570–571;
    K-3: 42, 62, 94, 212, 232, 380, 432, 638
Letter and Sound Place Mat, K-1: 555;
    K-3: 73, 391, 401, 411
Letter and word center,
    See **Learning centers**
Letter recognition,
    See **Concepts of print, Early literacy
    skills, Lowercase letters,
    Phonics/Decoding, Uppercase
    letters**
Letter songs, K-1: 182, 200, 232, 240, 250,
    282, 290, 300, 310, 356, 376, 386, 408,
    524, 544, 554; **K-2:** 42, 62, 94, 132, 212,
    232, 242, 256, 380, 400, 410, 432, 470,
    550, 570, 580, 594; **K-3:** 42, 62, 72, 94,
    132, 212, 232, 242, 256, 380, 390, 400,
    410, 432, 470, 542, 638
Letter/sound relationships,
    See **Phonics/Decoding**
Library Books,
    Are You There, Baby Bear? by
        Catherine Walters, **K-2:** 210–211,
        240–241
    Benny's Pennies, by Pat Brisson, **K-3:**
        40–41, 70–71
    A Birthday Basket for Tía, by Pat
        Mora, **K-2:** 40–41, 70–71
    The Body Book, by Shelley Rotner
        and Stephen Calcagnino, **K-1:**
        230–231, 272–273
    Bunny Cakes, by Rosemary Wells,
        K-1: 364–365, 384–385
    Butterfly, by Moira Butterfield, **K-2:**
        378–379, 408–409
    Career Day, by Anne Rockwell, **K-3:**
        210–211, 240–241
    Come Along, Daisy! by Jane Simmons,
        K-3: 378–379, 408–409
    The Crayon Box That Talked, by
        Shane DeRolf, **K-1:** 522–523,
        552–553
    Dear Juno, by Soyung Pak, **K-2:**
        92–93, 130–131
    Elmer, by David McKee, **K-2:**
        548–549, 578–579
    Fish Faces, by Norbert Wu, **K-3:**
        548–549, 576–577
    Good-Bye hello, by Barbara Shook
        Hazen, **K-3:** 92–93, 130–131
    Guess Who? by Margaret Miller, **K-3:**
        262–263, 300–301
    Hello Toes, Hello Feet! by Ann
        Whitford Paul, **K-1:** 180–181,
        208–209
    Hold the Anchovies! by Shelley
        Rotner, Julia Pemberton Hellums,
        K-1: 406–407, 444–445

I Took My Frog to the Library, by Eric
    Kimmel, **K-1:** 574–575, 612–613
Jazzbo and Googy, by Matt Novak,
    K-1: 122–123
Look Out Kindergarten, Here I Come!
    by Nancy Carlson, **K-1:** 106–107
So Say the Little Monkeys, by Nancy
    Van Laan, **K-2:** 600–601, 638–639
Swimmy, by Leo Lionni, **K-3:**
    598–599, 636–637
A Time for Playing, by Ron Hirschi,
    K-2: 262–263, 300–301
What's What? by Mary Serfozo, **K-3:**
    430–431, 468–469
Wonderful Worms, by Linda Glaser,
    K-2: 430–431, 468–469
Library/media center,
    See **Learning centers**
Listening,
    listening comprehension, **K-1:** 33, 57,
        91, 107, 123, 165, 181, 231, 341, 355,
        365, 407, 453, 509, 523, 575, 621;
        K-2: 25, 41, 93, 139, 195, 211, 221,
        263, 309, 365, 379, 389, 431, 439,
        533, 549, 559, 601, 609, 647, 671;
        K-3: 25, 41, 93, 195, 211, 263, 365,
        379, 399, 431, 439, 477, 533, 549,
        599, 645
    musical elements of language, **K-1:**
        24–25, 48–49, 132–133, 198–199,
        238–239, 248–249, 298–299,
        308–309, 414, 415, 422–423,
        468–469, 532–533, 542–543,
        582–583, 590–591, 636–637; **K-2:** 34,
        42, 52, 60–61, 62, 69, 72, 83, 86, 94,
        108–109, 132, 204, 209, 212, 222,
        230–231, 232, 239, 242, 256, 272,
        278–279, 302, 310, 318, 324–325,
        334, 372, 380, 398–399, 400, 410,
        432, 446–447, 456, 470, 486,
        492–493, 499, 500–501, 542, 550,
        568–569, 570, 580, 594, 610,
        616–617, 640, 648, 656, 662–663,
        672; **K-3:** 42, 60–61, 72, 94, 102, 118,
        132, 148, 162–163, 194–195, 230,
        256, 272, 302, 310, 424, 446–447,
        492–493, 502, 532–533, 608
    oral activities, participate in,
        conversations, **K-1:** 22, 30, 46, 54, 74,
        88, 104, 112, 120, 162, 178, 186, 196,
        206, 220, 228, 236, 246, 256, 270,
        278, 286, 296, 306, 338, 352, 362,
        372, 382, 396, 404, 412, 420, 428,
        442, 450, 458, 466, 474, 506, 520,
        530, 540, 550, 564, 572, 580, 588,
        596, 610, 618, 626, 634, 642 ; **K-2:**
        22, 38, 48, 58, 66, 68, 82, 90, 96, 98,
        106, 114, 120, 128, 136, 144, 152,
        160, 192, 208, 218, 226, 228, 238,
        252, 260, 268, 276, 282, 284, 298,
        306, 312, 314, 322, 330, 362, 376,
        386, 394, 396, 406, 420, 428, 434,
        436, 444, 452, 458, 466, 474, 482,
        490, 498, 530, 544, 546, 554, 556,

566, 574, 576, 582, 590, 596, 598,
604, 606, 614, 622, 636, 644, 652,
660, 668; **K-3:** 22, 38, 48, 68, 82, 90,
98, 106, 114, 128, 136, 144, 152, 160,
192, 208, 218, 228, 238, 252, 260,
268, 276, 298, 306, 314, 322, 330,
362, 376, 386, 396, 406, 420, 428,
436, 444, 452, 466, 474, 482, 490,
498, 530, 546, 556, 566, 574, 588,
596, 604, 612, 620, 634, 642, 650,
658, 666
discussions, **K-1:** 22, 24–25, 30, 32–33,
46, 48–49, 54, 56–57, 74, 76–77, 88,
104, 106–107, 112, 114–115, 120,
122–123, 162, 164–165, 178,
180–181, 186, 188–189, 196,
198–199, 206, 208–209, 212–213,
220, 222–223, 228, 230–231, 236,
238–239, 246, 248–249, 256,
258–259, 270, 272–273, 278,
280–281, 286, 288–289, 296,
298–299, 306, 308–309, 338,
340–341, 352, 354–355, 362,
364–365, 372, 374–375, 382,
384–385, 396, 404, 412, 418–419,
420, 428, 430–431, 442, 444–445,
450, 452–453, 458, 460–461, 466,
468–469, 474, 476–477, 506,
508–509, 520, 522–523, 530, 540,
542–543, 550, 552–553, 564,
566–567, 572, 574–575, 580,
582–583, 588, 590–591, 596,
598–599, 610, 612–613, 618,
620–621, 626, 628–629, 636–637,
642, 644–645; **K-2:** 24–25, 37, 40–41,
47, 50–51, 57, 60–61, 67, 70–71, 75,
84–85, 89, 92–93, 97, 100–101, 105,
108–109, 113, 116–117, 121,
130–131, 135, 138–139, 143,
146–147, 151, 154–155, 159,
162–163, 167, 194–195, 207,
210–211, 217, 220–221, 227,
230–231, 237, 240–241, 245,
254–255, 259, 262–263, 267,
270–271, 275, 278–279, 283,
286–287, 291, 300–301, 305,
308–309, 313, 316–317, 321,
324–325, 329, 332–333, 337,
364–365, 375, 378–379, 385,
388–389, 395, 398–399, 405,
408–409, 413, 422–423, 427,
430–431, 435, 438–439, 443,
446–447, 451, 454–455, 459,
468–469, 473, 476–477, 481,
484–485, 489, 492–493, 497,
500–501, 505, 532–533, 545,
548–549, 555, 558–559, 565,
568–569, 575, 578–579, 583,
592–593, 597, 600–601, 605,
608–609, 613, 616–617, 621,
624–625, 629, 638–639, 643,
646–647, 651, 654–655, 659,
662–663, 667, 670–671, 675; **K-3:** 37,
57, 67, 74, 84, 89, 97, 105, 113, 121,

use context clues, **K-3:** 240, 408

use personal experience, **K-1:** 91, 107, 181, 188, 189, 230, 231, 272–273, 280–281, 384, 430–431, 628–629; **K-2:** 41, 70, 108, 130, 154, 270, 388; **K-3:** 241, 278, 287, 301, 309, 379, 468, 568, 644

use picture clues, **K-1:** 33, 56, 90, 106–107, 164–165, 180–181, 258, 340, 364–365, 383, 431, 508, 574; **K-2:** 84, 116, 117, 254, 262, 300, 316, 364, 378, 408, 430, 468, 532, 592, 593, 600, 638, 654; **K-3:** 84, 92, 194, 240, 262, 286, 300, 301, 364, 378, 408, 430, 532, 548, 576, 598, 636

use text structure, **K-1:** 259, 461; **K-2:** 50, 100, 154, 194, 286, 316, 324, 332, 364, 422, 423, 476, 484, 558, 616, 646, 654, 655; **K-3:** 70

visualize, **K-2:** 155; **K-3:** 109

Students acquiring English,
See **English-Language Learners, Reaching All Learners**

Summarize,
See **Comprehension, Focus skills**

Swimmy, by Leo Lionni, **K-3:** 598–599, 636–637

Syllabication,
See **Phonemic awareness**

Take-Home Books, **K-1:** 202–203, 252–253, 302–303, 378–379, 424–425, 470–471, 546–547, 592–593, 638–639; **K-2:** 64–65, 110–111, 156–157, 234–235, 280–281, 326–327, 402–403, 448–449, 494–495, 572–573, 618–619, 664–665; **K-3:** 64–65, 110–111, 156–157, 234–235, 280–281, 326–327, 402–403, 448–449, 494–495, 616–617, 646–647, 654–655

Teacher Resources, K-1: vi-xxxii, 1–21, 86–87, 138–139, 142–161, 218–219, 268–269, 314–315, 316–337, 394–395, 440–441, 482–483, 484–505, 562–563, 608–609, 650–654, S2–S67, T1–T42, R2–R31; **K-2:** vi-xxxii, 1–21, 76–78, 80–81, 122–124, 126–127, 168–169, 170–191, 246–248, 250–251, 292–294, 296–297, 338–339, 340–361, 414–416, 418–419, 460–462, 464–465, 506–507, 508–529, 584–586, 588–599, 630–632, 634–635, 676–680, S1–S73, T1–T34, R1–R33; **K-3:** vi-xxxii, 1–21, 76–78, 80–81, 122–124, 126–127, 172–191, 246–248, 250–251, 292–294, 296–297, 342–361, 414–416, 418–419, 460–462, 464–465, 510–529, 582–584, 586–587, 628–630, 632–633, 676–677, S1–S73, T1–T30, R1–R33

Technology,

Internet/*The Learning Site,* **K-1:** 12, 152, 328, 496; **K-2:** R14–R15; **K-3:** 12, 182, 352, 520, R14–R15

Music CD, **K-1:** 24, 48, 52, 108, 174, 188, 198, 224, 308, 348, 366, 400, 468, 469, 516, 542, 636; **K-2:** 34, 52, 86, 204, 222, 230, 372, 424, 492, 500, 542, 568; **K-3:** 108, 154, 183, 230, 324, 329, 398, 532, 568, 591, 606, 614

Phonics Express CD–ROM, **K-1:** 175, 183, 211, 225, 233, 275, 349, 357, 367, 377, 409, 463, 517, 525, 535, 545; **K-2:** 35, 43, 53, 63, 87, 133, 205, 213, 223, 233, 243, 257, 373, 381, 391, 401, 411, 425, 433, 471, 479, 543, 551; **K-3:** 35, 43, 53, 63, 73, 86, 94, 205, 213, 223, 233, 243, 373, 381, 391, 401, 411, 425, 471

Text patterns,
See **Comprehension, Focus skills**

Text structures,

expository text, **K-1:** 56–57, 76–77, 90–91, 164–165, 222–223, 230–231, 258–259, 288–289, 272–273, 444–445; **K-2:** 194–203, 254–255, 262–263, 286–287, 300–301, 316–317, 364–365, 378–379, 408–409, 422–423, 430–431, 454–455, 468–469, 484–485; **K-3:** 24–25, 84–85, 116–117, 146–147, 210–211, 240–241, 262–263, 300–301, 430–431, 468–469, 548–549, 576–577

patterned text, **K-1:** 32–33, 114–115, 340–341, 430–431, 460–461; **K-2:** 22–33, 84–85, 116–117, 146–147, 194–203, 254–255, 286–287, 316–317, 364–365, 422–423, 454–455, 484–485, 532–533, 592–593, 624–625, 654–655; **K-3:** 40–41, 70–71, 92–93, 130–131, 194–195, 254–255, 286–287, 316–317, 364–365, 422–423, 454–455, 484–485, 532–533, 590–591, 622–623, 652–653

simple story structure, **K-1:** 106–107, 122–123, 280–281, 354–355, 362–365, 384–385, 452–453, 522–523, 552–553, 574–575, 612–613, 620–621; **K-2:** 40–41, 50–51, 70–71, 92–93, 100–101, 130–131, 138–139, 154–155, 162–163, 210–211, 220–221, 240–241, 270–271, 308–309, 388–389, 438–439, 476–477, 548–549, 578–579, 558–559, 600–601, 608–609, 638–639, 646–647, 670–671; **K-3:** 50–51, 138–139, 220–221, 270–271, 278–279, 308–309, 332–333, 438–439, 476–477, 644–645

Theme assessment, K-1: 7, 147, 323, 491; **K-2:** 7, 177, 347, 515; **K-3:** 7, 177, 347, 515

Theme projects,

All About Us" Chart, **K-1:** 152

"Animal Family" Posters, **K-2:** 182

Animal Parade, **K-2:** 520

Classroom Aquarium, **K-3:** 520

Come to Our "Town!" **K-3:** 12

Explorer's Log, **K-3:** 352

"Fabulous Food" Fair, **K-1:** 328

Give a Bug Talk! **K-2:** 352

"Helping Hands" Mural, **K-2:** 12

"Here's Our School!" Book, **K-1:** 12

"Neighborhood Songs" Concert, **K-3:** 182

A Silly Puppet Show, **K-1:** 496

Theme Resources, K-1: 2–3, 142–143, 318–319, 486–487; **K-2:** 2–3, 172–173, 342–343, 510–511; **K-3:** 2–3, 172–173, 342–343, 510–511

Theme review, K-1: 139, 315, 483, 651; **K-2:** 169, 339, 507, 677; **K-3:** 169, 339, 507, 675

Themes,

Animal Adventures, **K-2:** 508–677

Animal Families, **K-2:** 170–339

Around the Table, **K-1:** 316–483

Around the Town, **K-3:** 1–169

Bug Surprises, **K-2:** 340–507

Exploring Our Surroundings, **K-3:** 340–507

Family Ties, **K-2:** 1–169

Getting to Know You, **K-1:** 1–139

I Am Special, **K-1:** 140–315

Neighborhood Helpers, **K-3:** 170–339

Silly Business, **K-1:** 484–651

Under the Sea, **K-3:** 508–675

Think-Alouds, K-1: 32, 33, 56, 106, 114, 163, 164, 176, 180, 208, 222, 230, 232, 259, 262, 272, 289, 310, 340, 353, 364, 398, 406, 444, 452, 460, 508, 522, 552, 574, 590, 612, 620, 637, 644; **K-2:** 24, 25, 40, 51, 61, 70, 84, 85, 93, 101, 109, 116, 117, 130, 138, 146, 147, 155, 162, 194, 195, 210, 211, 220, 221, 230, 240, 241, 254, 255, 262, 263, 270, 271, 286, 287, 300, 301, 308, 317, 364, 378, 389, 408, 409, 430, 438, 446, 447, 454, 455, 468, 469, 476, 484, 501, 532, 548, 549, 558, 578, 579, 592, 600, 608, 624, 638, 646, 654, 662, 670; **K-3:** 24, 25, 40, 41, 50, 51, 70, 71, 84, 85, 88, 92, 100, 104, 108, 109, 116, 117, 130, 131, 138, 139, 142, 146, 147, 154, 158, 162, 206, 211, 216, 220, 240, 241, 254, 255, 262, 266, 270, 278, 286, 300, 301, 308, 309, 316, 332, 378, 379, 408, 422, 430, 439, 446, 454, 455, 476, 477, 484, 485, 492, 493, 501, 532, 533, 548, 549, 558, 569, 577, 590, 598, 606, 614, 615, 622, 636, 637, 644, 645, 653, 661, 668, 669

A Time for Playing, by Ron Hirschi, **K-2:** 262–263, 300–301

Acknowledgments

Big Books

For permission to reprint copyrighted material, grateful acknowledgment is made to the following sources:

Boyds Mills Press, Inc.: From Anne to Zach by Mary Jane Martin, illustrated by Michael Grejniec. Text copyright © 1996 by Mary Jane Martin; illustrations copyright © 1996 by Michael Grejniec.

Candlewick Press Inc., Cambridge, MA: The Shape of Things by Dayle Ann Dodds, illustrated by Julie Lacome. Text © 1994 by Dayle Ann Dodds; illustrations © 1994 by Julie Lacome.

Dutton Children's Books, a division of Penguin Putnam Inc.: Peanut Butter and Jelly: A Play Rhyme, illustrated by Nadine Bernard Westcott. Illustrations copyright © 1987 by Nadine Bernard Westcott.

Harcourt, Inc.: Look Closer by Brian and Rebecca Wildsmith. Copyright © 1993 by Brian and Rebecca Wildsmith. *Moo Moo, Brown Cow* by Jakki Wood, illustrated by Rog Bonner. Text copyright © 1991 by Jakki Wood; illustrations copyright © 1991 by Rog Bonner.

HarperCollinsChildrensBooks, a division of HarperCollins Publishers, Inc.: Does a Kangaroo Have a Mother, Too? by Eric Carle. Copyright © 2000 by Eric Carle. *I Read Signs* by Tana Hoban. Copyright © 1983 by Tana Hoban.

Hyperion Books for Children, an Imprint of Disney Children's Book Group, LLC: Warthogs in the Kitchen: A Sloppy Counting Book by Pamela Duncan Edwards, illustrated by Henry Cole. Text © 1998 by Pamela Duncan Edwards; illustrations © 1998 by Henry Cole. Originally published in the United States and Canada by Hyperion Books for Children.

Little, Brown and Company (Inc.): Off We Go! by Jane Yolen, illustrated by Laurel Molk. Text copyright © 2000 by Jane Yolen; illustrations copyright © 2000 by Laurel Molk.

North-South Books Inc., New York: Five Little Ducks: An Old Rhyme, illustrated by Pamela Paparone. Illustrations copyright © 1995 by Pamela Paparone.

Orchard Books, New York: Walking Through the Jungle by Debbie Harter. Text copyright © 1997 by Barefoot Books; illustrations copyright © 1997 by Debbie Harter.

G. P. Putnam's Sons, a division of Penguin Putnam Inc.: Mice Squeak, We Speak by Arnold Shapiro, illustrated by Tomie dePaola. Text copyright © 1984 by World Book, Inc.; illustrations copyright © 1997 by Tomie dePaola. Originally titled "I Speak, I Say, I Talk."

Jackie Silberg, Miss Jackie Music Co.: Music from "All the Fish" (Retitled: "Splash in the Ocean!"), adapted by "Miss Jackie" Silberg. Music copyright © 1977 by Miss Jackie Music Co.

Simon & Schuster Books for Young Readers, Simon & Schuster Children's Publishing Division: Pass the Fritters, Critters by Cheryl Chapman, illlustrated by Susan L. Roth. Text copyright © 1993 by Cheryl Chapman; illustrations copyright © 1993 by Susan L. Roth.

Library Books and Theme Books

For permission to reprint copyrighted material, grateful acknowledgment is made to the following sources:

Atheneum Books for Young Readers, an imprint of Simon & Schuster Children's Publishing Division: Cover and illustrations by Michael Bryant from *Good-Bye Hello* by Barbara Shook Hazen. Illustrations copyright © 1995 by Michael Bryant. Cover and illustrations by Yumi Heo from *So Say the Little Monkeys* by Nancy Van Laan. Illustrations copyright © 1998 by Yumi Heo.

Boyds Mills Press, Inc.: Cover and illustrations by Michael Grejniec from *From Anne to Zach* by Mary Jane Martin. Illustrations copyright © 1996 by Michael Grejniec.

Candlewick Press Inc., Cambridge, MA: Cover and illustrations by Julie Lacome from *The Shape of Things* by Dayle Ann Dodds. Illustrations © 1994 by Julie Lacome.

Dial Books for Young Readers, a division of Penguin Putnam Inc.: Cover and illustrations from *Bunny Cakes* by Rosemary Wells. Illustrations copyright © 1997 by Rosemary Wells.

DK Publishing, Inc., New York: Cover and illustrations by Nadine Bernard Westcott from *Hello Toes! Hello Feet!* by Ann Whitford Paul. Illustrations copyright © 1998 by Nadine Bernard Westcott.

Dutton Children's Books, a division of Penguin Putnam Inc.: Cover and photographs by Thomas D. Mangelsen from *A Time for Playing* by Ron Hirschi. Photographs copyright © 1994 by Thomas D. Mangelsen. Cover and illustrations from *Are You There, Baby Bear?* by Catherine Walters. Copyright © 1999 by Catherine Walters.

HarperCollinsChildrensBooks, a division of HarperCollins Publishers, Inc.: Cover and illustrations from *Guess Who?* by Margaret Miller. Copyright © 1994 by Margaret Miller. Cover and illustrations by Lizzy Rockwell from *Career Day* by Anne Rockwell. Illustrations copyright © 2000 by Lizzy Rockwell.

Henry Holt and Company, Inc.: Cover and photographs from *Fish Faces* by Norbert Wu. Photographs copyright © 1993 by Norbert Wu.

Hyperion Books for Children, an Imprint of Disney Children's Book Group, LLC: Cover and illustrations by Henry Cole from *Warthogs in the Kitchen: A Sloppy Counting Book* by Pamela Duncan Edwards. Illustrations © 1998 by Henry Cole. Originally published in the United States and Canada by Hyperion Books for Children. Cover and illustrations from *Jazzbo and Googy* by Matt Novak. Copyright © 2000 by Matt Novak.

Alfred A. Knopf, Inc.: Cover and illustrations from *Swimmy* by Leo Lionni. Illustrations copyright © 1963 by Leo Lionni; illustrations copyright renewed 1991 by Leo Lionni.

Little, Brown and Company (Inc.): Cover and illustrations from *Come Along, Daisy!* by Jane Simmons. Copyright © 1998 by Jane Simmons. Originally published in Great Britain by Orchard Books, 1998.

Lothrop, Lee & Shepard Books, a division of William Morrow & Company, Inc.: Cover and illustrations from *Elmer* by David McKee. Illustrations copyright © 1968 by David McKee.

Margaret K. McElderry Books, Simon & Schuster Children's Publishing Division: Cover and illustrations by Keiko Narahashi from *What's What?* by Mary Serfozo. Illustrations copyright © 1996 by Keiko Narahashi.

The Millbrook Press: Cover and illustrations by Loretta Krupinski from *Wonderful Worms* by Linda Glaser. Illustrations copyright © 1992 by Loretta Krupinski.

Penguin Putnam Books for Young Readers, a division of Penguin Putnam Inc.: Cover and illustrations by Tomie dePaola from *Mice Squeak, We Speak* by Arnold Shapiro. Illustrations copyright © 1997 by Tomie dePaola. Reprinted by permission of World Books, Inc. Originally titled "I Speak, I Say, I Talk."

Random House Children's Books, a division of Random House, Inc., New York: Cover and illustrations by Bob Barner from *Benny's Pennies* by Pat Brisson. Illustrations copyright © 1993 by Bob Barner. Cover and illustrations by Michael Letzig from *The Crayon Box that Talked* by Shane DeRolf. Illustrations copyright © 1997 by Michael Letzig.

Scholastic Inc.: Cover and photographs by Shelley Rotner from *The Body Book* by Shelley Rotner and Stephen Calcagnino. Photographs copyright © 2000 by Shelley Rotner. Cover and photographs by Shelley Rotner from *Hold the Anchovies! A Book about Pizza* by Shelley Rotner and Julia Pemberton Hellums. Photographs copyright © 1996 by Shelley Rotner.

Simon & Schuster Books for Young Readers, Simon & Schuster Children's Publishing Division: Cover and illustrations by Paul Johnson from *Nature Chains: Butterfly* by Moira Butterfield. Copyright © 1991 by Teeney Books Limited. Cover and illustrations by Cecily Lang from *A Birthday Basket for Tía* by Pat Mora. Illustrations copyright © 1992 by Cecily Lang.

Viking Children's Books, a division of Penguin Putnam Inc.: Cover and illustrations from *Look Out Kindergarten, Here I Come!* by Nancy Carlson. Copyright © 1999 by Nancy Carlson. Cover and illustrations by Blanche Sims from *I Took My Frog to the Library* by Eric A. Kimmel. Illustrations copyright © 1990 by Blanche Sims. Cover and illustrations by Susan Hartung from *Dear Juno* by Soyung Pak. Illustrations copyright © 1999 by Susan Hartung.

Big Book of Rhymes and Songs

For permission to reprint copyrighted material, grateful acknowledgment is made to the following sources:

Dial Books for Young Readers, a division of Penguin Putnam Inc.: "I Am" from *It's Raining Laughter* by Nikki Grimes. Text copyright © 1997 by Nikki Grimes.

David Higham Associates: "Kitchen Sink-Song" by Tony Mitton from *Poems Go Clang! A Collection of Noisy Verse.* Text © 1997 by Tony Mitton.

Homeland Publishing (CAPAC), a division of Troubadour Records Ltd.: Lyrics by Raffi and D. Pike from "Everything Grows" in *Raffi's Top 10 Songs to Read* by Raffi. Lyrics © 1987 by Homeland Publishing (CAPAC), a division of Troubadour Records Ltd. "Wheels on the Bus" and "Down By the Bay" (traditional) from *Rise and Shine* (1982) and *Singable Songs for the Very Young* (1976) by Raffi.

LADYBUG Magazine: "Winter Birds" by Ben Kenny from *LADYBUG* Magazine, January 1999, Vol. 9, No. 2. Text © 1999 by Benjamin C. Kenny. Lyrics from "Five Speckled Frogs" in *LADYBUG* Magazine, June 1994, Vol. 4, No. 10. Lyrics © 1994 by Carus Publishing Company.

Little, Brown and Company (Inc.): "Los pescaditos" / "The Little Fishes" from *Los pollitos dicen/The Baby Chicks Sing* by Jill Syverson-Stork and Nancy Abraham Hall. Lyrics copyright © 1994 by Jill Syverson-Stork and Nancy Abraham Hall.

Ludlow Music, Inc., New York, NY: From "Mary Was a Red Bird" ("Mary Wore Her Red Dress"), collected, adapted, and arranged by Alan Lomax and John A. Lomax. Lyrics TRO - © copyright 1941 (Renewed) by Ludlow Music, Inc.

The McGraw-Hill Companies: "Fuzzy Wuzzy, Creepy Crawly" from *Hey Bug!* by Lillian Schulz.

Marian Reiner, on behalf of Aileen Fisher: "When It Comes to Bugs" from *I Wonder How, I Wonder Why* by Aileen Fisher. Text copyright © 1962, 1990 by Aileen Fisher.

Westwood Creative Artists, on behalf of Dennis Lee: From "The Kitty Ran Up the Tree" in *Jelly Belly* by Dennis Lee. Text copyright © 1983 by Dennis Lee. Published by Macmillan of Canada.

⌐ Sunshine State Standards & Grade Level Expectations

1.0   The student uses the reading process effectively.

Benchmark	Grade Level Expectations	Page(s) or Location(s) Where Taught
LA.A.1.1.1:	The student predicts what a passage is about based on its title and illustrations. **The student:**	
	1. uses titles and illustrations to make oral predictions.	**Vol. 1:** 32, 43, 56, 106, 126, 164, 180, 230, 340, 354, 364, 398, 425, 430, 452, 508, 547, 574, 620, 636 **Vol. 2:** 50, 60, 108, 210, 262, 332, 364–365, 378, 398, 438, 446, 493, 532, 548, 558, 568, 600, 608, 646, 662, 670 **Vol. 3:** 24, 40, 50, 60, 92, 100, 194, 300–301, 364, 378, 430, 532, 598
LA.A.1.1.2:	The student identifies words and constructs meaning from text, illustrations, graphics, and charts using the strategies of phonics, word structure, and context clues. **The student:**	
	1. understands how print is organized and read (for example, locating print on a page, matching print to speech, knowing parts of a book, reading top-to-bottom and left-to-right, sweeping back to left for the next line).	**Vol. 1:** 22, 24, 33, 43, 46, 53–54, 57, 70, 76–77, 90–91, 104, 110, 112, 114–115, 118–119, 120, 130, 132–133, 136, 162, 164–165, 174, 176, 178, 180, 182–183, 186, 190, 198, 202–203, 205–206, 212, 220, 222, 224, 226–227, 230, 232, 234, 242, 244–245, 248, 252–253, 254, 258, 262–263, 270, 274, 278, 282, 286, 292, 294–295, 298–299, 304, 312, 338, 350, 354, 358, 360, 362, 366, 368, 374–375, 379–380, 382, 386, 388–389, 396, 398, 400, 408, 417–418, 419, 422, 424–425, 432–433, 435, 442, 444, 446, 450, 455–456, 458, 460–461, 462–463, 464, 466, 468, 470–471, 474, 478–479, 480, 506, 524, 526, 530, 532, 534, 536, 538, 546, 550, 572, 577, 584, 590, 593, 596, 600–601, 612, 614–615, 622–623, 626, 630, 636, 638, 639, 641, 645, 647 **Vol. 2:** 22, 24, 34, 38, 42, 47, 52, 62, 65, 67–68, 70, 75, 82, 84, 86, 90, 97–98, 106, 108, 110–111, 112, 114, 120, 132, 135, 141–142, 146, 148–149, 150, 152, 154, 156–157, 158, 162, 164–165, 192, 194, 204, 206, 208, 218, 222, 230, 236, 238, 240, 254, 288–289, 262, 268, 272–273, 274, 276, 278–279, 280–281, 282–283, 286–287, 288–289, 290–291, 298, 302, 310, 314, 318, 324–325, 326–327, 328, 330, 332, 335–336, 337, 362, 364, 372, 376, 380, 382, 386, 390, 392, 398, 402–403, 404–405, 422, 424, 426–427, 428, 430, 441, 443, 446, 448–449, 451, 455–456, 457, 459, 473, 479–480, 481, 484, 486–487, 488–489, 490, 492, 494–495, 496, 500, 502, 503, 530, 532, 544, 546, 552, 562, 565, 568, 572, 574, 590, 594, 598, 600, 618–619, 622, 628, 636, 640–641, 648, 649, 650, 656–657, 658, 660, 664–665, 666–667, 668, 673 **Vol. 3:** 22, 24, 34, 36, 42, 44, 52, 54–55, 56, 62, 64–65, 68, 86, 89, 92, 104, 108, 110–111, 121, 132, 141–142, 146, 148–149, 150–151, 154, 156–157, 158, 162, 164–165, 192, 194, 204, 206, 212, 214, 222, 224–225, 226, 230, 232, 234–235, 252, 254, 258, 260, 262, 267–268, 270, 274, 276, 281–282, 291, 298, 311–312, 314, 316–317, 319, 322, 326, 328, 330, 334–335, 362, 364, 372,

		374, 380, 386, 392–393, 394–395, 398, 402–403, 420, 422, 427, 430, 436, 440–441, 446, 448–449, 458–459, 479, 484, 486–487, 488–489, 494–495, 496, 500, 502–503, 530–531, 532, 544, 556, 562, 570–571, 574, 588, 592, 595–596, 600, 604, 608, 614, 617, 619–620, 622, 625–626, 638, 647, 652, 654–655, 656, 662–663, 668, 670–671
	2. knows the names of the letters of the alphabet, both upper and lower case.	**Vol. 1:** 46, 48, 50–51, 52–53, 57, 68–69, 72–73, 74, 77–78, 79, 81, 88, 102, 104, 112, 128, 162, 174–175, 176–177, 182–183, 190–191, 200–201, 206, 210–211, 220–222, 224–225, 232–233, 236, 240–241, 246, 250–251, 254–255, 256, 260, 261, 274–275, 277–278, 282–283, 285, 288, 290–291, 296, 306, 310–311, 312–313, 348–349, 356–357, 358, 360, 366–367, 368–369, 370, 376, 380, 386–387, 396, 400–401, 402–403, 404, 408–409, 416–417, 422, 433, 446–447, 454–455, 456, 457, 458, 463, 466, 468, 479, 516–517, 519–520, 524–525, 534, 535, 538, 543–544, 550, 554–555, 564, 576, 577, 580, 584–585, 592–593, 601, 638 **Vol. 2:** 22, 34, 42–43, 47–48, 52, 57, 62–63, 72–73, 87, 94–95, 97, 102, 106, 114, 118–119, 121, 132–133, 141–142, 149, 152, 160, 165, 192, 204–205, 208, 212–213, 215, 218, 222–223, 225, 232–233, 238, 242–243, 252, 255–256, 257, 260, 264, 268, 274, 276, 280, 298, 300, 306, 314, 322, 330, 362, 372, 380–381, 383, 390, 393, 400–401, 406, 410–411, 420, 423–424, 425, 440–441, 450, 457, 466, 470–471, 474, 478–479, 480–481, 482, 487, 490, 498, 503, 530, 543–544, 545, 550–551, 552–553, 556, 560–561, 564, 566, 570–571, 576, 581–582, 590, 595, 596, 598, 602, 606, 612, 622, 636, 650, 652, 660, 674 **Vol. 3:** 34–35, 42–43, 52–53, 62–63, 66, 72–73, 82, 86–87, 94, 98, 102, 106, 113, 118–119, 128, 132–133, 136, 140–141, 142, 144, 149, 152, 160, 165, 192, 204–205, 207, 212–213, 222–223, 225, 232–233, 236, 238, 242–243, 245, 256–257, 258, 264, 272–273, 284, 288, 306, 311–312, 319, 321, 335, 362, 372–373, 376, 380–381, 390–391, 393, 396, 400–401, 404, 406, 410–411, 413, 420, 424, 427–428, 432–433, 434, 436, 440, 452, 457, 459, 466, 470, 471, 474, 478–479, 480, 482, 487, 490, 498, 503, 542–543, 546, 550, 556, 563, 566, 604, 612, 639, 642, 646–647, 648, 650, 656, 658, 666, 671
	3. knows the sounds of the letters of the alphabet.	**Vol. 1:** 104, 112, 179, 182–183, 197, 200, 201, 210–211, 229, 232–233, 236, 240–241, 250–251, 255, 260–261, 282–283, 285, 290–291, 310–311, 353, 356–357, 367–368, 369, 376–377, 378, 382, 386–387, 405, 408–409, 416–417, 432–433, 446–447, 454–455, 456, 458, 462–463, 466, 470, 478–479, 524–525, 544–545, 554–555, 576, 577, 584–585, 588, 592–593, 595–596, 601, 614, 616, 630, 634, 646 **Vol. 2:** 22, 39, 42–43, 47, 62–63, 72–73, 83, 94–95, 102–103, 106, 110, 118–119, 132–133, 140–141, 148–149, 153, 164–165, 209, 212–213, 215, 225, 232–233, 242–243, 256–257, 264–265, 268, 272–273, 274, 280, 283, 288–289, 298, 302, 306, 310, 312, 318, 322, 326, 330, 380–381, 400–401, 406, 410–411, 440–441, 448–449, 456, 457, 470–471, 474, 478–479, 481–482, 486–487, 490–491, 502–503, 550–551, 556, 570–571, 581, 590, 594–595, 600, 602–603, 606, 610, 622, 626–627, 641, 649, 657, 660, 663, 672–673 **Vol. 3:** 22, 42–43, 62–63, 66, 68, 72–73, 75, 82, 94–95, 98, 102–103, 106, 110, 113–114, 118–119, 132–133, 140–141, 144, 148–149, 153, 164–165, 212–213, 232–233, 236–237, 238, 242–243, 245, 256–257, 264–265, 272–273, 280, 288, 310–311, 312, 315, 318–319, 321, 323, 326, 334–335, 362–363, 376, 380–381, 383, 385–386, 390–391, 396, 400–401, 404, 406, 410–411, 413, 428, 432–433, 436, 440–441, 445, 448, 452, 456–457, 471, 478–479, 482, 486–487, 491, 502–503, 530, 542–543, 550–551, 560–561, 570, 574, 578–579, 596, 600, 604, 608, 612, 619, 624–625, 638–639, 646, 650, 654–655, 659, 671

4. understands the concept of words and constructs meaning from shared text, illustrations, graphics, and charts.	**Vol. 1:** 26–27, 31, 77, 88, 90–91, 100–101, 102–103, 111, 114–115, 116–117, 131, 132, 163–164, 165, 176, 178, 181, 184, 186, 188, 192–193, 194, 199, 202, 212, 222–223, 226, 242–243, 244, 246, 248–249, 252–253, 254, 259, 263, 272–273, 276–277, 289, 294, 298–299, 312–313, 340, 348, 358, 361, 362, 368–369, 371, 374–375, 378–379, 382, 396, 399, 402, 404, 406–407, 412, 420, 423, 425, 430, 444–445, 463, 468, 477, 533, 567, 598–599, 613, 640, 645 **Vol. 2:** 25, 36, 40, 44, 51, 54, 58, 60, 64–65, 71, 92, 101, 104, 109–110, 112, 116, 131, 133–134, 150, 156, 162, 214–215, 216, 221, 224–225, 226, 230–231, 234–235, 241, 244, 252, 254–255, 266, 282, 286–287, 300–301, 327, 336, 365, 384, 392, 402, 404, 409, 422–423, 427, 430, 447, 450, 468–469, 471–472, 476–477, 480, 485, 488, 494, 500, 544, 552, 562–563, 569, 593, 601, 614, 617, 627, 636, 639, 644, 650, 652, 654–655, 660, 666, 673–674 **Vol. 3:** 38, 44–45, 50, 54, 58, 64, 85, 88, 101, 104, 109–110, 112, 116, 131, 133, 142, 150, 156, 159, 162, 208, 214–215, 216–217, 218, 220, 224, 226, 228, 231, 234, 241, 244, 258, 271, 276, 280, 286, 312–313, 314, 317, 320, 322, 325, 328–329, 330, 332, 382, 384, 388–389, 392–393, 394, 402, 409, 412, 422–423, 431, 434, 447–448, 449, 469, 471, 478, 488, 494, 500, 546, 552–553, 562, 570, 590–591, 594, 598, 603, 607, 614, 616, 618, 623, 637, 639, 646, 656–657, 662
5. understands basic phonetic principles (for example, knows rhyming words; knows words that have the same initial and final sounds; knows which sound is in the beginning, middle, end of a word; blends individual sounds into words).	**Vol. 1:** 47, 55, 75, 105, 113, 131, 163, 179, 182–183, 185, 187, 190, 196–197, 200–201, 207, 210–211, 221, 227, 229, 232–233, 236–237, 240–241, 247–248, 249–250, 251, 255, 257, 260–261, 279, 282–283, 287, 290–291, 297, 305, 307, 310–311, 339, 353, 357, 363, 373, 376–377, 383, 387, 388, 397, 405, 413, 416–417, 424, 429, 432–433, 443, 447, 451, 454–455, 459, 462–463, 467, 469–470, 475, 478–479, 525, 531, 541, 545, 551, 555, 565, 576, 577, 581, 583, 585, 587, 589, 592, 593, 597, 600–601, 611, 614–615, 619, 622–623, 627, 630–631, 633, 635, 637, 640, 645–646, 647 **Vol. 2:** 22–23, 25, 39, 43, 48–49, 59, 63, 69, 72–73, 83, 85, 91, 94–95, 99, 102–103, 110, 115, 118–119, 120–121, 129, 137, 140–141, 145, 148–149, 153, 156, 161, 164–165, 192–193, 209, 212–213, 219, 229, 232–233, 239, 242–243, 244, 253, 256–257, 261, 264–265, 268–269, 272–273, 274, 279–280, 283, 285, 288–289, 299, 302–303, 307–308, 310–311, 315, 318–319, 321, 323, 326, 331, 333–334, 335, 363, 376–377, 380–381, 387, 397, 401, 407, 410–411, 421, 429, 432–433, 437, 440–441, 445, 448, 453, 456–457, 467, 474–475, 478–479, 481–482, 483, 486–487, 491, 494, 499, 502–503, 531, 547, 551, 557, 567, 571, 577, 580–581, 591, 594–595, 599, 601–602, 603, 607, 610–611, 615–616, 618, 623, 626, 637, 640–641, 643, 645, 648–649, 653, 656–657, 658, 661, 664, 669, 672–673 **Vol. 3:** 39, 42–43, 49, 58–59, 62–63, 69, 71–72, 73, 75, 83, 90–91, 94–95, 97–98, 99, 102–103, 106–107, 110, 112, 113, 114–115, 117–118, 119, 129, 137, 140–141, 144–145, 148–149, 153, 156, 161, 164–165, 193, 209, 212–213, 219, 226, 228–229, 232–233, 237–238, 239, 242–243, 245, 253, 256, 257, 261, 264–265, 269, 272–273, 277, 280, 285, 288, 299, 302–303, 307, 310–311, 312, 314–315, 318–319, 322–323, 326, 330–331, 334–335, 363, 376–377, 380–381, 385–386, 387, 389–390, 391, 394, 396–397, 399–400, 401, 406–407, 410–411, 413, 421, 428–429, 432–433, 436–437, 440–441, 444–445, 447–448, 453, 456–457, 467, 475, 478–479, 482–483, 486–487, 494, 499, 502–503, 531, 543, 547, 550–551, 557, 559–560, 561, 567, 575, 578–579, 589, 592–593, 596, 600–601, 605, 607–608, 609, 612–613, 616, 619, 621, 624–625, 635, 638, 643, 646–647, 650–651, 654–655, 659, 667, 670–671

	6. understands that print conveys meaning.	**Vol. 1:** 26–27, 30, 88–89, 90–91, 100–101, 102–103, 120, 130, 178, 181, 184, 194, 206, 209, 212, 223, 226, 230–231, 239, 244, 246, 248–249, 254, 272–273, 276, 304, 350, 358, 362, 368–369, 370, 372, 375, 378–379, 380, 382, 388, 399, 402, 407, 444, 445, 518, 538, 602 **Vol. 2:** 57, 130–131, 139, 156, 216, 226, 230–231, 260, 300–301, 305, 365, 379, 409, 430, 435, 442, 444, 447, 468–469, 472, 477, 494, 606, 614, 622, 636, 639, 660, 673 **Vol. 3:** 47, 68, 104, 130–131, 139, 156, 217, 258, 262–263, 266, 298, 304, 306, 309, 312–313, 317, 328, 332–333, 422–423, 431, 442, 469, 494, 574, 594, 636–637, 662
LA.A.1.1.3:	The student uses knowledge of appropriate grade-, age-, and developmental-level vocabulary in reading. **The student:**	
	1. identifies high frequency words.	**Vol. 1:** 32, 56, 192–193, 202–203, 242–243, 248–249, 252–253, 254, 292–293, 295, 340, 358–359, 369, 379, 417, 422, 425, 455, 468, 470–471, 526–527, 537, 539, 546–547, 577, 593, 639 **Vol. 2:** 44–45, 54–55, 64–65, 110–111, 128, 141, 152, 157, 214–215, 216–217, 224–225, 228, 238, 265, 280–281, 282–283, 284, 312, 316, 326–327, 382–383, 393, 403, 405, 422, 441, 448–449, 466, 479, 495, 530, 542, 552–553, 562–563, 568–569, 572–573, 574, 618–619, 644, 664–665, 668, 672–673 **Vol. 3:** 44–45, 54–55, 58, 64–65, 68, 90, 106, 110–111, 128, 136, 141, 152, 157, 160, 214–215, 224–225, 230, 234–235, 255, 258, 280–281, 300, 304, 306, 311, 314, 317, 319, 322, 330, 383, 392–393, 402–403, 431, 448–449, 466, 469, 474, 490, 495, 498, 552–553, 562–563, 565, 570–571, 617, 625, 634, 642, 658, 663, 666
	2. identifies words that name persons, places, or things and words that name actions.	**Vol. 1:** 26–27, 28, 44, 57, 69, 72, 76–77, 81, 134, 162, 180, 184, 194, 209, 223, 244, 259, 273, 294, 308–309, 313, 339, 379, 382, 396, 423, 428, 430, 435, 445, 477, 533, 543, 570, 582, 603, 615, 624, 628 **Vol. 2:** 36, 46, 56, 66, 68, 71, 74, 221, 238, 244, 252, 287, 308, 337, 365, 375, 384, 427, 450, 459, 469, 472, 480, 485, 488, 562, 574, 593, 614, 617, 619–620, 621, 624, 647, 650, 652, 658, 660 **Vol. 3:** 101, 104, 150, 155, 159, 231, 255, 267, 298, 301, 303, 305–306, 312–313, 389, 594, 598, 603, 607, 614, 618–619, 623, 626
	3. identifies and sorts common words from within basic categories (for example, colors, shapes, foods).	**Vol. 1:** 23, 44, 114, 117–118, 164, 181, 199, 204, 222–223, 228, 231, 234, 239, 254, 258–259, 276, 289, 309, 359, 410, 418, 425, 445, 518, 527–528, 537, 553, 583, 598–599, 602, 613 **Vol. 2:** 70, 84, 218, 230–231, 255, 485, 533, 544, 566, 600, 628, 666 **Vol. 3:** 25, 37, 88, 120, 244, 409, 412, 422–423, 431, 577
	4. uses a variety of sources to build vocabulary (for example, word walls, other people, life experiences).	**Vol. 1:** 45, 90, 100–101, 103, 117–118, 119, 178, 181, 184, 188, 206, 212, 221, 223, 226, 239, 244, 249, 299, 309, 338, 350, 352–353, 359, 362, 366, 369, 372–373, 374–375, 379–380, 382, 388, 396, 402, 405, 408, 418, 431–432, 433, 478–479, 506, 527–528, 536–537, 601, 614, 623, 631, 646–647 **Vol. 2:** 36, 44, 105, 112, 134, 136, 164–165, 214–215, 216, 224–225, 234, 237, 272–273, 274, 283, 288–289, 383, 392–393, 396, 427, 432, 457, 472, 487, 502–503, 533, 553 **Vol. 3:** 44–45, 54–55, 97, 112, 128, 139, 149, 163–164, 165, 214–215, 225–226, 244, 280, 301, 303–304, 305, 313, 320, 325, 334–335, 383, 385, 393–394, 412, 434, 466, 487, 502–503, 552–553, 563, 594, 616, 634, 655, 670–671

	5. develops vocabulary by discussing characters and events from a story.	**Vol. 1:** 44, 114–115, 116, 132, 165, 176, 181, 209, 222, 231, 258–259, 273, 289, 350, 354, 364, 371, 379, 384–385, 402, 407, 423, 425, 430–431, 445, 468, 508, 533, 553, 583, 613, 645 **Vol. 2:** 36, 61, 71, 85, 92, 101, 104, 130–131, 134, 139, 147, 221, 231, 236–237, 241, 271, 301, 325, 365, 382, 399, 409, 422, 447, 450, 468–469, 477, 485, 549, 579, 593, 596–597, 617, 619, 638–639, 666, 670 **Vol. 3:** 50–51, 60, 85, 101, 130, 139, 147, 221, 224, 241, 255, 271, 280, 300–301, 308–309, 312, 316, 320, 332–333, 382, 384, 388–389, 392, 409, 422–423, 431, 447, 468, 477, 485, 501, 533, 559, 591, 598, 607, 614, 616, 618, 636, 645, 653, 669
LA.A.1.1.4	The student increases comprehension by rereading, retelling, and discussion. **The student:**	
LA.A.1.1.4.K.1	1. uses strategies to comprehend text (for example, retelling, discussing, asking questions).	**Vol. 1:** 107, 123, 165, 181, 208–209, 231, 258, 281, 341, 355, 365, 375, 379, 399, 407, 425, 444–445, 453, 552, 599, 620–621, 644 **Vol. 2:** 24–25, 40–41, 51, 60, 70–71, 84–85, 92–93, 100–101, 116, 130, 138–139, 147, 155, 159, 163, 195, 221, 240–241, 255, 271, 309, 336, 365, 388–389, 395, 404, 408–409, 431, 439, 447, 454, 477, 501, 549, 559, 601, 609, 625, 638, 647, 651, 659, 665, 671 **Vol. 3:** 24–25, 41, 67, 70, 84, 92–93, 100–101, 109, 139, 146–147, 194–195, 210–211, 220, 231, 240–241, 245, 254, 262–263, 270, 278–279, 286–287, 300–301, 305, 309, 316–317, 332–333, 364–365, 378–379, 408–409, 430, 439, 447, 455, 477, 481, 484–485, 492, 532–533, 549, 555, 558, 565, 573, 576, 590, 598–599, 602, 623, 645, 649, 652–653, 660–661, 668

READING

2.0 The student constructs meaning from a wide range of texts.

Benchmark	Grade Level Expectations	Page(s) or Location(s) Where Taught
LA.A.2.1.1:	The student determines the main idea or essential message from text and identifies supporting information. **The student:**	
LA.A.2.1.1.K.1	1. knows the main idea or essential message from a read-aloud story or informational piece.	**Vol. 1:** 33, 57, 72, 123, 126, 164, 273, 341, 355, 361, 406, 444, 473, 509 **Vol. 2:** 51, 67, 70, 116, 131, 195, 263, 365, 379, 389, 395, 408, 431, 451, 469, 533, 578–579, 592, 609, 621, 647, 671 **Vol. 3:** 25, 41, 61, 70, 84–85, 131, 147, 195, 211, 230, 240–241, 263, 279, 300–301, 332, 365, 408, 454, 485, 533, 549, 576, 590, 599, 653
LA.A.2.1.2:	The student selects material to read for pleasure. **The student:**	
	1. selects material to read for pleasure (for selects materials to read for pleasure.	**Vol. 1:** 129 **Vol. 2:** 329 **Vol. 3:** 57, 89, 97, 105, 113, 121, 337, 603, 611
LA.A.2.1.3:	The student reads for information to use in performing a task and learning a new task.	

	The student:	
	1. supports oral and written responses with details from the informative text.	**Vol. 1:** 230, 273, 355, 365, 384, 621 **Vol. 2:** 135, 266, 301, 365, 413, 431, 473, 484 **Vol. 3:** 135, 146, 263, 301, 305, 409, 430–431, 473, 548, 577
LA.A.2.1.4:	The student knows strategies to use to discover whether information presented in a text is true, including asking others and checking another source. **The student:**	
	1. understands that illustrations reinforce the information in a text.	**Vol. 1:** 70, 106, 118, 119, 122, 125, 126, 180, 198, 208, 230, 272, 288, 340–341, 365, 379, 384–385, 398–399, 431, 444, 480, 598 **Vol. 2:** 40, 84, 117, 166, 210, 241, 252, 254–255, 262, 300, 336, 364–365, 378–379, 408–409, 430, 504, 593, 608, 624, 638, 654–655 **Vol. 3:** 24, 40, 85, 92, 166, 194, 210, 240, 262–263, 286, 300–301, 309, 336, 364, 378, 408, 422, 430, 455, 473, 504, 532, 548, 576, 598–599, 622, 636, 641, 652–653, 672
LA.A.2.1.5:	The student uses simple materials of the reference system to obtain information. **The student:**	
	1. knows alphabetical order of letters.	**Vol. 1:** 50, 78, 174, 177, 190, 224, 274, 442 **Vol. 2:** 22, 34, 38, 52, 58, 68, 86, 106, 207, 237, 362, 372, 427 **Vol. 3:** 284, 444, 459
	2. uses pictures, environmental print (for example, signs, billboards) and people to obtain information.	**Vol. 1:** 90–91, 100–101, 102–103, 112, 118–119, 120, 130, 162, 178, 206, 228, 236, 277, 286, 296, 306, 362, 369, 372, 382, 449–450, 458, 474, 528–529, 617, 629 **Vol. 2:** 52, 128, 130, 136, 160, 192, 208, 218, 226, 228, 260, 266, 268, 276, 306, 314, 322, 330, 376, 386, 396, 406, 420, 452, 466, 468, 474, 482, 490, 498, 552, 554, 604, 621, 629, 636, 644, 652, 668 **Vol. 3:** 48, 82, 90, 98, 106, 114, 121, 128, 130, 136, 144, 152, 160, 192, 208, 218, 260, 268, 276, 362, 376, 386, 406, 436, 451, 466, 468, 474, 482, 488, 490, 498, 546, 556, 566, 588, 604, 612, 620, 634, 636, 642, 650, 658, 666
	3. asks "how" and "why" questions about a topic	**Vol. 1:** **Vol. 2:** 109, 195, 435, 659 **Vol. 3:** 447, 656

WRITING

1.0 The student uses writing processes effectively.

Benchmark	Grade Level Expectations	Page(s) or Location(s) Where Taught
LA.B.1.1.1:	The student makes a plan for writing that includes a central idea and related ideas. **The student:**	
	1. uses prewriting strategies (for example, drawing pictures, recording or dictating questions for investigation).	**Vol. 1:** 44, 80, 101, 107, 115, 129, 242, 245, 254, 276, 368–369, 378, 385, 389, 403, 407, 426, 448, 548–549, 556, 567, 579, 594, 602, 632, 640–641, 648

		Vol. 2: 88, 103, 109, 206, 234, 241, 311–312, 337, 381, 384, 389, 401, 404, 423, 427, 431, 443, 505, 575, 582–583, 596, 604–605, 612, 642–643, 658–659, 666–667 **Vol. 3:** 46, 275, 303, 305, 313, 328, 412
	2. generates ideas through brainstorming, listening to text read by teacher, discussing.	**Vol. 1:** 176, 184, 284, 350, 360, 362, 418, 448, 456, 464, 548–549, 556 **Vol. 2:** 96, 134, 226, 236, 442, 472, 574, 666 **Vol. 3:** 36, 46, 134, 206, 216, 266–267, 298, 309, 312, 320, 374, 434, 472, 544, 554, 572, 610, 626, 640, 657
LA.B.1.1.2:	The student drafts and revises simple sentences and passages, stories, letters, and simple explanations that • express ideas clearly; • show an awareness of topic and audience; • have a beginning, middle, and ending; • effectively use common words; • have supporting detail; and • are in legible printing. **The student:**	
	1. dictates messages (for example, news, stories).	**Vol. 1:** 46, 54, 74, 244, 263, 530, 540, 549, 579, 632 **Vol. 2:** 51, 88, 96, 120, 151, 236, 287, 320, 426, 433, 442–443, 480, 574, 612, 628 **Vol. 3:** 104, 142, 258, 282, 298, 374, 399, 404–405, 409, 426, 442, 618
	2. uses basic writing formats (for example, labels, lists, notes, captions, stories, messages).	**Vol. 1:** 44, 72, 80, 102, 110, 128–129, 176, 183–184, 204, 212, 233, 244, 254, 262–263, 284, 294, 304, 312, 350, 360, 368, 372, 278, 380, 385, 388–389, 409–410, 418, 434, 449, 470, 518, 556, 570, 579, 586, 603, 640–641, 648 **Vol. 2:** 36, 43, 46, 51, 56, 63, 66, 71, 74, 88, 96, 104, 112, 120, 128, 156, 158, 166, 206–207, 213, 216, 226, 233–234, 236, 241, 244, 259, 265, 271, 274, 279–280, 282, 289–290, 304, 311–312, 319–320, 321, 336, 375, 381, 384, 394, 401–402, 404–405, 412–413, 423, 426, 431, 434–435, 450, 459, 472, 480, 489, 494, 496, 504, 554, 575, 582–583, 596–597, 620–621, 642–643, 650, 658, 667 **Vol. 3:** 36, 64, 66, 74, 88, 95–96, 101, 103, 104–105, 112, 120–121, 142, 167, 206, 213–214, 226, 234, 236, 241, 244, 255, 258, 265, 274–275, 279, 282–283, 287, 290, 303–304, 305, 311–312, 313, 319–320, 337, 374, 381–382, 384, 389, 394, 399, 402, 404, 409, 412, 423, 426, 433, 442, 447, 450, 458, 489, 494, 496, 544, 580, 593–594, 595, 601–602, 609–610, 618, 626, 662
	3. demonstrates ability to sequence events during shared writing exercises.	**Vol. 1:** 263, 341, 370, 456, 464, 632 **Vol. 2:** 51, 120, 142, 166, 236, 280, 412, 504, 620 **Vol. 3:** 56, 104, 255, 298, 404, 426, 442, 602
	4. revises by adding details to pictures, dictation, or letters.	**Vol. 1:** 178, 254, 464, 472 **Vol. 2:** 46, 56, 66, 74, 112, 142, 150, 166, 236, 480, 488, 504 **Vol. 3:** 104, 142, 150, 480, 488, 648, 656
LA.B.1.1.3:	The student produces final simple documents that have been edited for • correct spelling; • appropriate end punctuation; • correct capitalization of initial words, "I," and names of people; • correct sentence structure; and • correct usage of age-appropriate verb/ subject and noun/pronoun agreement.	

	The student:	
1.	uses spelling approximations in written work.	**Vol. 1:** 101, 115, 233, 284, 360, 389, 426, 449, 457, 470, 642 **Vol. 2:** 36, 46, 56, 66, 71, 74, 104, 120, 142, 158, 166, 258–259, 274, 279, 373, 384, 391, 404, 413, 431, 433, 435, 443, 450, 459, 480, 496, 641–642, 643, 649–650, 657 **Vol. 3:** 64, 74, 88, 95, 103–104, 105, 121, 158, 206, 226, 234, 244, 255, 258, 265–266, 267, 274–275, 279, 282–283, 290, 320, 374, 394, 402, 405, 412, 423, 426, 433–434, 442, 447, 450, 458, 472, 480, 496, 549, 554, 562, 564, 580, 594–595, 602, 610, 618, 626, 640, 648
2.	uses directionality of print in writing (including but not limited to left-to-right, top-to-bottom, spacing between words).	**Vol. 1:** 110, 115, 128–129, 135–136, 202, 212, 225–226, 233, 244–245, 252, 254, 262–263, 284, 304, 312, 356, 360, 366, 368, 370, 378, 389, 396, 404, 410, 417, 419, 426, 428, 434, 449, 455, 470, 473, 480, 538, 556, 577, 593, 615, 623–624, 631 **Vol. 2:** 35–36, 43, 46, 53, 56, 63, 66, 71, 74, 87–88, 96–97, 104, 120, 134, 142, 150, 156, 158, 165–166, 206–207, 213, 216, 226, 233–234, 236, 241, 244, 258–259, 265, 271, 274, 279, 282–283, 287, 289–290, 304, 311–312, 317, 319, 321, 326, 329, 336, 374–375, 381, 384, 389, 401–402, 404–405, 412–413, 423, 426, 431, 433–434, 435, 442–443, 450, 458–459, 480, 488, 494, 496, 503–504, 505, 554, 574, 582, 596–597, 612, 620–621, 636, 641–642, 643, 649–650, 657–658, 667–668 **Vol. 3:** 46, 48, 64, 66, 74, 87–88, 95–96, 103–104, 105, 112, 114, 120–121, 134, 142, 158, 165, 167, 206, 214, 216, 226, 234, 236, 241, 244, 255, 258, 265–266, 267, 274–275, 279, 282–283, 287, 290, 298, 303–304, 305–306, 309, 311–312, 314, 319–320, 328, 330, 335, 337, 375, 381–382, 384, 389, 394, 399, 402, 404–405, 409, 412, 423, 426, 433–434, 442, 447, 450, 458, 480, 494, 496, 503, 554, 562, 580, 593–594, 595, 601–602, 610, 618, 626, 640, 648, 662, 671, 673
3.	identifies and attempts to use end punctuation (for example, the period, question mark, exclamation point).	**Vol. 1:** 109, 184, 212, 228, 254, 256, 404, 556, 578 **Vol. 2:** 46, 56, 66, 71, 74, 120, 142, 158, 166, 234, 290, 304, 316–317, 426, 434, 442, 458, 480, 496, 504, 650 **Vol. 3:** 64, 88, 96, 103, 112, 121, 234, 258, 266–267, 274–275, 282–283, 290, 298, 303–304, 328, 396, 402, 450, 458, 480, 496, 554, 594, 602, 610, 618, 648

WRITING

2.0 The student writes to communicate ideas and information effectively.

Benchmark	Grade Level Expectations	Page(s) or Location(s) Where Taught
LA.B.2.1.1:	The student writes questions and observations about familiar topics, stories, or new experiences. **The student:**	
	1. dictates or writes with pictures or words/ letters a narrative or informative piece about a familiar experience or text.	**Vol. 1:** 184, 262, 350–351, 360, 385, 448, 518, 553, 616 **Vol. 2:** 120, 150, 259, 282, 458, 488, 575, 620, 642–643, 658 **Vol. 3:** 206, 298, 336, 374, 458, 549, 559, 572, 626
	2. contributes ideas during a shared writing activity.	**Vol. 1:** 102, 110, 120, 128, 184, 186, 194, 212, 234, 244, 254, 263, 284, 294, 304, 341, 350, 352, 360, 362, 370, 372, 380, 382, 402, 410, 415, 456, 464, 472, 506, 520, 538, 578, 580, 610, 618, 624, 626, 632, 634, 640

		Vol. 2: 36, 56, 74, 88, 96, 104, 120, 134, 142, 244, 266, 274, 282, 374, 404, 426–427, 433, 442, 450, 472, 480, 544, 564, 574, 590, 598, 604, 606, 612, 614, 628, 636, 652, 666, 674 **Vol. 3:** 66, 104, 134, 142, 216, 236, 258, 298, 304, 306, 312, 314, 322, 328, 330, 384, 404, 426, 434, 442, 472, 480, 564, 572, 602, 618, 626, 640, 648
LA.B.2.1.2:	The student uses knowledge and experience to tell about experiences or to write for familiar occasions, audiences, and purposes. **The student:**	
	1. dictates and writes with pictures or words to record ideas and reflections.	**Vol. 1:** 52, 88, 104, 110, 118, 120, 128–129, 130,136, 162, 176, 178, 184, 186, 196, 204, 206, 212, 220, 226, 228, 234, 236, 246, 256, 263, 270, 278, 286, 306, 350, 360, 362, 372, 382, 415, 442, 448, 450, 456, 458, 466, 474, 480, 548, 570, 578, 586, 594, 602, 624, 632, 640–641, 648 **Vol. 2:** 22, 36, 38, 46, 48, 51, 56, 58, 66, 68, 74, 82, 88, 90, 96, 98, 104, 106, 112, 114, 120, 136, 152, 158, 160, 166, 192, 208, 216, 218, 226, 228, 236, 238, 244, 252, 260, 268, 274, 276, 284, 290, 298, 304, 306, 312, 314, 317, 322, 330, 336, 362, 374, 376, 384, 386, 396, 406, 412, 420, 426, 428, 434, 436, 444, 450, 452, 458, 466, 472, 474, 482, 490, 496, 498, 504, 544, 554, 564, 572, 574, 582–583, 596, 603–604, 605, 612, 620, 636, 642, 644, 650, 652, 658, 660, 666, 668, 674 **Vol. 3:** 22, 36, 38, 46, 48, 56, 66, 74, 82, 88, 90, 96, 98, 104, 106, 112, 114, 120–121, 128, 134, 136, 152, 158, 160, 166, 192, 206, 208, 216, 218, 226, 236, 238, 244, 252, 258, 260, 266, 268, 274, 276, 282–283, 284, 290, 303, 305, 309, 362, 374, 376, 384, 386, 394, 404, 406, 420, 426, 428, 442, 444, 450, 452, 458, 466, 472, 474, 480, 490, 496, 498, 504, 530, 544, 546, 556, 564, 566, 580–581, 588, 594, 596, 602,604, 610, 612, 618, 620, 634, 640, 642, 648, 650, 658, 666
LA.B.2.1.3:	The student uses basic computer skills for writing, such as basic word processing techniques such as keying words, copying, cutting, and pasting; using e-mail; and accessing and using basic educational software for writing. **The student:**	
	1. uses basic computer skills for writing (including but not limited to using a mouse, locating numbers/letters on keyboard, turning computer on/off, and locating and opening application icon).	
LA.B.2.1.4:	The student composes simple sets of instructions for simple tasks using logical sequencing of steps. **The student:**	
	1. dictates or writes simple informational texts (for example, descriptions, labels, lists).	**Vol. 1:** 44, 72, 80, 101–102, 110, 128, 176, 194, 212, 226, 231, 234, 244, 254, 312, 350, 362, 370, 375, 399, 403, 409–410, 423–424, 426, 428, 449, 470, 518, 538, 570, 594, 640, 648–649 **Vol. 2:** 36, 46, 56, 66, 71, 74, 104, 112, 207, 213, 216,226, 233–234, 237, 266, 271, 274, 287, 326, 329, 381, 384, 401–402, 404, 412, 423, 427, 431, 433, 450, 459, 472, 488, 489, 544, 554, 582, 596–597, 604, 621, 628, 666, 673–674

		Vol. 3: 64, 88, 101, 103, 105, 112, 134, 150–151, 234, 255, 266–267, 275, 279, 282, 290, 389, 393, 402, 404, 409, 423, 431, 433–434, 447, 472, 488–489, 564, 594–595, 618, 626

LISTENING, VIEWING, AND SPEAKING

1.0 The student uses listening strategies effectively.

Benchmark	Grade Level Expectations	Page(s) or Location(s) Where Taught
LA.C.1.1.1:	The student listens for a variety of informational purposes, including curiosity, pleasure, getting directions, performing tasks, solving problems, and following rules. **The student:**	
	1. follows two-step oral directions.	**Vol. 1:** 24–25, 29, 44, 47, 50–51, 53, 68, 73, 75–76, 77, 79–80, 89, 91, 101, 108–109, 111, 113, 121, 131, 176, 183, 185, 188–189, 209, 211, 221, 233, 237–238, 239, 241, 243, 248, 251, 255, 259, 271, 275, 288, 291–292, 295, 308, 311, 339, 349, 351, 358, 368–369, 371, 373, 378, 387, 397, 401, 407, 409–410, 418, 425–426, 427, 429–430, 431–432, 434, 454, 461–462, 478, 481, 507, 517, 526, 533, 535, 539, 549, 555, 557, 578, 587, 589, 592, 595, 597, 600, 602, 641, 643, 649 **Vol. 2:** 35, 37, 44, 53–54, 56–57, 66, 73–74, 99, 110, 115, 118, 135, 137, 145, 148, 164, 167, 205–206, 214–215, 217, 223–224, 225, 230–231, 234–235, 241, 257–258, 272–273, 277, 285, 288–289, 290, 304, 323, 336, 377, 381, 397, 404, 412–413, 424–425, 426–427, 429, 439, 443, 456, 458, 473, 475, 483, 486, 502, 504, 533, 543, 545, 547, 561, 563, 575, 577, 583, 595, 597, 599, 605, 607, 610–611, 613, 615, 618, 621, 623, 625–626, 642–643, 644–645, 650–651, 653, 655, 664, 666–667 **Vol. 3:** 39, 63–64, 67, 73, 88, 91, 97, 99, 110, 113, 115, 118, 135, 145, 148, 164, 167, 207, 209, 226, 233–234, 243, 245, 261, 264, 274–275, 277, 285, 299, 302–303, 315, 325, 334, 337, 378, 391, 393–394, 401–402, 411, 413, 424, 427, 437, 451, 458, 473, 483, 486, 502, 547, 565, 619, 621, 627, 641, 651, 654, 670, 673
	2. listens to oral language in different forms (for example, stories read aloud, audio tapes, nursery rhymes, songs).	**Vol. 1:** 24, 42–43, 48, 56, 90, 100, 106, 114–115, 119, 121–122, 124–125, 131, 132, 133, 164–165, 177–179–180, 182, 185, 188–189, 194, 198, 200, 207–208, 222, 230, 232, 235, 237–238, 247–248, 258, 262, 272, 276, 280, 298, 308, 340, 353–354, 355, 364–365, 373–374, 375, 384, 405–406, 408, 415, 422–423, 430–431, 435, 444, 452, 460, 464, 468–469, 476, 481, 508–509, 522, 524, 532, 542, 544, 552, 566, 574, 582, 590, 598, 612, 620–621, 628, 636, 644, 648 **Vol. 2:** 24, 39–40, 42, 50, 59–60, 61–62, 69–70, 83–84, 92, 100, 108, 116, 118, 121, 130, 134, 138, 143, 146, 150–151, 154, 159, 161, 167, 194, 209–210, 212, 220, 227, 230, 232, 240, 242, 245, 254, 262, 264, 270, 278–279, 282, 286, 291, 300, 305, 308, 313, 316, 320, 324–325, 332–333, 336, 364, 377, 380, 382, 388, 397–398, 399–400, 408, 422–423, 430, 432, 438, 443, 446, 451, 454, 468, 476, 484, 488, 492, 499, 532–533, 558, 560, 568, 578, 596, 600, 608–609, 616, 624–625, 638–639, 643, 646, 655, 662–663, 666, 670 **Vol. 3:** 24, 34, 40, 52, 92, 100, 108, 116, 118, 130, 134, 138, 146, 150, 161, 194, 204, 210, 220, 222, 254, 262, 270, 274, 278, 285–286, 291, 316, 325, 332, 364, 372, 380, 388, 398–399, 408, 422, 430, 432, 438, 446, 454, 468, 476, 484, 499, 532, 542, 548, 568, 590–591, 598, 606, 610–611, 614, 622, 624, 636, 644, 652, 667, 673

LA.C.1.1.2:	The student recognizes personal preferences in listening to literature and other material.	
	The student:	
	1. knows personal preferences for listening to literature and other material (for example, nursery rhymes, songs, stories).	**Vol. 1:** 220, 442, 473, 549, 618, 641 **Vol. 2:** 298, 505 **Vol. 3:** 162, 167, 500, 604, 668
LA.C.1.1.3:	The student carries on a conversation with another person, seeking answers and further explanations of the other's ideas through questioning and answering.	
	The student:	
	1. follows rules of conversation (for example, taking turns speaking and listening).	**Vol. 1:** 68, 88–89, 91, 100, 102, 104, 106–107, 111–112, 120, 130, 162, 165, 178, 185–186, 196, 205, 206, 208, 220, 227–228, 230, 236, 255–256, 258, 263, 270, 278, 286, 289, 296, 306, 338, 339, 352, 355, 361, 362, 364–365, 371–372, 374, 382, 383–384, 396, 404, 412, 420, 422, 426, 428, 442, 450, 458, 466, 474, 506, 508–509, 520, 525, 530, 540, 550, 572, 575, 578, 580, 586, 588, 596, 610, 618, 626, 634, 642 **Vol. 2:** 22, 38, 48, 58, 82, 90, 98, 106, 113–114, 144, 152, 160, 192, 195, 207–208, 218, 220, 226, 228, 238, 245, 252, 260, 268, 276, 298, 301, 305–306, 314, 322, 330, 362, 364, 376, 378–379, 382, 386, 392, 396, 298, 406, 420, 428, 436, 439, 442, 444, 450, 452, 455, 466, 474, 481–482, 490, 498, 530, 546, 565–566, 590, 598, 606, 614, 622, 636, 643–644, 646, 651–652, 655, 660, 668, 671 **Vol. 3:** 22, 41, 47–48, 55, 58, 68, 82, 90, 98, 106, 114, 128, 136, 144, 152, 160, 192, 208, 211, 217–218, 225, 228, 238, 241, 252, 260, 268, 276, 284, 287, 306, 313–314, 322, 326, 328, 330, 332–333, 362, 376, 386, 393, 396, 406, 409, 413, 420, 428, 443, 451, 459, 466, 474, 482, 490, 498, 530, 555–556, 574, 581, 588, 604, 612, 620, 634, 642, 650, 658, 666
LA.C.1.1.4:	The student retells specific details of information heard, including sequence of events.	
	The student:	
	1. listens for specific information, including sequence of events.	**Vol. 1:** 25, 108, 124, 341, 349, 353–354, 355, 365, 370, 372–373, 460–461, 477, 480, 518, 552, 644 **Vol. 2:** 24, 51, 61, 70, 162–163, 230, 240, 286, 305, 320, 328, 399, 408, 500–501, 533, 578, 592, 600, 608, 624, 639, 646, 670 **Vol. 3:** 57, 162–163, 227, 254, 278, 308, 333, 408, 493, 500–501, 505, 591, 606, 623, 669, 673

LISTENING, VIEWING, AND SPEAKING

2.0   The student uses viewing strategies effectively.

Benchmark	Grade Level Expectations	Page(s) or Location(s) Where Taught
LA.C.2.1.1:	The student determines the main idea in a nonprint communication.	

	The student:	
LA.C.2.1.1.K.1.	1. understands the main idea in a nonprint communication.	**Vol. 1:** **Vol. 2:** 324 **Vol. 3:** 61, 497, 622
LA.C.2.1.2:	The student recognizes simple nonverbal cues, such as use of eye contact, smiles, simple hand gestures.	
	The student:	
	1. understands simple nonverbal cues (for example, smiling, gesturing).	**Vol. 1:** **Vol. 2:** 40, 148, 324, 332, 382, 486 **Vol. 3:** 92, 148, 263, 325, 486, 603, 614, 622, 654

LISTENING, VIEWING, AND SPEAKING

2.0 The student uses speaking strategies effectively.

Benchmark	Grade Level Expectations	Page(s) or Location(s) Where Taught
LA.C.3.1.1:	The student speaks clearly and at a volume audible in large- or small-group settings.	
	The student:	
	1. speaks clearly and uses appropriate volume in different settings (for example, choral speaking, informal conversations, shared readings).	**Vol. 1:** 100, 108, 177, 207, 227, 262, 271, 281, 295, 365, 376, 383, 386, 388, 389, 405, 408, 416, 421, 422, 453–454, 458, 477, 508, 516, 540, 564, 576, 592, 594, 620 **Vol. 2:** 57, 67, 105, 118, 139–140, 212, 214, 218, 224, 227, 232, 234–235, 242, 245, 267, 280, 284, 304, 334, 385, 395, 398–399, 427, 440, 444, 459, 477–478, 596, 601, 616, 643, 647, 658–659, 663, 671 **Vol. 3:** 37, 96, 101, 139–140, 194–195, 207, 283, 287, 291, 298, 310, 318, 320, 323, 329, 413, 434, 458, 477–478, 545, 603, 645–646
LA.C.3.1.2:	The student asks questions to seek answers and further explanation of other people's ideas	
	The student:	
	1. asks and responds to questions.	**Vol. 1:** 24, 27, 30, 33, 46, 49, 54, 57, 74, 88, 90–91, 102, 104–105, 106–107, 114–115, 123, 125, 130, 132, 162, 165, 178–180–181, 182, 186–187, 188, 196, 198, 206, 210, 220, 223–224, 228–229, 230–231, 234, 236, 246, 248, 256–257, 258, 270, 272–273, 274, 278–279, 280, 281, 282, 284, 286, 288, 290, 293, 296, 306, 310, 338, 340–341, 348–349, 352, 355, 358, 362, 364, 366, 368, 372, 374, 378, 382, 384, 396, 398–399, 400–401, 402–403, 404–405, 406–407, 408, 412, 420, 422, 423, 425–426, 428, 430, 433–434, 435, 442–443, 446, 450–451, 452–453, 456, 458, 460, 463–464, 466–467, 468, 474, 476, 479, 506, 508–509, 516–517, 518, 520–521, 522–523, 530, 532–533, 534–535, 536, 540–541, 542, 550–551, 553, 564–565, 566–567, 572, 575, 580–581, 583, 584, 586, 588, 590, 596–597, 598, 601, 610–611, 612–613, 614, 618, 621, 626–627, 628, 634, 642, 645 **Vol. 2:** 22, 24–25, 34–35, 36, 40–41, 42, 45, 48–49, 50–51, 52–53, 55, 58, 61–62, 68, 70–71, 72, 82–83, 84–85, 86–87, 90, 92–93, 94, 98, 100–101, 102, 106–107, 108–109, 114–115, 119, 130, 132, 136, 144, 146, 149–150, 152, 154, 160, 165, 192–193, 194–195, 204–205, 208, 210–211, 212, 215, 219, 221–222, 223, 225,

		228–229, 230–231, 232, 238, 239, 240, 242, 252, 253, 254, 255, 256, 260, 262–263, 264, 266, 268–269, 271, 273, 276, 278, 282, 284–285, 289, 291, 298–299, 300, 306–307, 309, 314–315, 316, 320, 322, 324, 328, 330–331, 332, 362–363, 364–365, 372–373, 376–377, 379, 382–383, 386–387, 388–389, 390–391, 392–393, 396–397, 398–399, 406–407, 408, 410–411, 420–421, 422, 424–425, 428, 430, 436, 438–439, 444–445, 446–447, 452, 454, 457, 466, 468, 470, 474, 482, 484, 487–488, 490, 492, 498, 503, 530, 532–533, 542–543, 546–547, 548, 550, 555–556, 557–558, 559–560, 561–562, 564–565, 566–567, 568–569, 570, 572, 576, 579, 590, 592–593, 594, 598, 600–601, 604–605, 606, 608–609, 611, 614, 616–617, 618, 627, 636–637, 638, 640, 644, 646, 648, 652–653, 654–655, 656, 659–660, 662, 668–669, 670–671 **Vol. 3:** 22, 25, 34–35, 38–39, 40–41, 42, 48, 50–51, 52–53, 58, 62, 68–69, 71–72, 82, 84, 86–87, 90, 92–93, 94, 98, 101–102, 106–107, 114, 117, 119, 128, 130, 132, 136, 144, 146, 149–150, 152, 154, 160, 165, 192, 195, 204–205, 208–209, 210–211, 212, 218, 220, 222–223, 228, 232, 238–239, 242, 252–253, 255, 256, 258, 260, 262, 264, 268–269, 270, 273–274, 276, 279, 284–285, 287, 301, 304–305, 306, 308, 314, 316–317, 322, 324, 330, 332, 335, 362, 365, 372–373, 376–377, 378–379, 386, 388, 390, 396, 399–400, 406–407, 408, 410, 420–421, 422–423, 424, 428, 430–431, 438–439, 440, 447, 452, 454, 457, 466, 468, 470, 474, 482, 484, 487–488, 490, 498, 503, 530, 533, 542, 546, 548–549, 550, 556, 568, 574–575, 588, 590, 598–599, 602, 604–605, 607, 612–613, 618, 620–621, 634, 636, 638, 642, 650, 652, 655–656, 658, 666
LA.C.3.1.3:	The student speaks effectively in conversations with others. **The student:**	
	1. uses basic speaking vocabulary to convey a message in conversation (for example, numbers, adjectives, action words, shapes, colors, categories).	**Vol. 1:** 45, 91, 100–101, 103, 107, 112, 114–115, 116–117, 118–119, 132, 137, 181, 188, 192–193, 206, 209, 223, 226–227, 228, 231, 235, 239, 242, 246–247, 254–255, 258, 278, 340–341, 350, 361–362, 365 372, 375, 379, 396, 403, 407, 410–411, 418, 422, 426–427, 428, 434–435, 445, 449–450, 465, 506, 539, 556, 571, 575, 579–580, 602, 613, 629, 633, 640 **Vol. 2:** 61, 70, 85, 93, 101, 104, 109, 112, 120, 128, 195, 208, 218, 236, 245, 274, 365, 375, 385, 404, 408, 422, 427, 430–431, 442, 455, 564, 579, 593, 596–597, 598, 601, 604, 606, 608–609, 614, 616, 618, 636, 639, 643–644, 646, 652, 658, 666, 668, 670–671, 675 **Vol. 3:** 44, 85, 101, 214, 224, 237, 245, 258, 267, 271, 282, 298, 382, 384, 389, 392, 395, 409, 412–413, 422, 427, 443, 451, 615
LA.C.3.1.4:	The student uses eye contact and simple gestures to enhance delivery. **The student:**	
LA.C.3.1.4.K.1	1. uses eye contact and appropriate gestures to enhance oral delivery.	**Vol. 1:** 189, 238–239, 308, 361, 476–477 **Vol. 2:** 61, 83, 154, 163, 492, 501 **Vol. 3:** 71, 154, 329, 398, 660–661

1.0 The student understands the nature of language.

Benchmark	Grade Level Expectations	Page(s) or Location(s) Where Taught
LA.D.1.1.1:	The student recognizes basic patterns in and functions of language (patterns such as characteristic sounds and rhythms and those found in written forms; functions such as asking questions, expressing oneself, describing objects or experience, and explaining). **The student:**	
	1. knows patterns of sound in oral language (for example, rhyming, choral poetry, chants).	**Vol. 1:** 47, 55, 105, 108, 113, 133, 163, 181, 187, 221, 227, 237, 248, 255, 279–280, 287, 297, 307–308, 354–355, 356, 374–375, 376, 383, 416, 453, 469, 524, 532, 576, 583, 587, 590–591, 592, 614–615, 619, 622–623, 628, 630–631, 633, 637, 646 **Vol. 2:** 25, 107, 140, 155, 161, 163, 194, 212, 232, 242, 279, 302–303, 310–311, 318–319, 321, 333, 432, 440, 446, 478, 493, 499–500, 501, 531, 550, 570, 601–602, 610, 616, 640–641, 643, 648–649, 656–657, 662–663, 672 **Vol. 3:** 60, 70, 112, 115, 117, 140, 155–156, 161–162, 194, 230–231, 302, 310, 317–318, 325, 329, 331, 334, 364, 397–398, 478, 486, 493–494, 499–500, 502, 592–593, 597, 600, 606, 608–609, 624, 638, 646, 654, 662, 664, 667, 670
.	**2.** knows different functions of language (for example, expressing oneself, describing objects).	**Vol. 1:** 90–91, 101–102, 103, 125, 186, 304 **Vol. 2:** 51, 71, 104, 109, 147, 317, 485, 639 **Vol. 3:** 206, 231, 236, 374, 384, 404, 435, 443, 615
LA.D.1.1.2:	The student recognizes the differences between language that is used at home and language that is used at school. **The student:**	
	1. recognizes the differences between less formal language that is used at home and more formal language that is used at school and other public settings.	**Vol. 1:** 177 **Vol. 2:** 51 **Vol. 3:** 664

2.0 The student understands the nature of language.

Benchmark	Grade Level Expectations	Page(s) or Location(s) Where Taught
LA.D.2.1.1:	The student understands that word choice can shape ideas, feelings, and actions. **The student:**	
	1. understands that word choice can shape ideas, feelings, and actions (for example, story language, descriptive words).	**Vol. 1:** 114, 179, 188 **Vol. 2:** 51, 60, 109, 240–241, 263, 320, 638–639 **Vol. 3:** 109, 237, 623

LA.D.2.1.2:	The student identifies and uses repetition, rhyme, and rhythm in oral and written text. **The student:**	
	1. uses repetition, rhyme, and rhythm in oral and written texts (for example, recites songs, poems, and stories with repeating patterns; substitutes words in a rhyming pattern).	**Vol. 1:** 24–25, 26, 42, 48–49, 52, 77, 108, 116, 131, 133, 179, 182, 200, 207, 221, 232, 237–238, 244–245, 247–248, 249–257, 259–260, 271, 274, 282, 292, 297–298, 307–308, 313, 354, 356, 376, 383, 400, 408, 415, 416, 422, 446, 452–453, 454, 460–461, 462, 468, 476, 516, 524, 532, 576, 583, 584, 590–591, 592, 600, 614, 620, 622, 630, 636–637, 641 **Vol. 2:** 24–25, 42, 50, 62, 83, 86, 94, 118, 121, 132, 140, 154, 161–162, 163, 194, 204, 209, 212, 222, 230, 232, 235, 239, 241–242, 272, 279, 288, 302, 310, 318, 321, 333–334, 364, 372, 398–399, 422–423, 438, 440, 446, 451, 456, 470, 478, 492–493, 497, 499–500, 501, 505, 550, 558, 568–569, 570, 580, 602, 610, 616, 640, 648, 654–655, 656, 662–663, 672 **Vol. 3:** 61–62, 86, 94, 112–113, 118, 132, 140, 155, 159, 161–162, 220, 230–231, 232, 254, 256, 264, 285, 291, 302, 310, 318, 329, 331, 364, 380, 388, 390, 398, 400, 405, 410, 422, 432, 446, 454–455, 470, 478, 492–493, 499–500, 533, 568–569, 572–573, 589, 592, 600, 606, 614, 624, 627, 646, 656, 660–661, 664
LA.D.2.1.2:	**2.** understands the use of alliteration.	**Vol. 1:** **Vol. 2:** **Vol. 3:** 377, 590, 656, 664
LA.D.2.1.3:	The student recognizes that use of more than one medium increases the power to influence how one thinks and feels. **The student:**	
LA.D.2.1.3.K.1	**1.** understands that the use of more than one medium can influence how one thinks and feels (for example, music, illustrations).	**Vol. 1:** 194, 198 **Vol. 2:** 300 **Vol. 3:** 291
LA.D.2.1.4:	The student knows various types of mass media (including billboards, newspapers, radio, and television). **The student:**	
LA.D.2.1.4.K.1	**1.** knows various types of mass media (for example, film, video, television).	**Vol. 1:** 235 **Vol. 2:** 121, 291, 659 **Vol. 3:** 108, 591

LITERATURE

1.0 The student understands the common features of a variety of literary forms.

Benchmark	Grade Level Expectations	Page(s) or Location(s) Where Taught
LA.E.1.1.1:	The student knows the basic characteristics of fables, stories, and legends. **The student:**	
LA.E.1.1.1.K.1	**1.** knows a variety of familiar literary forms (for example, fiction, nonfiction, picture books, fairy tales).	**Vol. 1:** 31, 132, 180, 220, 231, 263, 298, 354–355, 374, 379, 415, 422, 444, 448, 452–453, 460, 473 **Vol. 2:** 64–65, 100, 108, 110, 146, 156, 211, 255, 282, 298, 301,

		326–327, 365, 378, 388, 398, 402, 408–409, 430, 438, 448, 451, 454, 476, 484, 494, 505, 558–559, 596, 601, 608, 616, 638, 658, 662, 667, 670 **Vol. 3:** 50, 84, 100, 108–109, 218, 254, 263, 270, 280, 402, 408, 422, 431, 438, 446, 448–449, 492, 606–607, 614, 616, 640, 648, 652, 660–661, 664
LA.E.1.1.2:	The student identifies the story elements of setting, plot, character, problem, and solution/resolution. **The student:**	
	1. knows the sequence of events, characters, and setting of stories (for example, read-aloud stories).	**Vol. 1:** 32–33, 107, 114, 123–124, 125, 128–129, 165, 181, 208–209, 281, 340, 354–355, 364–365, 384, 399, 448, 460, 473, 477, 522, 566–567, 574, 599, 612, 617, 620–621, 625, 644 **Vol. 2:** 37, 41, 51, 70–71, 84–85, 93, 100–101, 105, 117, 138, 147, 155, 162–163, 167, 195, 211, 220–221, 227, 230, 236, 238, 240, 244, 271, 275, 281, 308–309, 316, 329, 333, 379, 385, 389, 394, 395, 412, 439, 454, 476–477, 493, 501, 505, 532, 548–549, 558–559, 564–565, 578–579, 601, 609, 613, 620, 625, 638, 642, 647, 659, 670–671 **Vol. 3:** 93, 100–101, 116, 138–139, 155, 163, 254–255, 271, 278–279, 287, 308–309, 317, 408–409, 422, 438–439, 454–455, 476–477, 485, 501, 599, 602, 606–607, 622, 641, 644–645, 652–653, 669

LITERATURE

2.0 The student responds critically to fiction, nonfiction, poetry, and drama.

Benchmark	Grade Level Expectations	Page(s) or Location(s) Where Taught
LA.E.2.1.1:	The student uses personal perspective in responding to a work of literature, such as relating characters and simple events in a story or biography to people or events in his or her own life. **The student:**	
	1. relates characters and simple events in a read-aloud book to own life.	**Vol. 1:** 33, 57, 80, 107, 129, 164, 181, 184, 199, 230–231, 249, 272, 284, 360, 365, 385, 424, 445, 453, 481, 523, 529, 532, 548, 557, 571, 575, 582, 594, 603, 617, 628, 649 **Vol. 2:** 41, 57, 60, 70, 75, 96, 108, 110, 113, 117, 134, 143, 194, 226, 267, 270, 271, 280, 282, 304, 317, 365, 388–389, 423, 447, 481, 544, 554, 564, 592, 597, 604, 629, 650–651, 658, 662, 666, 670 **Vol. 3:** 89, 93, 97, 143, 240, 259, 263, 267, 278, 283, 287, 301, 308–309, 316, 365, 379, 405, 427, 481, 558, 611, 615, 627
	2. uses a variety of personal interpretations to respond to stories and poems (for example, talk, movement, music, art, drama, writing).	**Vol. 1:** 26, 108, 115, 123, 185, 189, 194, 205, 209, 212, 213, 244, 245, 305, 308, 351, 355, 385, 398, 399, 403, 407, 411, 423, 424, 430, 431, 449, 453, 465, 469, 476, 477, 480, 509, 529, 533, 543, 546, 548, 557, 571, 603, 617, 621, 625, 645 **Vol. 2:** 75, 105, 110, 113, 131, 151, 155, 159, 217, 227, 245, 267, 291, 305, 315, 336, 337, 385, 395, 399, 435, 472, 489, 493, 497, 549, 555, 575, 579, 583, 596, 597, 605, 618, 620, 625, 629, 639, 642, 643, 647, 651, 654, 658, 659, 662, 663, 666, 675 **Vol. 3:** 57, 71, 105, 109, 131, 151, 155, 159, 221, 227, 259, 263, 271,

LA.E.2.1.2:	The student recognizes rhymes, rhythm, and patterned structures in children's texts.	275, 290, 325, 337, 395, 405, 455, 469, 489, 497, 545, 569, 577, 591, 603, 611, 637, 649, 657, 665
	The student:	
	1. knows rhymes, rhythm, and patterned structures in children's text (for example, poetry, prose).	**Vol. 1:** 24, 132–133, 244, 252–253, 259, 274, 281, 355, 375–376, 422, 452–453, 460–461, 468–469, 476 **Vol. 2:** 24–25, 50, 146, 154, 162, 194, 212, 232, 235, 242, 278–279, 316, 325, 333, 364, 382, 422–423, 439, 446, 451, 484, 492–493, 500, 559, 574, 616, 619, 646, 664–665, 666 **Vol. 3:** 112, 154–155, 162, 167, 194, 364, 398, 422, 446, 454, 492–493, 500–501, 558, 606, 623, 627, 640, 660–661, 664, 669, 673